ECONOMIC ISSUES:
Readings and Cases

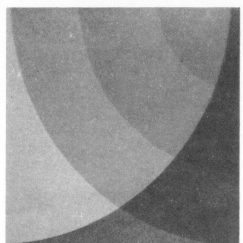

Campbell R. McConnell
PROFESSOR OF ECONOMICS, UNIVERSITY OF NEBRASKA

ECONOMIC ISSUES:
Readings and Cases, Third Edition

McGRAW-HILL BOOK COMPANY

New York · St. Louis · San Francisco · London · Sydney · Toronto · Mexico · Panama

ECONOMIC ISSUES: READINGS AND CASES

Library of Congress Catalog Card Number 69-17452

1 2 3 4 5 6 7 8 9 0   BABA   7 5 4 3 2 1 0 6 9 8

To Lauren, Curt, and Beth

Preface

There is a rather general and at least partially justified feeling that students of the principles of economics are led through the desert of analysis up to the oasis of current issues, but then not allowed to drink. A primary objective of this volume is to allow the student to drink deeply of current economic controversy through a readily accessible collection of materials which cover a wide range of policy-oriented topics.

This new third edition represents a substantial revision of its predecessor. One-third of the readings in this edition are new.

The readings have been selected and arranged in terms of the organizational structure of McConnell's *Economics*, fourth edition. I trust, however, that the selections can be readily used to supplement any standard textbook on the principles of economics. An outline which relates each reading to relevant text chapters is found on page xvii for the convenience of those who use the readings with McConnell's *Economics*. A list of the readings by author is also provided on page xiii for quick reference.

The selections are organized around five major headings: (1) economics and economic institutions, (2) macroeconomics, (3) microeconomics, (4) domestic economic problems, and (5) international economics and comparative systems. It is hoped that, in addition to providing a means for expanding, illustrating, and generally enriching the principles course, this volume will also prove useful in courses on current economic and social problems, and that particular selections will be relevant to a wide variety of more specialized courses in economics and other social disciplines. The majority of the readings can be profitably read by the interested layman who has not benefited from formal course work in economics.

The table of contents reflects the continued emphasis of this edition upon economic issues and policy-oriented topics. In many cases opposite positions on issues of current importance are presented in consecutive readings. Such wide-ranging topics as creeping inflation, the wage-price guideposts, the causes of unemployment, the structure of expansionary fiscal policy, the performance of monetary policy, the relationship between market structure and technological progress, the monopoly problem, our social security system, the social responsibility of businessmen, the guaranteed annual income, the economic role of government, the free-trade issue, the debate over flexible exchange rates, and current balance of payment policies are all analyzed from decidedly different points of view. Other readings simply present and explore specific problem areas: the population explosion, the corporation's role in society, fiscal federalism, the importance of debt, environmental pollution, racial discrimination, urbanization, disarmament, and so forth. A number of other readings are included because they constitute valuable case studies. In addition to readings on the Great Depression and Brazil's hyperinflation, case studies of the economies of Soviet Russia, France, China, and the Honduras are presented, as are a number of incisive case studies of the various market structures. A few readings are included primarily because they represent eloquent extensions of topics which are treated briefly, if at all, in introductory texts.

The full text from which each selection has been taken is available in most well-equipped libraries. Each reading has had to pass the stringent test of being both stimulating and comprehensible to the average college sophomore. Furthermore, a conscious effort has been made to use materials which will extend, rather than duplicate, that which is covered in basic textbooks. No serious attempt has been made to use the volume as a vehicle for introducing the unwary sophomore to the great economists and their works, although the writings of a number of universally known scholars have been included.

Most selections have been shortened—some substantially—but a deliberate effort has been made to safeguard them against distortion or loss of continuity. In a few instances empirical data have been updated. Because this volume is designed for beginning students rather than research scholars, I have taken the liberty of omitting footnotes from the selections and of adding subtitles.

The editorial introductions which precede each selection are designed to state the basic theme or conclusions of the reading and to relate it to other readings or to the formal body of economic analysis.

As in prior editions, I have continued to include several questions and study suggestions at the end of each selection. Some questions simply focus attention upon the basic points or arguments of each article and force the reader to ponder these points. Other questions attempt to relate the readings to basic material found in standard textbooks on the principles of economics. Still other questions force the student to compare different views and value systems. It is hoped, too, that these questions will provide the instructor with a ready means of gauging the conscientiousness and comprehension of his students.

My indebtedness is obviously great. First and foremost I am greatly obligated to the various authors and publishers who have generously permitted the reprinting of their works in this volume. Furthermore, my colleagues at the University of Nebraska have been most generous in guiding me to basic issues and relevant materials in their areas of specialty. Their assistance has undoubtedly contributed substantially to the quality and comprehensiveness of this volume.

Campbell R. McConnell

Contents

PART THREE • MICROECONOMICS: MARKETS, PRICES, AND RESOURCE ALLOCATION

PART FIVE • THE INTERNATIONAL ECONOMY AND COMPARATIVE ECONOMIC SYSTEMS

Contents by Author

Suggested Reading Assignments for
McConnell: *Economics*, 4th ed.

Reading Number ECONOMIC ISSUES, 3rd ed.	Chapter Number ECONOMICS, 4th ed.
1	2
2	1, 2
3	3
4	2, 20, 43
5	4, 5
6	7
7	8
8	8
9	6, 9
10	6, 9
11	9
12	11
13	11
14	11, 19
15	11
16	11
17	11, 12
18	11, 12
19	12, 13
20	14, 19
21	14
22	14
23	14, 19
24	15
25	16, 17, 18
26	18
27	18
28	22
29	22
30	22
31	20
32	22
33	21
34	22
35	22
36	23, 27
37	26
38	27
39	29
40	30
41	30
42	28
43	28, 30
44	28, 30
45	31, 32
46	33
47	27, 34
48	27, 34
49	34
50	34
51	35

ECONOMIC ISSUES:
Readings and Cases

PART ONE
ECONOMICS AND
ECONOMIC INSTITUTIONS

Reading 1

The Economic System

Howard R. Bowen, President, State University of Iowa

In this introductory reading Howard R. Bowen addresses himself to several questions fundamental to an understanding of economic science. What are the means of production? Why must these means be subject to some form of social control? What institutions comprise the economic system? Answers to these queries provide us with the background needed to pursue and relate to one another the many specific problems and issues dealt with in ensuing readings.

Economics is about the economic system. The first step in the study of economics is to obtain a clear conception of what the economic system is and what it does.

The economic system may be defined as the framework of institutions by which the use of the means of production and of their products is socially controlled.

MEANS OF PRODUCTION

Virtually all human ends are achieved through the action of human beings within an environment. The sole means available for the attainment of human ends are thus, (1) human beings with all their characteristics and potentialities, and (2) the various features of their environment. Not all of these means, however, can be regarded as means of production, otherwise the economic system would encompass all human activities and interests. The means of production are distinguished by two qualities: (1) the capacity to contribute to the production of transferable goods and (2) scarcity.

Only those human beings are regarded as means of production who are capable of contributing to the production of transferable goods, i.e., goods which can be enjoyed by other individuals. Thus, an individual capable of contributing to the production of food, books, clothing, medical service, dramatic performances, or any of a host of similar goods, is regarded as a means of production. This implies that certain individuals (e.g., invalids, infants, and "unemployables") are excluded from the category of means of production. Their activities (e.g., sleeping, eating, getting exercise, playing) yield enjoyments which are restricted to themselves and do not add to the satisfaction of others. The distinction between human beings who are capable of producing transferable goods and those who are not is important, because the productive power of those who possess this capacity is of direct interest not only to themselves but also to the members of the social group generally. The capacity of an individual to yield transferable goods makes him a part of the reservoir of available social resources.

Only those human and environmental means are regarded as means of production which are scarce relative to the amount of them which could be used to advantage. The exclusion of freely available means is to be explained not by the unimportance of such copious goods as air or natural gas in certain areas, but by the

From Howard R. Bowen, **Toward Social Economy**, Holt, Rinehart and Winston, Inc., New York, 1948, pp. 2–8, 52–53, abridged. Reprinted by permission.

fact that the use of these means is a matter of almost complete indifference—a matter to which men need give little attention. The utilization of scarce means, on the other hand, requires care, frugality, foresight, and administration, because the employment of these means for any one purpose is always at the sacrifice of some valued alternative use. The very attribute of scarcity implies that all possible uses cannot be achieved, that some uses must be foregone, and that the actual use must be selected after a comparison of possible alternatives. The administration of scarce means, which is called *economizing*, is a matter of great social importance.

Scarcity, as a criterion of the means of production, is chiefly relevant to the environmental means. Human beings, if capable of producing transferable goods, are generally scarce in the sense that more of them could be used advantageously if available. This does not imply, however, that they are in fact always so used—as all of us who have lived through the [Great Depression of the] 1930s know.

To summarize, the means of production include those human beings and features of the environment which, because they are capable of yielding transferable goods and are scarce, are of vital social concern and must be administered with care and frugality.

NEED FOR SOCIAL CONTROL

For two reasons the use of the means of production must inevitably be controlled in some way through social processes or agencies.

First, the scarcity of the means of production frequently leads to conflicts of interest among individuals and groups. The possession of these means (or their products) by any one person or group necessarily lessens the amount available to others. This conflict of interest, which may range from mild rivalry to armed strife, must, in the interests of peace and security, be resolved by some form of social control over individuals. Conflict arises not only in regard to the use of land, forests, minerals, fishing rights, and water-power rights, but also in regard to the use by some individuals or groups of the services of other individuals or groups—as in slavery, serfdom, imperialism, or employer-employee relationships.

Second, efficient use of the means of production requires organized, coordinated, and cooperative action on the part of virtually all persons in society. Though production could be carried on by each individual for his own use in the manner of Robinson Crusoe, cooperation makes possible division of labor and specialization. Cooperative production is, therefore, technically superior in the sense that greater output is possible with a given supply of the means of production. Division of labor implies that each productive agent is used for only one or a few types of operations in the production of any given product. This requires that the means of production be organized so that each may perform its service in the right way, at the right time, and to the right extent. Specialization, on the other hand, implies that the production of each good is carried on in separate organizations or even that different stages in the process of producing each good are carried on separately. Some arrangement must be made, then, to ensure that each line of production is pursued in the right way, at the right time, and to the right extent. In short, in order to achieve the technical advantages to be gained from division of labor and specialization, it is necessary that the social group arrange for organizing, guiding, and controlling the productive process so that the essential coordination and teamwork can be achieved. Any society that wishes to gain the advantages of cooperative production must provide or evolve a system of controls over the use of the means of production. Even the so-called "laissez-faire system," which attempts to maximize individual freedom in the use of the means of production, is based on highly developed and socially sanctioned rules regarding the use of these means. These rules, of course, are largely identified with the system of "private property" with all its implications.

The scarcity of the economic means combined with the technical superiority of division of labor and specialization makes of production a social and cooperative process, and necessitates some form of *social control* over the use of productive means. Consequently, any advanced society which hopes to be cohesive, stable, and efficient, must possess customs, laws, or other socially sanctioned usages for regulating the use of its means of production. These institutions, taken together, constitute its economic system.

ECONOMIC INSTITUTIONS

Since the activities of individuals in the use of the means of production are regulated, at any given time and place, through the institutions then and there prevailing, the precise manner in which a society will use its means of production will depend upon and be determined by the character of its economic institutions. For example, a change in the practices relating to inheritance of wealth will alter the distribution of control over the means of production and change the distribution of income. The enactment of legislation for the regulation of electric power enterprises will likely result in altering the quantity of electricity produced, or the incomes of the owners of the affected properties. The development of collective bargaining in labor relations will probably influence the supply of labor, the technical organization of production, and the distribution of income. The adoption of a code of professional ethics by physicians will influence the availability of medical service to various classes and the income of physicians. Free public education with numerous scholarships for the less well-to-do will tend to alter the distribution of incomes. The introduction of widespread consumer credit will increase the consumption of relatively expensive durable goods. The imposition of progressive taxes will reduce the rate of capital accumulation. The substitution of "central planning" for private enterprise will alter the relative quantites of goods produced. A religious taboo will reduce the consumption of affected articles. The custom of generous philanthropy will increase the amount of means devoted to religion, scientific research, education, or art. The sanctification of particular methods of production will prevent the adoption of more efficient methods and restrict the amount of the total social product. The social disapproval of leisure, combined with asceti-

cism, will make for rapid accumulation of capital. A strong spirit of nationalism will encourage the application of a large portion of the means of production to military purposes. These and many other possible illustrations indicate how completely the use of the means of production is determined by the customs, conventions, and practices—the institutions—of the group, and how any institutional change is likely to bring about a change in the use of the means of production.

The almost complete dependence of the economic process upon the character of the extant institutions means that economics is primarily a study of institutions and of their workings. Even traditional classical economics is of this type, its particular subject matter being the institutions associated with one or more of the variants of laissez-faire capitalism.

The economic process varies, from one time or place to another, to the extent that economic institutions are different. At different periods of history and in different parts of the world, economic systems have varied in almost every detail. There is little in common, for example, between the economic system of a Melanesian native group, the Aztec empire, a Greek city state, an English medieval manor, modern America, or modern Russia. Each of these economic systems represents a configuration of institutions almost totally unlike that of any of the others, yet each has a practicable means by which the fundamental tasks of the economic order have been accomplished. A close study of these systems would reveal, moreover, that no one of them has ever been completely static, and that each emerged as a result of an evolutionary process. It is only reasonable to suppose, then, that the various systems in operation today will gradually become modified until they, too, will have been transformed into new and different systems.

QUESTIONS AND STUDY SUGGESTIONS

1. How are the means of production defined? Why must these means be subject to some form of social control?
2. How do institutions affect economic processes? Why is economics "primarily a study of institutions and their workings"?

Reading 2

Economic Policy

Douglas C. Hague, Professor of Applied Economics, Sheffield University
Alfred W. Stonier, Senior Lecturer in Political Economy, University College, London

Douglas C. Hague and Alfred W. Stonier illustrate in this reading how economic policies are formulated, and provide valuable insights concerning the extent to which policies are scientific and the criterion by which policies can be judged "good" or "bad." We find, through an extended illustration of economic policy with respect to the distribution of income, that policy creation itself is fraught with ample room for controversy and disagreement because value judgments—as opposed to facts—are ultimately involved.

Two lessons suggested by this reading are particularly relevant for all the many areas of controversy discussed in the remainder of this volume. First, the character of a given problem may legitimately be viewed quite differently by different persons. For example, a given income distribution might be viewed by some (the very poor) as much too unequal and by others (the very rich) as not unequal enough. Second, even where agreement exists about the specific character of a problem, various observers may favor quite different remedies. All may agree, for example, that a given nation's income is too unequally distributed. However, some may, for good reasons, favor redistributing income through taxation and public expenditure policies; that is, they might advocate highly progressive taxes and programs of public spending and transfer payments designed to supplement the living levels of the poor. Others, for equally persuasive reasons, might want to limit drastically the inheritance of wealth or to alleviate the economic and noneconomic barriers which now might make it difficult for the children of the poor to enter higher-paid occupations. In short, economic problems breed controversy. Important economic problems are rarely susceptible to treatment by a universally accepted policy.

In their professional, as distinct from their private, life, economists are rarely dogmatic about the kind of economic policy which "ought" to be followed in a country. Certainly no economist has the right to feel that his particular professional knowledge gives him the right to lay down the law about the most desirable economic policies. A knowledge of economics cannot make a man's mind up for him; it can only help him to make his mind up for himself, by showing up the flaws in the assumptions and the logical reasoning of any argument that he may put forward. The basic reason for this somewhat surprising modesty on the part of economists is that to make policy prescriptions inevitably means making "value judgments." It means producing recommendations that cannot be justified by pure scientific analysis but depend on one's own feelings and views.

It is important that economists should always

From Douglas C. Hague and Alfred W. Stonier, **The Essentials of Economics**, Longmans, Green & Co., Inc., New York, 1955, pp. 157–167, abridged. Reprinted by permission.

make it quite clear that their policy recommendations are in no way "scientific." For the ordinary man, who knows that economics is a specialized science, may well be led into thinking that a particular recommendation is "scientific" merely because it is expressed in the economist's special jargon. Perhaps even more important is the danger that the economist himself may produce confused results if he tries to combine economic analysis with political propaganda. It is always so much easier to reach the conclusion one wants to reach rather than the conclusion one *ought* to reach. This is particularly so if one has a strong preconceived idea, based on one's political views, of the result one would like to achieve.

Economists typically smuggle in a few value judgments about which the opinion of modern economists is strongly agreed. For example, we accept the common view that a monopoly which earns high profits and charges high prices is "wrong." Similarly, it is generally implied that mass unemployment is "bad," and a deliberate policy of curing unemployment by a budget deficit is "good."

Here we shall try to show the kind of policies which present-day economists prescribe, and how far these policies can be justified on a strictly scientific basis. First, we must discuss the criterion by which economists class economic policies as "good" or "bad." This criterion is simple. Economists usually assume that a policy is "good" if it helps to increase the "economic welfare" of the community. By economic welfare, or well-being, they mean the satisfaction which the community derives from consuming goods and services. It follows that the "best" economic policy will be that which "maximises economic welfare." In other words, the "best" policy is that which gives the greatest possible satisfaction to the community through the consumption of goods and services.

Economists therefore make their policy recommendations on the assumption that the main concern of any Government is to "maximise" satisfactions in its own country by using its "scarce resources" to the best possible advantage. There will be qualifications to this aim, because such a simple goal cannot be the only end of a modern community. Such qualifications will emerge as we proceed.

POLICY TOWARD INCOME DISTRIBUTION

Let us begin by discussing a problem which can be solved on the basis of this simple assumption that the Government wishes merely to "maximise economic welfare." In modern economies there is much redistribution of income through progressive taxation, because it is generally felt that greater equality of incomes than would otherwise exist is desirable. This view is based, first, on the desirability of mitigating want as such, and, second, on the need to abolish extremes of wealth and poverty and so eliminate class distinctions based on the possession of very high incomes. We shall now show the way in which economists can justify contentions about the most desirable distribution of income in a society.

Let us begin by hunting for a reasonable hypothesis on which to base the analysis. There are various views which one can take. First, there are many people who sincerely believe that an equal distribution of income is either unequivocally good or unequivocally bad. There is no arguing with such an approach. Other people try to avoid making any judgment at all about such a difficult question as what the "best" distribution of the national income is. They believe in an economics which is entirely free from such absolute judgments. We cannot agree with that view; for one *can* say something about the "best" income distribution without being "unscientific."

THREE ASSUMPTIONS

We shall base our analysis on three assumptions. The first two are assumptions of fact; the third is a judgment of value. The first assumption of fact is this. If all prices are constant, a rise of, say, $1 in an individual's income will increase his satisfactions. A further increase of $1 in his income will again increase his satisfactions, but it will do so by a smaller amount. In other words, there exists what we may call the "law of diminishing satisfaction from extra income." The richer the man is, the less satisfaction will a given extra amount of money, say $1, give him.

This first assumption, we have said, is a fact and not a value judgment. It is a fact for the following reason. Let us assume that a man has an income of $100. It is only reasonable to suppose that when he spends this $100 he buys those goods which are most desirable to him. He will buy those goods first which he wants most. He wishes to obtain the greatest possible satisfactions from spending his $100; and if the goods he buys were not the most satisfying combination possible, he would not buy them. The goods which he does *not* buy *must* give him less satisfaction than those which he does buy. They clearly do not give greater satisfactions or he would have bought them instead.

There can therefore be no doubt that the second absolute increment in income which any consumer receives gives him less satisfactions than did the previous (equal) increment. Otherwise, he would have bought the second group of goods first. It follows that the satisfactions derived from spending equal increments in income decrease for all of us as we become richer.

The second assumption is also an assumption of fact, though it would be difficult to prove conclusively. Our first assumption has enabled us to see what successive increments of income are worth to any individual; we now need some way of making comparisons between individuals in order to see which people deserve the biggest incomes and which the smallest. What can we say about the capacity of different people to enjoy income? It seems rather rash to maintain that human beings are all completely unlike each other. There must be some similarities between different human beings, otherwise they would never all be called "human beings." Indeed, it seems far more reasonable to argue that all human beings are alike than to argue that all are different. Our second assumption is therefore that, in their ability to derive satisfaction from spending their incomes, people are all very similar. For we must always remember one thing. Whilst we may disagree wholeheartedly with the claim that "all men are born equal" in their capacity to enjoy spending their incomes, there is no need to insist that anyone who says that they are "all equal" is a lunatic. More than this, if a rich man denies that all men are much the same as each other, and claims instead that the rich are exquisite and the poor intolerable, is he not just being conceited? There are also those equally misguided people who seem to believe that the poor are all capable of leading a good life and that the rich are all wicked and insensitive to true enjoyments.

It is, of course, obvious that all people are *not* completely identical. Some people prefer smoking cigarettes to pipe-smoking; others prefer eating sweets to eating chocolates. But it certainly does not follow that, just because people like different things, a man cannot derive the same satisfactions from a dollar spent in one way as another man derives from spending a dollar in a different way. It may be impossible to prove that one man derives more enjoyment from Mendelssohn's Violin Concerto than another man obtains from Beethoven's Violin Concerto. But there is no reason why, in fact, they should not both be equally satisfied.

Let us assume for the moment that our second assumption takes the strict form of saying that all people are *identical,* not in their particular tastes, but in their capacity to enjoy income. It then follows that if one takes $1 from a richer man and gives it to a poorer man, one has increased the total satisfaction of the country. For since we are assuming that all men are identical, the principle of "diminishing satisfaction from extra income" shows that the richer man values his "marginal" dollar less highly than the poorer man does. The process of redistribution of income should consequently go on until all incomes are exactly equal. Only in this way can one "maximise the satisfactions of the community." For only at this stage will it be impossible to increase welfare by taking money from those with incomes which are above average, thereby giving more satisfaction to the new recipient than the income gave originally to the man from whom it is now taken away.

If one assumes that all consumers are identical, it follows that "national satisfaction" will be at a maximum when all incomes are equal. In fact, of course, such a bald contention is too strong. Our assumption that all people are *identical* was only made temporarily as a strict version of our real assumption, namely, that all people are very similar. If one makes this latter assumption, however, complete equality of incomes is likely to be quite close to the "best" position. If the state wishes to attain "maximum welfare," incomes should, apparently, only vary within a very narrow range.

This conclusion depends not only on our second assumption of fact, that all men are mentally similar in their ability to enjoy income, just as they are physically similar. It also depends on a judgment of value, namely, that if people are, in fact, mentally similar they ought all to be treated in a similar fashion—by being given similar incomes. Even if our second assumption of fact is wrong, however, this policy recommendation may still be correct. Even if all men are "not equal" in their ability to enjoy incomes, it is, nevertheless, still right to treat them as though they are. This is our value judgment.

MODIFICATIONS AND COUNTERARGUMENTS

Our conclusion may be wrong; if it is, it is the task of those who believe in inequality of income to make a better case for inequality. There is a very important point here. If one asked people whether or not they agreed with equality of incomes, one would usually find that equality was popular with the poor and anathema to the rich. On the other hand, if one asked a rich man whether he would still believe in inequality of income, even if it meant that he had to become very poor, one would be unlikely to find him maintaining his position. Self-interest would usually force him to agree that, rather than be a pauper, he would be content to allow greater equality of income. With rich people, the belief in inequality in incomes is not really a belief in inequality *as such;* it is more likely to be based on the realisation that with greater equality of income they would be much worse off.

There is, however, a different and very powerful argument against equality of incomes, especially where this is achieved by means of redistributive taxation. This is the "incentives" argument. Many modern countries redistribute income from rich to poor by means of a highly progressive tax system; and a progressive income tax will probably reduce incentives to work—especially at high levels of income, where rates of tax are also very high. There is a real danger that less work will be done by those people who earn the highest incomes if a sharply progressive tax system is used to redistribute income. Similarly, progressive income taxes may discourage the rich from using their savings to help in the financing of real investment in industry.

Perhaps those who bemoan the damaging effects of a highly progressive tax system are being too gloomy. But there is certainly no reason to suppose that incentives to work and save are left completely unchanged by progressive taxes. The whole difficulty of this problem is that few hard facts are known. It is therefore quite possible that, in a world where the only politically acceptable method of redistribution of the national income is through the tax sys-

tem, the desire to make the distribution of the national income more equal may also mean that the national income itself is smaller than it might have been. In other words, it is quite possible that we can either choose to give the working class a larger share of a national income that is growing only slowly, because incentives are blunted by progressive taxation; or perhaps we can choose to give them a smaller share of a national income that is growing very rapidly, unhampered by any "disincentive" effects of progressive taxes. As we have said, there is no absolute proof that this really is the choice confronting us. But the "incentives" argument—that we have the choice between a small share in a larger (and growing) income and a large share in a smaller (and static) income—is certainly a perfectly respectable one.

A further argument against equality of income is that it will reduce the savings of the community. The rich will not be able to save "out of their superfluity." Money which would have been saved by a rich man will probably, if incomes are made more equal, be spent by a poorer one. Thus, at times when progress in the economy depends on large savings to finance investment in industry, considerable inequality of income may be desirable. For there are likely to be more savings when incomes are unequal than when they are equal.

The important thing here, however, is to realise that there are two quite independent arguments which economists can put forward about the distribution of income. The first is that an *equal* distribution of a *given* income will "maximise welfare" at the present. The second is that an *equal* distribution of income may mean that the national income fails to grow as rapidly as it would have done with greater inequality. There is no way of reaching a final judgment without relying almost wholly on one's own opinions and feelings. The really important thing is to realise, as is all too rarely done in current discussions, that there are these two viewpoints from which the problems of income distribution can be approached, and that they tend to lead to different conclusions.

CHOICE BETWEEN UNEMPLOYMENT AND INFLATION

Another choice which seems to confront most governments today is that between unemployment and inflation. Pursuing a full employment policy is rather like walking along a tightrope. On one side lies deflation and depression; on the other side lies inflation and rising prices. Unless the government possesses an as yet undreamed-of-ability, it is likely that the task of maintaining full employment without inflation will prove too difficult for it. In practice, the choice is usually between an employment policy that is too weak, and does not completely abolish all unemployment, and a policy that is so strong that it causes some inflation. In these circumstances, the economist is often asked to say which is worse, unemployment or inflation.

Most people are agreed that unemployment is unequivocally bad. The "economics of waste," where men and machines are idle and where all the social problems of unemployment arise, is something that the post-war generations in all countries are determined never to experience.

But what of the alternative—inflation? It is much harder for economists to say anything about this; but they can at least point to a negative conclusion. Once full employment has been reached, one cannot increase standards of living by increasing people's money incomes. These increased incomes will merely be swallowed up in rising prices; and no one will be any better off in real terms. The only way to raise real incomes is to increase the nation's *productivity*. Nevertheless, there seems to be common acceptance of the view that *if* full employment does imply a certain measure of mild inflation, then that inflation is the price which must be paid to avoid the kind of mass unemployment that occurred in the 1930s. Whether inflation will itself lead to equally grave economic and social problems as those arising from mass unemployment, time alone can tell. At present, given the choice, most people in Great Britain seem to prefer inflation to unemployment.

THE COMPENSATION PRINCIPLE

We conclude by discussing one piece of technical apparatus which economists have developed in an attempt to solve policy problems without needing to make value judgments. Most economic policies cannot be put into operation without benefiting some people at the expense of others. This immediately raises the problem: how can we compare the loss suffered by one person, A, with the gain accruing to another person, B? Such a problem will arise in making all the most interesting practical policy decisions. For example, governments often have to decide whether to tax Peter in order that Paul's food may be subsidised, his rent reduced, or his children sent to school free. Economists have therefore devised a test by which, given sufficient information, they can show whether the gain to the one person will exceed the loss to the other. This test is known as the "compensation principle." The "compensation principle" says that if a new policy makes A so much better off that he could "compensate" B for the loss which the policy causes to him, *and yet* still be better off than originally, then the policy would increase "welfare." If the gainer cannot so "compensate" the loser, then the policy would decrease the satisfactions of the community.

The simplest way of looking at the compensation principle is this. Assume that a policy change is made, and that A becomes better off at the expense of B. The State now levies a money tax on A which just cancels out the benefit which he has received; similarly, the government pays a money grant to B which just cancels out the loss that he suffered by the change in policy. The question now is, will the government be able to take more money away from A in taxes than it has to pay to B? If so, A has gained more than B has lost. In other words, A would gain so much from the change that he could "bribe" B not to object to the change and still remain better off than he would have been without the change. The policy change has unequivocally increased "welfare."

To put the point more generally, if a policy change makes some people in a country better off and others worse off, has it increased the "total welfare" of the country? The answer is that it *has* increased welfare if those who have gained from the change can "bribe" the losers not to reverse the change, and yet these gainers remain better off because of the new policy, even after they have paid the "bribes." The compensation principle shows that, in this particular instance, the policy change would benefit the community as a whole.

We can now explain the traditional case for free international trade, a case which has always had the support of economists. With the simple kind of assumption that we are using, the position is that the removal of an import duty would be desirable if it left the community as a whole better off. This would be the case where the consumers who benefited from lower prices of imports after the tariff had been removed were able to "compensate" the industries which suffered a loss of income because of the increase in foreign competition, and yet these consumers remained better off because of the change to free trade. Most economists think that this could happen. Of course, if the gainers *could not* compensate the losers without themselves being worse off than when the tariff was in existence, the change to free trade would not be a change for the better.

Unfortunately, even the compensation principle does not completely remove the need for value judgments. The economist can now say that the import duty should be abolished and compensation paid *if necessary*. But the decision whether to pay that compensation still has to be taken; and it is not a decision which can be made on purely economic grounds. One has to face up to the fact that, in economics, there is hardly ever any clear-cut evidence on the desirability or otherwise of a given policy. The economist can certainly help the politician by explaining, as best he can, the true facts of the situation and the probable results of any change in policy. But the final decision cannot be made by the economist as such. The responsibility for the final decision on any economic policy must always lie with the politician and the citizen.

QUESTIONS AND STUDY SUGGESTIONS

1. What basic criterion do economists use in deciding whether a given economic policy is "good" or "bad"? Explain the problems involved in applying this criterion to the view that incomes should be more equally distributed.

2. What assumptions are invoked in analyzing the question of what is the "best" distribution of income? Which are based upon facts? Upon values? Comment: "One *can* say something about the 'best' income distribution without being 'unscientific.'"

3. Explain the arguments which can be made in favor of considerable inequality in income distribution. How does time enter into any comparison of the arguments for and against greater income equality?

4. What is the "compensation principle"? Explain its application. What difficulties might be encountered in applying this principle in solving specific policy problems?

Reading 3

The Division of Labor

Adam Smith, *The Wealth of Nations* (1776)

Specialization—the division of labor—is a basic feature of every economic system, regardless of its ideological framework or stage of development. This reading is an excerpt from Adam Smith's *Wealth of Nations* which, although published in 1776, still constitutes the classic statement of the advantages of specialization to society.

The greatest improvement in the productive powers of labour, and the greater part of the skill, dexterity, and judgment with which it is any where directed, or applied, seem to have been the effects of the division of labour.

The effects of the division of labour, in the general business of society, will be more easily understood, by considering in what manner it operates in some particular manufactures. It is commonly supposed to be carried furthest in some very trifling ones; not perhaps that it really is carried further in them than in others of more importance: but in those trifling manufactures which are destined to supply the small wants of but a small number of people, the whole number of workmen must necessarily be small; and those employed in every different branch of the work can often be collected into the same workhouse, and placed at once under the view of the spectator. In those great manufactures, on the contrary, which are destined to supply the great wants of the great body of the people, every different branch of the work employs so great a number of workmen, that it is impossible to collect them all into the same workhouse. We can seldom see more, at one time, than those employed in one single branch. Though in such manufactures, therefore, the work may really be divided into a much greater number of parts, than in those of a more trifling nature, the division is not near so obvious, and has accordingly been much less observed.

THE PIN FACTORY

To take an example, therefore, from a very trifling manufacture; but one in which the division of labour has been very often taken notice of, the trade of the pin-maker; a workman not educated to this business (which the division of labour has rendered a distinct trade), nor acquainted with the use of the machinery employed in it (to the invention of which the same division of labour has probably given occasion), could scarce, perhaps, with his utmost industry, make one pin in a day, and certain could not make twenty. But in the way in which this business is now carried on, not only the whole work is a peculiar trade, but it is divided into a number of branches, of which the greater part are likewise peculiar trades. One man draws out the wire, another straights it, a third cuts it, a fourth points it, a fifth grinds it at the top for receiving the head; to make the head requires two or three distinct operations; to put it on, is a peculiar business, to whiten the pins is another; it is even a trade by itself to put them into the paper; and the important business of making a pin is, in this manner divided into about eighteen distinct operations, which, in some manu-

From Adam Smith, **The Wealth of Nations**, Random House, Inc., New York, 1937, pp. 3–11, abridged.

factories, are all performed by distinct hands, though in others the same man will sometimes perform two or three of them. I have seen a small manufactory of this kind where ten men only were employed, and where some of them consequently performed two or three distinct operations. But though they were very poor, and therefore but indifferently accommodated with the necessary machinery, they could, when they exerted themselves, make among them about twelve pounds of pins in a day. There are in a pound upwards of four thousand pins of a middling size. Those ten persons, therefore, could make among them upwards of forty-eight thousand pins in a day. Each person, therefore, making a tenth part of forty-eight thousand pins, might be considered as making four thousand eight hundred pins in a day. But if they had all wrought separately and independently, and without any of them having been educated to this peculiar business, they certainly could not each of them have made twenty, perhaps not one pin in a day; that is, certainly, not the two hundred and fortieth, perhaps not the four thousand eight hundredth part of what they are at present capable of performing, in consequence of a proper division and combination of their different operations.

ADVANTAGES OF SPECIALIZATION

This great increase of the quantity of work, which, in consequence of the division of labour, the same number of people are capable of performing, is owing to three different circumstances; first, to the increase of dexterity in every particular workman; secondly, to the saving of the time which is commonly lost in passing from one species of work to another; and lastly, to the invention of a great number of machines which facilitate and abridge labour, and enable one man to do the work of many.

Improved Dexterity

First, the improvement of the dexterity of the workman necessarily increases the quantity of the work he can perform; and the division of labour, by reducing every man's business to some one simple operation, and by making this operation the sole employment of his life, necessarily increases very much the dexterity of

the workman. A common smith, who, though accustomed to handle the hammer, has never been used to make nails, if upon some particular occasion he is obliged to attempt it, will scarce, I am assured, be able to make above two or three hundred nails in a day, and those too very bad ones. A smith who has been accustomed to make nails, but whose sole or principal business has not been that of a nailer, can seldom with his utmost diligence make more than eight hundred or a thousand nails in a day. I have seen several boys under twenty years of age who had never exercised any other trade but that of making nails, and who, when they exerted themselves, could make each of them, upwards of two thousand three hundred nails in a day. The making of a nail, however, is by no means one of the simplest operations. The same person blows the bellows, stirs or mends the fire as there is occasion, heats the iron, and forges every part of the nail. In forging the head too he is obliged to change his tools. The different operations into which the making of a pin, or of a metal button, is subdivided, are all of them much more simple, and the dexterity of the person, of whose life it has been the sole business to perform them, is usually much greater. The rapidity with which some of the operations of those manufactures are performed, exceeds what the human hand could, by those who had never seen them, be supposed capable of acquiring.

Saving of Time

Secondly, the advantage which is gained by saving the time commonly lost in passing from one sort of work to another, is much greater than we should at first view be apt to imagine it. It is impossible to pass very quickly from one kind of work to another, that is carried on in a different place, and with quite different tools. A country weaver, who cultivates a small farm, must lose a good deal of time in passing from his loom to the field, and from the field to his loom. When the two trades can be carried on in the same workhouse, the loss of time is no doubt much less. It is even in this case, however, very considerable. A man commonly saunters a little in turning his hand from one sort of employment to another. When he first begins the new work he is seldom very keen and hearty; his mind, as they say, does not go to it, and for some time he rather trifles than applies to good purpose. The habit of sauntering and of indolent careless application, which is naturally, or rather necessarily acquired by every country workman who is obliged to change his work and his tools every half hour, and to apply his hand in twenty different ways almost every day of his life, renders him almost always slothful and lazy, and incapable of any vigorous application even on the most pressing occasions. Independent, therefore, of his deficiency in point of dexterity, this cause alone must always reduce considerably the quantity of work which he is capable of performing.

Machinery

Thirdly, and lastly, every body must be sensible how much labour is facilitated and abridged by the application of proper machinery. It is unnecessary to give any example. I shall only observe, therefore, that the invention of all those machines by which labour is so much facilitated and abridged, seems to have been originally owing to the division of labour. Men are much more likely to discover easier and readier methods of attaining any object, when the whole attention of their minds is directed towards that single object, than when it is dissipated among a great variety of things. But in consequence of the division of labour, the whole of every man's attention comes naturally to be directed towards some one very simple object. It is naturally to be expected, therefore, that some one or other of those who are employed in each particular branch of labour should soon find out easier and readier methods of performing their own particular work, wherever the nature of it admits of such improvement. A great part of the machines made use of in those manufactures in which labour is most subdivided, were originally the

inventions of common workmen, who, being each of them employed in some very simple operation, naturally turned their thoughts towards finding out easier and readier methods of performing it. Whoever has been much accustomed to visit such manufactures, must frequently have been shown very pretty machines, which were the inventions of such workmen, in order to facilitate and quicken their own particular part of the work. In the first fire-engines, a boy was constantly employed to open and shut alternately the communication between the boiler and the cylinder, according as the piston either ascended or descended. One of those boys, who loved to play with his companions, observed that, by tying a string from the handle of the valve which opened this communication to another part of the machine, the valve would open and shut without his assistance, and leave him at liberty to divert himself with his play-fellows. One of the greatest improvements that has been made upon this machine, since it was first invented, was in this manner the discovery of a boy who wanted to save his own labour.

It is the great multiplication of the productions of all the different arts, in consequence of the division of labour, which occasions, in a well-governed society, that universal opulence which extends itself to the lowest ranks of the people. Every workman has a great quantity of his own work to dispose of beyond what he himself has occasion for; and every other workman being exactly in the same situation, he is enabled to exchange a great quantity of his own goods for a great quantity, or, what comes to the same thing, for the price of a great quantity of theirs. He supplies them abundantly with what they have occasion for, and they accommodate him as amply with what he has occasion for, and a general plenty diffuses itself through all the different ranks of the society.

QUESTIONS AND STUDY SUGGESTIONS

1. Explain why economists take the position that the division of labor entails a more efficient allocation or utilization of society's scarce resources.

2. What are the specific advantages in having workers specialize?

Reading 4

The Population Problem: Myths and Realities

Dennis H. Wrong, Professor of Sociology, New York University

Perhaps no problem, aside from that of nuclear conflict, has elicited more concern than world population growth. Indeed, concern is warranted because the economic well-being of man depends in good measure upon the relationship between human resources (population) and property resources (land, capital, and technology). In this reading Dennis H. Wrong seeks to distinguish the facts from the fallacies—the myths from the realities—of the population problem. In so doing he probes the causes of the world population upsurge, possible political implications, and economic consequences in both advanced and underdeveloped countries.

In recent years the rapid growth of world population has come to loom as one of the great problems of the age. Vivid and ominous metaphors like the "population explosion," the "population bomb," or the "swarming of the earth" are by now part of the familiar vocabulary of public awareness—so familiar, indeed, as to have created the impression that we have a firm understanding of the danger. Yet because population trends are inseparably related to such emotion-laden matters as the role of women and the position of the family in society, to sexual practices and moral doctrines, and to the comparative sizes of national, religious, and racial groups, there has been a general reluctance to press hard upon the conventional wisdom embodied in the prevailing metaphors. Thus the way has been left clear for a host of misconceptions to flourish about the causes and consequences and control of population growth. These misconceptions, moreover, are held both by the "optimists" who refuse to regard population growth as a profound threat to human welfare, and by the "alarmists" who have for so long considered themselves voices crying in a wilderness of indifference and prejudice that they have become prone to shrill exaggerations and the brandishing of scare statistics.

PERVASIVENESS OF THE PROBLEM

Perhaps the most common of all the misconceptions concerning the so-called population explosion is that it poses a problem only to the economically underdeveloped, non-Western part of the world. Although most Americans take it for granted that their numbers will continue to increase steadily, they are not apt to regard this increase as amounting to anything so threatening as an "explosion" and are inclined to use the latter term only with reference to the larger countries of Asia. Yet the United States, as well as several other Western countries, have maintained rates of population growth since World War II equaling or exceeding those of many underdeveloped areas. The American rate of increase during the past decade, for example, has been as high as that of India and higher than Japan's. Moreover, the comforting belief that rapid population growth is a danger only to the underdeveloped world holds only if one adopts a thoroughly catastrophic perspective. Continued population

From Dennis H. Wrong, "Population Myths," **Commentary**, November, 1964, pp. 61–64, abridged. Reprinted from **Commentary** by permission; copyright © 1964 by the American Jewish Committee.

increase in the United States may not threaten us with imminent mass starvation and civil disorder, but it does strain our human and material resources, and aggravate our most serious social problems.

FALLING DEATH RATE

A second widespread misconception concerning the world population explosion is that it has resulted from a rise in the birth rate in the countries of rapid growth. This notion stems from a confusion between postwar American growth and the quite different pattern of growth in the underdeveloped countries. For in these latter countries the crucial factor has not been a "baby boom" such as we experienced here after the war, but rather a sharp drop in the death rate. In other words, while the level of fertility has remained the same or declined only slightly, a far higher proportion of infants is being kept alive by "death control" in the form of newly adopted medical and public-health measures. The survival of two newborn babies where previously only one survived is the immediate, demographically explosive consequence of the introduction of those measures, rather than an increase in the longevity of adults. Although the effects on population increase of this decline in infant mortality are identical to those of a rise in the birth rate, the "mindless breeding" of the "Asian masses" has nothing to do with the issue—tasteless and irrelevant references to sex as the "Indian national sport" notwithstanding.

But why have Asians, Africans, and Latin Americans failed to adopt birth control to balance the effects of death control? Is the problem, as is sometimes suggested, a matter of illiterate, superstitious, church-ridden peasants fatalistically clinging to past customs and incapable of following the Western example by adjusting their behavior to a new demographic situation? Here again a misconception —and a self-righteous one—is at work, for the demographic situation in the underdeveloped countries is unlike anything in Western population history. In Ceylon—to take the standard, and only slightly extreme, case—the death rate recently dropped as much in a single year (1947) as it did over a full fifty years in the West during the period when the latter was going through its own modernization process. It took nearly a century of declining mortality and rapid population growth before fertility

began to decline in the West; little wonder, then, that reproductive behavior in much of the underdeveloped world (where mortality levels are by now only a little higher than in the West) has not yet adjusted itself to the effects of death control. Unlike the contemporary underdeveloped nations, moreover, the West in its time had migration outlets to absorb part of its growth. And finally, the European states were never as large in absolute terms nor as densely settled as the major underdeveloped countries are today.

POPULATION AND POLITICAL POWER

Still another common misconception is that the balance of power in world politics is likely to be altered by the rapid growth in the population of the underdeveloped world. In the past, this idea often inspired apprehensions with a racist tinge (the "yellow peril" and the "black hordes"); nowadays, it more usually inspires "wave-of-the-future" rhetoric. The truth, however, is that in the nuclear age sheer numbers can no longer turn a nation into a major world power; indeed, the rapid growth of population in the underdeveloped countries actually *reduces* both their military and their industrial potential. To be sure, defenders of the view that national power in some last analysis still rests on population size insist—in an effort to adapt this thesis to the facts of nuclear technology—that only large and wealthy nations can support a considerable nuclear defense establishment. But this claim loses any plausibility it may seem to have when one considers the destructive power of even a few "old-fashioned" nuclear bombs, or when one recalls the one-sided, unbalanced patterns of economic growth which totalitarian regimes such as those of Russia and China are able to sustain in order to build up their armaments.

Does the population explosion, then, pose *no* problem to the world? Are the forebodings to which it has given rise utterly unjustified? Since the pace of world population growth has been quickened by the spread of death control rather than by an increase in human fertility, are we not entitled to regard an extra thirty years of life as an unqualified blessing conferred upon us by modern technology? If death control results in a larger population, why should this be of concern to anyone except a few aesthetes, haters of crowds, and those people who (as *Time* once suggested) prefer birds and animals to human beings? The answer is that the population explosion remains a monumentally serious problem even though some of the fears to which it gives rise are groundless, and even though it is the result of a technical revolution that is beneficial in other respects. In order to grasp its true nature and dimensions, one must begin by distinguishing clearly between its long-run and short-run effects.

LONG-RUN AND SHORT-RUN EFFECTS

Looking several centuries ahead, it is impossible to escape the conclusion that world population growth *must* eventually come to an end. One can argue, as do the "optimists," that new inventions, new sources of food, the marvels of science and technology in general, are capable of achieving gains in productivity that could support a vastly larger population than at present. But to grant that this is in principle possible is a very different matter from assuming that the benefits of such technological progress will in fact be made available in a short time to all of the world's peoples. The optimists are nowhere more optimistic than in their readiness to assume that increases in productivity that are now, or will shortly become, technically *possible* are likely to be *actually* achieved in this world of wars and national and imperial rivalries. Moreover, glowing estimates of future advances in productivity usually concentrate on possible gains in food production, ignoring the fact that human beings, however well-fed, also need *space*. Never-ending population growth would ultimately lead to a shortage of space even if the problem of food supply were solved.

Let us go further, however, and concede to the optimists the feasibility of a hypothetical world of planetary colonization, of human settlements underground and raised above the ground, of food acquired from the oceans or grown in high-yield chemical solutions. Let us concede also that such a world might feed its much larger population *more* adequately than we are fed today on earth. Is it not obvious that even *this* world could only continue to be viable if rapid population growth were to cease? For no matter what science and technology may achieve, the time must come when only stabilization of numbers will avoid disaster.

Alarmist writers on the population problem,

on the other hand, are not always clear as to the nature of the disaster they predict if population growth should continue. Frequently, they draw depressing pictures of a future in which the entire surface of the earth has been converted into a human anthill. By extrapolating present growth rates into the future, they suggest that we are heading toward such a world. Yet far more probable than the continuation of population growth to the point where we are faced with an anthill world, is the cessation of growth as a result of a rise in the death rate long before such a level of density is reached. The real issue, therefore, is *how* present growth rates will be lowered: will we be forced to abandon the low mortality we now enjoy and suffer a sharp rise in the death rate, or alternatively, will we cut back on population growth by learning to control our breakaway fertility? For the disaster with which the population explosion actually threatens us is not that we will one day be standing shoulder to shoulder on the earth's surface, but that we will lose our control over death and return to the kind of population stability (based on high mortality and fertility) prevailing in pre-modern societies.

In the short run, however, it is the effect of rapid growth on economic development that is the essence of the problem. Strangely, economic development and technical progress are often seen as alternatives to actions and policies designed to arrest population growth. We should, it is sometimes argued, concentrate on encouraging economic progress instead of worrying about birth-control campaigns, for economic progress will obviously permit more people to live at a higher standard of living. In its crudest form, this argument poses more food as an alternative to fewer people. But an odd distortion is involved here. Social scientists who advocate governmental birth-control policies do not see such policies as an *alternative*, but rather as a *prerequisite*, to economic development, no less essential to development than, say, the construction of dams and heavy industry.

A modern version of the optimistic position contends that as agrarian peasant societies are modernized, population growth will be slowed up by the mass adoption of family limitation under the new circumstances of urban living, open class systems, and greater material welfare. (This, of course, is what happened when the West achieved modernization.) But high rates of population growth in underdeveloped societies may swamp and destroy all programs for economic development by diverting resources needed for capital investment to meeting spiralling consumer demands.

THE UNDERDEVELOPED COUNTRIES

There is a further point of contrast between Western experience and the present situation of the underdeveloped world. Along with the faster decline in the latter's death rate, the greater density and size of its present population, and the lack of migration outlets, some sociologists and demographers have also pointed to the fact that the fertility levels prevailing today in the *tiers monde* are higher than was the case at the beginning of modernization in the West. They relate these higher levels to crucial differences between the Western family system and the so-called joint or consanguineal family systems of Asia and Africa, which are far more conducive to early marriage and to continuous childbearing through the wife's reproductive period. However, the importance of this particular difference may have been overstressed, for the underdeveloped countries possess several advantages over the West so far as prospects of succeeding quickly at fertility reduction are concerned. In the first place, they have achieved national independence in an era when a strong state, assuming full responsibilities for social welfare, has become the norm. Moreover, their traditional religions and value-systems, while containing many injunctions in favor of large families and high fertility, have never made a prime doctrinal tenet of pro-natalism combined with sexual asceticism to the degree that Christianity has—and all branches of Christianity, not merely the Roman Catholic Church. Even the absence of a strong secular humanitarian and libertarian tradition which frowns upon practices like sterilization and abortion (not to speak of infanticide) is an advantage from the standpoint of attaining fertility control. Latin America, the most rapidly growing region and the one with the highest birth rates, is, of course, an exception to these generalizations since its culture and social structure are largely an offshoot of Western civilization. Yet the very fact that it is an exception suggests that the linkage between high fertility and the joint family system may have been overstressed.

Given that modernization may be delayed and even prevented by the "premature" adoption of one of its essential features—namely death control—the underdeveloped countries can no more afford to follow a *laissez-faire* policy with respect to population growth than they can with respect to capital accumulation and economic growth itself. But once one speaks of the necessity of state policies designed to cope with population growth, further issues arise. It cannot be assumed that "voluntary" birth-control policies on the Japanese or Indian model are the only ones likely to be adopted: the ominous possibilities of man-made famines and even of direct genocide as means of reducing not population growth but existing over-population are already firmly established in the repertory of 20th-century politics.

But it is by no means certain that mass genocide, demographically motivated wars, or even the milder policy of holding back death-control measures (which *may* be what China is now deliberately doing) could successfully "solve" the population problem. A temporary rise in mortality might facilitate rapid economic development, which would then lead to the adoption of family planning. But more probably, the result would be a cycle of wars, civil strife, mass bitterness, and apathy that would themselves retard or prevent economic development.

BIRTH CONTROL

As for the more benign ways of lowering fertility, some of them seem almost as offensive to Western sensibilities as a deliberate increase in the death rate. Western social scientists and medical specialists have generally favored the voluntary use of chemical or mechanical contraceptives by individual couples (the method that is chiefly responsible today for maintaining the relatively low levels of fertility in the Western world itself). But it is beginning to appear that abortion and sterilization may have more appeal to some peoples as forms of birth control than the advanced contraceptive techniques of the West. Nor is it necessarily the case that "the pill"—the yet-to-be perfected oral contraceptive so often seen as the solution to population control in the underdeveloped world—will have greater appeal. In Japan, a decline of 50 percent in the birth rate in the decade from 1947 to 1957 was achieved largely by means of abortion, which was legalized in 1948. Since 1955, the number of abortions has dropped without a concomitant rise in the birth rate, which suggests that Japanese couples are learning to substitute other methods of birth control. Whether the new methods are mainly contraception or sterilization, however, remains open to dispute. Be that as it may, it seems likely that sterilization will become the favored method of achieving an initial reduction in the birth rate in countries as dissimilar as India and some of the Latin American nations. And since the goal of antinatalist policies in the underdeveloped world must be to achieve fertility decline *before* rather than after the achievement of full social and economic modernization, it ill behooves Westerners to frown on the adoption of methods like sterilization and abortion. The underdeveloped countries cannot afford to delay fertility reduction until after they have attained the benefits of modernization, and perhaps contraceptive birth control will itself have to be viewed as one of these benefits.

THE QUALITY OF LIFE

The issue of whether American aid to underdeveloped countries should include advice on birth-control techniques is largely responsible for the fact that the population explosion has become a subject of public debate in this country. Formulating the problem in terms of distant and for the most part non-Christian peoples has doubtless served to moderate potentially rancorous religious differences within the United States concerning these matters. However, it has also allowed us to evade the question of whether it is desirable that the American population should itself continue to soar at its postwar rate. Among the few professional demographers who have confronted this question are Lincoln and Alice Day. Their recently published book, *Too Many Americans*,

is refreshingly free from the strident alarmism that characterizes the writings of so many of the amateurs who have dealt with the subject. The Days readily concede that American population growth does not threaten us with the prospect of eventual famine or even declining living standards, for the almost universal practice of birth control among Americans provides a kind of built-in check on further growth should population pressure begin to depress standards of living. It is rather the "quality of life" that is threatened by ever-growing numbers of people: outdoor recreational areas are destroyed; air and water pollution spreads; traffic jams and urban congestion become more common; and the need for centralized administrative controls to provide services to a steadily enlarging clientele reduces personal freedom. The authors might also have stressed that population growth aggravates a great many other social problems we face: unemployment due to automation; the piling up of the poor in urban and rural backwaters; the strain on educational facilities; spiralling racial tensions.

Yet the Days are surely correct in distinguishing sharply between the drastic economic impact of population growth in the underdeveloped world and its less tangible effects on the quality of life in the United States. Catholics and others who take an absolutist position on population issues may go on advancing arguments designed to minimize the role of population growth in retarding economic progress in the underdeveloped world, but the arguments will remain dubious. For when all the misconceptions are cleared away, it becomes brutally apparent that there is no alternative to a decline in population growth, and that the only ways to achieve such a decline are birth control or a relaxation of death control. It is to the credit of the absolutists that they at least draw back from insisting starkly that the latter alternative be chosen.

QUESTIONS AND STUDY SUGGESTIONS

1. What major myths or fallacies are connected with the population problem?
2. Contrast the causes and potential effects of rapid population growth in the advanced and underdeveloped countries. What is the relationship between economic progress and population growth?
3. How do the "optimists" and "alarmists" view the resolution of the population problem in the long run?

Reading 5

The Price System

Lawrence C. Murdoch, Jr., Federal Reserve Bank of Philadelphia

The price system is perhaps the most fundamental institution of a capitalistic economy. This reading provides a simple and incisive explanation of how a competitive price system would function. However, because business firms and labor unions have acquired varying degrees of market power, the price system is actually less responsive to consumer wants than would be the case with "completely free enterprise." Furthermore, big business and labor unions cause a divergence between private and social interests. Finally, government modifies the price system by providing certain goods and services which the price system is incapable of producing, by altering the distribution of income, and by boosting demand as needed to correct for mass unemployment.

One day in the fall of 1961 a clerk dropped twelve letters in the mail. They were all on White House stationery and they all carried the same message. President Kennedy was writing to ask the presidents of our major steel companies not to raise their prices.

In Detroit recently we have seen a single union negotiate wages for an entire industry. It will happen again when the steel workers' contract comes up for renewal. In fact, such negotiations are going on all the time.

To most of us these are not momentous events.

But these events—the letters, the union-management negotiations—have a large significance for all Americans. They point up the kind of changes that take place in our economic system and one of the characteristics of our system—namely, adaptability to change.

The changes have been gradual and may not be too noticeable, but the economic system we call free enterprise today is different than it was yesterday.

For one thing, it isn't quite so free as it used to be. Some people think this is good, some

think this is bad. It certainly has happened for understandable reasons.

In order to see where our society is now, we should take a look at what it might be like if we had completely free enterprise.

COMPLETELY FREE ENTERPRISE

How would such an economy work? For one answer, let's flash back to Scotland in the year 1776. At the University of Edinburgh, Adam Smith is writing a book. He is writing about an invisible hand. He says everybody has an invisible hand on his shoulder leading him to his job and on shopping trips.

Smith said people work best in their own self-interest. So let them do just that and all society will benefit. It was almost by magic, as if an invisible hand were at work.

Hands off business! Smith told the government. Let people out of their strait jackets. With complete freedom, efficient firms and individuals will prosper and the inefficient will fail.

The invisible hand—or at least the muscle on

From **The Price System,** Federal Reserve Bank of Philadelphia, January, 1962. Reprinted by permission.

the invisible hand—is prices. Prices are what make a free enterprise system operate.

Adam Smith said that free prices would insure that factories produced the things people wanted most. Here's how it would happen.

Let's say people especially wanted hunting boots and there weren't many around. People would be willing to pay more—and the price of hunting boots would rise.

Making and selling hunting boots would become more profitable and more companies would go into the business. They would be able to pay higher wages and could attract workers away from less profitable industries. Workers, you see, are sellers—they sell their labor—and, of course, they want to get the highest possible price.

The makers of hunting boots would also be able to pay higher prices for machinery and higher interest for loans. So the output of hunting boots would increase because the boot makers were able to bid men, money, and machines away from less profitable industries. And what would these industries be? Why the ones that made things people didn't want so much.

Now, suppose people suddenly changed their minds about hunting boots—lost interest and weren't buying as many. Profits would decline. Some companies would leave the business; some workers would find jobs making something that was more in demand. Production of hunting boots would fall. Producers would try to attract more buyers by cutting prices.

You see how prices going up and going down might keep production in line with demand. And it could work for bread or watches or anything.

Free prices also would insure that things would be produced in the most efficient way.

Take the case of two firms making the same product—toothpaste. One firm is very efficient, the other is not. The efficient firm would be able to make toothpaste at much less cost and, as a result, it could either charge a lower price or make a bigger profit. In either case, the efficient firm could eventually put the inefficient one out of business.

Free prices would also reward good workers and provide an incentive for them to do their best.

The most skilled, most experienced workers and managers are the most valuable to their employers and they would get higher wages—in a free enterprise economy, that is. With their higher wages, they could buy more goods and service than the less efficient workers could.

It sounds pretty desirable, doesn't it? Freely moving prices making sure that the things people want most are produced, in the most efficient way, and that the best workers are better paid.

But that's not all. A free enterprise economy would steam along at full employment. The production and demand for all things would balance at a point where there would be jobs for everyone.

As we said, it was all due to each of us doing what is best for us individually and to prices moving freely in markets where individual buyers and sellers had no control. Everybody had to accept the prices that supply and demand set.

Prices still do a large part of the job that they were supposed to do. But their actual behavior is different in ways that are important, and merit exploration.

Several things have happened. In some cases our society has tried to improve the free price system. We have asked governments to take over some jobs the price system did poorly. In other instances we—employers, workers, consumers, and taxpayers—have tried to circumvent the free price system for very understandable reasons.

THE BUSINESSMAN

Self-interest, as indicated above, has always been a motivating force in our price system. Since the verdict of supply and demand could make or break a business, it is understandable that businessmen tried to gain some influence over prices at which they buy and sell.

Firms must make a profit or they fail. Making a profit is selling something for more than it costs to make it—and it's not as easy as it sounds.

Suppose your competitor finds a way to make and sell something cheaper than you can. You have to go along or you lose your customers. But unless you also get your costs down, there will be no more profits. And pretty soon, no more business. So you try to create a market at your price.

But how? You can't fix a price for a product

if someone else can sell the same thing for less. One way is to make your product different or at least seem different.

Suppose your company makes salt—just plain salt. You must sell at the free market price for salt, whatever it may be.

Then you get an idea. You add a secret ingredient—or you package it more attractively. Your product is now different. You don't have to sell at the price of just plain salt any more.

Firms have also gained some control over their prices by growth and merger. Large firms usually have more influence over price than small firms because they produce such a large percentage of the total supply of a product. Large firms can buy their supplies cheaper because they buy in great quantities. Large firms can advertise more. These are some of the factors that tend to give them more say over the prices at which they sell.

Large firms often take the lead in setting prices for an industry. Smaller firms usually don't want to take on the "big boy" in a price war so their prices often fall into line.

Influence over prices is greater in some industries than in others—although most businesses have little influence over prices.

Where price influence is strong, a drop in demand usually does not bring about a simultaneous drop in prices. There is one bug, however. Since prices don't fall with demand, production falls more sharply.

THE WORKER

Adam Smith felt that wages as well as prices should be determined freely. It would happen like this. When there were more workers than jobs, wages would fall. Cheaper labor would then encourage hiring and sooner or later everybody would find work at the new lower wage level. When jobs were plentiful relative to workers, wages would rise. Where wages were highest, relatively, labor—the better workers in fact—would be attracted.

But workers, too, hesitated over putting complete trust in the market system. They, also, have tried to control the price of their services. No one can do this by himself so workers have joined together in unions. Workers have long expected collective bargaining to raise their income, taking it for granted that a higher price for labor means larger payrolls.

Today, pretty largely, the wages of workers are determined—either directly or indirectly—by union-management negotiations. As a result, wages are likely to reflect the bargaining power of unions as well as workers' skill and experience.

This is one of the reasons wage rates no longer fall when demand for labor slackens. This, of course, is what the workers set out to accomplish. There is one bug, however. Since wages don't fall when demand does, employment drops perhaps more than it might otherwise.

THE GOVERNMENT

Governments, too, have been interfering with the free price system. Private demand and prices do not do some jobs at all, such as running an army or providing police and fire protection. Various governments have taken over these jobs.

We said that the free price system is supposed to reward the best workers. But what about the inefficient workers and those who can't work at all? We can't let them starve, so governments often care for those who can't make a go of it under the price system.

Adam Smith said that recessions in business were not the result of the price system itself, but because the price system was not completely free to do its work. The prescription for recession was for government to keep hands off the economy. The free price system would cure itself in time, it was reasoned.

Then came the deep, prolonged depression of the 1930s. Economists of the Adam Smith school thought the Depression was the result of imperfections in the free price system. Unemployment existed because wages were too high, they said. Get those wages down, get government out of business and there will be enough new demand for labor to put all workers back on the job.

Other economists took a different approach. They emphasized demand and de-emphasized prices and wages. In effect, they said leave prices and wages as they are and get people back to work by boosting demand.

Boosting demand was a job for the government, they said. Government was called on to abandon its traditional hands-off policy and do something.

Well, government did step in then and has in every recession since. Basically, government tries to spend more when others—businessmen and consumers—are spending less. This extra spending helps to buoy business and employment. And, of course, it also keeps prices from falling, putting less burden on the price system to adjust the economy.

In conclusion, the theory of freely fluctuating prices, considered essential by Adam Smith and other economists, has never been practiced faithfully and precisely. Partly by evolution, partly by purposeful action, business, labor and government have gained some influence over prices. Actually, therefore, prices and wages are not so responsive to changes in demand as is sometimes theoretically assumed.

QUESTIONS AND STUDY SUGGESTIONS

1. As Adam Smith envisioned it, how would a price system characterized by "completely free enterprise" negotiate the efficient production of those goods which consumers wanted most?
2. In what specific ways does the price system now deviate from "completely free enterprise"? What are the economic implications of these deviations?
3. Discuss the several ways in which government modifies or supplements the functioning of the price system.

Reading 6

Consumer Spending: The Inverted Wedding Cake Theory

Federal Reserve Bank of Philadelphia

Readings 6–11 provide us with important insights about the character and functioning of the three major aggregates of our economy—consumers, businesses, and government. In Reading 6 the notion that material wants are satiable is rejected and changes in the character and composition of consumer spending which have occurred as our society has become increasingly affluent are outlined. We find that the pattern of consumer wants has shifted from food and shelter to durable goods, and finally to education, services, and travel. The next level of consumer wants may well emphasize the social goods and services provided through government.

From "Consumer Spending: The Inverted Wedding Cake Theory," **Business Review**, Federal Reserve Bank of Philadelphia, March, 1964. Reprinted by permission.

A well-known explanation of our recent below-potential rate of output is that the American consumer is sated with goods. Total demand is said to be lethargic because so many families have all the houses, cars and washing machines they need.

SATIABILITY OF WANTS?

At first thought, this argument seems in conflict with common sense. We know human wants are capable of almost infinite expansion. Once the income to satisfy a certain want becomes available, another appears quickly. When a starving man gets a meal, he begins to think about an overcoat; when an executive gets a new sports car, visions of country clubs and pleasure boats dance into view.

So how can consumers be sated? Yet the argument persists—and our production rate is below potential.

Old-time economists observed that patterns of consumer spending changed as income increased over the long sweep of history. Perhaps this also is true in short periods of time. The myriad wants of individuals can be grouped loosely into several basic levels. Recent experience seems to indicate that when income is available to satisfy one level another level appears very quickly. The levels build up like the layers of a cake. Since each new level involves a greater number of increasingly complex wants, the layers might resemble an inverted wedding cake.

Thus consumers can be sated at one level of wants but not in the over-all sense. Even this may have an important effect on growth, however.

FIRST AND SECOND LEVELS: NECESSITIES

The first and most fundamental level of wants involves food. Once this want is satisfied, a second level appears—clothing and some sort of shelter. Since these physical wants are essential to survival, they often are called "necessities." By the end of World War II, necessity wants were satisfied and on a replacement basis for a great majority of our population. In 1946 consumers spent about 23 percent of their budget on food and 15 percent for clothing. The most recent figures are 18 percent and 10 percent, respectively. People are devoting a larger share

of income to housing today than they did in 1946 but this reflects the great increase in suburban home ownership, a relative luxury compared to basic shelter.

THIRD LEVEL: DURABLES

Then in the early postwar period a third level appeared. In it were such things as automobiles, appliances and new houses. People were unable to satisfy such wants during the depression for lack of income, and during the War for lack of production. In the latter 1940s, production met pent-up demand and easy credit in the market place. A decade-long buying spree resulted and the economy enjoyed substantial prosperity.

By 1957 or 1958 this third tier of wants was fairly well satisfied. There was one car on the road for every two people over 18; more than 90 percent of all homes had major appliances, almost two-thirds of all families owned their homes. Most durable goods and houses purchased since the 1950s have been to take the place of an older item already in use. In spite of the recent glowing reports from Detroit, consumers are using less than 5 percent of their budget to purchase automobiles, compared with 6.1 percent in 1955 and 5.5 percent in 1950.

FOURTH LEVEL: "LIFE ENRICHMENT"

Then, in the late 1950s, a fourth level of wants received increasing emphasis. It could be called the "life-enriching" strata. If the other levels might be said to feature physical satisfactions—the nourishment, comfort, safety and transportation of the human body—this one emphasizes psychological needs such as recognition, achievement, and self-realization. This fourth level includes a tremendous variety of goods and services, many with a strong element of "luxury." Among them are vacation trips, hunting and fishing paraphernalia, the best medical and dental care, hi-fi, "Ivy League" college education, entertainment, domestic help, hobbies and all manner of things cultural. Luxury versions of basic necessities also are covered here: gourmet foods, professionally decorated homes by Sears, Roebuck or Dorothy Draper, and the latest styles in clothing.

We don't mean to imply that the consumer

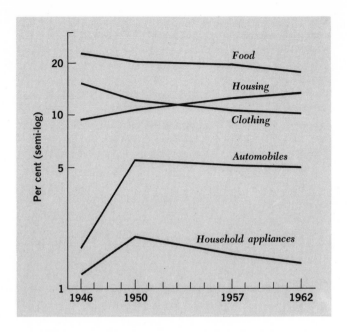

Figure 6–1. Spending for various items as a percentage of total consumer outlays.

never before bought such items or that he is no longer interested in things on the first three levels. The point is that the average family is devoting a significantly larger percentage of its income to satisfying these fourth-level wants. From 1957 to 1962 personal income increased 26 percent. In comparison, expenditures for medical expenses increased 40 percent; foreign travel, 47 percent; higher education, 80 percent.

Because there is a great variety of almost interchangeable goods and services on the fourth level, demand does not seem to have the single-minded focus that it does on the lower levels. There is no substitute for food, clothing and shelter if you haven't any; neither is there an effective substitute for an automobile or television set if you have your heart set on one. On the other hand, many fourth-level luxuries are substitutable, one for another. A vacation trip to Atlantic City could well be a last minute replacement for an outboard motor boat. Or you could easily change your mind and grill a steak in the backyard instead of taking the family out to a restaurant.

With consumers devoting a greater portion

of their budget to such mercurial wants, marketing has become more difficult. The consumer of today is harder to figure out, more difficult to anticipate, harder to sell. Possibly our economy would grow faster if more marketing and advertising efforts were raised from a type of "hammering" appropriate for the third level to relatively sophisticated and subtle fourth-level appeals.

The step up to the fourth level means that a greater percentage of total consumer spending is devoted to services which bulk large there, while goods dominate the first three levels. As a result 41 percent of the consumer budget now goes for services compared to 32 percent in 1946.

A FIFTH LEVEL?

Will consumers raise their sights to a fifth level of wants as their income increases, or will they continue to embrace a never-ending procession of luxuries and personal services—many still to be invented—on the fourth level?

A fifth level probably would involve wants that can be achieved best by collective action.

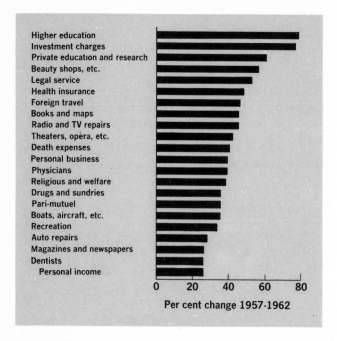

Figure 6–2.   The fast-growing fourth level of consumption.

In other words, consumers may be spending more of their incomes on taxes with which to pay for Government action against such universal enemies as disease, ignorance, crime and prejudice. Indeed the trend has already begun. In 1957, federal and state and local personal taxes paid came to 12 percent of personal income. In 1962 the figure had risen to 13 percent with the state and local bite increasing most rapidly. It is likely that this trend will continue as reductions in federal income taxes are more than offset by growth in tax rates levied by other units.

After filling our stomachs, our clothes closets, our garages, our teeth and our minds, we now may seek to insure the health, safety and leisure to enjoy more fully the good things on the first four levels.

QUESTIONS AND STUDY SUGGESTIONS

1. Briefly describe the five levels of consumer spending. Relate these levels to the satiability of consumer wants. Does available evidence suggest that the satiability of consumer wants is a cause of slow economic growth?

2. What is the probable impact upon (*a*) resource allocation and (*b*) the role of the public sector of the economy as consumers move to higher levels of wants?

Reading 7

The Corporation and the American Future

Andrew Hacker, Professor of Government, Cornell University

In a very real sense the economy of the United States is "corporate capitalism"; the increasing concentration of economic power in the hands of a relatively few giant firms is making the corporation a very powerful, perhaps even dominant, force in our society. In Reading 7 Andrew Hacker ponders the question: "Whom does the power of the corporation represent?" His answer is that the giant corporation reflects the curious circumstance of power without people. "The corporation . . . is power—the power of productive assets—without a human constituency." The implications of this phenomenon for the character of our economy and the individuals which comprise it are then perceptively examined.

Since the end of World War II the corporate form has emerged as the characteristic institution of American society. Its rise has rendered irrelevant time-honored theories of politics and economics, and its explosive growth has created a new breed of man whose behavior can no longer be accounted for by conventional rules of conduct.

There is still time for reflection on these developments. America is not yet dominated by the corporate way of life; indeed, were this so we would all be painfully aware of the fact, and discussion of it would be superfluous. As matters now stand the corporation is central to the nation's economy. The 150 largest own two-thirds of the productive assets of the nation.

But there remains a substantial segment of the economy that cannot be called corporate in any meaningful sense. The small business community stands alongside corporate America, and it still embraces most of the working and entrepreneurial population. Indeed, the 100 largest manufacturing corporations employ less than six million persons out of the total labor force, and the 500 largest provide jobs for only about four million more. The preponderance of employed Americans, then, do not owe their livelihoods directly to corporate America, and it will be some time before even a simple majority of them do.

Yet all signs are that the future lies with the great corporate institution. It is growing in wealth, in size, in power. No one can seriously contend that there will be a rebirth of small business or a contraction of corporate growth. The corporation, to be sure, is not at this time the typical institution of our economy or our society. There are too many other social and economic forms, noncorporate in character, to permit the assertion that General Motors or United States Steel represents our institutional life today. Refuge must rather be taken in the suggestion that the corporation is "prototypical"—typical not of what exists now, but rather of that which will be at some future time. To study the corporate form, therefore, is to speculate on the America of a generation yet to

From Andrew Hacker, "The Corporation and the American Future," **Challenge**, January, 1964, pp. 14–17. Reprinted by permission from **Challenge**, the Magazine of Economic Affairs.

come. From contemporary reality must be extrapolated the trends that will become increasingly accentuated.

CASE OF AMERICAN ELECTRIC

The problem, which extends beyond the simple one of definition, may be illustrated by an imaginary conversation taking place not too many years from now. The setting and the topic of the discussion happen to be political, but the dialogue would take much the same form were it extended to other spheres where corporate power is exercised.

By 1972 American Electric had completed its last stages of automation: employees were no longer necessary. Raw materials left on the loading platform were automatically transferred from machine to machine, and the finished products were deposited at the other end of the factory ready for shipment. AE's purchasing, marketing and general management functions could be handled by 10 directors with the occasional help of outside consultants and contractors.

Beginning in 1962 AE's employee pension fund had started investing its capital in AE stock. Gradually it bought more and more of the company's shares on the open market, and by 1968 it was the sole owner of AE. As employees became eligible for retirement—some of them prematurely, due to the introduction of automation—the fund naturally liquidated its capital to provide pensions. But instead of reselling its AE shares on the open market, the fund sold the stock to AE itself, which provided the money for pensions out of current income. By 1981 the last AE employee had died and the pension fund was dissolved. At this time, too, AE became the sole owner of its shares. It had floated no new issues, preferring to engage in self-financing through earnings.

By 1982 the 10 directors decided that AE would be well served by the passage of legislation restricting the imports of certain electrical equipment. They therefore secured the services of a public relations firm specializing in political campaigns. The objective was to educate the public and sway grassroots sentiment so that Congress would respond by passing the required bill. The public relations firm was given a retainer of $1 million and authorized to spend up to $5 million more on advertising and related activities.

Within months the public began to hear about the dire consequences that would follow the importation of alien generators. National security, national prosperity and the nation's way of life were threatened by a flood of foreign goods. The public relations firm placed several hundred advertisements in newspapers and magazines, and almost a thousand on television. At least 50 citizens' committees "spontaneously" arose to favor the legislation, and over 200 existing groups passed resolutions in its support. Lectures were given to women's clubs and films were shown in high schools. By the end of the year—an election year—public sentiment had been aroused and hardly a Congressman was unaware of the popular ferment.

The bill was introduced in both chambers and a good majority of Senators and Representatives, abiding by the wishes of their constituents, voted for it. The President signed the bill and it became law. AE's profits were substantially higher the following year.

THE INVESTIGATION

A group of Senators, however, were curious about what had been going on and they decided to investigate AE's foray into the political arena. One of the directors was happy to testify, for he knew that no law had been violated. No bribes had been offered, certainly, and no contributions to legislators' campaigns had been made. Toward the end of the inquiry, after all of the techniques employed by the company and the public relations firm had been brought out, the following colloquy took place:

Director: . . . And if we undertook these educational and political activities, it was our view that they were dictated by the company's best interests.

Senator: Now when you say that these campaigns were on behalf of the "company's" interests, I am not clear what you mean. Were you acting for your stockholders in this instance?

Director: I am afraid, Senator, that I cannot say that we were. You see, American Electric has no stockholders. The company owns all its stock itself. We bought up the last of it several years ago.

Senator: Well, if not stockholders, then were you acting as a spokesman for American Electric's employees—say, whose jobs might be endangered if foreign competition got too severe?

Director: No, sir, I cannot say that either. American Electric is a fully automated company and we have no employees.

Senator: Are you saying that this company of yours is really no more than a gigantic machine? A machine that needs no operators and appears to own itself?

Director: I suppose that is one way of putting it. I've never thought much about it.

Senator: Then, so far as I can see, all of this political pressure that you applied was really in the interests of yourself and your nine fellow directors. You spent almost $6 million of this company's money pursuing your personal political predilections.

Director: I am afraid, Senator, that now I must disagree with you. The 10 of us pay ourselves annual salaries of $100,000, year in and year out, and none of us receives any bonuses or raises if profits happen to be higher than usual in a given year. All earnings are ploughed back into the company. We feel very strongly about this. In fact, we look on ourselves as civil servants, in a way. Secondly, I could not say that the decision to get into politics was a personal wish on our part. At least eight of the 10 of us, as private citizens that is, did not favor the legislation we were supporting. As individuals most of us thought it was wrong, and not in the national interest. But we were acting in the company's interest, and in this case we knew that it was the right thing to do.

Senator: And by the "company" you don't mean stockholders or employees, because you don't have any. And you don't mean the 10 directors, because you just seem to be salaried managers which the machine hires to run its affairs. In fact, when this machine gets into politics—or indeed any kind of activity—it has interests of its own which can be quite different from the personal interests of its managers. I am afraid I find all this rather confusing.

Director: It may be confusing to you, Senator, but I may say that it has been quite straightforward to us at American Electric. We are just doing the job for which we were hired —to look out for the company's interests.

POWER WITHOUT PEOPLE

Far-fetched, to be sure, but how much so? Already, A. A. Berle tells us, the pension fund of one large corporation is buying up the stock of its parent company and is close to having a controlling interest. This corporation, he writes, "has self-contained control, and management is thus responsible to itself." Needless to say, the productive enterprise that can function without employees is not yet a reality. But automation is abolishing jobs and there is no guarantee that new positions will be created in their stead.

The questions put to corporate spokesmen center on the problem of who is represented in the exercise of corporate power, whether that power is at work in the political arena or any other segment of society. There remains in many American minds the belief that power should be representative, that the ability to control resources should act in the name of human beings if it is to be legitimate. The corporation, however, is power—the power of productive assets—without a human constituency. It has interests to promote and defend, but they are the interests of a machine more than those of the people who guide, and profit from, its workings. The managers who sit astride the corporate complexes do indeed have power; but it is the power bestowed on them by the resources of the enterprises they tend. Executives come and go, and their terms of office in the top positions are surprisingly short. But the productive assets remain, continually developing new interests to be safeguarded and new demands to be fulfilled.

The increasing irrelevance of people may be illustrated by some references to the role of the stockholder. To begin with, approximately a third of all stock purchases are held for less than six months. Thus an appreciable fraction of those who are the legal owners of corporate America are not permanent constituents of the firms in which they happen to hold shares, but rather transient investors with no sustained interest in the fortunes of the companies bearing the names on their stock certificates.

Even more important, it is no longer true that the significant owners of corporation stock are human beings whose interests are represented in the exercise of corporate power. Stockholders are now more and more not people but institutions, many of them also corporate in structure. If it is proposed that a corporation "represents" the owners of its shares, it will soon emerge that many of these owners are insurance companies, universities, banks, foundations, pension funds and investment houses. These institutions do, of course, have interests. But, again, they are not the interests of people.

That power may be rendered legitimate by demonstrating its representative quality has always been one of the foundations of democratic theory. If power is exercised by—and within—government agencies and voluntary associations, it can usually be shown that officials are elected by constituents who have consented to the uses of authority and who cast equal votes in determining the personnel and often the policies that are to prevail. Authority may be delegated rather than direct, and consent may be tacit rather than active, but the presumption remains that power in public and private life has a representative base.

SOCIAL PLURALISM

Correlative to this is the familiar pluralist model: a society composed of a multiplicity of groups and a citizenry actively engaged in the associational life. Some measure of equilibrium among forces is assumed, and if there is conflict it results in compromises not overly oppressive to any of the participants. And the groups with which we are dealing are presumed to be voluntary associations consisting of individual citizens who join together to further their common interests. Well suited to this scheme are the myriad professional, occupational, religious and other groups which speak in their members' names. Were groups such as the American Medical Association, the United Automobile Workers, the National Association for the Advancement of Colored People and the American Legion the only participants in the struggle for political and economic preferment, then the sociology of democracy would continue as an effective theory. For in cases like these it may still be assumed, in spite of tendencies toward bureaucratization, that the power of these associations is simply an extension of the individual interest and wills of their constituent members.

But when General Electric, American Telephone and Telegraph, and Standard Oil of New Jersey enter the pluralist arena, we have elephants dancing among the chickens. For corporate institutions are not voluntary associations of individuals, but rather associations of assets, and no theory yet propounded has declared that machines are entitled to a voice in the democratic process.

THE INVESTMENT DECISION

The fulcrum of corporate power, in the final analysis, is the investment decision. And the uses of capital for investment purposes are decided by small handfuls of corporate managers. They decide how much is to be spent; what products are to be made; where they are to be manufactured; and who is to participate in the processes of production. A single corporation can draw up an investment program calling for the expenditure of several billions of dollars on new plants and products. A decision such as this may well determine the quality of life for a substantial segment of society: men and materials will move across continents; old communities will decay and new ones will prosper; tastes and habits will alter; new skills will be demanded and the education of a nation will adjust itself accordingly; even government will fall into line, providing public services necessitated by corporate developments.

The American corporate system continues, in major outlines, to be capitalist in structure. Talk of a welfare state, of a mixed economy, even of a managerial revolution is of limited utility, for the fact remains that the major decisions in the economy are private. These decisions are made within closed circles, and public agencies may not intrude in any effective way.

Experience has thus far shown that public agencies set up to regulate private enterprise are soon brought to a close sympathy with the industries they were supposed to be regulating. This should occasion no great surprise. Corporations are powerful and they will use their resources to maintain a favorable climate for themselves. This is the politics of capitalism. It is not at all expressive of a conspiracy but rather a harmony of political forms and economic interests on a plane determined by the ongoing needs of corporate institutions.

NO MIDDLE GROUND

Are there alternatives to corporate capitalism? Few voices are heard nowadays suggesting the public ownership of major industries, and it is just as well, for the odds are that nationalization would end in disillusionment. The problem is that there is no real middle ground. This was known to both Adam Smith and Karl Marx, but it is a fact hard to swallow in an age that seeks reason along the course of moderation.

Suppose that America followed the British pattern and nationalized a few industries such as railroads, electricity and coal mines. But instead of becoming agencies of the public interest, these industries would soon enter service as handmaidens of the private sector of the economy. For the preponderance of economic power would remain in corporate hands, and the effective efforts would be made to ensure that the industries in the public sector were suitably docile and did not serve as vehicles for serious planning that might jeopardize corporate interests.

On the other hand, there is the extreme proposal that the state nationalize all industry, thus once and for all destroying private economic power. This was and is the Marxian prescription, offered with the full understanding that the old order must be felled with one stroke if the new is to rise from its ashes. But the problems of irresponsibility in corporate America are minor compared with those of totalitarianism, and the Marxist alternative to capitalism is hardly one that those who have known a free society can be expected to embrace with enthusiasm.

Hence the frustrations that mark any search for a middle ground. We hear much of regulation, of intervention, of planning on the part of government. But, to take only the last, who are to be the planners? What is to be their source of power, as against their legal authority, and who will give force to their decisions? And is it possible to prevent corporate institutions from seducing, capturing and otherwise infiltrating those who are mandated to plan the economy in the public interest?

THE SECOND AMERICA

The American people were not asked to consent to the rise of the corporation, yet they have had to adjust their lives to the imperatives of this pervasive institution. Not a few citizens have been recruited to corporate careers, and for them recent years have been a period of prosperity and progress. The new middle class has thus far found higher incomes and enhanced status, economic security and interesting work in the corporate world. To them society appears rational and they have few problems that can specifically be called "public" or "political." If this constituency of the corporation were able to embrace the whole of the working population, then despite the increased concentration of power it could at least be suggested that corporate America was bestowing its largesse upon all. But this is not the case.

There are losers as well as winners in the growth of corporate organization and technology. Not all who work for corporations have secure, let alone ascending, careers. The unskilled and the untrained continue to be hired at hourly wages, and then only for those hours when their services are required. Many of the unemployed are, indeed, corporate unemployed: they have been laid off from jobs they once had with corporations or have not been hired for jobs that corporate technology has been able to abolish.

By the same token trade unions are in decline, a development at least partly attributable to corporate technological innovations that have swelled the number of white-collar workers as a proportion of the employed population. Indirectly, and to some extent directly, corporate decisions have therefore both increased unemployment and diminished the role of unions. The latter consequence is a serious blow to the doctrine of social pluralism, for organized labor has been traditionally counted upon as a source of countervailing power against the strength of corporate management. Insofar as they are weakened, they deprive society of yet another check to the power of the corporation.

It may well be that two Americas are emerging, one a society protected by the corporate umbrella and the other a society whose members have failed to affiliate themselves with the dominant institutions.

What of this second America? In part it will consist of small businessmen and other independent spirits who manage to do well without corporate attachments. But, more importantly, it will be comprised of the unemployed, the ill-educated and the entire residue of human beings who are not needed by the corporate machine.

Little thought has been given to these people. How are they to earn their livings and support themselves? How will they maintain their self-esteem? If this pool grows to substantial proportions, if it finds political leadership, if it gives vent to its resentments and frustrations—then, and perhaps then only, will a force arise to challenge the great corporate institutions. For then power will meet power, the power of a mass movement confronting the power of the machine. The discard heap the machine itself created may arise to devour its progenitor.

This revolution—with or without violence, whether from the left or from the right—will only be averted if the corporation can make room in its environs for those who demand entry. Has it the jobs, the resources, the will and the imagination to achieve this? Thus far corporate America has escaped open attack be-cause the new technology is not yet at the point where its victims outnumber its beneficiaries.

But technology advances according to rules of its own, and support for the machine will diminish as accelerated automation contracts the corporate constituency. In this event the second America, the society of losers, may grow in numbers and power with increasing rapidity. The outcome may not be a pleasant one.

QUESTIONS AND STUDY SUGGESTIONS

1. What are the implications of the "power without people" problem which the author poses?

2. Explain: "The fulcrum of corporate power, in the final analysis, is the investment decision."

3. Analyze the alternatives to corporate capitalism. How does corporate capitalism affect the doctrine of social pluralism?

Reading 8

Private—But Not for Profit

Charles E. Lindblom, Professor of Economics, Yale University

The rapid growth of such nonprofit, private organizations as various foundations, mutual insurance companies, savings and loan associations, Blue Cross, private universities and research institutes, consumer and farmer cooperatives, and so forth, has been an important development in our economy in recent years. Because the "nonprofit sector" employs substantial quantities of resources, purchases a significant portion of total output, and frequently competes with the private sector, Charles Lindblom feels it is highly relevant to raise serious questions about the goals and operation of these nonprofit organizations. Who owns these institutions? How do they differ from private, profit-seeking enterprises? To whom are they responsible? What, if anything, compels these institutions to function with reasonable efficiency?

From Charles E. Lindblom, "Private—But Not for Profit!" **Challenge**, March–April, 1966, pp. 20–23. Reprinted by permission.

Excluding those who volunteer their services, one out of 20 job holders in the U.S. works for private nonprofit organizations, and these organizations purchase about $34 billion worth of goods and services. This constitutes a sizable chunk of our economy, and indications are that it is getting bigger. But what makes nonprofit organizations run? Do they draw their energies from something like the profit motive? Or are they propelled by public spirit?

The answers are less than obvious. The distinction between the private and the public sectors is always a fuzzy one. Clearly, these sectors cannot be distinguished by the importance of what they produce. The production of food, medical services and transportation—in each of which the public has an enormous stake—is largely in the private sector. But in some states much less important services, such as liquor retailing and the provision of recreational facilities, are partly in the public sector.

Nor does "public" mean governmentally controlled while "private" means free of control. "There is no unregulated industry." Moreover, because government-owned enterprises are customarily given a substantial grant of autonomy on the assumption that they will continue to be disciplined by market forces, the rigor of government control may be no greater for a government-owned enterprise than for a private corporation. It was often claimed, for example, that the effectiveness of government control over the Bank of England actually declined as a result of its nationalization in 1946.

CHARACTERISTICS OF NONPROFIT ORGANIZATIONS

It looks as though the public-private distinction has to be drawn, therefore, according to the lines of formal ownership. Into the public sector go all those enterprises owned by local, state or national government; into the private sector go all those owned by private parties.

But who owns Columbia University? Who owns Blue Cross? Who owns the RAND Corporation? They are owned neither by person nor institution. Again, therefore, the public-private distinction eludes us.

Organizations like Columbia University, the RAND Corporation and others that produce educational, scientific, medical, insurance and other services are owned neither by government nor by proprietors or stockholders. Asking who owns them is like asking who owns the State of California, the City of New York or the United States government.

The comparison is, on second thought, striking. It is as though these nonprofit organizations were little governments themselves. Like governments, they are often self-perpetuating institutions, administered by persons who somehow become officials in them without exercising any claims of ownership over them; they discharge functions in which some "public" has an interest; and they are sovereign in that they take orders neither from another institution nor from proprietors or stockholders. Indeed, they are so much like governmental organizations that some of them—a local chamber of commerce, for example—often pass for a branch of government.

But they are also like ordinary private corporations: they are run by a small group of top executives; they recruit labor competitively in the market; they often sell a product or a service in the open market; and they take on the characteristic names, structure of titles, and organizational forms of ordinary private business to a degree that almost completely obscures the difference between them and private enterprises. They are so much like ordinary private businesses that some of them—savings and loan associations, and mutual insurance companies, for example—are often assumed to be part of the private profit-seeking banking and insurance business.

Precisely who do we have in mind when we talk of nonprofit organizations? A recent study, "The Pluralistic Economy," by Eli Ginzberg, D. L. Hiestand and B. G. Reubens, classifies nonprofit organizations in this way: mutual insurance companies, savings and loan associations, trade associations, chambers of commerce, professional societies, farmers' cooperatives, consumer cooperatives, trade unions, private colleges or universities, foundations, voluntary hospitals, research organizations, churches, social clubs, Blue Cross and Blue Shield, and museums and libraries.

Consider how many of these organizations offer goods or services that are sold, or could be sold, by a profit-seeking enterprise. Insurance and savings and loan organizations offer such services. So do farmers' and consumer cooperatives, private schools and universities, hospitals, research organizations, Blue Cross and Blue Shield, museums and libraries. Trade associations and labor unions often include marketable services to their members among their other functions.

While foundations are less like ordinary business enterprises, some do publish and distribute marketable books and journals, and many provide a kind of service that is much like banking. Like private bankers, the foundations receive applications for funds to support projects; they review the merits of each request; they judge whether an investment in the proposed project will be fruitful; and they then finance the more likely projects. They typically differ from ordinary bankers, of course, in that they expect neither interest nor repayment.

Further removed from ordinary profit-seeking enterprises are social clubs and churches. But they, too, provide services, often even potentially marketable ones, to their members.

Ties between the nonprofit sector and other sectors of the economy run in all directions. Foundations, for example, often allocate much of their funds to other nonprofit organizations, like hospitals and universities. On the other hand, trade associations are often dependencies of profit-seeking enterprises and sell or give their services exclusively to them. Research organizations are drawn on heavily by both profit-seeking firms and government. Some, like the RAND Corporation, were established explicitly to serve governmental needs. Most of the output of the nonprofit sector goes, however, directly to individual consumers rather than to other productive sectors of the economy.

SIMILARITIES TO PROFIT SEEKERS

In trying to understand the useful role of nonprofit organizations in our economy, it is important to note that the profit-seeking sector of the economy is itself nonprofit in at least one important sense. Organized big business in the U.S. is governed by salaried managers whose incomes are more dependent on salaries, bonuses and other perquisites than on their share of dividends to owners.

Thus the manager of a big corporation is not much motivated by effective pressures from stockholders, from whose controls he has in large part escaped. Nor, because his income does not vary directly with profits, has he an immediate, direct and obvious interest in profit maximization. The standards he tries to meet are those of the managerial group of which he is himself a member, and his income and advancement depend on his reputation in the eyes of his colleagues rather than on profits. And they will judge him not only by the profits he makes for his company, but also by sales volume, by innovations he achieves in product or method, and by many other evidences they have of his competence, including his ways of meeting the particular problems of his company.

There is not much difference, then, between his motives and those of top management in Blue Cross or in a university or trade union. All these managers are alike, playing a conventionalized game with a prescribed method of scoring, valid only because it is in fact agreed to within the management community.

SOME DIFFERENCES

But if the profit-seeking sector and the nonprofit sector are so alike, what differences separate them?

The most obvious difference is, of course, that in the profit-seeking sector the users of the service pay the bills, while in the nonprofit sector others either share them or pay them. The "consumer" of the services of the Ford Foundation may be either the scholar whose work is subsidized or the public for whose benefit the research is undertaken. But it is the estate of Henry Ford that pays the bills. By contrast, it is the consumers of automobiles who pay the bills for the Ford Motor Company. Hence, the most obvious difference between the profit and nonprofit enterprise is that the nonprofit enterprise is established by people who wish to see more of a particular good or service produced than the beneficiaries of that service are willing or able to pay for. A nonprofit organization, in other words, is a device for the private subsidization of the production of selected goods and services.

Many nonprofit organizations, such as universities, derive only part of their income from their "customers" and need other contributions to remain afloat. But they do not wish to ignore the great contribution of "sales" to their solvency and program.

What about those nonprofit organizations that presumably can survive—or in fact do survive—exclusively on the proceeds from the sale or product of their services? The RAND Corporation, for example, can presumably support itself entirely through earnings from the research it provides for the U.S. Air Force and other agencies. Some colleges are wholly dependent on tuition payments, while some hospitals are wholly dependent on charges made to their patients. In these cases, what purpose is served by the nonprofit form of organization?

From the point of view of the organization itself, the answer is that the nonprofit status carries with it certain legal privileges. Nonprofit organizations typically do not pay income, property and certain other taxes; they escape liability for contributions for unemployment compensation and social security; they are not subject to the legal obligations to bargain with unions that govern private profit-seeking companies; and they enjoy certain other minor privileges and favors of government.

SOCIAL PURPOSE

But this does not help us decide whether any useful social purpose is served by the nonprofit form of organization for those enterprises that can or do support themselves wholly by sales of services. Perhaps the legal privileges granted to such organizations are a mistake.

Do the policies followed by nonprofit organizations—those capable of supporting themselves from sales receipts—differ from profit-seeking businesses? Both organizations will be greatly disciplined by their customers, for they can survive only if they satisfy these customers. Both will be regulated in countless ways by government. In both cases there will be a residual area for the exercise of discretionary managerial authority. But insofar as the manager of the nonprofit organization can exercise discretion, he will be guided by somewhat different and less commercial considerations than the profit-seeking manager for whom accumulation of capital, profit making, sales maximization and cost reduction are prominent themes.

To be sure, the distinction can easily be overdrawn. Nonprofit organizations often seek, for no good reason at all, growth for growth's sake and come to act very much like sales-promoting private entrepreneurs. And the profit-seeking entrepreneur often sees a long-term virtue in a passion for the quality of his products.

The difference remains, however. Most of us believe, for example, that nonprofit pharmaceutical houses (should there be such) would not exercise the discretion that consumer ignorance and government inattention grant to them to promote the sale of dubious and potentially dangerous or fatal medicines simply because it is profitable to do so. The nonprofit form is useful, therefore, whenever we want to restrain or weaken certain commercial compulsions and temptations, as is often the case especially in education, health and research work.

STANDARDS OF PERFORMANCE

Still, there are standards we can apply to the performance of nonprofit organizations. Viewing them as business enterprises, we can ask: Are they efficient? Viewing them as little governments, we can ask: Are they responsible? Neither question has ever claimed much attention in the United States. No large group has ever been greatly concerned with whether the charitable donations of those who support various nonprofit enterprises are efficient in producing results. It is the donors' business to worry about that, we have apparently thought.

But donors themselves have been little concerned. Sometimes they are not at all concerned because they are dead, the nonprofit organization being supported by an estate. In a distressing number of cases, moreover, living donors wish simply to discharge their moral obligations by a gift of suitable size, and do not care whether the donation ever bears fruit. In fact, through such devices as the United Fund, they both escape from having to choose carefully among alternative organizations and excuse the recipient organization from accounting to them for an efficient use of funds.

Cornuelle, in his recent book on the nonprofit sector, "Reclaiming the American Dream," reports the case of a school for poor mountain boys spending so much per pupil that it would have been cheaper to send them all to Eton and pay their travel cost to England. His judgment is: The independent sector "seems to drift, moving blindly and without discipline. Its power lies raw and undeveloped. It often seems listless, sluggish, passive and defensive. The commercial and government sectors have outrun it."

Presumably the nonprofit organizations that

sell their product are relatively more efficient. But the disciplinary power of dissatisfied consumers is strong or weak depending upon the alternatives to which the dissatisfied can turn. For hospitals, the choice is often limited in any one area; for colleges and universities, choice is increasingly limited by the disparity between the size of the college-age population and number of available institutions. Choice is also limited when services provided by an organization are tied to membership in a business association, trade union, church or club.

Even when customers are free to reject an unsatisfactory product from a nonprofit organization, the organization itself may still be kept afloat by contributions. Cornuelle has suggested that the nonprofit sector needs the discipline of competition with government, but even he recognizes the tendency for government and the nonprofit sector to mark out their own separate spheres rather than to compete.

SOCIAL RESPONSIBILITY

Nor is the public much concerned about whether these little "governments" discharge their functions with a sense of social responsibility. Since nonprofit organizations do not enjoy powers of compulsion over the citizenry, what they do and how they do it is thought to be the private affair of the organizations themselves and of their donors. But can we pass over the question of responsibility in the case of a huge organization such as the Ford Foundation that is dominant enough in its field to change substantially the character of American universities? We have not begun to think through the problem of social responsibility of those nonprofit organizations powerful enough to matter.

The problem of responsibility becomes poignant when we reflect that one of the great virtues of the profit-seeking enterprise is, paradoxically, its irresponsibility. The business enterprise in the marketplace is an institution free to pursue objectives, like the production of yachts, of no use to the majority. It is also an instrument for proceeding heartlessly with innovation by throwing the cost of innovation— in the form of destroyed jobs, for example— onto people who are powerless to veto the decision to innovate. In these respects, the business enterprise is a device for escaping the constraints that direct democratic control over decisions would impose: and this kind of irresponsibility, though it poses problems, is endorsed almost everywhere. The same kind of irresponsibility is also to be endorsed for the nonprofit sector and for the same reasons.

But this does not mean that any and all kinds of irresponsibility are to be applauded in either the profit or nonprofit sector.

Here, of course, there can be no question about whether management ought to serve the public interest. The question is: What public interest and by whom defined? If not by government and not solely by the standards of the management community, by whom or what and how?

QUESTIONS AND STUDY SUGGESTIONS

1. What do you feel are the basic advantages and disadvantages of (a) profit-seeking and (b) nonprofit organizations from society's point of view?
2. Discuss the problems involved in measuring the performance of nonprofit institutions.
3. To whom is a private profit-seeking firm responsible? To whom is a unit of government responsible? To whom is a nonprofit organization responsible?

Reading 9

The "Primrose Path" of Centralism

National Association of Manufacturers

Readings 9 and 10 present two divergent views on the economic role of government. The conservative view of the National Association of Manufacturers in Reading 9 holds that government—particularly the Federal government—is playing much too large a role in our economy. Centralism entails a myriad of specific undesirable consequences, as, for example, the inefficient administration of the "truly national tasks," the excessively high cost of Federal programs, the necessity of punitive tax rates, and the destruction of the balance of powers between the Federal government and the states. Most important, however, is the fact that the rationale of centralism imposes no effective limitations upon the powers of the Federal government; hence, "there is no natural stopping place short of a monolithic, completely authoritarian state." Thus the greatest danger of the centralist philosophy is that it poses a fundamental threat to individual freedoms. "Centralism, under a cloak of humanitarianism, is really contemptuous of the ability of the people to think for themselves, to handle their own affairs, and to solve their own problems."

In little more than 100 years the United States has developed from a primarily agricultural economy into the world's leading industrial nation. Our standard of living is higher than that of any other country. We are the recognized leaders of the free world. And the outlook is for further growth and a continuing improvement in our living standards.

Much depends, however, on the relationship between the government and the economy. Historically, we have in the main adhered to the principles of a free enterprise economy. The action of prices in the free market has determined the goods and services that were produced, allocated resources among industries, adjusted consumption to supply and distributed the product among the members of society. Individual ambition has been regarded as the most universal, reliable, and powerful of human motives, and each individual has enjoyed freedom of action to satisfy his wants and to make voluntary decisions concerning his economic problems as he deemed best. It has generally been held that the aggregate of such decisions would result in wiser solutions of the economic problems of our society than would decisions imposed by an outside agency.

Yet, among those calling themselves "liberals" today, there is articulate support of the "outside agency" approach, and the agency which they consider most competent, and to be primarily relied upon, to solve all problems on almost all subjects is the federal government. In this writing, the doctrine of extreme reliance on the federal government is called "centralism."

As such attitudes spread, correct perspective on the relation of government activity to our

From Government Economy Committee, National Association of Manufacturers, **The "Primrose Path" of Centralism**, New York, 1960, abridged. Reprinted by permission.

economic growth becomes increasingly important. The high cost of the federal government, the growing size and scope of its organization and operations, and the mounting criticism of its performance of essential national services in face of the Communist menace and increasing world tensions, are matters which gravely concern the security of the nation and the well-being of its citizens. And the impact of federal policies on our economic life is of utmost significance to our purpose, our strength and our future.

FEDERAL RESPONSIBILITIES

The broad national purpose in establishing the form of government under which we have lived since 1789 was never better stated than in the Preamble to the Constitution:

We, the people of the United States, in order to form a more perfect union, establish justice, insure domestic tranquility, provide for the common defense, promote the general welfare, and secure the blessings of liberty to ourselves and our posterity, do ordain and establish this Constitution of the United States.

The people, the states, and the United States were thus recognized as collaborators in this organization of a new political and social order. They were made jointly responsible for successful achievement of the national purpose here proclaimed and each party to the compact had its own sphere of performance. Certain powers, with accompanying responsibilities, were delegated to the United States, to be exercised by the Congress, and with conscious effort to limit the authority and scope of the central government, those powers, with their accompanying responsibilities, which were not delegated by the Constitution to the United States, nor prohibited by it to the states, were reserved to the states respectively, or to the people.

The intention was to establish a balance between the powers, responsibilities, and rights of central and state governments, respectively. While a completely static balance was never visualized, it was expected that insistence by the states and by the federal government upon their respective constitutional rights and responsibilities would be a check on too great concentration of power at either point. However, for two reasons the federal government has become increasingly important since the Civil War.

The first of these is that during the first half of the 20th Century the two most devastating wars in the world's history occurred. Our participation in these wars involved an expansion of the federal administrative and fiscal structure which could not be reduced immediately, after either event, to the pre-war level. This sheer quantitative enlargement of the federal government could have been dealt with in time, however, by insistent state pressure for restoration of better balance in their favor.

The second reason for relative state inaction has been more serious and more insidious. It was the emergence, in the depression of the 1930s, of a political and economic philosophy which, since then, has been increasingly claimed as the criterion of good public policy by a number of academicians, politicians and other opinion makers, who in turn have convinced a good many citizens. The philosophy of centralism has thus provided the rationalized basis for the steady expansion of the size, power, and cost of the federal government. But it has eroded the sense of responsibility of the states and diminished their zeal to fulfill their constitutional destiny as sovereign members of a union of states. It has caused the people to forget that they are the residual repository of sovereignty under the Constitution.

Centralism provides grants and loans to persons and to states and their political subdivisions. It participates in the support of non-federal governmental functions and of private economic activities. Instead of creating an economic climate which would help citizens and communities by motivating them to help themselves, centralism makes use of distress and natural state-by-state differences to spread and strengthen federal power. Centralism nourishes itself by weakening the strength and independence of the states and their political subdivisions. It entrenches itself by redistributing among the less productive, the income and wealth of the highly productive, the savers and the investors. It fosters, doles, and feeds dependency, because it thrives on them.

Centralism recognizes no effective limitations on federal powers, which means that while this doctrine is operative and persuasive in the formulation of public policy, the road is open for unrestricted federal expansion. As centralism strengthens, state sovereignty diminishes.

Unless a popular reaction against centralism is generated and made manifest, there is no natural stopping place short of a monolithic, completely authoritarian state.

CONSEQUENCES OF CENTRALISM

Even without further expansion, the doctrine of centralism has resulted in a federal government structure too big for competent management, too powerful for the best relationship between the people and their government, and too grasping of both resources and responsibilities to permit the fullest flowering and independence of the private economy. Some of the salient evidence of this indictment is summarized herewith.

1. Diversion of Attention and Effort from the Truly National Tasks

The most serious consequence of centralism is one which has received little attention. Apparently overlooked, or at least disregarded, in the hastening course of centralist headway is a factor vital to the defense and survival of the nation. This is the diversion of the time and energy of federal officials—the Executive and the Congress—into so many byways of purpose that efficient discharge of those duties and functions which *only* the federal government can carry out have suffered.

2. Excessive Cost of Centralism

A second serious consequence of overloading federal officials with matters that belong elsewhere is the heavy cost which such a policy has imposed on the people. It is axiomatic that the most expensive way to get anything done is for the federal government to do it. There are various reasons for this result:

First, the full cost of federal undertakings is often not set out in the beginning. Popular acceptance is more easily obtained by under-estimates of cost, by small initial appropriations and expenditures which get the project under way without too much objection. Once the commitment has been made, the cost estimates go up and up, the time schedule for completion is extended, and after it is too late the people discover that the programs and projects which seemed at first to be good bargains are anything but that.

Second, Washington must operate by remote control, which is seldom highly efficient. Supervision must filter down through various bureaucratic layers which delay and impede decision making. Federal appropriations for various programs tend to be more lavish than would be provided if financial responsibility were located closer to the job to be done.

Third, wage and hour requirements, which are based on standards prevailing in metropolitan areas, increase materially the cost of federally-aided construction projects for small communities. The people will discover how deeply this two-edged sword cuts if they allow themselves to be drawn into any scheme for general federal aid to school construction.

Fourth, the people tend to be more tolerant of large federal appropriations and more unconcerned about excessive costs because of the persistent illusion that federal money is "free money." However painfully aware they may be in general of the heavy federal tax burden, the penalty of excessive cost of specific programs is seldom brought home to them. The real impact is concealed by the lack of connection, in the Congressional procedures, between spending and taxing legislation. In city councils and state legislatures, this connection is more clearly and quickly identified, and hence the relation of program benefit and cost is more soberly weighed. This is why the battle cry of the pressure groups is—"On to Washington, for that is where the money is easy to get."

3. Retention of Restrictive, Punitive Tax Rates

The cost involved in supporting government programs so unlimited as to deal with any and every problem or difficulty that may affect individuals or communities naturally becomes a justification for the retention or imposition of excessive tax rates. Furthermore, under the influence of centralism, the pressure is always to keep spending in pace with revenues, and professions of concern about the weight of the tax load are washed out by putting tax rate reform at the bottom of any list of things to be done with the government's finances.

4. Expansion of Federal Power through Grants, Loans or Subsidies

The objective of centralism is expansion of federal power and control. The underlying rationalization of this objective is a conviction that the federal government should lead and support the people. This necessarily implies a distrust of state and local governments, and a belief that citizens are too dilatory in action and deficient in grasp to face the issues which centralist planners deem important.

The depression of the 1930s left a framework of fiscal relationships between the federal government and the states, and the government and the people, which provided an ideal opportunity for the centralists. Various federal grant, loan and subsidy programs established in that period as rescue operations to meet economic emergencies faced by the states and the people, offered ready-made patterns and specific tools for centralist purposes. Where the major emphasis of these original programs was relief, a shift of focus was apparent in their extension and in the introduction of new aid programs. The new theme was "the general public interest." A persuasive but mechanistic justification accompanied this. It was that these federal programs were needed and undertaken "to stimulate initiation" by states, communities or individuals of certain activities deemed desirable.

From its beginning, centralism expansion faced potential resistance by the states against federal invasion of governmental areas presumably reserved to them by the Constitution. But it was forestalled by a purposeful use of the aid pattern already established. The states, in effect, were "bribed" to withhold resistance, and successive extensions of centralism were "bought" with the federal funds or credit extended. Aid programs now cover a wide range of purposes, many of which cannot be demonstrated as matters of federal concern except under a centralist interpretation of national government for promoting the public welfare.

5. The Dominance of Minority Groups

Centralism thrives on the principle of "divide and rule," which means in the present connection an immoderate encouragement of minority groups. The purpose of legislative action at any governmental level is to deal with matters deemed to require attention from the standpoint of the general public interest. The active supporters or opponents of specific legislative proposals before a city council, a state legislature, or the national Congress ordinarily number many fewer than the entire group that would be affected by particular legislative measures. However, the privilege of any individual or group to present their views to government is protected by the constitutional right of petition.

From this standpoint, a minority has as good standing as a majority, and of course in the aggregate the several minorities do comprise the majority. The growing disposition to associate success at the polls with beneficial attitudes toward the interests of organized, articulate minority groups has had increasingly undesirable results.

Logrolling among minority groups, even when their respective objectives may be in conflict, is a profitable undertaking for those concerned because it virtually always leads to more federal spending on all of the projects involved. Examples abound of this sacrifice of the general public interest to specific minority commitments. Thus, the costly agricultural subsidy program needs Congressional support from the urban districts, where the projects of slum clearance and urban renewal need the help of farm state votes.

6. Demotion of the States as Sovereign Entities

The ultimate expression of centralism is the monolithic, authoritarian state, which brooks no impediment to total power. One of Hitler's first acts in his march toward dictatorship was abolition of most of the powers, duties, and functions of the several German states. The proponents of centralism would reduce the American states to the status of provinces. They deride "states' rights" as an obsolete shibboleth and are openly scornful of the states' capacity to discharge their responsibilities. They disregard the fact that while there is in this country no intentional design to dictatorship, the influence of centralism if not abated, will lead to a vesting of total power somewhere—whether the lodgment might be with the Congress or with a "strong man" in the executive branch, or with the army. The momentum of centralism has been for some time a threat to the balance between federal and state jurisdictions, and as the federal government becomes more powerful, its encroachment upon the states becomes more serious.

7. Business Competition with Taxpaying Citizens

As a further means of expanding federal control and domination, centralism presses for extension of government controlled and operated public power and credit enterprises, the operations of which never yields a net income for general purposes equal to that which could be realized in private hands. It has long been recognized that control of the sources of energy by government assures domination of the energy users. Conservation of natural resources has served as a means, and a cloak, for this key invasion of the private economy. Popular support has been obtained by favoring service-users at the expense of taxpayers. Furthermore:

a. Federal ownership and operation of public power facilities undermines the state and local tax base by exemption of federally owned plant and equipment from the local tax rolls. In the few cases where payments are made "in lieu" of taxes, these are no more than token amounts by comparison with the local tax revenues that are collected from comparable privately owned property;

b. The income base for federal taxation is depleted;

c. The funds for government business enterprises are provided by appropriations, or by Treasury advances at interest rates below the cost of borrowed funds. The terms of repayment to the Treasury, where provided for, are unrealistically long;

d. The lack of a profit motive as a spur to efficient management is paralleled, in the case of government enterprises, by the absence of an obligation to conserve the capital. If a government enterprise impairs its capital by incurring losses in operation, this impairment is made good by another appropriation or a Treasury loan at an interest rate below cost.

BRINGING GOVERNMENT BACK HOME

The theme of this study is that security for the nation and for the individual citizens in this dangerously critical period in world affairs depends upon, and requires, that the national responsibility be limited to the truly national tasks. All services and functions pertaining to the economic progress and welfare of the people except those which can be performed only by the federal government should be handled by a lesser jurisdiction if they are properly governmental in character, or left to private initiative. This conclusion is diametrically opposed to the thesis of centralism, which seeks to achieve security and economic progress through continued expansion of federal authority. The battle line is thus clearly drawn. Under centralism there is no logical stopping place in the extension of federal power and control short of a monolithic, authoritarian state. The attack must be directed to reversal of this trend by bringing government back home.

THE CONFLICT BETWEEN AUTHORITY AND FREEDOM

Centralism is also a matter of serious concern to the people as a threat to the preservation of balance between authority and freedom. It has often been said that government means total authority within whatever bounds its jurisdiction extends. There can be no partial acceptance of government's will, no option to the citizens to obey or disobey. The wider the scope of government's operations, the larger the area within which the individual has no choice but to obey, and the smaller the area within which he is free of government restraint or compulsion. We need enough government to assure a peaceful, orderly community at home and to provide for security against foreign aggression; but we dare not have so much government that personal liberties are imperiled and the economic basis of individual self-support is destroyed through excesses of expenditure, taxation, and regulation.

This dilemma is real. As stated so clearly by Woodrow Wilson fifty years ago—"The history of liberty is the history of the limitation of governmental power, not the increase of it."

The insistence of centralists that government must do more and more for more people ignores the menace to freedom that is involved in such a policy. Expanding government beneficence means expanding government authority, which in turn means more regimentation both of the beneficiaries and of those on whom the increasing costs are levied. The centralism program of doing more and more for the people rests not on concern, but on distrust. It holds that they will not face up to their problems and that only a super-government can support and guide the nation. Centralism, under a cloak of humanitarianism, is really contemptuous of the ability of the people to think for themselves, to handle their own affairs, and to solve their own problems.

Centralism furthers its ends by exaggeration. It thrives on "crises," and facts are largely superfluous. The campaign for massive federal support of education, for example, is being waged by exaggerating the alleged "crisis" in school construction and teachers' salaries, and by disregarding the facts as to the real accomplishments by state and local action without federal aid. The crisis technique is widely used because the "immediate need" thesis swings people away from a thoughtful weighing of the facts to the quick and easy out of more federal spending.

If freedom is conquered here, it will be conquered as it was in Russia and China, by the aggrandizement of government and the parallel decay of popular will and capacity to resist.

Centralism weakens natural resistance to governmental encroachment by spreading distrust of private, local, and state action, by undermining confidence in the private enterprise system, by extolling Soviet central planning, and by the specious pleading that most of our personal and governmental problems are too big for any agency but the federal government.

Our job, as citizens of a republic and disciples of the creed of individual worth and freedom, is to challenge the premises of this doctrine and to take the initiative by attacking its vulnerable points. We should constantly drive home the gravity of the conflict between centralism and personal freedom. We should emphasize that the people can have more from now on, including recognition of individual human dignity and preservation of hard-won personal freedoms, under an economic system of free, private enterprise with a minimum of government control and intervention, and with moderate tax rates, than they can possibly have under punitive tax rates and a political and economic system of government direction, dole, and domination.

QUESTIONS AND STUDY SUGGESTIONS

1. What reasons, according to the NAM, underlie the growth of the Federal government in the economy? What are the consequences of a philosophy of "centralism"?

2. What reasoning lies behind the NAM's conclusion that "it is axiomatic that the most expensive way to get anything done is for the federal government to do it"? Do you agree with this conclusion?

3. Carefully evaluate: "The wider the scope of government's operations, the larger the area within which the individual has no choice but to obey, and the smaller the area within which he is free of government restraint or compulsion."

Reading 10

Why Government Grows

Michael D. Reagan, Professor of Political Science, University of California at Riverside

In sharp contrast to the NAM's position, Michael D. Reagan takes a much more liberal stand with respect to the economic role of government in this reading. His basic point is that the absolute and relative growth of the public sector is the result of the voters' demands for more social goods and services and for the solutions to problems with which the private sector is unable to cope. More specific reasons for the growth of government include: changes in population size and composition which have necessitated greater government spending on welfare programs and education; urbanization and industrialization which have increased interdependence and made the individual less economically self-sufficient; and rapid technological advance which has increased the need for government action in protecting consumers from fraudulent and dangerous products.

The size of government and the amount it spends, runs the argument of many conservatives in the United States, is determined simply by the personal biases of those in office at a particular time.

The President, particularly but not exclusively if he is a Democrat, is the focal point of such discussions in this age of executive leadership in the legislative process. From FDR's "New Deal" to LBJ's "Great Society," those who dislike activist government have blamed the articulators in the White House for the growth of the federal budget and the expansion of public programs. It is at least implicitly assumed by such critics that if Presidents were less personally expansionist and less articulate, we would have much smaller government.

There are many reasons for doubting these assumptions, the first and simplest being that government continued to grow even during an eight-year period presided over by a President who was neither expansionist nor, thought many, especially articulate. Thus fiscal 1952 saw federal budgetary expenditures of $65.3 billion, while for 1959 the comparable figure was $80.3 billion.

If one assumes that governmental growth at any level derives essentially from the preferences of the chief executive, then statistics on state and local expenditures would indicate that we have an extremely expansionist-minded group of mayors and governors: between 1954 and 1966 state expenditures rose from $15.8 billion to $38.2 billion, and local government expenditures from $17.8 billion to $43.5 billion.

Since governments continue to grow, at every level, regardless of party, and over considerable periods of time and changes of people, one must either assume that all political

From Michael D. Reagan, "Why Government Grows," **Challenge**, September–October, 1965, pp. 4–7. Reprinted by permission. Statistical data updated by editor.

leaders are empire builders and that all legis-latures are supine, or that there are some deeper reasons.

DEMOCRATIC ACTION

The most important *general* factor in explain-ing the growth of public programs in the United States is simply that we are a democ-racy—i.e., that ours is an open political system which responds to public demands. Further-more, the two-party competitive system which we enjoy also means that both parties exercise initiative in pointing out social problems and offering solutions—in the hope that the voters will be attracted to that party which seems to be offering the best solutions. This is to look at the matter crassly. But I also believe that a high proportion of our national political leadership had an intrinsic interest in improv-ing the human quality of our society, quite apart from personal political dividends.

Annual growth in the National Park Service and the Forest Service, and the recent creation of a Bureau of Outdoor Recreation, for exam-ple, all attest to increased public demand for recreational facilities. The traveling American vacationer does not like it when he pulls into camp and finds all places taken for the night by early afternoon. Increased private affluence directly causes demands for increased public expenditure. Purchasers of the seven or eight million passenger cars being sold annually cer-tainly want decent roads to drive them on. The ability of this particular public interest to over-come conservative ideology was manifested when the Eisenhower Administration changed the federal share in the $40 billion interstate highway program from 50 percent to 90 per-cent.

At the local level, does any intelligent citi-zen really expect his town or city fathers to provide *only* police and fire protection? More often than not there are substantial demands for new school buildings and more specialized teachers, for parks and playgrounds and the staff to take care of the children playing in them, for modern sewage disposal facilities, improved streets and parking garages, etc. While we do not enjoy the added tax burden necessary to pay for the services we demand, it is generally a better risk for the elected offi-cial to provide the services than to keep taxes down at the expense of the public needs. It is we the people, in short, who are expansionist;

and it is our open democratic system that makes the government react accordingly.

Conservative ideology, incidentally, is con-tradictory on this point. Typically, the federal government is charged with arbitrary self-extension, with imposing itself on an unwilling people. Simultaneously, both the President and the Congress are attacked for "demagoguery" and "pandering to the masses" when they do respond to electoral demands for new programs and larger public outlays. One cannot have it both ways. Every individual may feel on occa-sion that the public (i.e., everyone except him-self) is demanding something that it should not; but we should appreciate that responsive-ness to public demands, even those of which we may not approve, is a sign that democracy is alive.

"NATIONAL SECURITY STATE"

National security is, in turn, the largest single specific cause of growth in the federal budget. For fiscal 1968 it is estimated that defense will take 46 cents of every federal budgetary dol-lar, veterans four cents, and fixed interest charges (most of this on debt incurred in World War II and the Korean conflict) nine cents. Space programs, which many people think of as primarily related to national se-curity (although this may not, in fact, be the case), take another three cents. Other inter-national activities account for three cents. These total 65 percent of the federal govern-ment's total expenditures. Trust funds (social security, interstate highways, etc.) take another 27 cents, leaving 8 cents for agriculture and all other domestic activities. In terms of federal expenditure, ours is more a "national security state" than a "welfare state."

Not only have national security expenses in-creased, but a broadening of the security con-cept to include many nonmilitary programs has also led to an increase in the complexity of government. Economic aid and technical assis-tance, overseas propaganda and information activities, the Peace Corps and the Food for Peace Program are but a few of the enlarged range of activities associated with the extended modern concept of national security.

POPULATION AND THE PUBLIC SECTOR

But even if there were no new programs, gov-ernment would continue to grow just to pro-vide existing services to a rising population which in just 25 years has grown from 132.5 million to 195 million.

The character of services needed, however, is not a constant, for the age distribution of the population and the urbanization pattern have created new social needs, hence, pressures for new programs. Changes in age composition account for the demand for medical care for the aged, for example. Thanks to advances in medicine and public health in this century, the over-65 group has jumped from nine million in 1940 to 17.6 million in 1965.

At the other end of the spectrum, the age group under 14 has grown from 30 million to 68 million in the past 25 years. This is a fact not unrelated to the emergence of the aid to dependent children program as a major factor in welfare expenditures. Further, a current under-21 population of 87 million explains the explosive growth in educational expenditures and the increasing demands each year for federal aid to education.

Taking those under 21 and those over 65 together, we have 104 million persons. This leaves approximately 90 million in the economically productive age group of 21 to 65. Perhaps the fact that the latter group is now a minority of the population—and, of course, far from all of this group are employed—largely explains the general increase in public services. Urban society's lack of economic opportunity for children and the aged, as compared with an agricultural society, adds greatly to the burdens of those in the middle. In such circumstances, an equitable distribution of services probably requires collective provision. Thus the changes in the *character* of the population are a vital factor in explaining governmental growth.

URBANIZATION AND INDUSTRIALIZATION

Concomitant with the increased population is the even more significant fact of how that population lives and makes a living. Technology, in its manifestations of industrialization and urbanization, creates problems that Thomas Jefferson did not have to face: unemployment, housing, public health, economic power to be regulated, transportation needs, etc. The informal social controls that sufficed in the face-to-face relationships of a small town and with the simpler products of an agricultural age are no longer adequate. They have increasingly to be supplemented, if not supplanted, by formal controls. Let us look at a few examples of the consequences on government of the industrialization-urbanization complex.

With unemployment constantly running at close to five percent, and threatening to go higher rather than lower under the combined impact of an expanding 18 to 21 age population and automation, we might start with the unemployment compensation program. The need for government to provide a supporting framework for individuals and families is not the result of an alleged loss of "moral fiber," but of the interdependence of industrial employment and the living patterns of an urban society.

In earlier times, people were literally more self-sufficient than it is possible for them to be today: the farm family grew its own food, made some of its own clothing and built its own shelter. Children contributed economically by working in the fields. There was not the same dependence on cash income that there is today. Grandparents could be cared for within the home and continue to be useful members of the family. Even when industrialism began to make some headway, the son who went off to the city could still return to the family farm if he lost his job or became ill.

Contrast the situation today: Production and consumption are divorced. The man does not work on his own farm but for an organization. The family does not produce its own food, clothing and shelter, but has members performing specialized tasks for cash incomes, which are then exchanged for the family's needs. Loss of cash thus means loss of all sustenance. The family farm is no longer there to fall back upon. Industrial employment is subject to fluctuations against which no individual can protect himself. Given the consequences of unemployment and this inability to guard against it by one's own actions, some form of social insurance to maintain cash income during periods of nonemployment is an absolute necessity. During the 1958 and 1961 recessions, it turned out that the state programs were insufficient because of the large number of persons who exhausted the time limits of assistance.

TECHNOLOGY AND THE CONSUMER

Consider also drug regulation and other forms of consumer protection which have received recognition since 1961 by the creation of a Consumer Advisory Council and a White House Special Assistant for Consumer affairs. In his 1962 message on consumer problems, President Kennedy said:

Ninety percent of the prescriptions written today are for drugs that were unknown 20 years ago. Many of the new products used every day in the home are highly complex. The housewife is called upon to be an amateur electrician, mechanic, chemist, toxicologist, dietitian and mathematician—but she is rarely furnished the information she needs to perform these tasks proficiently. . . . The consumer typically cannot know whether drug preparations meet minimum standards of safety, quality and efficacy.

Because the buyer cannot satisfactorily be his own testing service in a complex industrial technology, a new function emerges for government. The more we rely upon science for health, the greater the importance of regulation to protect us against the worthless and the dangerous. Given the cost of medical care and the human cost of false hopes raised by over-touted medicines, the 1962 extension of the Food and Drug Administration's responsibility to cover the effectiveness as well as the safety of drugs cannot be viewed as unjustified.

TRANSPORTATION AND RESOURCES

Take transportation. The Interstate Commerce Commission, one of the oldest federal agencies, was formed in 1887. The Civil Aeronautics Board came into being in 1938 with the rise of commercial aviation, and the Federal Aviation Agency in 1958 to meet safety and technical problems of air traffic, airport planning and control systems. In recent years, short-range transportation in and around cities went unplanned as our cities grew and the automobile multiplied. The result: chaos. The governmental response: the Urban Mass Transportation Act of 1964, which authorizes federal assistance to state and local governments in planning, developing and improving local mass transit systems.

Because an industrial society uses natural resources in great quantities and in complex ways, the development of those resources has become a matter of high governmental concern. This concern is manifested, for example,

in the postwar creation of the Office of Saline Water and the Office of Coal Research, both in the Department of the Interior, to conduct technical and economic research.

I am sure that each of us could multiply these examples. The point is simply that part of the price of a technological civilization is an expansion of governmental activities to cope with the social by-products of advancing technology.

PERSONAL INTERESTS

So far we have discussed the impact of impersonal developments upon governmental growth. But there are also important personal elements of who gets what and of community values. Business competition in the United States has frequently taken a political form. Typically this occurs when one economic interest, feeling itself weaker in the marketplace than another, demands legislation to redress the balance. The Robinson-Patman Act and fair trade laws are consequences of such infighting within the private sector.

More generally, it can be shown that practically all of the major regulatory programs have been the result of group conflicts in which one disadvantaged (from an economic power standpoint) business group makes a demand that another be regulated. The antitrust laws and the original rationale of the Interstate Commerce Commission fall into this category.

Even more interesting, some public agencies and programs are the result of demands by a group that *itself* be regulated! Assignment of radio frequencies to broadcasters by the Federal Communications Commission began when the broadcasters themselves asked for an end to the chaos they had been creating. The established airlines wanted the Civil Aeronautics Board's licensing of routes to regulate competition. Similarly with the formerly exempt truckers, who asked for inclusion in ICC licensing in the 1950s in the hope that the rate of new entries (i.e., competition) would be reduced.

On at least one occasion we have had the curious phenomenon of a private interest group demanding that what the government wanted to keep voluntary be made compulsory. I refer to the oil import curbs established by President Eisenhower. In that case, the "majors" wanted voluntary controls only, but the domestic "independents," fearing, of course, the impact of imports on domestic production, insisted that the regulatory program be a mandatory one. While one might say that the underlying factor in such developments is technological, the immediate cause of governmental action is the demands of groups of people—people who generally oppose expansion of the public sector.

CHANGING VALUES

It would, of course, be possible for society to ignore its problems or assume that private action is sufficient to handle them. Facts and situations do not create their own public programs. These result from objective situations *plus* the subjective factor of the community's reaction—and that reaction changes as value patterns change.

When unemployment was thought of, in Spencerian terms, as the just punishment of the shiftless and lazy, no one thought to provide public protection. When *caveat emptor* was the slogan of the day, we did not create consumer advisory groups. When equality was seen in legalistic dimensions only, we did not initiate economic and educational programs to counteract the social inequalities of opportunity that arose from a child's environment. Recent battles over the form of medical care for the elderly illustrate the continuing battle between a set of values that supports the means test and a competing set of values that holds such tests to be inconsistent with the human dignity of our older citizens.

At the risk of oversimplification, it seems fair to say that in the 20th century American society has undergone a basic shift in values from an individualistic, antigovernment value pattern to one that might be called socially (some would say socialistically) oriented. Economic calamity is seen as man made rather than God given, and our concept of democracy now includes the use of government as a collective representative of the people in tackling the problems that some men's actions have made for others.

As recent criticisms of the Area Redevelopment Administration and the successor Appalachian aid program have stressed, however, all the humanitarianism in the world can accomplish little without effective techniques for directing social forces toward the desired goal. In this sense, the understanding of man and social processes that the social sciences are providing is a prime prerequisite to effective public action.

But more than that, increased knowledge is itself a factor that impels us to take action, for we feel an obligation to *use* our knowledge to improve the quality of life. I suppose this reflects the activist philosophic temper of the United States. Whatever the deeper psychology may be, the fact is plain that the extensive government programs since 1946 for stabilizing the economy and stimulating its growth are the combined result of community values (involuntary unemployment is bad) and of modern economic knowledge (the development of national income and input-output analysis).

In short, we the people—what we know, what we do, what we want and how we feel about ourselves and our society—are the basic cause of government growth. Political leaders are our instruments, perhaps often the catalysts of action; but their arbitrary will is the least of the reasons for the continued expansion of the public sector in the United States.

QUESTIONS AND STUDY SUGGESTIONS

1. Explain how (*a*) population growth, (*b*) industrialization and technological advance, and (*c*) urbanization have contributed to the expansion of the public sector of the economy.
2. How might a two-party political system contribute to the growth of government's economic role?
3. Carefully contrast Professor Reagan's philosophy of the economic role of government with that of the NAM (Reading 9). What do you consider to be the strong and weak points of each view? To which position do you subscribe?

Reading 11

The Financial Dilemma of American Federalism

Morgan Guaranty Trust Company

Historically, Federal, state, and local governments have collaborated in providing social goods and services. But in recent years state and local governments have found it increasingly difficult to perform their traditional functions because of inadequacies in their tax systems. The result has been growing Federal participation in such fields as highway construction, education, and urban problems which traditionally have been reserved for state and local action. Reading 11 analyzes a recent tax-sharing proposal designed to improve state and local finances and to strengthen our system of fiscal federalism. The proposal calls for the Federal government to share on a continuing basis some portion of its tax revenues with state and local governments. This tax sharing will take the form of "no strings attached" grants based upon population size.

The system of government called federalism is America's special contribution to the art of political organization. Involving as it does a division of political authority between a central government and state governments, it was, when inaugurated in 1787, a unique creation in a period characterized either by unitary governments with strongly centralized authority or loose confederations with little effective centralized power. To the framers of the Constitution, federalism represented a workable means of reconciling the clear need for unified action in fields such as defense and foreign affairs with the widespread wish to keep most of the ordinary civil functions of government firmly under the control of the states.

WASHINGTON'S GROWING ROLE

American federalism has, of course, undergone very significant changes since its creation. Over the decades, the national government has tended to assert authority ranging far beyond that explicitly conferred on it originally. And in the legal contests that have been fought because of this, the courts have decided largely in favor of the national government. As a result, the national government is now deeply involved in a wide range of activities that initially seemed to be reserved to the states and, inferentially, to local bodies deriving their powers and rights from the states.

The good and bad in this evolution are difficult to assess. The unqualified assertion that all past additions to Washington's authority were unfortunate and unnecessary clearly lacks historical perspective. Much of the centralization of power that has occurred probably has to be accepted as unavoidable in the light of the social and economic changes that have come about in the last 180 years. Many problems, national in character, clearly exist in a complex industrial society of almost 200 million persons that simply could not have been foreseen when population numbered less than four million and was sustained chiefly by family farming.

From "The Financial Dilemma of American Federalism," **The Morgan Guaranty Survey**, Morgan Guaranty Trust Company, September, 1966, pp. 4–11, abridged. Reprinted by permission.

It does not follow, however, that *all* additions to national power have been necessary or desirable, or that continuing enlargement of national authority should go unchallenged. Many problems—for example, those relating to education, urban transit, and neighborhood improvement—retain a distinctly local or regional character. Yet it is in precisely those areas that Washington's role is most rapidly expanding. Significantly, these accretions to national power are justified not by a claim that Washington has superior "know-how" or greater efficiency in these matters, but by the frankly acknowledged inability of state and local governments to muster the fiscal resources needed to solve the problems they face. In short, Washington simply is acting to fill a void. In filling this fiscal void, however, it is effecting an important new transformation in American federalism.

The malapportionment of many state legislatures undeniably has been an important contributing factor to the growth of Washington's participation in state and local affairs. Dominated by rural legislators, many states simply have not given adequate recognition to the difficulties of cities and suburban areas. Consequently, local officials have turned increasingly to Washington for help. Court-ordered reapportionment of state legislatures surely will alter this picture. And this change in itself will do much to revitalize grass roots politics. To be truly effective, however, state legislatures will need command over vastly improved fiscal resources to meet their own needs and those of local governments, which rely on state legislatures for financial support.

FISCAL DILEMMA

Elements of the fiscal dilemma facing state and local governments can be seen in relevant fiscal data. State and local government expenditures rose over 230 percent from 1950 to 1965. The factors behind this rise in outlays are well known—among them, a large increase in population; a shift in the population's age distribution in the direction of youthful and elderly persons for whom schools, hospitals, and other essential services had to be expanded; a desire to catch up on numerous programs postponed first because of depression and then because of World War II.

By virtually any yardstick, the rise in state and local government expenditures has been impressive. They have risen faster than has the gross national product, and far faster than Washington's spending. Yet the backlog of unmet needs remains great, and pressures for new and improved services are likely to mount in the future. Total state and local government spending, which ran at about $93 billion in 1965, seems likely to approach the $130-billion mark by 1970.

State and local governments have made substantial efforts to meet their revenue needs from their own sources. Tax revenues alone rose 224 percent from 1950 to 1965. And further increases in state and local tax receipts are certain in the future. For a variety of reasons, however, it seems exceedingly doubtful that state and local bodies will be able to produce revenues equal to the added expenditures they will be called upon to make. The temptation to turn to Washington for help is thus virtually certain to persist.

CALLING THE TUNE

Almost exclusively, the national government's financial aid to states and localities currently comes as specific "grants-in-aid" for designated activities, such as highway building or public welfare. The share of state and local spending financed by grants rose from 9 percent in 1950 to 12 percent in 1965, and could go to 17 percent by 1970, if newly enacted programs develop as anticipated. Literally scores of individual programs are in operation—over sixty in the Office of Education alone. Most grants entail fairly detailed compliance with conditions established by Congress in enacting programs covered. Some financial grants to local governments totally bypass state governments—a particularly flagrant violation of the logic of American federalism.

Helpful as grants are in making possible needed public services, they thus strike powerfully at important pillars of federalism. Paying the piper entails inevitable prerogatives, and it is a good presumption that, in order to obtain funds, states and localities increasingly will be doing those things Washington most wants done—and doing them in prescribed ways. What will certainly emerge is the imposition across the country of flat national standards that disregard regional differences. This, for instance, is tending to occur in pollution abatement efforts. There is a very real risk that the political stature of states and localities will be permanently diminished by this combination of specific directive and growing financial dependence. And in the process, the role of states as proving grounds for what Justice Brandeis called "novel social and economic experiments" surely will be circumscribed. Additionally, public service in state and local governments could become even less attractive than it now is to citizens of energy and ability.

These trends and their implications deserve more explicit public recognition than they have so far received. Far from inexorable, they can be arrested, and perhaps reversed, without damage to existing and prospective programs of public service.

FISCAL MISMATCH

The essence of the problem is what Professor Walter W. Heller, former Chairman of the Council of Economic Advisers, has called a "fiscal mismatch," in which the national government retains a dominant hold on high yielding revenue sources, such as income taxes, while state and local governments with less satisfactory revenue sources are asked to provide more and better services for rapidly expanding populations.

Closer examination of some of the obstacles states and localities encounter in attempting to enlarge their revenues provides revealing insight into the nature of that fiscal mismatch. Property taxes and revenues from sales and gross receipts taxes together account for a very sizable proportion of state and local government receipts—over 43 percent in 1965—and yields from both have risen substantially since 1950. With good prospects for growth in the economy in the years ahead, receipts from these major sources can be expected to grow further. To a considerable extent, however, increases in these revenues have been achieved through higher tax *rates*, and it may be difficult because of mounting taxpayer opposition to adopt similar rate increases in the future. It is therefore questionable whether receipts from property and sales taxes will grow as rapidly in the future as they have so far in the postwar years.

Heavier tax rates on residential property and retail sales encounter particularly powerful opposition from labor unions and "liberal" groups generally. Neither revenue sources, they say,

takes sufficient account of individual ability to pay; both assertedly fall most heavily on those of relatively modest means, who normally spend a large proportion of their incomes for housing and items covered by sales taxes. Property and sales taxes in this view are regressive, hence bad.

These criticisms probably overstate the case against property and sales taxation. With essentials such as food largely excluded, sales taxes are far less regressive than opponents claim. And studies indicate that property taxes tend to be assessed roughly in proportion to income rather than regressively. Nonetheless, it is true that intensified use of sales and property taxation would tend to reduce the over-all progressiveness of the national-state-local tax structure.

States and localities also face serious practical impediments to intensified use of most of their other revenue bases. One key obstacle stems from the competitive struggle among states and localities to attract new industry and to keep that which they already have. Governors and mayors throughout the land hesitate to raise tax levels for fear of giving neighboring locales an edge in this contest. For example, the possibility that New York would lose its major stock exchange if higher stock transfer taxes were enacted was a troubling consideration in deliberations earlier this year over a comprehensive new revenue program to meet the city's growing needs. And in state after state new devices have been adopted to reduce tax burdens on immigrant industries in an effort to encourage economic development.

Finally, of course, the very heavy burden of federal taxation is a major roadblock to increased state and local revenues, probably the most serious obstacle of all. Against the background of high federal tax rates, even the most marginal rise in state and local levies is likely to seem onerous and to arouse intense opposition.

Compensating for these difficulties by recourse to borrowing obviously has its limits. State and local governments have already borrowed heavily to meet their financial requirements, sending their debt from $24.1 billion in 1950 to $99.5 billion in 1965. And interest payments on debt have been a rapidly rising component of state and local government outlays. Many jurisdictions have already begun to encounter constitutional limitations on indebtedness; and many have had to employ costly devices, such as revenue bonds, to side-step such restraints. Aside from the legal difficulties, sound financial practice would counsel against allowing too much of the state and local financing burden to fall on debt.

RESOLVING THE MISMATCH

In contrast to the fiscal problems of state and local governments, Washington—because of a progressive income tax structure and sustained prosperity—is enjoying a remarkable revenue escalation. And until the heating up of the Viet Nam conflict and the swelling of Great Society undertakings, it appeared for a while that its tax take might be so great as to create problems of "fiscal drag" on the economy.

A logical solution to the quandary of fiscal mismatch would be the development of a workable means of allocating to states and localities a significant proportion of the revenue harvest reaped by Washington. For revenue sources such as personal and corporate income are not, after all, inherently "national." Washington's commanding hold on them grew largely out of pressing revenue needs created by war. By retaining that hold even after external threats subsided, it has preordained the increasing dependence of state and local governments that threatens the survival of meaningful federalism.

A practical approach to this problem need not be complex. There are a number of feasible alternatives for achieving the desired reallocation. One, a proposal for the automatic sharing of revenues between state and national governments along lines suggested by Professor Heller and Mr. Joseph A. Pechman of the Brookings Institution, is embodied in legislation already introduced in Congress. Co-sponsored by Senators Javits and Hartke, it would "establish the sharing of certain federal tax receipts by the states" through a "Tax Sharing Fund" equal each year to 1 percent of the aggregate taxable income reported during the prior calendar year on individual income tax returns. Most of the fund's resources would be distributed to the 50 states in proportion to population and tax "efforts," as indicated by the ratio of state and local revenues collected to personal income in each state; part would be reserved for supplementary distribution to relatively poor states, as measured by per

capita income. Breaking sharply with traditional grants-in-aid, revenue transfers under the bill would be largely without strings attached—the only strictures being fairly broad ones, such as prohibitions against using funds for racially segregated activities. Individual states could thus exercise wide discretion in using any funds received, choosing expenditure targets in accordance with their particular insights into state and local problems.

Although a modest first step, this proposal has great appeal as a way of expanding necessary government services without simultaneously extending Washington's involvement in peculiarly state and local problems. It goes to the root of the fiscal dilemma plaguing state and local governments by providing a revenue source that would tend to grow rapidly as the economy expands and incomes increase. It would help free states from the compulsion to look over their shoulders at what neighbors are doing to attract industry before undertaking needed spending programs. At the same time, it holds out the prospect that poorer states will obtain the revenues they need to establish at least the minimum standards of education and other services that are essential in a fluid society. Long-term planning by states and localities in meeting public service needs would also be facilitated by revenue sharing, since the regular and continuous flows of funds into a specially designated trust fund would eliminate the uncertainties characteristic of the annual appropriation process.

CRITICISMS OF THE PLAN

Revenue sharing has, nonetheless, encountered powerful opposition. Spokesmen for urban areas oppose the proposal out of the conviction that cities' problems have chronically been neglected by state legislatures distributing funds, and that untied allotments to states would simply prolong those injustices. Any assistance Congress is able to provide can, in their view, best be channeled through direct grants to urban areas where problems of population, pollution, and traffic congestion are most serious. In addition, there is an uneasy feeling among city officials that revenue sharing would undermine existing federal grants-in-aid to cities. Another group of critics argues that it is wrong to divorce the responsibility for collecting taxes from their use. In this view, the national government should either continue to tax and spend or else should reduce its tax take to afford leeway for states and localities to increase theirs. Other people simply contend that tax rates at all levels of government are too high and that the case for increased public services is not valid. If Washington has revenues above and beyond its current needs, it is asserted, the proper course of action would be federal tax reduction or debt retirement, not the creation of yet another plan for separating taxpayer and dollar. Still other opponents argue that revenue sharing would merely allow state and local governments to relax their efforts to improve their own revenues.

Some of these contentions admittedly contain elements of validity. There may, for example, be merit to cities' claims that they have been given financial short-shrift by state legislators in the past. But there is every reason to expect that legislative reapportionment on the state level will in the future assure that state funds will be more equitably distributed. Worry about the disruptive impact on existing grants-in-aid also appears exaggerated, given the sheer momentum of these programs. In principle, the contention that it would be preferable to reduce federal tax rates to permit room for higher levies by states and localities is unassailable. As a practical matter, however, it must be recognized that it is far more efficient to have one income tax collector rather than 50 for states plus countless others for localities. There are just no economies of scale in the latter arrangement. An insistence that tax reduction and debt retirement be given absolute priority has undeniable appeal. One scarcely need be a full-fledged Galbraithian, however, to sense that there are substantial areas of neglect in the public sector of the economy, ranging from serious deficiencies in anti-pollution efforts to ineffective programs for unsnarling traffic movements. Finally, despite the political hurdles that have stood in the way, state and local officials have enacted an impressive array of new revenue measures in the postwar period. And so great will be revenue needs in the future that it is gratuitous to charge that state and local officials will falter in efforts to enlarge their own revenue sources if a tax sharing plan is enacted.

It may be objected that an accurate and equitable determination of a state's revenue "effort" is impractical. Some states rely more heavily than others on taxes that place a relatively large burden on lower income groups. Thus, ostensibly equal "effort" levels could represent very different burdens from state to state on taxpayers in similar income groups. Nevertheless, revenue sharing, by relieving financial stresses on all states and localities could at least help arrest the growth of disparities in tax burdens.

Not all of the criticisms of revenue sharing can be fully refuted, and there can be no doubt that revenue sharing falls short of perfection. The importance of revitalizing the role of state and local governments in the federal system is so overriding, however, that whatever validity those criticisms retain loses much of its force.

THE TAX CREDIT ALTERNATIVE

Revenue sharing, of course, is not the only means whereby the fiscal strains of state and local governments could be relieved. The most frequently recommended alternative is a program of tax credits that would permit taxpayers to deduct from their computed federal tax liability the amount of taxes paid to state and local governments. This effect is already achieved in some degree under present procedures which allow taxpayers to include numerous state and local levies among deductions claimed on their federal income tax forms, thereby partially offsetting state and local tax burdens. The tax credit would allow a far greater, or perhaps complete, offsetting of those burdens. This would make it a lot more likely that states and localities would increase their own taxes. Complete offsetting would largely overcome the inhibitions states now have about putting themselves at a competitive disadvantage in scaling up their tax rates. It needs to be recognized, of course, that a complete offset could have a troublesomely disruptive effect on Washington's budget process, since federal receipts could become acutely sensitive to the varying revenue actions of states and localities. Some limitation on the extent of the tax credit is therefore probably a practical necessity. Even so, the idea of a more generous offset than now exists has much to recommend it and deserves sympathetic consideration along with revenue sharing.

The primary difference in end result between the two is that the tax credit approach would not directly entail special consideration for lower income states, as provided in the Javits-Hartke version of revenue sharing. The case for this special consideration derives from the fact that the need for public services tends to be greatest in precisely those states where the base of taxable income is lowest. In many instances, these states are now making, contrary to common allegations of laxity, efforts that are disproportionately heavy. In Mississippi, for example, revenues collected by state and local governments per $1000 of personal income received in the state are far above the national average; so are state and local expenditures per $1000 of personal income. Yet the State has need for sharply upgraded services; and other states are in similar predicaments.

Representatives of some of the more affluent states object to revenue sharing precisely because of its redistributive feature. But their objections tend to be self-defeating, since a proposal that did not provide some redistribution probably could not muster the support needed to carry it through both houses of Congress. Firm opposition to redistribution could deny needed fiscal relief to both affluent states and their lower-income counterparts.

A TIME TO BEGIN

Increasing the fiscal resources of state and local governments cannot of itself be expected to solve all of the problems confronting them. Many problems, particularly in localities, arise from deficiencies in administration and certainly in some instances from simple ineptitude. A better fiscal base from which to work, however, should be of considerable help to states and localities in enabling them to streamline their operations. Together with the invigoration that can be expected from reapportionment, revenue sharing—or perhaps some combination of it with the tax credit or other alternatives—has enormous potential for making state and local governments more vital factors in American federalism. An approach of this sort holds out the best hope of arresting the drift toward unitary government.

QUESTIONS AND STUDY SUGGESTIONS

1. What is the nature of the "fiscal mismatch" between the Federal government, on the one hand, and state and local governments, on the other?
2. What are the advantages and disadvantages of (a) specific or conditional grants-in-aid and (b) the Heller-Pechman tax-sharing proposal?
3. What are the criticisms of the tax-sharing proposal? Compare the "tax credit alternative" with the tax-sharing proposal. Which do you favor? Why?

PART TWO

MACROECONOMICS:
THE BUSINESS CYCLE,
STABILIZATION POLICIES,
AND ECONOMIC GROWTH

Reading 12

The Valley of Darkness

Arthur M. Schlesinger, Jr., Albert Schweitzer Professor of the Humanities, City University of New York

The word "depression" has only vague and remote connotations to the reader who has grown up during the prolonged period of prosperity which has characterized our economy since the early 1940s. One may read of a "sluggish economy," "necessary inventory adjustments," "mild down-swings," or even "recessions" without comprehending the devastating impact of the full-scale, prolonged economic nightmare that was the Great Depression of the 1930s. In this reading Arthur M. Schlesinger, Jr., vividly reconstructs "The Valley of Darkness" through which our economy faltered for an entire decade. Here we encounter the ugly panorama of a depressed society: empty and silent factories, groups of disillusioned and angry out-of-work men, hungry and ill-clothed children, wage rates of 8 or 10 cents per hour, and the brooding omnipresence of political and social chaos. Here is revealed the paradox of a society most abundantly endowed with property and human resources, yet failing to feed and clothe its popula-tion—the grotesque paradox of poverty amidst plenty.

By the spring of 1930 at least 4,000,000 Amer-icans were unemployed. Breadlines began to reappear in large cities for the first time since 1921—lines of embarrassed men, shuffling pa-tiently forward for a chance at a piece of bread and a cup of coffee. In New York City it was reported in March that the number of families on relief had increased 200 percent since the crash in October. The municipal lodging houses were now crowded; nearly half of the first 14,000 admitted were first-timers; and the city was letting homeless men sleep on the municipal barge as it tied up at the dock at night, where the icy wind whipped across the East River. In Detroit, said William Green of the A. F. of L., "the men are sitting in the parks all day long and all night long, hundreds and thousands of them, muttering to them-selves, out of work, seeking work."

"THE PROCESSION OF DESPAIR"

Across the country the dismal process was beginning, ushering in a new life for millions of Americans. In the twenties wage earners in general had found ample employment, satis-faction in life, hope for the future. Now came the slowdown—only three days of work a week, then perhaps two, then the layoff. And then the search for a new job—at first vigorous and hopeful; then sober; then desperate; the long lines before the employment offices, the eyes straining for words of hope on the chalked boards, the unending walk from one plant to the next, the all-night wait to be first for pos-sible work in the morning. And the inexorable news, brusque impersonality concealing fear: "No help wanted here" . . . "We don't need nobody" . . . "Move along, Mac, move along."

From Arthur M. Schlesinger, Jr., **The Crisis of the Old Order, 1919–1933**, Houghton Mifflin Company, Boston, 1957, pp. 1–5, 167–176, 248–251, abridged. Reprinted by permission.

And so the search continued, as clothes began to wear out and shoes to fall to pieces. Newspapers under the shirt would temper the winter cold, pasteboard would provide new inner soles, cotton in the heels of the shoe would absorb the pounding on the pavement, gunny sacks wrapped around the feet would mitigate the long hours in the frozen fields outside the factory gates. And in the meantime savings were trickling away. By now the terror began to infect the family. Father, no longer cheery, now at home for long hours, irritable, guilty, a little frightened. Sometimes the mother looked for work as domestic, chambermaid or charwoman; or the children worked for pennies after school, not understanding the fear that was touching them, knowing that they must do what they could to help buy bread and coffee.

As savings end, borrowing begins. If there is life insurance, borrowing on that, until it lapses; then loans from relatives and from friends; then the life of credit, from the landlord, from the corner grocer, until the lines of friendship and compassion are snapped. Meat vanishes from the table; lard replaces butter; father goes out less often, is terribly quiet; the children begin to lack shoes, their clothes are ragged, their mothers are ashamed to send them to school. Wedding rings are pawned, furniture is sold, the family moves into ever cheaper, damper, dirtier rooms. In a Philadelphia settlement house a little boy of three cried constantly in the spring of 1930; the doctor examined him and found that he was slowly starving. One woman complained that when she had food her two small children could barely eat; they had become accustomed to so little, she said, that their stomachs had shrunk. In November the apple peddlers began to appear on cold street corners, their threadbare clothes brushed and neat, their forlorn pluckiness emphasizing the anguish of being out of work. And every night that fall hundreds of men gathered on the lower level of Wacker Drive in Chicago, feeding fires with stray pieces of wood, their coat collars turned up against the cold, their caps pulled down over their ears, staring without expression at the black river, while above the automobiles sped comfortably along, bearing well-fed men to warm and well-lit homes. In the mining areas families lived on beans, without salt or fat. And every week, every day, more workers joined the procession of despair. The shadows deepened in the dark cold rooms, with the father angry and helpless and ashamed, the distraught children too often hungry or sick, and the mother, so resolute by day, so often, when the room was finally still, lying awake in bed at night, softly crying.

WINTER, 1931

And so the nation staggered into the second winter of the depression, and unemployment began to settle into a way of life. The weather was glorious much of the winter—clear, light air, brilliant sunlight, dry, frosty snow. But the cold was bitter in unheated tenements, in the flophouses smelling of sweat and Lysol, in the parks, in empty freight cars, along the windy waterfronts. With no money left for rent, unemployed men and their entire families began to build shacks where they could find unoccupied land. Along the railroad embankment, beside the garbage incinerator, in the city dumps, there appeared towns of tarpaper and tin, old packing boxes and old car bodies. Some shanties were neat and scrubbed; cleanliness at least was free; but others were squalid beyond belief, with the smell of decay and surrender. Symbols of the New Era, these communities quickly received their sardonic name: they were called Hoovervilles. And, indeed, it was in many cases only the fortunate who could find Hoovervilles. The unfortunate spent their nights huddled together in doorways, in empty packing cases, in boxcars.

At the breadlines and soup kitchens, hours of waiting would produce a bowl of mush, often without milk or sugar, and a tin cup of coffee. The vapors from the huge steam cookers mingling with the stench of wet clothes and sweating bodies made the air foul. But waiting in the soup kitchen was better than the scavenging in the dump. Citizens of Chicago, in this second winter, could be seen digging into heaps of refuse with sticks and hands as soon as the garbage trucks pulled out. On June 30, 1931, the Pennsylvania Department of Labor and Industry reported that nearly one-quarter of the labor force of the state was out of work. Clarence Pickett of the Friends found schools where 85, 90, even 99 percent of the children were underweight, and, in consequence, drowsy and lethargic. "Have you ever heard a hungry child cry?" asked Lillian Wald of

Henry Street. "Have you seen the uncontrollable trembling of parents who have gone half starved for weeks so that the children may have food?"

And still unemployment grew—from 4,000,000 in March 1930 to 8,000,000 in March 1931. And, more and more, the community found the relief problem beyond its capacity to handle. Local fiscal sources were drying up; local credit was vanishing; towns and counties found they could tax or borrow less and less. Some states had constitutional prohibitions against the use of state funds for home relief. And states too were on the verge of exhausting their tax possibilities; the general property tax had almost reached its limit, and, as income fell, the income tax, for the few states that had it, brought in declining amounts.

As the number of unemployed grew, the standards of relief care declined. More and more it seemed as if the burden was too great for individual communities to carry longer. In the fall of 1931 Governor Franklin D. Roosevelt of New York established a state emergency relief administration; other states followed this example. Effective relief, said William Allen White in September 1931, would be "the only way to keep down barricades in the streets this winter and the use of force which will brutalize labor and impregnate it with revolution in America for a generation."

And so, through the winter of 1931–32, the third winter of the depression, relief resources, public and private, dwindled toward the vanishing point. In few cities was there any longer pretense of meeting minimum budgetary standards. Little money was available for shoes or clothing, for medical or dental care, for gas or electricity. In New York City entire families were getting an average of $2.39 a week for relief. In Toledo the municipal commissary could allow only 2.14 cents per meal per person per day. In vast rural areas there was no relief coverage at all. "I don't want to steal," a Pennsylvania man wrote Governor Pinchot, "but I won't let my wife and boy cry for something to eat . . . How long is this going to keep up? I cannot stand it any longer . . . O, if God would only open a way."

THE FARMER

The shadow fell over the cities and towns; it fell as heavily over the countryside. Farmers had already drawn extensively on their savings before 1929. The Wall Street explosion only made their situations worse by diminishing even more the demand for farm products. And, where industry could protect its price structure by meeting reduced demand with reduced output, farmers, unable to control output, saw no way to maintain income except to increase planting. Total crop acreage actually rose in 1930 and showed no significant decline in 1931.

The burden of agriculture adjustment thus fell not on production but on price. The figures were dramatic. Between 1929 and 1934 agricultural production declined 15 percent in volume, 40 percent in price; industrial production 42 percent in volume, 15 percent in price. The relative stability of industrial prices worsened the farmers' terms of trade; the ratio of the prices the farmer received to the prices he paid plunged from 109 in 1919 (in terms of 1910–14 prices) and 89 in 1929 to 64 in 1931. Corn slid down to 15 cents, cotton and wool to 5 cents, hogs and sugar to 3 cents, and beef to 2.5 cents. A farmer who chewed one thick plug of Drummond a day required almost a bushel of wheat a day to keep him in chewing tobacco. It took 16 bushels of wheat—more than the average yield of a whole acre—to buy one of his children a pair of $4 shoes. Net farm income in 1932 was $1.8 billion—less than one-third what it had been three years earlier. So appalling a slump left many farm families with little income, and many with no income at all.

The farmer's obligations—his taxes and his debts—had been calculated in terms of the much higher price levels of the twenties. A cotton farmer who borrowed $800 when cotton was 16 cents a pound borrowed the equivalent of 5,000 pounds of cotton; now, with cotton moving toward 5 cents, he must pay back the debt with over 15,000 pounds of cotton. And, while the farmer's income fell by 64 percent, his burden of indebtedness fell a mere 7 percent. In the meantime, fences were standing in disrepair, crops were rotting, livestock was not worth the freight to market, farm machinery was wearing out. Some found it cheaper to burn their corn than to sell it and buy coal. On every side, notices of mortgage foreclosures and tax sales were going up on gate posts and in county courthouses. William Allen White summed it up: "Every farmer, whether his farm is under mortgage or not, knows that with farm products priced as they are today, sooner or later he must go down."

The southwestern drought only intensified the sense of grievance. In January 1931, several hundred tenant farmers presented themselves at the Red Cross in England, Arkansas, and asked for food. They included whites and Negroes, and some carried rifles. When the Red Cross administrator said that his supply of requisition blanks had been exhausted, the mob marched on the stores and seized their own flour and lard. "Paul Revere just woke up Concord," said Will Rogers, "these birds woke up America."

A. N. Young, president of the Wisconsin Farmers' Union, warned the Senate Agriculture Committee early in 1932: "The farmer is naturally a conservative individual, but you cannot find a conservative farmer today. He is not to be found. I am as conservative as any man could be, but any economic system that has it in its power to set me and my wife in the streets, at my age—what else could I see but red."

"The fact is today," Young told the Committee, "that there are more actual reds among the farmers in Wisconsin than you could dream about. . . . They are just ready to do anything to get even with the situation. I almost hate to express it, but I honestly believe that if some of them could buy airplanes, they would come down here to Washington to blow you fellows all up."

1932

And the economic decline continued. National income, which had been $87.4 billion in 1929, fell with the value of the dollar to $41.7 billion in 1932. Unemployment rose: 4 million in 1930, 8 million in 1931, 12 million in 1932—nearly one out of every four workers in the nation seeking a job. Net investment in 1931 was minus $358 million (in 1929 prices); the next year it fell to a disheartening minus $5.8 billion. The Federal Reserve Board index of manufacturing production went down from 110 in 1929 to 57 in 1932; wage payments from $50 billion to $30 billion. And, as prices and income fell, the burdens of indebtedness—farm mortgages, railroad bonds, municipal and state debts—became insupportable.

Statistics reflected only dimly the human reality. The year 1932 brought new anguish. By spring, when United States Steel made its second large wage slash, the attempt to maintain pay scales had pretty well foundered. By the end of the year, the weekly wage in iron and steel averaged 63 percent less than in 1929. The Pennsylvania Department of Labor reported in July 1932, that wages had fallen to 5 cents an hour in sawmills, 6 cents in brick and tile manufacturing, 7.5 cents in general contracting. In Malvern, Arkansas, lumber workers received 10 cents an hour; women in Tennessee mills were paid as little as $2.39 for a 50-hour week. In lighter industries, conditions were even worse. The Connecticut Commissioner of Labor recorded in the summer of 1932 the existence of over one hundred sweatshops hiring young girls for as little as 60 cents to $1.10 for a 55-hour week. A family of six, including four children, were found stringing safety pins on wires late into the night for four or five dollars a week. And it was increasingly hard for decent employers to continue paying 1929 wages while competitors were cutting their labor costs in half. The entire wage structure was apparently condemned to disintegration.

RELIEF

But a job, even in sweatshops, was still better than unemployment; for the patchwork of relief was visibly collapsing. The need had never been greater. New people were crowding the offices, God-fearing members of the middle class who had not dreamed that they would one day stand drearily in line for a handout. As the applicants increased and the resources diminished, standards of assistance went down. By 1932 only about one-quarter of the unemployed were actually receiving relief, limited in the main to food, with sometimes a little fuel. Voluntary funds had almost given out; 90 percent of relief came from public funds; and these funds too were diminishing. RFC aid was too meager and unreliable for advance planning. As a consequence, the administration of relief was on a disaster basis. "We of the cities have done our best," said the mayor of Toledo in the spring of 1932, but "we have failed miserably."

In New York City, those lucky enough to get on the rolls at all were averaging $2.39 per family per week; and the city's relief fund could take care of only about half the unemployed heads of families. A group of Latin Americans and Portuguese Negroes found refuge in a deserted Armour packing plant on West 30th Street, climbing to the top floor at night by rope ladder. Other unemployed built shacks in the bed of the abandoned reservoir in Central Park. They called it Hoover Valley and scavenged for a living almost under the shadow of the glittering, half-empty skyscrapers on their southern horizon.

In Chicago, one out of every two workers was without a job. Municipal employees went for months without pay. From May 1931, the Chicago Public Library could not afford a single new book. Socialists and Communists organized demonstrations among the 700,000 unemployed. It might be better for Washington to send $150 million to Chicago now, Mayor Anton Cermak vainly suggested in June 1932, than to send federal troops later.

The Philadelphia Community Council described its situation in July 1932 as one of "slow starvation and progressive disintegration of family life." In the Pennsylvania coal fields, miners kept up a subdued battle against starvation, freezing in rickety one-room houses, subsisting on wild weed-roots and dandelions, struggling for life in black and blasted valleys. In Kentucky they ate violet tops, wild onions, and the weeds which cows would eat (one wrote, "as cows won't eat a poison weeds"), while wan children attended school without coats, shoes, or underclothes. In Logan and Mingo Counties of West Virginia, according to Clarence Pickett's testimony before a House committee, people were breaking into storehouses and stealing supplies. "I would steal before I would starve," interjected Congressman Kent Keller of Illinois. "I think all of us would probably," replied the Quaker official, adding hastily: "I don't know whether you want that in the record."

In Oakland, California, four-year-old Narcisson Sandoval, who had been living on refuse, died of starvation, while her brothers and sisters were rushed to a hospital on the verge of death. In Northampton, Massachusetts, Anthony Prasol, the father of eight children, killed himself because he had no hope of work or assistance. Faith in life itself seemed to be ebbing away; the national birthrate for 1931

was 17 percent below 1921 and 10 percent below 1926.

INAUGURATION DAY, 1933

The White House, midnight, Friday, March 3, 1933. Across the country the banks of the nation had gradually shuttered their windows and locked their doors. The very machinery of the American economy seemed to be coming to a stop. The rich and fertile nation, overflowing with natural wealth in its fields and forests and mines, equipped with unsurpassed technology, endowed with boundless resources in its men and women, lay stricken. "We are at the end of our rope," a weary President Hoover at last said, as the striking clock announced the day of his retirement. "There is nothing more we can do."

Saturday, March 4, dawned gray and bleak. The darkness of the day intensified the mood of helplessness. "A sense of depression had settled over the capital," reported the *New York Times*, "so that it could be felt." In the late morning, people began to gather for the noon ceremonies, drawn, it would seem, by curiosity as much as by hope. As they waited, they murmured among themselves. "What are those things that look like little cages?" one asked. "Machine guns," replied a woman with a nervous giggle. "The atmosphere which surrounded the change of government in the United States," wrote Arthur Krock, "was comparable to that which might be found in a beleaguered capital in war time." The colorless light of the cast-iron skies, the numb faces of the crowd, created almost an air of fantasy.

The fog of despair hung over the land. One out of every four American workers lacked a job. Factories that had once darkened the skies with smoke stood ghostly and silent, like extinct volcanoes. Families slept in tarpaper shacks and tin-lined caves and scavenged like dogs for food in the city dump. In October the New York City Health Department had reported that over one-fifth of the pupils in public schools were suffering from malnutrition. Thousands of vagabond children were roaming the land, wild boys of the road. Hunger marchers, pinched and bitter, were parading cold streets in New York and Chicago. On the countryside unrest had already flared into violence. Farmers stopped milk trucks along Iowa roads and poured the milk into the ditch. Mobs halted mortgage sales, ran the men from the banks and insurance companies out of town, intimidated courts and judges, demanded a moratorium on debts. When a sales company in Nebraska invaded a farm and seized two trucks, the farmers in the Newman Grove district organized a posse, called it the "Red Army," and took the trucks back. In West Virginia, mining families, turned out of their homes, lived in tents along the road on pinto beans and black coffee.

IMPENDING REVOLUTION

In January, Edward A. O'Neal, an Alabama planter, head of the Farm Bureau Federation, bluntly warned a Senate committee, "Unless something is done for the American farmer we will have revolution in the countryside within less than twelve months." Donald Richberg, a Chicago lawyer, told another Senate committee a few weeks later, "There are many signs that if the lawfully constituted leadership does not soon substitute action for words, a new leadership, perhaps unlawfully constituted, will arise and act." William Green, the ordinarily benign president of the ordinarily conservative American Federation of Labor, told a third committee that if Congress did not enact a thirty-hour law, labor would compel employers to grant it "by universal strike." "Which would be class war, practically?" interrupted Senator Hugo Black. "Whatever it would be," said Green, "it would be that. . . . That is the only language that a lot of employers ever understand—the language of force." In the cities and on the farms, Communist organizers were finding a ready audience and a zealous following.

Elmer Davis reported that the leading citizens of one industrial city—it was Dayton, Ohio—had organized a committee to plan how the city and the country around could function as an economic unit if the power lines were cut and the railroads stopped running. Over champagne and cigars, at the Everglades in Palm Beach, a banker declared the country on the verge of revolution; another guest, breaking the startled silence, advised the company to "step without the territorial boundaries of the United States of America with as much cash as you can carry just as soon as it is feasi-

ble for you to get away." "There'll be a revolution, sure," a Los Angeles banker said on a transcontinental train. "The farmers will rise up. So will labor. The Reds will run the country—or maybe the Fascists. Unless, of course, Roosevelt does something."

But what could he do? In February 1933, the Senate Finance Committee summoned a procession of business leaders to solicit their ideas on the crisis. Said John W. Davis, the leader of the American bar, "I have nothing to offer, either of fact or theory." W. W. Atterbury of the Pennsylvania Railroad: "There is no panacea." Most endorsed the thesis advanced by the permanent elder statesman Bernard Baruch: "Delay in balancing the Budget is trifling with disaster." And, as they spoke their lusterless pieces, the banks began to close their doors. "Our entire banking system," said William Gibbs McAdoo in exasperation, "does credit to a collection of imbeciles."

But bankruptcy of ideas seemed almost as complete among the intellectuals. "My heartbreak at liberalism," wrote William Allen White "is that it has sounded no note of hope, made no plans for the future, offered no program." On the eve of the inaugural, a leading American theologian pronounced an obituary on liberal society. His essay was written, said Reinhold Niebuhr, on the assumption that "capitalism is dying and with the conviction that it ought to die." Let no one delude himself by hoping for reform from within. "There is nothing in history to support the thesis that a dominant class ever yields its position or its privileges in society because its rule has been convicted of ineptness or injustices." Others, in their despair, could only yearn for a savior. Hamilton Fish, the New York congressman, spoke for millions when he wrote to Roosevelt late in February that in the crisis we must "give you any power that you may need."

The images of a nation as it approached zero hour: the well-groomed men, baffled and impotent in their double-breasted suits before the Senate committee; the confusion and dismay in the business office and the university; the fear in the country club; the angry men marching in the silent street; the scramble for the rotting garbage in the dump; the sweet milk trickling down the dusty road; the noose dangling over the barn door; the raw northwest wind blasting its way across Capitol plaza.

QUESTIONS AND STUDY SUGGESTIONS

1. What was the effect of the Great Depression upon (*a*) employment; (*b*) the birth rate; (*c*) farm prices and output; (*d*) industrial prices and output; (*e*) wages and wage rates; (*f*) nutritional and housing standards; and (*g*) the burden of agricultural debts?

2. Comment on (*a*) the adequacy of the relief that state and local governments gave the unemployed; (*b*) the despair and sense of terror that developed among the unemployed as the Depression deepened; (*c*) the violence and the growing disrespect for law and order; (*d*) the likelihood of the violent overthrow of capitalism and the United States government; and (*e*) the absence of suggestions for means of halting the Depression.

Reading 13

When Inflation Runs Wild: The Case of Brazil

Charles T. Stewart, Jr., Research Professor of Economics, George Washington University

The Great Depression of the 1930s portrays one extreme of the business cycle. This reading, on the other hand, is a fascinating case study of the inflationary pole of the cyclical spectrum. In modern Brazil we find that, because of a variety of inappropriate government policies, dramatic increases in the price level and an equally drastic deterioration in the value of the monetary unit have occurred. The effects of Brazil's hyperinflation are manifold: the volume and composition of saving is substantially distorted; producers lack a reliable standard of value requisite to rational decision making; the quality of service has seriously deteriorated in regulated industries; and, perhaps most important of all, there has been a deterioration in the moral fiber of the nation.

From Charles T. Stewart, Jr., "When Inflation Runs Wild," **Nation's Business**, January, 1965, pp. 79–81, © 1964, Nation's Business—the Chamber of Commerce of the United States. Reprinted by permission.

Take a country that:

1. Continuously gives huge subsidies to consumers.

2. Legislates large increases in wages and fringe costs.

3. Allows enormous government deficits.

4. Has official corruption on a grand scale.

5. Speeds up the money-printing presses.

6. Harshly regulates its utility industries.

And you have an example of galloping inflation.

This has happened in one of our neighboring countries—Brazil, a nation with 80 million people and a land area as large as the United States, where inflation in the past year probably has exceeded 100 percent. (The cost of living increased 13 times over since 1958.)

This has not been brought on by war or natural catastrophe but by public policies which have stopped the growth of people's income and which nearly led to a communist takeover.

DISAPPEARING COINS

One of the first things the visitor notices in Brazil is the absence of coins. The reason is simple. With rapidly rising prices and consequent diminishing buying power of the cruzeiro, the brass and silver coins in circulation became more valuable for their metal content than for their purchasing power and were promptly melted. Cheaper aluminum coins minted to replace them in turn soon became worth melting for their metal content.

The denominations of most of these coins would now be the equivalent of anywhere from one thousandth to one tenth of a cent—hardly worth loading down one's pockets.

Not only have all coins disappeared, but small denomination paper money is seldom used. Even five-cruzeiro notes, which are worth about three tenths of a penny, are fairly rare. Those still found are old and torn; no more in these lower denominations are being printed.

The visitor will also learn that he does not always get the exact change for some of his purchases; nor is he expected to pay the exact amount listed. For example, in purchasing 22 cruzeiros worth of stamps—which until recently were enough to send a postcard air-mail to the United States—20 cruzeiros might be accepted or, conversely, one might receive 80 cruzeiros worth of change for a hundred-cruzeiro note.

Considering that 100 cruzeiros are worth about six cents, it is not surprising that salespeople accept underpayments of a few cruzeiros or give excess change in similar amounts.

BILLFOLDS ARE OBSOLETE

Another early discovery of a visitor to Brazil is that pocketbooks are obsolete. Until a few months ago the largest note in circulation was 1,000 cruzeiros, which at one time represented more than $100 (U.S.) but currently is worth about 60 cents.

The traveler cannot cram an ordinary billfold with much more than $10 worth of currency. To carry sizable amounts of cash he literally must stuff a briefcase or a plain paper bag.

Some 5,000-cruzeiro bills (worth around $3) are being printed but these are still scarce and much in demand because they permit carrying a somewhat larger amount of cash in a more compact package. Just counting change is a time-consuming operation employing millions of man-hours every month.

Just as coins are out, so are coin-operated machines. Taxi meters are a problem. In some the highest amount which can be registered is not sufficient for a long ride. As prices rise and taxi rates are adjusted accordingly, cab drivers receive printed cards which indicate the calculations to be made from the meter readings.

The tourist may be surprised to find large price differences for the same item in different stores. The resident, however, knows that identical items in the same store may be listed at widely different prices; one item may be half the price of another. The reason:

As goods come into stock they are priced in accordance with their cost at the time. A few weeks later wholesale places may be up 20 percent and new stock coming in is listed at a substantially higher price. The rate of inflation is so rapid that many store managements do not think it worth their while to reprice all their items; they prefer to keep small stocks and leave the items as originally priced until sold. The buyer may therefore obtain a bargain by shopping around.

Government efforts at retail price control— on meat and sugar, for instance—collapsed quickly when stores almost overnight ceased to stock items which they feared could be sold only at a loss. The legal interest rate ceiling of

12 percent a year is meaningless. Violation is not direct but via subterfuge—adding on extra charges, not listed as interest, that nevertheless boosts the cost of borrowing.

INSURANCE AND SAVING

With substantial and unpredictable inflation there can be no life insurance business as we know it. In fact, there is no market for any kind of long-term insurance which depends upon the stability in the value of a policy for years ahead. Individuals who wish to protect their families may take out a heavy accident insurance policy a few months at a time. As one policy expires a new policy with higher premiums and a higher cruzeiro total is taken out.

It might seem that under these circumstances little money would be deposited in banks, which pay six percent a year, whereas the loss in the purchasing power of money recently has been higher than that per month.

Nevertheless, some individuals put their savings in bank accounts because they are unaware of the impact of inflation. More, however, do so rather than to hold amounts in cash, on which there is no interest, in the anticipation of shortly investing the funds more productively.

Often considerable time elapses before these funds are invested; meanwhile, a substantial share of their value evaporates. There is incentive to keep checking account balances as small as possible, to delay payments as long as possible, to speed up receipts and to spend these receipts before they decline in purchasing power.

TAX EVASION

It is impossible to raise the salaries of public employees to keep pace with inflation. Instead, many government workers, and most teachers, take other jobs and collect two or more paychecks. They get full-time government pay for part-time work.

Rapid inflation also promotes tax evasion. Even if the taxpayer is brought to heel some years later, by then the tax due, even with penalty, is a fraction of the original burden. Tax evasion in turn increases government deficits and in some cases increases tax rates, which may encourage further evasion and inflation in a vicious spiral.

Indicating the magnitude of the problem, 23 revenue agents were arrested this past August in São Paulo, which has one of the best administrations in Brazil, and charged with corruption. The following week voluntary tax payments increased 75 percent. Now that corrupt officials are being fired, careers are being wrecked and some of the worst offenders are ending up in jail, tax evasion is on the wane.

PRODUCER PROBLEMS

Whatever the problems of the consumer in facing inflation, they are dwarfed by those confronting the producer. With costs increasing rapidly and unpredictably, the producer finds it hazardous to make firm price commitments on advance orders.

Unpredictable fluctuations in the exchange rate, added to these other problems, make estimates of future costs almost impossible. Many export opportunities have been turned down because they involve commitments at firm dollar prices many months in advance of delivery.

The producer can do little to minimize his cost uncertainties by purchasing large amounts ahead of need. The lack of bank credit except for short periods, and the very high cost of such short-term credit, forbid tying up too much in large inventories.

MINIMUM WAGE CAUSES INFLATION

The major cost item, namely labor, is tied to statutory minimum wages; many other cost items are linked by escalator agreements to minimum wages.

Such minimums, which are changed periodically by the federal government and which vary not only from state to state but even in the same state between the capital city and the interior, directly influence the pay of a substantial proportion of workers. Changes in pay may be of the order of 50 or even 100 percent.

The obstacles which inflation creates for longer-term cost estimates and pricing policy have their impact also on investment. It is difficult to determine what the productivity of new investment will be, or even what the size of markets themselves will be by the time investments are completed.

The unavailability of bank credit of more than 120 days and the four to six percent monthly rates of interest strongly discourage investment with borrowed funds. Equity capital is very scarce, partly because of the tremendous uncertainties multiplied by inflation and partly because of the lack of legal protection for minority stockholders.

EFFECT ON PUBLIC UTILITIES

Perhaps the most distorting effects of inflation have been in transport, communications and power, services provided either by government or utilities whose rates are subject to government regulation. The process of rate adjustment to cost increases is often slow. When the impact of inflation on costs is added to political pressures to keep consumer prices low, the adjustment request becomes obsolete long before it is granted. New investment and even maintenance suffer in consequence. The firm has neither the profits nor the incentives to invest.

Railroads have been caught in this vicious spiral for many years. As a result the major role in general transport has been assumed by buses and trucks. This is true even though railroad rates are extremely low, often below operating costs. But the consequent lack of investment and inadequate maintenance make freight deliveries so unreliable that more expensive truck shipment is almost universally preferred.

Even in the case of buses, rate regulation in some cases discourages development of new routes and improvement of service. Coastal shipping plays a minimal role in freight movement because of excessive loading and unloading costs and delays which are largely the result of the labor situation in the major ports.

Air transport, which is carrying an increasing share of freight as well as passengers, is in a more favorable position, essentially because rate regulation is done by the Air Force which is more prompt in handling requests for adjustments than other regulatory agencies. The difference in rate adjustment is shown by the fact that air travel from Porto Alegre to São Paulo is approximately five times as expensive as the bus fare.

The situation in transport is duplicated in communications. Postal rates are preposterously low and postal service is absurdly unreliable and slow. Many letters never reach their destination. As a result various substitutes for postal service have been developed. In the major urban centers most firms maintain messenger boys to pick up and deliver messages and packages in person rather than depending upon the postal service.

Telephone and telegraph services are equally inadequate. Messengers substitute for urban telephone communications as well as for mail. The capacity of urban telephone systems is overtaxed. It is very often difficult to obtain a line; interurban telephone calls in particular may take hours to complete. Telephone rates, of course, are extremely low.

The same situation prevails in the national telegraph system. The rates for telegrams are far below their true cost. Service is completely unreliable. A telegram between São Paulo and Tio often takes two weeks to arrive. Under such conditions, of course, no urgent messages can be sent through the national telegraph and a number of private companies have set up their own networks which provide prompt service at many times the cost of the national telegraph.

In electric power, the process of rate adjustment has improved and is now handled quite promptly. Still, the years of inflation with regulated rates and the tendency to set rates to provide little profit—since the power companies were usually foreign-owned—have left their mark in terms of inadequate capacity and lack of incentives to increase capacity. Many firms have their own generators—often imported, operated on imported fuel and producing high-cost electricity—to insure against failures and shortages of power in the public distribution network.

Low utility rates encourage consumption, aggravate shortages and worsen service. Where services to households are provided at a fixed fee irrespective of volume of consumption, as in the case of telephone service, additional consumption is free, further increasing excess demand. The substitutes which have developed to circumvent the shortages—captive power plants, private courier services, trucking in place of ship and rail—are in most cases higher in cost. Thus demand inflation and cost inflation reinforce each other.

RECENT REFORMS

The new government of President Castello Branco is attempting the politically difficult job of reversing the policies which brought about this mess.

Large subsidies on wheat and gasoline have

been eliminated; postal rates and railroad tariffs have been raised to cover costs. These measures mean an immediate rise in prices but in the longer run should help put a damper on inflation by curtailing excess demand and by slashing the federal budget deficit.

Measures discriminating against foreign capital have been eliminated, leading to leftist charges of Yankee domination. The number of government employees is being cut down by attrition. Besides revenue agents, many corrupt officials, including generals, state governors and national legislators, are being prosecuted.

All these measures hurt some groups and create enemies. The most unpopular measure of all, perhaps, is government restraint of wage increases; yet wage restraint is the critical test which will measure the success of the government in reestablishing price stability.

Brazilian leaders are convinced that inflation control is a necessary condition for resuming rapid economic growth.

QUESTIONS AND STUDY SUGGESTIONS

1. What have been the underlying causes of Brazil's inflation? Explain how demand and cost inflation have reinforced one another.
2. What impact has Brazil's hyperinflation had upon (a) money as a medium of exchange and store of value; (b) business planning and decision making; (c) the efficient use and allocation of resources; and (d) the moral fiber of the nation?
3. Analyze the economic effects of inflation upon Brazil's public utility industries. Why has the quality of services frequently deteriorated?

Reading 14

Progress towards Economic Stability
Arthur F. Burns, Professor of Economics, Columbia University

Is the American economy of the late 1960s and 1970s susceptible to a business recession comparable to that of the thirties or to a hyperinflation such as that experienced by Brazil? Or do we enjoy a "depression-proof" economy? Arthur Burns contends in this reading that the United States has made substantial progress toward achieving a more stable economy. This progress has been the result of a composite of structural, policy, and attitudinal changes within our society. For example, the growth of corporate enterprise, the expansion of the public sector of the economy, the evolution

From Arthur F. Burns, "Progress towards Economic Stability," **American Economic Review**, March, 1960, pp. 1–19, abridged. Reprinted by permission.

of the social security system, shifts in the occupational allocation of the labor force away from cyclically volatile industries, and changes in consumer behavior are all important changes in the organization and structure of our economy which have made it more immune to cyclical instability. The development and improved use of both monetary and fiscal policies have provided us with an impressive arsenal of anticyclical weapons. Finally, the widespread expectation that government will act with reasonable promptness and decisiveness to check sizable recessions and inflations injects an element of economic confidence into our society which was obvious by its absence a third of a century ago. Burns's conclusion is not that the business cycle has been eliminated, but that future variations in business activity can be expected to be less severe than those of the past.

The American people have of late been more conscious of the business cycle, more sensitive to every wrinkle of economic curves, more alert to the possible need for contracyclical action on the part of government, than ever before in our history. Minor changes of employment or of productivity or of the price level, which in an earlier generation would have gone unnoticed, are nowadays followed closely by laymen as well as experts. This sensitivity to the phenomena of recession and inflation is a symptom of an increased public awareness of both the need for and the attainability of economic progress.

It is a fact of the highest importance, I think, that although our economy continues to be swayed by the business cycle, its impact on the lives and fortunes of individuals has been substantially reduced in our generation. More than twenty-five years have elapsed since we last experienced a financial panic or a deep depression of production and employment. Over twenty years have elapsed since we last had a severe business recession. Between the end of the second world war and the present, we have experienced four recessions, but each was a relatively mild setback. Since 1937 we have had five recessions, the longest of which lasted only 13 months. There is no parallel for such a sequence of mild—or such a sequence of brief—contractions, at least during the past hundred years in our own country.

Nor is this all. The character of the business cycle itself appears to have changed, apart from the intensity of its over-all movement. We usually think of the business cycle as a sustained advance of production, employment, incomes, consumption, and prices, followed by a sustained contraction, which in time gives way to a renewed advance of aggregate activity beyond the highest levels previously reached. We realize that changes in the price level occasionally outrun changes in production, that employment is apt to fluctuate less than production, and that consumption will fluctuate still less; but we nevertheless think of their movements as being roughly parallel. This concept of the business cycle has always been something of a simplification. For example, during the early decades of the nineteenth century, when agriculture dominated our national economy, occasional declines in the physical volume of production, whether large or small, had little effect on the number of jobs and sometimes had slight influence even on the flow of money incomes. As agriculture diminished in importance, the nation's production, employment, personal income, consumption, and price level fell more closely into step with one another and thus justified thinking of them as moving in a rough parallelism. In recent years, however, and especially since the second world war, the relations among these movements have become much looser.

The structure of an economy inevitably leaves its stamp on the character of its fluctuations. In our generation the structure of the American economy has changed profoundly, partly as a result of deliberate economic policies, partly as a result of unplanned developments. In considering problems of the future, we can proceed more surely by recognizing the changes in economic organization which already appear to have done much to blunt the impact of business cycles.

CHANGES IN BUSINESS ORGANIZATION

In the early decades of the nineteenth century the typical American worker operated his own farm or found scope for his energy on the family farm. Governmental activities were very limited. What there was of industry and commerce was largely conducted through small firms run by capitalist-employers. Corporations were rare and virtually confined to banking and transportation. As the population grew and capital became more abundant, individual enterprise expanded vigorously but corporate enterprise expanded still more. An increasing part of the nation's business therefore came under the rule of corporations. By 1929, the output of corporate businesses was already almost twice as large as the output of individual proprietorships and partnerships. The gap has widened appreciably since then. Corporate profits have therefore tended to increase faster than the incomes earned by proprietors, who still remain very numerous in farming, retail trade, and the professions. Fifty years ago the total income of proprietors was perhaps two and a half times as large as the combined sum of corporate profits and the compensation of corporate officers. By 1957 this corporate aggregate exceeded by a fourth the income of all proprietors and by two-thirds the income of proprietors outside of farming.

The great growth of corporations in recent decades has occurred preponderantly in industries where the firm must operate on a large scale to be efficient and therefore must assemble capital from many sources. But a corporation whose stock is held publicly and widely has a life of its own, apart from that of its owners, and will rarely distribute profits at the same rate as they are being earned. While profits normally respond quickly and sharply to a change in sales and production, the behavior of dividends is tempered by business judgment. In practice, dividends tend to move sluggishly and over a much narrower range than profits. Corporations have therefore come to function increasingly as a buffer between the fluctuations of production and the flow of income to individuals. In earlier times the lag of dividends was largely a result of the time-consuming character of corporate procedures. More recently, the advantages of a stable dividend—especially its bearing on a firm's financial reputation—have gained increasing recognition from business managers. Meanwhile, modern trends of taxation have stimulated corporations to rely more heavily on retained profits and less on new stock issues for their equity funds,

and this development in turn has facilitated the pursuit of stable dividend policies. Thus the evolution of corporate practice, as well as the growth of corporate enterprise itself, has served to reduce the influence of a cyclical decline of production and profits on the flow of income to individuals.

INCOME TAXATION

The expansion and the means of financing of governmental enterprise, especially since the 1930s, have had a similar effect. The increasing complexity of modern life, a larger concept of the proper function of government, and the mounting requirements of national defense have resulted in sharp increases of governmental spending. Fifty years ago the combined expenditure of federal, state, and local governments was about 7 percent of the dollar volume of the nation's total output. Governmental expenditures rose to 10 percent of total output in 1929 and to 26 percent in 1957. This huge expansion of governmental enterprise naturally led to increases in tax rates and to an energetic search for new sources of revenue. In time, taxes came to be imposed on estates, gifts, employment, sales, and—most important of all—on the incomes of both corporations and individuals. Fifty years ago customs duties still yielded about half of the total revenue of the federal government, and none of our governmental units as yet collected any tax on incomes. Twenty years later, personal and corporate income taxes were already the mainstay of federal finance. Subsequently, the activities of the federal government increased much faster than local activities and taxes followed suit. By 1957 the income tax accounted for nearly 70 percent of federal revenue, 8 percent of state and local revenue, and a little over half of the combined revenue of our various governmental units.

This dominance of the income tax in current governmental finance, together with the recent shift of tax collection toward a pay-as-you-go basis, has measurably enlarged the government's participation in the shifting fortunes of the private economy. During the nineteenth century, taxes were not only a much smaller factor in the economy, but such short-run elasticity as there was in tax revenues derived almost entirely from customs duties. Hence, when production fell off and private incomes diminished, the accompanying change in governmental revenues was usually small. In recent years, however, governmental revenues have become very sensitive to fluctuations of business conditions. When corporate profits decline by, say, a billion dollars, the federal government will collect under existing law about a half billion less from corporations. When individual incomes decline by a billion, the federal government may be expected to collect about $150 million less from individuals. State income taxes accentuate these effects. In short, when a recession occurs, our current tax system requires the government to reduce rather promptly and substantially the amount of money that it withdraws from the private economy for its own use. The result is that the income from production which corporations and individuals have at their disposal declines much less than does the national income.

SOCIAL SECURITY SYSTEM

Moreover, the operations of government are now so organized that the flow of personal income from production is bolstered during a recession by increased payments of unemployment insurance benefits. Unemployment insurance was established on a national basis in 1935, and the protection of workers against the hazards of unemployment has increased since then. Not all employees are as yet covered by unemployment insurance and the benefits, besides, are often inadequate to provide for essentials. Nevertheless, there has been a gradual improvement in the ability of families to get along decently even when the main breadwinner is temporarily unemployed. At present, over 80 percent of those who work for a wage or salary are covered by unemployment insurance, in contrast to 70 percent in 1940. The period over which benefits can be paid to an unemployed worker has become longer and the typical weekly benefit has risen in greater proportion than the cost of living. Furthermore, arrangements have recently been concluded in several major industries whereby benefits to the unemployed are supplemented from private sources.

Other parts of the vast system of social security that we have devised since the 1930s have also served to support the flow of personal income at times when business activity is declining. Payments made to retired workers kept increasing during each recession of the postwar period. The reason is partly that workers handicapped by old age or physical disability experience greater difficulty at such times in keeping their jobs or finding new ones and therefore apply for pensions in somewhat larger numbers. Another factor has been the intermittent liberalization of statutory benefits. But the most important reason for the steady increase of old-age pensions is the maturing of the social security system. In 1940, only 7 percent of people of age 65 and over were eligible for benefits from the old-age insurance trust fund, in contrast to 23 percent in 1948 and 69 percent in 1958. The trend of other public pension programs and the various public assistance programs has also been upward. Between 1929 and 1957 the social security and related benefits paid out by our various governmental units rose from 1 percent of total personal income to 6 percent. In 1933, with the economy at a catastrophically low level, these benefit payments were merely $548 million larger than in 1929. On the other hand, in 1958—when business activity was only slightly depressed—they were $4.4 billion above the level of 1957. Even these figures understate the difference between current conditions and those of a quarter century ago, for they leave out of account the private pensions which are beginning to supplement public pensions on a significant scale.

As a result of these several major developments in our national life, the movement of aggregate personal income is no longer closely linked to the movement of aggregate production. During the postwar period we have had several brief but sizable setbacks in production. For example, in the course of the recession of 1957–58, the physical output of factories and mines fell 14 percent, the physical output of commodities and services in the aggregate fell 5.4 percent, and the dollar volume of total output fell 4.3 percent. In earlier times personal incomes would have responded decisively to such a decline in production. This time the government absorbed a substantial part of the drop in the dollar volume of production by putting up with a sharp decline of its revenues despite the need to raise expenditures. Corporations absorbed another part of the decline by maintaining dividends while their undistributed profits slumped. In the end, the aggregate of personal incomes, after taxes, declined less than 1 percent and the decline was over before the recession ended.

Although the details have varied from one case to the next, a marked divergence between the movements of personal income and production has occurred in each of the postwar recessions. Indeed, during 1953–54 the total income at the disposal of individuals defied the recession by continuing to increase. This unique achievement was due to the tax reduction that became effective soon after the onset of recession as well as to the structural changes that have reduced the dependence of personal income on the short-run movements of production.

CHANGES IN INDUSTRY AND LABOR FORCE

When we turn from personal income to employment, we find that the imprint of the business cycle is still strong. During each recession since 1948, unemployment reached a level which, while decidedly low in comparison with the experience of the thirties, was sufficient to cause serious concern. But although the fluctuations of employment have continued to synchronize closely with the movements of production, the relation between the two has been changing in ways which favor greater stability of employment in the future.

As the industrialization of our economy proceeded during the nineteenth century, an increasing part of the population became exposed to the hazards of the business cycle. Manufacturing, mining, construction, freight transportation—these are the strategic industries of a developing economy and they are also the industries in which both production and jobs have been notoriously unstable. Shortly after the Civil War, the employees attached to this cyclical group of industries already constituted 23 percent of the labor force. Employees of industries that have remained relatively free from cyclical unemployment—that is, agriculture, merchandising, public utilities, financial enterprises, the personal service trades, and the government—accounted for another 32 percent. The self-employed in farming, business, and the professions, whose jobs are especially steady, made up the rest or 45 percent of the work force. This was the situation in 1869.

Fifty years later, the proportion of workers engaged in farming, whether as operators or hired hands, had shrunk drastically, and this shrinkage was offset only in part by the relative gain of other stable sources of employment. Consequently, the proportion of employees in the cyclical industries kept rising, decade by decade, and reached 36 percent in 1919.

Clearly, the broad effect of economic evolution until about 1920 was to increase the concentration of jobs in the cyclically volatile industries, and this was a major force tending to intensify declines of employment during business contractions. Since then, the continued progress of technology, the very factor which originally was mainly responsible for the concentration in the cyclical industries, has served to arrest this tendency. The upward trend of production in manufacturing and the other highly cyclical industries has remained rapid in recent decades. However, advances of technology have come so swiftly in these industries as well as in agriculture that an increasing part of the nation's labor could turn to the multitude of tasks in which the effectiveness of human effort improves only slowly where it improves at all. Thus the employees of "service" industries constituted 24 percent of the labor force in 1919, but as much as 44 percent in 1957. The proportion of self-employed workers in business and the professions, which was 9.4 percent in the earlier year, became 10.6 percent in the later year. True, these gains in types of employment that are relatively stable during business cycles were largely canceled by the countervailing trend in agriculture. Nevertheless, the proportion of employees attached to the cyclically volatile industries has not risen since 1919. Or to express this entire development in another way, the proportion of workers having rather steady jobs, either because they work for themselves or because they are employed in industries that are relatively free from the influence of business cycles, kept declining from the beginning of our industrial revolution until about 1920, and since then has moved slightly but irregularly upward.

Thus, the changing structure of industry, which previously had exercised a powerful destabilizing influence on employment and output, particularly the former, has ceased to do so. The new stabilizing tendency is as yet weak, but it is being gradually reinforced by the spread of "white-collar" occupations throughout the range of industry. For many years now, the proportion of people who work as managers, engineers, scientists, draftsmen, accountants, clerks, secretaries, salesmen, or in kindred occupations has been increasing. The white-collar group, which constituted only 28 percent of the labor force outside agriculture in 1900, rose to 38 percent in 1940 and to 44 percent in 1957. Workers of this category are commonly said to hold a "position" rather than a "job" and to be paid a "salary" rather than a "wage." Hence, they are often sheltered by a professional code which frowns upon frequent firing and hiring. Moreover, much of this type of employment is by its nature of an overhead character and therefore less responsive to the business cycle than are the jobs of machine operators, craftsmen, assembly-line workers, truck drivers, laborers, and others in the "blue-collar" category. For example, during the recession of 1957–58, the number of "production workers" employed in manufacturing, who approximate the blue-collar group, declined 12 percent, while the employment of "nonproduction workers," who approximate the white-collar group, declined only 3 percent. This sort of difference has been characteristic of recessions generally, not only the most recent episode, and on a smaller scale it has also been characteristic of industry generally, not only of manufacturing.

It appears, therefore, that changes in the occupational structure of the labor force, if not also in the industrial structure, have been tending of late to loosen the links which, over a considerable part of our economic history, tied the short-run movement of total employment rather firmly to the cyclical movement of total production, and especially to the cyclical movement of its most unstable parts—that is, the activities of manufacturing, mining, construction, and freight transportation. This stabilizing tendency promises well for the future, although up to the present it has not left a mark on records of aggregate employment that is comparable with the imprint that the stabilizing influences we discussed previously have left on personal income. In the postwar period, as over a longer past, the number of men and women at work, and even more the aggregate of hours worked by them, has continued to move in fairly close sympathy with the fluctuations of production.

We can no longer justifiably suppose, however, when employment falls 2 million during a recession, as it did between July 1957 and July 1958, that the number of people who receive an income has declined by any such figure. In fact, the number of workers drawing unemployment insurance under the several regular plans rose about 1.3 million during these twelve months, while the number of retired workers on public pensions rose another million. Hence, it may be conservatively estimated that the number of income recipients increased over 300 thousand despite the recession. In the other postwar recessions our experience was fairly similar. In other words as a result of some of the structural changes on which I dwelt earlier the size of the income-receiving population has grown steadily and escaped cyclical fluctuations entirely.

CHANGES IN CONSUMER SPENDING

Turning next to consumer spending, we must try once again to see recent developments in historical perspective. The fact that stands out is that the impact of business cycles on consumption has recently diminished, while the effects of consumption on the business cycle have become more decisive.

In the classical business cycle, as we came to know it in this country, once business investment began declining appreciably, a reduction of consumer spending soon followed. Sometimes the expansion of investment culminated because the firms of one or more key industries, finding that their markets were growing less rapidly than had been anticipated, made an effort to bring their productive capacity or inventories into better adjustment with sales. Sometimes the expansion culminated because the belief grew that construction and financing costs had been pushed to unduly high levels by the advance of prosperity. Sometimes it culminated for all these or still other reasons. But whatever the cause or causes of the decline in investment, it made its influence felt over an increasing area of the economy. For a while consumer spending was maintained at a peak level or even kept rising. But since businessmen were now buying on a smaller scale from one another, more and more workers lost their jobs or their overtime pay, financial embarrassments and business failures became more frequent, and uncertainty about the business outlook spread to parts of the economy in which sales and profits were still flourishing. If some consumers reacted to these developments by curtailing their spending in the interest of caution, others did so as a matter of necessity. Before long, these curtailments proved sufficient to bring on some decline in the aggregate spending of consumers. The impulses for reducing business investments therefore quickened and the entire round of events was repeated, with both investment and consumption declining in a cumulative process.

As the contraction continued, it tried men's patience, yet in time worked its own cure. Driven by hard necessity, business firms moved with energy to reduce costs and increase efficiency. Consumers whose incomes were declining often saved less or dissaved in order not to disrupt their customary living standards. Hence, even if sales and prices were still falling, profit margins improved here and there. In the meantime, bank credit became more readily available, costs of building and terms of borrowing became more favorable, the bond market revived, business failures diminished, and the investment plans of innovators and others began expanding again. When recovery finally came, it was likely to be led by a reduced rate of disinvestment in inventories or by a new rush to make investments in fixed capital. At this stage of the business cycle, consumer spending was at its very lowest level, if not still declining.

Many of these features of earlier business cycles have carried over to the present. However, the behavior of consumers in the postwar recessions has departed from the traditional pattern in two respects. In the first place, consumers maintained their spending at a high level even after business activity had been declining for some months, so that the tendency of recessions to cumulate was severely checked. During the recession of 1945 consumer spending actually kept increasing. In each of the later recessions it fell somewhat; but the decline at no time exceeded 1 percent and lasted only a quarter or two. In the second place, instead of lagging at the recovery stage of the business cycle, as it had in earlier times, consumer spending turned upward before production or employment resumed its expansion. Not only have consumers managed their spending during recessions so that the cumulative process of deflation has been curbed, but consumer spending has emerged as one of the active factors in arresting recession and hastening recovery.

This new role of the consumer in the business cycle reflects some of the developments of the postwar period that we considered earlier, particularly the greatly enhanced stability in the flow of personal income, the steady expansion in the number of income recipients, and the relative increase in the number of steady jobs. It reflects also the improvements of financial organization and other structural changes which have strengthened the confidence of people, whether acting as consumers or investors, in their own and the nation's economic future. Whatever may have been true of the past, it can no longer be held that consumers are passive creatures who lack the power or the habit of initiating changes in economic activities. There is no harm in thinking of consumer spending as being largely "determined" by past and current incomes, provided we also recognize that the level of current incomes is itself shaped to a significant degree by the willingness of people to work hard to earn what they need to live as they feel they should. The evidence of rising expectations and increased initiative on the part of consumers is all around us. It appears directly in the rapidly rising proportion of women in the labor force, in the sizable and increasing proportion of men who hold down more than one job, in the slackening of the long-term decline of the average work week in manufacturing despite the increased power of trade unions, as well as indirectly in the improvement of living standards and the great upsurge of population. Indeed, the expansive forces on the side of consumption have been so powerful that we must not be misled by the cyclical responses of consumer spending, small though they were, to which I referred earlier. There are no continuous records of inventories in the hands of consumers; but if such statistics were available, we would almost certainly find that consumption proper, in contrast to consumer spending, did not decline at all during any of the postwar recessions.

In view of these developments in the realm of the consumer, it is evident that the force of any cyclical decline of production has in recent years been reduced or broken as its influence spread through economy. Production has remained unstable, but the structure of our economy has changed in ways which have limited the effects of recessions on the lives of individuals—on the numbers who receive an income, the aggregate of personal incomes, consumer spending, actual consumption, and to some degree even the numbers employed. It is, therefore, hardly an exaggeration to assert that a good part of the personal security which in an earlier age derived from living on farms and in closely knit family units, after having been disrupted by the onrush of industrialization and urbanization, has of late been restored through the new institutions that have developed in both the private and public branches of our economy.

CHANGES IN BANKING

In concentrating, as I have thus far, on the changes of economic organization which have lately served to reduce the impact of business cycles on the lives of individuals, I have provisionally taken the cyclical movement of production for granted. Of course, if the fluctuations of production had been larger, the impact on people would have been greater. On the other hand, the stabilized tendency of personal income and consumption has itself been a major reason why recent recessions of production have been brief and of only moderate intensity. Many other factors have contributed to this development. Among them are the deliberate efforts made in our generation to control the business cycle, of which I have as yet said little.

In earlier generations there was a tendency for the focus of business thinking to shift from the pursuit of profits to the maintenance of financial solvency whenever confidence in the continuance of prosperity began to wane. At such times experienced businessmen were prone to reason that it would shortly become more difficult to collect from their customers or to raise funds by borrowing, while they in turn were being pressed by their creditors. Under the circumstances it seemed only prudent to conserve cash on hand, if not also to reduce inventories or accounts receivable. Such efforts

by some led to similar efforts by others, in a widening circle. As pressure on commodity markets, security markets, and on the banking system mounted, the decline of business activity was speeded and the readjustment of interest rates, particularly on the longer maturities, was delayed. More often than not the scramble for liquidity ran its course without reaching crisis proportions. Sometimes, however, as in 1873, 1893, and 1907, events took a sinister turn. Financial pressures then became so acute that doubts arose about the ability of banks to meet their outstanding obligations and, as people rushed to convert their deposits into currency, even the soundest banks were forced to restrict the outflow of cash. With the nation's system for making monetary payments disrupted, panic ruled for a time over the economy and production inevitably slumped badly.

It was this dramatic phase of the business cycle that first attracted wide notice and stimulated students of public affairs to seek ways and means of improving our financial organization. The Federal Reserve Act, which became law under the shadow of the crisis of 1907, required the pooling of bank reserves and established facilities for temporary borrowing by banks. The hope that this financial reform would ease the transition from the expanding to the contracting phase of business cycles has been amply justified by experience. But the Federal Reserve System could not prevent the cumulation of financial trouble during business expansion. Nor could it prevent runs on banks or massive bank failures, as the Great Depression demonstrated. The need to overhaul and strengthen the financial system became increasingly clear during the thirties and led to numerous reforms, among them the insurance of mortgages, the creation of a secondary market for mortgages, the insurance of savings and loan accounts, and—most important of all—the insurance of bank deposits. These financial reforms have served powerfully to limit the propagation of fear, which in the past had been a major factor in intensifying slumps of production.

CHANGES IN ATTITUDES

But more basic than the financial innovations or any other specific measures of policy has been the change in economic and political attitudes which took root during the 'thirties. The economic theory that depressions promote industrial efficiency and economic progress lost adherents as evidence accumulated of the wreckage caused by unemployment and business failures. The political belief that it was best to leave business storms to blow themselves out lost its grip on men's minds as the depression stretched out. In increasing numbers citizens in all walks of life came around to the view that mass unemployment was intolerable under modern conditions and that the federal government has a continuing responsibility to foster competitive enterprise, to prevent or moderate general economic declines, and to promote a high and rising level of employment and production. This new philosophy of intervention was articulated by the Congress in the Employment Act of 1946, which solemnly expressed what had by then become a national consensus.

In recent times, therefore, the business cycle has no longer run a free course and this fact has figured prominently in the plans of businessmen as well as consumers. During the 1930s, when the objectives of social reform and economic recovery were sometimes badly confused, many investors suspected that contracyclical policies would result in narrowing the scope of private enterprise and reducing the profitability of investment. These fears diminished after the war as the government showed more understanding of the need to foster a mood of confidence so that enterprise, innovation, and investment may flourish. In investing circles, as elsewhere, the general expectation of the postwar period has been that the government would move with some vigor to check any recession that developed, that its actions would by and large contribute to this objective, and that they would do so in a manner that is broadly consistent with our national traditions. This expectation gradually became stronger and it has played a significant role in extending the horizons of business thinking about the markets and opportunities of the future. The upsurge of population, the eagerness of consumers to live better, the resurgence of Western Europe, the revolutionary discoveries of science, and the steady flow of new products, new materials, and new processes have added impetus to the willingness of investors to expend huge sums of capital on research and on the improvement and expansion of industrial plant and equipment. Some

of these influences have also been effective in augmenting public investment. The fundamental trend of investment has therefore been decidedly upward. The private part of investment has continued to move cyclically; but it is now a smaller fraction of total national output and it has displayed a capacity to rebound energetically from the setbacks that come during recessions.

IMPROVED MONETARY POLICY

The specific measures adopted by the government in dealing with the recessions of the postwar period have varied from one case to the next. In all of them, monetary, fiscal, and housekeeping policies played some part, with agricultural price-support programs assuming special prominence in one recession, tax reductions in another, and increases of public expenditure in still another. Taking a long view, the most nearly consistent part of contracyclical policy has been in the monetary sphere. Since the early 1920s, when the Federal Reserve authorities first learned how to influence credit conditions through open-market operations, long-term interest rates have tended to move down as soon as the cyclical peak of economic activity was reached, in contrast to the long lags that were characteristic of earlier times. Since 1948 the decline of long-term interest rates in the early stages of a recession has also become more rapid. This change in the cyclical behavior of capital markets reflects the increased vigor and effectiveness of recent monetary policies. Inasmuch as optimism, as a rule, is still widespread during the initial stages of an economic decline, a substantial easing of credit, provided it comes early enough, can appreciably hasten economic recovery. This influence is exerted only in part through lower interest rates. Of greater consequence is the fact that credit becomes more readily available, that the money supply is increased or kept from falling, that the liquidity of financial assets is improved, and that financial markets are generally stimulated. The effects of easier credit are apt to be felt most promptly by smaller businesses and the home-building industry, but they tend to work their way through the entire economy. There can be little doubt that the rather prompt easing of credit conditions, which occurred during recent setbacks of production, was of some significance in keeping their duration so short.

BUSINESS POLICIES

Business firms have also been paying closer attention to the business cycle, and not a few of them have even tried to do something about it. These efforts have been expressed in a variety of ways—through the adoption of long-range capital budgets, closer control of inventories, and more energetic selling or some relaxation of credit standards in times of recession. I do not know enough to assess either the extent or the success of some of these business policies. Surely, business investment in fixed capital has remained a highly volatile activity—a fact that is sometimes overlooked by concentrating attention on years instead of months and on actual expenditures instead of new commitments. There is, however, strong evidence that the businessmen of our generation manage inventories better than did their predecessors. The inventory-sales ratio of manufacturing firms has lately averaged about a fourth less than during the 1920s, despite the increased importance of the durable goods sector where inventories are especially heavy. The trend of the inventory-sales ratio has also moved down substantially in the case of distributive firms. This success in economizing on inventories has tended to reduce the fluctuations of inventory investment relative to the scale of business operations and this in turn has helped to moderate the cyclical swings in production. Not only that, but it appears that the cyclical downturns of both inventories and inventory investment have tended to come at an earlier stage of the business cycle in the postwar period than they did previously, so that any imbalance between inventories and sales could be corrected sooner. Since consumer outlays—and often also other expenditures—were well maintained during the recent recessions of production, the rising phase of inventory disinvestment ceased rather early and this naturally favored a fairly prompt recovery of production.

Thus, numerous changes in the structure of our economy have combined to stimulate overall expansion during the postwar period and to keep within moderate limits the cyclical declines that occurred in production. Indeed, there are cogent grounds for believing that these declines were even more moderate than our familiar statistical records suggest. The line of division between production for sale and production for direct use does not stand still in a dynamic economy. In the early decades of the industrial revolution an increasing part of our production was, in effect, transferred from the home to the shop and factory. This trend has continued in the preparation of foods, but in other activities it appears on balance to have been reversed. The great expansion of home ownership, the invention of all sorts of mechanical contrivances for the home, longer vacations, the general eagerness for improvement, if not also the income tax, have stimulated many people to do more and more things for themselves. Consumers have become equipped to an increasing degree with the capital goods they need for transportation, for the refrigeration of food, for the laundering of clothes, as well as for entertainment and instruction. They have also been doing, on an increasing scale, much of the carpentry, painting, plumbing, and landscaping around their homes. Such activities of production are less subject to the business cycle than the commercial activities which enter statistical reports. Yet these domestic activities have undoubtedly been expanding rapidly, and perhaps expanding even more during the declining than during the rising phase of the business cycle. Hence, it is entirely probable that the cyclical swings of production have of late been smaller, while the average rate of growth of production has been higher, than is commonly supposed.

SUMMARY

It is in the nature of an economic vocabulary to change slowly, when it changes at all. We keep speaking of the price system, the business cycle, capitalism, socialism, communism, and sometimes we even refer to the "inherent instability" of capitalism or of communism; but the reality that these terms and phrases are intended to denote or sum up does not remain fixed. I have tried to show how a conjuncture of structural changes in our economy has served to modify the business cycle of our times. Some of these changes were planned while others were unplanned. Some resulted from efforts to control the business cycle while others originated in policies aimed at different ends. Some arose from private and others from public activities. Some are of very recent origin and others of long standing. The net result has been that the intensity of cyclical swings of production has become smaller. The links that previously tied together the cyclical movements of production, employment, personal income, and consumption have become looser. And, as everyone knows, the once familiar parallelism of the short-term movements in the physical volume of total production, on the one hand, and the average level of wholesale or consumer prices, on the other, has become somewhat elusive.

To be sure, special factors of an episodic character played their part in recent business cycles, as they always have. For example, a pent-up demand for civilian goods was highly significant in checking the recession of 1945. The tax reduction legislated in April 1948 helped to moderate the recession which began towards the end of that year. The tax cuts announced soon after business activity began receding in 1953 merely required executive acquiescence in legislation that had been passed before any recession was in sight. Again, the sputniks spurred the government's response to the recession of 1957–58. Special circumstances such as these undoubtedly weakened the forces of economic contraction at certain times; but they also strengthened them at other times. In particular, governmental purchases from private firms have not infrequently been an unsettling influence rather than a stabilizing force. We need only recall the drop of federal expenditure on commodities and services from an annual rate of $91 billion in the early months of 1945 to $16 billion two years later, or the fall from $59 billion to $44 billion soon after the Korean hostilities came to a close. The ability of our economy to adjust to such major disturbances without experiencing a severe or protracted slump testifies not only to our good luck; it testifies also to the stabilizing power of the structural changes that I have emphasized.

It seems reasonable to expect that the structural changes in our economy, which have recently served to moderate and humanize the business cycle, will continue to do so. The growth of corporations is not likely to be checked, nor is the tendency to pay fairly stable dividends likely to be modified. The scale of governmental activities will remain very extensive, and so it would be even if the communist threat to our national security were somehow banished. Our methods of taxation might change materially, but the income tax will remain a major source of governmental revenue. Governmental expenditures might fluctuate sharply, but they are not likely to decline during a recession merely because governmental revenues are then declining. The social security system is more likely to grow than to remain stationary or contract. Private pension arrangements will multiply and so also may private supplements to unemployment insurance. Our population will continue to grow. The restlessness and eagerness of consumers to live better is likely to remain a dynamic force. Research and development activities will continue to enlarge opportunities for investment. Governmental efforts to promote a high and expanding level of economic activity are not likely to weaken. Private businesses will continue to seek ways to economize on inventories and otherwise minimize the risk of cyclical fluctuations in their operations. Employment in agriculture is already so low that its further decline can no longer offset future gains of the service industries on the scale experienced in the past. The spread of white-collar occupations throughout the range of industry will continue and may even accelerate. For all these reasons, the business cycle is unlikely to be as disturbing or troublesome to our children as it once was to us or our fathers.

This is surely a reasonable expectation as we look to the future. Yet, it is well to remember that projections of human experience remain descriptions of a limited past no matter how alluringly they are expressed in language of the future. A lesson of history, which keeps resounding through the ages, is that the most reasonable of expectations sometimes lead nations astray. If my analysis is sound, it supports the judgment that the recessions or depressions of the future are likely to be appreciably milder on the average than they were before the 1940s. It supports no more than this. In view of the inherent variability of business cycles and our still somewhat haphazard ways of dealing with them, there can be no assurance that episodic factors will not make a future recession both longer and deeper than any we experienced in the postwar period. Nor can there be any assurance that the conjuncture of structural changes on which I have dwelt will not be succeeded by another which will prove less favorable to economic stability.

QUESTIONS AND STUDY SUGGESTIONS

1. Professor Burns contends that the structure of the American economy has changed in recent years "to blunt the impact of the business cycle." Indicate the changes which have occurred in each of the following spheres to reduce the extent of economic fluctuations: (*a*) business organization; (*b*) taxation; (*c*) government expenditures; (*d*) industry and the labor force; (*e*) consumer spending; (*f*) banking; (*g*) economic and political attitudes; and (*h*) monetary policy.

2. Using the answer prepared for question 1, explain *precisely how* each of the changes listed has had the effect of reducing fluctuations in personal income, employment, consumption, or production.

3. Has the reduced impact of the business cycle been the result of discretionary monetary and fiscal policy or the result of a greater tendency toward built-in stability?

4. What does the author mean by "special factors of an episodic character"? What role have these special factors played, and what role does Professor Burns believe they will play in future business cycles?

5. Does Professor Burns believe that the changes which have led to greater stability will be reversed in the future or that they will continue to produce a tendency toward even greater economic stability? Explain the reasons for his belief.

Reading 15

Creeping Inflation: The Pickpocket of Prosperity

Federal Reserve Bank of Philadelphia

Many economists would agree with Arthur Burns's assessment (Reading 14) of our progress toward greater economic stability. At the same time they would argue that modest, but persistent, inflation and unemployment still constitute first-rank economic problems. Thus it is that the problem of "creeping inflation," a 2 or 3 percent annual rise in the general price level, has been accorded detailed appraisal in the postwar period. The

From "Creeping Inflation: The Pickpocket of Prosperity," **Business Review**, Federal Reserve Bank of Philadelphia, August, 1957. Reprinted and updated by permission.

next two readings present sharply contrasting evaluations of creeping inflation. The first view, expressed by the Federal Reserve Bank of Philadelphia in Reading 15, is that, despite its "seductive charm," creeping inflation is a very shaky foundation upon which to base sound economic progress. On the one hand, when compounded over a number of years, the arbitrary adverse effects of creeping inflation upon fixed-income receivers, savers, and creditors become quite severe. More important, on the other hand, is the fearsome possibility that, thanks to the "cost-push" pressures created by an environment of mild inflation, creeping inflation might readily evolve into hyperinflation.

A simple act of inflation is to blow air into a toy balloon. Kids love it. A more sophisticated form of inflation is to blow too much money into the economy. Some adults love it because it creates a feeling of prosperity.

Not prosperity, but a feeling of prosperity. For what does it profit a man if he gets twice as much money, when it costs three times as much to live?

Money bewitches people. They fret for it, and they sweat for it. They devise most ingenious ways to get it, and most ingenuous ways to get rid of it. Money is the only commodity that is good for nothing but to be gotten rid of. It will not feed you, clothe you, shelter you, or amuse you unless you spend it or invest it. It imparts value only in parting. People will do almost anything for money, and money will do almost anything for people. Money is a captivating, circulating, masquerading puzzle.

Ask an economist about money and you may be sorry. He will tell you that money is a medium of exchange, a standard of value, a store of value, and a standard of deferred payments. See what we mean!

How money works as a medium of exchange we first discovered at a tender age when we found with great delight that pennies buy lollipops. As we became bigger operators, we developed bigger wants that required bigger money. Bigger wants are taken care of nicely with $2\frac{1}{2}$ inch by 6 inch paper portraits of various notables—Washington for a dollar, Lincoln for five dollars, Hamilton for ten, and so on. These are freely passed from hand to hand with almost total disregard as to whose portrait is worth what. That's what "medium of exchange" means.

The claim that money is a standard of value is one of those things. If money were the standard of value that it is supposed to be, the same amount of money would always buy the same amount of goods. But it doesn't. We know from recent experience that the dollar is slipping because it takes more of them to get the essentials of life. The one-dollar silver certificate is identified as one dollar no less than 15 times on the face and 10 times on the back —and so it is. But in the market place, it's not the dollar it used to be. The dollar is a standard of value but not a stable standard like a yard or a gallon or a ton.

The claim that money is a store of value also requires some apology. When you check a suitcase full of personal belongings at a baggage counter, you get a ticket or a claim check and go about your business confident that you can reclaim the bag upon surrender of the ticket. If, upon doing so, you find that half of your clothing and other personal effects have been removed, you would set up a big howl, saying, "I've been robbed." In like manner, if you tucked $100 under the mattress several years ago for safekeeping, you find you have been robbed because those dollars buy less in today's markets.

As a standard of deferred payment, money also leaves considerable to be desired. The investor that today buys a 10-year bond for $1,000 is entitled to $1,000 in 1973, but who knows what the purchasing power of the dollar will be in 1973? If the dollar will be worth more than it is at present, the investor makes a speculative gain; if it will be worth less, he will suffer a speculative loss. The dollar can be as fickle in the future as it has been in the past.

Living as we do in a money economy there is nothing for free. Everything costs money. Everything has its price, and the price is always so much money. Now money, as has already been insinuated, does not always behave as it should and the telltale evidence of the misbehavior of money is the behavior of prices.

THE BEHAVIOR OF PRICES

Prices seldom stand still for any length of time. When the housewife goes to market she may observe that coffee and potatoes cost a cent or two less than the week before, and that pork and butter cost two or three cents more. A price-conscious housewife is also quick to observe similar changes in department-store merchandise. At the same time that prices of linens and yardgoods may be falling, the prices of men's shirts and children's shoes may be rising. That's the way life is.

Price changes are the inevitable result of changing conditions of demand and supply in markets where freedom of competition prevails. Increasing demand or diminishing supply tends to bring about higher prices, and decreasing demand or increasing supply tends to bring about lower prices. Moreover, changing prices are not only passive results of changes in supply and demand but also active causes thereof. Rising prices stimulate production and discourage demand, and falling prices encourage demand and discourage production.

Prices are the automatic regulators that tend to keep production and consumption in line with each other. In the performance of this function, however, it is quite common for the prices of some goods and services to be rising while the prices of others are falling, and that is the point we wish to stress here.

THE MISBEHAVIOR OF MONEY

When prices of everything are going up, it is not because everything is worth more, but because the dollar is worth less. The value of a good is its power to command another good in exchange for itself. If a pencil costs 10 cents and a pen costs a dollar, it means that a pen is worth ten pencils, or a pencil is worth one-tenth of a pen. Should prices of everything double, then pens would sell for $2 and pencils for 20 cents each. Ten pencils would still exchange for one pen, and inasmuch as prices of all things have doubled, their exchange ratios or value remain the same. But something has happened to the value of the dollar. It has been cut in half. That's inflation.

Again, should prices of everything be halved

it would not be because everything is worth less but because the dollar is worth more. That's deflation. During a period of inflation, prices rise and the dollar loses purchasing power. During a period of deflation, prices fall and the dollar gains purchasing power.

How money misbehaves is shown by Figure 15–1 with only two lines. The line labeled "Consumer prices" is the official consumer price index compiled by the Bureau of Labor Statistics, and it measures the changes in prices of goods and services purchased by families of city wage earners and salaried clerical workers. The index is based upon prices of about 300 items in 46 cities. In short, the line shows how the cost of living rises and falls with respect to a base period (1947–1949 = 100) to which the line is anchored.

The other line labeled "Purchasing power of the dollar" is the same story translated so that it shows what happens to the value of the dollar when consumer prices rise and fall. You can see that the two lines are reciprocal, as indeed they must be because when the cost of living rises, the purchasing power of the dollar falls and it takes more dollars to maintain your standard of living. When consumer prices fall, the purchasing power of the dollar rises and it takes fewer dollars to buy the goods and services to which you are accustomed.

Now look what has happened during the past three and one-half decades. In the years of the Great Depression from 1930–1933, consumer prices took quite a slide. You can see what World War II did to the cost of living. Note the rise in consumer prices from 1940 to 1943. After the end of the war, consumer prices took another big jump. They seemed to have reached a plateau in the stretch between 1952 and 1955, after which they again started moving upward. The index rose from 60 in 1940 to 128 at present, which means that we now pay one dollar for what cost only 47 cents in 1940. World War II caused most of the inflation.

WAR, WEAPONS, AND WAMPUM

Producing weapons for war is inflationary. Output of civilian goods is reduced to a minimum as productive facilities are pressed into the making of weapons. The gainfully employed, however, receive wages for their work regardless of whether they make bazookas or butter. But civilians don't spend their money for

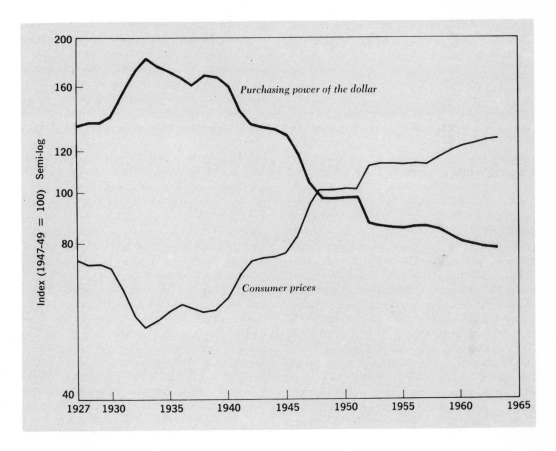

Figure 15–1.   What changing prices do to the buying power of the dollar.

munitions, so the extra bazooka money which is not taken away from them in taxes churns up prices in the butter market despite desperate efforts to prevent it. War always fills the purse faster than the pantry.

War is inflationary in still another way—the way it is paid for, or rather the way it is not paid for. The cost of the war not raised by taxes is borrowed by selling bonds. Government bonds bought by people, savings banks, insurance companies, commercial and industrial corporations come out of savings, and such bond buying is not inflationary.

Not so the buying of bonds by commercial banks. The bonds they buy feed the fires of inflation because they do not buy bonds out of their savings but out of money which they create. The money comes right off the keyboard of the bookkeeping machine in the bank. Technically, such money is called "demand deposits" against which the borrower can draw checks.

"THERE SHE BLOWS!"

After World War II a lot of the Government bonds were turned into money, and that can be done faster than making automobiles, so there was more inflation. People cashed their bonds at the banks, lenders sold Governments to make loans, and the Federal Reserve as the ultimate buyer under the support program supplied the high-powered reserve dollars needed to support the swelling money supply.

Inflation seems to be an inevitable by-product of war. This is confirmed by the long-run record of wholesale prices, shown in Figure 15–2. All the mountain peaks are the handiwork of Mars. Germany, after World War I, had an inflation that out-flated all inflations. Printing presses turned out paper marks by the trainload, and the cost of living rose 1,200 billion times. Mortgages, bonds, and other long-term contracts became absolutely worthless, and life insurance policies were not

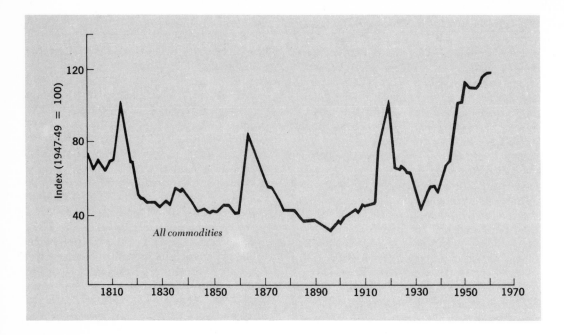

Figure 15–2.   A long look at wholesale prices.

worth the postage required to notify the company of the decease of the policy holder. What started out as just a little inflation wound up in complete collapse and chaos.

To be sure, no one is advocating that we go on a gigantic inflationary fling and wreck our economy like the Germans wrecked theirs. But why not try a little inflation, just a few cents worth a year—an "ever normal" debasement of the dollar, a planned inflationary prosperity?

THE CHARM OF CREEPING INFLATION

Creeping inflation has charm, seductive charm. It is a delusion, but such a delightful delusion. It affords an apparently easy way out of so many of the daily difficulties that confront us.

Creeping inflation sends up prices on the securities markets, farmers wishing to sell out get fancy prices for their farms, businessmen find it easier to make profits that come from inventory appreciation and higher selling prices, and workers get higher wages. The prosperity doesn't ring true, but it rings the cash registers because there is more money around. People on fixed incomes do not share in the additional money unless they own a share or two of stock, in which case they get a whiff of prosperity.

Creeping inflation is a monetary patent medicine, an economic elixir. It is a soothing compound containing syrup sweet to the taste, and alcohol to dull the senses. Recommended doses: 2 to 3 percent a year. It is good for all diseases of the body economic. Will prevent falling pricitis, underflourishment, profit deficiency, and inventory indigestion. Creeping inflation is a habit-forming economic tranquilizer.

Because creeping inflation wears a false face of prosperity, many people are easily fooled by it. First, it is tolerated, then it is accepted, and finally it is rationalized. In fact, the rationalizing has already begun. We are told that the country is confronted with a choice of three evils. We must accept enough unemployment to keep labor costs from rising, or impose direct Government controls over wages and prices, or embrace creeping inflation. The first is socially undesirable, the second is politically impossible in times of peace—which leaves creeping inflation as the least of three evils. So goes the argument.

Is it true that we must choose some form of evil? To say so does not necessarily make it so. It has not been proven that the only solution to heavy unemployment is ever-rising prices. On the contrary, if inflation is allowed to run its course we may ultimately precipitate unemployment of really serious proportions.

THE PICKPOCKET OF PROSPERITY

Simply because all our business reckoning is done in dollars, it is so easy to fall for the fallacy that more dollars bring more prosperity. The essence of prosperity is not more dollars, but more goods and services. We can consume only what we produce. If we want to consume more, we must produce more—and there is no money magic that will enable us to consume more than we produce.

Currently we—all 185 million of us—are producing and consuming goods and services at the rate of $521 billion a year. Last year we were producing and consuming at the rate of $504 billion. With pride we point to the $17 billion increase. But that was in dollars, and don't forget that consumer prices rose over 1 percent during the past year, so a large part of the increased prosperity was phoney. Well over $7 billion of the gain was nullified by the depreciation in the purchasing power of the dollar. And yet there are a lot of grown-up people who still believe in Santa Claus. Confusing money with wealth, they think that if everybody has more money everybody is better off.

Well, suppose the Government were to adopt a policy of creeping inflation, say, 3 percent a year so frequently advocated. Consider the factory worker, head of a family, making $6,000 a year. Knowing that the cost of living will rise 3 percent each year, he will demand an escalator clause so that his wages will go up automatically with the rising cost of living. By so doing he contributes to further inflation because contracts of this kind cause price increases to spread far and wide.

Consider the school teacher, age 40, whose only income is his salary. What a dreary prospect creeping inflation holds for him! A 3 percent yearly increase in the cost of living is tantamount to an annual cut in salary. Creeping inflation picks his pocket year after year. When he is 65 and ready to retire, his dollars will have shrunk to 47 cents, and a $3,000 annual retirement income will have less than $1,500 purchasing power. Government workers, hospital employees, social service workers and many other salaried people will have their pockets picked in this kind of "prosperity."

Creeping inflation makes suckers out of savers. It would systematically pick the pockets of the over 100 million holders of life insurance policies, the 15 million savings and loan shareholders, the 14 million employees with pension rights under private plans, the 66 million people covered by social security, and the 67 million with savings deposits in commercial and savings banks. It is a delusion to think that creeping inflation—a mere 2 or 3 percent a year—does no harm. A 2 percent annual rise, compounded, would double the price level about every 35 years. *A 3 percent annual rise would double prices about every 23 years.*

Moreover, there is a world of difference between a fortuitous creeping inflation, such as we are now having, and a planned creeping inflation. Suppose the Government were to accept as a national policy the inevitability of a 2 or 3 percent annual inflation. As citizens would come to know that the Government is not only accepting but seeking a slow and steady depreciation of the dollar, they would realize that there is no point in holding insurance policies or putting money into savings accounts, savings bonds, and other forms of dollar assets. Instead of saving, they would put their money into real estate, commodities, equity securities, and other forms of investment that ride with the rising tide of inflation. It would make us a nation of speculators rather than savers.

It is naive to believe that a deliberate policy of 2 or 3 percent inflation could be maintained indefinitely. Inflation, by its very nature, feeds on itself, and it would not be long before creeping inflation would accelerate to running inflation and ultimately galloping inflation. Moreover, if we are simple-minded enough to believe that a little inflation brings a little prosperity, then why not double the inflation and double the prosperity? Having gone that far, let's redouble the inflation and redouble the prosperity. If more money is the royal road to prosperity, it is easy to make ourselves fabulously wealthy.

Inflation, whatever and wherever it is tolerated, is a pickpocket of prosperity, and the bigger the inflation the bigger the pocket-picking.

THE COURSE OF CREEPING INFLATION

Pocket-picking is going on right now, all around us. The cost of living has already gone up 20 percent above the 1947–49 base period, as shown by the "All items" line in Figure 15–3. As might be expected, some items rose more briskly than others. The clothing dollar was the best behaved and the food dollar also

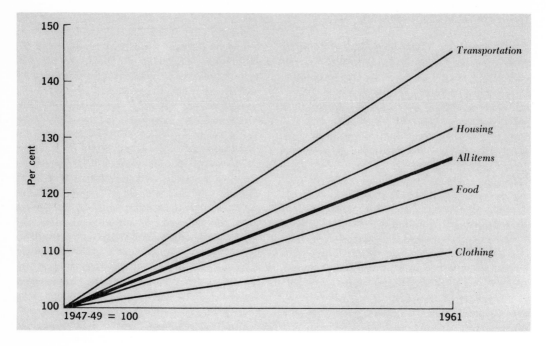

Figure 15–3.   The cost of living marches uphill.

did not get too far out of line. The bad actors were housing, which includes rent, and transportation costs. These costs rose 32 and 46 percent respectively.

For four years we seemed to have achieved price stability. From 1952 to early 1956 the cost of living held very steady. Rents rose during this period but the declining cost of food helped to keep the over-all average on a fairly even keel.

Early in 1956, however, the cost of living resumed its upsurge and all of the components, including food, joined in the advance. In June 1957 the cost of living was about 5 percent above the March 1956 level when the uphill march began. That is a very high rate of depreciation for the American dollar.

CAUSES OF CREEPING INFLATION

Currently, the critics can't agree as to the causes of our creeping inflation. One group says it is basically demand pulling prices higher, and the other group says it is rising costs pushing prices higher. Let us examine the debate between the "demand-pullers" and the "cost-pushers." The demand-pullers stress the fact that we have in our economy three great groups of spenders—namely, consumers, business, and government—whose combined actions exert a powerful pull on prices.

The country's 185 million consumers, as a group, have a lot of pull. They stepped up their expenditures from $233 billion in 1953 to a current annual rate of $339 billion. Most people love to spend and will do so at the drop of a down payment.

Governments are easy spenders. They spend $109 billion a year for things no one can possibly object to—common defense and general welfare. But defense and welfare are costly commodities with bigger price tags each year.

Businessmen are courageous spenders. The amount of money they put into new plants and equipment since the end of World War II has amazed everybody including the businessmen themselves. In the past four years, they have spent over $180 billion for this purpose, and this year they are spending at the rate of $46 billion. Businessmen, governments, and consumers are a powerful trio of demand-pullers, and it is hardly becoming for any one of them to hold the others responsible for contributing toward inflation.

TABLE-THUMPING THEORY OF WAGES

Creeping inflation is also aided and abetted by a vast army of cost-pushers. The country's 75 million workers are potential cost-pushers, and the 18 million organized workers are organized cost-pushers. Fed up with having their pockets picked by the rising cost of living, workers demand more wages. Fearful of what higher wage costs will do to their profit margins, employers resist the demands of workers. Then starts the collective bargaining—the democratic process of table thumping. In due time an agreement is reached, and the betting on the sidelines is on the question of how much prices will be raised as a result of the higher wages.

It should not be necessary to raise prices if the wage increases do not rise faster than the increases in labor productivity. That all the wage increases taking place are "necessary" is both alleged and denied. In any event, it appears that price increases always follow on the heels of wage increases, and because wages are the largest cost component in so many industries it is difficult to escape the conclusion that rising wages have something to do with creeping inflation.

Moreover, some of the wage agreements have escalator clauses that gear the wage rates right into the cost of living. An escalator clause provides that for every change of so many decimal points in the Bureau of Labor Statistics index of consumer prices, the workers shall automatically get an increase or decrease of so many cents in their basic wage rates. Sooner or later the increased costs of production break out in higher prices. Then the workers in escalated industries are entitled to another automatic pay increase. More and more unionized workers are jumping on the escalator bandwagon, and you can see why.

INFLATION AUTOMATION

Wage escalation is automated inflation without vacuum tubes, transistors, or printed circuits. It is built-in inflation. Once installed it is automatic, requires no servicing or adjustment, never wears out. It has no moving parts except wages and the cost of living. Rising costs of living drive up wages, and rising wages drive up the cost of living.

The cost-pushers are only seeking to escape the ravages of inflation. Workers are trying to preserve their standard of living, and businessmen are trying to preserve their profit margins. But in pushing up prices, both of them are helping to bring about the very thing they seek to avoid. Everybody's price is someone else's cost.

Is creeping inflation caused by demand-pullers or cost-pushers? It is not a case of one or the other; both forces are at work. Trying to assess their relative importance in the current inflationary climate is like trying to determine which blade of the scissors does most of the cutting. But we do know that demand-pullers and cost-pushers together are cutting down the dollar.

Whether demand-pulling or cost-pushing, the inevitable side-car of rising prices is money —sufficient money to support the rising prices. How eagerly and easily banks accommodate the demand for more money has already been observed, and currently businessmen are borrowing heavily. Prices, however, are not solely dependent upon how much money is at work but also upon how hard the money supply is working. Money goes round and round from butcher to baker to lipstick maker, and the same amount of money going around twice as fast has the same effect on prices as twice the amount going around at the former rate of circulation. In 1956, for example, the money supply increased only 1 percent, but it circulated 8 percent faster. That helped inflation to creep.

THE CURE FOR CREEPING INFLATION

We need not be unduly concerned about the relative merits of the push-or-pull argument. One thing we do know, and know full well, is that there can be no inflation without an overabundance of money that leaves a gap between total spending and the available supply of goods. Dollars without goods do no good.

Sometimes it is advocated that the best way to close the gap is to produce more goods. Increased production alone, however, will not solve the problem because extra output means extra input. The additional man-hours and the extra flow of materials together with increased profit on the extra output will yield additional income—so we have not made any progress toward licking inflation. The gap remains.

A more effective way is to remove the surplus money that's doing the damage to the dollar. Making money scarcer means people will have to pay more to borrow it. Money, like everything else, has its price and the price is the interest rate.

The interest rate is determined in the credit market in the same way that the price of steers is determined in the cattle market. Droves of steers stampeding the market depress prices; a big demand in the face of light shipments boosts prices. In the credit market, borrowers —consumers, businessmen, and governments— seek funds from the lenders: insurance companies, mutual savings banks, savings and loan associations, and commercial banks.

When the borrowers want more funds than the available supply of the lenders, interest rates go up and money is said to be "tight," in the jargon of the trade.

The Federal Reserve is commended by some and condemned by others for allowing money to get tight and for raising the discount rate, which is the interest that commercial banks must pay when they borrow from the Fed. Control over the money supply is exercised by regulation of the reserves available to commercial banks so that growth in the money supply will not put excessive pressure on the demand for goods and services available.

In restricting the supply of money and credit, spending borrowed funds is discouraged because of the increased price of money— the higher rate of interest. In effect, higher-priced money is substituted for higher-priced goods. The available supply of money and credit then goes to those who are willing to pay the higher price for borrowed money. So money becomes "tight" not through an actual reduction in the supply of money and credit but because of increased demand of borrowers. Had the Federal Reserve obliged with enough credit to satisfy all the demands, it would have added greatly to inflationary pressures without adding to the supply of goods, and prices would have shown an even greater rise.

Tight money is said to pinch the small busi-nessman and to interfere with the construction of much-needed schools, roads, and housing. So it does, but so do rising prices or direct rationing. There is no painless way to stop inflation. If it is allowed to continue unchecked, ever-higher prices and ever-rising costs will hurt more people and hurt them harder than tight money.

UNCLE SAM'S SPENDING

It is difficult, if not impossible, to curb creeping inflation without some help from Uncle Sam. He is a big operator who spends at a rate in excess of a billion dollars a week, and that has a terrific impact on our economy. Like so many of us, he finds it hard to live within his income and when he doesn't, he adds to the inflationary pressures.

Money taken from us in the form of taxes reduces our spending power, to be sure, but if the Government spends the money, inflationary pressure is not *reduced* one whit. If the Government spends more money than it takes from us in taxes, inflationary pressures are increased.

Uncle Sam could really be helpful in the fight against inflation if he learned not only to live within his income but to have a good surplus when inflation threatens. If the Federal Government wants stable money and lower interest rates, it can have them by reducing its expenditures and its heavy demands on the money market.

In days gone by, unscrupulous sovereigns debased their currencies by nicking the coin of the realm, which had disastrous results. By tolerating creeping inflation—which is the pickpocket of prosperity—we could go down the same road. With mass prosperity and mass savings, economic welfare requires a dollar that is kept sound both as a medium of exchange and a store of value. Which would you rather have —a stable economy built on a stable dollar or a wobbling economy built on a woozy dollar?

QUESTIONS AND STUDY SUGGESTIONS

1. Explain each of the functions of money. How might inflation interfere with the capacity of money to fulfill these functions efficiently?
2. Explain: "When prices of everything are going up, it is not because everything is worth more, but because the dollar is worth less."

3. Why might the production of war goods be especially inflationary? Explain why government bond sales to commercial banks might be more inflationary than bond sales to individuals and business corporations.

4. What is the difference between a "fortuitous" and a "planned" creeping inflation? Why might this difference be important? Distinguish between "demand-pull" and "cost-push" inflation. What are escalator clauses?

5. Comment on the statement: "There is no painless way to stop inflation." Comment: "Everybody's price is someone else's cost."

6. Discuss the recommended cure for creeping inflation.

Reading 16

How Bad Is Inflation?

Sumner H. Slichter, late Professor of Economics, Harvard University

The late Sumner Slichter concludes in this reading that creeping inflation might not be as bad as it is frequently pictured. On the contrary, all things considered, mild inflation might be clearly preferred to the relevant alternatives. More specifically, Slichter reasons that creeping inflation is a necessary concomitant of a prosperous, expanding economy. Stated differently, long-run price stability can be achieved only at the cost of chronic unemployment or drastic government intervention in collective bargaining. The goals of economic freedom and full employment conflict with that of price stability, according to Slichter, and the best choice is to make price stability subservient to the other two more crucial goals. Furthermore, there is no real reason why mild inflation need blossom into uncontrolled galloping inflation; indeed, there are good reasons why our economy will remain aloof from an "inflationary psychosis." In short, the economic injustices and hyperinflationary potential of creeping inflation have been exaggerated and viewed without regard for the relevant alternatives. "How Bad Is Inflation?" Not so bad at all!

"The recent decline in consumer spending," said a conference of distinguished Americans, "is only a lull in a continuing inflation that threatens the stability of the national economy and the security of the entire Western World."

This view of inflation is typical of hundreds of statements that have been made during the past few years. It reflects the uncritical and almost hysterical fear that the thought of inflation arouses in a large part of the commu-

From Sumner H. Slichter, "How Bad Is Inflation?," **Harper's Magazine**, August, 1952, pp. 53–57, abridged. Reprinted by permission.

nity. It also reflects failure to see some of the problems that confront the country and that can be solved best through a slow rise in prices.

It is, of course, true that extreme inflation is disastrous, and that many countries have experienced it during the past thirty years. The great inflation in Germany in the early twenties is the one that is best known in this country. Not only did the German inflation wipe out the savings of millions of people but it badly reduced the efficiency of the economy. When prices are doubling every few weeks or less, as they were doing in Germany, no one can afford to take time to plan his expenditures carefully. The lack of careful planning was especially wasteful in the case of outlays for machinery and buildings.

But the extreme sort of inflation experienced by Germany is not easily started, and it is not likely to occur here. To produce the German type of inflation there must be lack of faith in the capacity of the government to perform the ordinary job of governing. What is likely to happen in the United States is a *slow* rise in prices—a rise interrupted frequently by small or moderate recessions, but nevertheless a rise. Of course, even a small increase of 2 percent or 3 percent a year, though hardly enough to be noticed at any given moment, is sufficient to cause substantial injustice. For example, a rise of only 2 percent a year will reduce the purchasing power of the dollar by 45 percent in thirty years, so that the pension or life insurance that one started to buy in one's youth will have lost nearly half its purchasing power before one has reached the age of retirement.

COST OF PRICE STABILITY

The obvious injustices of even a slow long-term rise in prices lead many people to insist that such a rise must be prevented—that nothing but a stable price level will be satisfactory. At the risk of being called an irresponsible and dangerous thinker, let me say that in the kind of economy possessed by the United States a slowly rising price level is actually preferable to a stable price level. The reason for this conclusion is that the maintenance of a stable price level would conflict with other important interests of the country. For example, the maintenance of a stable price level in the long run would require that the country considerably relax its efforts to keep business recessions

as mild as possible. Furthermore, the maintenance of a stable price level would require the acceptance of chronic unemployment or drastic intervention by the government in the relations between employers and employees.

The champions of a stable price level do not seem to be aware of the conflicts between the goal which they advocate and other desirable goals. Indeed, they are so impressed by the injustices caused by inflation that they fail to see that serious injustices would have to be imposed in order to keep the price level stable —injustices even greater than those which would accompany a slowly rising price level. Let us look more closely at the reasons for believing that a slowly rising price level is preferable to a stable one.

INFLATION AND PROSPERITY: INCOMPATIBLE?

Suppose that the desire of the people of the United States to raise their standard of consumption were so strong that the demand for goods slightly exceeded the supply of goods. The productive capacity of industry would be fully used. Practically every man, woman, and child who wished to work would have a job, enterprises as a whole would not lack for customers, and there would be a strong incentive for industry to enlarge its capacity. Would this be a bad state of affairs? I do not believe that most people would regard it as bad. They like demand to be large enough to strain the productive capacity of industry and to provide jobs for all job seekers. *And yet the situation that I have described would be inflationary.* The excess of demand over supply would cause prices to creep upward.

In a vigorous and dynamic economy in which consumers are eager to live better, and in which producers are good at bringing out new and improved articles and have efficient sales organizations, the situation that I have described is likely to exist for much of the time. But these periods of vigorous demand, in which the price level usually rises slowly, are interrupted from time to time by business recessions. When sales start to fall off, should the community stand aside and let the recession develop without restraint? Or should the community take vigorous steps to combat the depression and to keep it as mild as possible?

Everyone knows today that the country will

not tolerate a policy of doing nothing about recessions. And in the divided world of today, in which every recession in business gives opportunities for Communist activity, it is imperative that the United States avoid severe or even moderate recessions. Since this country is such a large part of the world's economy, producing about 40 percent of the world's goods and consuming nearly as much, even a moderate drop in business here would dangerously disrupt the economies of other free countries.

But the policy of keeping recessions as mild as possible is incompatible with the ideal of long-run stability of the price level. In order for the price level to remain stable in the long run, the fall in prices that accompanies each recession must be great enough to cancel out the rise in prices during the preceding boom. If the country halts each recession fairly promptly, prices will not fall sufficiently to wipe out the rise of the former boom. Hence each revival of business will start from a higher price level than the previous revival, and the long-term movement of prices will be slowly upward. Although a slow climb of prices would create injustice by diminishing the purchasing power of pensions, insurance, and some savings, let us not overlook the fact that recessions also create injustice. A drop in prices sufficiently severe to cancel the rise of prices in the preceding boom would be accompanied by severe unemployment. People who were eager and able to work would have to remain idle while the demand for goods was being allowed to drop until some earlier price level had been restored. Hence the cost of long-run stability of prices would be the unnecessary unemployment and loss of output that accompany recessions sufficiently severe to cancel the price rise of the previous booms.

PRICE STABILITY AND COLLECTIVE BARGAINING

The problem of a wise price policy is complicated by the rise of powerful trade unions in recent years. The bargaining power of unions naturally varies with the demand for goods and labor. At some point short of full employment the bargaining power of most unions becomes so great that they are able to push up money wages faster than the engineers and managers can increase output per man-hour. The ability of unions to raise money wages is enhanced by stiff taxes upon corporate profits. Since a large part of any wage advance would diminish the tax liability of the employer, and to that extent cost him nothing, his incentive to resist the wage demands of unions is weakened.

The ability of unions to raise wages faster than the engineers and managers raise output per man-hour confronts the community with two more or less unpleasant possibilities. One possibility is that the rise in labor costs might come out of profits instead of being passed on in the form of higher prices. But the number of men that employers are willing to hire depends upon their success in making money. Hence a drop in profits would mean fewer jobs and more unemployment. The increase in unemployment would weaken the bargaining power of unions. After unemployment had reached a certain level, probably around 4 or 5 percent of the labor force, the unions would not be able to raise wages faster than the average advance in output per man-hour. Hence rising wages would no longer produce an increase in labor costs and unemployment. The community, however, would get stable labor costs only by sacrificing the output of several million men—that is, by accepting a lower standard of living.

Another possibility is that the community might attempt to protect itself against rising labor costs by placing legal restrictions on collective bargaining. Such restrictions would be most difficult to enforce, and they would, of course, involve much sacrifice of freedom on the part of both employees and employers. Most people would probably regard this remedy as worse than the disease.

Confronted with the unpleasant choice of chronic unemployment or government regulation of collective bargaining the community is likely to decide that prices should be encouraged to rise sufficiently to offset the rise in labor costs. This policy would mean a slowly rising price level and all of the injustices that go with it. It would, however, enable the community to avoid the disadvantages of chronic unemployment or of government regulation of collective bargaining.

Cannot ways be developed of limiting the bargaining power of unions so that free collective bargaining would be preserved but so that unions would be unable to impose a cost inflation on the community? I have seen no promising proposals. The prohibition of industry-wide bargaining, which has been suggested, would probably hurt employers more than unions. The Swedish trade unions are now wrestling with the tendency for collective bargaining to inflate labor costs and thus indirectly to inflate prices. The Swedish unions are proposing tax changes which, they hope, will stiffen the resistance of employers to the unions' wage demands. Their proposals do not seem to me to be very promising, but the fact that the unions have made them is significant. It may seem startling for unions to attempt to build up the bargaining power of employers—but the union leaders are faced with a novel problem. They find that agreements among unions to practice restraint in pressing for higher wages break down after several years, and neither the leaders nor the members like the tendency for rising wages to push up prices.

GALLOPING INFLATION UNLIKELY

Is not a slowly rising price level bound soon to become a galloping inflation? If people expect prices to rise, will they not prefer to own goods rather than cash, bank deposits, mortgages, or bonds? As more and more people attempt to shift from money and fixed dollar assets into goods, will not the price level increase faster than before, and will not this faster rise stimulate still more people to buy goods, real estate, and stocks? Hence is not even a creeping rise in prices dangerous?

It is true that all extreme inflations started out as slow and creeping ones, but it is not true that a slow advance in prices easily becomes a rapid rise. One reason is that the prospect of a general increase in prices does not mean that the price of any particular article will rise. Hence the expectation of a general advance may not be effective in getting people to buy specific goods. A second reason is that styles are constantly changing and goods are constantly being improved. Each of these conditions limits buying in advance of needs. A third reason is that the purchases by enterprises and individuals are restricted at all times by uncertainties concerning the size of their future incomes. Finally, and most important, both business concerns and individuals are limited in buying by the size of their present incomes. Enterprises and individuals may go into debt in order to spend more than their incomes, but willingness to incur debt is limited, and the increase in indebtedness can be controlled by proper credit policies. Hence, with reasonably strict credit policies, the rate at which prices rise can be controlled.

DANGERS OF INFLATION EXAGGERATED

These remarks make plain that when I point out that the goal of stable prices conflicts with other desirable goals and that the country has problems which can best be solved by permitting a slow rise in prices, I am not opposing all efforts to control inflation. Indeed, the more successfully the country checks recessions, the more willing it must be to keep the rise of prices during booms to the minimum required by rising labor costs. Hence successful fights against recessions increase the need for strict credit policies during booms.

Although a slowly rising price level will cause substantial injustice, the magnitude of the injustice should not be exaggerated. People will be able to protect the purchasing power of most of their savings by investing in real estate and stocks, and by keeping their savings banks accounts to a minimum. Mutual funds offer the small saver a way of diversifying his investment in stocks. The cost of life insurance and pensions will, of course, be considerably increased because, if prices rise, people will need more insurance and larger pensions. More than offsetting these injustices, however, will be the avoidance of the unemployment that is necessary in order to keep prices stable. The net advantage to the country of a slowly rising price level over a stable one is the greater amount of employment, and hence the greater amount of production and the higher standard of consumption, that are made possible by a slowly advancing price level.

QUESTIONS AND STUDY SUGGESTIONS

1. What are the consequences of maintaining a stable price level in the long run? Why, according to Professor Slichter, would each of these consequences come about?

2. Why is it concluded that prosperity and price stability are basically incompatible goals?
3. Why is wage bargaining by unions judged to be inflationary?
4. Contrast this article with the preceding article on each of the following points: (*a*) the compatibility of prosperity and price stability; (*b*) the relative importance of inflation as an economic problem; (*c*) the role of unions in the inflationary process; and (*d*) the likelihood that creeping inflation will give rise to galloping inflation. Which overall view of inflation do you think is the more accurate?

Reading 17

Unemployment and Deficient Demand

Walter W. Heller, Professor of Economics, University of Minnesota

The fact that the economic cost of unemployment is great behooves government to formulate policies designed to achieve a full-employment level of output. What should be the specific character of these policies? The answer to this question obviously depends upon the causes of unemployment. And on this matter there has recently been ample controversy. The crux of this controversy is revealed in Readings 17 and 18. In Reading 17 Walter W. Heller, former Chairman of the Council of Economic Advisers, reveals the government's general position. Although structural considerations undoubtedly contribute to unemployment, available evidence indicates that the major cause of persistent unemployment is a deficiency of aggregate demand. To achieve full employment, therefore, aggregate demand must be stimulated. This can best be done, according to Heller, by reducing taxes.

Recent discussions may have generated an impression of greater disagreement among the Nation's economists about the origins and solutions of the employment problem than actually exists. For in fact, the great majority of those who have studied the matter carefully would agree with the Administration's view that our excessive unemployment today cannot be traced to a single cause nor eliminated by a single cure. Rather, it has a mixture of causes which must be dealt with by a mixture—an amalgam of cures.

From **Economic Report of the President, 1964**, Washington, January, 1964, pp. 166–174, 182–183, abridged.

TYPES OF UNEMPLOYMENT

One problem, and a central one, is that total expenditures in the economy—total demand for goods and services—are not sufficient to generate an adequate total number of jobs. We can, for convenience, call this kind of unemployment "demand-shortage" unemployment. In our view, demand-shortage unemployment can and must be attacked by vigorous policies—principally tax reduction—to raise the total demand for goods and services.

Another problem is that the characteristics of our available workers—their locations, skills, education, training, race, sex, age, and so on—do not fully match the characteristics employers are seeking in filling the jobs that are available (or that would be available at full employment). In a dynamic, changing economy there is always some of this mismatching, and we call the unemployment that results from it "frictional." But when the pockets of such unemployment become large and stubborn—especially when they impose chronic burdens on particular disadvantaged groups and regions—we speak of the unemployment problem as "structural."

This type of unemployment is also a serious problem, which requires major policy actions to overcome its corrosive effects. Structural problems are not new. And the available evidence does not show that the proportion of our total unemployment problem that we label "structural" has increased significantly, nor that its character has materially changed. But this in no way diminishes the need for attacking these structural problems with vigorous policies —principally education, training and retraining, and special regional programs—to match the supply of labor skills more closely to the changing demand for labor skills.

Along with demand-shortage and structural unemployment, one also hears a great deal about the problem of "technological unemployment"—of men being put out of work by machines and, more particularly, by the process which has come to be called "automation." This is, indeed, a serious and continuing problem. But two points should be emphasized at the outset.

First, "technological unemployment" is not a third form of unemployment, separate from the other two. Rather, it expresses itself through these other forms. Technological change causes obsolescence of skills and therefore produces some of the mismatching between available workers and jobs that we call "structural" unemployment. Moreover, by raising output per worker, technological change is one of the principal sources of growth in our *potential* total output or GNP—which, if not matched by corresponding growth in *actual* GNP, opens a gap in demand and thereby causes demand-shortage unemployment.

Second, those who maintain that the economy now faces a problem of "technological unemployment" that is somehow new, and more formidable than in the past implicitly assert that the rate of technological change has recently speeded up. Unless this is the case, the problem is not new—it has always been with us and has not proved to be a long-run problem for the economy as a whole. The continuing process of rapid technological change, which has constituted the very core of the American economy's strength and progressiveness for at least 150 years, has always put particular workers and businesses out of jobs and required particular adjustments that have been difficult and sometimes painful. It poses a new general problem for the economy only if technological change becomes so rapid that the demand adjustments and labor market adjustments it requires cannot be accomplished by the economic processes of the past.

These, then—demand-shortage elements, structural elements, and a possible aggravation of both by accelerated technological change— are the principal ingredients of the unemployment problem. It would be unwise and imprudent to ignore any of these ingredients either in diagnosing the problem or in prescribing remedies.

The primary attack on high unemployment must be through fiscal measures to speed the growth of total demand and thereby to create new job opportunities. But this need not—indeed, must not—impede a simultaneous attack on our stubborn structural problems. The two approaches are not merely complementary; they are mutually reinforcing. On the one hand, training and other programs to facilitate labor mobility can ease and speed the process by which demand-stimulated increases in output are translated into increases in employment. On the other, since structural maladjustments tend to flourish in slack markets, a vigorous expansion in demand helps cut structural problems down to size.

UNEMPLOYMENT AND TAX REDUCTION

The American economy has been plagued with persistently excessive unemployment for 6 years. The unemployment rate has been 5 percent or more for 71 consecutive months. Since 1957, it has averaged 6 percent. Even in the face of annual advances of about $30 billion in GNP (annual rate), unemployment has not been diminishing. Thus, although GNP rose from $556.8 billion in the third quarter of 1962 to $588.5 billion in the third quarter of 1963, the unemployment rate remained the same in both quarters. And even with a prospective increase of $100 billion in the GNP rate from early 1961 to early 1964 (a rise of 20 percent in current dollars and about 15 percent in constant dollars), the unemployment rate will have come down only about 1½ percentage points in that 3 year period.

The persistence of this high level of unemployment is sometimes cited as evidence of structural difficulties which will blunt the effect of the proposed $11 billion tax cut now being considered by the Senate Finance Committee and make it difficult to reach the interim full-employment goal of 4 percent unemployment, let alone our ultimate goals beyond the 4 percent level. The structural problem will be examined in some detail later in this statement. But here, several points should be noted to indicate why the road to 4 percent unemployment is clearly open to demand-powered measures.

1. The pre-1957 postwar performance of the U.S. economy gives ample evidence of its ability to achieve 4 percent and even lower levels of unemployment without excessive strain.

2. The availability of 1.1 million excess unemployed workers (even by the modest 4-percent criterion and not counting the labor force drop-outs resulting from slack job opportunities) and of substantial excess capacity (even after large gains, the average operating rate in manufacturing is running at only 87 percent of capacity) demonstrates that we are still suffering from a serious shortage of consumer and investment demand.

3. There are virtually no signs of economic tension, of the barriers that would divert the force of demand stimulus away from higher output, more jobs and higher incomes into higher prices—there are no visible bottlenecks in the economy, wage rate increases have been the most moderate in the postwar period, and the record of price stability in recent years has been outstanding.

In reference to the first point, the unemployment rates in the first postwar decade deserve a further word. In the period of vigorous business activity in 1947 and 1948, unemployment averaged 3.8 percent of the labor force. After the recession of 1949 and the recovery of 1950, the rate was relatively stable from early 1951 to late 1953, averaging 3.1 percent. Since that time, the rate has drifted upward. In the period of stable unemployment from mid-1955 to late 1957, unemployment averaged 4.3 percent, an increase of more than one-third above the 1951–53 period. In the first half of 1960, unemployment averaged 5.3 percent, nearly one-fourth above the 1955–57 level. Following the recession and recovery of 1960–61, the rate fluctuated within a narrow range averaging 5.6 percent in 1962 and 1963 to date, a little higher than early 1960. Looking at the 1947–57 period, the average unemployment rate was below 4 percent in each of the following years: 1947, 1948, 1951, 1952, and 1953, and below 4½ percent in 1955, 1956, and 1957.

When one looks behind these figures to get a grasp of the economic conditions that produced them, the most notable difference between the pre-1957 and post-1957 periods is found in the strength of market demand. In the first postwar decade, markets were strong. Backlogs of consumer demand had to be worked off. The demands of the Korean conflict had to be met. Outmoded plants and equipment had to be replaced or modernized, and capacity had to be enlarged. Deficiencies in housing, office facilities, and public works had to be made up.

But 1957 marked a watershed. In the ensuing period, demand has slackened at a time when our labor force growth has been accelerating in response to the postwar jump in the birth rate. Business fixed investment dropped off from 10–11 percent of the GNP to only 9 percent—indeed, the level of such investment in 1962 barely struggled back to its level in 1956, while GNP was rising by nearly one-fifth (both in constant prices).

Thus, the clearest and most striking change since 1957 is the weakening of demand. So the clearest and most urgent need today is to remove the overburden of taxation which is retarding the growth in demand to full employment levels. Income tax rates enacted to finance war and fight inflation—though reduced in 1954—are still so high that they would yield a large surplus of revenues over expenditures if we were at full employment today. They are, in short, repressing demand and incentives in an economy operating well short of its capacity.

To avoid misunderstanding, it is important to stress that any employment program would be unbalanced and incomplete without determined measures (a) to upgrade and adapt the skills and education of the labor force to the more exacting demands of our advancing technology and (b) to facilitate the flow of workers from job to job, industry to industry, and place to place. Nevertheless, our principal reliance for a return to the 4 percent-or-better levels of unemployment we took for granted in the early postwar period must be on measures to boost demand for the products of American industry and agriculture.

PERSISTENT PROBLEMS OF STRUCTURAL UNEMPLOYMENT

The tax cut would thus increase demand to levels consistent with a 4 percent rate of unemployment. It would ease our most pressing unemployment problems. But no one can assume that our worries about unemployment would then be over. Some of its most distressing and inequitable aspects would remain.

To be sure, tax reduction will create new jobs in every community across the Nation and expand employment in every industry. The overwhelming majority of American families will benefit directly from the income tax cuts that will accrue to 50 million tax-paying individuals and 600,000 tax-paying corporations. Their direct rise in after-tax income will soon be translated, through the marketplace, into stronger markets for all kinds of goods and services and a quickening of the business pulse in all communities. With average working hours already at a high level, this added demand and activity will in large part be translated, in turn, into additional jobs, and income for the unemployed. Thus, the non-taxpaying minority will, in a very real sense, be the greatest beneficiaries of the tax program.

Experience clearly shows (1) that the unemployment rate will decline for every major category of workers and (2) that the sharpest declines will occur where the incidence of unemployment is the highest: among teenagers, the Negroes, the less-skilled, the blue-collar groups generally.

But even so, the unemployment rates of many groups will still be intolerably high. Back in 1957, for instance, when the average unemployment rate was just over 4 percent for the whole economy, the rates were much higher for many disadvantaged groups and regions—e.g., 10.8 percent for teenagers, 8.0 percent for nonwhites, 9.4 percent for unskilled manual workers, and 11.5 percent for workers in Wilkes-Barre–Hazleton, Pennsylvania.

These *high specific unemployment rates, which persist even when the general rate falls to an acceptable level,* are the essence of the problem of structural unemployment. Even a fully successful tax cut cannot solve problems like these by itself. They require a more direct attack.

To reduce the abnormally high and stubborn unemployment rate for Negroes requires a major improvement in their education and training and an attack on racial discrimination. To reduce the persistent high rate for the unskilled and the uneducated groups demands measures to help them acquire skills and knowledge. To reduce excessive unemployment associated with declining industries and technological advance requires retraining and relocation. To reduce high unemployment in distressed areas of Pennsylvania, Michigan, Minnesota, and elsewhere calls for special measures to rebuild the economic base of those communities and assist their workers.

Both the Administration and the Congress have recognized that these measures must be taken concurrently with measures to expand aggregate demand. Coal miners in Harlan County are structurally unemployed *now,* and so are Negro and Puerto Rican youths in New York City. Yet, programs to reduce structural unemployment will run into severe limits *in the absence of an adequate growth of demand,* i.e., in the absence of rapid expansion of total job opportunities. Such expansion is needed to assure that retrained and upgraded workers, for example, *will* find jobs at the end of the training period and *will not* do so at the expense of job opportunities for other unemployed workers. As structural programs create new and upgraded skills, they will in some cases fit the participants for jobs that had previously gone begging. But for the most part, the needed jobs must be created by expansion of total demand.

Quite apart from the human significance of structural unemployment, it also has great economic importance. For only as we reduce structural and frictional unemployment can we achieve the higher levels of total output which would be associated with unemployment rates below our 4 percent interim target. The Council emphasized this point in its 1963 *Annual Report* (p. 42), as follows:

Success in a combined policy of strengthening demand and adapting manpower supplies to evolving needs would enable us to achieve an interim objective of 4 percent unemployment and permit us to push beyond it in a setting of reasonable price stability. Bottlenecks in skilled labor, middle-level manpower, and professional personnel [now] tend to become acute as unemployment approaches 4 percent. The result is to retard growth and generate wage-price pressures at particular points in the economy. As we widen or break these bottlenecks by intensified and flexible education, training, and retraining efforts, our employment sights will steadily rise.

Every worker needlessly unemployed represents a human cost which offends the sensibilities of a civilized society. But each worker needlessly unemployed also represents a waste of potential goods and services, which even an affluent society can ill afford. More intensive measures to attack structural unemployment are necessary to reduce the unemployment rate not merely to 4 percent, but beyond.

HAS STRUCTURAL UNEMPLOYMENT INCREASED?

The preceding section addressed itself to structural unemployment as a human and social problem and considered its role in the process of lowering the unemployment rate to and below 4 percent. But it is also appropriate to ask: has structural unemployment increased to such an extent since 1957—the last time unemployment was near 4 percent—that it will impede the expansionary effects of demand-creating measures in general and the tax cut in particular?

The answer is clear: The evidence we have assembled and the tests we have made do not support the thesis that, over-all, the incidence of structural unemployment has increased in importance since we last achieved high employment. There may be some problems that seem more serious today than earlier; but in other areas we have probably progressed.

Expansion of the economy in response to a stepping-up of the growth of demand will not be impeded by pockets of surplus labor existing in a limited number of categories—we have always had distressing surpluses in certain categories, and the tax cut will not fully eliminate them. Economic expansion could eventually be impeded by shortages in strategic categories of skills and training, but the statistical evidence reveals no such shortages enroute to 4 percent unemployment.

It is difficult to believe that an economy that was able to absorb the dramatic shifts needed to convert to war production in World War II, and that operated at unemployment levels as low as 1.2 percent during that war and more recently (1953) at 2.9 percent, could not move rather readily, over the space of 2 or 3 years, to our interim target of 4 percent unemployment.

Our own recent economic history assures us of the economy's ability to adapt to rapid change. Additional assurance along this line is found in the experience of other countries whose systems and values are similar to our own. During the past decade, the Western European economy has undergone staggering structural changes. France and Belgium have adjusted to the decline of important mining areas, Germany to the inflow of millions of refugees from the East, and Italy to the problem of absorbing large numbers of poorly educated rural migrants into urban occupations. And all of Western Europe has adjusted to the replacement of obsolete capital, and of productive methods often unchanged for a century or more with machinery and methods geared to the most advanced technology in the world. The advance of productivity has been revolutionary. During the 1950s, output per manufacturing worker increased 2¼ times as fast in

Germany as in the United States, 3 times as fast in France, and 4 times as fast in Italy. In their adjustment to these changes the Europeans, though they may have other advantages, did not have the advantage of a labor force nearly as well educated, as well trained, as mobile, or as flexible as ours.

Nonetheless, the Europeans have maintained unemployment rates considerably lower than ours. After adjustment for conceptual differences, the unemployment rate in 1960 was 1.0 percent in Germany, 1.9 percent in France, and 4.3 percent in Italy. In Italy and Germany these low rates represented a considerable improvement over earlier postwar experience, and the higher Italian rate has subsequently declined materially.

The major explanation for such low unemployment rates in economies undergoing such profound transitions lies in the maintenance of a very high level of demand. During the 1950s the average annual growth rate in France was 4 percent, in Italy, 6 percent, and in Germany, over 7 percent—and both Italy and France have had even higher rates so far in the 1960s. This experience demonstrates beyond any doubt that, under the stimulus of adequate demand, and with the aid of active labor market policies, modern economies are sufficiently resilient to absorb poorly educated workers, to adapt to skill shortages, and to adjust to rapid technological change in a manner which maintains extremely low unemployment rates. This European experience—which in broad outline has been matched in Japan—reassures us that, once high and growing demand presses our capacity, we too will adapt to rapid change and maintain our economic health.

Structural unemployment is a human and an economic problem that we must attack by every means available. But the expansion of total demand through tax reduction remains the crucial central element in our attack upon unemployment.

QUESTIONS AND STUDY SUGGESTIONS

1. What evidence and comparisons are used by the author to back his contention that current unemployment is largely due to a deficiency of aggregate demand?

2. How might a higher level of aggregate demand help resolve problems of structural unemployment which now exist?

Reading 18

Unemployment and Structural Changes

Charles C. Killingsworth, Professor of Labor and Industrial Relations, Michigan State University

The deficient-demand thesis of Reading 17 is not universally accepted. A number of respected economists feel that structural changes are the main source of recent unemployment. In Reading 18 Charles C. Killingsworth makes a strong and eloquent case for the structural view. In particular, he argues that available evidence suggests that substantial changes have recently in the structure of the demand for labor. We need more scientists, technicians, and other highly trained personnel and fewer blue-collar workers. But the composition of labor supply has only partially adjusted to this change in demand. The result is a serious labor market imbalance, the remedy for which lies in greater investment in the training and education of human resources rather than increases in aggregate demand which will inevitably be frustrated by shortages of high-level manpower.

Automation, especially in its advanced forms, fundamentally changes the man-machine relation. Such a change is not unprecedented in economic history. The assembly line, as it replaced earlier techniques, helped to create literally millions of simple, repetitive jobs that could be learned in a few hours or a few days. Anybody who had two hands, two eyes, and a capacity to endure monotony could do the work.

AUTOMATION AND JOBS

Today we have the electric eye, the iron hand, the tin ear, and the electronic brain. We also have the know-how to tie them together in self-regulating systems that can perform an enormous variety of jobs. There are two major results. One is a great reduction in the number of simple, repetitive jobs where all you need is your five senses and an untrained mind. The

other result is a great increase in the number of jobs involved in designing, engineering, programming and administering these automatic production systems. Industry needs many more scientists, engineers, mathematicians, and other highly trained people, and many fewer blue-collar workers.

Between 1957 and 1962 production workers in manufacturing declined by nearly a million, while nonproduction workers increased by about a third of a million. The net change was a reduction of about 600,000 in employment.

Not all of the increase in white-collar employment in manufacturing was due to automation, of course, and not all of the newly hired employees were scientists and engineers. But the changing composition of employment was partly due to automation.

In an economy in which so many patterns are changing rapidly, broad averages and grand totals may conceal more than they re-

From **Nation's Manpower Revolution:** Hearings before the Subcommittee on Employment and Manpower of the Committee on Labor and Public Welfare, 88th Cong., 1st Sess., Washington, 1963, part 5, pp. 1470–1480, abridged.

veal. I think that this is especially true of the effects of automation and the concomitant changes of today. Let us take as an example the figures showing total civilian employment since 1949. Unemployment crept upward during the latter part of this period—first two notches up, then one notch down, and then another two notches up. In 1951–53, the average was about a 3 percent rate of unemployment. In 1962–63, the average has been almost double that, or between 5½ and 6 percent.

It is not self-evident from these figures that any part of this creeping unemployment problem is due to automation or other basic changes in the patterns of the economy. There is eminent authority to the contrary. The President's Council of Economic Advisers has repeatedly declared that automation and "structural unemployment" are not responsible for the gradual creep of unemployment above the 4 percent level of 1957. For example, the 1963 report of the Council includes the following passage (p. 25):

The problems of structural unemployment—of imperfect adaptation of jobs and workers—are persistent and serious, and they are thrown into bold relief by the prolonged lack of sufficient job opportunities over the past 5 years. *But these problems of adaptation have not constituted a greater cause of unemployment in recent years than in earlier periods.* The source of the high unemployment rates in recent years, even in periods of cyclical expansion, lies not in labor market imbalance, but in the markets for goods and services. [Emphasis not in original.]

This analysis of the unemployment problem —that it is caused primarily by a lagging growth rate—is the basis for the administration's emphasis on a large tax cut as the top-priority item in the program to "get the economy moving again." Chairman Walter Heller of the CEA has repeatedly said that there is a good prospect that the tax cut would reduce unemployment to the 4 percent level.

I think that it can be demonstrated that the Council is the victim of a half-truth. The lagging growth rate is only a part of the problem, and it may not be the most important part. I think that it is extremely unlikely that the proposed tax cut, desirable though it is as a part of a program, will prove to be sufficient to

reduce unemployment to the 4 percent level. Perhaps it is true that in politics you can't get everything all at once. But I feel compelled to say that my analysis leads me to the conclusion that the administration's economic program is seriously incomplete. It gives woefully inadequate attention to what I regard as a key aspect of the unemployment problem of the 1960s; namely, labor market imbalance.

LABOR MARKET IMBALANCE

Let me preface my own analysis of those figures with a brief restatement of my argument to this point. The fundamental effect of automation on the labor market is to "twist" the pattern of demand—that is, it pushes down the demand for workers with little training while pushing up the demand for workers with large amounts of training. The shift from goods to services is a second major factor which twists the labor market in the same way. There are some low-skilled, blue-collar jobs in service-producing industries; but the most rapidly growing parts of the service sector are health care and education, both of which require a heavy preponderance of highly trained people.

I have already presented some figures showing the changing patterns of demand for labor. These changing patterns of demand would not create labor market imbalance, however, unless changes in the supply of labor lagged behind. We turn now to the figures which show that such a lag has in fact developed.

Table 18–1 shows the relationship between rates of unemployment and levels of education of males 18 and over in 2 years—1950 and 1962.

The overall unemployment rate was substantially the same in both years—6.2 in 1950, and 6.0 in 1962. But there was a redistribution of unemployment between these 2 years. The unemployment rates at the top of the educational attainment ladder went down, while the rates at the middle and lower rungs of the ladder went up substantially. The most significant figure in this table, I think, is the one showing the very large decrease in the unemployment rate of college graduates.

It is important to note that all of the improvement in the unemployment situation in 1962, as compared with 1950, was concentrated in the elite group of our labor force— the approximately 20 percent with college

Table 18-1.   EDUCATION AND UNEMPLOYMENT, APRIL, 1950 AND MARCH, 1962 (males, 18 and over)

Years of school completed	Unemployment rates		Percentage change, 1950 to 1962
	1950	1962	
0 to 7	8.4	9.2	+9.5
8	6.6	7.5	+13.6
9 to 11	6.9	7.8	+13.0
12	4.6	4.8	+4.3
13 to 15	4.1	4.0	−2.4
16 or more	2.2	1.4	−36.4
All groups	6.2	6.0	−3.2

training. In all of the other categories, which have about 80 percent of the labor force, unemployment rates were substantially higher in 1962 than in 1950. These figures, I contend, substantiate the thesis that the patterns of demand for labor have been twisted faster than the patterns of supply have changed, and that as a result we had a substantially greater degree of labor market imbalance in 1962 than in 1950.

In all likelihood the official unemployment statistics substantially understate the size of the labor surplus of men with limited education. If we found jobs for most of those now officially reported as unemployed, the news of improving opportunities would undoubtedly bring back into the labor force many men who are not now counted as members of it. Unfortunately, we cannot count on the same flexibility of supply at the top of the educational scale. Even the most extreme pressures of demand cannot pull the participation rate much about 98 or 99 percent, which (as just stated) is the current rate in some college-trained age groups.

AGGREGATE DEMAND AND MANPOWER BOTTLENECKS

Our overall unemployment rate has now been above 5 percent for more than 5 years, and we cannot be sure what effects a substantial increase in spending by consumers, businesses and Government (i.e., an increase in aggregate demand) would have on the patterns of employment, unemployment, and labor force participation just discussed. Many respected economists believe, as one of them once put it, that

the hard core of unemployment is made of ice, not rock, and that it would melt away if overall demand rose high enough. As already noted, the Council of Economic Advisers has virtually guaranteed that the administration's tax cut program—which in its current version would put about $11 billion in the hands of consumers and businesses—would reduce unemployment to an "interim target" rate of 4 percent by 1966. This line of reasoning assumes (either implicitly or sometimes explicitly) that no serious bottlenecks of labor supply would appear before the achievement of the overall unemployment rate of 4 percent. I seriously question the validity of this critically important assumption under the labor market conditions of today and the foreseeable future.

The benefits of a decline in the overall rate of unemployment appear to be quite unevenly distributed among the educational attainment groups that we have been considering. The year 1957 was the last one in which we had an unemployment rate as low as 4 percent. It is instructive to see how the patterns of unemployment changed from 1950, when the overall rate was above 6 percent, to 1957, and then again to 1962, which had about the same overall rate as 1950. This comparison is made in two forms in Table 18–2. This table shows the actual unemployment rates for the various educational attainment groups in those 3 years, and it also expresses the unemployment rate for each group in each of the 3 years as a ratio of the rate for all of the other groups combined. (Thus, the 0 to 7 years of education group had an unemployment rate about 50 percent higher than all other groups combined in 1950; its rate was more than double the rate

Table 18–2.   ACTUAL AND RELATIVE UNEMPLOYMENT RATES BY EDUCATIONAL ATTAINMENT, APRIL, 1950, MARCH, 1957, AND MARCH, 1962 (males, 18 and over)

| | Unemployment rates | | | | | |
| | Actual percentages | | | Relative* | | |
Years of school completed	1950	1957	1962	1950	1957	1962
0 to 7	8.4	6.9	9.2	154	203	170
8	6.6	4.4	7.5	108	110	132
9 to 11	6.9	4.7	7.3	115	120	142
12	4.6	3.0	4.8	70	67	75
13 to 15	4.1	2.7	4.0	64	64	65
16 or more	2.2	0.6	1.4	34	14	21
All groups	6.2	4.1	6.0	*	*	*

* The relative unemployment rate is the ratio between the percentage unemployment rate for a given educational attainment group and the percentage unemployment rate for all other groups at the same point in time.

for all other groups in 1957; and its rate was 70 percent higher in 1962.)

Clearly, unemployment at the bottom of the educational scale was relatively unresponsive to general increases in the demand for labor, while there was very strong responsiveness at the top of the educational scale. The percentage unemployment rate for college graduates in 1957 merits close attention. It was an almost incredible 0.6 percent. I have queried the experts in the Bureau of Labor Statistics on this figure, and they assure me that they have no less confidence in it than in the other 1957 figures. Surely a figure as low as that represents what is sometimes called "overfull" employment—i.e., demand which seriously exceeds supply.

Bear in mind that the unemployment rates for the lower educational attainment groups (those with 80 percent of the men) are now higher than in 1950, and that the unemployment rate for college graduates is now substantially lower than in 1950. Also bear in mind that the labor force participation rate figures strongly suggest a large and growing "reserve army"—which is not counted among the unemployed—at the lower educational levels, and that there is no evidence of any such reserve of college-trained men. Finally, bear in mind the differences between the lower end of the educational scale and the upper end in responsiveness to overall decreases in the unemployment rate.

When you put all of these considerations to-

gether, I believe that you are ineluctably led to the conclusion that long before we could get down to an overall unemployment rate as low as 4 percent, we would have a severe shortage of workers at the top of the educational ladder. This shortage would be a bottleneck to further expansion of employment. I cannot pinpoint the level at which the bottleneck would begin to seriously impede expansion; but, on the basis of the relationships revealed by Table 18–2, it seems reasonable to believe that we could not get very far below a 5 percent overall unemployment level without hitting that bottleneck.

CONCLUSIONS

The most fundamental conclusion that emerges from my analysis is that automation and the changing pattern of consumer wants have greatly increased the importance of investment in human beings as a factor in economic growth. More investment in plant and equipment, without very large increases in our investment in human beings, seems certain to enlarge the surplus of underdeveloped manpower and to create a shortage of the highly developed manpower needed to design, install, and man modern production facilities.

As we have all heard over and over again, the outlook for high school dropouts is bleak indeed. Exhortations, no matter how well meant, are not going to cure this problem, and neither will the token fund set aside by President Kennedy for grants to local units for experimental programs in this area. But here again dollars alone are not the answer. We need many more highly skilled teachers, counselors, and social workers. These, too, are in very short supply. Many other present shortages of highly trained manpower, in the private sector of the economy as well as in the public, could be cited. Unquestionably these shortages would be intensified and new ones would appear if we moved closer to full utilization of our economic potential.

To my mind, the greatest shortcoming of the administration's program for reducing unemployment is the failure to recognize the crucial need to break the trained manpower bottleneck.

I would give a considerably higher priority to the stimulation of investment in human beings than I would to such measures as the proposed tax cut. But I would still rate the tax cut as important. Denying that the tax cut is the "ultimate weapon" against unemployment is not denying that it can make some contribution to the reduction of unemployment. After all, even to get below a 5 percent unemployment rate would be a considerable achievement today. But a really effective attack on the complex problem of unemployment requires a whole arsenal of powerful weapons.

And we don't have all the time in the world. Human history has been described as a race between education and catastrophe. In the past dozen years, education has been falling behind in that race.

QUESTIONS AND STUDY SUGGESTIONS

1. What arguments and evidence does the author present to substantiate his view that current unemployment is caused by changes in the structure of labor demand?

2. What do each of the two positions on the causes of current unemployment—the deficiency-of-demand view and the structural view—imply with respect to the kind of public policies required to achieve full employment?

Reading 19

Keynes and the New Economics
The Editors of *Time*

John Maynard Keynes was the most influential—and perhaps the most controversial—economist of modern times. Keynes's major contribution was to undermine the classical notion that a market economy would automatically tend to produce at full employment. He argued that private de-

From "We are All Keynesians Now," **Time**, December 31, 1965, pp. 64–67, abridged. Copyright © Time, Inc., 1965. Reprinted by permission.

mand might be deficient and, if prosperity was to be maintained, government would be obliged to adopt policies to bolster aggregate demand. Keynesian economics is now widely accepted and is the intellectual mainspring for the stabilization policies of most advanced capitalistic systems. As one prominent economist has put it: "We are all Keynesians now."

The ideas of economists and political philosophers, both when they are right and when they are wrong, are more powerful than is commonly understood. Indeed the world is ruled by little else. Practical men, who believe themselves to be quite exempt from any intellectual influences, are usually the slaves of some defunct economist.
—*The General Theory of Employment, Interest and Money*

Concluding his most important book with those words in 1935, John Maynard Keynes was confident that he had laid down a philosophy that would move and change men's affairs. Today, some 20 years after his death, his theories are a prime influence on the world's free economies, especially on America's, the richest and most expansionist. In Washington the men who formulate the nation's economic policies have used Keynesian principles not only to avoid the violent cycles of prewar days but to produce a phenomenal economic growth and to achieve remarkably stable prices. In 1965 they skillfully applied Keynes's ideas—together with a number of their own invention—to lift the nation through the fifth and best, consecutive year of the most sizable, prolonged and widely distributed prosperity in history.

By growing 5 percent in real terms, the U.S. experienced a sharper expansion than any other major nation. Even the most optimistic forecasts for 1965 turned out to be too low. The gross national product leaped from $628 billion to $672 billion—$14 billion more than the President's economists had expected. Among the other new records: auto production rose 22 percent, steel production 6 percent, capital spending 16 percent, personal income 7 percent and corporate profits 21 percent. Figuring that the U.S. had somehow discovered the secret of steady, stable, noninflationary growth, the leaders of many countries on both sides of the Iron Curtain openly tried to emulate its success.

KEYNES'S CENTRAL THEME

Basically, Washington's economic managers scaled these heights by their adherence to Keynes's central theme: the modern capitalist economy does not automatically work at top efficiency, but can be raised to that level by the intervention and influence of the government. Keynes was the first to demonstrate convincingly that government has not only the ability but the responsibility to use its powers to increase production, incomes and jobs. Moreover, he argued that government can do this without violating freedom or restraining competition. It can, he said, achieve calculated prosperity by manipulating three main tools: tax policy, credit policy and budget policy. Their use would have the effect of strengthening private spending, investment and production.

When Keynes first propagated his theories, many people considered them to be bizarre or slightly subversive, and Keynes himself to be little but a left-wing mischief maker. Now Keynes and his ideas, though they still make some people nervous, have been so widely accepted that they constitute both the new orthodoxy in the universities and the touchstone of economic management in Washington. They have led to a greater degree of government involvement in the nation's economy than ever before in time of general peace. Says Budget Director Charles L. Schultze: "We can't prevent every little wiggle in the economic cycle, but we now can prevent a major slide."

KEYNESIAN POLICIES

By and large, Keynesian public policies are working well because the private sector of the economy is making them work. Through the 1964 tax cut, government gave business the incentive to expand, but it was private businessmen who made the decisions as to whether, when and where to do it. Washington gave consumers a stimulus to spend, but millions of ordinary Americans made the decision—so vital to the economy—as to how and how much to spend. For all that it has profited from the ideas of Lord Keynes, the U.S. economy is still the world's most private and most free-enterprising. Were he alive, Keynes would certainly like it to stay that way.

The recent successes of Keynes's theories have given a new stature and luster to the men who practice what Carlyle called "the dismal science." Economists have descended in force from their ivory towers and now sit confidently at the elbow of almost every important leader in government and business, where they are increasingly called upon to forecast, plan and decide.

First the U.S. economists embraced Keynesianism, then the public accepted its tenets. Now even businessmen, traditionally hostile to government's role in the economy, have been won over—not only because Keynesianism works but because Lyndon Johnson knows how to make it palatable. They have begun to take for granted that the government will intervene to head off recession or choke off inflation, no longer think that deficit spending is immoral. Nor, in perhaps the greatest change of all, do they believe that government will ever fully pay off its debt, any more than General Motors or IBM find it advisable to pay off their long-term obligations; instead of demanding payment, creditors would rather continue collecting interest.

THE NEW ECONOMICS

Though Keynes is the figure who looms largest in these recent changes, modern-day economists have naturally expanded and added to his theories, giving birth to a form of neo-Keynesianism. Because he was a creature of his times, Keynes was primarily interested in pulling a Depression-ridden world up to some form of prosperity and stability; today's economists are more concerned about making an already prospering economy grow still further. As Keynes might have put it: Keynesianism + the theory of growth = The New Economics. Says Gardner Ackley, chairman of the Council of Economic Advisers: "The new economics is

based on Keynes. The fiscal revolution stems from him." Adds the University of Chicago's Milton Friedman, the nation's leading conservative economist, who was Presidential Candidate Barry Goldwater's adviser on economics: "We are all Keynesians now."

KEYNES'S LIFE

Far from being a socialist left-winger, Keynes (pronounced canes) was a high-caste Establishment leader who disdained what he called "the boorish proletariat" and said: "For better or worse, I am a bourgeois economist." Keynes was suspicious of the power of unions, inveighed against the perils of inflation, praised the virtue of profits. "The engine which drives Enterprise," he wrote, "is not Thrift but Profit." He condemned the Marxists as being "illogical and so dull" and saw himself as a doctor of capitalism, which he was convinced could lead mankind to universal plenty within a century. Communists, Marxists and the British Labor Party's radical fringe damned Keynes because he sought to strengthen a system that they wanted to overthrow.

Keynes was born the year Marx died (1883) and died in the first full year of capitalism's lengthy postwar boom (1946). The son of a noted Cambridge political economist, he whizzed through Eton and Cambridge, then entered the civil service. He got his lowest mark in economics. "The examiners," he later remarked, "presumably knew less than I did." He entered the India Office, soon after became a Cambridge don. Later, he was the British Treasury's representative to the Versailles Conference, and saw that it settled nothing but the inevitability of another disaster. He resigned in protest and wrote a book, *The Economic Consequences of the Peace*, that stirred an international sensation by clearly foretelling the crisis to come.

He went back to teaching at Cambridge, but at the same time operated with skill and dash in business. The National Mutual Life Assurance Society named him its chairman, and whenever he gave his annual reports to stockholders, the London Money Market suspended trading to hear his forecasts for interest rates in the year ahead. He was also editor of the erudite British *Economic Journal*, chairman of the *New Statesman and Nation* and a director of the Bank of England.

Keynes began each day propped up in bed, poring for half an hour over reports of the world's gyrating currency and commodity markets; by speculating in them, he earned a fortune of more than $2,000,000. Money, he said, should be valued not as a possession but "as a means to the enjoyments and realities of life." He took pleasure in assembling the world's finest collection of Newton's manuscripts and in organizing London's Camargo Ballet and Cambridge's Arts Theater. Later, the government tapped him to head Britain's Arts Council, and in 1942 King George VI made him a lord.

Part dilettante and part Renaissance man, Keynes moved easily in Britain's eclectic world of arts and letters. Though he remarked that economists should be humble, like dentists, he enjoyed trouncing countesses at bridge and Prime Ministers at lunch-table debates. He became a leader of the Bloomsbury set of avant-garde writers and painters. At a party at the Sitwells, he met Lydia Lopokova, a ballerina of the Diaghilev Russian ballet. She was blonde and buxom; he was frail and stoop-shouldered, with watery blue eyes. She chucked her career to marry him. His only regret in life, said Keynes shortly before his death of a heart attack, was that he had not drunk more champagne.

THE WHOLE ECONOMY

The thrust of Keynes's personality, however strong, was vastly less important than the force of his ideas. Those ideas were so original and persuasive that Keynes now ranks with Adam Smith and Karl Marx as one of history's most significant economists. Today his theses are the basis of economic policies in Britain, Canada, Australia and part of Continental Europe, as well as in the U.S.

Economics is a young science, a mere 200 years old. Addressing its problems in the second half of its second century, Keynes was more successful than his predecessors in seeing it whole. Great theorists before him had tried to take a wide view of economic forces, but they lacked the 20th century statistical tools to do the job, and they tended to concentrate on certain specialties. Adam Smith focused on the

marketplace, Malthus on population, Ricardo on rent and land, Marx on labor and wages. Modern economists call those specializations "microeconomics"; Keynes was the precursor of what is now known as "macroeconomics"—from the Greek *makros,* for large or extended. He decided that the way to look at the economy was to measure all the myriad forces tugging and pulling at it—production, prices, profits, incomes, interest rates, government policies.

For most of his life, Keynes wrote, wrote, wrote. He was so prolific that a compendium of his books, tracts and essays fills 22 pages. In succession he wrote books about mathematical probability (1921), the gold standard and monetary reform (1923), and the causes of business cycles (1930); each of his works further developed his economic thinking. Then he bundled his major theories into his magnum opus, *The General Theory,* published in 1936. It is an uneven and ill-organized book, as difficult as *Deuteronomy* and open to almost as many interpretations. Yet for all its faults, it had more influence in a shorter time than any other book ever written on economics, including Smith's *The Wealth of Nations* and Marx's *Das Kapital.*

KEYNES AND CLASSICAL ECONOMICS

Keynes perceived that the prime goal of any economy was to achieve "full employment." By that, he meant full employment of materials and machines as well as of men. Before Keynes, classical economists had presumed that the economy was naturally regulated by what Adam Smith had called the "invisible hand," which brought all forces into balance and used them fully. Smith argued, for example, that if wages rose too fast, employers would lay off so many workers that wages would fall until they reached the point at which employers would start rehiring. French Economist Jean Baptiste Say embroidered that idea by theorizing that production always creates just enough income to consume whatever it produces, thus permitting any excesses of demand to correct themselves quickly.

Keynes showed that the hard facts of history contradicted these unrealistic assumptions. For centuries, he pointed out, the economic cycle had gyrated from giddy boom to violent bust; periods of inflated prosperity induced a speculative rise, which then disrupted commerce and led inexorably to impoverished deflation. The climax came during the depression of the 1930s. Wages plummeted and unemployment rocketed, but neither the *laissez-faire* classicists nor the sullen and angry Communists adequately diagnosed the disease or offered any reasonable remedies.

By applying both logic and historical example to economic cycles, Keynes showed that the automatic stabilizers that economists had long banked on could actually aggravate rather than prevent a depression. If employers responded to a fall-off in demand by slicing wages and dumping workers, said Keynes, that would only reduce incomes and demand, and plunge production still deeper. If bankers responded to a fall-off in savings by raising interest rates, that would not tempt penniless people to save more—but it would move hard-pressed industrialists to borrow less for capital investment. Yet Keynes did not despair of capitalism as so many other economists did. Said he: "The right remedy for the trade cycle is not to be found in abolishing booms and keeping us permanently in a semi-slump; but in abolishing slumps and thus keeping us permanently in a quasi-boom."

THE MANAGEMENT OF DEMAND

The key to achieving that, Keynes perceived, is to maintain constantly a high level of what he called "aggregate demand." To him, that meant the total of all demand in the economy—demand for consumption and for investment, for both private and public purposes. His inescapable conclusion was that, if private demand should flag and falter, then it had to be revived and stimulated by the only force strong enough to lift consumption: the government.

The pre-Keynesian "classical" economists had thought of the government too. But almost all of them had contended that, in times of depression, the government should raise taxes and reduce spending in order to balance the budget. In the early 1930s, Keynes cried out that the only way to revive aggregate demand was for the government to cut taxes, reduce interest rates, spend heavily—and deficits be damned. Said Keynes: "The State will have to exercise a guiding influence on the propensity to consume partly through its scheme

of taxation, partly by fixing the rates of interest, and partly, perhaps, in others ways."

A few other economists of Keynes's time had called for more or less the same thing. Yet Keynes was the only one with enough influence and stature to get governments to sit up and pay attention. He was the right man at the right time, and his career and fame derived largely from the fact that when his theories appeared the world was racked by history's worst depression and governments were desperately searching for a way out.

Contrary to the Marxists and the socialists, Keynes opposed government ownership of industry and fought those centralists who would plan everything ("They wish to serve not God but the devil"). While he called for conscious and calculated state intervention, he argued just as passionately that the government had no right to tamper with individual freedoms to choose or change jobs, to buy or sell goods, or to earn respectable profits. He had tremendous faith that private men could change, improve and expand capitalism.

HIS CRITICS

Like any genius, Keynes had plenty of faults and shortcomings. Even his admirers admit that he could be maddeningly abstruse and confusing. His few outright critics feel that, while he knew how to buoy a depression-stricken industrial economy, he offered little in the way of practical information about how to keep a prosperous modern economy fat and secure. Keynesian theories are certainly unworkable in the underdeveloped nations, where the problem is not too little demand but insufficient supply, and where the object is not to stimulate consumption but to spur savings, form capital and raise production.

Such critics as former U.S. Budget Director Maurice Stans still worry that Keynes makes spenders seem virtuous and savers wicked, and thus subtly threatens the nation's moral fiber. Other doubters contend that earlier obscure economists originated some of the ideas that Keynes popularized, and that all he did was wrap them up in a general theory. But even his severest detractors bow to his brilliance, use the macroeconomic terms and framework that he devised, and concede that his main theories have largely worked out in practice.

QUESTIONS AND STUDY SUGGESTIONS

1. How did Keynes's theories differ from those of classical economics? Specifically, what were Keynes's major criticisms of the classical theory of employment?

2. Comment: "Critics have generally attacked Keynes as being a liberal or radical, but in fact he was a conservative."

Reading 20

Problems in Stabilization Policy

James R. Schlesinger, The RAND Corporation

In Reading 20 James R. Schlesinger provides us with a revealing comparison of fiscal policy "in theory" and "in practice." Early proponents of fiscal policy embraced a perfectionist view of it; that is, they envisioned fiscal policy as a means to the simultaneous and permanent achievement of full employment and price level stability. Both economic and political limitations have shattered this perfectionist vision. On the economic front, such problems as the partial incompatibility of the goals of full employment and price stability (noted by Slichter in Reading 16) and the inability of fiscal policy to adjust the composition of aggregate demand to the productive capacity of individual industries have become evident. Political obstacles have also been formidable. The reluctance of Congress to achieve a budgetary surplus renders fiscal policy of doubtful use in controlling inflation. Potential political and social frictions inhibit fiscal action which reapportions the tax burden. Government expenditures which rise during recession are frequently not reversible during inflation. All these complications have changed perfectionist attitudes toward fiscal policy and have made its limitations increasingly evident. Attitudes toward fiscal policy are now being altered in two other respects. First, we are coming to recognize that there exists a great variety of specific tax and government expenditure policies from which to choose in deriving and applying fiscal policy. Second, our mixture of policies to achieve overall stabilization is further broadened by the innumerable ways in which fiscal measures can be blended with monetary policy and debt management policy.

From James R. Schlesinger, "Emerging Attitudes toward Fiscal Policy," **Political Science Quarterly**, March, 1962, pp. 6–18, abridged. Reprinted by permission.

It is clear that the proponents of fiscal policy have obtained the substance of their desires, while leaving to their rivals only empty forms and slogans. Consequently, it would seem that the former have won a great victory, and that they would be content to see their dreams fulfilled. Paradoxically, however, this is not the case. Although the use of fiscal policy in achieving stability is universally accepted today, the hopes of those who originally formulated it have gone unfulfilled. For various reasons our method of employing fiscal weapons, our attitudes toward fiscal policy, and our experience with employment programs, have all proved to be something of a disappointment to them.

ECONOMIC LIMITATIONS

The goal of the formulators of full employment programs was not merely the *mitigation* but the virtual *elimination* of economic fluctuations. If, through the use of the fiscal weapon, aggregate demand could be more or less precisely matched to potential supply, then no (competent) man need be more than temporarily unemployed. And the original proponents did believe that fiscal policy might be employed so flexibly. By varying expenditures or the tax structure whenever deflationary or inflationary pressures became apparent, full employment without inflation could be permanently achieved. This attitude towards employment policy, which may be called the perfectionist view, supplied the initial impulse for the Employment Act in this country. Since proponents of these policies would not be satisfied with mere palliatives, the automatic stabilizers, which could only mitigate but not eliminate fluctuations, were viewed as desirable but insufficient. To achieve a permanent state of full employment, the automatic stabilizers would have to be supplemented by discretionary fiscal policy, flexibly employed. In the view of their critics, this "attempt to drain the last dregs of employment out of the system" was likely to do more harm than good. They thought that discretionary fiscal policy too ambitiously employed was characterized by inherent defects which the formulators of the programs had to perceive. Time has proved the skeptics to have been very perceptive.

Part of the difficulty of the perfectionist view lay in the economic realm. The biggest error, perhaps, was the failure to appreciate the strong upward pressure on wages, costs, and prices which would exist under full employment conditions. American theorists underestimated the strong preference on the part of individual unions to preserve their autonomy rather than to observe a general wage-price formula. They overestimated the willingness of pressure groups in general to exercise self-restraint in the public interest. They overestimated both the effectiveness and public tolerability of the control of prices in "bottleneck sectors." Consequently, they failed to appreciate adequately the tendency of demand to leak off into higher wages and prices rather than into expanded output, once the sanction of unemployment was removed. One apparent effect of a full-employment guarantee has been to make a steady rise in the price level inevitable.

Advocates of the employment programs failed to perceive another defect in the perfectionist view. Although it is a very powerful instrument, fiscal policy is also a *crude* one and may not be sufficiently subtle to achieve the *delicate* kinds of adjustment required in an economy which is dependent upon the *voluntary* action of individuals to achieve necessary adjustments. This type of difficulty is shown most clearly in the case of unemployment in export industries, which depend after all upon foreign buyers. An expansionary fiscal policy, by raising domestic costs and prices and making domestic goods less attractive to foreign purchasers, may actually magnify rather than diminish the problem of unemployment in the export industries—to say nothing of intensifying any balance of payments difficulties which may exist.

Even within the domestic economy, fiscal policy may be incapable of dealing with the problem of structural unemployment. When changes occur in consumer preferences or in the pattern of industrial production, the shift in the structure of output is likely to create a declining industry concentrated in a particular region. This is the problem of the depressed area about which fiscal policy can do little. Any increase in aggregate demand brought about by an expansionary fiscal policy is likely to result in continued unemployment in the depressed area, associated with a rise in the price level in other sectors of the economy. The problem in this case is that the simple Keynesian model upon which fiscal policy is based may be misleading. Aggregate supply may be equated to aggregate demand in the over-all sense, without the hoped for results, since demand may be concentrated upon industries in which capacity is insufficient, while unemployment continues in those industries against which consumer preferences have been shifting. In West Virginia, for example, the chief industry, coal, has suffered simultaneously from: a) a substantial fall-off in foreign demand since 1957; b) a gradual diminution of demand on the part of domestic consumers; and, c) improvements in the methods of coal-mining which have diminished the need for miners. Unemployment in West Virginia remains high, on account of the reluctance of the population to move away from their homes despite the shrinkage of employment opportunities. Irrespective of the statements of office seekers on the campaign trail, there is really very little that the federal government can do about this condition, short of *directing* industrial investment into the state. Due to the handicaps of location under which West Virginia labors, the effect of an expansionary fiscal policy on its unemployment problem will be modest at best.

POLITICAL REALITIES IN A DEMOCRACY

Failure to take account of its economic limitations has not, however, proved to be the chief drawback to fiscal policy in the postwar period. A far graver defect was the failure of its proponents to recognize the limits to its political workability, especially in the context of the American political system. Under *ideal* conditions, it could be expected that flexible use of fiscal policy could prevent unemployment, except for very short periods, outside of depressed areas. But such a result presupposes that the nation's fiscal machinery is controlled by rational and detached experts uninfluenced by pressures, interests, or impassioned controversies. Such is not the case, although at one time fiscal theorists naively assumed that it was. The nation's fiscal policy is decided by members of Congress subject to the strong and somewhat irrational demands of ordinary voters and of special interest groups. The practical results have consequently diverged considerably from the expectation of those who formulated the employment programs. As a result,

since early in the postwar period, discretionary fiscal policy has been viewed with some skepticism by all except academic observers.

The most obvious of fiscal policy's political difficulties is its asymmetry or lopsidedness. According to the original conception, fiscal policy was intended to be a dual-purpose weapon, effective in dealing with excessive as well as insufficient demand. In times of inflation, budgetary surpluses would restrain total expenditures and ease inflationary pressures, just as in times of depression, demand was maintained by a budgetary deficit. In practice, nothing has been so hard to attain or to retain as a budgetary surplus. Paying taxes is burdensome and unpleasant to the voters, so that Congress is under constant pressure to reduce taxes. Moreover, expanded expenditures are quite satisfying to whatever groups are benefited, and Congress is under steady pressure to increase its outlays. Under these circumstances it is difficult even to balance the budget in times of prosperity, let alone obtain a surplus (which incidentally helps to explain the aura of fiscal rectitude which came to be built up around the balanced budget rule). Fiscal policy readily serves as a stimulant in periods of depression, but not as a restraint in periods of excessive demand. Whenever a surplus appears, there is a strong tendency either for expenditures to creep up or for tax cuts to be given—either action intensifying the pressure and throwing a larger burden on monetary policy.

There is a second facet to the lopsidedness of fiscal policy. If the onset of a recession brings about discretionary increase of expenditures on the part of the government, vested interests are created in such expenditures and, with the return of prosperity, it becomes difficult to reduce them. Associated with the reluctance to increase tax rates, the result could be perennially unbalanced budgets. Moreover, permanent increases in federal expeditures in recession, even if matched by an increase in taxes in prosperity, might mean that a rising proportion of national output is incorporated into the government sector—a condition which is not consistent with the political goals of a good many citizens. This tendency of government expenditures to creep up in recession without receding in prosperity is sometimes referred to as the "ratchet effect"—it has made political conservatives, at any rate, suspicious of the aggressive use of fiscal policy.

THE TAX STRUCTURE

The assumption of fiscal theorists that the tax structure is far more flexible than conditions really warrant creates another difficulty. Theorists may view the tax structure as a technical instrument to be used for the manipulation of demand. The public, however, tends to regard the tax system as a matter of balanced rights and responsibilities, based upon justice and equity. Continued variation of tax rates may undermine the willingness to pay taxes upon which, in the final analysis, the effectiveness of fiscal policy depends. The willingness to pay taxes, particularly income taxes, is not a universal phenomenon. It could be that the attempt to overuse the fiscal instrument might destroy the delicate structure upon which it rests. At some point in the future the public may come to appreciate the desirability of viewing taxation simply as a device for influencing expenditures in the private sector. It clearly does not do so at the present time, thus making it hard to increase taxes or to reimpose them once they have been removed.

A barrier to the kind of flexibility envisaged by the theorists arises from the fact that any variation of the tax structure may mean a shift in the *distribution* of the tax burden among different classes of citizens and taxpayers. Any change in the tax structure which forces a reappraisal of the appropriateness of relative burdens almost inevitably breeds both intense political controversy and a degree of social friction which is disturbing. Each group's notion of equity in the tax structure is based upon the (tacit) belief that a larger share of the burden should be shifted to others—labor pleads for higher exemptions, while business pleads for a lower corporate income tax. It is for this reason that a wise rule-of-thumb in public finance is that "an old tax is a good tax." Avoiding changes in the tax structure means avoiding the reawakening of controversy and harmful passions. Fiscal theorists who urge continuous modification of the tax structure ignore the fact that fiscal policy is only in some respects a *general* control. Both tax and expenditure policies operate by directly affecting the interests of specific groups which are likely to feel resentful when those interests have been damaged. Continued modification of the tax structure may lead to social controversy, a feeling of ill usage, a decline in morale which weakens the social fabric, and, by weakening the willingness to pay taxes, may undermine the fiscal policy instrument itself.

CLUMSINESS OF FISCAL POLICY

Even more than the economic difficulties, the political clumsiness of discretionary fiscal policy has increased the reluctance to employ it aggressively in counteracting mild downturns, and has made it almost impossible to use fiscal policy effectively in dealing with inflationary pressures. To be sure, this defect refers only to discretionary fiscal policy rather than to the automatic stabilizers which do not require either precise forecasting or rapid and frictionless adjustments brought about through cumbersome political machinery. Only when a gross maladjustment exists between aggregate demand and supply, is it clear that discretionary fiscal policy can be employed. The tricky problems thus arise when one tries to decide what to do in in-between situations in which the automatic stabilizers have failed to prevent more unemployment developing than one would desire, yet the unemployment has not gone deep enough to warrant the risks of discretionary fiscal policy. Both the inflexibility of expenditures in the downward direction (the ratchet effect) and the political frictions generated by variation of the tax structure have made all postwar administrations loath to employ fiscal policy in as flexible a way as the academics of the 'forties hoped.

In one respect fiscal policy has revolutionized budget policy, in another it has left conditions surprisingly unchanged. Although the rule of the *annually* balanced budget has met its end, in fact if not in fiction, it has proved to be impossible to frame budget policy solely in terms of "functional finance" or "the economic requirements of particular conditions." Such concepts provide too elastic a criterion for budget policy, and it is for this reason that the balanced budget remains relevant as an aspiration, if not as a rule. Democracies appear to be reluctant to discipline themselves. The projected balancing of a target budget for conditions of full employment provides a disciplinary value in a society in which the public is inclined to overlook the fact that costs must be paid—a disciplinary value which the original proponents of fiscal policy may have treated too lightly.

VISTAS OF THE FUTURE

In two other respects attitudes toward fiscal policy have been changing rapidly. First, we have come to recognize that a given level of effective demand may be obtained through an incredible variety of fiscal devices which can be fitted together in an array of distinct patterns of tax and expenditure policies. Secondly, we have learned that fiscal policy does not exist in a vacuum; it must be effectively coordinated with monetary and debt management policies in order to achieve the nation's goals; whatever they may be. These two changes are closer together than one might think, for together they represent a departure from stale ideological controversy which has enormously broadened the range of the potential components of the nation's policy-mix.

The first point requires some amplification. In contrast to a widespread view of fifteen years ago that the "marginal propensity to save" was too "high" to permit reliance on the tax reduction route to stimulate total expenditures, tax reduction is today viewed as an effective instrument for stimulating not only consumption but investment as well. Peacetime levels of taxation much higher than were anticipated in the 'forties have meant that the leeway for stimulating expenditures through tax reduction is much greater than hitherto. These higher levels of taxation have meant that a large share of tax revenues has come from the lower and middle income groups; consequently a reduction in taxes may more easily stimulate mass consumption expenditures than was anticipated earlier. Moreover, upper income groups are more willing to consume out of increased after-tax incomes than was believed possible even ten years ago. The recognition of the expansibility of consumption is most vividly illustrated by the shift of the main focus of the critics of our economic system from "the mature economy" to the "affluent society"—that is, a shift from a view that the propensity to consume is too low to the view that it is too high. In addition, the abandonment of the notion that the volume of investment is "autonomously" determined has meant recognition that it is not at all difficult to stimulate additional *investment* expenditures via the tax reduction route. Particularly is this true when fiscal policies of a somewhat wider scope, including tax credits for investment expenditure or more

generous treatment of depreciation allowances, are considered.

The widening range of activities which it is regarded as appropriate for the government to support has meant a similar broadening of opportunities on the expenditures side. In the depression the choice lay between traditional public works which provided tangible results and relief expenditures which did not. Expenditures resulting in tangible benefits now include the housing program, slum clearance, and a greater expanded conception of resource development. With respect to expenditures for intangible benefits the government may now spend for education, for unemployment compensation and for a variety of welfare measures, without indulging in the leaf-raking fiction that there is a direct *quid pro quo*. In light of the broadened array of fiscal weapons, increasingly there are differences concerning the appropriate mixture of fiscal devices to achieve a given level of demand.

The second point reflects the recognition that monetary policy and the closely allied debt management policy can have a substantial influence on effective demand. Moreover, fiscal and monetary policies are closely associated in determining the availability of capital funds, and the allocation of resources as between consumption and investment. In the days when monetary policy was regarded as hopelessly ineffective, the problem of coordination could be blithely ignored. Now it is seen that a tighter fiscal policy permits a more lenient monetary policy, and vice versa. For effective monetary policy the problem of debt management must be under control, both with respect to its structure and its trend, and the trend of the debt reflects government surpluses and deficits, that is, fiscal policy. Thus there is a question of choice involved in the policy-mix. Accepting the goal of full employment, one can choose either to emphasize or deemphasize fiscal policy depending on whether one wishes to place a smaller or greater burden on monetary and debt management policy respectively.

Put together, both the centrifugal tendency for the scope of fiscal policy to widen and the centripetal tendency for it to become more closely intertwined with monetary and debt management policy in the over-all policy-mix have vastly increased the number of possible combinations of policy ingredients to achieve a given policy goal. Figure 20–1 illustrates this

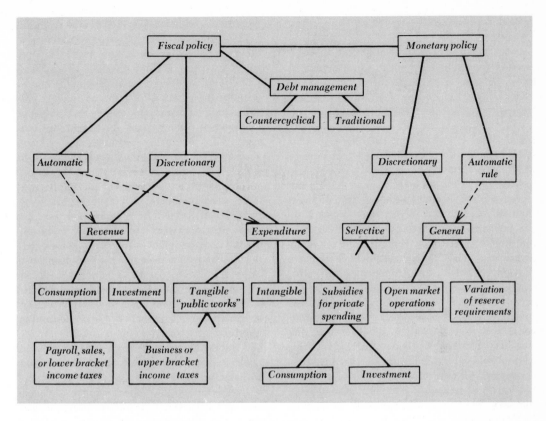

Figure 20–1.   Possible policy ingredients for stabilization.

range of possibilities. On the highest level, a choice must be made between emphasizing fiscal policy and emphasizing monetary policy. Just below these two policy areas, not quite independent but not altogether dependent, is debt management, more subordinate to monetary than to fiscal policy but still reflecting immediate budgetary pressures. One may attempt to use debt management countercyclically or one may have the more modest and traditional Treasury objective of managing it "for its own sake."

Within the area of fiscal policy, one has a variety of choices. One may choose to rely exclusively on automatic stabilizers (accompanied by flexible monetary policy) or one may attempt to use discretionary fiscal policy. Under the latter heading there will be an opportunity to emphasize the revenue or the expenditure side (just as would be the case for automatic stabilizers, though not to the same degree). If the emphasis is placed on the revenue side,

a choice will be made between influencing demand by affecting consumption, which implies variation of sales-type taxes, payroll taxes, or lower bracket income taxes, or by influencing investment, which implies changes in business taxes, upper bracket income taxes or depreciation policies. (Relying on investment changes must mean, of course, considerable reliance on monetary policy.) On the expenditure side, a choice may be made between changing expenditures for tangibles or for intangibles, or the decision might be made directly to subsidize private consumption or investment.

Monetary policy, though it remains wholly discretionary at the present time, may also be subdivided. One may rely on general controls, or one may make some use of selective controls. Under the heading of the traditional quantitative weapons, a choice will have to be made between emphasizing open-market operations or utilizing changes in reserve requirements in determining monetary strategy.

VALUE JUDGMENTS

In choosing the ultimate policy-mix, value judgments are unavoidable. As a general, if not universal, rule, the political right with its deep distrust of concentration of power, particularly in the government, has tended to favor monetary policy over fiscal policy. When fiscal policy is employed, the preference is for total reliance on the automatic stabilizers. If discretionary fiscal policy is employed, the preference is for reliance on changes on the revenue side, especially those that stimulate investment activity. When expenditures must be adjusted, it is preferred that increases be for tangibles (such as roads) rather than intangibles (welfare benefits broadly construed). Curiously enough, in the case of subsidies the right has little aversion to subsidizing investment outlays, but a deep repugnance for subsidizing consumption outlays, although as a rule, subsidization of private expenditures is preferred to increased state activity.

The political left tends in the other direction. Fiscal policy, even discretionary fiscal policy, is *preferred* to monetary and debt management policies. Changes on the expenditure (that is, increases) are preferred to changes on the revenue side. If changes on the revenue side are accepted, the preference is normally toward stimulating mass consumption rather than investment. There is no aversion to expenditures for intangibles. Subsidization of certain types of private consumption seems highly desirable, but direct subsidization of private investment is viewed with extreme suspicion. In employing monetary policy, the left, unlike the right, has some partiality for the selective controls, and has a preference for higher reserve requirements with open-market purchases by the Federal Reserve, while the right prefers lowered reserve requirements.

At the present time, it should be emphasized, most of the disputes superficially concerning stabilization policy are really about value judgments on issues other than stabilization. When labor unions insist that recession should be fought by lowering sales or first bracket taxes, increased expenditures or subsidies, and looser money, but also insist that *reversal* of these policies is *not* the proper way to fight inflation (but rather business and upper bracket income taxes should be increased and selective controls on spending adopted), plainly the argument is not over stabilization *per se* but rather over increased consumption, decreased income inequality, and the appropriate role of the state. Similarly, when the political right recommends diminished progressivity of the income tax in *inflation* and in *deflation*, this clearly is not a question involving stabilization policy alone. Both sides are likely to insist that failure to adopt their particular remedies will be destabilizing, but that is the merest window dressing. Any detached observer will note a variety of ways of skinning the stabilization cat. Stability can be achieved through a vast number of combinations of policy measures, each one of which will reflect a different set of value judgments. The greater variety of fiscal devices and the increased flexibility of fiscal policy, in combining it with monetary or debt management policies, has increased the latitude for controversy over issues different from, but still unhappily confused with, the appropriateness of using fiscal policy for stabilization purposes.

QUESTIONS AND STUDY SUGGESTIONS

1. Explain the "perfectionist view" toward fiscal policy. Note both the economic and political problems involved in applying fiscal policy. Explain the significance of the "lopsidedness of fiscal policy" and the "ratchet effect."

2. What difficulties does the author believe are encountered in using the tax structure as a fiscal policy tool?

3. Explain (*a*) the different fiscal devices; (*b*) the different monetary devices; and (*c*) the different combinations of monetary and fiscal devices that can be used to influence effective demand. What specific kinds of monetary and fiscal policy, in the author's opinion, are preferred by the political right and by the political left?

Reading 21

Stabilization Policy: Historical Record and New Directions

Council of Economic Advisers

Reading 21 is a succinct summary of two decades of experience under the Employment Act of 1946. The CEA sketches the historical background out of which the act evolved and discusses the various applications of fiscal and monetary policy designed to realize the objectives of the act. Stabilization policy has had to contend with new problems not envisioned by framers of the Employment Act, for example, "the problem of inadequate demand in expansion" and the tendency of inflation to occur prior to the realization of full employment. In recent years stabilization policy—the "new economics"—has emphasized the realization of the economy's growth potential rather than the mere mitigation of the ups and downs of the business cycle.

There were great expectations and not a few qualms when the Employment Act was signed into law on February 20, 1946, following enactment by heavy bipartisan majorities in both houses of Congress.

THE ACT AND ITS BACKGROUND

The legislation of 1946 set forth the following declaration of policy:

The Congress declares that it is the continuing policy and responsibility of the Federal Government to use all practicable means consistent with its needs and obligations and other essential considerations of national policy, with the assistance and cooperation of industry, agriculture, labor, and State and local governments, to coordinate and utilize all its plans, functions, and resources for the purpose of creating and maintaining, in a manner calculated to foster and promote free competitive enterprise and the general welfare, conditions under which there will be afforded useful employment opportunities, including self-employment, for those able, willing, and seeking to work, and to promote maximum employment, production, and purchasing power.

In making this declaration, the Congress recognized that the billions of independent spending and saving decisions of a free economy could well result in levels of total demand either short of full employment or in excess of productive capacity. Furthermore, it took the view that Government policies could play a constructive role in improving the stability and balance of the economy.

The Act was a product of the experiences of the Great Depression and World War II. The Depression shook but did not destroy the faith in an automatic tendency of the economy to find its proper level of operation. In the early 1930s, public works and other antidepression programs were justified as temporary "pump priming," to help the private economy get back on its track after an unusual and catastrophic derailment. And the departure from orthodox fiscal principles was made with regret and without complete consistency. The Government expenditures explicitly designed to combat de-

From **Economic Report of the President, 1966**, Washington, pp. 170–184, 186, abridged.

pression necessarily increased budget deficits; but this implication was veiled by financing these outlays through an "extraordinary" budget. Meanwhile, taxes were raised, and salaries and housekeeping expenditures cut in the regular budget, thereby reducing the over-all stimulation of Government measures.

The relapse of the economy in 1937 into a sharp decline from a level still far below full employment gave rise to conflicting interpretations. To some, it proved that pump priming and Government deficits had undermined the confidence of the business community and thereby only worsened the situation. Others, however, concluded that it pointed to the need for larger and more sustained fiscal and monetary actions to revive the economy. In drawing this conclusion, economists were buttressed by the writings of J. M. Keynes, who offered a theoretical explanation of the disastrous depression. The Keynesian conclusions received additional support during World War II because they offered a satisfactory explanation of why the high deficit-financed defense expenditures of that period not only wiped out unemployment but went beyond to create inflationary pressures.

Memories of the disastrous 1930s were very much in the public mind as World War II was drawing to an end. Many active proponents of "full employment" legislation in 1945 and 1946 feared a relapse into depressed levels of economic activity like those of the 1930s, once military spending ended. They looked toward Federal public works spending as a peacetime replacement—at least, in part—for the wartime defense outlays.

The opponents of "full employment" legislation had several reservations and objections. Some feared that it would mean a statutory blessing for perpetual budgetary deficits, soaring public expenditures, and massive redistribution of income from upper to lower income groups. There were doubts that Government actions could and would on balance raise employment; and there were fears that these actions would lead to regimentation and would jeopardize the free enterprise system. The proponents of legislation, on the other hand, argued that the Act would merely provide a setting essential to the proper functioning of the free enterprise system because a depressed economy heightened social tensions, discour-

aged innovation and initiative, dulled competition, and undermined confidence.

The legislation which finally emerged from this discussion wisely abstained from diagnosing depression as the disease and public works as the cure, but instead concentrated on establishing the principle of continuing Government responsibility to review and appraise economic developments, diagnose problems, and prescribe appropriate remedies. And it placed major responsibility squarely upon the President, who was asked to discuss his execution of that responsibility in an Economic Report to be transmitted to the Congress at the start of each year.

The Act also established two agencies—the Council of Economic Advisers in the Executive Branch and the Joint Committee on the Economic Report (later named the Joint Economic Committee) of the Congress—with interrelated but separate responsibilities. These institutions have each filled a vital and previously missing role in their respective branches of Government—they have provided a coordinated overview of the economic impact of the entire spectrum of Government tax, expenditure, monetary, and other activities. To maintain the emphasis on advice and coordination, the Joint Economic Committee was not given any substantive legislative responsibility nor the Council any policy-executing duties. Both agencies have participated actively in the counsels of Government; both have conscientiously striven for a thoroughly professional economic competence and approach in their respective reports and recommendations; and both have contributed to the public understanding of economic issues.

Today's economic policies reflect the continuing impact of the Employment Act in all the years since its inception. And our accumulating experience is certain to be reflected in the policies of the future. This discussion reviews the development of policy in the past 20 years.

AVOIDING DEPRESSIONS AND BOOMS

The Congress proved wise in its decisions to state goals broadly and to concentrate on continuing review, analysis, and proposals, since the specific problems that actually arose were somewhat different from those which many supporters of the Employment Act had anticipated.

Although an important part of the impetus for the Employment Act derived from the prolonged depression of the 1930s and the resulting fear of stagnation in the American economy, this problem did not prove to be the primary challenge to economic policymaking under the Act. Indeed, immediately after World War II, excess-demand inflation proved to be the key problem. Subsequently, policy was focused on the age-old problem of limiting the size and duration of cyclical swings. Only much later and in a much different and milder form did stagnation arise as a live issue.

Thus, much of our experience under the Act consisted of policy actions to combat recession—lest it turn into depression—and to contain excess demand pressure—lest it generate inflationary boom.

COMBATING RECESSIONS

A series of relatively short and mild recessions required Government attention in the postwar period. The problem of cyclical declines was not unexpected by the framers of the Employment Act, nor was it new to the American economy. In the period between 1854 (the beginning of the business cycle annals of the National Bureau of Economic Research) and World War II, we had experienced 21 periods of recession or depression. Our postwar record is blemished by 4 additional periods of contracting economic activity—1948–49, 1953–54, 1957–58, and 1960–61.

Compared with the previous cyclical record, the postwar recessions have been far shorter, considerably milder, and substantially less frequent. During the past 20 years, the economy has spent a total of 42 months, or 18 percent of the time, in periods of recessions, far less than the 43 percent applicable to the 1854–1939 era.

Discretionary Policies

This improvement in the postwar record of the economy was aided by the deliberate discretionary steps taken by the Government to modify the impact of business downturns and thereby to prevent cumulating declines into depression. The speed and force of these actions—in both the fiscal and monetary areas—varied among the recessions. Thus, in 1949

little new fiscal action was taken, partly because inflation was viewed as a key problem even during the decline, and partly because Government measures taken the previous year were expected to have a considerable impact on the economy: the tax reductions of 1948 were supplying large refunds, and large expenditure increases were forthcoming under the recently enacted Marshall Plan. The Federal Reserve did act to reduce reserve requirements in a series of steps during the spring and summer of 1949, reversing a two-year rise in short-term interest rates.

In 1953–54, as military outlays declined and aggregate activity retreated, the principal expansionary influence came from previously scheduled reductions of corporate and personal income taxes. But some new action was taken to reduce excise taxes and to speed up expenditures. All three major instruments of monetary policy—reserve requirements, the discount rate, and open market operations—were used to encourage the expansion of credit-financed expenditures. Meanwhile, the Administration planned larger fiscal steps that might be taken if the recession seemed likely to be prolonged. Significantly, in 1954, the bipartisan character of expansionary fiscal policies was established for the first time, as the Republican Administration of President Eisenhower adopted measures that had previously been linked to the New Deal and Keynesian economics.

In 1958, the recession was considerably deeper than its two postwar predecessors and both the Eisenhower Administration and the Congress were more vigorous in taking action. An important concern of earlier years—that business confidence might be disturbed by Government recognition of a recession—seemed insignificant since the sharp recession was obvious to all.

Several important measures were taken. The benefit period for unemployment compensation was temporarily extended. Grants to States under the Federal highway program were enlarged and accelerated, and other programs in the budget also were expanded or rescheduled to provide an earlier stimulative effect. The Government also acted to spur housing activity by financial operations in the mortgage market and by altering terms on Government-guaranteed home mortgages. The important measures were launched near, or after, the trough of the recession. Thus, in retrospect, policy helped most to strengthen the early recovery rather than to contain or shorten the recession. Nevertheless, in view of the general recognition that the Government would be running a substantial deficit in any case, these additions to Federal outlays were a significant reflection of changed attitudes toward the role of fiscal policy.

Monetary policy also played a constructive role in the 1957–58 recession, once the monetary authorities moved to ease credit 3 months after the peak in economic activity. Thereafter, Federal Reserve actions contributed to a revival in housing and other investment by promoting a sharp reduction in interest rates, both short- and long-term.

The first fiscal measures to deal with the 1960–61 recession were taken with the inauguration of President Kennedy in January 1961, when the recession had just about run its course. Nevertheless, improvements in the social insurance system, rescheduling of Federal expenditures, and expanded programs (including defense and space) were an important stimulus to the recovery during 1961. In contrast to the delay in taking fiscal measures, the Federal Reserve reversed a tight money policy early in 1960, prior to the downturn.

Not all discretionary changes in taxes or expenditures have contributed to economic stability. Indeed, some steps taken to pursue national security or social goals had destabilizing economic impacts, which were not always appropriately offset. Previously scheduled payroll tax increases took effect in 1954, 1959, and 1962, and drained off purchasing power in recession or in initial recovery. In 1953, defense outlays declined and triggered a recession before offsetting expansionary policies were adopted.

Structural Changes for Stability

On the whole, discretionary fiscal and monetary actions made a distinct positive contribution in limiting declines. Even more important in this respect was the strengthened inherent stability of the postwar economy.

In large measure, this can be traced simply to the greater size of the Government relative to the total economy: that is, the increased importance of Government expenditures—both purchases of goods and services and transfer payments. Government outlays do not participate in the downward spiral of recession; because of its borrowing capacity, the Federal Government—unlike businesses and households—can maintain its spending in the face of declining income receipts. Although State and local governments do not have equal immunity from the need to tighten their belts, they have been able to maintain their growing spending programs relatively unaffected during the mild postwar recessions.

When private incomes and employment decline, purchasing power is automatically supported by both a decline of Federal revenues and an increase in unemployment compensation payments. Transmission of the virus of deflation is thus impeded. During postwar recessions, the progressive Federal personal income tax has not had to demonstrate its full stabilizing effectiveness because of the mildness of dips in personal earnings. There have, however, been sharp declines in corporate incomes; the Federal Treasury has shared about half of the drop in profits, thereby helping to bolster dividends and to cushion cash flow, and hence investment outlays.

A number of improvements in our financial structure were developed in the 1930s to assure that financial collapse and declines in economic activity would not generate a vicious downward spiral as they did after 1929. These important financial mechanisms include Federal insurance of private deposits; the separation of commercial and investment banking functions; the Federal Reserve's increased ability to provide banks with reserves in time of crisis; and the joint work of the Federal Reserve and the Securities and Exchange Commission to reduce harmful speculation in the stock market. The very existence of these structural changes has contributed to stability by improving confidence.

With the help of the more stable structure of the economy, recessions in the postwar era have been limited to declines in investment spending (and, in 1953–54, Federal outlays). Consumer incomes have not declined significantly, and hence households have maintained their spending in recession. With the nearly two-thirds of GNP represented by consumer expenditures insulated from decline and with a solid foundation of public outlays, declines in private investment have not cumulated. In contrast, the Great Depression generated a decline of consumer outlays of 40 percent from 1929 to 1933, and the shrinkage of consumer markets aggravated and reinforced the collapse in investment spending.

CONTAINING INFLATIONARY PRESSURES

The desirability of price stability was clearly recognized in the legislative discussion of the Employment Act. But few considered the danger of postwar inflation nearly as great as the opposite danger of relapse into depression. The legislation itself emphasized the objectives of using resources fully and attaining high employment. It did not explicitly label price stability an objective of policy, although this was implicit in the Act and fully reflected in the policies of every Administration. Nevertheless, concern has been expressed at times that policies for "maximum employment" might allow demand to press too hard on available resources, thus biasing the American economy toward inflation.

In the wartime environment, inflationary pressures of excess demand had been suppressed by direct controls on prices and by rationing. It turned out, however, during the years immediately following World War II that these measures had served partly to postpone—rather than to eliminate—significant demand pressures. Substantial backlogs of demand emerged in the 1946–48 period. Consumers and businesses possessed large accumulations of liquid assets to finance the rebuilding of their depleted stocks of household appliances, machinery, and equipment, and their houses and plants.

Thus, contrary to expectations, the initial years of the postwar era were marked by excessive rather than inadequate demand. In this environment, living standards of consumers, the productivity of labor, and the capacity of businesses rose rapidly. But so did the price level, with a jump of 31 percent in consumer prices from June 1946 to August 1948. Automatic fiscal stabilizers helped to contain the growth of private after-tax incomes, and were reflected in budgetary surpluses during the period. The economic policymaking machinery set up under the Employment Act may have moderated pressures to cut taxes drastically. Meanwhile, monetary policy was tied to a policy of supporting Government bond prices and was not free to combat inflation.

During the Korean war, however, the Government acted vigorously to counter inflationary tendencies close to their source. The March 1951 Federal Reserve-Treasury "accord" unleashed monetary policy. Selective controls on consumer instalment credit and on home mortgages were instituted. The enactment of three large increases in income and profits tax rates in 1950 and 1951 is one of the better examples of timely fiscal policy. These actions reflected, in part, recommendations by the Council of Economic Advisers and hearings and reports of the Joint Economic Committee.

Right after the outbreak of hostilities, prices had risen sharply in a flurry of consumer and business buying and, as a result, prices and wage ceilings had been imposed early in 1951. Once the restraining influence of over-all fiscal and monetary policies was fully felt, there was little pressure on the ceilings, and the economy was able to meet the peak defense demands of the emergency without inflationary strain.

The immediate postwar period and the early months of the Korean war are the two blemishes of clearly excessive demand on our postwar record. Apart from these two intervals, wholesale prices have shown a net increase of only 2 percent in the postwar era. In 1956 and 1957, the only other periods of marked price increases, over-all demand was not generally excessive. That inflation raised new issues, which are discussed below. In view of the whole postwar record, it can hardly be said that the Employment Act has biased policy toward inflation.

EVOLVING PROBLEMS AND POLICIES

During the postwar era, the American economy has remained free of the malignant diseases of depression and run-away inflation. And the rate of economic growth has considerably exceeded its long-term average. The objectives of the Employment Act, however, have not always been fully met. In particular, experience has demonstrated that the avoidance of depression did not guarantee the achievement of "maximum employment" and the avoidance of excess-demand booms did not assure the maintenance of price stability.

INADEQUATE DEMAND IN EXPANSION

The strength of private demand in the early postwar years and then again immediately after the Korean war led to a reassessment of the tasks of stabilization policy. After a decade of postwar experience, suspicions arose that the typical problem would be to contain rather than to stimulate private demand.

Any such conclusion was soundly refuted by the facts of the ensuing years. With the backlogs met, and with a marked decline in the rate of family formation, private demand weakened in the late 1950s. The economy's performance weakened correspondingly because Government did not act to compensate. Thus, while unemployment had averaged 4.2 percent of the civilian labor force in the first postwar decade, it remained above that level every month between late 1957 and October 1965, averaging 5.7 percent.

The problem of inadequate demand in expansion, which became the primary focus of fiscal action in the 1960s, was a new challenge to policymaking under the Employment Act. In the first postwar decade, each time the economy advanced or rebounded from a recession, it reached the neighborhood of full employment. The policymakers had been ready in the early postwar years to deal with non-cyclical problems of submerged prosperity or stagnating production. They had seen maximum employment as a moving target which could be maintained only through a substantial growth of output. Both the Council of Economic Advisers and the Joint Economic Committee had given these issues repeated attention in the late 1940s and early 1950s. But until the late 1950s, no experience had been encountered to distinguish the problem of full employment from that of cyclical prosperity.

Then came a sequence of disturbing events: the 1957–58 recession followed a year of slow advance; the 1960–61 recession began from a peak far below full employment; and the expansion that began in 1961 seemed to be running out of steam after little more than a year.

During the initial years of this period, Government policy maintained vigilance against excessive buoyancy of demand when that was no longer the problem. Restrictive fiscal and monetary actions choked off the recovery of 1958–60. The shift to an expansionary fiscal policy by the Kennedy Administration early in 1961 was designed primarily to initiate a thriving recovery. A determined policy strategy to assure complete recovery was first formulated when the economy faltered in 1962.

The combination of fiscal stimuli to consumer demand and direct tax incentives to investment, together with monetary actions permitting an ample rise in credit, promoted a vigorous and sustained expansion after 1963. The inherent strength of both consumption and investment demand appeared in a new light, once the Revenue Act of 1964 exerted its invigorating influence.

INFLATION AT LESS THAN FULL EMPLOYMENT

Another problem encountered at times during the postwar era has been the tendency of prices to rise even in the absence of over-all excess demand pressures. This tendency reflects structural characteristics of the American economy. The economy is not made up of fully competitive labor and product markets in which large numbers of buyers and sellers interact and respond passively to prices. On the contrary, in many industries both unions and businesses exercise a considerable degree of market power. As a first result, wages and prices are both somewhat rigid in a downward direction. To the extent that prices rise more readily in response to excess demand than they decline in the face of excess supply, the price level is given an upward bias, which can become particularly acute if there are sharp shifts in demand among various sectors of the economy. Secondly, because of market power, some firms augment increases in costs originating elsewhere and unions can escalate their wage demands if prices begin to rise. Third, firms can use a strong market position to widen margins in a period of prosperity even if there are no upward pressures on their costs. Fourth, in the nature of the collective bargaining process, key wage bargains in some industries may tend to establish a pattern applied elsewhere. In particular, if the industries with key wage bargains happen to have excess demands and very strong profits, the pattern will tend to pull wages upward more rapidly throughout the economy.

An important, broadly oriented study by the

Joint Economic Committee analyzed the workings of these important influences in the 1956–57 inflation. In that period, excess demands that were present in machinery and equipment, automobile, and metals industries led to price increases that were not offset elsewhere. Large wage settlements in these industries with high demand and high profits had pattern-setting effects on many other contracts, thus adding to costs on a broad front.

Rising prices that originate from such a process can affect expectations, jeopardize the stability and balance of an expansion, and create inequities and distortions just as readily as demand inflation. But measures to restrain these price increases by reducing over-all demand will enlarge unemployment and impair the productivity record so important to cost-price stability over the longer run. Policies to improve the operations of markets, increase resource mobility and accelerate technical change can help to increase the economy's resistance to rising prices. But in a world where large firms and large unions play an essential role, the cost-price record will depend heavily upon the responsibility with which they exercise the market power that society entrusts to them.

The need for responsible private action was brought to public attention in the Economic Reports of President Eisenhower's second Administration. Through the major innovation of the guideposts in the Kennedy and Johnson Administrations, this need has since been focused and developed into a national policy to enlist the force of public opinion to maintain cost-price stability. The emergence of such a policy has been all the more important in recent years because of the balance of payments problem that has persisted alongside the domestic need for more expansion.

ECONOMIC POLICY TODAY

Two decades of economic analysis and policy experience have shaped the development of a revised economic policy. By some, current policy has been labeled the "new economics." It draws heavily on the experience and lessons of the past, and it combines both new and old elements. Current policy represents a coordinated and consistent effort to promote balance of over-all supply and aggregate demand—to sustain steady balanced growth at high employment levels with essential price stability.

This approach to policy has several key aspects, not entirely novel by any means. First, it emphasizes a continuous, rather than a cyclical, framework for analyzing economic developments and formulating policies. Stimulus to demand is not confined to avoiding or correcting recession, but rather is applied whenever needed for the promotion of full-utilization and prosperity. Second, in this way, it emphasizes a preventive strategy against the onset of recession. Third, in focusing on balance of the economy, this policy strategy cannot give top priority to balance in the budget. When private investment threatens to outrun saving at full employment, a Government surplus is needed to increase total saving in the economy while restrictive monetary policy may also be called for to restrain investment outlays. When, as in recent years, private saving at full employment tends to outrun actual private investment, the balance should be corrected by budget deficits and expansionary monetary policy. Fourth, it considers the budget and monetary conditions in the framework of a growing economy, recognizing that revenues expand and thereby exert a fiscal drag on demand unless expansionary actions are taken; similarly, it recognizes that money and credit must expand just to keep interest rates from rising. Fifth, this strategy emphasizes the use of a variety of tools to support expansion while simultaneously pursuing other objectives. Manpower policies, selective approaches to control capital outflows, as well as general fiscal and monetary measures, are all part of the arsenal. Sixth, it calls for responsible price-wage actions by labor and management to prevent cost-inflation from impeding the pursuit of full employment. Finally, it makes greater demands on economic forecasting and analysis. The job of the economist is not merely to predict the upturn or the downturn but to judge continuously the prospects for demand in relation to a growing productive capacity.

THE NATURE OF CYCLICAL INSTABILITY

An industrial economy is vulnerable to cumulative upward and downward movements in activity, so evident in our long-term record. While they can have diverse specific causes, these cyclical fluctuations can be explained as the result of imbalances between the rate of growth of productive capacity and the rate of growth of final demands that make use of productive capacity.

During periods of prosperity, a considerable part of the Nation's output is used to increase productive capacity through investment in plant and equipment and business inventories. If demand keeps pace, sales expand and the new capacity turns out to be profitable. Businessmen find that their decisions to increase capacity have been validated and they continue to pursue expansionary investment policies. If, on the other hand, inventory stocks are built up far in advance of need—on the basis of overly optimistic sales forecasts or as an inflation-hedge—businessmen will subsequently wish to cut back their rate of accumulation. Similarly, if outlays for business fixed investment add to productive capacity faster than demand expands, overheads on new capital cut into profits, inducing business firms to trim their capital outlays. Even if businessmen continue to add somewhat to their productive capacity, the mere decline in the rate of expansion can mean an absolute reduction in the demand for capital goods and for output to go into inventories. Payrolls and purchasing power are thereby curtailed and a decline in total demand can result. Thus a slowdown in economic activity is converted into a definite downturn—a recession or depression.

Imbalance can arise because businessmen in the aggregate invest too much and overbuild, creating more capacity than the economy can—even at best—put to productive use. Or alternatively it can stem from "underbuying," a growth of final demand too slow to make use of even moderate additions to capacity. In principle, cyclical movements can also be triggered by overbuilding of new homes and consumer durables.

Overbuilding of inventories—partly encouraged by expectations of rising prices—was probably the key factor in the first postwar downturn, which occurred in 1948. That experience demonstrated that a situation of high total demand could deteriorate rapidly into recession without any change in the basic underlying factors in the private economy or any restraining shift in public policy. In 1953, the sharp decline in defense outlays reduced final demands and precipitated recession; productive capacity became temporarily excessive and investment spending declined. In 1956–57, rapid growth of productive capacity was associated with an investment boom; meanwhile, final demands grew very slowly. It is not possible to deliver a clear verdict on whether more vigorous growth of final demand would have justified the high investment levels then obtaining. But with the slow growth of demand that actually occurred, there was an abrupt decline in plant and equipment spending as well as inventory investment in 1957. In 1959–60, the rate of expansion of capacity (including inventories) was not excessive measured against the capabilities of the economy; the failure of the economy to support that growth of capacity must be attributed to "underbuying," the inadequate expansion of final demand, in an environment of restrictive fiscal and monetary policies.

In the future as in the past, policies to avert recession cannot wait until imbalances develop and the signs of a downturn are clear. The fact that economic activity is rising cannot be an assurance of continued growth if the expansion is too slow to match the growth of productive capacity. Nor can a strong level of investment be relied on to sustain expansion if it threatens an excessive growth of productive capacity. Recognizing these tasks, Government must apply its fiscal and monetary policies continuously to sustain and support a balanced expansion, sometimes by moderating the strength of an excessive investment boom, sometimes by adding to the strength of lagging final demand. The best defense against recession is a policy to sustain continued expansion. In a free economy, fluctuations in private demand will inevitably occur, and the Government will not always have the wisdom or the ability to counteract them. Continued expansion cannot be guaranteed, but recurrent recession need not be accepted as a necessary fact of economic life.

POLICY FOR A GROWING ECONOMY

In order to achieve the goal of maximum employment, the Government must coordinate all its policies to take account of the persistent growth of the economy's potential output.

The Problem of Fiscal Drag

One consequence of economic growth is that budgetary policies become more restrictive if they stand still. If tax rates are unchanged, Federal revenues will grow continuously as the economy expands. Meanwhile, if Federal expenditures are held constant in the face of growing revenues, the Federal budget will exert a continuing "fiscal drag" on private demand.

Either increased expenditures or reduced tax rates can offset this influence. A total of these two types of stimulative actions which exactly matched the dollar amount of normal revenue growth would provide a precise offset to fiscal drag.

A simple mechanical offset to fiscal drag is not, however, a satisfactory rule for fiscal policy. When aggregate demand threatens to exceed the supply capacity of the economy, some fiscal drag should be allowed to operate. On the other hand, waning strength in private demand points to fiscal action that would more than offset the drag, effecting a desirable decline in the high-employment surplus.

Furthermore, tightness or ease of monetary policy is important in determining appropriate fiscal actions. There is an analog to drag in the monetary area: A growing economy generates rising demands for liquid assets and increasing needs for borrowing. If monetary policies stand still in the sense of holding supplies unchanged, continually tighter credit conditions and higher interest rates will be the result.

Accelerating Growth

The growth of the economy is a major influence on policy; the opposite side of the coin is the major role of policy in influencing potential economic growth. The larger the amount of current output invested in physical and human resources, the more rapidly productivity and the productive capacity of the economy will increase.

A number of policy choices can speed growth by shifting resources into various types of investment. Public investment in human and physical resources can yield rich returns in more rapid economic growth. Some public investments, such as those on research and development, encourage complementary private investment. Outlays for manpower training improve labor skills and productivity. Throughout our history, investment in education has been one of the key contributors to growth. Private investment in plant and equipment is a key determinant of our industrial capacity. It can be stimulated by easing monetary policies. It can also be encouraged by selective tax reductions, such as the investment credit and depreciation reform of 1962 and the reductions in corporate tax rates in 1964 and 1965.

When the economy is below full employment, any stimulative measure is likely to add to private investment, thereby contributing to the growth of potential, as well as to actual, output. But, at full employment, more resources can be devoted to capital formation only if current consumption is restrained. A policy strategy to accelerate growth may therefore point to higher personal income taxes or similar measures to hold consumption below what would otherwise be appropriate.

Choices of Tools

Economic policy has many tools available in pursuing the goals of full employment, rapid growth, price stability, and balance of international payments. The full range of economic objectives must be reflected in the selection of policies to meet particular circumstances.

Policy instruments differ in their impact. Sometimes policy tools can advance the economy toward more than one goal. For example, manpower policies help to maintain price stability at high employment and to promote economic growth. Conflicts may occur, however. For example, high interest rates impinge particularly on investment both at home and abroad, hence somewhat reducing foreign capital outflows but also reducing aggregate demand and slowing economic growth. In the case of potential conflicts, instruments must be used more selectively; for example, moderate changes in interest rates can be supplemented by taxes on foreign investment, like the Interest Equalization Tax.

The potential for timely results differs for various policy instruments. Monetary policy can be altered readily, although its full economic impact will not be immediate. While some restraint or speedup in Federal outlays can be applied by Executive authority alone, tax rate changes must, of course, be approved by the Congress. The speed of congressional action on tax changes has varied. It acted rapidly to increase taxes in 1950, and to reduce excise taxes both in 1954 and 1965. On the other hand, it took 13 months to enact the comprehensive Revenue Act of 1964. Tax revision can help to avoid the necessity for abrupt changes in Federal expenditures, which could require stopping a project before its conclusion or starting a new one with inadequate planning.

Given the possibility for achieving needed short-run stimulus or restraint through changes in taxes, transfer payments, or monetary policy, decisions on expenditures for public services can rest on basic judgments of costs and benefits of public and private spending. The availability of this choice permits resources to be devoted to the highest priority uses.

CONCLUSION

As the primary objective set by the Employment Act is being reached, new problems move to the fore and are receiving increasing attention in public policy. These include the efficient use of the Nation's human and natural resources, the conquest of poverty and suffering, the reconstruction of our cities, and the many other tasks. And undoubtedly in the pursuit of the goals of the Employment Act during the next 20 years, policymakers will encounter a new range of problems, no more completely foreseeable now than were the issues of today in 1946.

While important problems remain, we are nonetheless at an historic point of accomplishment and promise. Twenty years of experience have demonstrated our ability to avoid ruinous inflations and severe depressions. It is now within our capabilities to set more ambitious goals. We strive to avoid recurrent recessions, to keep unemployment far below rates of the past decade, to maintain essential price stability at full employment, to move toward the Great Society, and, indeed, to make full prosperity the normal state of the American economy. It is a tribute to our success under the Employment Act that we now have not only the economic understanding but also the will and determination to use economic policy as an effective tool for progress.

QUESTIONS AND STUDY SUGGESTIONS

1. Describe the historical background and economic context against which the Employment Act of 1946 was passed. Comment: "Keynesian economics and its policy implications have been bipartisan."
2. What are the implications of a growing public sector for economic stability?
3. Discuss the problems of "inadequate demand in expansion" and "inflation at less than full employment." How has macroeconomic policy been used in dealing with these problems?
4. Explain: "Cyclical fluctuations can be explained as the result of imbalances between the rate of growth of productive capacity and the rate of growth of final demands that make use of productive capacity."
5. What are the main characteristics of the "new economics"?

Tax Cuts versus Increases in Government Spending: Two Views

If the economy encounters a recession, an expansionary fiscal policy is in order. But should this policy take the form of tax reductions or increases in government spending? The view of the Kennedy-Johnson administrations was that unemployment is due to a deficiency of aggregate demand (Reading 17) and that tax reduction is the best means of stimulating demand to achieve full employment. In Reading 22 we find the late President Kennedy extolling the merits of tax cuts as a means of increasing consumption and investment and stimulating private initiative and incentives. In contrast, John Kenneth Galbraith favors increases in government expenditures as the best fiscal avenue to full employment. Galbraith bases his view on essentially two points. First, he feels that much of our current unemployment is structural (Reading 18) and not due to a deficiency in demand. Second, he feels that increases in spending are needed to meet acute social needs in such areas as education, air and water pollution, urban decay, and so forth. The United States, Galbraith contends, suffers from acute shortages of certain social goods and services which can only be overcome through increases in government spending (see Readings 63 and 64).

First View: The Case for Tax Reduction

John F. Kennedy, President of the United States

There are a number of ways by which the Federal Government can meet its responsibilities to aid economic growth. We can and must improve American education and technical training. We can and must expand civil research and technology. One of the great bottlenecks for this country's economic growth in this decade will be the shortage of doctorates in mathematics, engineering, and physics. A serious shortage with great demand and undersupply of highly trained manpower. We can and must step up the development of our natural resources.

But the most direct and significant kind of Federal action aiding economic growth is to make possible an increase in private consumption and investment demand—to cut the fetters which hold back private spending. In the past, this could be done in part by the increased use of credit and monetary tools—but our balance-of-payments situation today places limits on our use of those tools for expansion. It could also be done by increasing Federal expenditures more rapidly than necessary—but such a course would soon demoralize both the Government and our economy. If Government

Excerpts from a speech by President John F. Kennedy before the Economics Club of New York, Dec. 14, 1962. Reprinted in the **Congressional Record**, Jan. 15, 1963.

is to retain the confidence of the people, it must not spend more than can be justified on grounds of national need or spent with maximum efficiency.

NEED FOR TAX REDUCTION

The final and best means of strengthening demand among consumers and business is to reduce the burden on private income and the deterrents to private initiative which are imposed by our present tax system—and this administration pledged itself last summer to an across-the-board, top-to-bottom cut in personal and corporate income taxes to be enacted and become effective in 1963.

I am not talking about a "quickie" or temporary tax cut, which would be more appropriate if a recession were imminent. Nor am I talking about giving the economy a mere shot in the arm, to ease some temporary complaint. I am talking about the accumulated evidence of the last 5 years that our present tax system, developed as it was, in good part, during World War II to restrain growth, exerts too heavy a drag on growth in peacetime—that it siphons out of the private economy too large a share of personal and business purchasing power—that it reduces the financial incentives for personal effort, investment, and risk taking.

In short, to increase demand and lift the economy, the Federal Government's most useful role is not to rush into a program of excessive increases in public expenditures, but to expand the incentives and opportunities for private expenditures.

NONINFLATIONARY TAX CUTS

If the economy today were operating close to capacity levels with little unemployment, or if a sudden change in our military requirements should cause a scramble for men and resources, then I would oppose tax reductions as irresponsible and inflationary and I would not hesitate to recommend a tax increase, if that were necessary. But our resources and manpower are not being fully utilized; the general level of prices has been remarkably stable; and increased competition, both at home and abroad, along with increased productivity will help keep both prices and wages within appropriate limits.

The same is true of our balance of pay-

ments. While rising demand will expand imports, new investment in more efficient productive facilities will aid exports and a new economic climate will both draw capital from abroad and keep capital here at home. It will also put us in a better position, if necessary to use monetary tools to help our international accounts. But, most importantly, confidence in the dollar in the long run rests on confidence in America, in our ability to meet our economic commitments and reach our economic goals. In a worldwide conviction that we are not drifting from recession to recession with no answer, the substantial improvement in our balance-of-payments position in the last 2 years makes it clear that nothing could be more foolish than to restrict our growth merely to minimize that particular problem, because a slowdown in our economy will feed that problem rather than diminish it. On the contrary, European governmental and financial authorities, far from threatening to withdraw gold, have urged us to cut taxes in order to expand our economy, attract more capital and increase confidence in the future.

TAX CUTS, DEFICITS, AND SURPLUSES

But what concerns most Americans about a tax cut, I know, is not the deficit in our balance of payments but the deficit in our Federal budget. When I announced in April of 1961 that this kind of comprehensive tax reform would follow the bill enacted this year, I had hoped to present it in an atmosphere of a balanced budget. But it has been necessary to augment sharply our nuclear and conventional forces, to step up our efforts in space, to meet the increased cost of servicing the national debt and meeting our obligations, established by law, to veterans. These expenditure increases, let me stress, constitute practically all of the increases which have occurred under this administration, the remainder having gone to fight the recession we found in industry, mostly through the supplemental employment bill, and in agriculture.

We shall, therefore, neither postpone our tax cut plans nor cut into essential national security programs. This administration is determined to protect America's security and survival and we are also determined to step up its economic growth. I think we must do both.

Our true choice is not between tax reduction, on the one hand, and the avoidance of large Federal deficits on the other; it is increasingly clear that no matter what party is in power, so long as our national security needs keep rising, an economy hampered by restrictive tax rates will never produce enough revenues to balance our budget just as it will never produce enough jobs or enough profits. Surely the lesson of the last decade is that budget deficits are not caused by wildeyed spenders but by slow economic growth and periodic recessions and any new recession would break all deficit records.

In short, it is a paradoxical truth that tax rates are too high today and tax revenues are too low and the soundest way to raise revenues in the long run is to cut rates now. The experience of a number of European countries has borne this out. This country's own experience with tax reduction in 1954 has borne this out.

And the reason is that only full employment can balance the budget and tax reduction can pave the way to full employment. The purpose of cutting taxes now is not to incur a budget deficit, but to achieve the more prosperous, expanding economy which will bring a budget surplus.

I repeat: our practical choice is not between a tax-cut deficit and a budgetary surplus. It is between two kinds of deficits; a chronic deficit of inertia, as the unwanted result of inadequate revenues and a restricted economy, or a temporary deficit of transition, resulting from a tax cut designed to boost the economy, increase tax revenue and achieve—and I believe this can be done—a future budget surplus. The first type of deficit is a sign of waste and weakness. The second reflects an investment in the future.

Second View: The Case for Increased Government Spending

John Kenneth Galbraith, Professor of Economics, Harvard University

I was never as enthusiastic as many of my fellow economists over the tax reduction of last year. The case for it as an isolated action was undoubtedly good. But there was danger that conservatives, once introduced to the delights of tax reduction, would like it too much.

Tax reduction would then become a substitute for increased outlays on urgent social needs. We would have a new and reactionary form of Keynesianism with which to contend.

This remains a danger. It would already be a grave one if Secretary McNamara had not done such a brilliant job of getting control of military expenditures. This has given some margin for increasing expenditures on social requirements. But we must continue to be wary of tax reduction at a time when so many public tasks of such urgency are awaiting attention.

I am not quite sure what the advantage is in having a few more dollars to spend if the air is too dirty to breathe, the water is too polluted to drink, the commuters are losing out on the struggle to get in and out of the cities, the streets are filthy, and the schools are so bad

that the young, perhaps wisely, stay away, and hoodlums roll citizens for some of the dollars they saved in taxes.

TAX CUTS AND UNEMPLOYMENT

In fact, this kind of economic policy defeats even the goal of full employment. For, increasingly, the problem of employment is not a deficiency of demand but unemployability that results from deficient education, preparation, or unrelieved social squalor. The unemployed today consist overwhelmingly of three overlapping groups.

The unemployed are the uneducated; it was last year 8.4 percent for those with less than 8 years of schooling and negligible for those with 16 years or more. I may say here that this figure understates the proportion of the uneducated who are unemployed because they have a greater tendency than the better educated to withdraw from the labor market and not be listed as jobseekers.

The unemployed are the young—those with-

From **January 1965 Economic Report of the President:** Hearings before the Joint Economic Committee, Congress of the United States, 89th Cong., 1st Sess., Washington, 1965, part 2, pp. 13–15, abridged.

out training, work skills or a foot in the labor force; teenage unemployment was 15 percent of jobseekers in this category last year and the Economic Report rightly calls this unemployment "the greatest test now confronting . . . our general economic and manpower policies." And the unemployed are the Negroes; Negro unemployment last year was more than twice that for whites.

The primary remedy for this unemployment is not to create demand, that is important, but rather it is better education, more job training, more deliberate job creation for youngsters and an equal break in education and employment for Negroes.

And, since we are dealing here with a seamless web, it means communities with better recreation, better welfare workers, better housing, better law enforcement, less squalid surroundings and an end to the Negro ghettos.

Tax reduction, which puts a few more spendable dollars in the pockets of the comparatively well to do, does nothing to make the unemployable more employable. And it also exposes the question of the quality of employment.

By sufficiently expanding demand, we can draw some semiliterate youngsters off the street and into jobs. Then official employment figures will look better. But this is something I would like to stress—they will be lousy jobs and those who hold them will be the first to be discharged when a machine comes along that can do the work better.

The test is not alone jobs but the preparation of people for high quality employment.

And not even employment is the only test of an economy. We want better communities and better services not alone because these insure more employable people but because they make life better.

FEDERAL REVENUES AND STATE PROBLEMS

The great economic anachronism of our time is that economic growth gives the Federal Government the revenues while, along with population increase, it gives the States and especially the cities the problems. The one unit of government gets the money.

The other gets the work. This adds to the danger that we will reduce Federal taxes at a time when States and especially localities are struggling with ever greater needs. It adds also to the urgency of Federal aid for specific local functions or a system of providing general Federal assistance to local government. It argues against Federal tax reduction while local government struggles ever more desperately with the disparity between needs and revenues.

In short, there is a right way and a wrong way of attacking the problem of maintaining a high level of demand and an adequate rate of growth. The wrong way, which could become very popular with all who have a short-run orientation to their own pocketbook, is by tax reduction even though at the expense of needed public services. The right way is to provide for needed public services.

TAX CUTS: THE WRONG COURSE

For many years now, economists have distinguished between a progressive fiscal policy that promoted economic expansion and an old-fashioned fiscal policy that balanced the budget and accepted the inevitability of recession and unemployment.

Liberals could be identified by their support of a progressive fiscal policy; conservatives were marked by their myopic insistence on a balanced budget. The distinction is no longer applicable. The need to sustain the level of demand is now common ground between men of widely varying political temperament and taste.

But demand can be maintained by reducing taxes and ignoring social need. This is reactionary Keynesianism. Or it can be maintained by improving education, taking account of the problems of our cities and having compassionate regard for the needs of the less fortunate. This is the progressive policy. It will also be quite a bit more controversial. It has often been observed that economists, when they become noncontroversial, are usually either wrong or not doing anything.

I do not doubt that the President and his advisers are modern liberals. No President in recent times has put so many of our social needs on the agenda as President Johnson. I would hope, however, that the Congress, guided by this view of what is reactionary and what is progressive, will support and encourage the Executive in the proper course.

To meet social needs is the right course. To reduce taxes at the expense of social needs is the wrong course.

QUESTIONS AND STUDY SUGGESTIONS

1. Why did President Kennedy favor tax cuts, rather than increased government spending, as a means for stimulating the economy? What rationale prompts Professor Galbraith to take the opposite position? More specifically, why does Galbraith feel that tax cuts may be of little assistance in reducing unemployment?
2. Distinguish between "a chronic deficit of inertia" and "a temporary deficit of transition." Explain how a tax cut which immediately gives rise to a "deficit of transition" might actually induce a budget surplus over time.
3. Why does Galbraith favor a program of general Federal assistance to state and local governments?

Reading 23

Stabilization Policy: Some Unconventional Suggestions

Alvin H. Hansen, Professor of Political Economy, Emeritus, Harvard University

In this reading a senior American economist, Alvin H. Hansen, suggests that our stabilization arsenal might be further strengthened by the addition of a number of specific new weapons. For serious consideration he proposes the following: (1) Automatic or semiautomatic adjustments should be applied to the first income bracket so that tax collections will vary directly with such criteria as the levels of employment, industrial production, or investment, to strengthen the built-in stability of the tax system. (2) Accelerated depreciation should be administered countercyclically to dampen investment fluctuations. (3) An anti-inflationary tax should be applied to abnormal spurts in capital goods outlays. (4) A generous Federal unemployment insurance system should be enacted to supplement the existing state systems. (5) The procyclical character of advertising outlays might be corrected by making advertising costs tax-deductible during a downswing, but nondeductible during inflation. (6) Public representation through government in all significant collective-bargaining negotiations is necessary and justified in view of the full-employment commitments government has given labor and management. (7) The specific problem of the rising price of services, which lies in obstinate scarcities

From **Economic Issues of the 1960's** by Alvin H. Hansen, pp. 31–39. Copyright, 1961. McGraw-Hill Book Company, New York. Reprinted by permission.

of medical care, low-cost housing, and urban transportation, can be resolved only through "drastic reforms" brought about by an expanding
public sector. Overall, these proposals amount to a provocative assault
upon the tendency to look upon society's present anticyclical arsenal as
adequate and complete.

I have argued that the twelve years from 1948 to 1959 inclusive have in fact been years of substantial price stability despite the Korean spurt and the investment boom of 1956–1957. Still the record could have been somewhat better, particularly if we could have avoided that last spurt. Our record in the past dozen years is in fact not a bad one, but I think we can do better both with respect to full employment and with respect to price stability.

THINGS NOT TO DO

There are some things we are now doing about inflation that we ought not to do. We should stop trying to scare the wits out of people about this inflation issue. Fortunately the public puts little stock in this alarmist talk about the "tinder of inflation lying all about us." If the public really did take these statements seriously, there could be unfortunate consequences. Our people, however, have a sound common sense about such matters. And while this hysteria probably doesn't do us much harm, let us hope that we shall have less of it in the future.

Another thing we should not do: We should not make the inflation issue primarily a matter for monetary policy. Excessive use of the monetary weapon would force us fairly rapidly into very high rates of interest. We should indeed repeal the arbitrary 4¼ percent interest-rate ceiling. But we should pursue monetary, fiscal, and other policies designed to soften the upward pressure on interest rates.

We should not fasten upon the Federal Reserve System a mandate to maintain stable prices. It couldn't be done anyway. A mandate that could be fulfilled could be very damaging to the Federal Reserve. Moreover the goals we seek are far too complex, and often conflicting, to permit such a mandate.

Another thing: We should stop being afraid to use specific and direct controls, namely real estate and consumer credit controls. These controls strike precisely at the points where the battle is raging. They are not blunderbuss gunshots. Installment credit jumped 45 percent from 1954 to 1957. These controls should be restored to our anti-inflation arsenal. The administration of these controls could doubtless be improved. For one thing, Professor Arthur Smithies has suggested that we regulate the lending authorities involved, in a manner analogous to the regulation of commercial banks.

We should stop using the inflation scare as a political whip to keep much-needed governmental expenditures down. Government outlays should be decided on their own merits quite regardless of the inflation issue. And once decided upon, taxation should be adjusted to the budgetary requirements of a balanced economy. This may or may not be a balanced budget. Taxes are indeed the main bulwark against inflation. If we are to meet at all adequately our growing public needs, we shall, I believe, need higher tax rates. The 1954 tax rates are not sacrosanct, though both of our political parties seem so to regard them. We should moreover do a better job of tax collection. We should tap dividends and interest at the source, as we now do wages and salaries. We should tighten up on expense accounts and depletion allowances.

There is no platform that politicians would rather run on than one calling for a cut in taxes. But this is the last thing that any responsible statesman should advocate in a time of urgent public needs. Mind you, I do not mean that we should not have a flexible anticyclical tax policy. A crying need in this country, as our recent experience shows, is to place far less reliance upon a flexible interest-rate policy and more reliance upon a flexible tax policy. A reform urgently needed, which would add immeasurable strength to our built-in stabilizers, would be to "devise a politically acceptable means of automatically varying tax rates with the ups and downs of economic activity."

AUTOMATIC TAX-RATE ADJUSTMENT

We should introduce an automatic or semiautomatic system of tax-rate adjustment in the first income tax bracket, so that the rate would rise and fall according to agreed-upon criteria of employment, degree of capacity utilization, industrial production, and rates of investment. Such first-bracket rate adjustments would in time come to be looked upon as just as natural and normal a procedure as the long-familiar interest-rate adjustment. As an accepted policy instrument, it should cause no surprise; indeed it should be expected. It should become routine procedure. Primary reliance should be placed upon this adjustment mechanism.

Tax-rate adjustment has a great advantage over monetary policy in the respect that it acts almost instantaneously, while monetary policy begins to become really effective only after the general liquidity of a rich community has to a considerable degree been exhausted. Tax-rate adjustments become quickly effective in view of our system of collection at the source.

Such a reform would be a long step forward. Not only would we have added a powerful anticyclical weapon to our arsenal; we should also be able, by relying less on the monetary weapon, to achieve a more stable and also a lower long-term rate of interest—a matter of no small importance for growth and progress.

COUNTERCYCLICAL ACCELERATED DEPRECIATION

Related to a flexible tax program is the matter of accelerated depreciation. This was introduced into our tax system in 1954. I heartily agree that accelerated depreciation is a powerful and highly desirable method of stimulating investment. But I deprecate the fact that we do not administer it in a countercyclical manner. The privilege of accelerated depreciation was one of many factors that caused the abnormal spurt of investment in 1955–1957—a rate of investment, as Chairman Martin of the Federal Reserve Board rightly said, that was not maintainable.

If we really mean to do something about short-run price increases, we shall have to iron out the fluctuations in investment. This is crucial in any short-run anti-inflation program. A cyclically adjusted system of accelerated depreciation could do *something* to smooth out these extreme fluctuations. Such a program could take the milder form of deferment of depreciation allowances, or it could take the more drastic form of complete denial. Canada introduced the deferment plan in April, 1951, in an effort to check the Korean boom. The deferment was in effect for nearly two years.

After the inflationary pressures had eased off, the deferment regulation was withdrawn. Thus an anticyclical policy was in fact pursued.

In March, 1960, West Germany changed the depreciation allowances on producers' equipment. From 25 percent of value in the first year, the rate was cut to 20 percent. For subsequent years the rates were similarly reduced. Also the depreciation rates for houses were cut from 10 percent in the first two years to 7½ percent, and for subsequent years the rates were reduced.

AN ANTI-INFLATIONARY TAX ON INVESTMENT

And just as accelerated depreciation can be employed to stimulate investment when capital outlays are abnormally low, so a *tax* on investment could be employed to choke off such unhealthy and abnormal investment spurts as that of 1955–1957. In 1952 Sweden introduced a special tax on investment on industrial buildings, machinery, and equipment. The tax was employed during the years 1952–1953 as a means of checking an excessive burst of investment. In the recession of 1954 the tax was rescinded. But again at the beginning of the 1955–1957 investment boom a special tax of 12 percent was imposed on industrial investment.

Contrast this anticyclical policy with anti-inflationary monetary policy. Anticyclical monetary policy has the serious disadvantage that sharp increases in the rate of interest profoundly affect capital values. In the nineteenth century that was not any serious matter. Property was not then held primarily in the form of securities. In the nineteenth century stiffer interest rates mainly affected the holding of stocks of commodities. Changes in the rate of interest thus had an immediate impact on commodity prices. And on the other hand, capital values were not seriously disturbed. Today the situation is quite different. It is simply obsolete thinking to argue that interest-rate policy can play the same role today that it did in the nineteenth century.

In contrast a cyclically adjusted tax on investment acts to deter abnormal spurts of investment without affecting the interest-rate structure and capital values. Moreover, small new and growing businesses can be exempted from the investment tax. In contrast, restrictive monetary policy tends in fact to discriminate against new business ventures.

ADVERTISING AND INFLATIONARY PRESSURES

Countercyclical fluctuations in advertising outlays would clearly be desirable from the standpoint of business itself, and from the standpoint of the economy as a whole such countercyclical movements would contribute to stability. Unfortunately, advertising expenditures tend to fluctuate *with* the cycle and thus serve to intensify instability and to add to the inflationary pressures in boom times. Consideration might be given to countercyclical adjustment of advertising as an allowable business expense in calculating income taxes.

The postal rates on advertising materials circulated through the mails could be sharply increased. This form of advertising appears to be an effective means of stimulating bizarre and wasteful types of expenditure. The great bulk of this material does indeed, it appears, go into the wastepaper basket. As such, it is a drag on the Post Office Department and must be regarded as a public nuisance. Nevertheless, it appears to be a highly profitable form of advertising, and this suggests that it does increase private expenditures and so adds to inflationary pressures in boom periods. It should be added that advertising over the telephone is equally objectionable and is indeed an invasion on privacy.

Pay TV and radio would make it possible to eliminate advertising altogether from television and radio broadcasting. This form of advertising is peculiarly obnoxious and is increasingly interfering with orderly programing. And there can be no doubt that it contributes not a little to inflationary pressures.

A general curtailment of aggregate advertising outlays would reduce private expenditures and so help to free resources for national security, for public investment in human and natural resource development, and for much-needed public services. Advertising, by creating inflationary pressures, prevents useful, even essential, public outlays.

GOVERNMENT'S ROLE IN COLLECTIVE BARGAINING

Finally, there is one obvious thing that can be done and should be done about the problems of the wage-push and of administered prices. The public should be represented at every important collective-bargaining table. Collective bargaining is indeed here to stay and we welcome it. Large business units are here to stay and we welcome them. American opinion has veered to the position, I think rightly, that big units contribute to efficiency. But is it not sheer madness to continue the obsolete fiction that the public has no stake in collective bargaining in a society so highly interdependent as ours? If no agreement can be reached, the government should recommend a settlement. The facts about wages, costs, and profits should be made public. No corporation should be allowed to raise prices for a period of, say, six months after the agreement has been put into effect.

Suggestions similar to those I have discussed have been cold-shouldered by both management and labor. This suggests a kind of arrogant disdain of the public interest which the American people will not long tolerate. Now that the government offers management and labor the protective canopy of full-employment policies, powerful trade unions and giant corporations can scarcely claim the right to raise wages and prices in the dark. The public has a right to know the facts and to throw in its weight at the bargaining table.

WHAT TO DO WITH THE RISING COST OF SERVICES

The reforms I have been suggesting apply primarily to the wholesale price index. The consumer price index is something else again. It keeps creeping up, owing to the rising cost of services—transportation services, hospital and medical care, and house rent. Stabilizing the commodity index would not completely stop the rise in services. If we really mean to do something about this, drastic reforms in the fields of medical care, low-cost and middle-income housing, and urban transportation will have to be undertaken. We are reluctant to do these things. There are scarcities here to be overcome. But the answer will involve an enlarged role of government—a further extension of the welfare state.

The problem of inflation will require continuous study, and we shall learn by experience. We do not know what are the tolerable limits of creeping inflation. We do not know what constitutes reasonable price stability. We do not know how serious are the conflicts that will emerge in the pursuit of our various goals

—the goals to stability, growth, and our international obligations. Compromises there will be. Price stability within viable limits will remain a matter of concern. The public will demand this of any administration in Washington. In this matter the American people and their government can, I believe, be depended upon to act in a reasonably responsible manner. The danger lies not in this direction. The danger lies rather in complacency. What is needed is not the banker mentality of caution, but rather the entrepreneurial spirit of adventure, of bold experimentation. I leave it to the reader to see if he can scan on the horizon that kind of leadership.

QUESTIONS AND STUDY SUGGESTIONS

1. Why does Professor Hansen argue that we should "place far less reliance upon a flexible interest-rate policy and more reliance upon a flexible tax policy" to achieve price level stability? More specifically, why is it argued that an automatic system of adjusting the tax rate on the first income bracket is a more effective stabilizing technique than is monetary policy?
2. What is accelerated depreciation? How might it be used countercyclically?
3. Why is an anti-inflationary tax on investment, as opposed to a tight money policy, recommended as a means of controlling inflationary spurts of investment spending?
4. How might advertising expenditures be made countercyclical?
5. What are Professor Hansen's recommendations with respect to (a) potentially inflationary collective bargaining and (b) the rising prices of services?

Reading 24

Debt and Economic Stability

Rudolph A. Peterson, President of Bank of America

Individual households and businesses are inclined to look upon debt with anxiety and alarm or, at best, to regard it as a necessary evil. But the basic theme of this reading is quite to the contrary: in a modern complex economy a growing aggregate debt (private and public) is a requisite of

From Rudolph A. Peterson, "Debt in the New Economic Environment," **Challenge**, December, 1964, pp. 15–19, abridged. Reprinted by permission from **Challenge**, the Magazine of Economic Affairs, 475 Fifth Avenue, New York, N.Y. 10017.

continuing prosperity and economic growth. Simply put, in an expanding economy the volume of saving will increase. Therefore, if total spending—and consequently output and employment—is to be sustained, this saving or its equivalent must be obtained and spent by consumers, businesses, and government. The process by which this is achieved is debt creation. Furthermore, the author explodes some of the major myths surrounding debt by explaining that debt is not too high in our economy; debt has not expanded more rapidly than our ability to sustain it; and the Federal debt is not a major economic problem.

I am not under any illusion that the myths about debt have never been exposed, but somehow fears of further debt extension live on. This seems to be the case even when there is no problem of deterioration in the quality of credit. These fears may not have done particular damage a century and a half ago, when most of our forebears were a pretty independent lot. Today, however, in the new environment of essential interdependence of people, the proper extension of debt performs a vital function.

The environment in which most of us will have to live is one in which our daily sustenance depends on the performance of our fellowmen as well as of ourselves. In our society, this means dependence on the smooth and continuous functioning of a sensitive market mechanism that responds to money expenditure. In order to keep in healthy operation the delicate interplay of millions of independent economic decisions, balancing actions by society are needed. In addition, this new environment continually requires gigantic investment of capital to provide a rising level of living for an increasing population. Savings need to be generated in great volume and efficiently converted into investment.

POSITIVE ROLE OF DEBT

There would, of course, be no need for debt today if everyone's "wants" ,coincided identically with the supplies of goods available, and if individuals were self-sufficient or at least provided for their purchases and investments out of their own individual savings. But neither is the case. The efficient transfer of funds from savers to investors in our complex economy involves extensive use of financial intermediaries. And, in some cases, more than one financial intermediary is interposed. This situation gives rise to a growth in debt claims greater than the expansion of real savings and investment. With the increased size and complexity of our financial system, this divergence increases.

Thus, debt is an essential element of the modern world. True, it can grow too fast or too slowly. Its uses can be badly distributed, or its quality impaired, with sad consequences for the nation. Basically, however, under the conditions which prevail today, debt must grow in order for the economy to prosper.

There is a special reason for the growth of debt in the new environment of overwhelming market interdependence. In this kind of economy, total income cannot be allowed to fall over any long period of time without disrupting the markets. This means that total money expenditures cannot be allowed to decline more rapidly than prices fall. But prices do not readily move downward. Therefore, when some elements in the economy spend less than their incomes, other elements must spend more than their incomes to keep the markets balanced. Some of this balance is provided by spending funds previously saved; much of it is provided by new debt extensions. Most of the borrowing is undertaken without any thought of its economic effects. If the economy is working properly, however, the borrowing will provide a necessary balance.

It is particularly important in today's new environment that leaders of thought and action appreciate the *positive* role that debt can and does play. If the necessary balancing actions of society are to be effective, quick and adequate response of debt to changes in savings is required. If this response is not forthcoming from original savers and from final borrowers, it should come from commercial banks and other private financial intermediaries. If it does not come from those private institutions, it must come from the Federal Reserve System or the public treasuries. In any event, when debt extension is needed for the health of the economy, there should be no time-consuming hesitations as a result of false fears concerning debt.

Setting aside the question of debt quality, let us look specifically at four of these fears— the mythology of debt in the United States. These fears are expounded over and over again at banquet tables. The speaker warns of the dire results of reckless spending and heedless prodigality. He hints at the awful day of reckoning when we shall have to repay. He righteously denounces the burden we are leaving to our children. He castigates the federal government as the prime source of this hideous evil of debt. And, finally, he urges us to mend our ways, get out of debt, and be saved. The speech has a moral ring to it. It has some of the elements of a revival meeting in its fervor.

None of us will argue that the incurring of debt should be done without prudence and caution. Most of us are continually concerned about safeguarding the quality of credit. In the cold light of banking experience, I can testify that there *are* moral issues involved in debt, and ethical aspects, the preservation of which is basic to our society. But these proper considerations tend often to be glossed over in the enthusiastic denunciations of debt as such. The banquet speech is wrong, not because there are no seeds of truth in the general concern about debt, but because so much of the sermon is devoted to aspects which are not true. I want to look at four of these questionable propositions or myths.

FOUR DEBT MYTHS

Myth Number One: Debt in the United States is too high. There is no question about the fact that total net debt in this nation is huge. It passed the trillion-dollar mark near the end of 1962. But absolute figures are deceptive. Bigness is not badness per se. One cannot say that debt is too high except in relation to the *effects* of debt and in light of reasonable criteria as to when the negative effects become unbearable.

One of the most serious results of an "excessive" volume of outstanding debt is the reduced ability to expand debt further. This causes trouble for the economy, paradoxically, not because of the absolute size of the debt outstanding, but because of the *insufficient* size of the new debt flotations.

In this sense, total net debt in the United States is not excessive. The change in outstandings last year [1963] was at an all-time high— $76 billion—following the previous high in 1962 of $73 billion. These changes in outstandings substantially exceed the records posted during World War II.

Based upon this fact, I would say that there is no apparent dearth of credit in this country. Nor are there any signs that credit as a whole is approaching a breakdown. There is every expectation that we can continue a reasonable expansion of our debt if the proceeds are used productively.

Myth Number Two: Debt in the United States has grown many times more rapidly than our nation's ability to pay it off. There is certainly no question that net debt in the United States has grown rapidly. The present level of debt is six times what it was in 1929 and has grown by $687 billion just since the end of World War II. This represents a compound growth rate of about 5.7 percent from 1945.

But the country has also grown tremendously since 1929 and since the end of World War II. The United States has 67 million more people than it had at the start of the Great Depression, and some 50 million more than at the end of the war. Therefore, while total debt grew at a rate of 5.7 percent, net per capita debt has grown since 1945 at a compound rate of 3.9 percent.

When we talk about "the ability to pay off the current total debt," we are dealing with still another distortion. Implicit in the prospect of "paying off total current debt" is the idea that the total debt could suddenly be called, and that there would be an immediate shift of real assets from debtors to creditors. There are at least three flaws in this concept.

First, we have no comparative spreads of maturities of our existing and previous debt. It is clear, however, that total debt does not require immediate repayment, but, rather, prolonged periods for settling these obligations.

Second, if the past is any indication of the future, a large but unknown part of current net debt will be extended or renewed, thus further prolonging the period in which debt would have to be paid off. It is indeed possible to maintain perpetual debt as the refunding operations of some of our most prudently managed corporations prove.

Third, any dramatic effort to shift resources

suddenly and burdensomely from debtors to creditors would surely run into popular and political obstacles which would probably make it impossible to effect such a sudden shift.

Moreover, in recent years the average American citizen has increased his capacity to pay a dollar of maturing debt in two respects, and one of these changes has grown more rapidly since 1929 than has total net debt.

First is the increase in the "paying power" of goods and services. This has been caused by the increase in prices—inflation, in other words—which, in turn, reflects the gradual decline in the purchasing power of money. Over the years total net debt in the United States has grown at just about the same rate as current dollar gross national product—a little more since 1929, a little less than World War II. There is no really adequate measure of changes in all the relevant market values so that it is virtually impossible to "deflate" the debt accurately. Using the widest measure of price change, however—the so-called GNP deflator—it was twice as costly in terms of goods to repay a dollar of debt in 1929 as it is today. In other words, the physical volume of the things we would have to do without in order to pay off a dollar of debt in 1964 is only about half what it was at the 1929 peak of prosperity. While inflation may raise legitimate ethical and economic questions about redistribution of real assets between creditors and debtors, it nonetheless clearly reduces the real cost to the individual debtor of repaying existing debt. Total net debt per person expressed as an index of the volume of goods and services required to pay it off has grown since 1945 at a compound rate of seven-tenths of one percent. This is substantially less than our economy's growth rate.

There is a second and even more relevant concept of the cost of repaying individual money obligations. This is the cost in terms of human effort. Since 1929 tremendous strides have been made in the productivity of the U.S. economy. Man-hours required to pay off a dollar of debt have been reduced considerably. It is roughly estimated that total man-hours worked in the recession year 1960 were about 25 percent greater than during the prosperity year 1929, while real output was nearly 150 percent greater. Real output per man-hour worked, therefore, has probably at least doubled since 1929. If this is the case, the human

effort cost of repaying the debt in 1963 would be about half as great as the "paying power" figures shown. This would indicate that the real per capita cost of repaying total net debt is lower today than it was in 1929, and that the number of man-hours required has dropped by more than 25 percent since 1945.

Myth Number Three: The recent high growth of the federal debt is a major problem. A basic difficulty here is that some critics of federal debt look at it out of context, with no reference to total net debt—or they fail to differentiate between the two. Between 1929 and 1945 the bulk of the changes in total net debt were, indeed, accounted for by the growth in federal debt. During those years there was some justification for confusing the two or considering them as one.

However, net federal debt outstanding at the end of 1963 was little higher than at the end of 1945, which was, of course, one of the peak years in history. Federal debt grew by only $9 billion during this period, while the rest of the total net debt grew by $679 billion. Clearly, the federal government is far from leading the debt extension parade.

Debt of state and local governments has contributed about eight times as much to the growth of total net debt since the war as has federal government debt. The main contributor, however, has been the private sector of our economy—corporations and individuals. Altogether, governmental entities added $74 billion to the total of net debt in the postwar period, compared with $613 billion added by the private sector. Certainly, the growth of federal debt since the war has been minor compared with the growth of private debt.

From the standpoint of taxable income, which represents a rough estimate of the potential for paying off the federal debt, we are in a far easier position today than we were at the end of World War II. At that time, net federal debt was nearly one-third higher than total personal and corporate income combined. Last year, net federal debt was barely half as large as personal and corporate income in the United States. Except for three recession years, the annual growth of this "tax base" since 1945 has been several times as great as the growth in net federal debt. Moreover, the extensive assets under federal ownership could well be considered as an offset to federal debt in calculating whether that debt has grown too high to be managed. In view of these facts, can we properly consider the existence, the magnitude or the rate of growth of federal debt a serious problem for the United States?

Myth Number Four: Federal debt must be reduced, or, at the very least, cannot be allowed to expand further. It is little wonder that this is a popular myth. A gross federal debt of well over $300 billion is awesome to contemplate. Yet we must come to grips with the fact that $1 billion or $300 billion are units of counting with which we measure our economic universe in much the same way we use light years to measure the physical universe. Our economic universe is already immense and is growing with each passing day. Our annual output of goods and services is well over half a trillion dollars, and our national wealth can be conservatively estimated in the neighborhood of $1.5 trillion. Both figures could double in a generation or so.

It is against these astronomical figures that the federal debt should be considered. And when so considered, it becomes a good deal less frightening. Hence, all of the arguments I have previously stated relative to debt—its relation to GNP; its relation to taxable income; its relation to the real cost of repayment—are all applicable to the concern that federal debt must be reduced.

There are other reasons why this is not an acceptable proposition. In the first place, we must never forget that government obligations are an asset to their holders. Indeed, under ordinary circumstances, the purchasers of government bonds, notes, certificates or bills consider these investments more valuable than the money they give up for them. As long as this valuation holds good, does the economy as a whole necessarily gain by wiping out these assets through debt liquidation?

Moreover, some debt possesses a liquidity which facilitates private business transactions. Millions of individuals have achieved some sense of financial security through their holdings of "E" bonds, for example. Increased flotations of Treasury bills have been partly responsible for holding some corporate funds in this country rather than adding to the deficit in our balance of international payments. Federal National Mortgage Association issues—included in the previous figures on federal debt along with the obligations of other federal agencies—have provided a flexibility which the mortgage market would not otherwise have had. It is misleading to look upon federal debt instruments as unmitigated evils.

Finally, there is no more reason for extinguishing federal debt than permitting corporate debt, for example, to be renewed. Many corporations of great stature and financial strength operate with substantial volumes of outstanding debt on a seemingly perpetual basis. Provided the funds obtained from investors or lenders are productively invested by the borrower, there is no cause for them to be deleted from the financial structure of the businesses. Similarly with federal debt. It will often be desirable and economic for a maturing federal issue to be rolled over rather than paid off. The wisdom of such action cannot be judged sweepingly in advance, but only in the light of circumstances prevailing at the moment.

The sum and substance of these arguments is that the question of reducing federal debt or of expanding it further should not be determined by absolute size of the debt, but by the economic impact that will result. It is the functioning of the economy that counts.

Here the new environment bears most directly on the problem of debt. The overwhelming dependence of the men, women and children of this nation on the stable functioning of markets means that the preservation of the order and efficiency of these markets is vital to the preservation of the society itself. The proper rate and direction of extension of total net debt is basic to the smooth functioning of our markets. And net federal debt operations can form a key catalytic element in the expansion of total debt.

This does not mean that federal debt expansion need be a large part of the whole, but it must occur when needed. It does not mean that Treasury financing operations are crucial, independent of the Federal Reserve actions which determine the *net* impact of federal debt on the economy. Nor does it mean that the financing flows themselves are the most important part of the federal contribution; the tax and expenditure impacts which federal debt flotations make possible may be even more important. What it does mean is that federal expenditure and tax policy is a stout staff on which our economy must lean from time to time, and emotional attitudes toward debt should not be allowed to interfere with that support when the necessity arises. Unrealistic limitations to the quick expansion of federal debt when required for the health of the total economy, and unreasoning pressures to reduce federal debt regardless of the economic impact of such action, seem out of place in a sound, modern economy.

These, then, are the principal elements of the mythology of debt. I hope I have succeeded in placing a cloud of suspicion over their intellectual sanctity, because these myths may bar the door to the possibilities of wiser and more flexible use of federal debt as an instrument of economic policy.

QUESTIONS AND STUDY SUGGESTIONS

1. Why is debt essential in the "new economic environment"? Briefly analyze the four myths of debt.
2. How have inflation and productivity increases affected the nation's ability to pay off its total debt?
3. How does the Federal debt compare with (a) private debt and (b) the debt of state and local governments? Explain this recent statement by Professor Kenneth E. Boulding: "I think a strong case can be made that at the present the national debt is dangerously low, as it is about the same proportion of the GNP that it was in 1929. . . . I suspect myself that we probably need a fairly sharp increase in the national debt, perhaps a doubling within 10 years, if we are to avoid serious deflation and unemployment."

Reading 25

Interest Rates, Monetary Policy, and the Economy

Board of Governors of the Federal Reserve System

In this reading the interest rate is envisioned as being determined by the demand for and supply of loanable funds. The demand for and supply of loanable funds are in turn determined by saving and investment decisions and the expectations of consumers and businesses. The purpose of mone-

From **The Federal Reserve System: Purposes and Functions,** 5th ed., Washington, 1963, pp. 107–111, 116–125, abridged. Reprinted by permission.

tary policy—open-market operations and changes in reserve requirements and the discount rate—is to manipulate the supply of loanable funds and therefore the interest rate in the interest of full employment and price stability.

Interest rates are the prices paid for use of credit. The instruments of monetary policy have an influence on the economy in part through their impact on these prices. But in a market economy many factors go into the formulation of interest rates. They are established in the credit market by the interplay of the many forces of demand and supply, including the impact on credit supply associated with the use of monetary policy instruments. The pricing function of interest rates is to bring the supply of and demand for funds into balance. In this process interest rates influence the volume and composition of available loan funds and their allocation among competing economic activities.

Variations in interest rates exert incentive and disincentive effects on individual seekers and suppliers of funds. These effects derive directly from the pricing role of interest rates and indirectly from their role as capitalization rates by means of which future streams of income may be translated into present-day capital values.

DIFFERENCES AMONG INTEREST RATES

Reflecting the many purposes and situations that give rise to borrowing and lending, there is a wide variety of loans and investments in credit markets, each bearing an interest rate. Some interest rates are relatively high, and some relatively low. The particular level for each security reflects the distinctive characteristics of the obligation, the particular class of borrowers using it, and the preferences that lenders and investors may show for it.

Observable differences in market interest rates are affected by a wide variety of factors. Among the most important are the maturity structure of market instruments, that is, whether short- or long-term; the market's evaluation of differences in factors related to risk, including the business experience of borrowers and the kinds of assets or guarantees that back up their obligations; whether the loan is large, readily negotiable in form, and

often traded in the market, or whether it is relatively small, less negotiable, and seldom traded; tax exemption features; and the varying supplies that lenders make available in given circumstances for different uses.

FACTORS IN INTEREST RATE CHANGES

Variations in the supply of and demand for loanable funds of enough strength to change the level and maturity structure of market interest rates are usually the joint product of a number of underlying economic forces. Insofar as the maturity structure of interest rates is concerned, it is influenced by the comparative liquidity of credit market instruments; by the degree to which liabilities and functions of different financial institutions influence their preferences for short- and long-term securities; by expectations of active market participants about future rates; and by the relative supply of securities outstanding in different maturity categories.

All of these forces are continuously working on the maturity composition of market interest rates. Sometimes they tend to reinforce each other, but at other times they may be offsetting.

For instance, an increase in the outstanding amount of short-term U.S. Government securities available to the nonbank public and a decrease in the outstanding amount of long-term securities would tend—if no other forces were at work—to raise short-term and lower long-term interest rates. This tendency might be reinforced by market expectations. On the other hand, offsetting changes in the market's demand for securities may well occur over time as a result of changing institutional preferences or the persistence of countervailing expectations. In a well organized and flexible credit market, dynamic adjustments are constantly under way as temporary market factors give way to more lasting influences.

In fact, because of competitive relations in the credit market, the various market interest rates generally respond together to changes in fundamental economic forces, though some rates move more readily, more rapidly, and more extensively than others. Basic influences on the central tendency shown by all rates—that is, on the average level of interest rates—include changes in the nation's saving and investment propensities, changes in market expectations as to the future course of economic activity and of prices, and changes in the flow of bank credit and money.

Saving-Investment Process

From a saver's point of view the rate of interest can be viewed as a price that translates present saving into future buying power. For example, at a 5 percent annual interest rate, $100 saved from present income will exchange for $105 after a year. Meanwhile, since the saver has not spent his $100—that is, has refrained from current consumption to this extent—his saving permits resources to be used to an equivalent dollar amount for the nation's investment in plant and equipment, durable goods, and housing (or in net foreign investment).

A nation's saving represents the amount by which its members have refrained from using income to buy goods and services to be consumed currently. The investment of this saving, which represents expenditures for tangible wealth (plus or minus the net change in claims on foreigners), increases the economy's capacity to produce goods and services in the future. This increase, when realized, takes the form of added output of goods and services from which borrowers are able to pay the interest earned by the nation's saving.

Interest is, on the one hand, an earning on saving and, on the other, a cost of investment in buildings, equipment, or other capital goods. Movements of interest rates, therefore, can be said to reflect the balancing of saving and investment tendencies at given levels of output and prices. But the demand for investment in relation to the economy's willingness to save also affects a nation's real output as well as the market prices of the goods and services that have been produced. The extent of influence depends on the economic and financial organization of a country, on the phase of its economic cycle, and on specific economic conditions at the time.

In recession periods the plant facilities of a country turn out a volume of goods and services below their capacity. In these circumstances an increase in investment demand relative to the supply of saving is likely to lead to the financing of a larger volume of real investment, and thus to increased output and rising real income. The rise in real income from the expanded investment demand will generally be accompanied by an increase in saving. This will limit any tendency for interest rates to rise, and saving and investment may be brought into balance at little net advance in either interest rates or in the level of prices for goods and services.

In times of economic boom, however, when plant capacity is fully or almost fully utilized, investment demand in excess of available saving works progressively to intensify upward pressures on interest rates and price levels. Under these conditions the extent to which saving may be increased out of a rise in output and real income is necessarily limited.

Role of Expectations

Shifts in expectations of businesses and consumers as to the future course of prices, production, and income affect saving, investment, and interest rates. Two kinds of effects can be distinguished. First, there are the very short-run effects, felt mainly in short-term markets and not closely related to basic tendencies in saving and investment. Second, there are the longer-term effects on saving and investment, which have a more pervasive and sustained impact on interest rates.

How shifts in business expectations may affect interest rates in the short run is illustrated by what typically happens in credit markets in the early stages of a cyclical recovery. Under these conditions interest rates—particularly short-term rates—usually rise faster than basic demand-supply developments warrant. This rise is influenced by prospects of rapid expansion in economic activity, high and rising demands for credit, and a possible shift in Federal Reserve System operations from being appreciably stimulative to being less stimulative and eventually restraining.

Conversely, market expectations that the near-term economic outlook is unfavorable may precipitate a sharp decline in short-term rates.

At such times prospects will loom large for a significant reduction in borrowing demands and for an increase in the supply of funds as a result of more active bank credit expansion under the stimulus of monetary policy. Interest rate movements of this short-term type may slow down markedly, or even be reversed, if it becomes evident that the market's expectations are not to be realized.

Longer-run effects of expectations may include dislocations in the saving-investment process and may thereby have more enduring effects on conditions in credit markets. For example, upward pressures on interest rates and commodity prices become and remain intensified during periods when high capacity utilization is accompanied by widely prevalent expectations of inflation. In such periods potential borrowers are stimulated to obtain immediate financing in order to beat the expected higher costs of business plant and equipment in the future. Investors also take steps to protect themselves against the expected inflation. For instance, they purchase inflation hedges such as equities and land rather than debt obligations, and they also borrow to finance these purchases.

When inflationary expectations are modified, the process is reversed. Investors' preferences for debt obligations relative to equities become stronger; yields on equities tend to rise; and upward pressures on interest rates are displaced by declining tendencies.

Money and Bank Credit

Fluctuations in market rates of interest are affected not only by changes in the saving-investment process and in the economy's expectations but also by changes in the supply of bank credit and money. When bank credit expands, banks buy securities and make loans for financing economic activity, and this adds directly to the supply of funds available. Thus interest rates may fall in response to this expansion in supply.

When bank credit expands, the supply of money typically rises. Increases in the supply of money not matched by increases in the public's desire to hold cash have one of two effects or some combination of them. As one alternative, the supply of funds in credit markets may rise further as the public attempts to substitute other financial assets for cash; if so, downward pressures on market rates of interest may be accentuated. As another, consumers and businesses may spend larger amounts on goods and services as they try to reduce the amount of cash they hold.

Interactions

The factors influencing the supply of and demand for loanable funds and the levels of interest rates—that is, the money supply, saving and investment, and expectations—are not independent of each other. The behavior of one is influenced by and impinges on the movements of the others. Changes in interest rates, output, and prices are a product of their joint effects.

When economic activity declines and investment demand falls relative to saving, interest rates tend to fall. At such times reserve banking actions to increase the availability of credit and the supply of money will make for easier credit market conditions, declining interest rates, and a financial environment and expectations favorable to a revival in economic activity.

When the economy is at a high level of capacity utilization, when demands for goods and services tend to exceed the capacity to produce them at current prices, and when investment demand is outrunning the propensity to save, prices and interest rates tend to rise. Under these circumstances reserve banking actions will generally be designed to keep credit and monetary expansion in line with the economy's growing capacity to produce and thereby to contain inflationary pressures.

Unlimited expansion of bank credit and money in these conditions, in order to satisfy all demands for credit at pre-existing interest rates, would enlarge the dollar amount of both saving and spending without relieving the shortage of real resources. It would thus result mainly in rising prices and expectations of further rises. It would not check, except perhaps temporarily, a pronounced tendency for interest rates to rise. Thus for monetary policy to be an effective influence toward stable prices and sustained economic growth, interest rates need to fluctuate in response to variations in economic activity, the supply of saving, and investment demands.

FEDERAL RESERVE ACTIONS AND INTEREST RATES

Federal Reserve policy, which has its immediate impact on the availability of bank reserves, affects market interest rates in several ways. The main influence of monetary policy on interest rates is exerted by the increase or decrease in the supply of funds in the market that results from multiple expansion or contraction of bank credit based on fractional reserve requirements. On the average, however, only a small share of aggregate credit demand is satisfied through the bank credit expansion that is associated with growth in money supply. Available estimates indicate that the share so satisfied averaged about 6 percent annually during the decade ending in 1962.

The Federal Reserve can initiate a change in bank reserves through its open market operations or, when appropriate and feasible, by changes in reserve requirement percentages. Federal Reserve purchases and sales of Government securities in the open market, of course, have some immediate impact on interest rates. By conducting most of its operations in short-term securities, the market for which is much broader than markets for longer issues, the System tends to minimize this immediate impact. Purchases have been made, however, in the intermediate- and long-term area in an effort to reduce even further the downward pressures on short-term rates at times when this has appeared to be desirable, such as in periods when short-term capital outflows have been intensifying a balance of payments problem.

Since open market operations in securities of either short or long maturity bring about larger changes in the supply of funds—through multiple expansion or contraction of bank credit—their basic impact is on rates in all sectors of the market, which come to be affected in some degree. Flexible adjustment between short- and longer-term interest rates is an essential aspect of a responsive credit market. Such a market continuously reflects evolving borrower and lender preferences in the commitment of financial resources into the future. Continuous market adjustments enable the nation's financial institutions to function effectively in the public interest, as they mobilize the saving of numerous individuals and others and channel the funds into investments.

The Federal Reserve discount rate is related to and interacts with interest rates in the market. As was explained earlier, the Federal Reserve discount rate is kept in close alignment with short-term interest rates in order to avoid giving member banks either too much or too little incentive for using a facility that is intended to meet banking contingencies and temporary needs for reserve funds. While the discount rate is administered in relation to the level and structure of market interest rates, market rates themselves are primarily the product of the forces of demand for and supply of credit, including of course the effect of other Federal Reserve actions affecting bank reserves.

Because of psychological factors in the market, bank credit and monetary policy may have some effect on interest rates in addition to, and even prior to, those resulting from changes in bank reserve positions. However, interest rate movements prompted by expectations of prospective reserve banking action are not likely to be long sustained unless accompanied by changes in basic supply and demand conditions.

The course of interest rates is necessarily affected by reserve banking action, as monetary policy influences the availability of bank reserves and the flow of bank credit and money in response to developments in domestic economic activity and in the balance of payments. Reserve banking operations, however, attempt to interfere as little as possible with investor, lender, and borrower decisions as to the specific commitment of financial resources over time.

QUESTIONS AND STUDY SUGGESTIONS

1. Why is there a variety of interest rates? What is the "maturity composition" of interest rates?
2. What effect do changes in business and consumer expectations have upon interest rates?

3. Describe the impact of "the nation's saving and investment propensities" upon the interest rate. Explain how an increase in the demand for funds for investment would affect real output and interest rates during (*a*) a period of recession and (*b*) a period of full employment.
4. Discuss in detail how the monetary policies of the Federal Reserve affect the interest rate and the level of economic activity.

Reading 26

Monetary Policy: Rules or Discretion? Two Views

Should the monetary authorities—the Board of Governors of the Federal Reserve System—enjoy more or less complete discretion in managing the money supply? Or should Congress impose a specific monetary rule or guideline upon the Fed which forces it to increase the money supply at some fixed rate (for example, a rate equal to the projected growth of real GNP) each year? This is one of the most debated issues in the area of monetary management. Reading 26 presents two sharply divergent views on the subject.

Milton Friedman is a persuasive advocate for a monetary rule. He argues that historically the monetary authorities have generally taken actions which have contributed to economic instability; in particular, the Fed has tended to overreact to changes in economic activity through a failure to allow for time lags between the initiation of their policy actions and the impact of these policies upon the economy. The record of monetary policy can be improved, Friedman contends, "by adopting publicly the policy of achieving a steady rate of growth" in the money supply.

Other monetary experts disagree with Professor Friedman's prescription. Lester Chandler holds that the relationship between the money supply and aggregate demand (the immediate determinant of output and the price level) is a variable one because the velocity of money changes secularly, cyclically, and in response to interest rate fluctuations. Hence, an annual increase in the money supply based upon the projected growth of real GNP will not necessarily result in an increase in aggregate demand sufficient to realize precisely the potential growth in real output. Thus a monetary rule could easily foster unemployment or inflation. Professor Chandler concludes that there exists "no workable alternative to discretionary monetary actions."

First View: The Case for a Monetary Rule

Milton Friedman, Professor of Economics, University of Chicago

My own studies of monetary history have made me extremely sympathetic to the oft-quoted, much reviled, and as widely misunderstood, comment by John Stuart Mill. "There cannot . . . ," he wrote, "be intrinsically a more insignificant thing, in the economy of society, than money; except in the character of a contrivance for sparing time and labour. It is a machine for doing quickly and commodiously, what would be done, though less quickly and commodiously, without it: and like many other kinds of machinery, it only exerts a distinct and independent influence of its own when it gets out of order."

True, money is only a machine, but it is an extraordinarily efficient machine. Without it, we could not have begun to attain the astounding growth in output and level of living we have experienced in the past two centuries —any more than we could have done so without those other marvelous machines that dot our countryside and enable us, for the most part, simply to do more efficiently what could be done without them at much greater cost in labor.

But money has one feature that these other machines do not share. Because it is so pervasive, when it gets out of order, it throws a monkey wrench into the operation of all other machines. The Great Contraction [Depression] is the most dramatic example but not the only one. Every other major contraction in this country has been either produced by monetary disorder or greatly exacerbated by monetary disorder. Every major inflation has been produced by monetary expansion—mostly to meet the overriding demands of war which have forced the creation of money to supplement explicit taxation.

WHAT MONETARY POLICY CAN DO

The first and important lesson that history teaches about what monetary policy can do— and it is a lesson of the most profound importance—is that monetary policy can prevent money itself from being a major source of economic disturbance. This sounds like a negative proposition: avoid major mistakes. In part it is. The Great Contraction might not have occurred at all, and if it had, it would have been far less severe, if the monetary authority had avoided mistakes, or if the monetary arrangements had been those of an earlier time when there was no central authority with the power to make the kinds of mistakes that the Federal Reserve System made. The past few years, to come closer to home, would have been steadier and more productive of economic well-being if the Federal Reserve had avoided drastic and erratic changes of direction, first expanding the money supply at an unduly rapid pace, then, in early 1966, stepping on the brake too hard, then, at the end of 1966, reversing itself and resuming expansion until at least November, 1967, at a more rapid pace than can long be maintained without appreciable inflation.

Even if the proposition that monetary policy can prevent money itself from being a major source of economic disturbance were a wholly negative proposition, it would be none the less important for that. As it happens, however, it is not a wholly negative proposition. The monetary machine has gotten out of order even when there has been no central authority with anything like the power now possessed by the Fed. In the United States, the 1907 episode and earlier banking panics are examples of how the monetary machine can get out of order largely on its own. There is therefore a positive and important task for the monetary authority—to suggest improvements in the machine that will reduce the chances that it will get out of order, and to use its own powers so as to keep the machine in good working order.

A second thing monetary policy can do is provide a stable background for the economy— keep the machine well oiled, to continue Mill's analogy. Accomplishing the first task will contribute to this objective, but there is more to it than that. Our economic system will work best when producers and consumers, employers and employees, can proceed with full confi-

From Milton Friedman, "The Role of Monetary Policy," **American Economic Review,** March, 1968, pp. 12–17, abridged. Reprinted by permission.

dence that the average level of prices will behave in a known way in the future—preferably that it will be highly stable. Under any conceivable institutional arrangements, and certainly under those that now prevail in the United States, there is only a limited amount of flexibility in prices and wages. We need to conserve this flexibility to achieve changes in relative prices and wages that are required to adjust to dynamic changes in tastes and technology. We should not dissipate it simply to achieve changes in the absolute level of prices that serve no economic function.

In today's world, if monetary policy is to provide a stable background for the economy it must do so by deliberately employing its powers to that end. I shall come later to how it can do so.

Finally, monetary policy can contribute to offsetting major disturbances in the economic system arising from other sources. If there is an independent secular exhilaration—as the postwar expansion was described by the proponents of secular stagnation—monetary policy can in principle help to hold it in check by a slower rate of monetary growth than would otherwise be desirable. If, as now, an explosive federal budget threatens unprecedented deficits, monetary policy can hold any inflationary dangers in check by a slower rate of monetary growth than would otherwise be desirable. This will temporarily mean higher interest rates than would otherwise prevail—to enable the government to borrow the sums needed to finance the deficit—but by preventing the speeding up of inflation, it may well mean both lower prices and lower nominal interest rates for the long pull. If the end of a substantial war offers the country an opportunity to shift resources from wartime to peace time production, monetary policy can ease the transition by a higher rate of monetary growth than would otherwise be desirable—though experience is not very encouraging that it can do so without going too far.

I have put this point last, and stated it in qualified terms—as referring to major disturbances—because I believe that the potentiality of monetary policy in offsetting other forces making for instability is far more limited than is commonly believed. We simply do not know enough to be able to recognize minor disturbances when they occur or to be able to predict either what their effects will be with any pre-cision or what monetary policy is required to offset their effects. We do not know enough to be able to achieve stated objectives by delicate, or even fairly coarse, changes in the mix of monetary and fiscal policy. In this area particularly the best is likely to be the enemy of the good. Experience suggests that the path of wisdom is to use monetary policy explicitly to offset other disturbances only when they offer a "clear and present danger."

CONDUCTING MONETARY POLICY

How should monetary policy be conducted to make the contribution to our goals that it is capable of making? This is clearly not the occasion for presenting a detailed "Program for Monetary Stability"—to use the title of a book in which I tried to do so. I shall restrict myself here to two major requirements for monetary policy that follow directly from the preceding discussion.

The first requirement is that the monetary authority should guide itself by magnitudes that it can control, not by ones that it cannot control. If as authority has often done, it takes interest rates or the current unemployment percentage as the immediate criterion of policy, it will be like a space vehicle that has taken a fix on the wrong star. No matter how sensitive and sophisticated its guiding apparatus, the space vehicle will go astray. And so will the monetary authority. Of the various alternative magnitudes that it can control, the most appealing guides for policy are exchange rates, the price level as defined by some index, and the quantity of a monetary total—currency plus adjusted demand deposits, or this total plus commercial bank time deposits, or a still broader total.

Of the three guides listed, the price level is clearly the most important in its own right. Other things the same, it would be much the best of the alternatives—as so many distinguished economists have urged in the past. But other things are not the same. The link between the policy actions of the monetary authority and the price level, while unquestionably present, is more indirect than the link between the policy actions of the authority and any of the several monetary totals. Moreover, monetary action takes a longer time to affect the price level than to affect the monetary totals and both the time lag and the magnitude of effect vary with circumstances. As a result, we cannot predict at all accurately just what effect a particular monetary action will have on the price level and, equally important, just when it will have that effect. Attempting to control directly the price level is therefore likely to make monetary policy itself a source of economic disturbance because of false stops and starts. Perhaps, as our understanding of monetary phenomena advances, the situation will change. But at the present stage of our understanding, the long way around seems the surer way to our objective. Accordingly, I believe that a monetary total is the best currently available immediate guide or criterion for monetary policy—and I believe that it matters much less which particular total is chosen than that one to be chosen.

A second requirement for monetary policy is that the monetary authority avoid sharp swings in policy. In the past, monetary authorities have on occasion moved in the wrong direction —as in the episode of the Great Contraction that I have stressed. More frequently, they have moved in the right direction, albeit often too late, but have erred by moving too far. Too late and too much has been the general practice. For example, in early 1966, it was the right policy for the Federal Reserve to move in a less expansionary direction—though it should have done so at least a year earlier. But when it moved, it went too far, producing the sharpest change in the rate of monetary growth of the postwar era. Again, having gone too far, it was the right policy for the Fed to reverse course at the end of 1966. But again it went too far, not only restoring but exceeding the earlier excessive rate of monetary growth. And this episode is no exception. Time and again this has been the course followed—as in 1919 and 1920, in 1937 and 1938, in 1953 and 1954, in 1959 and 1960.

The reason for the propensity to overreact seems clear: the failure of monetary authorities to allow for the delay between their actions and the subsequent effects on the economy. They tend to determine their actions by today's conditions—but their actions will affect the economy only six or nine or twelve or fifteen months later. Hence they feel impelled to step on the brake, or the accelerator, as the case may be, too hard.

MONEY SUPPLY GROWTH RULE

My own prescription is still that the monetary authority go all the way in avoiding such swings by adopting publicly the policy of achieving a steady rate of growth in a specified monetary total. The precise rate of growth, like the precise monetary total, is less important than the adoption of some stated and known rate. I myself have argued for a rate that would on the average achieve rough stability in the level of prices of final products, which I have estimated would call for something like a 3 to 5 percent per year rate of growth in currency plus all commercial bank deposits or a slightly lower rate of growth in currency plus demand deposits only. But it would be better to have a fixed rate that would on the average produce moderate inflation or moderate deflation, provided it was steady, than to suffer the wide and erratic perturbations we have experienced.

Short of the adoption of such a publicly stated policy of a steady rate of monetary growth, it would constitute a major improvement if the monetary authority followed the self-denying ordinance of avoiding wide swings. It is a matter of record that periods of relative stability in the rate of monetary growth have also been periods of relative stability in economic activity, both in the United States and other countries. Periods of wide swings in the rate of monetary growth have also been periods of wide swings in economic activity.

By setting itself a steady course and keeping to it, the monetary authority could make a major contribution to promoting economic stability. By making that course one of steady but moderate growth in the quantity of money, it would make a major contribution to avoidance of either inflation or deflation of prices. Other forces would still affect the economy, require change and adjustment, and disturb the even tenor of our ways. But steady monetary growth would provide a monetary climate favorable to the effective operation of those basic forces of enterprise, ingenuity, invention, hard work, and thrift that are the true springs of economic growth. That is the most that we can ask from monetary policy at our present stage of knowledge. But that much—and it is a great deal—is clearly within our reach.

Second View: The Case against a Monetary Rule

Lester V. Chandler, Professor of Economics, Princeton University

I do not believe that Congress, or anyone else, can formulate specific operating guides that will promote selected economic objectives in anything like an optimum way. In fact, we would be fortunate indeed if the specific guides did not on many occasions lead us away from our chosen goals. And the more specific and binding the operating guides, the greater is the danger.

A specific operating guide would presumably be formulated and prescribed in terms of the behavior of some financial or monetary variable. For example, it might be stated in terms of a prescribed behavior of interest rates, or the behavior of total bank credit, or the behavior of the money supply, however defined. None of these is in itself an ultimate objective or of prime importance. Each assumes importance for policy purposes only to the extent that it is related in a reliable way to economic variables of greater importance—to such things as the behavior of aggregate demand for output and the responses of real output, prices and employment. For a specific operating guide couched in terms of some monetary or financial variable to be useful, you would have to be able to predict long into the future a constant relationship between that variable and the ultimate policy variable that does matter. I am convinced that this cannot be done.

Consider the much-publicized proposal that the money supply should be increased—week in, week out—at an annual rate approximating the growth potential of real GNP. The quantity of money is in itself of little importance. What is far more important is the behavior of total demand for output, or GNP at current prices. All the evidence indicates that there is not a constant relationship between the stock of money and the rate of flow of expenditures for output. Rather, the two are linked in a variable way by income velocity, or its inverse, the amount of money balances demanded by business and the public relative to their expenditures. These have fluctuated significantly both cyclically and over longer terms, and

there is no reason to expect that they will be stable in the future.

SECULAR GROWTH AND CYCLICAL CHANGES

There is good reason to believe that the American economy, with its rising capacity to produce, will need a secular increase in the money supply. But no one can forecast far in advance the rate of increase of the money supply that will be required to keep aggregate demand for output in line with the economy's capacity to produce. For example, the money supply, narrowly defined, has increased since 1947 at an average annual rate of about $2\frac{1}{2}$ percent, while GNP, or expenditures for output, has grown more than twice as fast, at an average rate of more than 6 percent. Thus, the average income velocity of money has grown at an annual rate of 3.4 percent, and from an arithmetic point of view has accounted for more than half of the rise of spending for output. It is difficult to account fully for this rise of income velocity, or greater economizing on money balances. A part is probably due to the general rise of interest rates. Some of this may disappear if interest rates fall to lower levels, though we do not know how much. Clearly, however, a considerable part of the increase stems from financial innovations of a more lasting nature, such as improved corporate cash management, invention of various competing financial instruments, and greater financial sophistication of households.

It is almost in the nature of things that we cannot forecast far ahead what further financial innovations will occur, how fast they will spread, or how much they will affect income velocity. There are, however, great potentialities in the spreading use of bank credit cards, instant credit, and computers. In view of such uncertainties, it would not seem wise to order the Federal Reserve to increase the money supply steadily at some predetermined rates.

Also damaging to the prescription of a steady rate of increase of the money supply

From **Standards for Guiding Monetary Action:** Hearings before the Joint Economic Committee, 90th Cong., 2d Sess., Washington, 1968, pp. 5–7, abridged.

are the cyclical variations in the income velocity of money. That income velocity does fluctuate in a procyclical manner, rising in booms and falling during recessions, is a well-documented fact. Even Professor Friedman admits this, though he plays down its significance. But it is significant. For example, even a 10 percent decline in income velocity–a fall from the present figure of about 4.4 per year to 4 per year–would be associated with a decline of more than $80 billion in the value of GNP, the money supply remaining constant. In effect, this is equivalent to a 10 percent reduction of the money supply, which would obviously be significant. Fluctuations of income velocity by 10 percent or more over the course of a cycle are by no means uncommon.

FLUCTUATING INTEREST RATES

If the rule of a steadily increasing money supply were adopted, income would continue to fluctuate over the business cycle, if for no other reason than because interest rates would fluctuate. It is highly significant that Professor Friedman stands almost alone in contending that income velocity and demands for cash balances are not significantly affected by changes in interest rates. Virtually all other investigators have found very significant effects. They differ somewhat on which interest rates are most influential and how great the responsiveness is, but all find that increases of interest rates reduce velocity. This assures that velocity will behave in a procyclical manner.

Consider, for example, the situation in 1966 when rapidly rising Government expenditures coincided with a strong investment boom. Interest rates would have risen sharply even if the money supply had been increasing at an annual rate of 3 or 4 percent. The rise of interest rates would have induced both business and the public to economize on their money balances, which yield no explicit return, and this would have been reflected in a rise of income velocity. Thus at the peak of interest rates, business and the public would be holding money balances relative to their expenditures which would continue to be satisfactory only so long as interest rates remained at that level. When the boom subsided and interest rates tended to fall, they would demand to hold more money relative to their expenditures, and their attempts to replenish their balances to the new and higher demanded levels would delay and retard the downward adjustment of interest rates and a general easing of money market conditions. Thus what could have been only a mild recession may be translated into a more serious recession or even into a depression, especially if an expansionary fiscal policy is not initiated.

CONCLUSION

I conclude, then, that while it may be feasible to provide more specific guides relating to the objectives of monetary policy, it is not feasible to formulate more specific and appropriate operating guides for the policy actions to be taken to promote those objectives.

I see no workable alternative to discretionary monetary actions. I say this despite the many shortcomings of discretionary policies–difficulties of forecasting, lags in the effects of monetary policies, and so on. The Federal Reserve has made mistakes and will doubtless make more. But one need not think that Federal Reserve officials and their staffs are infallible to believe that their discretionary actions based on flows of current information, on forecasts for the coming months and on continuous revision of those forecasts, will yield better monetary policies than those dictated by some inflexible rule formulated and prescribed months, or even years, in advance.

QUESTIONS AND STUDY SUGGESTIONS

1. What are Professor Friedman's two "requirements for monetary policy"?
2. Why does Friedman recommend the monetary rule that the money supply should be increased at a rate of 3 to 5 percent per year? Why shouldn't the rate be higher or lower? What are Professor Chandler's objections to the monetary rule?
3. Explain: "The two writers reach different positions on the advisability of a monetary rule because they differ as to the variability of the velocity of money."

Reading 27

The Need for an "Independent" Monetary Authority: Two Views

Criticism of the appropriateness and effectiveness of monetary policy frequently leads to questioning the relatively "independent" status of the Board of Governors of the Federal Reserve System within our governmental structure. This independence has several roots: for example, the long and staggered terms (fourteen years) of Board members mean that the Board's composition cannot be significantly altered during any one president's term of office; the Federal Reserve System is internally financed and not dependent upon congressional appropriations, and so forth. Is this independence from the executive and legislative branches of government desirable for the nation's overall stabilization policy? The purpose of Reading 27 is to present two sharply conflicting views on this question.

First View: The Merits of an "Independent" Monetary Authority

J. Dewey Daane, Member of the Board of Governors, Federal Reserve System

Taking a closer look at these three main threads in the current inquiry, namely, the relationship and role of the Federal Reserve within the framework of Government, the allegation of banker domination, and the monetary policy process, it will come as no surprise to you that I do not find much to agree with in these bills.

IDENTICAL GOALS

First of all, whatever the theoretical possibilities may be of a basic conflict between the Federal Reserve and the administration, the fact is that the relationship has been and is a harmonious one. In announcing his decision to reappoint Mr. Martin as Chairman of the Board of Governors, the President described the relationship in these terms:

As Chairman of the Board of Governors, Mr. Martin has cooperated effectively in the economic policies of this administration and I look forward to a constructive working relationship in the years ahead.

As you know, the Federal Reserve System is a fully independent agency of the U.S. Government but it is essential that there exist a relationship of mutual confidence and cooperation between the Federal Reserve, the economic agencies of the administration, including espe-

From **The Federal Reserve System after Fifty Years, Volume 2:** Hearings before the Subcommittee on Domestic Finance of the Committee on Banking and Currency, 88th Cong., 2d Sess., Washington, 1964, pp. 970–973, abridged.

cially the Secretary of the Treasury, and the President.

Mr. Martin has my full confidence and I look forward to continuing to work with him and his colleagues on the Board in the interest of a strong U.S. economy.

The Federal Reserve System, after all, is a public institution. Its policies evolve within the framework of general Government policies. The primary goals of monetary policy are identical to those of Government economic policy; we, too, are governed by the Employment Act of 1946. Thus the principal objective of monetary policy is to make a maximum contribution to the attainment of the national economic goals of an adequate rate of growth, sustained high levels of production and employment, and reasonable price stability. We, too, are seeking maximum employment, production, and purchasing power.

In recent years I have been in the administration as a part of the Treasury Department and its policies, and I have also previously been on the other side of the fence as a part of the Federal Reserve and its policies. Both institutions clearly have been working toward the same dual objectives, namely, the attainment of a satisfactory rate of growth with maximum employment, and the elimination of a serious balance-of-payments problem.

From my experience both at the Treasury and the Federal Reserve it may be helpful to you if I comment somewhat further on the effective working relationships which now exist between these two agencies. There are, of course, shades of difference in view between the Federal Reserve System and the Treasury from time to time, but the same thing may be said within either the Federal Reserve or the Treasury, and in my judgment these differences are healthy. The fact of the matter is, that in the formulation of monetary policy, the Federal Reserve is as responsive to the needs of Government finance as it either should be or can be, and the Treasury, in turn, is acutely conscious of the problems which its debt management operations create for the monetary authorities. I am quite certain from my experience on both sides of the fence that it would be unreasonable to hope for any significant improvement in the technical coordination of monetary policy and debt management through the consolidation of these functions under a single head.

DANGERS OF CENTRALIZATION

This then leaves as the only significant question whether the public interest would be better served by placing the formulation of monetary policy under the domination or the detailed direction of the Secretary of the Treasury. I am convinced that this would be most unfortunate—not just for the Federal Reserve and for the Treasury in the first instance, but more importantly for the Government and the people of the country in the longer run. Both the Treasury and Federal Reserve naturally reflect two different viewpoints related to their own particular responsibilities which need to be fully reflected in their respective spheres. These responsibilities should not be centralized. In my view, it is greatly to the advantage of the Treasury that it is able to make its debt management decisions in the light of a monetary policy which is determined independently by men of high qualifications, rather than place itself in the dilemma of having to generate both monetary and debt management policies simultaneously, which would require it somehow to insulate its thinking on monetary policy in some way from its obvious and desirable zeal to finance the debt as economically as possible. I have seen at first hand in other countries the dangers involved in downgrading or subordinating monetary policy.

Again, from my own experience in serving two Secretaries of the Treasury, both of whom were able and conscientious public servants but already overburdened in terms of the tremendous responsibilities thrust upon them, I question whether as a practical matter it would be feasible for the Secretary of the Treasury to participate fully in the formulation of monetary policy. Some alternative involving delegation of authority would have to be developed and I do not believe this would be desirable.

The present arrangements for the coordination of monetary policy with the other economic policies of Government are, in fact, very effective.

Second View: The Shortcomings of an "Independent" Monetary Authority

Harry G. Johnson, Professor of Economics, University of Chicago

The argument for an independent monetary authority has two facets to it. One is the political argument that an independent monetary authority is desirable to prevent Government from being able to indulge in its natural propensity to resort to inflation. The other, which is less explicitly political, is that a stable monetary environment is essential to the proper functioning of a predominantly free enterprise society, and that an independent monetary authority is essential to maintain such a monetary environment.

THE POLITICAL ARGUMENT

The first argument seems to me utterly unacceptable in a democratic country. Indirectly, it is an argument for establishing the monetary authority as a fourth branch of the Constitution, charged with the function of forcing the Legislature and the Executive to follow conservative economic policies involving the balancing of the budget and restraint on Government expenditures. In other words, it involves the establishment of a special position in Government for the owners of one form of property—owners of money and of assets fixed in terms of money—a position which is inconsistent with the principles of democratic equality and the presumption of democracy that the purpose of government is to serve the social good.

THE ECONOMIC ARGUMENT

Turning to the second argument, granted that a stable monetary environment is desirable, the question arises whether an independent monetary authority as presently understood is sufficient to provide such stability. The argument that it is assumes that, if free of control by the Executive and Legislature, the monetary authority will govern monetary policy in the light of the long-run best interests of the economy, and will conduct its policy with flexibility and efficiency in the short run. This assumption is not consistent with the historical evidence of the behavior of monetary authorities; the evidence is rather that central banks have done little if anything to restrain inflationary policies in wartime—and war and its aftermath have been the almost exclusive source of serious inflation in the major countries in the 20th century—while in peacetime they have displayed a pronounced tendency to allow deflationary policies on the average. Moreover—I refer here particularly to the behavior of the United States and Canadian central banks in the past decade—in the short-run conduct of policy they have tended to overreact to changes in the economy and to reverse their policy with a substantial delay, thereby contributing to the economic instability that their policies are intended to combat.

These defects are in my judgment inherent in the conception, constitution, and operating responsibilities and methods of an independent monetary authority, and are unlikely to be modified greatly by gradual improvement of the techniques of central banking on the basis of accumulated experience and research. For one thing, freedom of a central bank from direct political control does not suffice to render it insensitive to contemporary political opinion. On the contrary, its position as the one agency of economic policy formation outside the normal political structure both exposes it to subtle and sustained political pressures and forces it to become a political animal on its own behalf, devoting considerable effort either to justifying its policies by reference to popularity-esteemed objectives or to denying responsibility for economic conditions and passing the buck on to the Executive or the Legislature, the result being to obfuscate the policy choices that have to be made. Secondly, the position of the central bank as controller of the money supply inevitably must bias the monetary authority—except in times of national emergency such as war—toward emphasizing the pursuit of objectives connected with the value of money—resistance

From **The Federal Reserve System after Fifty Years, Volume 2:** Hearings before the Subcommittee on Domestic Finance of the Committee on Banking and Currency, 88th Cong., 2d Sess., Washington, 1964, pp. 1192–1194, abridged.

to domestic inflation, and preservation of the international value of the currency—to the underemphasis or neglect of other objectives such as high employment and economic growth. Thirdly, the methods of monetary management, which involve the central bank concentrating its attention on money market conditions and interest rates, and on member bank reserve positions and lending, rather than on the performance of the economy in general, are extremely conducive to the behavior pattern of overreaction and delayed correction of error already mentioned.

Because it concentrates on money market and banking phenomena, rather than the effects of its policies on the quantity of money and economic activity, and because the effect of monetary policy on the economy operates with a substantial lag, the central bank is extremely likely to push its policy too far and too fast before it realizes that the policy has taken effect and begins to consider moderating it; and because the realization of effectiveness comes late, it is likely to reverse its policy too sharply. In addition, the fact that the central bank stands in a special relation to its Government and domestic economy fosters the existence of an international fellow club member relationship among central banks, a relationship congenial to the formation and propagation of policy fads in central banking. It is only on the basis of fads in central banking opinion, I believe, that one can understand the emergence of the fear of runaway inflation as a dominant motif in central bank policy statements in 1957–58.

IN SUMMARY

My own view is that the pursuit of monetary stability through the separation of monetary management from other economic policy, and its placement under an independent authority, is an illusory solution to the problem. Instead, I believe that monetary policy should be brought under the control of the Executive and Legislature in the same way as other aspects of economic policy, with the administration bearing the ultimate responsibility for monetary policy as part of economic policy in general. In making this recommendation, I must admit that there is a danger of monetary mismanagement in the pursuit of political objectives; but I consider it preferable for such mismanagement to be a clear responsibility of the administration, and accountable to the electorate.

QUESTIONS AND STUDY SUGGESTIONS

1. Why does Mr. Daane feel it is undesirable that the men responsible for fiscal policy and debt management also determine monetary policy?
2. What does Professor Johnson mean when he argues that preoccupation of an independent monetary authority with the value of money will cause it to neglect other economic goals?

Reading 28

Guideposts for Noninflationary Wage and Price Behavior

Council of Economic Advisers

Traditionally, inflation has been the consequence of excess aggregate demand. But in recent years we have found that, as the economy approaches full employment, cost-push inflation tends to occur. Reading 28 sets forth the Federal government's guidepost for noninflationary wage and price behavior. Simply put, this guidepost says that increases in wage rates should be limited to the overall rate of increase in the nation's productivity. The rationale is that if the average hourly output of workers increases by, say 2 percent, businesses can increase wages by 2 percent without experiencing any increase in labor cost per unit of output. Because wage increases limited to productivity increases keep labor cost per unit of ouput constant, there is no reason for businesses to raise the prices of their products.

There are important segments of the economy where firms are large or employees well-organized, or both. In these sectors, private parties may exercise considerable discretion over the terms of wage bargains and price decisions. Thus, at least in the short run, there is considerable room for the exercise of private power and a parallel need for the assumption of private responsibility.

THE PUBLIC INTEREST

Individual wage and price decisions assume national importance when they involve large numbers of workers and large amounts of output directly, or when they are regarded by large segments of the economy as setting a pattern. Because such decisions affect the progress of the whole economy, there is legitimate reason for public interest in their content and consequences. An informed public, aware of the significance of major wage bargains and price decisions, and equipped to judge for itself their compatibility with the national interest, can help to create an atmosphere in which the parties to such decisions will exercise their powers responsibly.

How is the public to judge whether a particular wage-price decision is in the national interest? No simple test exists, and it is not possible to set out systematically all of the many considerations which bear on such a judgment. However, since the question is of prime importance to the strength and progress of the American economy, it deserves widespread public discussion and clarification of the issues. What follows is intended as a contribution to such a discussion.

Mandatory controls in peacetime over the outcomes of wage negotiations and over individual price decisions are neither desirable in the American tradition nor practical in a diffuse and decentralized continental economy. Free collective bargaining is the vehicle for the achievement of contractual agreements on wages, fringes, and working conditions, as well

From **Economic Report of the President, 1962,** Washington, January, 1962, pp. 185–190, abridged.

as on the "web of rules" by which a large segment of industry governs the performance of work and the distribution of rewards. Similarly, final price decisions lie—and should continue to lie—in the hands of individual firms. It is, however, both desirable and practical that discretionary decisions on wages and prices recognize the national interest in the results. The guideposts suggested here as aids to public understanding are not concerned primarily with the relation of employers and employees to each other, but rather with their joint relation to the rest of the economy.

WAGES, PRICES, AND PRODUCTIVITY

If all prices remain stable, all hourly labor costs may increase as fast as economy-wide productivity, without, for that reason alone, changing the relative share of labor and non-labor incomes in total output. At the same time, each kind of income increases steadily in absolute amount. If hourly labor costs increase at a slower rate than productivity, the share of nonlabor incomes will grow or prices will fall, or both. Conversely, if hourly labor costs increase more rapidly than productivity, the share of labor incomes in the total product will increase or prices will rise, or both. It is this relationship among long-run economy-wide productivity, wages, and prices which makes the rate of productivity change an important benchmark for noninflationary wage and price behavior.

Productivity is a *guide* rather than a *rule* for appraising wage and price behavior for several reasons. First, there are a number of problems involved in measuring productivity change, and a number of alternative measures are available. Second, there is nothing immutable in fact or in justice about the distribution of the total product between labor and non-labor incomes. Third, the pattern of wages and prices among industries is and should be responsive to forces other than changes in productivity.

ALTERNATIVE MEASURES OF PRODUCTIVITY

If the rate of growth of productivity over time is to serve as a useful benchmark for wage and price behavior, there must be some meeting of minds about the appropriate methods of measuring the trend rate of increase in productivity both for industry as a whole and for individual industries. This is a large and complex subject and there is much still to be learned. The most that can be done at present is to give some indication of orders of magnitude, and of the range within which most plausible measures are likely to fall (see Table 28–1).

There are a number of conceptual problems in connection with productivity measurement which can give rise to differences in estimates of its rate of growth. Three important conceptual problems are the following:

1. Over what time interval should productivity trends be measured? Very short intervals may give excessive weight to business-cycle movements in productivity, which are not the

Table 28–1.   ANNUAL RATES OF GROWTH OF OUTPUT PER MAN-HOUR, 1909 TO 1960 (based on establishment series)

Industry series	Average annual percentage change*			
	1909 to 1960	1947 to 1960	1947 to 1954	1954 to 1960
Total private economy	2.4	3.0	3.5	2.6
Nonagriculture	2.1	2.4	2.7	2.2
Nonmanufacturing	†	2.2	2.6	1.9
Manufacturing	†	2.8	2.9	2.9
Manufacturing corrected for varying rates of capacity utilization	†	2.8	2.8	3.1

* Computed from least squares trend of the logarithms of the output per man-hour indexes.
† Not available.
SOURCES: U.S. Department of Labor and Council of Economic Advisers.

relevant standards for wage behavior. Very long intervals may hide significant breaks in trends; indeed in the United States—and in other countries as well—productivity appears to have risen more rapidly since the end of the Second World War than before. It would be wholly inappropriate for wage behavior in the 1960s to be governed by events long in the past. On the other hand, productivity in the total private economy appears to have advanced less rapidly in the second half of the postwar period than in the first.

2. Even for periods of intermediate length, it is desirable to segregate the trend movements in productivity from those that reflect business-cycle forces. Where the basic statistical materials are available, this problem can be handled by an analytical separation of trend effects and the effects of changes in the rate of capacity utilization.

3. Even apart from such difficulties, there often exist alternative statistical measures of output and labor input. The alternatives may differ conceptually or may simply be derived from different statistical sources. A difficult problem of choice may emerge, unless the alternative measures happen to give similar results.

Selected measures of the rate of growth of productivity in different sectors of the economy for different time periods are shown in Table 28–1. Several measures are given because none of the single figures is clearly superior for all purposes.

THE SHARE OF LABOR INCOME

The proportions in which labor and nonlabor incomes share the product of industry have not been immutable throughout American history, nor can they be expected to stand forever where they are today. It is desirable that labor and management should bargain explicitly about the distribution of the income of particular firms or industries. It is, however, undesirable that they should bargain implicitly about the general price level. Excessive wage settlements which are paid for through price increases in major industries put direct pressure on the general price level and produce spillover and imitative effects throughout the economy. Such settlements may fail to redistribute income within the industry involved;

rather they redistribute income between that industry and other segments of the economy through the mechanism of inflation.

PRICES AND WAGES IN INDIVIDUAL INDUSTRIES

What are the guideposts which may be used in judging whether a particular price or wage decision may be inflationary? The desired objective is a stable price level, within which particular prices rise, fall, or remain stable in response to economic pressures. Hence, price stability within any particular industry is not necessarily a correct guide to price and wage decisions in that industry. It is possible, however, to describe in broad outline a set of guides which, if followed, would preserve over-all price stability while still allowing sufficient flexibility to accommodate objectives of efficiency and equity. These are not arbitrary guides. They describe—briefly and no doubt incompletely—how prices and wage rates would behave in a smoothly functioning competitive economy operating near full employment. Nor do they constitute a mechanical formula for determining whether a particular price or wage decision is inflationary. They will serve their purpose if they suggest to the interested public a useful way of approaching the appraisal of such a decision.

If, as a point of departure, we assume no change in the relative shares of labor and nonlabor incomes in a particular industry, then a general guide may be advanced for noninflationary wage behavior, and another for noninflationary price behavior. Both guides, as will be seen, are only first approximations.

THE GENERAL GUIDEPOST

The general guide for noninflationary wage behavior is that the rate of increase in wage rates (including fringe benefits) in each industry be equal to the trend rate of over-all productivity increase. General acceptance of this guide would maintain stability of labor cost per unit of output for the economy as a whole —though not of course for individual industries.

The general guide for noninflationary price behavior calls for price reduction if the industry's rate of productivity increase exceeds the over-all rate—for this would mean declining unit labor costs; it calls for an appropriate increase in price if the opposite relationship prevails; and it calls for stable prices if the two rates of productivity increase are equal.

MODIFICATIONS

These are advanced as general guideposts. To reconcile them with objectives of equity and efficiency, specific modifications must be made to adapt them to the circumstances of particular industries. If all of these modifications are made, each in the specific circumstances to which it applies, they are consistent with stability of the general price level. Public judgments about the effects on the price level of particular wage or price decisions should take into account the modifications as well as the general guides. The most important modifications are the following:

1. Wage rate increases would exceed the general guide rate in an industry which would otherwise be unable to attract sufficient labor; or in which wage rates are exceptionally low compared with the range of wages earned elsewhere by similar labor, because the bargaining position of workers has been weak in particular local labor markets.

2. Wage rate increases would fall short of the general guide rate in an industry which could not provide jobs for its entire labor force even in times of generally full employment; or in which wage rates are exceptionally high compared with the range of wages earned elsewhere by similar labor, because the bargaining position of workers has been especially strong.

3. Prices would rise more rapidly, or fall more slowly, than indicated by the general guide rate in an industry in which the level of profits was insufficient to attract the capital required to finance a needed expansion in capacity; or in which costs other than labor costs had risen.

4. Prices would rise more slowly, or fall more rapidly, than indicated by the general guide in an industry in which the relation of productive capacity to full employment demand shows the desirability of an outflow of capital from the industry; or in which costs other than labor costs have fallen; or in which excessive market power has resulted in rates of profit substantially higher than those earned elsewhere on investments of comparable risk.

OTHER CONSIDERATIONS

It is a measure of the difficulty of the problem that even these complex guideposts leave out of account several important considerations. Although output per man-hour rises mainly in response to improvements in the quantity and quality of capital goods with which employees are equipped, employees are often able to improve their performance by means within their own control. It is obviously in the public interest that incentives be preserved which would reward employees for such efforts.

Also, in connection with the use of measures of over-all productivity gain as benchmarks for wage increases, it must be borne in mind that average hourly labor costs often change through the process of up- or down-grading, shifts between wage and salaried employment, and other forces. Such changes may either add to or subtract from the increment which is available for wage increases under the over-all productivity guide.

Finally, it must be reiterated that collective bargaining within an industry over the division of the proceeds between labor and non-labor income is not necessarily disruptive of over-all price stability. The relative shares can change within the bounds of noninflationary price behavior. But when a disagreement between management and labor is resolved by passing the bill to the rest of the economy, the bill is paid in depreciated currency to the ultimate advantage of no one.

It is no accident that productivity is the central guidepost for wage settlements. Ultimately, it is rising output per man hour which must yield the ingredients of a rising standard of living. Growth in productivity makes it possible for real wages and real profits to rise side by side.

Rising productivity is the foundation of the country's leadership of the free world, enabling it to earn in world competition the means to discharge its commitments overseas. Rapid advance of productivity is the key to stability of the price level as money incomes rise, to fundamental improvement in the balance of international payments, and to growth in the nation's capacity to meet the challenges of the 1960s at home and abroad. That is why policy to accelerate economic growth stresses investments in science and technology, plant and equipment, education and training—the basic sources of future gains in productivity.

QUESTIONS AND STUDY SUGGESTIONS

1. What general wage-price policy does the Council of Economic Advisers suggest labor and management follow? Explain why this guidepost is noninflationary.

2. What problems might be involved in applying this guidepost? What exceptions are acknowledged by the CEA?

Reading 29

Wages and Prices by Formula?

Arthur F. Burns, Professor of Economics, Columbia University

The government's wage-price guidepost (Reading 28) is not universally accepted as either an effective or a desirable component of public policy. In Reading 29 Arthur F. Burns questions the usefulness of the guidepost. On the one hand, the application and administration of the guidepost entail numerous practical difficulties. On the other hand, it is Burns's position that the wage-price guidepost may have highly undesirable effects upon the economy. For example, application of the guidepost may thwart the operation of competitive forces and thereby dilute the efficiency of the economy. More important, it is held that the wage-price guideline may constitute a significant step toward outright government control over wages and prices.

Let us try to visualize a little more definitely how the CEA's wage-price guideposts, if they were generally and fully respected, would work out in practice.

WAGES AND PRICES

Statistical records stretching back into the nineteenth century demonstrate that, although the over-all productivity of our economy occasionally declines, its trend has been steadily upward. If this continues to be true, as we may reasonably suppose, general observance of the guidelines will result in higher wages every year, regardless of the stage of the business cycle or the level of unemployment or the state of the balance of payments. The rise of wages will be the same, on the average, in years of recession as in years of prosperity; but in any given recession the rise of wages could easily be larger than in the preceding years of prosperity. Furthermore, the average

From Arthur F. Burns, "Wages and Prices by Formula?" **Harvard Business Review**, March–April, 1965, pp. 55–64, abridged. Reprinted by permission.

wage will tend to rise in any given year by the same percentage in every firm, regardless of its profitability or the state of the market for different kinds of labor.

However, general observance of the guidepost for prices will not freeze individual prices or the relations among them. What it would tend to freeze is (1) the general level of prices and (2) the ratio of individual prices to unit labor costs of production. The tendency of the price-cost ratio to remain constant will be stronger in some industries than in others. Strictly speaking, the guidepost for prices specifies merely that the ratio of price to unit labor cost of production should not rise; it does not argue against a decline of the price-cost ratio. Hence, firms or industries experiencing a weak demand for their products or keen foreign competition may need to be content with prices that decline relative to their unit labor costs. On the other hand, firms or industries that are favored in the marketplace would be unable to raise prices relative to their unit labor costs even if their incoming orders were many times as large as their production. Nor would they be able to raise prices to compensate for increases in costs of production other than those of labor.

INCOME SHARES

The broad effect of these tendencies would be to keep more or less constant the percentage share of the national income—or of national output—going to labor. Changes in the use of capital relative to the use of labor, whether upward or downward, could still have a large influence on the size of the national income but not on the proportion of income accruing to labor. Unless major shifts occurred in the occupational or industrial distribution of employment, any fluctuation in labor's percentage share of the national income would be due primarily to the discrepancy between the movement of over-all productivity in a particular year and the corresponding trend increase. Nonlabor income, in the aggregate, would also tend to be a constant percentage of the national income.

It is well to bear in mind, however, that since profits are only a fraction of nonlabor income, the share of profits in the total national income could either rise or decline. In the postwar period, the amount paid by corpora-

tions on account of excises, customs duties, property taxes, licensing fees, and other indirect taxes has risen more rapidly than their net output. If this trend continues, the income share of investors in the corporate sector will tend to undergo a persistent decline, while that of labor will tend to remain constant.

THROTTLING OF COMPETITION

In the hypothetical economy that I have sketched, monopolies—whether of business or labor—would no longer have the power to push up the price level. Put more precisely, if trade unions and business firms complied voluntarily with the guidelines, they would relinquish any market power that they have not yet used or that they might gain in the future. This is worth noting, but it is not the main point.

The *fundamental* point of the preceding analysis is that general observance of the guideposts would throttle the forces of competition no less effectively than those of monopoly. The point is important because, unlike much of the rest of the world, the rivalry among U.S. business firms is very keen. Even in industries where a few corporations dominate the market —as in the case of automobiles, steel, and aluminum—each corporation competes actively against the others in its industry, against rival products of other industries, and against foreign suppliers. Competition in labor markets is also stronger than casual references to labor monopoly may suggest. After all, only a little over a fourth of the population working for wages or salaries is unionized, and many of the trade unions are weak. By and large, it is competition—not monopoly—that has vast sweep and power in our everyday life. Since free competitive markets would virtually cease to exist in an economy that observed the guidelines, this transformation of the economy merits serious reflection.

To be sure, compliance with the guidelines would be voluntary in the economy we are considering. That, however, may not mean much. For when economic freedom is not exercised, it is no longer a part of life. As far as I can see, an economy in which wages and prices are set voluntarily according to a formula suggested by the government would be almost indistinguishable from an economy in which wages and prices are directly fixed by governmental authorities. In either case—

. . . the movement of resources toward uses that are favored by the buying public would be impeded;

. . . the tendency to economize on the use of what happens to be especially scarce, whether it be materials or labor or equipment, would be weakened;

. . . since prices will no longer tend to equate demand and supply in individual markets, some form of rationing would need to be practiced.

In all likelihood, therefore, a shift from our present market economy to one of voluntary compliance with the guidelines would adversely affect efficiency. It would also adversely affect the rate of economic growth and the rate of improvement of the general standard of living.

ARE THE GUIDES WORKABLE?

This theoretical sketch of how our economy would work if the guidelines were generally and fully observed has blinked institutional factors—such as the adjustments caused by the disappearance of auction markets, the new role of trade unions, and so on. Moreover, our theoretical sketch has tacitly assumed that voluntary compliance with the guidelines is merely a matter of will. Life is not that simple. Even if everyone responded to the government's plea for "cooperation" and sought faithfully to act in accordance with the guidelines, it would frequently be difficult or actually impossible to do so.

There is, first of all, a vast gap in our statistical arsenal. To comply with the guideline for *wages*, businessmen would need to know the trend increase of the over-all output of the nation per man-hour. Once this highly complex magnitude had been estimated by the government, it would presumably be subjected to outside review, revised if need be, and accompanied by a specification of the boundaries of the year (if a year be the interval) to which it would apply. All firms dealing with labor, except those newly established, would then know what wage adjustment was expected of them.

Compliance with the *price* guideline would be infinitely harder. For this purpose, every company would need to know the trend increase in the productivity of its own industry and how this increase compares with the trend increase of over-all productivity of the econ-

omy. Such information is not generally available, nor is it readily usable.

APPLYING THE INDEXES

The productivity indexes now being published, besides being often out of date, lump together a great variety of products. In time, more detailed and more current indexes of productivity will doubtless be constructed, but there are limits to what is statistically feasible. Even if measures of this type become available for each of a thousand or ten thousand industries, much confusion or perplexity will still remain:

1. Should a manufacturer of bricks, for example, be guided in his pricing by an index of productivity for the stone, clay, and glass group or by an index confined to brick manufacture?

2. If the latter, is the pertinent index a nationwide measure, one confined to his region, or perhaps to his locality or plant?

3. How should a manufacturing firm proceed when its output is not standardized or when it makes a hundred different items, instead of just one product?

4. If the appropriate index is not available, as may long remain the case for many firms, especially in the service trades, what is the best "proxy" for it?

5. Will the judgment of a company's management on such issues, even if made entirely in good faith, be acceptable to others—such as its trade union, the Council of Economic Advisers, or the general public—who also seek only what is right?

Better statistics on productivity will reduce these difficulties; however, they cannot possibly remove them.

CHANGES IN WORK FORCE

Another puzzling problem would be posed by changes in the composition of labor that is used in industry. Consider, for example, the case of a company that has recently decided to employ more skilled workers of different sorts and less unskilled labor:

Since skilled labor is compensated at a higher rate, the average wage per hour that is paid by the company to its workers will go up, quite apart from any wage increase that may be needed for the individual grades of labor. Let us now suppose that the wage guidepost calls for an increase of, say, 3 percent. Then the company's employees will naturally expect an increase of this size in their individual rates of pay.

But may not the company's personnel executive, who has become steeped in the mathematics of the guidelines, properly insist that the average wage has already gone up this much or more on account of the more intensive use of skilled labor and that no increase of wage rates is therefore warranted by the government's guideline? Will the trade union's representative grasp this statistical subtlety? Will he not argue that the guideline requires an increase of 3%, that other organizations are putting through such increases, and that simple justice requires that the same be done by this company?

Suppose that the personnel executive perseveres and finally convinces the union's representative. Will the latter, in turn, be able to persuade the company's employees? Can we even be sure that the company's board of directors will be convinced by the argument of its personnel officer?

In view of modern trends that emphasize the use of higher skills, this sort of difficulty would be bound to occur frequently in an economy of voluntary compliance.

OTHER PITFALLS AND PUZZLES

Another problem that businessmen and trade-union leaders would need to face is whether the modifications of the guideposts that the Council of Economic Advisers has officially sanctioned apply in a particular case. In assuming, as I have, a general willingness to comply with the guidelines, I have not meant to abstract from human nature entirely. Since the modifications suggested by the Council are phrased in very general terms, men acting in good faith may feel that their situation is precisely the kind of rare case that permits some departure from the guidelines. But will business managers and labor leaders always or even frequently agree in their interpretation of what modifications are permissible? In any event, is it not likely that the modifications will turn out to be numerous, rather than, as now intended by the Administration, relatively few?

In view of these and many other problems that are bound to arise in practice, the guide-lines would prove unworkable over a very large segment of industry, even if everyone sought conscientiously to observe them. To deal with this critical difficulty, a new governmental apparatus might need to be established; its function would be to spell out detail rules and to interpret them in individual cases. Although there is no way of telling just how such an agency would work, it seems reasonable to expect that not a few of its clarifying rules and interpretations would be arbitrary, that its advisory rulings would at times involve considerable delay and thereby cause some economic trouble, and that the rulings themselves would have at least some inflationary bias. These factors inevitably cast a cloud over the preceding analysis of how an economy of voluntary compliance would function, but they hardly make the prospect more inviting.

SPECTER OF CONTROLS

I have as yet said nothing about the aspect of guidepost policy that has aroused the most skepticism—namely, the likelihood of general observance on a voluntary basis. In recent years unemployment has been fairly large, and many industries have had sufficient capacity to increase output readily. Under such conditions, upward pressure on prices cannot be great. Even so, the guidelines have been sharply criticized or defied by powerful segments of the business and labor community. The critical test of the inhibiting power of the guidelines will come, of course, when both labor and commodity markets become appreciably tighter—and this test may come soon. If the recent wage settlement in the automobile industry is at all indicative, expectations of a high degree of compliance with the guidelines are hardly warranted. Similar experiments in other countries also suggest that general price stability will not long be maintained through voluntary restraint.

But once the government in power has committed itself to a policy, it may become difficult to move off in a new direction. A strong commitment to the policy of the guidelines inevitably means that any extensive private defiance would, besides frustrating the government's anti-inflation policy, injure its prestige. There is always a possibility, therefore, that failure to comply voluntarily with the guidelines will be followed by some coercive measure. This might initially take the form, as has frequently been proposed, of a review by a governmental board of the facts surrounding the price or wage changes that are being contemplated. The thought behind proposals of this nature is that once the facts are clearly developed, the force of public opinion will ordinarily suffice to ensure "responsible" action by corporations and trade unions.

No one can be sure whether this expectation will be fulfilled. But if it is, the governmental review board will have virtually become an agency for fixing prices and wages. If, on the other hand, the board's reports were flouted with any frequency, the next step might well be outright price and wage fixing by the government. It would seem, therefore, that from whatever angle we examine the guidelines, direct controls pop up dangerously around the corner.

INCIPIENT REALITIES

This danger must not be dismissed as an illusion. Although the guidelines are still in their infancy, they have already hardened. Nor has the evolution of the Administration's thinking concerning the guidelines been confined to a literary plane. In April 1962, only three months after the announcement of the guidelines, the Administration moved sternly to force the leading steel companies to cancel the price increases that they had just posted. This interference with the workings of a private market had no clear sanction in law, and it caused consternation in business circles. Fortunately, a crisis was avoided by a prompt and concerted effort of the Administration, in which President Kennedy himself took the leading part, to restore business confidence.

Since then, the government has been more cautious. But it has continued to espouse the need for moderation in the matter of wages and prices, and now and then has even gently rattled its sword. Early in 1964 President Johnson requested the Council to reaffirm the guideposts. He emphasized his commitment to this policy by adding that he would "keep a close watch on price and wage developments, with the aid of an early warning system which is being set up." Last summer, when intimations of a rise in the price of steel appeared in the press, the President lost no time in declaring that such action would "strongly conflict with our national interest in price stability."

TOWARD SOUNDER POLICIES

As this account of recent history suggests, the guidepost policy may, under the pressure of events, move our nation's economy in an authoritarian direction. The danger may not yet be large, in view of prevailing political attitudes, but it could become serious in a time of trouble or emergency. And this is not the only risk, as I shall presently note. However, the fact that many citizens both within and outside government favor the guidelines must also be considered, for it means that they see smaller risks or larger advantages in this policy than I do.

It may readily be granted that the guidepost policy has the meritorious objective of blunting the power of monopolists to push up the price level. This is the feature of the policy that its proponents often stress. Indeed, they are apt to argue that it matters little in practice whether or not the bulk of the economic community pays any attention to the guidelines— as long as the major corporations and trade unions do so.

But if the guidelines are circumscribed in this fashion, they are still subject to the criticism of interfering with the competitive forces of the markets in which many major corporations actually operate. Moreover, the absence of a precise indication of what firms, industries, or trade unions are covered by the guidelines can create a mood of uncertainty that will militate against compliance. Not least important, the effectiveness of the guidelines in curbing inflation becomes doubtful when their application is restricted. For the very limitation on wage and price increases in the guideline sector of the economy would facilitate increases in the uncovered sector whenever an expansive economic policy generated a monetary demand that grew faster than the supply of goods and services.

Another argument frequently advanced in favor of the guideposts is that if they were in fact respected on a sufficient scale, then profit margins would tend to be maintained and the chances of prolonging the current business expansion would therefore be improved. This consideration is bound to count in men's thinking at a time when our nation is striving to reduce unemployment and to spread prosperity.

We must not, however, become so absorbed in today's problems that we overlook those that will haunt us in a later day. If the guidelines may stretch out the expansion now by helping to maintain the relatively high profit margins of prosperity, may they not at some later time stretch out contraction by serving to maintain the low profit margins of recession?

Let me add, also, that I recognize that the guideline policy was adopted by the Administration only after it had given serious consideration to alternatives. The thought of its economists apparently is that, in general:

1. Monetary and fiscal tools must be used to promote expansion as long as the economy is not operating at full employment.

2. Other devices must therefore be employed (in the absence of full employment) to prevent inflation.

3. Policies aiming to increase competition or to improve productivity cannot accomplish much in the short run or cannot be pushed hard for political reasons.

4. Direct controls of wages and prices cannot and should not be seriously considered under peacetime conditions.

5. Consequently, there is only one major way left for curbing immediate inflation—namely, through devices of exhortation.

6. And the guidelines for wages and prices are merely a promising specific application of the technique of exhortation.

LOCUS OF RESPONSIBILITY

Space will not permit me to unravel this complicated argument, but I at least want to suggest why I think it may be faulty. Once the government looks to trade unions and business firms to stave off inflation, there is a danger that it will not discharge adequately its own traditional responsibility of controlling the money supply and of maintaining an environment of competition. In the past our own and other governments have often found it convenient to blame profiteers, corporations, or trade unions for a rising price level. Only rarely have they pointed the finger of blame at their own policies—such as flooding the economy with newly created currency or bank deposits.

To the extent that the government relies on private compliance with its guidelines for prices and wages, it may more easily be tempted to push an expansive monetary and fiscal policy beyond prudent limits. Besides, it may fail to resist strongly enough the political pressure for higher minimum wages, larger trade union immunities, higher farm price supports, higher import duties, more import quotas, larger stockpiling programs, and other protective measures that serve either to raise prices or to prevent them from falling.

One of the major needs of our times is to give less heed to special interest groups and to reassert the paramount interest of consumers in vigorous competition. The political obstacles to reducing artificial props for prices are undoubtedly formidable. However, reforms of this type—supplemented by more stringent antitrust laws, effective enforcement of these laws, and reasonable steps to curb featherbedding—are likely to contribute more to the maintenance of reasonable stability in the general price level than will the guidelines for wages and prices on which we have recently come to rely.

QUESTIONS AND STUDY SUGGESTIONS

1. Discuss the author's major reservations and criticisms of the CEA's wage-price guidepost.
2. What practical problems might be encountered in applying the guideposts to specific firms and industries?
3. Explain the author's contention that the application of the wage-price guidepost will tend to (a) reduce competition; (b) increase government control over the operation of the economy; and (c) weaken monetary and fiscal policy.

Reading 30

Public Policies to Deal with Inflation Caused by Market Power

Emmette S. Redford, Professor of Government, University of Texas

In the reading, Emmette S. Redford deals with cost-push inflation—a problem which the existence of strong unions and big businesses poses for society as a whole. Inflation might result not only from an excess of total spending but also from the concentration of market power in the hands of both unions and businesses. The author outlines four possible methods of dealing with inflation caused by market power: (1) reliance upon such corrective forces in the economy as, for example, countervailing power and the social responsibility of unions and businesses; (2) the control of total demand through monetary and fiscal policy; (3) a more vigorous and comprehensive application of the antitrust laws; and (4) the withdrawal of the support of private monopoly by the Federal government. Discounting the potentialities of these four policies, Redford recommends that consideration be given to government surveillance, review, or, in the extreme, direct control of specific wage and price increases. He fully recognizes, however, that the political and administrative problems associated with public consideration of wage and price increases would be substantial.

This paper deals with the inflationary threat inherent in wage setting and pricing practices in large organizations of labor and capital. It states the problem of cost-push inflation, discusses generally and briefly the applicability and adequacy of various approaches in public policy to the problem, and points up the specific administrative problems involved in direct government limitation or surveillance of wage and price increases by organizations with considerable market power.

INFLATIONARY CONCENTRATIONS OF MARKET POWER

It can be assumed that there is a public interest in avoidance of inflation, and that inflation is manifested in the price level. There is also evidence now that inflation may be caused in two ways. One is through an increase in demand so as to put pressure upon the supply of goods, which is commonly referred to as demand or demand-pull inflation. The other is through an independent increase in wages or prices and is called sellers' or cost-push inflation.

Key economic decisions on wages and prices are now made for vital areas of the economy by organizations of great size and power. Wages are fixed by agreement between organizations; such wages are now often referred to as administered wages. Prices may be fixed by organizations in accord with objectives desired to be attained and such prices determine or influence the pricing levels for an industry or product; such prices are sometimes called ad-

From Emmette S. Redford, **Potential Public Policies to Deal with Inflation Caused by Market Power,** Study Paper No. 10 prepared in connection with the Study of Employment, Growth, and Price Levels, Joint Economic Committee, 86th Cong., 1st Sess., Washington, 1959, pp. 1–10, 27–29.

ministered prices. Whenever one or more organizations acting singly, concurrently, or jointly have the ability through the administration of wages or prices to exact more income for the amount and quality of labor, capital, commodity or service supplied than could be obtained in the absence of such organizational action, they may be said to have market power.

The effective exercise of market power may contribute to inflation in several ways. The first is through the downstream movement (the passing on) of the particular item of cost which is controlled. For example, market power over producers' prices of automobiles or steel will be reflected in succeeding stages of distribution and ultimately in consumers' costs. Because successive sellers often increase their dollars-and-cents markups more than the increase in their purchase costs, the amount of the price increase will swell as the commodity moves through successive stages of production and distribution. This pyramiding of prices through the pricing practices of successive groups of sellers enlarges the inflationary effect of original cost increases in producer industries. Second, market power may contribute to inflation if exercised under such conditions as to create a pattern to be followed in other industries, thus creating lateral downstream movements of pyramiding prices which further enlarge the effect of the original exercise of market power. This kind of enlargement of the effects of cost increases is now familiar as a result of the pattern-setting wage negotiation and the pattern-setting price movement of firms in a leadership position. Third, exercises of market power may give rise to repetitive cycles of wage-price or price-wage increases. These cycles, after the manner of the chicken and the egg cycle, may lead to an inflationary spiral which feeds upon itself. Thus three types of chain reaction may be created by the exercise of market power: the direct, pyramiding, downstream; the pattern-setting, pyramiding, lateral; and the wage-price or price-wage cycle.

There is, therefore, latent inflation in the existence of market power. When concentrations of power are sufficient to create market power these concentrations become inflationary concentrations of power; that is, they are capable of producing inflationary effects. This capability creates the threat of sellers' inflation. Whether such inflation actually develops will be dependent upon the exercise of market power in situations which create one or more of the types of chain reaction described above and upon the nonexistence of measures to counteract these effects.

BASIC APPROACHES IN POLICY

The existence of market power is now widely recognized as a cause for deep concern. The business community is concerned over the existence of this power in labor organizations. Thus, a statement prepared for the Chamber of Commerce of the United States says that "cost-induced inflation is becoming a very real possibility, if not an alarming probability," and finds the cause in the "monopoly power of organized labor." Labor organizations are concerned over the existence of the power in industrial organizations. The AFL-CIO Executive Council has declared:

The ability of the executives of the dominant corporations in strategic industries, such as steel, auto, and oil refining, to raise prices regardless of economic conditions in recent years, represents a major problem that must be solved if the Nation is to achieve relative price stability.

Others in a more independent position than either of these contending forces are concerned over the phenomena accounting for both statements, namely, the concentration of power in organizations.

Americans have always been concerned over concentrations of power. Once it was a concern over the concentration of political power. In the Constitution-framing period of our Nation, Americans learned how to limit power in two ways: by checking power with power through separation of powers, checks and balances, and federalism; and by direct limitations on the use of power through bills of rights and judicial review. In the following century Americans were alarmed over growing concentrations of private economic power. Again they learned how to use two methods for limiting power: by restraint on its growth and exercise through antitrust laws, and by direct limitation on rates of charge through regulatory agencies.

The problem of concentrated private power has now been presented in new ways. Unfortunately, there appears to be no simple way of dealing with it in its present forms. The policy issues are extremely complicated and baffling, and it is probable that the responsible Government official will find only partial answers and that even these will be found in several complementary approaches. It will be helpful to refer briefly to the several lines of approach which are proposed as answers to the problem of inflation or of concentrated power to see how far they may provide an answer to inflationary concentrations of private power. There are, in general, five lines of approach suggested for public policy.

Corrective Forces within the Economy

One line of approach suggested is that Government depend upon the corrective forces operating with the economy. Three types of argument are currently advanced in favor of this approach.

One argument is that society will be best protected by the conscience and restraint of those who possess market power. The argument has been set forth by A. A. Berle as the means of meeting the general problem of corporate powers. In his exposition the argument is not for a completely let-alone policy by Government, for it is assumed that the conscience of man can be buttressed by legal standards of trusteeship developed in courts or in legislatures.

It is likely that courts and legislatures will indeed develop additional standards of trusteeship for organizations of capital and of labor; at the same time, it may be doubted whether legal standards of trusteeship, whatever they may accomplish in meeting other problems of private power, can define standards of restraint on wage requests and price changes which can be made effective primarily through the conscience of men. A recent study of "Pricing in Big Business" reports that corporate officials appear to be sensitive to public reaction to their policies and to feel a sense of public responsibility, and that many of the large corporations tried to hold the price line following the end of World War II; assertions of similar attitudes among labor leaders have also been made; but it may nevertheless be too much to expect that management and labor will be able consistently to view specific questions of wages and prices in terms of public interests rather than of the interests of the groups which they are under compulsion to represent.

Another argument is that of countervailing power, which is that private concentrations of power beget opposed concentrations. The argument is supported by the fact that concentrations of labor have arisen to meet concentrations of capital and that concentrations of buyers or sellers have often arisen to meet concentrations of the other. The conclusion is drawn that the public is protected by a new check and balance system, that between organizations; to the extent that the new system works the public need not be concerned with the failure of the old checks and the balances assumed to operate in the competitive market. The wise course for Government to follow, it is suggested, is to support movements for the rise of countervailing power, as it did for labor through the National Labor Relations Act, or to aid those areas of the economy where countervailing power has not arisen, as it has done for agriculture.

Although countervailing power may be protection for the public, both critics and proponents of the idea have noted that it may not always exist or may not be operative. Large organizations of buyers and sellers may collaborate with each other and pass the cost to the consumer or freeze out competitors; many organizations are either not faced with opposing organizations of power or are faced with opposing organizations with too little strength to resist; in some industries vertical integration has extended the power of organizations all the way from the producer to the consumer. Yet the chief limitation on the protection of countervailing power is that noted by the original proponent of the idea. It is that in times when demand is high and relatively inflexible, buyers find little cause to resist the cost-push pressure of sellers. It becomes easier to accept the increased cost and pass it along. Even the will of the managers of industry to resist the demands of labor is weakened. Labor-management agreements become inflationary because there is no countervailing power in consumers. In other words, cost-push of labor, the market power of industry, and the demand-pull of buyers all contribute to upward movement of prices. It may be added that even the first two of these may sometimes, without demand sufficient to induce full use of capacity, lead to sectoral inflation. It is not likely, therefore, that policymakers will accept countervailing power as sufficient in itself to protect the public interest.

Still another argument is that of freedom of enterprise. This argument is often presented as a denial of the existence of effective market power. In this form, it is an argument that organizations cannot on a sustained basis exact an excess above what a free market will allow. Critics would answer that this is not true, or that even if it were true the power to exert temporary control or influence could set in motion a chain of inflationary forces. The argument for freedom of enterprise is also presented as a claim that, whatever may be the adverse effects of private market power, these cannot be as bad as the effects of public power exerted through legislatures and administrators. Presented in this way the issue appears to be between those who trust private power and those who trust public power. Many, however, will be interested in searching for ways by which public power may be exerted to avoid excessive uses of private power without leading into the main dangers in use of public power. This desire will lead to consideration of other approaches in policy.

Demand Controls

A second line of approach is through controls over demand, chiefly through monetary and fiscal measures.

The reason for support for this policy is that management of monetary and fiscal measures may dampen demand pressures and thus prevent sellers from obtaining price increases. But such measures are most effective for the highly competitive sectors of the economy and may "touch lightly, or even exempt," the markets where firms are large and prices are administered. To be effective in markets where there is concentrated market power, monetary and fiscal controls would probably have to be so drastic that they would create recession in the economy generally. It would be economically undesirable and politically infeasible to use monetary and fiscal controls on so drastic a scale.

There is increasing recognition, as stated at the first of this paper, that there are two broad elements in the problem of inflation. The demand-pull element may be met by general demand controls (monetary and fiscal measures) supplemented perhaps with selective demand controls (e.g., restrictions on installment buying or on inventory buildup). The cost-push element may require other types of controls especially adapted to the prevention or control of bridgehead situations which would have a major inflationary effect.

Antitrust

A third approach is maintenance or restoration of competition through antitrust.

A fuller realization of the potentials of antitrust could be one means of preventing inflation through exercise of market power. Alertness in detection and vigor in enforcement may narrow the range of collusive and coercive practices. Effectiveness in enforcement could be increased by granting the Department of Justice power to obtain information through civil investigation demands. Further barriers to concentration of power could be erected through legislation extending the antimerger provision of the Clayton Act to banks and by preventing mergers until these could be studied by a governmental agency. Adoption of some rather arbitrary legislative tests on legality of business conduct might simplify standards of enforcement and expand the role of antitrust. Selected industries of high concentration and chain-producing effects could be studied to see whether enlargement of competitive forces, either under existing or new laws, would be possible. Actions of a rather drastic type on the antitrust front could presumably prevent the development of situations which would lead to consideration later of much more drastic remedies, including price controls of some sort.

Nevertheless, the limitations of antitrust are of common knowledge. Periods of weak enforcement or of weakening judicial construction, limited funds for enforcement and prolonged litigation, loopholes such as those which have characterized section 7 of the Clayton Act, difficulties of unraveling tangled skeins of corporate relationship or of breaking apart a merged enterprise, judicial requirement of complete market analysis in place of acceptance of per se doctrines—these and other difficulties are known. More significant perhaps, the nature of the industrial problem has changed. Prevention of collusion and coercion, and of monopoly, does not mean that managerial leadership in high concentration situations cannot set the pattern of price and production in an industry. New adventures in antitrust along bold new lines might be required if the problem of market power was to be fully dealt with through this method.

Even more baffling are the issues presented by the proposals to solve the wage-push problem by expansion of antitrust prohibitions with respect to labor organizations. These proposals take two forms. One is to prevent the exercise of labor power to control product markets, as for example through maintenance of prices or prevention of entry of new employers. There is much argument for clarification and expansion of legal restriction on such exercises of labor power, but the practical problems in definition of types of action to be covered are difficult and this form of public action would in all probability not materially affect the potentialities for wage-push inflation. The second form of the proposals is for limitation on the market power of unions in negotiating wages and other labor benefits. Insofar as such proposals relate to labor practices, such as secondary boycotts and "hot cargo" clauses, the established approach in Government legislation is to seek to deal with these under the basic labor regulatory statute (Labor-Management Relations Act) rather than the basic business regulatory statutes (antitrust laws); Congress has already given considerable attention to problems of this kind. The plain fact is, however, that legislation on labor practices may have little effect upon the bargaining power of most big unions. Moreover, insofar as such proposals encompass limitation of industrywide or multiple-unit bargaining there are many problems. Some think marketwide bargaining is desirable. Some think it is preferable to whipsaw tactics through which a union threatens each employer in turn with a strike; a ban on multiple-unit bargaining would probably not be effective without a limitation on multiple-unit union organization. So drastic a step is not likely, for it runs counter to traditional public policy with respect to unionization and would meet powerful political opposition. There may, it may be concluded, be need for study of the applicability of the antitrust approach to new types of market power, but it is not likely that the problem of wage-push inflation will be met adequately by this approach.

Withdrawal of Government Support for Market Power

Another approach would be to retreat from governmental measures which have the effect of supporting or protecting private market power. This could include retreat from a considerable number of Government price-prop and price-protective measures.

Many Government policies tend to establish a protective shield around market power. Among those which may have this effect are the following:

(a) Protective tariffs and quotas.

(b) Resale price maintenance laws.

(c) Production controls for oil.

(d) Patent grants.

(e) Government—especially defense—purchasing and disposal policies.

(f) Safeguards for rights of unionization and collective bargaining.

(g) Protections against competition and rate reductions in regulated industries.

The listing of these measures underscores certain basic realities with respect to public policy affecting price levels. Public policy encompasses many objectives which may conflict with that of preventing inflation, including such objectives as national security, conservation of resources, and support of the purchasing power of various groups. The public official will take account of varied economic and non-economic objectives and make choices among policy objectives which are in conflict with each other.

It may be that developing consciousness of the potential impact of private market power on the economy will lead to more caution in creation of protective shields for private groups. On the other hand, it is apparent that the motivations which have led to the various public policies will not disappear and hence that there will be no general retreat from these policies. It may be expected that a government that is responsive through representative institutions will yield to many group demands which have the effect of sustaining or increasing price levels.

Public Consideration of Wage and Price Increases

The inadequacies of internal corrective forces, the ineffectiveness of demand-limiting controls of monetary and fiscal types as restraints upon sellers' inflation, the imperfections of antitrust law and ineffectiveness of antitrust enforcement, and the unlikelihood of general retreat from price-prop and price-protective policies probably account for the recent suggestions for public consideration of wage and price increases. The proposals for public consideration all look to some type of executive or administrative consideration of specific price and/or wage increases.

The proposals vary from mere surveillance and publicity to public determination for one or a few industries. They may be arranged to show an order of progression of increasing severity.

1. Notice. Firms of great size and power would be required to give notice of intention to increase prices to some public authority. Such proposals for notice always include one or more of the following means of public follow-up action.

2. Hearings. Hearings might accompany notice requirements being either (a) mandatory, or mandatory unless a finding of lack of necessity was made, or (b) optional, within the discretion of the public authority designated to hold hearings. Or hearings might be held in the absence of notice requirements whenever economic stability was, in the opinion of the President or other authority, threatened by a prospective price and/or wage increase. In the former case law would require notice and hearing; in the latter it would provide only for hearing on an intervention basis. Notice and hearing for a category of industries or products would require a standing agency to administer the hearing requirements; hearings on an intervention basis could be held by a standing agency or by ad hoc groups designated by the President or other authority. In this discussion consideration is given to the two possibilities of: (a) notice and hearing, and (b) hearing with requirement of notice.

3. Factfinding. A finding of facts could be made on the basis of facts (a) gathered in a study, or (b) obtained in a hearing, or (c) adduced in both ways. Thus, factfinding is possible with or without hearings.

4. Publication of findings. The mildest form of sanction for notice and hearing, hearing, or factfinding requirements would be the force of an informed public opinion. Publication of findings is, therefore, an essential feature of proposals for these forms of public participation.

5. Advisory opinions. Publication of findings could be accompanied by an advisory opinion or recommended decision. This means of increasing the extent of public participation has been included in various proposals.

6. Delay. Suspension of wage or price increases might be provided by law (a) for a period after notice, (b) until hearings were held or a factfinding or other report issued, or (c) for a period after the date of issuance of a report or advisory opinion.

7. Public decision. Utility-type control has been suggested for one or a few industries, particularly steel. This would mean refusal of permission to make proposed price increases. In addition, public decision might be substituted for collective bargaining in such industries where there was a threat of cost-push inflation. This would mean refusal of permission to make wage increases.

ADMINISTRATIVE AND POLITICAL PROBLEMS

The administrative difficulties to be faced in public effort to prevent the use of market power to produce inflationary increases in prices and wages would be tremendous. Over what industries, companies, or products would surveillance be necessary? Could the public effort be successful without surveillance over a wide range of American industry? Could public effort be pinpointed at the strategic centers from which new inflationary pressures would arise? Could public attention be brought to these centers in time to prevent the beginning of new inflationary chain effects? What type of public action would be needed? Would notice of prospective price and wage increases be necessary? If so, would exceptions to the requirements for notice be required to meet special situations in industry? What follow-up action would be taken after receipt of notice? Could the consideration of filings and the making of fact studies or holding of hearings be completed in the brief period within which judgment would be required? Would factfinding report, on hearings, and advisory recommendations carry real weight with the companies or unions seeking increases? What standards could be used in determining whether to investigate or hold hearings, what to pinpoint in factfinding or hearing reports, what recommendations to make? How could public participation be organized so as to produce confidence in reports but at the same time to produce enough support from the Government to carry weight with the parties affected? Could public authority be exercised with aggressive and continuing attention to public interests or would organs of administration become sluggish and weak in motivation? Would a continuing type of control, similar to utility control, be desirable for a few sectors of the economy? If so, for which sectors? Could agencies for administration of such controls maintain the independence and vigor needed for success?

Government surveillance of price and wage increases would have political effects. New issues in politics would be created and these would relate to matters of intense interest to parties. The pressures on Government from labor and investor interests would be increased, and the political struggle among groups might be intensified. The political resistance to adverse Government actions on wages and prices would be great, so great in fact that it could be expected that only the power and prestige of the Presidency could be expected to carry weight against the resistance. And allegations of Presidential partiality toward particular groups would be unavoidable.

The ultimate test of public surveillance would lie in the economic and social results. The surveillance would need to be exercised with consideration of multiple objectives, including not only that of price stability but the effects upon economic growth, employment, and purchasing power, national security, and justice to economic groups. To balance these objectives and give each its proper weight in a rapidly changing economy, and to conclude public consideration with the expedition required to avoid adverse effects on the economy, would constitute a large challenge to administrative and political authorities seeking to avoid inflationary wage and price increases.

The administrative difficulties and political consequences of public action, and the strong desire to maintain private decision on matters of wages and prices, has led to a great reluctance to consider means of public participation in these matters, even when production was impeded over a protracted period by a strike in a key industry. Patience may be an attribute of wisdom on matters of this kind. At the same time, the growth of market power leads inevitably to consideration of public participation. In the labor field provision for notice and for fact finding in emergencies is already part of public policy. The means of dealing with stoppage of industry, inflationary threats, and other types of situations created by the development of large organizations with economic power

will be one of the most difficult areas of policy in the future.

POLICY GUIDELINES

It may be hoped that the threats from concentrations of economic power may be met by a variety of Government policies. A prime need is more effective enforcement of antitrust laws and amendments of these laws to insure more complete attainment of their purpose. Government policies which tend to support and strengthen the market power of groups need to be considered in terms of their effects on the power of these groups over the economy. Such developments would aim toward correction and prevention of all the manifestations of market power and would lessen the need for consideration of public intervention on prices and wages. Yet it is unlikely that developments of these types will go far enough to prevent the existence of inflationary concentrations of market power. Since this is true, the means of restraining the use of market power toward inflationary ends has now begun to be considered. Some would warn, "Beware of beginnings"; others would advise, "Begin now to acquire knowledge and experience on the problem."

If a beginning toward public consideration of prices and/or wages which may have inflationary effects is desired, the following lines of policy may be the most feasible for effective administration and hence the ones on which consideration should be focused.

1. Establishment of a study center in the executive branch of the Government to analyze the effects of concentrated market power on prices and wages, to pinpoint the centers of concentrated power which have the largest potential for starting inflationary chain movements, and to recommend to the President and to the Congress policies for avoiding inflationary moves from centers of market power.

2. Requirement of notice of prospective changes in prices, or of wages which would lead to price increases, where such changes would issue from positions of power and would have a serious inflationary effect. The selection of industries, companies, or products for which this requirement would be imposed would need to be made carefully so as to limit the burden on Government and on economic organizations. It would probably be desirable for Congress to retain control over the selection, either through strict definition of categories to

be included, or through approval or veto powers over executive determinations on inclusion of specific industries, companies or products, or categories of these. In an area of evolving policy, continued congressional participation and executive-congressional cooperation may be both desirable and necessary.

3. Authorization to the President to set up fact-finding and hearing boards to study prospective price and/or wage increases and issue advisory statements or recommendations. A study center, on the basis of information obtained from notices or otherwise, could advise the President on the need for factfinding and hearing boards and could be authorized also to present facts and arguments to the boards. Whether the burden imposed upon the President by such requirements would be so large as to require consideration of establishment of other administrative arrangements would be revealed as the scope and frequency of public intervention was determined by experience or further policy decisions.

4. Development of a policy for the steel industry. Because of the inflationary record and potential of steel prices and wages, a policy for the steel industry alone could be considered as an alternative to requirements for a number of industries or products, such as are outlined under paragraphs 2 and 3 above. A policy for the steel industry might have the dual objective of avoiding inflationary effects of concentrated market power and of preventing stoppages of production. The alternatives of policy which could be considered extend over the whole range of possibilities discussed in this paper, including notice, factfinding, hearings, advisory opinions, and public determination in case of serious threat to the public interest.

QUESTIONS AND STUDY SUGGESTIONS

1. What are the two main types of inflation? Explain how market power might contribute to inflation.

2. Carefully evaluate (*a*) internal correctives, (*b*) monetary and fiscal techniques, (*c*) antitrust, and (*d*) the withdrawal of government support of market power as policies designed to alleviate inflation arising from the market power of unions and big businesses.

3. Discuss the various degrees of more direct governmental intervention in wage-price determination.

4. What administrative and political problems might be encountered in any effort by government to prevent market power from being exercised in an inflationary manner? What policy guidelines does Professor Redford offer to deal with these problems?

Reading 31

The Forces of Growth

Leonard S. Silk, Economics Editor, *Business Week*

Economic growth, of crucial importance for poor and rich nations alike, is clearly at the forefront of economic analysis. Economists today are devoting more time and effort to measuring, explaining, and meeting the problems associated with economic development than to any other single aspect of economics.

What makes an economy grow? What are "the forces of growth"? Leonard Silk tells us in this reading that, while the rate of investment is the primary and immediate determinant of economic growth, the ultimate determinants encompass a host of economic and cultural forces. Of these forces, the basic progenitor of investment and therefore of growth in recent years is "the growth of scientific and technical knowledge which culminates in new products, new processes, new resources." The author envisions our society in the midst of a research revolution which, assuming our research effort is adequately financed and efficiently administered, should stimulate the innovational investment upon which continued economic development depends.

What are the real forces that determine the growth of the economy? And to what extent can they be altered?

Scraps of various theories of economic growth have been littering our libraries for hundreds of years. But, after the middle of the nineteenth century, respectable economists abandoned the effort to understand growth and instead tried to turn economics into a neat, precise, deductive science like Newtonian physics. Growth was too messy—too full of historical, sociological, technological, political, geographical, "institutional" complexities.

The gold rush into the growth field by economists after World War II started theories of growth multiplying again. The rush was spurred on by political factors—first, the drive of the poor nations for economic development and, second, the great thrust forward of the

Soviet Union and the evolving competition between communism and capitalism. Its result has been the rediscovery of what the earlier writers, philosophers, historians, sociologists, and the classical economists had already learned.

This was that there are two basic sets of causes of growth:

One is the complex of cultural factors—including science, technology, population changes, religion, politics, social attitudes, class structure, and the intellectual and moral qualities of men: their skills, their imaginations, their drive, their courage.

The other is a set of economic factors—especially the possibility of accumulating capital and using it to make a profit.

These two sets of factors, cultural and economic, must cojoin if growth is to occur. The two come together in the act of investment; that is the genetic moment for economic growth.

What's more, there is a close and direct link between the rate of investment and the rate of economic growth. In the United Kingdom between 1950 and 1957, for example, gross investment stood at something over 13 percent of gross national product, and the annual rate of increase in GNP was below 3 percent. In Mexico, the United States, France, and Belgium, gross investment ran higher—between 16 and 17 percent of GNP; and in these countries GNP climbed at rates varying from just over 3 percent to just over 5 percent. In Japan, Venezuela, and the Soviet Union, on the other hand, gross investment reached such expansive rates as 25 to 29 percent of GNP; and the growth of GNP speeded up accordingly, ranging up to an 8 percent rate in Japan and above 9 percent in Venezuela. The correlation between rates of investment and rates of economic growth is by no means tight and consistent, but that there is an important causal link no economist would deny.

But if it is investment that plays so basic a role in economic growth, what causes investment to rise—or to sink?

AUTONOMOUS AND INDUCED INVESTMENT

Broadly, in considering what spurs on the investment process, economists have come to split investment into two categories—autonomous investment and induced investment. Economists use both terms without much precision. What they mean approximately, though, is this:

Investment is autonomous when it creates its own demand.

Investment is induced when it represents a response to preexisting demand that forces producers to increase capacity.

Another way of putting the difference would be to say that autonomous investment results primarily from noneconomic causes, from forces outside the economic system itself—that is, from the action of the various cultural forces that help to bring about economic growth.

Induced investment, by contrast, results primarily from economic factors—from changes in business activity, from the relationship of costs, prices, interest rates, profit margins, the ratios

between sales and capacity, and other forces within the economic system itself.

Autonomous investment—which, as we shall see, is the heart of the long-term growth problem—comes chiefly from:

1. The discovery of new techniques of production, such as the assembly line or the steam shovel; these cut production costs.

2. The development of new products, such as the automobile or the television set; these create new markets.

3. The development of new resources, such as petroleum or helium—a process usually stimulated by some technological advance (though at one time military conquest or exploration of distant lands played the leading role in bringing new resources to a nation's economy).

4. Population growth and migration, which may stimulate investment in housing, public utilities, "social capital."

5. War—hot or cold—which necessitates expansion of plant and equipment to produce defense goods or, for that matter in this age of total military, economic, diplomatic, psychological, foreign-aid competition, many other kinds of goods.

The last two factors—population growth and migration and war—may seem to come close to induced investment, or response to existing demands. But, essentially, they are noneconomic factors—"cultural" forces outside the operation of the economic system itself, and so are grouped with autonomous investment.

THE POWER OF NEW IDEAS

What has become increasingly clear is that the most important element in autonomous investment (whether sparked by population pressure, military dangers, idle curiosity, the instinct of workmanship, or the love of a dollar) is the growth of scientific and technological knowledge which culminates in new products, new processes, new resources—in other words, innovational investment. There we find the great progenitor of economic growth.

In the past the United States has had three great innovational pushes that have sent the economy climbing upward, each lasting about half a century. The first big push—based on cotton textiles, iron, and steam power—lasted from the end of the American Revolution until the 1840s. Then came the second push—based on the building of the railroads, and on steel—lasting until close to the end of the 1890s. The third thrust—powered by electricity and the automobile—got under way around the turn of the century, probably ended a few years ago.

The Research Age

It is going to be a lot harder, though, to fasten a label on the new innovational push that we have been experiencing since the end of World War II. That's because it has not been based on any one or two innovations that provide a convenient tag, but upon a whole flood of them.

These postwar innovations owe their origin to major scientific progress in nuclear and solid-state physics, organic and inorganic chemistry, electronics, engineering, the earth sciences, the biological sciences, mathematics. The important scientific work that led to breakthroughs—and innovations—in those fields stretched back through the war years and on through the years of apparent economic stagnation in the 1930s (when the work of scientists such as Einstein, Lawrence, Fermi, and Meitner was far from stagnating).

What will this new epoch be called? It's clearly an understatement to call it the atomic age, as people did at the end of the war. It's too narrow to call it the age of automation or cybernetics, as Norbert Weiner did. And it's much more than the space age. Because of its tremendous breadth, we might simply call it the research age, however vague the term, however subject to misuse.

Three Stages

This research revolution has happened so fast that it's hard to see it in perspective, to be sure that one isn't either exaggerating or underestimating the dimensions of the revolution. Science and technology now play so prominent a role in everyday life and in our business affairs that it seems inconceivable that only 400 years ago people shied away from Galileo and considered him a practitioner of the black art. Some scholars see the application of science and technology to industry as having come on in three stages. It is hard to find accurate tags for the stages, since they shade into one another. They might perhaps be called the stages of (1) the isolated inventor, (2) the organized investigators, and (3) the organized scientists.

1. Man had been inventive since the beginning of time, but not until he had collected a great deal of information about nature and perfected his processes of reasoning did he become "scientific." When inventors began to use the scientific method in the eighteenth century, the result was the industrial revolution. Large-scale mechanical manufacturing, which started in Britain, spread technology around the world. In this country, whole new industries sprang up from the inventions of such men as Eli Whitney, Robert Fulton, Elias Howe, Samuel F. B. Morse, Cyrus McCormick, Alexander Graham Bell, Charles Goodyear, John Wesley Hyatt, Thomas A. Edison, Charles M. Hall. The pace of inventing had enormously quickened in the nineteenth century from earlier periods. Alfred North Whitehead has put the matter this way:

What is peculiar and new to the [nineteenth] century, differentiating it from its predecessors, is its technology. It was not merely the introduction of some great isolated inventions. It is impossible not to feel that something more than that was involved. For example, writing was a greater invention than the steam-engine. But in tracing the continuous history of the growth of writing we find an immense difference from that of the steam-engine. We must, of course, put aside minor and sporadic anticipations of both; and confine attention to the periods of their effective elaboration. For scale of time is so absolutely disparate. For the steam-engine, we may give about a hundred years; for writing, the time period is of the order of a thousand years. Further, when writing was finally popularized, the world was not then expecting the next step in technology. The process of change was slow, unconscious, and unexpected.

In the nineteenth century, the process became quick, conscious, and expected. . . . The greatest invention of the nineteenth century was the invention of the method of invention.

2. But, though the method of invention was known, and the pace of inventions had greatly accelerated, the great technological contributors of the nineteenth century were mainly isolated geniuses who may themselves have known relatively little about science. In Germany, toward the end of the nineteenth cen-

tury, a second phase in the application of science to industry began. With a push from the Kaiser in the form of institutes, German science was encouraged to correct and enrich industrial processes. This was the beginning of organized research. The American effort in this second phase was slow in starting, because natural resources here were so plentiful that the idea of conservation or technological development of resources seemed rather unimportant. But the effort did begin at length in the laboratories of Arthur D. Little (1886), Eastman Kodak (1893), B. F. Goodrich (1895), General Electric Co. (1900), National Bureau of Standards (1901), E. I. du Pont de Nemours & Company (1902). By 1920, the number of such organized research laboratories was only 220. But during the 1920s and 1930s, we outstripped all competition in the organized application of science to manufacturing.

3. The third phase—in which basic science is emerging as the initiator and leader of industrial practice—is the astonishing one which has broken upon us, most obviously, since World War II, though its roots extend further back in time. The British scientist and novelist C. P. Snow observes that this new phase is certainly related to the great industrial revolution of the eighteenth to the early twentieth century, but he finds it ". . . far more deeply scientific, far quicker, and probably far more prodigious in its result."

This change comes from the application of real science to industry, no longer hit and miss, no longer the ideas of odd "inventors," but the real stuff.

Dating this second change is very largely a matter of taste. Some would prefer to go back to the first large-scale chemical or engineering industries, round about sixty years ago. For myself, I should put it much further on, not earlier than thirty to forty years ago—and as a rough definition, I should take the time when atomic particles were first made industrial use of. I believe the industrial society of electronics, atomic energy, automation, is in cardinal respects different in kind from any that has gone before, and will change the world much more.

War and Organized Research

Probably the greatest thing that sold industry on the new approach was the way organized research attacks paid off in World War II. By 1939 British scientists were moving into high places in their government and industry to attack a wide variety of problems. In this country the Office of Scientific Research and Development performed much the same function, and initiated many of the wonders that helped to win the war. Most dramatic and important of all was the Manhattan Project, which enlisted and coordinated the talents of many specialists in the quest for the atom bomb. Here time was the vital element; there was no question about how badly we needed the atom bomb. We organized to get it, and we got it. Similarly, in the chemical industry, there was urgent need to find a way synthetically to replace natural rubber, and a search was organized. Everybody with any knowledge about polymers was invited in on this one; some of the big chemical companies donated the services of whole groups of researchers for $1 a year. Again the search was successful, and the United States was able to build enough rubber plants to ease its dependence on imported rubber during the war. With these and such other great technological achievements as radar and the antibiotics, one can go a long way toward supporting the thesis that war—at least World War II—has been a powerful propellant of economic development.

THE REVOLUTION SPREADS

The research revolution has deepened and widened since the war. Nor is it only the big sensational things—headline-grabbers such as atomic reactors, hydrogen bombs, electronic computers, jet transports, atomic submarines, earth satellites—that have issued forth from this new innovational push. The list of new products that have staged a fast growth in the postwar period is long. Here are just some of the fastest-growing new products and new services, spawned by industrial research and development, that have helped push the economy upward at a rapid pace in the 1948–1958 decade:

Products with growth rates of 40 percent per year—or more:
Transistors
Titanium sponge
Power steering
Power brakes
Antibiotics
Television sets

Polyethylene
Styrene plastics and resins
Vitamins
Helicopters (nonmilitary)
Synthetic rubber
Butadiene
Synthetic detergents

Products with growth rates of 30 to 40 percent per year:
Television broadcasting stations
Ton-miles of air flown
Synthetic fibers (except rayon)
Electric driers
Automatic coffee makers
Argon
Room air conditioners
Tape recorders
Pentaerythritol

There's another side to this picture, however. You find it in the list of products that have shown a declining trend through the postwar period. Lumped together in this group are sheepskins, local transit, lead, cast-iron boilers, railroad passenger cars, anthracite coal, radiators and convectors, steam locomotives, tin, brick, woolen goods, tractor moldboard plows, work shirts, domestic heating stoves, creamery butter, black blasting powder, natural soap, textile bags—and other victims of technological change.

Many of these declining products represented innovations in their day (if you go back far enough, all of them did). And like them, each of the multitude of postwar innovations has its own life to live. Some will have a long and pretty steady period of expansion before they taper off. Others shoot up like a rocket, hit a ceiling, then perhaps drop back. Still others will keep booming upward for a long time.

This falling off of obsolescent products as technology changes is the reverse side of the innovation process on which the late Joseph Schumpeter built his theory of economic growth and business cycles. It is what Schumpeter called "creative destruction"—creative, because the ultimate effect of innovation is growth, not stagnation; capitalism is a system of economic change that, in his words, ". . . not only never is but never can be stationary."

This process of growth via technological progress and innovation is, of course, nothing new; long before Schumpeter, the early nineteenth-century Canadian economist John Rae —Adam Smith's foremost critic—built a theory of growth based on technological change and industrial innovation. And, economic theory apart, technological progress has played a major role in propelling this economy, and other economics, forward, particularly since the middle of the eighteenth century.

But what is new in our time is the multiplication of innovations—and the widespread recognition and systematic application by industry of the notion that new products and new processes are the key to a company's growth, an industry's growth, a nation's growth—and the recognition that, through systematically planned and administered research, we can count on the continuous development of innovations to keep the economic system expanding.

We do not know precisely what our laboratories will discover in the years ahead. But we do know that if we sponsor an adequate research program, they will make discoveries that call for new investment and generate greater production. Knowing this, we can, in a real sense, make innovation a deliberate program rather than a chance development and thus ensure future growth.

QUESTIONS AND STUDY SUGGESTIONS

1. What are the "two basic sets of causes of growth"?
2. State and explain the relationship between the rate of investment and the rate of growth.
3. Distinguish between "autonomous" and "induced" investment. What factors underline autonomous investment? Of these, which is deemed the most important?
4. Discuss the "research age" and its history. Describe the three stages through which science and technology have come to be applied to history.

Reading 32

Automation and Unemployment

National Commission on Technology, Automation, and Economic Progress

It is generally agreed that technological progress and full employment are both important contributors to economic growth. But are the two compatible? Is automation—the use of self-regulating and highly integrated machinery and equipment—a creator or a destroyer of jobs? This is a perplexing question which has salient implications for economic policy (Readings 17 and 18).

In 1965 the President appointed a National Commission on Technology, Automation, and Economic Progress. One of its mandates was to investigate the general question of the impact of automation upon employment. Reading 32 consists of excerpts from the Commission's report which summarize its findings on the recent historical relationship between automation and employment; project future adjustments in the structure of employment which will be induced in part by technological change; and detail a number of policy recommendations to facilitate those job shifts with which the labor force will be confronted in the years ahead.

At the end of the Korean war, unemployment began to creep upward from an average level of some 3 percent of the civilian labor force; it rose and fell with economic conditions, but stalled at higher levels at the peak of each succeeding business cycle. The explanation was sought by some in the dramatic technological changes that had occurred during the 1950s. It was not the first time that the possibility of persistent technological unemployment had been the focus of public discussion.

We believe that the general level of unemployment must be distinguished from the displacement of particular workers at particular times and places, if the relation between technological change and unemployment is to be clearly understood. The persistence of a high general level of unemployment in the years following the Korean war was not the result of accelerated technological progress. Its cause was interaction between rising productivity, labor force growth, and an inadequate growth of aggregate demand. This is firmly supported by the response of the economy to the expansionary fiscal policy of the past 5 years. Technological change, on the other hand, has been a major factor in the displacement and temporary unemployment of particular workers. Thus technological change (along with other forms of economic change) is an important determinant of the precise places, industries, and people affected by unemployment. But the general level of demand for goods and services is by far the most important factor determining how many are affected, how long they stay unemployed, and how hard it is for new entrants to the labor market to find jobs. The basic fact is that technology eliminates jobs, not work. It is the continuous obligation of economic policy to match increases in productive potential with

From the National Commission on Technology, Automation, and Economic Progress, **Technology and the American Economy**, vol. 1, Washington, 1966, pp. 9–31, 110–112, abridged.

increases in purchasing power and demand. Otherwise the potential created by technical progress runs to waste in idle capacity, unemployment, and deprivation.

GENERAL LEVELS OF UNEMPLOYMENT

Changes in the volume of unemployment are governed by three fundamental forces: the growth of the labor force, the increase in output per man-hour, and the growth of total demand for goods and services. Changes in the average hours of work enter in exactly parallel fashion but have been quantitatively less significant. As productivity rises, less labor is required per dollar of national product, or more goods and services can be produced with the same number of man-hours. If output does not grow, employment will certainly fall; if production increases more rapidly than productivity (less any decline in average hours worked), employment must rise. But the labor force grows, too. Unless gross national product (total final expenditure for goods and services corrected for price changes) rises more rapidly than the *sum* of productivity increase and labor force growth (again modified for any change in hours of work), the increase in employment will be inadequate to absorb the growth in the labor force. Inevitably the unemployment rate will increase. Only when total production expands faster than the rate of labor force growth *plus* the rate of productivity increase and *minus* the rate at which average annual hours falls does the unemployment rate fall. Increases in productivity were more important than growth of the labor force as sources of the wide gains in output experienced since 1947. These increases in potential production simply were not matched by increases in demand adequate to maintain steady full employment.

In the late 1950s, productivity and the labor force were increasing more rapidly than usual, while the growth of output was slower than usual. This accounts for the persistence of high unemployment rates.

Except for the recession years of 1949, 1954, and 1958, the rate of economic growth throughout this period exceeded the rate of productivity increase and employment rose. But in only 6 of the past 12 years was the growth rate high enough to offset both productivity increase and labor force growth. In the other 6 years unemployment rose.

But if part of the national purpose is to reduce and contain unemployment, arithmetic is not enough. We must know which of the basic factors we can control and which we wish to control. Unemployment would have risen more slowly or fallen more rapidly if (1) productivity had increased more slowly, or (2) the labor force had increased more slowly, or (3) hours of work had fallen more steeply, or (4) total output had grow more rapidly. These are not independent factors, however, and a change in any of them might have caused changes in others.

A society can choose to reduce the growth of productivity, and it can probably find ways to frustrate its own creativity. We believe this choice to be utterly self-defeating in its impact on living standards and wages. Although a reduction in the growth of productivity at the expense of potential output might result in higher employment in the short run, the long-run effect on employment would be uncertain and the long-run effect on the national interest would be disastrous. It may be possible to slow the growth of the labor force by encouraging later entry, earlier retirement, lower participation by some groups, or reduced hours of work. In the past, rising productivity has been realized partly through higher incomes and partly through reduced working time and shorter working life. This pattern is likely to continue.

The high unemployment that led to the formation of this Commission was the consequence of passive public policy, not the inevitable consequence of the pace of technological change. The experience of the economy during the life of this Commission is the best evidence that economic growth can continue to offset the growth of productivity and labor force and reduce unemployment further. We believe that continued reduction in unemployment is a feasible task and a matter of urgency for our society. We recognize that the task is a challenging one under the circumstances of the coming years.

We do not expect output per man-hour in the whole—private *and* public—economy to rise during the next decade at a rate substantially faster than the 2.8 percent a year characteristic of the postwar period. Some moderate acceleration may take place in the longer run. The growth of the labor force, however, is predictable and dramatic. The labor force will increase approximately 1.9 percent a year during the next 5 years, and almost as fast in the following 10 or 15 years. We expect a continued slow and irregular decline in hours of work. It follows that the output of the economy—and the aggregate demand to buy it—must grow in excess of 4 percent a year just to prevent the unemployment rate from rising, and even faster if the unemployment rate is to fall further, as we believe it should. Yet our economy has seldom, if ever, grown at a rate faster than 3.5 percent for any extended length of time. We have no cause for complacency. Positive fiscal, monetary, and manpower policies will be needed in the future as in the past. The Nation should not be lulled into forgetfulness by a short-run need for increased defense expenditures.

TECHNOLOGICAL CHANGE AND PARTICULAR UNEMPLOYMENT

Hidden beneath national averages is continuous movement into, out of, between, and within labor markets. In 1964, for instance, the average number of persons in the labor force was 74 million, with about 70 million employed and 3.9 million unemployed.

Some of the 14 million who experienced some unemployment in 1964 were new entrants to the labor force. Others were laid off only temporarily. But between one-third and one-half of those unemployed were permanently or indefinitely severed from their jobs; they were forced to find new employment, remain among the unemployed, or withdraw from the labor force. Thus the average number unemployed during a year understates the actual volume of involuntary displacement that actually occurred.

There are many causes of displacement. The demand for a product may decline, perhaps in a general cyclical downturn, perhaps because consumer tastes change. A new product or a newly invented process may capture a market from an existing producer. A company or an industry may change its location, perhaps in search of lower wage rates or raw material sources, or because a technological change in transportation affects the relative advantages of being near raw materials sources or near markets. An employer may find himself in an unfavorable competitive position because of technological backwardness, his own inefficiency, or for reasons beyond his control. A major technological development may displace an entire occupational group within a plant. An accretion of small changes may increase productivity more rapidly than output rises and attrition can absorb.

Displacement is implicit in the natural history of economic development, as the example of the United States shows. In the most primitive stages of growth, the labor force is concentrated on producing food and fibers; as the economy becomes more productive, there is a shift to the production of manufactured goods; then, as basic physical needs are satisfied, larger portions of the labor force are transferred (or displaced) to the production of a variety of services.

Employment shifts, whether by industry or occupation or by establishment, are only an indication, not a measure, of the displacement of individuals. Employment changes within an establishment may not enter the statistics at all. Jobs may disappear but the workers may be absorbed in other parts of the establishment. Employment in one firm may decline but be offset by increases in another, leaving industry totals unaffected. There are, however, offsetting forces. Some workers quit voluntarily, retire, or die. A fall in employment which does not exceed this attrition rate need not result in displacement. On the other hand, some of the voluntary quits may be in anticipation of layoffs and therefore represent a hidden displacement.

Nor is there a good measure of the distress caused by displacement. Everything depends on the difficulty with which a new job is obtained, its location, and relative attractiveness. If the economic environment is favorable and the displaced worker has attractive skills, the distress need not be great. If the contrary, the human costs of displacement may be high. Under the best of circumstances a loss of accumulated job rights and a lower wage are likely consequences. The most serious adjustment problems have resulted when massive displacement has occurred among workers with overspecialized skills in isolated areas without alternative sources of employment. Coal miners are a prime example. The most profound of all displacements has been that in agriculture, where, in the postwar period, a 5.7 percent annual rate of productivity increase accompanied by only a 1.4 percent increase in farm output has reduced farmowners and farm-workers from 8.2 million in 1947 to 4.8 million in 1964, or 42.3 percent. Those who left by the door marked "education" entered a new productive life. Too many, suffering from deficient rural educations, lacking skills in demand in urban areas, unaccustomed to urban ways, and often burdened by racial discrimination, exchanged rural poverty for an urban ghetto. How many of the 4.8 million workers who remain in agriculture are underemployed is conjectural, but the number is probably high.

SKILL, EDUCATION, AND UNEMPLOYMENT

Unemployment has been concentrated among those with little education or skill, while employment has been rising most rapidly in those occupations generally considered to be the most skilled and to require the most education. This conjunction raises the question whether technological progress may induce a demand for very skilled and highly educated people in numbers our society cannot yet provide, while at the same time leaving stranded many of the unskilled and poorly educated with no future opportunities for employment.

No confident answer can be given to this difficult and complex question. Our society is extending secondary and higher education to larger and larger fractions of the population, and, therefore, it is necessary that the number of suitable and rewarding jobs should increase correspondingly. Otherwise a different kind of frustration would result. We must, then, ask a much more subtle question: Is the demand for highly educated people outrunning the supply, and is the supply of unskilled workers outrunning the demand? It is intrinsically difficult to establish any answer because occupational content can change while the occupational title remains the same, and because it is often unclear which occupations make greater demands in skill and education. Even if we were confident that there were imbalances between skills demanded and skills supplied, it would not follow that the source of the imbalance is technological. Japan and Western Europe operate sophisticated industrial economies with educational profiles far inferior to our own, and there is reason to believe that a highly automated economy could be engineered to fit a variety of educational profiles. But that is not our problem. In the shorter run, whatever the general trend, there is no doubt that technological change may increase, decrease, or simply change the skills required in particular jobs. The result may be displacement.

There is little doubt that the occupational structure of the American labor force is changing and will continue to change. Perhaps the main reason for this is the rapid growth of those industries—education, finance, insurance, health, and business services—which employ predominantly white-collar and professional workers. Another reason is the rapid improvement in educational attainment itself. Technological change within industries does not seem to be the major factor, except as regards the declining employment of laborers. Whether changes in the demand for different skills are to a substantial extent placing the new jobs beyond the reach of those losing other jobs can best be assessed by examining the relationship between educational attainment and educational requirements.

Here, too, the evidence is at best fragmentary, but the Commission is impressed with labor market developments during the business expansion following the tax reduction of early 1964. As the general unemployment rate has fallen, the improvement has been greatest for those with the least education. In 1965, the unemployment rate for those with 8 years of schooling or less fell from 7.6 to 5.9 percent; for high school graduates with no further education, from 4.8 to 4.1 percent; and for a college graduate, only from 1.5 to 1.4 percent.

It is the proper function of a market to allocate resources, and in this respect the labor market does not function differently from any other. If the available resources are of high quality, the market will adjust to the use of high quality resources; if the quality is low, methods will be developed to use such resources. In an efficient market, the choice between low-skill and high-skill manpower and between labor-intensive and capital-intensive production methods is made on the basis of relative costs. Although employment of unskilled, untrained labor can be encouraged by lowering its cost relative to that of skilled, trained labor a better way would be to generate higher rates of economic activity. (In the same way, labor and machines "compete" with each other.) In a slack labor market employers must have some means of selecting among numerous applicants, and it is not surprising that educational attainment is often used as a convenient yardstick, regardless of its direct relevance to the requirements of the job.

We have found it useful to view the labor market as a gigantic "shapeup," with members of the labor force queued in order of their relative attractiveness to employers. If the labor market operates efficiently, employers will start at the head of the line, selecting as many as they need of employees most attractive to them. Their choice may be based on objective standards relating to ability, or on dubious standards of race, sex, or age; wage differentials may also be important; and formal education may be used as a rough screening device. The total number employed and unemployed depends primarily on the general state of economic activity. The employed tend to be those near the beginning and the unemployed those near the end of the line. Only as demand rises will employers reach further down the line in their search for employees.

TECHNOLOGY AND EMPLOYMENT: THE NEXT TEN YEARS

The structure of employment a decade ahead can be projected to a first approximation from present trends and foreseen technological developments. We provide only a summary here.

1. Given the projected growth of the labor force, the assumptions imply that 88.7 million persons would be gainfully employed in 1975, about 18.3 million more than in 1964—an average increase of nearly 1.7 million annually. (This compares with an average annual employment increase of 1.1 million between 1960 and 1965, and 1.8 million between 1964 and 1965.)

2. Farm employment is expected to decline by about 1 million and all other employment is expected to increase by more than 19 million, for a net employment gain of 18.3 million. For nonfarm "goods producing" industries—manufacturing, mining, and construction—a moderate increase in manpower requirements of 17 percent is projected, a rate of increase somewhat faster than during the 17-year period 1947–64. Requirements in the "service producing" sector as a whole—trade, finance, government, services, and transportation and public utilities—are expected to increase by 38 percent, somewhat faster than over the past 17-year period, and more rapidly than the goods producing industries.

3. The effect of these industry employment trends will be to continue recent trends in the industrial composition of the economy. Government and services will increase sharply as a percent of the total; contract construction and trade will also increase their share. On the other hand, the relative importance of manufacturing and transportation and public utilities will decline slightly, and the relative size of agriculture and mining will continue to decline sharply. Taking the broad "goods" and "services" sectors as a whole (and including in goods agriculture, with its self-employed as well as its wage and salary workers) the goods sector will decline from about 41 percent of all jobs in 1964 to 36 percent in 1975; the service sector will increase its share of manpower requirements from 59 to 64 percent. (If self-employed persons in nonagricultural industries were added to the above comparison, the services sector would have a slightly larger share in both years.)

4. Concern has been expressed that the impact of technological and industrial change will drastically curtail employment opportunities for less skilled workers. The principal conclusion is that the overall demand for less skilled workers will not decrease over this 11-year period, although it will decline somewhat as a percentage of the total. Needs for laborers in 1975 will be roughly the same as in 1964, although they will decrease from 5.2 to 4.2 percent of total manpower requirements.

5. The greatest increase in employment requirements will be for professional and technical workers; more than 4.5 million additional personnel will be required. The white-collar group as a whole is expected to expand by nearly two-fifths and to constitute 48 percent of all manpower requirements in 1975. The blue-collar occupations are expected to expand at less than half this rate, and will make up about 34 percent of all requirements. A rapid expansion in requirements for service workers is anticipated—a 35 percent increase in employment.

6. These changes in occupational requirements have significant implications for certain groups in the labor force. If nonwhites continue to hold the same proportion of jobs in each occupation as in 1964, the nonwhite unemployment rate in 1975 will be more than five times that for the labor force as a whole. In 1964, the unemployment rate of nonwhites was 9.8 percent, about twice that for whites. If

trends in upgrading the jobs of nonwhites continue at the same rate as in recent years, the nonwhite unemployment rate in 1975 would still be about 2½ times that for the labor force as a whole. Thus nonwhites must gain access to the rapidly growing higher skilled and white-collar occupations at a faster rate than in the past 8 years if their unemployment rate is to be brought down to the common level.

If all occupations have the same composition by age in 1975 as in 1964, opportunities for younger workers (aged 14–24) will be substantially fewer than the number in this age group seeking work. The unsatisfactory current relation of youth unemployment to total unemployment will worsen unless utilization patterns change. There is here a clear need for action.

It is at best difficult to separate the technological from other causes of the structural changes we have been describing. To the displaced employee, or even to the maker of public policy, the precise causes of displacement and unemployment may not even seem important. Because society gains from the flexibility and responsiveness which are the sources of displacement, it is society's responsibility to see that alternative opportunities are available and that blameless individuals do not bear excessive costs.

SUMMARY AND RECOMMENDATIONS

Unemployment tends to be concentrated among those workers with little education, not primarily because technological developments are changing the nature of jobs, but because the uneducated are at the "back of the line" in the competition for jobs. Education, in part, determines the employability and productivity of the individual, the adaptability of the labor force, the growth and vitality of the economy, and the quality of the society. But we need not await the slow process of education to solve the problem of unemployment.

The outlook for employment and adjustment to change in the next decade depends upon the policies followed. Uneven growth and decline of occupations and industries could, but need not, cause serious difficulties for the economy as a whole. The number of unskilled jobs will not decline, though unskilled jobs will continue to as a proportion of all jobs. Growth patterns in both the economy and the labor force provide an important warning: Unless Negroes

and, to a lesser degree, youth, are able to penetrate growing occupations and industries at a more rapid rate than in the past, their high unemployment rates will continue or even rise. Our society must do a far better job than it has in the past of assuring that the burdens of changes beneficial to society as a whole are not borne disproportionately by some individuals.

The more adequate fiscal policies of the past 2 years have proven their ability to lower unemployment despite continued technological change and labor force growth. Economic policy must continue, watchfully but resolutely, to reduce the general unemployment rate. We must never again present the spectacle of wartime prosperity and peacetime unemployment. The needs of our society are such that we should give major attention in our fiscal policies to public investment expenditures.

With the best of fiscal and monetary policies, there will always be those handicapped in the competition for jobs by lack of education, skill, or experience or because of discrimination. The needs of our society provide ample opportunities to fulfill the promise of the Employment Act of 1946: "a job for all those able, willing, and seeking to work." We recommend a program of public service employment, providing, in effect, that the Government be an employer of last resort, providing work for the "hard-core unemployed" in useful community enterprises.

Technological change and productivity are primary sources of our unprecedented wealth, but many persons have not shared in that abundance. We recommend that economic security be guaranteed by a floor under family income. That floor should include both improvements in wage-related benefits and a broader system of income maintenance for those families unable to provide for themselves.

To facilitate adjustment to change as well as to improve the quality of life, adequate educational opportunity should be available to all. We recommend compensatory education for those from disadvantaged environments, improvements in the general quality of education, universal high school education and opportunity for 14 years of free public education, elimination of financial obstacles to higher education, lifetime opportunities for education, training, and retraining, and special attention to the handicaps of adults with deficient basic education.

Adjustment to change requires information concerning present and future job opportunities. We recommend the creation of a national computerized job-man matching system which would provide more adequate information on employment opportunities and available workers on a local, regional, and national scale. In addition to speeding job search, such a service would provide better information for vocational choice and alert the public and policymakers to impending changes.

The public employment service is a key instrument in adjustment to technological and economic changes. But it is presently handicapped by administrative obstacles and inadequate resources. We recommend the now federally financed but State-administered employment services be made wholly Federal. This would bring them into harmony with modern labor market conditions. Then they must be provided with the resources, both in manpower and funds, necessary to fulfill their crucial role.

We recommend that present experimentation with relocation assistance to workers and their families stranded in declining areas be developed into a permanent program.

Displacement, technological and otherwise, has been particularly painful to those blocked from new opportunity by barriers of discrimination. The Commission wishes to add its voice to others demanding elimination of all social barriers to employment and advocating special programs to compensate for centuries of systematic denial.

Technological and economic changes have differential geographic impacts requiring concerted regional efforts to take advantage of opportunities and avoid dislocation. We recomment that each Federal Reserve bank provide the leadership for economic development activities in its region. The development program in each Federal Reserve District should include: (1) A regular program of economic analysis; (2) an advisory council for economic growth composed of representatives from each of the major interested groups within the district; (3) a capital bank to provide venture capital and long-term financing for new and growing companies; (4) regional technical institutes to serve as centers for disseminating scientific and technical knowledge relevant to the region's development; and (5) a Federal executive in each district to provide regional coordination of the various Federal programs related to economic development.

The responsibility of Government is to foster an environment of opportunity in which satisfactory adjustment to change can occur. But the adjustments themselves must occur primarily in the private employment relationship. The genius of the private adjustment process is the flexibility with which it accommodates to individual circumstances. Our report suggests areas for consideration by private and public employers, employees, and unions. We also recommend study of a reinsurance fund to protect pension rights and modifications of the investment tax credit to encourage employers to provide appropriate adjustment assistance. We also advocate a positive program by employers and unions to provide compensatory opportunities to the victims of past discrimination and stronger enforcement provisions in civil rights legislation relating to employment. Federal, State, and local governments are encouraged to conduct themselves as model employers in the development of new adjustment techniques.

Technology enlarges the capacities of man and extends his control over his environment. The benefits of increased productivity can and should be applied to combinations of higher living standards and increased leisure, improvements in the work environment, increased investment in meeting human and community needs, and assistance to less advantaged nations.

QUESTIONS AND STUDY SUGGESTIONS

1. In general, what is the Commission's overall conclusion as to the impact of technological change upon the rate of unemployment? Use the following formula—Labor force × productivity per worker = real GNP—to explain the high unemployment rates of the late 1950s.

2. Comment: "Technology eliminates jobs, not work."

3. What changes in the size and occupational distribution of the labor force does the commission anticipate by 1975?

4. Summarize and evaluate the commission's policy recommendations. Which of these do you think should be assigned the highest priority in minimizing unemployment over the next decade?

Reading 33

The Electric Car: Technological Progress and Economic Adjustment

Lloyd D. Orr, Associate Professor of Economics, Indiana University

While the development of new and improved products is a fundamental aspect of economic growth, major product innovation invariably threatens the position of existing industries and calls for important and painful reallocations of resources. In Reading 33 the anticipated development of the electric car is analyzed. The potential advantages of the electric car over gasoline-powered automobiles include not only greater durability, lower operating costs, and superior design for immediate consumers, but also diminished air pollution for society at large. The electric car, however, poses a serious threat to the market position of the Big Three of the automobile industry. The economies of scale in production and the dealer system which now serve as barriers to entry will be weakened or destroyed by the development of the electric car. The petroleum and auto service industries also stand to be adversely affected, but the electric utility industry can anticipate growth.

In 1915 Henry Ford and Thomas Edison abandoned an attempt to develop and produce an electric automobile. With this decision, made in favor of gasoline power, the development of electric propulsion systems for highway vehicles virtually ceased, although production on a limited scale continued through the years. Now, after over seventy years of refinement, gasoline-powered vehicles dominate the transportation of passengers in the United States.

Despite some fundamental weaknesses inherent in this complicated piece of machinery, it is the most efficient and flexible means of family transportation in most areas of the country.

There is much to recommend the electric automobile, but it has always had a fatal defect: an inadequate source of energy storage. The standard lead-acid battery with an energy storage capacity of 10 watt hours/pound is simply incapable of powering a vehicle over a

From Lloyd D. Orr, "The Electric Car: Economics and Technology," **Business Horizons,** Summer, 1967, pp. 47–56. Reprinted by permission.

range that would justify its use for any purpose other than urban travel. This limitation has made the electric car unattractive to virtually all potential customers.

Now it appears that recent developments in battery technology will overcome this problem, and that within the next five to ten years we will have batteries produced from low cost materials which, with an appropriate supporting service infrastructure, will be capable of propelling a significant proportion of our automobiles. These batteries are basically of two types. The sodium-sulfur battery being developed by the Ford Motor Company is claimed to have an energy density of 150 watt hours/pound and a virtually unlimited life-span. Metal-air batteries are being explored or developed by several companies, including General Electric, the Leesona Moos Corporation, a General Dynamics-Edison Electric Institute combination, and a Ford-Yardney Electric combination. These batteries are expected to have an energy density of 60–80 watt hours/pound.

Either system is easily capable of providing an adequate range for urban and suburban travel in a car of any dimensions from subcompact to full size. Estimates of their highway capabilities vary widely. Most of the differences in projections on highway range are traceable to differences in assumptions (usually not stated) concerning vehicle redesign, the proportion of the automobile's weight devoted to batteries, and the supporting structures (compressing, cooling, insulating, and protective devices) necessary to make the basic battery a practical operating unit.

Within the next five to ten years, metal-air batteries should be capable of propelling a specially designed vehicle for roughly 200 miles at an average highway speed of 60–70 miles per hour. If the Ford battery has an actual energy density as great as 100 watt hours/pound, including the required supporting structures, it should provide a practical highway range of at least 250 miles. With these ranges and proper highway service facilities, an electric automobile designed for the one-car family should be feasible.

If the new batteries can be recharged rapidly, charging facilities in the vicinity of restaurants will be required. Ford's sodium-sulfur battery is said to be rechargeable in as little as one-half hour. This arrangement would be ideal. If longer periods are required, battery exchange stations and standard battery packages will be needed. Battery stations have been labeled as too expensive by spokesmen for the Ford Motor Company, which expects that gasoline vehicles will dominate all but commuting and short-range delivery trips for the foreseeable future.

One can easily agree that costs of battery exchange will be *high* without accepting the conclusion that they will *prohibit* the development of a full-range vehicle. It is true that exchange stations will need a large inventory of batteries, the most expensive component of an electric automobile. The labor costs for each exchange are also likely to be higher than for refueling a gasoline vehicle. But this does not mean the costs *per mile traveled* will be higher. Suppose a battery exchange costs as much as 5 cents per mile. A privately owned passenger car seldom travels more than 500 miles per day. If such a car, electrically powered, has a range of 250 miles, it would require but one exchange each day with some help from recharging during stops for meals. Assuming an overnight charging cost of approximately 1 cent per mile, the average fuel cost per mile of highway travel would be 3 cents. This is little more than the 2½ cents it now costs for fuel and lubrication in full-size automobiles. Further, if the daily trip is less than 250–300 miles, no battery exchange would be needed, and the cost per mile would be around 1 cent. For the average driver who would exceed the 250–300 mile range only a few days each year, the electric car would be a bargain even if a battery exchange cost as much as 10 cents per mile. Vehicles that are constantly used for highway travel would be more efficiently powered by gasoline at this higher rate.

It would be a mistake to assume that development should be confined to commuter and special vehicles merely because electric automobiles will not quite match the range characteristics of gasoline-powered vehicles. A compact or full-size automobile with a 250-mile range will meet the needs of most families. It would have offsetting advantages that would attract many individuals who would not consider a tiny commuting vehicle. Frequent long-range travel, which might be inconvenient or expensive in an electric automobile, would not be a problem for the typical family. The rental of a gasoline automobile or use of public transportation are obvious solutions when a trip requires high daily mileage for a week or more and *if* highway recharging proves to have a high per mile cost.

Skeptics still point to difficult problems that remain to be solved before the full-range electric car can be mass produced and marketed. I do not intend to minimize the problems of development, but the number of serious and informed proponents appears to be increasing rapidly. With the development of motors and control devices that will give electric vehicles acceleration and speed characteristics similar to those of present automobiles, electric propulsion poses a serious threat to the dominance of the internal combustion engine. The growing enthusiasm is based on the current progress of research and development, and on the substantial private and social benefits that would follow the full development of electric propulsion systems.

ADVANTAGES OF ELECTRIC CARS

Less Air Pollution

The primary impetus for serious consideration of the electric vehicle is that air pollution would be reduced by substitution of electric motors for internal combustion engines. The estimates of economic loss stemming from air pollution have varied from $4 billion to $20 billion per year. Most of these estimates are little more than guesses, but there is no doubt that the economic costs are enormous and increasing. Even more important are the associated problems of comfort and welfare for our urban citizens. The photochemical smog produced by automotive exhausts is estimated to be responsible for 50 percent of the nation's air pollution and a much higher percentage of California's.

The point has been made that the switch to electric automobiles may merely substitute air pollution by the electric utility companies for air pollution by automobiles. This point ignores several relevant facts: (1) the pollution caused by a coal-burning generating plant for a given amount of automotive propulsion would be less than that caused by internal combustion engines under most circumstances; (2) the extra generating capacity is not likely to be located in the center of a metropolitan area; (3) the heavy use of off-peak power to refuel the elec-

tric automobile at night would significantly lower the cost of producing electric power and should make the installation of sophisticated smog control devices economically feasible; and (4) a growing proportion of new capacity in the electric utility industry is nuclear.

Exhaust control devices for gasoline-powered automobiles will improve over the next ten years. The effect will be reduction—but not elimination—of the pollutants in exhaust emissions. As the trend toward population and urban concentration continues, these devices may fail to alleviate the pollution problem to any significant extent. If our goal is to clear the air, rather than merely to hold the level of contaminants below lethal levels, then electricity will maintain a decided advantage as a propulsion system.

Durable Drive Components

A standard American automobile has approximately 15,000 parts. Electric automobiles will have significantly fewer parts and, more important, most of them will be durable and require little servicing. Despite immense refinement, the reciprocating internal combustion engine is still a machine inherently designed to create maintenance problems while in the process of rapidly tearing itself apart. Such engines would be replaced with electric motors that can run thousands of hours without maintenance and whose torque characteristics and reversibility eliminate the need for a transmission.

One motor for each rear wheel (as a minimum) eliminates the need for differentials and drive shafts. Because of efficiencies inherent in small motors, large cars will probably have a motor at each wheel. Two motors would end the need for snow tires and chains under most circumstances; four would enable the family sedan to pull out of situations that would mire the best of today's four-wheel drive vehicles operating through differentials. In addition, the only significant noise in an electric automobile will come from tires and wind at high speed.

In short, the electric car will be durable, simple, silent, and relatively maintenance free, with excellent traction and standing start acceleration, but with somewhat limited passing acceleration by today's standards. This highway power limitation should be of decreasing importance to the consumer as more and more four-lane highways are built.

Lower Operating Cost

Comparisons of operating cost must be conjectural since little is known about mass production economies for batteries and other components that are not yet fully developed. Initially, an electric vehicle will probably be more expensive than its gasoline counterpart. Not only are batteries likely to be expensive, but certain chassis components may have to be upgraded to provide compatibility with the more durable basic mechanical components. However, the significantly greater durability of the electric vehicle should ultimately lower its depreciation cost per mile of operation.

Currently, the average operating cost per mile of a full-size sedan driven 10,000 miles each year may be conservatively estimated at 10 cents. The operating cost of an electric vehicle should be substantially less than this. The per mile savings could easily be 1 cent on depreciation, $1\frac{1}{2}$ cents on fuel and lubrication, and $\frac{1}{2}$ cent on maintenance. Although these are rough estimates, the resulting per mile cost of 7 cents (70 percent of that for the gasoline vehicle) is probably not overly optimistic. The point is that the cost of automotive transportation should be reduced substantially. In 1965 the saving for the United States would have been approximately $21 billion if all passenger cars had been electric.

Public Appeal

Because batteries do not require critical placement in the electric automobile, the designer will have more freedom. He may produce aerodynamic design that will significantly increase the range at high speeds. Initially, however, the electric automobile will probably have to look and perform much like its gasoline counterpart in order to win public acceptance. The American consumer is wedded to his automobile in its present form as he is to no other product. How much of the sex and power image that is alleged to be associated with it can be transferred to the electric automobile cannot be predicted.

No one knows more about the appeal of the present automobile to the American consumer than Detroit. However, the view that the public cannot be induced to purchase a vehicle with performance and appearance characteristics similar to present automobiles, plus some substantial advantages, may represent wishful thinking. If the full-range vehicle can be developed, the consumer will be offered a full-size automobile with some extremely attractive characteristics, compared with the car he is currently driving, and at a per mile operating cost usually associated with the Volkswagen. The gasoline-powered automobile initially won out over the electric on grounds of practical superiority. Despite the mystique surrounding the noisy, smelly, vibrating piston engine, it will probably ultimately lose on these same grounds. With the inherent advantages of the electric automobile and the current prospects for its development (which could be enhanced by appropriate public policies), a preliminary consideration of the probable reaction and ultimate adjustment of the automobile industry to this important technological change is very much in order.

EFFECTS ON THE AUTO INDUSTRY

Despite the basic attractiveness of the electric automobile and probable solution of the problem of adequate range, the attitude of the automobile industry has been largely negative. The Chrysler Corporation has announced no serious development work. General Motors has produced an experimental prototype based on the Corvair. The acceleration and speed of this car are quite acceptable, but evidently it contains few major innovations that would lead to a practical, low-cost, mass-produced vehicle. Their public announcements on the feasibility of an electric vehicle have been uniformly discouraging.

Ford has done by far the most serious development work. Rather than produce prototypes on the basis of current technology, they have appropriately concentrated on basic research. Their development of the sodium-sulfur battery has already been mentioned. They have contracted with Yardney Electric for joint exploration of the metal-air battery potential, and are also investigating lightweight electric motors and solid state control components. Nevertheless, Ford insists that the electric car will have only urban and suburban capabilities for the foreseeable future, and that the internal combustion engine will be the dominant power source for automobiles for many years.

The attitude of the automobile industry toward electric propulsion, demonstrated by its public statements and the relatively small amounts it is spending on development, raises some interesting questions. Their attitude is probably determined by forces much more powerful than the problems of development, costs of tooling for production, or public acceptance, which are usually cited.

I do not wish to minimize these problems, but they need to be viewed in proper perspective. The costs of development may be high. If they are so high that the potential private gain to producers seems too small, then a question of public policy arises because of the tremendous social gains that would result from the adoption of electric automobiles.

Costs of tooling will undoubtedly be large, but the major retooling would be only for power train components. The construction of other components and assembly will remain basically unaltered, and the costs involved, although still substantial, must be viewed in comparison with the retooling expenditures that the automobile industry periodically makes for major model changes. High retooling costs are evidently not an unknown and frightening specter in Detroit.

Any industry faced with a fundamental change in its product has reason to be apprehensive. Much of the basis for its stability and ability to predict future trends may be destroyed. There are good reasons to believe that a shift to electric propulsion presents some particularly disturbing prospects for the automobile industry as it is presently structured.

Threatened Structural Changes

Three companies have dominated the production of automobiles in the United States since the 1930s. Joe S. Bain has described this perpetuation of concentrated economic power in terms of barriers that must be surmounted by those who might wish to enter the industry. The two most formidable barriers are economies of scale and the dealer system.

Economies of scale refer to the yearly production rate required to achieve the minimum cost per unit of output. In the automobile industry, they are of primary importance in the production of engines and bodies. Bain estimates that production levels of 300,000–600,000 units/year are required to gain the most important scale economies. To break into the industry, this means a substantial capital investment ($250–500 million), plus substantial "shakedown losses," plus the risk of never making the required market penetration.

A major innovation could markedly reduce this barrier to entry and thus diminish the advantage accruing to those currently producing automobiles. If the internal combustion engine is eliminated, major scale advantages would stem only from the production of bodies. It could be argued that scale economies are likely to be important in producing batteries or even motors. True, but there is no reason why these components need be produced by the automobile industry. Once the technology is developed, they are likely to become rather standard items; indeed, the need for exchange battery stations indicates that there *must* be battery standardization. A few battery and component producers could supply many companies that produce bodies and assemble the car. The competitive advantage in low-cost power trains may well be lost to the current automobile producers.

An even higher barrier to potential entry into the automobile industry is the dealer system. For a new company, a dealer system is hard to build from scratch. Dealers tend to be financially weak at the start and may have to be sustained for prolonged periods by a parent company, which is usually having financial difficulties of its own. A strong dealer system offers substantial advantages to the parent company in terms of local reputation, promotional activity, and service.

Maintenance is the vital, product differentiating service provided by the dealer. A dealer system with a high geographical density means good service and the availability of parts. The importance of this function in building sales may be emphasized by recalling one of the first questions asked of a driver of an unusual looking foreign car: "Where do you get parts and service?"

The electric automobile will radically change the importance of the maintenance function. Service will be required much less frequently, and the need for specialized parts on an emergency basis should decline markedly. If the product change stimulates new producers who use standardized batteries, motors, and control systems produced outside the automobile industry, then it is almost inevitable that supermarket dealerships, handling several makes of automobiles, will develop. The required parts inventories for these dealers would probably still be less than for a present dealer handling a similar volume of only one brand name. The large mail-order houses offer another possibility for substantial gains in marketing efficiency.

The automobile industry cannot fail to view with apprehension an innovation that threatens to weaken or destroy the two major foundations of its concentrated economic power. The battery is the crucial element, and most of its development is taking place outside the automobile industry. Battery producers are not likely to discriminate in favor of present automobile manufacturers. Consequently, automobile producers may lose a great portion of the production and marketing advantages they now enjoy. These comments are, of course, relevant only to the Big Three; American Motors will surely view the situation as an opportunity.

Effect on Planned Obsolescence

The substantially greater durability of the electric automobile is likely to have a pronounced effect on the concept of planned obsolescence. This must certainly be a disturbing prospect for the automobile industry. If redesign and other innovations encourage the average new-car buyer to trade every two years (as he now does) then, after a transition period, the market will be flooded with used cars that will refuse to parade into the junkyard at an age of 8 or 9 years (as they now do). A marked decrease in trade-in values will follow.

This effect, combined with the fact that maintenance costs will not rise as quickly with age as they do now, will discourage the new-car buyer from making frequent trades. Furthermore, the new-car buyer is likely to insist on more durable chassis-body components to accompany the naturally more durable mechanical components. He will either want to drive the car for an extended period himself or protect his investment for trade-in purposes. Stated in its simplest economic terms, a substantially decreased flow of new automobiles will be required to maintain the desired stock of vehicles once the transition period has been passed. The price mechanism will operate in the manner required to bring about this result.

The notion of more durable automobiles is usually greeted with cynicism: "Detroit will find a way to make them wear out." This view,

besides being unfair to the automobile industry, misses the point. Improvements in automobiles have moderately but steadily increased the miles they will travel with a given amount of maintenance. They are junked when the cost of maintenance (associated with the characteristics and complexities of the internal combustion engine) rises above the value of the vehicle for transportation. This wearing out process will take substantially longer with the electric automobile. Present competition in the automobile industry, plus additional competition from potential domestic and foreign producers, should be sufficient to ensure full exploitation of its basic durability.

The prospect of a relative decline in the production of automobiles, perhaps by a third or more, is a bleak one for the automobile industry. After the transition period, this would mean a smaller share of the gross national product for the industry and slower absolute growth. There are, however, forces that would tend to offset this decline. The greater durability demanded for chassis-body components will raise the per unit price. Also, it would be surprising if the consumer did not use part of his savings in the cost of automotive transport to buy an automobile of higher quality. We should not expect the romance of the American consumer with his automobile to decline with the switch to electric propulsion, although the characteristics of the relationship will probably change.

The switch to electric propulsion must be viewed as contrary to the self-interest of the automobile industry. The technical and production problems that must be solved before a full-range vehicle can be produced and marketed are formidable, but their solution is a near certainty. A comprehension of the negativism toward the full-range vehicle displayed by the Big Three must include an understanding of the potential changes in industrial and marketing structure.

In my view the industry is in some danger of being engulfed by its own success. It has been so successful in providing for the transportation of the American citizen and in absorbing threats to the direction of its main thrust that it may regard itself as insulated against even the most fundamental challenge. The smoothness with which it handled the phenomenon of the compact car was an incredible exercise in production and marketing. Marginal entrants were driven from the field by the entrance of the Big Three compacts in 1960. Increases in size and horsepower then gradually led to an abandonment of the economy market. American Motors recently found itself in a position to fill the vacuum (much as it did in 1956) with an $1,850 Rambler American.

However, the electric vehicle represents a challenge of an entirely different order. The social and private advantages offered by this innovation are important enough to induce substantially different attitudes toward automotive transportation. Ford seems to realize this. They are definitely in the mainstream of developmental work. If we can judge General Motors and Chrysler by their public pronouncements, they are displaying a rigidity that could have unfortunate consequences. If the innovation is successful and they are unprepared, there would be substantial losses. If they are able to forestall or substantially delay the innovation, then society as a whole would be denied important benefits.

EFFECT ON OTHER INDUSTRIES

Other related industries, of course, would be affected by the electric automobile. The oil, electric utility, and automotive service industries are three prime examples. A major research effort will be required to study potential effects, but some comments can be made now.

The oil industry will face a loss of sales that could approach 30 percent of its present volume of fuels in the United States (this is the approximate percentage of motor fuels used by cars). It does not include the substantial loss in the sale of motor oil. In the short run, a major adjustment problem will obviously arise. New markets must be found and the structure of output altered accordingly. In the long run, the effect will be a highly beneficial conservation of the earth's limited oil resources.

Management in the electric utility industry is likely to welcome the problems created. Most refueling of electric automobiles will take place at night when this industry has a large volume of excess capacity. The capital expansion required to produce the vast increase in power consumption will therefore be relatively modest, and power for the electric vehicle should be very cheap. An associated benefit should be a reduction in the cost of power for other industrial and domestic uses.

The electric utility industry should realize that its best interests are closely associated with the development of a full-range vehicle that depends completely on batteries. If development is confined to commuter vehicles, then almost all one-car families will be forced to rely on gasoline power. Consumers do not buy cars to meet their "average daily requirements." They buy them to meet "peak load" range and capacity needs. Many will rationally reject a small commuting vehicle, even as a second car. We should, therefore, expect the electric utilities to engage in a concerted effort to bring about battery standardization, highway battery exchange stations, development of quick recharge batteries, and other systems necessary for a practical highway vehicle.

The automotive service industry, on the other hand, will go through a period of decline and reorientation; problems of transition will undoubtedly be serious. An industry that now suffers from a shortage of skills will be faced with a surplus of employees and a difficult retraining problem.

APPROPRIATE PUBLIC POLICY

The possibilities for reducing air pollution that are associated with the electric automobile have generated governmental interest in its development. It is therefore appropriate to assess the role that the federal government can play in connection with this innovation. Most of the items discussed here are already under consideration by federal agencies or committees of Congress.

Thorough development is the key to a successful electric automobile. Private resources devoted to development, however, will be largely based on calculations of private gain. The advantages to the automobile industry appear to be quite limited: basic technical knowledge will provide them with a hedge against potential competition from new entrants into the industry and a commuter car provides a partial answer to the problem of air pollution and thus reduces the criticism leveled at their main product. Even these potential gains have induced only Ford to make a substantial developmental effort. The potential for gain to the electric utility industry is large. In my opinion, their approach to development has been timid, given the size of the market for electric power that would accompany this innovation.

If the gains to purchasers in terms of low cost and convenience of transportation and the gains to society in terms of air pollution control are important—as they clearly are—then an excellent case can be made for a public subsidy to solve the technical problems more quickly and suitably. My own view is that technical development is inevitable, but that the time required to realize its full potential can be shortened by many years through governmental subsidy. Widespread public acceptance of electric propulsion will depend on the development of versatile full-range vehicles. Detroit will not energetically pursue this development unless there is a threat of stiff competition. Government subsidy of research and development will provide the technological basis for the emergence of the required competition.

The certainty and the speed of transition will depend to a great extent on the coordination of battery and propulsion components development with the tooling, service infrastructure, and electric power production necessary to support the mass production and marketing of an electric vehicle. If I am to purchase such a vehicle, I must be assured that the battery stations or charging facilities are available for highway refueling. Ways in which the government might aid in projecting these needs and coordinating the development of facilities need to be explored.

The problems associated with such a major shift in industrial structure are serious. A thorough knowledge of the nature and extent of these difficulties needs to be developed so that their social and private costs can be minimized. The government should acquire an understanding of these difficulties at an early stage in order to ease the burden of transition, rather than react to events as they occur.

The development of a full-range electric vehicle that is attractive to the consumer will be more effective in reducing the problem of air pollution than an entire phalanx of federal, state, and local controls. Government regulation is likely to prohibit the use of internal combustion engines in many areas, and require the expense of sophisticated emission control devices and inspections to ensure a proper functioning of combustion and exhaust systems.

There are few innovations on the horizon that offer comparable benefits to our citizens—both individually and collectively. Such an innovation should be given every possible encouragement. We have an opportunity both to hasten its implementation and to reduce the costs associated with transition.

QUESTIONS AND STUDY SUGGESTIONS

1. What are the current technological obstacles to the development of the electric car? Discuss the private and social benefits which may be derived from the electric car.

2. What are the major obstacles which now block the entry of new firms to the automobile industry? What effects might the development of the electric car have upon these barriers in particular and the present automobile industry in general?

3. Discuss the potential impact of electric cars upon the petroleum, electric utility, and automobile service industries.

4. Discuss the author's public policy recommendations and their underlying rationale.

Reading 34

Growth Prospects for a Mature Economy

Charles T. Stewart, Jr., Research Professor of Economics, George Washington University

This reading is concerned with this question: Is it necessary and inevitable that an advanced economy such as the United States encounter a declining rate of economic growth? There are three related avenues of thought which suggest that economic stagnation may well occur in a mature economy. First, the increasing importance of capital-saving production techniques may weaken the level of investment spending. Second, the shift of workers from manufacturing industries, where the rate of productivity increase is high, to service industries, where the rate of productivity increase is low, will reduce the economy's overall rate of productivity increase. Third, as the maturing economy becomes more affluent, consumers find themselves increasingly satiated with goods and services and, therefore, consumption expenditures decline. The author critically examines these three arguments and concludes that the United States' future growth prospects are far from dismal.

Must an advanced economy slow down like a man of advancing years? Must we be content with a snail's pace of economic growth and productivity gain? Many think so and marshal impressive arguments. The danger is that these views will be accepted and that people will readjust their thinking and actions to slow growth and to a rapid closing of the economic gap between ourselves and other nations.

The pessimistic way of thinking follows three lines of argument: (1) a decline of investment opportunities leading to secular stagnation; (2) the increasing share of services in our economy and slow productivity gains in the service industries; and (3) satiation of wants leading to stagnation of consumer demand.

However, abundant evidence indicates that future growth can be rapid, and that no slowdown is in sight, and that there is no necessity in the age of nations as there is in the years of man.

MATURE ECONOMY

The mature economy hypothesis, child of the 1930s, stated that the end of the frontier meant a decline in profitable investment opportunities. Private savings would tend to exceed available private investment, with a resulting decline in spending, income, and employment. The nation could be saved from chronic mass unemployment only by public works and other government expenditures to compensate for the inadequacy of private investment.

Much has happened since the 1930s to discredit the secular stagnation-mature economy hypothesis. The miracles of electronics, the development of computers, the widening industrial uses of the atom—to mention just a few—

From Charles T. Stewart, Jr., "Growth Prospects for a Mature Economy," **Business Horizons**, Spring, 1964, pp. 31–38, abridged. Reprinted by permission of the author and Indiana University.

explode the belief that we are running out of new inventions and opportunities for business innovation.

THE NEW STAGNATION THESIS

But the pessimists are a hardy lot who have refurbished their theories to cope with new realities. They point out that even if the pace of technological progress has not slowed, nor the opportunities for new investment declined, capital requirements have fallen. We have learned to produce new goods or expand capacity with less capital than previously needed. Highly refined tools, improved managerial techniques, and the automation of production processes have increased output from a given amount of capital equipment. The oxygen-injection technique in steel making is an outstanding example of a capital-saving technique that, with a very small investment, permits a doubling of the output of blast furnaces. Thus, rates of investment needed to achieve full employment increase excess capacity so much that they are succeeded by long periods of investment decline and chronic unemployment.

Of course, much truth can be seen in this streamlined version of the stagnation thesis. Private investment as a share of GNP has declined; even in absolute terms investment falls below the 1956–57 level, but it is primarily based on the conventions of statistical measurement. By investment we count investment in plant and equipment, omitting nearly all the $16 billion spent on research and development —an amount that has mushroomed from a mere $3 billion a decade ago. (Much of this, admittedly, is defense-oriented, with limited commercial payoffs.)

We also neglect most of the business expenditure invested in skilled employees, without whom the new tools, processes, and products would be useless. The postwar period has witnessed not so much a decline in investment per unit of output as a shift from the tangible investment in plant and equipment to the less tangible yet equally productive and job-making investment in research and in new skills.

TERTIARY REVOLUTION

The second school of growth retardation emphasizes the changing structure of the economy. As productivity increases, labor and capital shift from the primary industries—agriculture in particular—to the secondary industries or manufacturing. In backward countries, 80 percent of the labor force is engaged in agriculture; in the United States, the corresponding figure is less than 8 percent, and even this share is declining. This shift—made possible by large gains in agricultural productivity—rapidly accelerates the growth rate of the country and results in expansion of the manufacturing sector, whose average productivity is high. This is what happened in Russia, Japan, and other countries that started late in the industrial revolution.

The United States has moved beyond this stage to the tertiary revolution. Manufacturing is no longer a growing sector; we have enough of many goods, and productivity advances in goods-producing industries permit output increases without gains in employment. Only large defense expenditures have prevented a substantial decline in manufacturing jobs. These now account for less than 25 percent of total employment, the lowest proportion since 1940, and the trend is down. A larger share of our rising incomes is spent on services, and employment and investment grow in the tertiary, or service, sector of the economy. But productivity gains tend to be slow in services, and, therefore, their expansion at the expense of the goods-producing sectors slows down the average productivity gain and the rate of economic growth. This, at least, is the pessimistic verdict.

DIVISION BY SECTORS

The facts allow a more optimistic interpretation. First, the statistics misrepresent the shift between sectors. The 80 percent engaged in agriculture in backward countries devotes much time to construction, agricultural processing, manufacture, and services that advanced and specialized farming delegates to the industrial and services sectors. For every person directly engaged in farming in our country, roughly one more is engaged indirectly—manufacturing the tractors that have replaced horses and mules, refining the fuels that have replaced animal feed, providing the transportation, storage, marketing, and processing that in the past were in part performed by the farmer. Thus, perhaps 16 percent, not 8 percent, of our labor force is still engaged in agriculture—directly or indirectly.

Much the same process of specialization has occurred in manufacturing. A large share of many of the service industries functions in support of manufacturing: banking and finance, transportation and utilities, warehousing and wholesaling. Much of the shift of expenditures and employment to services reflects a growth of specialized services and a reduction in the range of functions performed by manufacturers. Only the growth in those services geared to households, and supplying the demands of other consumer-oriented service industries, can properly be said to be a response to changing patterns of final demand with rising per capita incomes.

POSTWAR PRODUCTION

Second, the spectacular rise in the service sector is mainly a delayed response to depression and war, rather than a secular trend. Consumers were starved for goods in the 1930s because of depressed economic conditions; this deficiency continued during the war and early postwar period because of shortages. If we compare the share of services in total output or employment in the 1940s with the share in the 1950s, we can note a substantial shift to services—particularly services to households and government. On the other hand, a comparison of the share of employment in manufacturing with the share in services in the late 1920s and in the late 1950s shows almost no change in the ratio. Service employment was 2.05 times manufacturing employment in the period 1925–29 and 2.20 times in 1955–59.

Thus, the major shift to services in the postwar period is nothing but a catching up with the situation prevailing in the 1920s. During the late 1940s and early 1950s, households stocked up on their deferred needs for consumer goods and bought new goods whose availability had been delayed by the war and postwar shortages. Once this replacement and stocking up had been largely accomplished, the share of manufacturers in consumer demand and in output and employment declined.

There is another way of looking at the composition of output. Manufactured goods produced today are quite different from those produced in the 1920s. Specifically, goods sold to households have a much higher proportion of embodied services now than they did during the 1920s. Foods are much more highly processed; prepared, even pre-cooked, frozen foods have replaced the staples such as flour and the raw and unprepared vegetables of previous decades. When account is taken of the large growth of services built into the highly processed goods being sold to households, it is unquestionably true that services are a substantially large share of output and employment now than they were in the 1920s and that a long-term trend points toward a services-based economy.

PRODUCTIVITY IN SERVICES

It is often assumed that this trend toward services is bound to reduce our rate of productivity gain, because big gains are in goods-producing industries, not in services. This conclusion is unwarranted. First, we cannot foresee precisely what sectors will experience the largest productivity gains. Second, we do know that many of the gains, currently and in the immediate future, are in the area of office procedures and operations that are more important in many service industries than in manufacturing. Third, a slow gain of productivity in services is primarily a consequence of our inadequate yardsticks. These yardsticks do not fully account for quality improvements of particular importance in services—such as medical care or teaching, which absorbs a large part of our labor force. Nor do we have any comprehensive measure of quality improvement in government services, which are included in productivity statistics on a cost-of-production basis.

One reason for the common belief that productivity gains in services can only be limited is the assumption that most services are labor-intensive and offer limited opportunities for greater capitalization. On the contrary, it is clear enough that utilities and transportation services are very highly capitalized.

The statistical bias in favor of tangible capital overlooks the greatly improved quality of service provided by the refined technical skills of people rendering personal services—such as teachers and physicians—as well as the skills of those engaged in policy making—for example, government officials. Our lack of adequate measures for intangible products excuses the prevalent belief in their low productivity gain.

Many opportunities for rapid productivity growth in consumer services exist that are only open for developed countries with very high per capita incomes. For example, the distribution industry in the United States has experienced high absolute productivity and rapid gains in productivity but still offers much scope for improvement. Recent gains and future prospects, however, depend on: (1) the universal availability of passenger cars, large home refrigerators, and deep freezers; (2) the universality of consumer credit; (3) multiple media of mass communication; (4) large home storage facilities; (5) the two-day weekend; (6) suburbanization; and, in effect, (7) high per capita incomes. Large gains are within sight in the huge education industry following breakthroughs in learning theory. The extent of the gains is a function of the number of people attending schools, which is much higher in the advanced countries than in the backward countries.

SATIATION

The last reason alleged why our nation is doomed to grow slowly in the future seems perverse; the reasoning is that slow growth is a result of rapid productivity gain. According to this school of thought, as real incomes rise a point is reached where wants do not expand proportionally and people do not spend enough of their incomes to maintain high levels of employment, investment, and income. While the stagnation theory of the 1930s emphasized inadequate investment opportunities, the satiation thesis of the 1960s foresees inadequate consumption opportunities. The reasoning generalizes from Adam Smith's observation that "the desire of food is limited in every man by the narrow capacity of the human stomach" and Engel's finding that as income rises the share of income spent on food declines. The same observations apply to any other specific item of consumption; a person reaches a limit to the number of symphony concerts he is willing to hear, the amount of education he is willing to absorb, and the number of cars he is prepared to own. The fallacy lies in generalizing from specific instances of satiation to a satiation level of real income. As new products are developed and old ones improved, new wants are created or old wants, which could not have previously been met, can be exercised.

To support the income satiation hypothesis,

we would need evidence of a declining share of disposable income spent on goods and services. Despite a doubling and tripling of real incomes since the turn of the century, the share of disposable income consumed is about the same today as it had been, as far back as our records go. No matter how rapid future productivity gains are, satiation will not become a threat until the share of income spent begins to decline.

THE WORKWEEK

A second piece of evidence that might support the satiation hypothesis is a changing balance of demand between work and income and leisure. The decline in the workweek, which has proceeded for more than a century, has, in fact, slowed down. Current demands for a shorter workweek are paired to the postulate of no decrease in pay. Even then, the motivation is clearly fear of unemployment rather than a satiation of desires. A greater demand for leisure per se would be inconclusive, because it may be wanted for increased enjoyment of the fruits of labor. It is the increased willingness to sacrifice income, or to reduce income gains, that would be supporting evidence. But there is no sign of it on the economic scene.

It is paradoxical to observe that the hours worked by people in the advanced countries tend to be more, not fewer, than the hours worked in underdeveloped countries. To some extent, this may be a question of opportunity for work rather than an underdevelopment of wants. Also, it may partially be a more favorable relationship between the returns of labor and the prices of goods. Whatever the fundamental reason or reasons, present evidence does not indicate a problem of satiation and resulting slowdown in the rate of economic growth.

SUMMARY

Logically, the three sources of pessimism conflict. The prospect of satiation is based on expected rapid gains in productivity. Slowdown comes from the demand side. Expectations that productivity gains will be modest, or may slow down with advances in technology and changes in economic structure, emphasize the supply side. The more validity in the satiation thesis, the less important any adverse consequences of technological leadership and a shift to tertiary industries become.

Although none of the fears is entirely baseless, the evidence in their support is not solid and much contravening evidence exists. The fear of declining investment opportunities, popular in the 1930s, seems absurd today in view of what has happened since then. This fear is also negated by future prospects for rapid technological advance issuing from the research revolution of our time. Investment in plant and equipment as a share of GNP may decline but intangible investment—in skills and in research and development—will increase. Many investment opportunities are open to us that are closed to underdeveloped countries, and other opportunities are limited to advanced countries with very high per capita income. The fear that other nations will close the gap between themselves and the United States seems no more realistic than a fear that the gap between advanced and backward nations will continue widening.

The shift of labor and capital from goods-producing to service industries has been much exaggerated; much of it is no more than a return, after a depression and war, to patterns prevailing in the 1920s. Nevertheless, the trend exists and will continue. It need not adversely affect the rate at which we increase per capita incomes, for great productivity advances are in the offing for many services. The sluggish performance of some service industries in productivity gain reflects the inadequacy of our statistical measures for intangible products and quality improvements.

The fear that satiation of consumer demand is in the offing, bringing unemployment and economic slowdown as a consequence of rapid productivity gain, lacks empirical support. For generations Americans have promptly adapted their spending patterns to rising levels of income and spend as large a share of their income today as they ever did. Furthermore, people have not shown an increased willingness to trade work, and income from work, for added leisure.

It would be foolish to argue that we have nothing to fear; but neither can we argue that America has already reached, or must soon enter, a stage of low and declining growth rates. No inexorable law limits human inventiveness or the expansion of human wants, or drives less advanced nations to overtake those in the forefront of technology and living levels. Determinism has limited bearing on the course of human affairs, and future growth is still largely a matter of choices and alternatives.

QUESTIONS AND STUDY SUGGESTIONS

1. Why do some economists take the position that rapid technological progress might cause the rate of economic growth to decline?
2. Discuss (a) the satiation hypothesis and (b) the tertiary revolution, emphasizing their alleged impact upon economic growth.
3. What arguments are used by the author in refuting the notion that the growth rate will inevitably decline in a mature economy?

Reading 35

Economic Growth and Human Well-Being

Walter A. Weisskopf, Professor of Economics, Roosevelt University

In this thought-provoking essay Walter A. Weisskopf charges that our economic behavior and political actions suffer from an overinfatuation with economic growth. The basic theme of this reading is that an expanding GNP is not by any means the equivalent of an improvement in human well-being. Preoccupation with economic goals—particularly an expanding GNP—has caused our society to neglect and to sacrifice those noneconomic wants which are crucial to improved human well-being. Here we encounter a disturbing plea to seek balance, stability, and harmony in our lives by putting the economic objective of growth into better perspective.

The modern social sciences abound with findings about the bad effects of modern industrial society. It is not necessary to present a complete catalog of this criticism here. Suffice it to mention the lack of community and solidarity, the impersonality of human relations, the other-directed conformism of man in the "lonely crowd," the anomie or rulelessness caused by modern rationalism, the estrangement of modern urban man from nature, his alienation from himself through his subjection to the market, his becoming an annex to the machine, his loss of individuality through subjection to the gigantic establishments of production and consumption. What is important to understand is that modern sociology and social psychology are actually criticizing *the detrimental effects of our economic system although it has given wealth to the masses.* However, economists to whom, since Adam Smith, this wealth was an unquestionable goal are still making the same assumptions; they have by-passed this criticism instead of assimilating it into their thought.

SCIENCE OF WELL-BEING

A new "science" of human well-being is needed. Such a discipline may examine the possibility that a person, a family, a group, or a nation can have too much wealth and income and too much economic growth and productivity. It may consider that the way in which wealth is produced, distributed, and consumed can, in itself, be a blessing but also a destructive way of life. We shall have to develop a new discipline of human well-being which will teach people when to work and when and how to rest; when it is wise to refrain from getting more even if one can "afford" it; and how to resist the temptations of modern mass production and consumption should physical and mental health require it. This is not a restriction of economic freedom but the extension of rationality into the sphere of individual living.

Such a science of human well-being should start with simple assumptions. They can be listed as follows:

From Walter A. Weisskopf, "Economic Growth and Human Well-being," **The Quarterly Review of Economics and Business**, Summer, 1964, pp. 17–29, abridged. Reprinted by permission.

1. The principle of balance.
2. The principle of real costs.
3. The principle of direct negative effects.
4. The principle of balance between means and ends.

All these principles have to be considered whenever a question of economic policy arises.

REAL COSTS

The principles of *balance* and of *real costs* are closely interrelated. Real costs arise from all human endeavors because human time and energy are limited—because man is a finite being. Our life on earth lasts only a limited time and we are not omnipotent; therefore, everything we do and accomplish implies the sacrifice of something we give up by allocating our limited time and energy in a specific way. This is a broader version of the scarcity concept used in economic reasoning; it could also be called the principle of sacrificed alternatives. However, it should not only be applied to goods and services; it means more than the sacrifice of more steaks to more cars under full employment. It is a general characteristic of finite human existence: embracing one mode of life implies the sacrifice of another one.

In economic reasoning only those costs are considered which consist of the sacrifice of alternative goods and services that cannot be produced for the market under the existing conditions. However, there are human potentialities and needs which are not related to the procurement of goods and services and cannot be satisfied by producing for and by buying and selling in the market. Love; friendship; primary, warm, close, affectionate human relations; the experience of beauty; the pursuit of truth; and worship are of this nature. It is often reasoned by economists that these aspects of human existence are covered by "leisure." This, however, is merely a negative concept, defined as the absence of work and production. It is then assumed that an economy which provides sufficient leisure will also provide sufficient time and energy for the fulfillment of noneconomic aspirations. This is by no means necessarily the case because the mere absence of work does not imply automatic fulfillment of these noneconomic needs.

These noneconomic needs which cannot be satisfied by more production for the market are the real costs of economic growth and of the striving for more and more goods and services.

A society which allocates most of the activity of its members to the production of goods will prevent the fulfillment of needs and aspirations which are thus neglected. The members of such a society will consider nonmarket activities as inferior and less important aspects of life. Parents, peer groups, authorities, and educational media, instill the idea that whatever has no market value has hardly any value at all. The meaning of life in our society depends on the experience of participating in production for the market. This leads to the neglect of noneconomic values and of the real costs of economic growth.

BALANCE

These sacrificed ways of life, however, may be required to balance and equilibrate human existence. The principle of *balance* is derived from biology. It refers to an ecological situation in which various organisms and species determine each other's sizes and keep each other in equilibrium. Rachel Carson, in her spectacular book *The Silent Spring*, has recently popularized this concept. The concept of balance, in its broadest meaning, implies that human well-being requires an equilibrium of forces which are opposed to each other in such a way that they are the opposite sides of the same entity, like the two poles of the earth. Reason and emotion, consciousness and the unconscious, body and mind—these are examples for such polar antinomies which have to be balanced in order to establish human health and well-being.

Our overemphasis on economic growth and acquisition leads to a disturbance of the balance of our existence. Because of the principle of scarcity, the excess of time and energy used for the procurement of goods and services for the market must, by necessity, lead to neglect of all those faculties and modes of life for which not enough time and energy are left. Human existence is thereby disequilibrated.

Our excessive economic orientation sharpens all those value-attitudes which are necessary for economic growth. Thus, our mode of life is characterized by an overemphasis on intellectual reasoning, an exclusive directedness toward manipulation and control of the outer world, and a compulsive drive toward activism. We are sacrificing those alternative faculties and attitudes which cannot contribute to an increase in wealth. This has resulted in an atrophy of emotions and feelings, a neglect of the inner world, and a deterioration of our capacity for a receptive orientation toward the universe, nature, and our human environment, and thereby, of our aesthetic and religious faculties.

Too much economic growth tends to destroy the balance between activistic effort and receptivity, doing and being, grasping and receiving, conscious intentional effort and passive inner experience, and between reason and feeling. This destructive effect is wrought by excessive *individual* striving for acquisition as well as by the exclusive emphasis on *national* economic growth. Unless an increase in the national income is counterbalanced by some gains in these neglected dimensions, such an increase may actually cause a decline in human well-being.

Economists usually assume that wants are unlimited and that, therefore, there is no upper limit to consumption. This runs counter to the wisdom of all ages before the industrial revolution. In antiquity and in the Middle Ages the expansion of "needs" was considered as unhealthy and "bad." The principle of balance requires the conception of an optimal supply of goods and services. This idea seems to have been completely abandoned in economic reasoning. Introspection and observation indicate that people may be surfeited with goods. Man's limited time and energy may be inadequate to adjust to an ever increasing amount and variety of goods.

Less than fifty years ago a person could reach the economic goals of his life when he married, bought and furnished a house, educated his children, and accumulated some savings for his old age. Today he is lured further and further away from rest and satisfaction by more and more new goods and gadgets; they keep him tied to the leash of work and acquisition until he is buried without ever having reached a moment of peace where he could look back to his work and say: It is good.

If ours is an "achieving society" it must give to people at least once in a while the feeling of having achieved their goal. An economy bent on continuous individual and social growth and expansion makes the experience of achieving a goal difficult if not impossible and leads to an unbalanced existence. The neuroses of the "status-seekers" and of the "pyramid-climbers" are symptoms of this disequilibrium. There-

fore, we may approach a stage of economic development where people may get tired of a way of life which prevents them from ever reaching an economic goal. In order to restore a balance they may refuse to absorb additional wealth and turn to other pursuits.

The principle of balance can also be applied to the *rate* of growth and economic change. The market economy has been compared to a gale of creative destruction. An increasingly faster rate of change is a characteristic of our present economy. Although much attention is paid to the difficulties of adjustment to a rapidly changing economy, there is hardly any discussion of an optimal rate of change. Is there a limit to the degree of economic change to which man can adjust? Is there a limit beyond which economic change, even if desirable in terms of more output, becomes intolerable for individuals and detrimental to well-being? It is, of course, difficult to give an answer to this question in quantitative terms; but it should be established that change is not always a gain but can inflict discomfort and suffering.

If modern industrial man may have found roots in a stable environment, economic change may uproot him again. The general feeling of insecurity and lack of community that pervades our society may have its roots in the continuous changes and their threat to physical and mental stability. The modern economy forces man into a pattern of extreme flexibility and detachment. He has to be continuously on the alert and adjust himself to the changing frontiers of production, jobs, and consumption. This has made him into a lonely member of a crowd. Economic change may sever the ties to habitat and neighborhood; it may cut apart the bonds of friendship and human relations. The great attention paid to human relations in industry is a consequence of the lack of attachment and involvement that continuous change requires. Definitely there can be too much change and too fast a rate of change. The principle of balance requires an equilibrium between change and stability. This should be kept in mind by those who consider economic growth unequivocally desirable.

DIRECT NEGATIVE EFFECTS

The *direct negative effects* of economic growth must also be taken into account in an examination of human well-being in the industrial economy. It is hardly an exaggeration to assume that almost any increase in production brings about a decrease in well-being in some other direction. Air and water pollution, smoke, smog, poisoning of crops, noise, dirt, ugliness of cities, destruction of the landscape, and the strains of rush-hour traffic are well-known examples. These negative effects are an essential characteristic of our production methods and should be taken into account when we plan for economic growth. It is characteristic of our attitudes that national income accounts do not include these negative effects. Thus they present an overly optimistic picture. An additional chemical plant will increase the gross national product; the water pollution caused by the same plant will not be accounted for and thereby the increase in real income will be overstated. But this is more than a faulty accounting method; it is a basic flaw in our attitude toward economic progress and human well-being which ought to be corrected.

MEANS AND ENDS

The principle of *balance between means and ends* is disturbed by the utilitarianism of our economic reasoning and attitudes; in technology and in business, only the end counts. In technology the so-called economic principle requires that the maximum effect be accomplished with the minimum effort; in business it requires that the greatest total revenue be produced with the minimum cost. The means and the way in which the goals are accomplished are depreciated. The opposite spirit is expressed in Matthew 16:26—"For what is a man profited if he shall gain the whole world and lose his soul?" A goal, even if beneficial in itself, can be vitiated by the bad effects of the means of accomplishing it. This principle can be applied to economic activity; the way in which output is produced and income earned is relevant to well-being and its negative effects may wipe out the positive effects of the increase in output and income.

The problem involved in the balance of means and ends can be illustrated by a comparison between play and work. In play and in games the way that leads to the goal is as important as, or more important than, the goal itself; in work it is only the goal that counts. Bertrand de Jouvenel has made this distinction very clear:

Play is the activity which procures satisfaction in such a way that the goal is merely the final point of such activity; labor is the activity which is only justified by its end.

This is especially true in our economy; labor and work are experienced as a disagreeable burden which is only justified by the goal of production and income. All civilizations which preceded industrial society considered labor as a curse and a burden. Under the impact of the Protestant ethic and of the achieving society, systematic productive work acquired the dignity of an end in itself and of a way of life. This attitude, however, required a great amount of repression and instinctual abnegation. In pre-industrial capitalism this was mitigated by the fact that the worker worked in his own house with his own tools and was master of his time. Also, commercial relations were not yet separated from human relations; suppliers and customers were friends and neighbors. Furthermore, the "instinct of workmanship" was satisfied so far as the worker produced a complete product.

However, the growing mechanization and division of labor in modern times again reduced work from an end in itself to a burdensome means of livelihood. Our economy has become an impersonal master; the slavery imposed by men has been replaced by the slavery imposed by machines and by the organization of labor. There is little pleasure and well-being connected with the work of the great majority of our employees and workers. Its only subjective *raison d'être* is the earning of an income and its only social rationale is the increase in the gross national product. That means that most of our waking hours are spent in an activity abhorrent to us and detrimental to our well-being.

But even if work in the modern economy were more pleasant and more self-satisfying, the utilitarian attitude which extolls future ends above the presently used means would prevent us from enjoying it in the here and now. We are forced, by our economic system, to think, plan, and care continuously for the future, so that we are prevented from living in and enjoying the present. Our constant orientation toward future goals takes us "out of ourselves," out of our present existence; but actual zest for living is possible only so far as one can live in the present.

POLICY IMPLICATIONS

If these principles were applied in welfare economics, we would arrive at policy recommendations which would often be different from those usually made by economists. The obsessive preoccupation with the growth and the rate of growth of the gross national product—I propose to call it GNP fetishism—stems from the neglect of these basic principles governing human well-being. The GNP is not used as a limited statistical device, but as a yardstick of welfare and performance and as a goal of national policies. GNP figures, conjectural and tentative at best, are watched by businessmen and politicians alike. Their decline or allegedly insufficient growth is experienced as a national calamity; and the comparison of the growth rates of Eastern and Western nations has become a matter of international competition.

After what has already been said, it is obvious that the GNP cannot be used as a measure of well-being and not even of performance. Not only does it leave out services which do not enter the market but it cannot include any of the disequilibrating, negative effects and costs discussed here. The fact that the statistical measurement of these negative effects and real costs is difficult or impossible is no excuse for ignoring them. After all, economic thought made its greatest strides long before it became mathematical and statistical.

Income Distribution

One of the reasons why economists consider growth of the GNP as a desirable policy goal is that it seems to provide a quantitative yardstick for policy decisions. Here, as so often in the modern sciences, the method determines not only the object but also the goal. The disadvantages of using GNP in policy decisions lies precisely in its purely quantitative character. Well-being depends not merely and predominantly on quantity but on quality. In respect to the GNP this means that its composition matters more than its size or its growth rate. Galbraith has asserted that the public sector of our economy is starved in comparison with the private sector. Here, a qualitative yardstick is applied to national income. This can be done on a wider scale. Up to now we

have been plugging for more and more in the mistaken belief that this will also take care of the problem of psychologically and socially undesirable allocation. However, we should begin to ask the question, More and more of what? It matters less how large the GNP is than of what it is composed.

If more attention were paid to the qualitative aspects and to the composition of the GNP, economists might turn again to the problem of *income distribution*. Galbraith has pointed out that we are escaping into the relatively simple policy of advocating growth to solve the problems of stability, security, and a more equal distribution. Our GNP does not necessarily have to be larger but it should be more justly and more equally distributed. Although the GNP has increased continuously, this has not achieved sufficiently equal distribution. We have to work actively toward this goal. This will require, among other things, an increase in the free services and in the formation of social capital from which the economically underprivileged benefit more than the higher income groups. This in turn will require a different allocation of resources from the one that our present mixed system has brought about. Merely advocating an increase of the GNP and hoping that this will remedy the problem of unequal distribution is facile escapism.

The reason for this preoccupation with size and growth in the aggregate and for the neglect of composition and distribution is not hard to find. It is much easier and requires less revolutionary changes if one confines oneself to the stimulation of the aggregate income than if one advocates policies for reallocation and redistribution. Here the congenital conservatism of economic reasoning comes to the fore. Reallocation can take place in the present circumstances only through government activity. To bring about a reallocation of resources seems to require such stringent governmental activity—taxing and spending—that few economists would dare to advocate it under the present political conditions.

Growth and Employment

However, a higher GNP and a faster rate of growth are also advocated to bring about full employment. To justify a higher GNP and a higher growth rate by the necessity of full employment implies a radical reversal of economic reasoning. Economics started with the assumption that need satisfaction is the goal of the economy and that employment and utilization of resources is necessary because we need more goods and services. There is nothing inherently desirable in the full utilization of resources, unless they serve to produce needed goods and services.

If one demands a higher GNP to accomplish full employment, production and resource utilization become the end and consumption the means. More goods have to be produced in order to employ more people. More people can be employed only if more goods are consumed. The natural relation between production and consumption is reversed; now it is assumed that higher production is desirable to keep factories, machines, and people at work. Thus a vicious circle is created; people must consume in order to work. This does not make any sense. It does not make sense to increase the GNP and its growth rate *merely* in order to employ people. Employment is desirable only if the goods produced by it are needed.

This is again a problem of channeling men into occupations where they are needed. If this is impossible the only reason for employing people is the humanitarian principle that a minimum of living standards should be guaranteed to everybody. This is why we pay unemployment compensation, relief, and subsidies. Unless the unemployed can be used to produce needed goods it does not make sense to employ them by overstimulating the entire economy and by putting an additional strain on *all* members of society through a faster rate of growth. This is like giving benzedrine to an already overactive person.

This way of dealing with unemployment, however, is rooted in our attitude toward income. There is a deep reluctance to pay out rewards and to distribute purchasing power except for work and additional production. This is not due to fear of inflation, which could be dealt with by monetary and fiscal measures; it is due to the subliminal remnants of the labor ethic according to which those who do not work should not eat. Although we have consciously abandoned this idea in our social legislation, we still adhere to the belief that income should only be a reward for production. This belief is reinforced by the fact that in industrial society only work in a traditional type of occupation gives meaning to life. We could easily grant to the unemployed sufficient purchasing power to live in relative comfort if they would not feel useless and excluded from a meaningful life without a job.

This will require the serious task of reeducation if our economy should become more and more automated. Serious students of automation predict that in the near future only a minority will find work in our economy. If this should prove correct we will have to change traditional attitudes toward work. This may not require that people will have to do entirely without work; but new types of activity and new ways of life will have to develop. It may be that all those activities which up to now have been considered as inferior, such as contemplation, meditation, worship, education, artistic activities, and aesthetic pursuits, will assume a primary importance.

QUESTIONS AND STUDY SUGGESTIONS

1. Briefly state the author's major theme. Specifically, why might economic growth differ from an improvement in human well-being?
2. Explain: "Our overemphasis on economic growth and acquisition leads to a disturbance of the balance of our existence."
3. Why might it be important to achieve the optimum, as opposed to the most rapid, rate of economic growth?
4. What are the policy implications of a "science" of human well-being?

PART THREE

MICROECONOMICS: MARKETS, PRICES, AND RESOURCE ALLOCATION

Reading 36

Marginal Analysis: The Case of Continental Air Lines

Leonard S. Silk and Daniel B. Moscowitz

Perhaps the fundamental characteristic of capitalism is its basic reliance upon an elaborate system of product and resource markets. These markets —some highly competitive, others less so—are the fundamental mechanism by which scarce resources are allocated among alternative employments. Hence, in good measure an understanding of capitalism is synonymous with an understanding of markets.

Economists employ marginal analysis in explaining and comparing the price-output decision of firms operating under a variety of more or less competitive market situations. In this reading the character of marginal analysis is succinctly revealed as we discover how Continental Air Lines has expanded its profits by applying the marginal approach in its decision making.

Continental Air Lines, Inc., last year filled only half the available seats on its Boeing 707 jet flights, a record some 15 percentage points worse than the national average.

By eliminating just a few runs—less than 5 percent—Continental could have raised its average load considerably. Some of its flights frequently carry as few as 30 passengers on the 120-seat plane. But the improved load factor would have meant reduced profits.

For Continental bolsters its corporate profits by deliberately running extra flights that aren't expected to do more than return their out-of-pocket costs—plus a little profit. Such marginal flights are an integral part of the over-all operating philosophy that has brought small, Denver-based Continental—tenth among the 11 trunk carriers—through the bumpy postwar period with only one loss year.

THE MARGINAL APPROACH

This philosophy leans heavily on marginal analysis. Put most simply, marginalists maintain that a company should undertake any activity that adds more to revenues than it does to costs—and not limit itself to those activities whose returns equal average or "fully allocated" costs.

The approach, of course, can be applied to virtually any business, not just to air transportation. It can be used in consumer finance, for instance, where the question may be whether to make more loans—including more bad loans —if this will increase net profit. Similarly, in advertising, the decision may rest on how much extra business a dollar's worth of additional advertising will bring in, rather than pegging the advertising budget to a percentage of sales

Adapted from "Airline Takes the Marginal Route," **Business Week**, April 20, 1963, pp. 111–113. Reprinted by permission.

—and, in insurance, where setting high interest rates to discourage policy loans may actually damage profits by causing policyholders to borrow elsewhere.

The economist who understands marginal analysis has a full-time job in undoing the work of the accountant. This is so because the practices of accountants—and of most businesses—are permeated with cost allocation directed at average, rather than marginal costs.

In any complex business, there's likely to be a big difference between the costs of each company activity as it's carried on the accounting books and the marginal or "true" costs that can determine whether or not the activity should be undertaken.

The difficulty comes in applying the simple "textbook" marginal concept to specific decisions. If the economist is unwilling to make some bold simplifications, the job of determining "true" marginal costs may be highly complex, time-wasting, and too expensive. But even a rough application of marginal principles may come closer to the right answer for business decision-makers than an analysis based on precise average-cost data.

Proving that this is so demands economists who can break the crust of corporate habits and show concretely why the typical manager's response—that nobody ever made a profit without meeting all costs—is misleading and can reduce profits. To be sure, the whole business cannot make a profit unless average costs are met; but covering average costs should not determine whether any particular activity should be undertaken. For this would unduly restrict corporate decisions and cause managements to forgo opportunities for extra gains.

MARGINALISM IN A NUTSHELL

The essence of marginal decision-making can be readily summarized by an illustration. Shall Continental run an extra daily flight from City X to City Y? Suppose the fully allocated costs of this flight are $4,500; out-of-pocket costs of the flight are $2,000; and the flight should gross $3,100. Management's decision is to run the flight. It will add $1,100 to net profit—because it will add $3,100 to revenues and only $2,000 to costs. Overhead and other costs, totaling $2,500 [$4,500 minus $2,000], would be incurred whether the flight is run or not. Therefore, fully allocated or "average" costs of

$4,500 are not relevant to this business decision. It's the out-of-pocket or "marginal" costs that count.

Continental's approach is this: It considers that the bulk of its scheduled flights will have to return at least their fully allocated costs. Overhead, depreciation, insurance are very real expenses and must be covered. The out-of-pocket approach comes into play only after the line's basic schedule has been set.

Then Continental goes a step further to see if adding more flights will contribute to the corporate net. Similarly, if it is thinking of dropping a flight with a disappointing record, Continental puts it under the marginal microscope: "If your revenues are going to be more than your out-of-pocket costs, you should keep the flight on."

By "out-of-pocket costs" Continental means just that: the actual dollars that Continental has to pay out to run a flight. It gets the figure not by applying hypothetical equations but by circulating a proposed schedule to every operating department concerned and finding out just what extra expenses it will entail. If a ground crew already on duty can service the plane, the flight isn't charged a penny of their salary expense. There may even be some costs eliminated in running the flight; they won't need men to roll the plane to a hangar, for instance, if it flies on to another stop.

Most of these extra flights, of course, are run at off-beat hours, mainly late at night. At times, though, Continental discovers that the hours aren't so unpopular after all. A pair of night coach flights on the Houston-San Antonio-El Paso-Phoenix-Los Angeles leg, added on a marginal basis, have turned out to be so successful that they are now more than covering fully allocated costs.

ALTERNATIVE COSTS

Continental uses an alternative cost analysis closely allied with the marginal concept in drawing up schedules. For instance, on its 11:11 p.m. flight from Colorado Springs to Denver and a 5:20 a.m. flight the other way, Continental uses Viscounts that, though they carry some cargo, often go without a single passenger. But the net cost of these flights is less than would be the rent for overnight hangar space for the Viscount at Colorado Springs.

And there's more than one absolute-loss flight scheduled solely to bring passengers to a connecting Continental long-haul flight; even when the loss on the feeder service is considered a cost on the long-haul service, the line makes a net profit on the trip.

Continental's data handling system produces weekly reports on each flight, with revenues measured against both out-of-pocket and fully allocated costs. Continental uses these to give each flight a careful analysis at least once a quarter. But those added on a marginal basis get the fine-tooth-comb treatment monthly.

There are times, though, when the decisions dictated by the most expert marginal analysis seem silly at best, and downright costly at worst. For example, Continental will have two planes converging at the same time on Municipal Airport in Kansas City, when the new schedules take effect.

This is expensive because, normally, Continental doesn't have the facilities in Kansas City to service two planes at once; the line will have to lease an extra fuel truck and hire three new hands—at a total monthly cost of $1,800.

But, when Continental started pushing around proposed departure times in other cities to avoid the double landing, it began to look as though passengers switching to competitive flights leaving at choicer hours, would lose Continental $10,000 worth of business each month. The two flights will be on the ground in Kansas City at the same time.

QUESTIONS AND STUDY SUGGESTIONS

1. What is marginal analysis? Explain how it is used by Continental Air Lines in deciding whether particular flights should be added or dropped.

2. How can a flight which fails to cover its average or fully allocated costs be profitable?

Reading 37

Costs and Prices in Launderettes

T. Kempner, Lecturer in Applied Economics, University of Sheffield

In this reading the economist's analytical tools are used in analyzing the price-output behavior of the British launderette industry. We find a mixture of both competitive and monopolistic forces influencing price. Each local launderette has a local monopoly, and prices are generally set by an association of launderette operators; yet each operator's monopoly power "is strictly limited by the many alternative methods of washing." Costs are

From T. Kempner, "Costs and Prices in Launderettes," **The Journal of Industrial Economics**, June, 1960, pp. 216–228, abridged. Reprinted by permission.

classified as fixed, recurring fixed, wage, and variable. Because fixed costs are dominant, it is found that average or per unit cost falls continuously over the relevant range of output. Thus we find, in this particular instance, that the profit-maximizing output of the firm is *not* the output at which marginal revenue equals marginal cost (indeed, there is no such point); rather, each launderette is prompted "to increase the utilization of plant (and thus the number of washes) during normal business hours." This reading provides us with an intriguing example of how the economist's concepts of cost and demand (price) can be employed in understanding the operation of a particular real-world industry.

This paper is an attempt to explain the behavior of costs and prices in a particular case. In economic literature there is a lack of detailed information to show exactly what happens to costs and prices in practice. This example is a very simple one. It is about the "Launderette" shops which have sprung up in large numbers in Britain over the last ten years. This is not a history of the growth of the launderette industry. My interest is in the explanation of cost and price levels. Much can be learned from detailed investigation of particular firms and industries and in this way the theory of the firm can be amplified and made more realistic.

I chose the launderettes, first, because there are no multiproduct complications and, second, because the cost and price data which I needed were made available to me by Bendix Home Appliances Ltd. From this information I hoped that it would be possible to draw up cost and revenue schedules.

GENERAL BACKGROUND

Self-service launderettes have become a familiar feature of most shopping centres. They are small retail shops with between 8 to 20 washing machines and 2 to 3 spin dryers (or extractors). The customer, with the guidance of the shop's staff, puts the washing into the machine and starts the process. Soap is added as indicated by lights. No other action is needed and the machine performs its tasks automatically. For most of the washing time it is possible for the customers to do other shopping. Three different washing processes are available. The first is a hot wash of up to 170° F. and takes approximately 36 minutes. During this time the machine will wash twice, rinse four times and extract water four times. The second method is the same as the first, but

the temperature of the water is not allowed to rise above 110° F. The third alternative is a short cycle of 18 minutes at a temperature of between 95–100° F. and consists of one wash, two rinses and two extractions. When the machine has done its job, the wet washing can be put into a separate spin dryer. Two applications of about 1 minute each are sufficient to prepare laundry for ironing.

The plant and equipment needed will consist of the shop itself, the washing machines and extractors, counters, scales and chairs. Behind the scenes are the hot water plant, equipment for water treatment and water pumps. The capacity and cost will, of course, vary with the number of washers installed.

Most launderettes look as though they all belong to one retail chain—there are over 1200 of them. In fact they are separately owned, but the similarity of their appearance is due to their main suppliers—Bendix Home Appliances Ltd. The majority of self-service launderettes in this country have been started with the advice and equipment of this company.

A fully automatic washing machine was a comparative novelty just after the war. The main object of the Bendix Company at that time was, and still is, to boost the sales of washing machines direct to domestic buyers. It was realized that this objective could be helped by the establishment of launderettes to serve as a demonstration of what the machines could do. The result was that there occurred a big expansion both of launderettes and of direct sales to the domestic market. But the launderettes are, as it were, the shop window: the bulk of the sales of washing machines is to private buyers. This does not mean, however, that the Bendix Company has no interest in the launderettes beyond their establishment. Far from it. Close contact is maintained and advice regularly given.

THE BACKGROUND TO PRICES

The price situation in this industry and its description is an essential setting for the analysis of costs which follows.

The price per wash is almost uniform for each launderette. The history of price policy is sufficiently short and uncomplicated to make it possible to attempt an explanation. Initially and for a number of years after their introduction the price was 35 cents per wash. This was based chiefly on the known costs in relation to the estimated use of the equipment. The estimate was not entirely a shot in the dark because of the experience gained at an experimental launderette in Queensway. With an estimated use of between 60 percent to 70 percent during hours of opening, 35 cents seemed to give an adequate return on capital and it was a price which appeared reasonable in relation to a number of other factors which are examined below.

First, direct costs vary with the extent of utilization. Costs per unit increase rapidly at less than 50 percent of the output possible in a 5½-day week. Soon after 50 percent they become constant per unit. Further details are in the cost section below.

Second, competition from other washing methods has to be taken into account. There is very little, if any, direct competition between one launderette and another. It has been a deliberate policy on the part of the Bendix Company not to encourage the establishment of launderettes in areas where an existing business can be endangered. Careful surveys of proposed sites are made, designed, among other things, to show the effects of a new shop on the surrounding launderettes. However, an alteration in the price per wash by a particular launderette would not necessarily mean that it would gain business from or lose it to another. It has been found that most customers use a launderette if it is available in their usual shopping centre. If the local price rises appreciably, they will not be prepared to make a special journey to the next nearest launderette. So up to a point the local shop has a monopoly—but a monopoly which is strictly limited by the many alternative methods of washing.

A part of the price policy is the influence which the trade as a whole tries to exert over its members. They have their own local associations and are quick and vocal in their resentment of anyone who alters the common price or standard. This kind of influence is more potent than is generally acknowledged. It is true that the strong-minded can stand out against such pressures. But the majority of people are neither strong enough to go against the tide nor do they feel an urge to innovate or experiment with prices or methods contrary to the established pattern. Inertia is one of the most important elements in price policies.

The tendency then is for a uniform price at all levels of output. So far the only change in price has been from 35 to 39 cents and was caused by increases in costs over a period. (The increase was accepted by most launderettes after negotiation with local associations and a national delegate meeting.) The average revenue curve for the firm and the industry is therefore a horizontal straight line. Price will not vary with output.

A few launderettes still charge the old price of 35 cents. Both cost and demand factors seem to be jointly responsible for this. In some areas rents and wages are lower than the national average. The chief cause of the lower costs seems to be that in these areas employment is less full than in the rest of the country. Costs and prices have been more stable. In these places the justification for pushing prices up to 39 cents has been largely absent. At the same time the possibility of doing so was also lacking; for many proprietors believed that their customers would not be prepared to pay a higher price.

The market for washers direct for home use has expanded greatly since the war. The machines used in launderettes are more efficient than the majority of those available to the domestic purchaser; the former can take a bigger load at a time and a controlled and regular supply of hot water is also available. The shops also have large and very effective spin dryers. Two opposing considerations are at work here. It is probable that in time the housewife will become more appliance-minded. The first tendency is for an increasing number of people to use launderette facilities. Against this, more and more households will try to buy their own equipment, not only because people believe (not necessarily correctly) that it is more convenient, but also because they like gadgets or because their neighbours have them.

There is no firm basis for guessing which tendency will dominate. At present launderettes are still increasing the number of their customers, though naturally at a slower rate than in the early years. It is probable that within the next ten years demand for launderette services will stabilize and after that cease to expand.

COSTS

An analysis was made of the initial and running costs of a unit of 8 washers and one of 15 washers; the results are given in Table 37–1 and in Figures 37–1 and 37–2.

A standard production period of a week of 5½ days, or 49 hours, was used as a measure of performance. This standard period can be used as a measuring rod. Each proprieter hopes to use the equipment as much as possible during the 49 hours the shop is open. Full utilization would mean some 1100 washes per

week for the 15 unit and about 578 for the 8 unit. This is the limit of the output which can be achieved without overtime. A standard period was also needed for the following reasons: First, I wanted to observe the behaviour of costs at different levels of output. This is especially important because variable costs alter disproportionately with changes in output. Second, the use of the standard period would show how costs change when output increases above the limit of output possible in the normal working week of 5½ days or 49 hours. Third, the standard period makes it easier to allocate fixed costs to total output. I used a week because it was convenient, but a month or 3 months would have done just as well. However, a week because it is so short, largely overcomes the possibility of changes in factor costs. Of course, the cost situation described below will alter whenever factor prices change

Figure 37–1.   Total costs and revenue for a launderette.

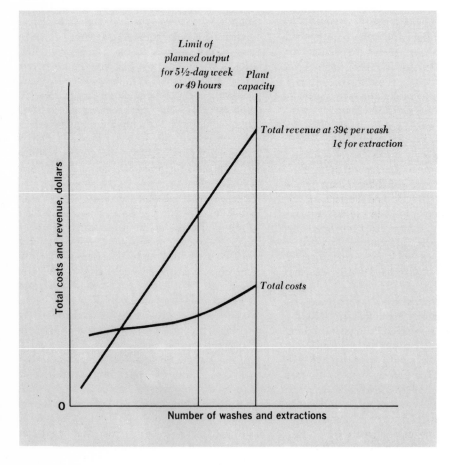

Total costs were divided into four parts: fixed costs, recurring fixed costs, wage costs and variable costs. The main problem here was how to divide up total costs in a way which would accurately reflect the time element (or life) of some of these costs. This is the problem: certain costs, which I have called fixed costs, are the initial expenses associated with the setting up of the business. Some of these, like the preliminary legal expenses are once-for-all costs; others like expenditure on plant and equipment will last for a number of years before replacement of worn-out or obsolete parts becomes necessary. Fixed costs must be allocated to total output, but this cannot be known until after the equipment has come to the end of its use. Only then can one know accurately the length of its life, the total output which it helped to make, and its scrap value. Accountants and cost accountants meet this problem every day. Their method, which I have followed here, is to make an estimate, usually a conservative one, of the expected life of the capital items and then allocate a proportion of the total cost to a particular period. In this case the Bendix Company advises amortization over a period of eight years. Accepting this, it only remains to apportion fixed costs over the eight-year period. I have used the "straight line" method of depreciation—an equal amount every year. The year was further divided into fifty-two weekly periods.

Fixed costs (non-recurring) then consist of the expenses of setting up in business. There are likely to be variations according to local circumstance, but a reasonable amount would be $14,560 for a 15 unit and $8,120 for the 8 unit. These amounts include the washers, extractors, oil-fired heating units, furnishings and equipment, decoration, preliminary advertising, and legal expenses. Over eight years amortization would be $36.40 and $19.60 per week respectively.

Recurring fixed costs include rent, rates, supervision, accounting, maintenance, advertising, insurance, stationery and sundries. I have distinguished these items from the fixed costs in the previous paragraph, because, although they must be paid if the business is to keep going, nevertheless unlike the other fixed items, they must be paid and paid again at regular, and *short*, intervals. Also recurring fixed costs can be allocated to output with far greater accuracy than the once-for-all fixed costs.

Wage costs are also shown seperately because they are neither true variable nor fixed costs. The 8 washer unit needs one full- and one part-time attendant; the 15 unit two full-time attendants. In the former case I have assumed that each attendant is paid at the rate of $16.80 per week; in the latter at a rate of $22.40 per week, both for a normal working week of 5½ days without overtime. In practice wage costs are fixed costs both up to the limit of planned output for a 5½ day week and also for a period of up to one week (or such other time as may be necessary for labour to be fired and hired). But beyond the point of capacity thus defined overtime must be paid. When overtime is paid wage costs will rise with output like variable costs.

Lastly, variable costs. These include fuel, electricity, water, soap and softening salts. Variable costs increase with output, but not proportionately. Largely because of variations in fuel costs, variable costs per unit go up considerably as output declines below 50 percent of planned output of a 49 hour week. On the other hand at above 50 percent there is little further change in variable costs and they rise proportionately with output. The figures which were made available to me show that at about 60 percent of planned output and over, variable costs per unit were approximately five and one-half cents. Below 50 percent costs per unit increased rapidly so that, for example, at 20 percent of planned output they had risen to approximately ten cents. A tabulation of these types of costs for an 8 washer unit is shown in Table 37–1.

I have not included an item for "normal profit" in the costs. The concept of normal profits is of considerable use in the pure analysis of the theory of the firm. However, I felt unable to use it in this case because I could not define it clearly enough for practical purposes.

The cost-revenue position for a launderette is summarized in Figures 37–1 and 37–2. The main conclusions which can be drawn from the data can be briefly stated.

Total revenue increases at a faster rate than total costs. This was so not only up to the limit of planned output of 578 washes, but beyond it. This fact is reflected in decreasing average costs. Moreover the decrease in average costs continued even when output had been increased up to 150 percent of normal capacity.

Table 37–1.   COSTS FOR AN EIGHT-WASHER UNIT PER WEEK (in dollars)

Output (washes)	Total fixed costs	Total recurring costs	Wage costs	Total variable costs	Total costs	Average variable costs	Average costs
100	$19.60	$33.60	$25.20	$10.06	$ 88.46	$0.101	$0.88
150	19.60	33.60	25.20	11.81	90.21	0.079	0.60
200	19.60	33.60	25.20	13.42	91.82	0.067	0.46
250	19.60	33.60	25.20	16.77	95.17	0.067	0.38
300	19.60	33.60	25.20	18.37	96.77	0.061	0.32
350	19.60	33.60	25.20	19.40	97.80	0.055	0.28
400	19.60	33.60	25.20	22.17	100.57	0.055	0.25
450	19.60	33.60	25.20	24.94	103.34	0.055	0.23
500	19.60	33.60	25.20	27.71	106.11	0.055	0.21
550	19.60	33.60	25.20	30.48	108.88	0.055	0.20
600	19.60	33.60	27.02*	33.25	113.47	0.055	0.19
650	19.60	33.60	28.84*	36.02	118.06	0.055	0.18
700	19.60	33.60	30.66*	38.79	122.65	0.055	0.175
750	19.60	33.60	32.48*	41.56	127.24	0.055	0.17
800	19.60	33.60	34.30*	44.33	131.83	0.055	0.165
850	19.60	33.60	37.10†	47.10	137.40	0.055	0.162
900	19.60	33.60	39.90†	49.88	142.98	0.055	0.159

* Overtime at time and a quarter.
† Overtime at double time.

By that time the shop would be open until very late at night! In practice this does not happen, but I tried the device of increasing output to see whether costs per unit would increase. They would not do so. Not even when I assumed that the late shift would be paid overtime rates at double time.

Costs behave in the way they do because most of them are fixed irrespective of output. Moreover variable costs, because of the effect of technical economies of scale, decline rapidly per unit of output during the early stages of production and then become constant. Wage costs are the only items which increase per unit after the limit of planned output has been reached, but they are too small a proportion of total costs to affect the decrease of average costs. Managerial diseconomies of scale, which in traditional models could be relied on to help increase average costs, do not really apply in this case.

However, it is largely unreal to assume that there will be much overtime working. It is usual for a launderette to work at between 60 percent to 70 percent of the output possible in a normal 5½ day week. Apart, possibly, from a late evening once a week for late shoppers there is little justification for evening opening.

OUTPUT AND SALES POLICY

The output and sales policy of a launderette is of special interest because it involves fundamental problems of economic theory. Unfortunately I can do no more at this stage than to state some of these problems. Very briefly, in the usual theory of the firm there will be a tendency for output to be determined by a point where marginal cost and marginal revenue are equal and price is not less than average cost in this position. Of course, this implies that, to begin with, marginal increments of output will add more to revenue than to cost but that eventually this position will be reversed. Consequently, there will be a level of output when an additional unit of output adds as much to revenue as to costs. This is the point of equilibrium because further output will increase marginal costs per unit more than marginal revenue. The theoretical model is one of great power and simplicity.

The difficulty comes when one tries to fit the output and sales policy of a launderette into this traditional framework. Average costs, for the reasons given above, decreased up to the limit of plant capacity and price does not change with the level of sales. At no level of

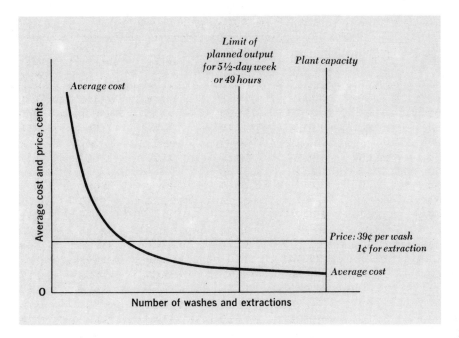

Figure 37–2.   Average costs and price for a launderette.

output up to the point of plant capacity did marginal costs and marginal revenue become equal.

The last paragraphs should not be taken as an attack on the existing theory of the firm. With the launderettes this result is caused by the special relationship between different items of costs. Yet we are in no position to say that this is an unusual exception which is unlikely to occur again in other industries. Only further research can tell us. My own view is that we may find completely different cost (and price) conditions in different industries.

Output Goal

In the circumstances at what level of output will the launderette aim? In practice the object appears to be the very simple one of trying to increase the utilization of the plant (and thus the number of washes) during normal business hours. And although I tried hard to find a more sophisticated explanation of sales policy, I did not succeed. I can do no more than briefly outline some of the things a launderette proprietor will do (or could do) to increase profits. He knows that total revenue increases faster than total costs and so his first efforts will be to in-

crease sales. The staff will be encouraged to go out of their way to be helpful to customers. Small additional services will be rendered: for example, some of the machine-minding operations will be done by the shop's staff for those customers who have much shopping to do.

Very little is known about the effect of advertising expenditure. Some advertising is done locally at the time when a new shop is opened, but for a going concern selling costs of this type are very small indeed. Possibly they could with advantage be increased even though the market which any one launderette can tap is limited strictly by geographical considerations.

Price Alterations

It is possible for individual launderettes to alter the national price of 39 cents, although for reasons given earlier they are unlikely to do so. As explained earlier, the current price is geared to costs and the expected total demand. There is nothing very scientific about the price, but it does seem to give an acceptable income to the proprietor. An increase to, say, 42 cents might give bigger profits at the moment, but the market has to meet competition from other sources, particularly the domestic washers. The effect of a fall in price is equally doubtful. To be effectively noticed it would require a big fall—10 or even 14 cents. Yet to justify a drop in price of between one-quarter to one-third would need a very big expansion of business indeed.

One unsolved question is that of off-peak pricing. So far as my information goes this has not been tried. My inquiries to a number of proprietors show that they do not think that they could gain any benefit from this method of pricing. They say, first, that the total number of customers is unlikely to be sufficiently influenced by off-peak reductions to make it worth while. It might simply shift the peaks and cause loss of revenue. Secondly, the customers may resent this form of discrimination. Many of their clients have worked out a time of the week (or booked an appointment) when they can be sure of a machine and when they can get a part of the operation done by the staff while they do their shopping. While I am not entirely convinced of this argument, I do not feel capable of challenging their estimate of the elasticity of demand for their product; nor of underwriting an experiment even for the furtherance of economic knowledge.

Cost Reductions

The industry is much more interested in reductions in costs because these would have a known and immediate effect. On the whole such reductions can only be achieved by an improvement in the techniques used. The equipment suppliers conduct research into the problems of better and cheaper equipment and its more profitable utilization. This does not preclude the proprietor from making his own improvements if he has the technical or commercial ability.

CONCLUSIONS

The cost schedules for the firms in this little industry show a situation where average total costs continue to fall up to the limit of planned output and, indeed, beyond it to the point of plant capacity. It was explained that the average cost curve failed to turn up and assume a U shape because of the special proportional relationship between variable costs and the other cost items: variable costs fell per unit of output as output increased from zero, but soon after 50 percent of planned output they became constant per unit. Even overtime failed to stop the continuing decline of average costs because they were too small a part of the total costs.

When this situation is allied with a constant price per unit irrespective of the level of sales, it becomes impossible for marginal cost and marginal revenue to intersect at any output up to plant capacity. For each launderette output will be increased as much as possible, for every increase in output adds more to revenue than to costs.

It would indeed be unwise to build a theory on one small and very simple example. Yet one wonders to what extent these cost and price situations are reproduced in other businesses. It may be that decreasing average costs, over ranges of output which are physically possible, are more common than was once believed possible and that a U-shaped short-run cost curve is only a special case. But before we can be sure one way or the other, much more detailed research into individual examples is necessary.

QUESTIONS AND STUDY SUGGESTIONS

1. Which of the four basic market structures—pure competition, monopolistic competition, oligopoly, or pure monopoly—best describes the British launderette industry? Specifically note both competitive and monopolistic elements which are evident in the industry. Describe the competitive relationship between launderettes and the purchase of automatic washers for home use.

2. Describe the fourfold breakdown of costs used by Professor Kempner, and illustrate each type of cost.

3. Most textbooks portray the typical firm's average-cost curve as being U-shaped. Account for the fact that the average-cost curve of launderettes continues to decline as output increases.

4. Using Figure 37–2, explain why, under the price-cost conditions which characterize the British industry, marginal cost and marginal revenue will never intersect to indicate an equilibrium level of output? What is the actual output goal of a launderette operator?

Reading 38

The British Hosiery Industry

A. G. Pool, Professor of Economics, University of Leicester
G. Llewellyn, Research Assistant in Economics, University of Leicester

The British hosiery industry, described and analyzed in this reading, is in fact a case study in pure and monopolistic competition. The industry closely fits the textbook models of these market structures. Economies of scale are relatively unimportant, and barriers to entry are virtually non-existent. As a result, the number of sellers is quite large and production is unconcentrated. There is no evidence of collusion among either sellers or buyers. The standardized character of the product makes some segments of the hosiery industry almost purely competitive; in other segments product differentiation makes the industry monopolistically competitive. Considerable light is thrown upon price-cost relationships in the industry. While firms profess to use many different cost formulas as a basis for price setting, the actual prices charged are narrowly circumscribed by market conditions. The performance of this highly competitive industry is essentially that which economic theory enables us to predict. There are no excess profits, and firms of most efficient size produce at their most efficient rates of output.

The manufacture of hosiery in Great Britain is commonly regarded as a competitive industry. No evidence of monopolistic or restrictive practices among hosiery manufacturers has been cited in any of the official reports concerned with monopoly in British industry; and those engaged in the industry assert that the multiplicity of genuinely independent firms, the ease with which new firms can establish themselves, and the complete absence of agreements seeking to regulate prices and output, make it virtually impossible for the individual firm, or for any group of firms, to exercise monopoly power.

THE INDUSTRY DEFINED

The "hosiery and other knitted goods trade" comprises all those firms that are engaged

From A. G. Pool and G. Llewellyn, **The British Hosiery Industry: A Study in Competition,** Leicester College and Leicester University Press, Leicester, 1955 and 1958, abridged. Reprinted by permission.

mainly in the *knitting* of goods, that is to say, the industry is defined not by the raw materials used (which include cotton, wool, silk, and the modern synthetic fibres) nor by the form or purpose of the product (which includes hose, underwear, outerwear, gloves, scarves, and other kinds of clothing), but by the nature of the *process*. Thus "hosiery" comprises every kind of knitted product, and not only hose in the narrow sense.

STRUCTURE OF THE HOSIERY INDUSTRY

A fundamental condition for the existence of effective competition within any industry is that there should be a large number of independent firms supplying closely substitutable products to a common market. There must be no concentration of a large part of the industry's production in the hands of a single firm or a small group or combination of firms; for such a concentration would enable a dominant firm or group to act as a "price leader" and set the pace for the whole industry. Nor must the firms in the industry produce commodities so dissimilar in character that they are regarded by buyers as quite distinct and imperfectly substitutable goods; for a low degree of substitutability between the products of different firms would virtually turn each firm into a monopolistic producer of a unique and distinctive commodity.

A major characteristic of the hosiery industry, which makes for a high degree of competitiveness, is the prevalence of small and medium-sized firms. This is illustrated in Table 38–1, an analysis by size of the "larger" establishments (employing more than 10 persons each) in 1951. Of the 1,094 "larger" establishments in the United Kingdom 21.1 percent employed from 11 to 24 persons, 50.0 percent from 11 to 49, and 73.7 percent from 11 to 99. When to the "larger" establishments we add a further 307 establishments (not shown in Table 38–1), which in 1951 employed fewer than 11 persons, we find that nearly four-fifths of the hosiery establishments in the United Kingdom employed fewer than 100 persons. At the other end of the scale very few really large firms are to be found: only 2.7 percent of the "larger" establishments in 1951 employed more than 499 persons and only 0.6 percent employed more than 999.

Establishments employing from 100 to 499

Table 38–1.   SIZE DISTRIBUTION OF HOSIERY ESTABLISHMENTS IN THE UNITED KINGDOM IN 1951

Average number employed	Number of establishments	Number of persons employed	Net output ($000)
11–24	230	4,055	$ 5,513
25–49	316	11,169	15,352
50–99	260	18,411	26,648
100–199	146	20,197	30,136
200–299	53	12,797	19,085
300–399	42	14,490	21,104
400–499	17	7,498	11,480
500–749	17	10,675	17,035
750–999	6	4,727	9,870
1,000 and over	7	12,763	26,015
Totals	1,094	116,782	182,238

persons in 1951, though less than a quarter of the total number, accounted for nearly a half of the total employment and produced nearly 45 percent of net output; and those establishments employing 500 workers or more, though only a little over 2 percent of the total, were responsible for 29 percent of the industry's net output and for 24 percent of the total employment. At the other end of the scale, the smaller establishments employing from 11 to 99 persons, which as we have seen made up about three-quarters of the total, produced 26 percent of net output and accounted for 28.9 percent of the total employment.

Compared with the other textile industries, small establishments, especially those employing fewer than 50 workers, account for an appreciably larger part of the aggregate output of the hosiery industry. Surprisingly enough, this is also true of the larger establishments, employing 1,000 workers or more; it is the medium-sized establishments, with from 100 to 499 workers, that are proportionately less important in the hosiery trade where they account for rather less than half the total output.

ENTRY CONDITIONS

Several factors account for the preponderant influence of small- and medium-sized firms in the manufacture of hosiery. The industry has always been, and still is, one in which it is possible, and indeed easy, to commence production in a very small way. The conditions affecting the entry of new firms into the industry will be considered in detail later in this report. Here we may summarize the main factors by saying that large hosiery firms differ from small primarily in having more machines and workers *of the same kind,* not in carrying further the specialization of men and machines; hence the technical economies of scale are comparatively slight and do not prevent the smaller firms from holding their own in competition with the larger. Further, in many sections of the industry, though not in all, new knitting machines can be purchased for less than one thousand dollars apiece, so that the man with experience of the industry and a modest capital of, say, fourteen thousand dollars has a reasonable expectation of establishing himself and consolidating his position. And finally, no obstacles to new firms have been erected either by the state or by the industry itself. The result is that there is a continuous flow of new firms into the industry (and, of course, an exodus of firms whose proprietors fail to make sufficient profits to induce them to stay); and practically all the newcomers start on a very modest scale.

The only section of the industry that reveals a pronounced tendency towards large-scale production is that engaged in the manufacture of ladies' fully-fashioned hose, and even here a number of quite small firms are to be found. In the other sections the technical conditions of production make it possible for a multiplicity of small- and medium-sized businesses to hold their own in competition with few large firms.

Although there is a great deal of "product differentiation" in every branch of the industry, there are in each section scores of firms with machines that can be readily adjusted to produce goods that are very close substitutes for each other.

LACK OF CONCENTRATION

The most important conclusion to be drawn from this study of the size-structure of hosiery firms is that this is not an industry dominated by a few giant firms which set the pace for a sprinkling of small "hangers-on"; the degree of concentration in hosiery is slight compared with that of most other manufacturing industries. In 1953 the three largest hosiery units employed a little over 7½ percent of the total number of workers attached to the industry.

Thus the forces making for industrial concentration appear to have been fighting a losing battle in the manufacture of hosiery.

Amalgamation of firms, the process by which most of the giants of British industry have been built up, has had little influence on the structure of the hosiery industry. The few combinations that have been attempted have not been conspicuously successful, indeed compared with most manufactures, the hosiery industry is pervaded by a highly individualistic spirit. Out of 1,127 hosiery manufacturing firms listed in Skinner's Hosiery and Knit Goods Directory for 1953, 800 are managed by directors who, so far as we can tell, have no connection with the boards of any other firm; only 180 have directors who sit on the boards of other hosiery concerns, and a further 147 have directors connected with firms not engaged in the manufacture of hosiery. Of the three largest units in the industry, one owns no subsidiaries and none of its directors appears to be a member of any other board; while a second has a small number of subsidiaries but otherwise no apparent connection, through interlocking directorates, with any other concern. Only the third of the trio has connections with other hosiery and textile concerns, and these do not appear to be extensive. The comparative insignificance of interlocking directorates is further illustrated by the fact that of 3,053 hosiery directors (including sole proprietors and partners) listed in Skinner's Directory 2,622 held only a single directorate, and a further 299 only two directorates.

The individualistic and competitive spirit of the industry is seen also in the limited range of functions entrusted to its trade associations. Their functions are primarily those of collecting and disseminating commercial and technical information, negotiating with governmental bodies, co-operative research, and providing advisory services for member firms. But the *restrictive* functions exercised by the trade associations of many other industries are lacking; except for one dyers' association (which, strictly speaking, is outside the hosiery industry) the trade associations have no power to regulate prices or output or to allocate markets or contracts among members; they do not impose exclusive dealing contracts on the buyers of hosiery or operate "stop lists"; nor are rebates paid to those who confine their purchases to members of the association.

ENTRY OF NEW FIRMS INTO THE INDUSTRY

In their survey of the historical development of the industry the Working Party states that "access to the industry by a man of small or moderate means has always been remarkably easy and new entrants, their prospect of success based on the proved success of their employers and knowing the facilities and advantages of their own district, settled down one after the other as neighbours and competitors of their former masters." How far this is still true of the industry it is the purpose of this section of the report to make clear.

In order to study in detail the conditions affecting the establishment of new firms, we have attempted to trace as many as possible of the hosiery manufacturing concerns that have been started in the North-Midlands region since the end of the war and to obtain from them, by personal interview, information relating to production, employment, capital, and the like. The North-Midlands region covers a representative cross-section of the industry; well over half the industry, measured in terms of employment, is located within this region, Leicester and Nottingham being by far the largest centres; and all the main branches of the industry are represented in the region.

So far as we have been able to ascertain, seventy-nine new hosiery manufacturing firms were established in the region during the years 1945–53. As there were about 700 hosiery firms in the region at the end of 1953, postwar firms accounted for approximately 11.0 percent of the total. We have traced thirty-one hosiery manufacturing firms that went out of business during the years 1949–53 (excluding firms that were reconstructed or acquired by new proprietors).

The relative numbers of firms entering the different sections of the industry are a reflection less of the comparative pressure of the demands for different products than of comparative ease of entry. In the stocking trade, for example, by far the greatest pressure of demand since the war has been in the fully-fashioned, not the seamless, section. The demand for fully-fashioned stockings (usually of silk) was expanding rapidly before the war. That only six of the 75 new firms in the North-Midlands region have entered this section is almost certainly attributable to the amount of capital needed to equip a factory for the production of fully-fashioned hose and to the lack of factory premises suitable for the installation of large modern machines: a single new machine of the most modern type costs up to $56,000, and the opinion of the trade is that this is a branch of production in which there are considerable technical economies of scale not available for the small firm. Second-hand machines, which are usually of the older and obsolescent types, can be bought at lower prices than that mentioned, but there have been comparatively few of them on the market.

We have been able to examine the conditions affecting the establishment and growth of 67 of the 79 businesses founded since the war; these represent 85 percent of the total and include firms in all the main sections of the industry. Of the 67 more than a half started in business as private firms without limited liability—20 as sole proprietors and 16 as partnerships; the remaining 31 were all private companies. By the end of 1953 five of the sole proprietors and six of the partnerships had converted themselves into private companies, but not one of the 67 had become a public company. Without exception they were all small or very small businesses at the date of establishment; the largest had an initial payroll of 63, and 79 percent employed fewer than 11 persons each. Ten firms employed nobody other than their working proprietors or directors.

The six new firms producing full-fashioned stockings all began with second-hand machines and at the end of 1953 were still using such machines only. Five of these firms started with a proprietors' capital averaging $9,296 each, and ranging from $1,400 to $22,400; for the sixth no information about initial capital is available. Ten of the thirteen new firms in the seamless hose section had an average initial capital of $4,410 ranging from $3,360 to $5,600; no information is available about the other three. Three of these started with some new machines; the remainder had second-hand only.

The Knowledge Requirement

The manufacture of hosiery is not the kind of enterprise on which a man may safely embark with no other qualifications than native wit and general business experience; if the promoter of a new hosiery firm does not himself possess a technical knowledge of the industry he must secure the services of a technically qualified manager, on whom he will have to lean heavily. In practice, as one would expect, almost all the new firms have been promoted by men whose previous experience has been in the hosiery industry, predominantly on the technical side. Of the 67 new firms in the North-Midlands region all but three had among their proprietors or directors at least one with previous experience of the industry; in 29 of these the owners' experience had been entirely, or almost entirely, on the technical side, the bulk of them having been employed as machine operators or mechanics; in 5 firms all the promoters' experience had been predominantly non-technical—administrative, clerical, marketing, or advertising; and 30 firms had directors who, individually or collectively, had had both technical and non-technical experience of the industry.

The few who entered the industry from outside came from silk throwing, weaving, plastics, building, wholesaling, and co-operative retailing; at least one of these had a family connection with the hosiery industry and entered into partnership with a technically qualified relative. Thus, for all practical purposes it may be said that in the North-Midlands region the founders of new hosiery firms have been recruited wholly from within the industry; the establishment of new businesses has not been difficult for those who already knew their way around the industry, but, notwithstanding the high level of post-war prosperity, only an insignificant number of strangers to the industry have sought to found businesses in it. Hosiery manufacturing, unlike shop-keeping or catering, is not a trade in which the novice with a little capital and a lot of confidence is prepared to have a go.

Capital Requirements

For the initial financing of their ventures, the founders of new businesses have relied very largely on their own private capital, derived from such sources as savings, war gratuities, and the like. The banks come into the picture much more frequently once the firm is established, and it is clear from the balance sheets we have examined that the growth of many of the new firms has been partly financed with the aid of bank loans; but the part played by the banks in putting up the initial capital for entirely new hosiery ventures appears to have been very limited.

The most striking features of the capitalization of new hosiery firms are, first, the extremely small amounts of capital with which a number of ventures have managed to get going, especially in the earlier postwar years, and second, the wide range of the capitals with which this group of small private concerns have equipped themselves.

The initial capital ranged from as little as $134 up to $56,000. The arithmetical average of the original capitals of the 64 firms is $9,492, but this is not a truly representative figure since more than half of them started with less than $7,000 each. Fifty-six hundred dollars is both the median figure and the one that occurs most often (8 firms began with this amount of capital), and may be taken as the best single indication of the opening capital of the general run of new firms.

The amount of capital with which a hosiery manufacturer can establish himself in business depends on a great many factors, which vary from firm to firm; among these are the scale on which he proposes to operate, the amount of credit he can secure from yarn merchants, and the amount he must give to those who buy his output, whether he is buying his premises outright or renting them, whether he is buying second-hand or new machines, and whether he is paying for them cash down or in installments.

Patents

The exclusive use of certain techniques of production, protected by patents or secrecy, has in some industries been a means by which established firms have been able to prevent the entry of rivals, or at least to put newcomers at a serious technical disadvantage and reduce their chances of survival. We have found no evidence in the hosiery industry that new firms are faced with such obstacles. Large numbers of patents have, of course, been taken out for knitting and other machines by firms in the textile engineering industry. But it is the practice of the machine builders to sell their patented machines on the same terms to all hosiery manufacturers, whether old established or new; their patents limit the activities of rival machine builders but do not limit entry into the hosiery industry. If the building of machines and the manufacture of hosiery were combined in vertically integrated firms, the possession of a machine patent by a firm mainly interested in selling hosiery might conceivably restrict competition. But this kind of integration has not taken place; some of the machine builders produce small quantities of hosiery as a sideline, but their primary interest is to *sell* their machines, not to use them as a means of obtaining an exclusive market for their own hosiery products.

The patenting of a hosiery *product*, as distinct from a machine, could seriously hamper the establishment of new firms wishing to manufacture that product; a well-known historical example of this kind of restriction was the interlock process. Both the interlock fabric and the machinery for making it were protected by patents taken out in 1908 and 1909, and only three British manufacturers were licensed to use the process. The expiry of the patent in 1929 was followed by a remarkable expansion of this section of the industry; during the war years, according to the Working Party Report, 70 percent of the output of cotton hosiery goods were made of interlock fabric. At the present time there appear to be no patents restricting firms from manufacturing particular types of hosiery; the only legal limitations on the right of a new firm to produce goods indistinguishable from those of existing firms are those arising under the Trade Marks Acts.

Technology

In some industries the entry of new firms, though not restricted by legislation, trade associations, or patents, is nevertheless rendered difficult by the necessity for new firms to establish themselves on a very large scale if they are to have any hope of producing at a competitive level of costs. The normal process of growth, from infancy to full maturity, is out of the question for such firms. It is abundantly clear that the hosiery industry is not one in which the technical conditions of production afford such overwhelming advantages to the large-scale firm that the small man has no chance of establishing himself. There are certainly economies of scale in most, if not all, sections of the industry; but there is very little published evidence to show how large these economies may be. The Working Party referred

to the uncertainty in the industry itself about the optimum size of a production unit and stated that it had been unable "to ascertain clearly what significant difference in efficiency (if any) existed between firms from the point of view of size alone."

We may conclude, from our survey of the establishment and growth of new firms since the war, that the technical conditions of hosiery manufacture show no sign as yet of ending the traditional process by which the industry has maintained its own growth; new small firms are continually entering the industry, of which some may be expected to fall by the wayside while others will grow to full maturity. The minimum capital required by a new firm is still small enough to enable enterprising men of modest means to establish themselves with a reasonable prospect of success. There are no legislative restrictions on the entry of new firms, nor do the trade associations of the industry put any obstacles in the way of new entrants.

COMPETITION AND PRICE FIXING

The British hosiery industry is not a perfectly competitive industry in the sense in which that term is used nowadays by theoretical economists. For where "perfect competition" prevails the individual firm does not have a price *policy* at all. It can sell whatever output it chooses to produce at the current market price, which is determined by impersonal market forces; hence there is no point in its offering to sell goods at less than the price currently prevailing in the market. On the other hand it will sell nothing at all if it attempts to charge more than the prevailing price. Thus under "perfect competition" the individual firm is free to decide what its output shall be, but not what price it shall charge. For an industry to be characterized as competitive in this extreme sense certain conditions must be satisfied: all the firms within the industry must produce identical goods, so that the source from which the buyer takes his supply is a matter of complete indifference to him; there must be so many firms that no single producer can influence the level of the market price by varying his output; producers must not collaborate in any way to regulate prices, output or the entry of new firms; and every buyer and seller must be well informed about what is happening in the whole of the market.

Few competitive industries, if any, satisfy all the conditions of this theoretical model; perhaps those that approach it most closely are some branches of the agricultural industry. Where the conditions are not fully satisfied we have an industry in which competition is said to be in some degree "imperfect." Thus rival firms may offer to buyers products which, though serving the same purpose and going by the same name, differ in quality, style, colour, or packing, or in other respects that the consumer regards as significant. The producer then has to decide how much above or below the prices of his competitors' lines he can profitably fix the price of his own line. He is not tied, as under "perfect" competition, to a single market price, but finds that there is a range, narrow or wide according to the keenness of competition, within which he is free to settle his own price.

ROLE OF PRODUCT DIFFERENTIATION

The evidence cited so far shows that competition in the hosiery industry is not impaired either by restrictive agreements among firms or by the presence of a few large and dominant firms acting as price leaders. Of the factors making for some degree of "imperfect" competition in the industry much the most important is product differentiation. There are at least 150 separately named products turned out by the industry, from ankle socks to wraps, and in most of these there is an immense range of lines. They may be made of wool, cotton, nylon, rayon or other man-made fibres; the yarns may be coarse or fine; the number of stitches to the inch and the type of stitch can be varied; so can the colour, the style, the finish, the size, and the packing. In the outerwear section particularly, where fashion plays so large a part, even a small firm will design and try out in the market scores of "numbers" each year; one such firm informed us that twice a year it offered to the wholesaler through whom it marketed all its output about 100 different lines in ladies' dresses, of which generally 25 to 30 would be taken up by the wholesaler. There is a ceaseless search for new styles that will take the fancy of buyers, resulting in the production of a countless variety of lines. This variety is, however, by no means peculiar to the fashion trade in hosiery; for example, one of the firms interviewed, specializing in the manufacture of children's socks, uses 380 dif-ferent yarns (of varying material, count, and colour). This wide range of quality and style is naturally matched by a corresponding range of prices for goods that go by the same name: ladies' fully-fashioned nylon stockings, for example, may range in price (retail) from 69 cents a pair to $2.94, and for a pair of men's socks one can pay as little as 41 cents or as much as $2.31 (excluding the more expensive hand-knitted varieties that may run up to $3.85).

The problem facing the typical hosiery manufacturer is not always simply that of fixing a price for a product he has already decided to make. It is also in many cases that of deciding what style of product he can profitably make at a certain price. For such typical products as stockings and socks the range of retail prices is not continuous; prices are fixed at conventional points in the scale, and the intermediate prices are seldom used. Thus the conventional prices for fully-fashioned nylon stockings are 69 cents, 83 cents, and so on up the scale by intervals of 14 cents. Faced with such a price scale the manufacturer will realize that a line which, with distributors' margins added, would result in a retail price of say 90 cents is unlikely to find favour with distributors; if it is not rejected out of hand by the distributors he will have either to improve its quality, so that it can hold its own in competition with other lines selling retail at 97 cents, or to lower its cost (e.g., by using cheaper yarn or by cutting out some of the trimmings) so as to bring the price down to 83 cents. Many of the firms interviewed explained that it was not an uncommon experience to find, on estimating the cost of a line and quoting a price to the distributors, that they were asked to modify the specifications of the product so as to make it saleable at one of the conventional retail prices; simplifying the product and knocking 28 cents a dozen off the manufacturer's price might just enable it to find its place in a quality-price group where it would have a chance of selling well.

THE COST-PRICE RELATIONSHIP

In order to determine the most profitable price for a particular product the manufacturer would need to know both the shape of the demand curve for the product (i.e., what quantities he could sell at different levels of price) and the shape of the cost curve (*i.e.*, how his total costs would vary with the quantity produced). If, at the price he is currently charging, the demand is inelastic in the technical sense, it will pay him to raise the price, since, although he will then sell a smaller quantity, his total receipts will increase and his total costs will fall. On the other hand it will pay him to lower the price if the demand is so elastic that the sale of a larger output adds more to his total receipts than to his total costs.

As regards the relationship between demand and price, the firms we interviewed all showed an awareness of the fact that they must expect to sell less at a high price than at a low one; but we found little evidence of attempts to estimate the precise relationship between the level of demand and the level of price. Firms appeared to have pretty definite ideas about the upper limit of price beyond which demand could be expected to be so elastic that their products would be "priced out of the market." In selecting a price within the range below this upper limit the firms interviewed were mainly concerned to keep their order books well filled and their workers and machines working as nearly as possible up to capacity. If they found a new line selling more readily than they had expected when they first priced it, they did not increase the price but geared their production to make the most of the brisk demand. Many firms declared that once they had fixed the prices to be charged to wholesalers it would be difficult if not impossible to raise them (unless the increase were justified by higher production costs); and the loss of customers' goodwill might well make such a price increase unprofitable in the long run.

As regards the relationship between costs and output, the assumption commonly made by hosiery manufacturers is that an extension of productive capacity will cause total costs to increase more or less in proportion to output. Broadly speaking, there is not very much more specialization of workers and machines in large hosiery firms than in small. For example the same circular machines for knitting half-hose are used in large factories as in small; the only difference is that there are more of them. Similarly the knitters, linkers, stampers, and the rest of the ancillary workers are, in general, performing the same operations in the large firm as in the small. We have in the hosiery industry an example of what the economist calls fixed coefficients of production: the same knitting machines, the same sewing machines, the same knitters, and the same ancillary workers tend to be employed in more or less the same fixed proportions, irrespective of the size of the firm. Doubtless there are some economies of scale in the hosiery trade, especially on the managerial side. But for any given line the main items of cost per dozen—yarn costs and direct labour costs—are likely to vary very little with the size of the firm. Since these two items account for all but a minor part of total costs, the scope for economies of scale is generally considered to be very small.

We found the firms interviewed very conscious of the fact that an expansion of output up to the limits of their existing productive capacity would lower average costs, by spreading overheads further, and that production at less than capacity would raise average costs. A main aim of their pricing policy, accordingly, was to keep their machines and workers fully employed, since only in that way could they succeed in keeping their average costs down to the minimum that was technically achievable.

PRICING PRACTICES

All the interviewed firms prepared cost estimates, but they described in very different terms the use to which they put such estimates. At one extreme were a number of manufacturers who stated that their selling prices were normally equal to their estimated production costs plus a pre-determined profit margin, usually expressed as a percentage of total costs. Some of the firms in this group applied to all their products the same rate of mark-up; others differentiated the mark-up according to their judgment of the state of the market, lower rates being generally applied to standard lines than to novelties. At the other extreme were firms that first determined into which quality-price group each of their lines fell, and then calculated the price they could charge to retailers or wholesalers by deducting the usual dealers' margins from the "recognized" retail prices. Cost estimates enabled these firms to calculate the residual profit margins they could expect to secure, but played no direct part in determining the prices actually charged. In between these two groups was a third, comprising firms that calculated for each line what may be called a "costed price" or "target price"—costs plus an "acceptable" or "normal" profit margin—but nevertheless charged more or less than the "costed prices" according to their estimates of what the market would bear. For such firms costs plus "normal" profit margins were no more than a general guide to the prices actually charged; they were certainly not the sole determinant of selling prices.

At first sight it may seem puzzling that within the same industry there should be some firms apparently able to calculate their selling prices from ascertained costs, including a predetermined profit margin, and others unable to do more than calculate the residual profit remaining after deducting ascertained costs from selling prices fixed by the market. Some appear to be in the happy position of making their prices depend on the profit they choose to write into their calculation, while others have to adjust their production programme to prices that they are powerless to fix or even to influence directly. These contrasting positions become more understandable when it is remembered that what, for convenience, is called the hosiery industry really comprises a number of sections producing a great variety of products, which are sold in markets that vary considerably in competitiveness. The manufacturer of a highly profitable line in cashmere cardigans may, for a time, be the only firm marketing that product; he alone can settle its price, and he will naturally describe his pricing procedure as consisting of the addition of a profit margin to his estimated costs, the margin being one that is "acceptable" to him or that he thinks "the market will bear." At the opposite end of the spectrum of competition is the manufacturer of a standard line in plain grey half-hose, which he sells in a market supplied by scores of other manufacturers. He also has to attach a price to his product, but he finds that the only choice open to him is to charge whatever has come to be the "recognized" price established by the competitive forces of the market. Thus he will naturally declare that his costing system plays no part in determining his prices: it merely helps him to discover what profits he can expect to secure from different lines when sold at prevailing prices.

Whatever the motions gone through by individual manufacturers in the process of settling their prices, it is evident to us that the selling policy they all adopt is accurately described as one of charging what they think the market will bear. This formulation covers, at one end, the case where the manufacturer can only charge the recognized competitive market price (since the market will "bear" nothing more than this) and where the function of his cost estimate is simply to enable him to judge the residual profit margin the market price will yield him. At the other end it covers also the case where, there being a range of possible prices among which a choice has to be made, the manufacturer decides to include a mark-up of 12 percent in his calculation because he believes that the resulting price will be the most profitable one within the range open to him. In short the pricing policies of hosiery manufacturers constitute a continuous spectrum, which can only with artificiality be divided into apparently distinct categories.

GENERAL CONCLUSIONS

The main conclusions that emerge from this enquiry may be summarized as follows.

1. Although most of the conditions that make for effective competition are satisfied by the industry—multiplicity of producers and of buyers, technical conditions that enable small firms to hold their own in competition with large, ease of entry of new firms, and absence of collective regulation of prices and output—the immense variety of ways in which almost every kind of hosiery can be differentiated is a feature that is incompatible with "perfect competition," as that term is defined by the economist. The manufacturer of a line has to meet competition from the slightly different or significantly different lines offered by rival firms, and is compelled to fix his prices with due regard to the prices of these close substitutes. In an extreme case, where a number of firms produce lines that buyers consider to be indistinguishable, a uniform price is established by supply and demand and has to be accepted by each of the competitors. But in the typical case the manufacturer is able to choose among a number of possible prices: he has to have a price policy.

2. Almost every firm performs the operation of estimating the average cost per dozen of each line and of adding thereto what it considers to be a reasonable profit margin, so arriving at a calculated price based on cost. The price so calculated may become the actual selling price, if the firm's assessment of the

market situation (including the prices charged by competitors) leads it to believe that the calculated price is the one it can most profitably charge. But, to judge from the sample of firms we have interviewed, more often than not the selling price will differ from the calculated price; it will do so whenever the price that the market is judged to be able to bear is above or below the calculated price. In short, the manufacturer's choice of price is determined by his judgment of the market situation, not by his calculation. It would, in our view, accord more with the realities of the pricing process if the manufacturer calculated his expected *profit*, by subtracting estimated costs from the price actually charged, instead of adding estimated costs and a notional profit margin in order to arrive at a "price" that will probably not be the one actually charged.

3. Circumstances may for a time enable a firm to fix the price of a line at a level yielding unusually high profits; it may be the first to introduce a new style that takes the public's fancy; it may devise a cheaper method of producing a familiar product; or it may be supplying a market in which a temporary shortage of yarn creates a situation favourable to a limited number of manufacturers (*e.g.*, the market for fully-fashioned nylon stockings for some years after the war). But such abnormal profits are short-lived owing to the pervading influence of competition. Machines are readily adjusted to produce the lines that are found to be in greatest demand; and the introducer of a new style can expect to find it imitated by competitors within a few months and to have his innovation profits consequently pruned.

QUESTIONS AND STUDY SUGGESTIONS

1. Explain precisely what the authors mean by the hosiery industry. Describe the hosiery industry and the various segments of the industry using the following criteria: (*a*) the number of sellers and the extent of concentration among them; (*b*) the barriers to entry; (*c*) the number of buyers and the extent of concentration among them; (*d*) collusion among sellers; and (*e*) the amount of product differentiation.

2. To what extent are there economies of scale in the industry? What is the effect of these scale economies on the long-run average costs of a firm as it grows in size? What is the behavior of a firm's average costs in the short run as the firm expands its output toward capacity?

3. Explain the relationship between the ability of a new firm to enter the industry and each of the following: (*a*) the kind of prior business experience needed; (*b*) the amount of capital needed; (*c*) the activities of trade associations; (*d*) patented techniques of production; (*e*) patented products; and (*f*) economies of scale.

4. Is the British hosiery industry an example of pure competition, of monopolistic competition, of neither, or of both? Explain your answer.

Reading 39

The Economics of Advertising

L. G. Telser, Professor of Economics, University of Chicago

Advertising is a basic characteristic of most monopolistically competitive industries and of many oligopolistic industries. However, the alleged merits and demerits of advertising have long been debated, largely with little or no regard for empirical evidence. In Reading 39 Professor Telser draws heavily upon his own empirical work on the effects of advertising. The result is a dispassionate appraisal of the relationship between advertising and profits, the impact of advertising upon brand loyalty, and the effect of advertising upon competition.

High on the list of controversial economic topics stands advertising. The critics of advertising claim it abuses consumer confidence, shapes and sometimes vulgarizes taste, and creates abnormal, unjustified profits. To these critics advertising is the leading symbol of materialistic Western civilization and of capitalism in particular. There is once more talk of a tax on advertising and of limitations on the advertising of some products, particularly medicines and cigarettes. Nowadays there are few defenders of advertisers, and even these speak humbly and possibly without conviction. In intellectual circles it is risky to one's reputation of intelligence and/or honesty to defend advertising. This one-sided view of the subject is by itself a phenomenon deserving of serious study, but it lies outside the scope of my present task. What seems most lacking in the debate is an attempt to understand the functions of advertising, its uses, and its prevalence. Indeed, some aspects of advertising pose problems of considerable intellectual challenge, whose study will aid protagonists on all sides of the debate on advertising.

SOME PROBLEMS IN ADVERTISING

Advertising comes in many forms. Not all goods are advertised to the same extent, if at all, and different goods are advertised in different media. A conspicuous form of advertising is on television, and even larger sums in total are spent on advertising in the other media—newspapers, magazines, radio, billboards, and direct mail. Some commodities are more advertised in one medium than in another. For example, retailers generally concentrate their advertising in newspapers. Large mail-order houses use media with a national audience and spend large sums preparing and mailing catalogues. Some nationally distributed goods such as automobiles and cigarettes are advertised in many media, while others such as breakfast cereals are advertised mostly on television. Some commodities are not advertised at all, such as locomotives, contraceptives, and glass eye balls. Consumer goods are much more advertised than industrial products. What explains these differences in the usage of advertising by commodity and by media?

Reprinted from "Some Aspects of the Economics of Advertising," **The Journal of Business**, April, 1968, pp. 166–173, abridged, by permission of the University of Chicago Press. Copyright © 1968 by the University of Chicago.

Advertising outlays on a given commodity change over time. For example, in the 1920s cigarettes were more advertised than in the 1930s, and, more recently, cigarettes are again heavily advertised. Two breakfast cereals, General Mills' Wheaties and Kelloggs' Corn Flakes, were much more advertised than they are now. Kodak Instamatic cameras and Polaroid Land cameras are now more advertised than they will be in the future. What explains these changes over time?

Total advertising outlays as a percentage of national income show remarkable stability over time. In the United States this ratio has remained between 2 and 3 percent of national income annually, except for some changes over the business cycle. The percentage rises somewhat when business is slack and falls somewhat when business is more active. What explains the secular stability of this ratio and its behavior over the business cycle?

Advertising is only one means of promoting the sale of goods and services. Personal selling is the older method, and more is spent on salesmen than on advertising. Moreover, one cannot understand the determinants of advertising expenditures without considering the problem of explaining total selling outlays. There are wide differences in personal selling. In supermarkets there are salesmen who are little more than clerks; at auto dealers there are salesmen who are anything but clerks. Industrial-goods salesmen often provide their customers with technical advice, and detail men give physicians considerable information about drugs. Some goods are sold mainly through the efforts of salesmen, while others rely mainly on advertising and still others, notably drugs, depend on both personal selling and advertising. There is a logic to these methods of promotion. This is shown by a comparison between two independent sets of data on advertising in the 1930s, one collected in England by Kaldor and Silverman and the other in the United States by the Federal Trade Commission. Advertising as a percentage of sales for the same products in the two countries is remarkably close. This can be no coincidence. Basic factors inherent in the market, the product, and the tastes of consumers explain these similarities.

ADVERTISING AND PROFITS

Study of the problems just cited advances our understanding of the determinants of advertis-ing outlays and throws light on the contention that advertising is a means to abnormally high profits. In its most naive form this belief rests on some easily available statistics. The *Fortune* list of the five hundred largest companies gives the ten companies with the highest rate of return on invested capital. Frequent members of this list are such large advertisers as Gillette, Avon, American Home Products, and Alberto Culver. Other companies among the golden ten are those that spend large sums on research and development. The moral seems clear. The road to riches requires a firm to spend on research and development and advertising. Indeed, were matters really so simple, it would be hard to explain why all companies do not travel the same road to riches. Alas the figures are fallacious, because they cling to old-fashioned accounting conventions that define capital as consisting only of investments in tangible items such as plant, equipment, and inventories. However, the true capital of a company includes expenditures that yield a return long after the initial outlays. Advertising expenditures together with research and development have this property. Yet the typical balance sheet omits them. The relevant rate of return on the firm's true capital is much lower than the *Fortune* figures suggest. I shall return to the question of the profitability of advertising below.

A SHORT HISTORY OF ADVERTISING

To understand the present state of advertising, a brief glance at its history is helpful. Although we need not embark on a picturesque tour of the posters in the ancient world, we may recall that advertising is among the oldest of man's activities, probably first appearing in conjunction with the oldest profession. Advertising in its modern form began in England in the middle of the nineteenth century, together with the popular press. This is no accident. The large circulation of the penny newspapers provided a ready audience for advertising messages not long overlooked by businessmen. Proprietary medicines were among the first major advertisers in these newspapers, and more respectable products, such as tea, cocoa, and sewing machines, did not lag far behind. It is the United States that deserves the credit for the rapid improvement and development of advertising. A pioneer user was Kellogg, who originally promoted health foods as a proprietary remedy for alimentary problems but soon recognized the larger possibilities in selling his wares as breakfast cereals. The modern national advertising campaign can be said to have begun with the introduction of the first domestic blend of cigarettes, Camels, in 1913. Cigarette makers continued to innovate in advertising, particularly by their use of radio in the twenties and thirties.

Important changes in methods of distribution were helped by the emergence of advertising. The local shop and retailer played a smaller role, and self-service stores offering customers packaged, branded, and nationally advertised goods at lower prices grew rapidly. Competition among retailers became keener, because with the new sales methods it was easier for consumers to shop in several stores in search of the lowest price for a standard, branded item. At the same time, manufacturers became more involved in distribution. Kaldor and others claim that the heavier expenses of the new methods of promotion gave monopoly power to the manufacturer. This last point is important, and I shall have more to say about it.

DETERMINANTS OF ADVERTISING EXPENDITURES

To say that business firms advertise because they find this to be profitable, although true, does not advance our understanding of the subject. We must look more closely at the mechanism of advertising. To this end let us consider how advertisers choose media for a given product, say, baby food. Potential customers are mothers of babies. Hence the advertiser wants media whose audience includes a sizeable number of females in this category. Television programs such as baseball games might be less suitable than weekly comedy programs after 8:00 P.M. In general the advertiser will attempt to allocate the funds in his advertising budget among the various media so as to obtain the maximum number of potential customers for his product. This may seem obvious, yet it goes far in explaining why some products are more advertised than others. Some products have so few potential customers that it does not pay to advertise them in any media, for example, glass eye balls. Such products are more efficiently promoted in other ways—by the use of salesmen or simply by relying on the buyers ability to find the sellers for themselves, say,

with the help of directories. This also explains why industrial products are less advertised than consumer products. There are fewer customers of industrial products, and it would be wasteful to convey advertising messages to them via the standard media. If there are enough industrial customers to support a trade journal, this journal will also contain pertinent advertising. The same is true of hobbyists. It is probably better to advertise chess sets in a chess magazine than in *Life*. Indeed, without advertising many specialized magazines could not survive.

The same considerations explain the greater advertising of new than of established products. To illustrate, it is instructive to examine changes in advertising outlays on cigarettes during the past fifty years. At first cigarettes were a new product competing with cigars. During the twenties, advertising outlays were large and directed at women. By the thirties, penetration of both male and female markets had reached high and stable levels so that advertising outlays dropped to a point sufficient to maintain awareness among existing customers and to contact new potential customers as they came of age. After World War II there were new varieties—long cigarettes, filtered and mentholated ones, etc. To sell these new brands there were sharply increased advertising outlays. The ultimate reason for the appearance of the new brands was the connection between smoking and lung cancer and not the advertising in itself.

BRAND LOYALTY

It is widely believed that advertising can reduce competition by the creation of brand loyalty for the advertised brands. This proposition is testable by comparing the brand-share stability of two classes of products, one which is more advertised and the other which is little advertised. The brand shares in the heavily advertised product class should be more stable over time than brand shares in the little-advertised product group. I tested this proposition by comparing the share stability of a group of toiletries and cosmetics, a heavily advertised product class, with a group of food items, a much less advertised product class. Contrary to the hypothesis, brand-share stability is *lower* for the more advertised than for the less advertised group. The life-span of a brand in the cosmetic-toiletry category is shorter than for a product in the foods category. The explanation is clear. The high level of advertising results from the high frequency of introduction of new products in the cosmetic class. Far from creating brand *loyalty*, the high advertising outlays are the result of brand *disloyalty*. Consumers become dissatisfied with the existing brands of cosmetics, toiletries, and toothpaste and are constantly ready to test the promise of new varieties—promises hardly capable of fulfilment.

Similar reasoning explains the large sums spent in promoting drugs. There is frequent introduction of new drugs. To gain acceptance for these new products, the drug companies spend large sums on detail men and advertising. If the drug companies spent smaller sums in accelerating the acceptance of new products, they would obtain a lower rate of return and would also spend less on research and development.

The conclusion is that some of the large advertising outlays are explained by the rapid rate of introduction of new products. It also appears that advertising by itself seems incapable of maintaining consumer acceptance of a product that is found to be unsatisfactory.

ADVERTISING AND MONOPOLY

Closer study of the relation between advertising and competition is possible. One measure of competition in an industry, widely accepted by economists, is the concentration of sales among the four leading firms in the industry. The larger the share of the total going to the four leading firms, the less the competition. If advertising reduces competition, then there ought to be high levels of advertising in those industries in which the leading firms have a large share of total sales and low levels of advertising in industries where the leading firms have small shares. This seems to be true in some industries, for instance, soaps, cigarettes, and breakfast cereals, but it is false in other industries, drugs, and cosmetics. The best way to test the proposition is to examine the data for all consumer-product industries. Such an examination shows a negligible positive association between advertising intensity and concentration. In other words, the exceptions to the hypothesis nearly outweigh the conforming cases. Changes in concentration and advertising intensity ought to move in the same direction according to the hypothesis that advertising

lessens competition. The data for the period 1947–57 show, if anything, the opposite relation—an inverse association between changes in advertising intensity and changes in concentration.

The weakness of the hypothesis claiming a positive association between advertising and monopoly is shown by another fact. Industries that make industrial goods hardly advertise and yet may be highly concentrated. Thus if all manufacturing industries were examined to determine the relation between advertising intensity and the concentration of sales among the leading firms, no systematic pattern would emerge. Advertising levels are better explained by the factors I have discussed above than by the state of competition in the industry. Characteristics of the customers of the product, their number, and the cost of contacting them by various media are much more important in explaining the level of advertising.

Although a continuously high rate of profit year after year is a symptom of monopoly, occasional high profits are not, even if these may result from a successful advertising campaign. Some highly advertised consumer products strike the public fancy and yield a handsome return, and this can also happen to unadvertised goods for much the same reasons. Examples of the latter abound—best sellers, hula hoops, *Gone with the Wind,* and miniskirts. Neither Xerox nor IBM owes its profits to advertising. Conspicuous examples of success due to advertising are offset by the more numerous and unpublicized failures (the Edsel?). The result is an average rate of return.

Despite these facts there are some who believe that advertising is an unusually powerful money-maker. The case for a tax on advertising had better rest on firmer ground than the contention that advertising lessens competition, as evidenced by the high profits that advertising can generate—a position defended by Assistant Attorney General Donald Turner.

ADVERTISING AND NATIONAL INCOME

The stability of advertising outlays as a percentage of national income results from the stability of the determinants of these expenditures. The turnover of consumers, the number of potential customers, their characteristics, and the rate of introduction of new products all determine the number of advertising messages that the sellers of goods and services wish to convey. In addition to these real factors, advertising outlays depend on the prices charged by the media. These prices depend on costs as determined by the nature of the audience relevant to the advertiser and by the forces affecting the average price level in the economy. The result is stability in the ratio of advertising outlays to national income. This stability has persisted for the past forty years despite the appearance of new media that might provide scope for increased advertising outlays. It should be borne in mind, however, that the new media substitutes for the old and that competition among the media, together with increased efficiency, checks the price of advertising services.

The cyclical behavior of advertising outlays has an equally prosaic explanation. When business declines unexpectedly, budgeted advertising is not reduced at first. Hence advertising outlays rise relative to income. When business unexpectedly improves, advertising outlays do not rise simultaneously, so that advertising outlays as a percentage of income fall.

In a static economy there would be less advertising. Information about goods and services, terms of sale, and the identity of buyers and sellers would not become obsolete. Catalogues and directories would never be changed. People would continue to use the same things in the same way. To the extent that advertising conveys pertinent information about such changes, it facilitates economic growth.

CONSUMER PROTECTION

My analysis so far has dealt mostly with the more technical aspects of advertising. I have not said whether advertising is sufficiently informative, whether trivial product differences are overemphasized, whether advertising is truthful or deliberately misleading, whether there is too much advertising, whether the support of television out of advertising receipts debases the quality of television entertainment, and whether advertising stimulates too much useless change.

Central to many of these questions is the undeniable fact that as the economy grows richer it yields a larger array of complicated consumer goods. To purchase wisely requires a high degree of competence that only a specialist can acquire. This expertise cannot be obtained from a careful study of the content of advertising messages. The potential for abuse is present. Is it only the fear of government controls that checks the cupidity of the advertiser?

Surely not. To obtain the continued patronage of a satisfied clientele is often the goal of business enterprise, and not out of altruism. For experience has shown this to be the profitable course. Moreover, consumers can judge the quality of goods and services indirectly in many ways. They test the reliability of sellers through long experience. Department stores and mail-order retailers act in effect as expert buyers on behalf of their customers. These retailers have the knowledge to buy goods and get good value for their money. Competition forces them to sell these goods jointly with their expertise at reasonable prices. Nor is experience the sole mentor of consumers. Guaranties and warranties guard their interest. Finally, in cases of serious damage consumers can resort to the courts. Manufacturers of defective articles are liable for the damage they cause, and the risk of costly law suits increases their incentive to control the quality of their products. A wide reputation engendered by advertising in itself forces sellers to exercise closer watch on the quality of products. This can be understood by comparison with a state in which consumers of defective articles do not know the maker and, therefore, do not know who ought never be patronized again. It is interesting to note that one of the arguments in the Soviet Union for the recent introduction of advertising and brand names is the desire to give factories stronger incentive to improve the quality of consumer goods.

The market also meets the demand for information about consumer goods in direct ways. A few magazines specialize in reporting to their readers about the attributes of numerous articles by brand. Nevertheless, some kinds of potentially useful information are strangely absent. Thus advertisers rarely compare their own products directly with competing wares. Most advertising is mere puffing, and very little is critical. Magazines and newspapers are also deficient because they do not provide their readers with news about consumer products. Perhaps because of pressures from advertisers there are few columns containing news about consumer items, although this might be expected to have considerable interest to many readers. The only consumer products criticized in newspapers and magazines are plays, books, movies, and television programs.

Though experience acquaints consumers with the good and bad qualities of products, it is sometimes a slow and costly teacher. Partly for this reason there has never been sole reliance on market forces. Weights and measures were among the earliest subjects of government control. The government inspects, controls, and licenses many goods and services ranging from meats to elevators, drugs, and physicians. The Federal Trade Commission scrutinizes advertising and prosecutes for false or misleading statements. At the same time, advertising of a product is considered to confer an implicit warranty that makes the manufacturer liable for faulty performance. Sweeping rules for additional regulation cannot be laid down, and I believe that each case has to be judged on its merits.

QUESTIONS AND STUDY SUGGESTIONS

1. Critically discuss: "Advertising is a means to abnormally high profits."
2. Does advertising increase brand loyalty? Does advertising promote or diminish competition?
3. How do you explain the stability of advertising outlays as a percentage of the national income?

Reading 40

Oligopoly Pricing: Possible Strategies

Joseph P. McKenna, Professor of Economics, Boston College

Oligopolistic markets are not readily susceptible to precise analysis. A basic reason for this is that the small number of firms which characterizes such industries results in mutual interdependence and, therefore, uncertainty in decision making. That is, the consequences of any one firm's price-output decision are intimately and directly determined by the character of his rivals' decisions. In this reading Joseph P. McKenna uses a profits-payoff table to reveal the basic nature of this mutual interdependence and to outline a number of collusive and noncollusive strategies which might well evolve.

From **Intermediate Economic Theory**, by Joseph P. McKenna, copyright © 1959, Holt, Rinehart and Winston, Inc. Used by permission of the publishers.

Oligopoly is characterized by a specific form of uncertainty. Here the uncertainty depends upon the reactions of competitors, not upon unpredictable world conditions. Furthermore, this uncertainty is multilateral, for the outcome of each firm's actions depends upon the behavior of every other.

THE PAYOFF TABLE

We can, therefore, draw up a payoff table for each firm, showing its potential profit from each action of its own and of its opponents. For simplicity, let us assume that there are only two firms and limit their actions to changing prices. In such a case, we can put the payoff table for both firms on a single chart. In Table 40–1, the prices of firm A are listed along the left margin and the prices of firm B across the top. For every pair of prices, the profit of each firm is shown. A's profits are shown in the lower, white portion of each cell, B's profits in the upper, shaded portion. For example, if A sets a price of $0.80 and B a price of $0.70, A's profit will be $7000, B's profit $22,000. We have calculated this table so that the firms are not identical. In general B is a more profitable firm than A. We have also assumed that there is some degree of product differentiation, so that it is conceivable for a firm to make some profit even if its price is higher than that of its competitor.

SOME POSSIBLE STRATEGIES

Various courses of action in the face of uncertainty are possible. Here we will discuss only six of the most common.

1. Minimax

Each firm may wish to play it safe. It therefore considers the worst that can happen at each price it might set. A, for example, may lose $7000 if it charges $1.00, or $4000 if it charges $0.90. At $0.80 it is guaranteed a profit of at least $3000, and at $0.60 and $0.70 a profit of at least $2000. It will, therefore, choose $0.80, which guarantees at least $3000.

Similarly, B could calculate its worst possibilities at each price. There are, in order, $6000, $8000, $12,000, $10,000, −$6000, ranging from highest to lowest price. B will also choose $0.80, which guarantees at least $12,000.

Actually, since each will set a price of $0.80, A's profit will be $10,000 and B's profit $25,000.

2. Unwarranted Assumption

Sometimes a businessman believes that his opponents' prices will remain stable although his prices change. If A believes that B will con-

Table 40–1.   OLIGOPOLISTS' PROFIT (unit : $1,000).

Price of A \ Price of B	$1.00	.90	.80	.70	.60
$1.00	34 / 11	36 / 5	33 / 0	30 / −4	8 / −7
.90	26 / 18	28 / 15	31 / 5	24 / 0	6 / −4
.80	18 / 21	24 / 14	25 / 10	22 / 7	5 / 3
.70	10 / 16	17 / 13	18 / 11	20 / 8	−6 / 2
.60	6 / 8	8 / 6	12 / 5	10 / 4	−4 / 2

tinue to charge $0.80, it will find it better to charge $0.70, for that will increase its profit to $11,000. If B then feels that A's price will remain $0.70, B too will find it worthwhile to cut to $0.70, thereby increasing its profit from $18,000 to $20,000. This new position is stable, for neither finds it worthwhile to change prices further. Such behavior is rare because the businessman involved must be alert enough to maximize his profit, given his competitor's price, but naïve enough not to expect reaction from his competitor.

3. Price Rigidity

Assume it is each firm's expectation that its competitor will match price cuts but not price increases. This means that the firm in Table 40–1 expects to move up the column but down the diagonal. If A and B are both charging $0.80, A will foresee profits of $5000 at $0.90 and 0 at $1.00. If firm A cuts price, it expects a profit of $8000 at $0.70 and $2000 at $0.60. Since all of these profits are less than the $10,000 it can make by staying at $0.80, it will not change.

Firm B faces the same problem. From the $25,000 it can make by charging $0.80, price increases will diminish its profit to $24,000 or $18,000, and price cuts to $20,000 or a loss of $4000.

The "stickiness" of oligopolistic prices is evident here. If the two firms make this assumption, they will continue to charge whatever their prices happened to be when they first came into competition. Obviously, such prices must be explained by history rather than by current conditions alone.

4. Fusion

In an unregulated economy, the best policy for all firms is to unite. In this way, the firms can maximize their total profit and then divide it between them. With this policy, the firms in Table 40–1 will do best if each sets a price of $1.00, making a total profit of $45,000. Such fusion has been achieved by means of trusts and corporate mergers, and, in Europe, by cartels.

5. Collusion

Firms often agree to follow parallel courses of action while maintaining separate identities. Although such agreements are also illegal in the United States, they are often hard to detect. For example, let us suppose both firms have reached a price of $0.70 after a series of competitive price cuts. At this stage, the sales managers might lunch together and agree that each will raise prices to $0.90. The limit to such collusion is only the diversity of the firms in the industry. In this case, for example, B would rather have prices raised to $1.00, but A would not. Collusion occasionally fails because there is no single action that is best for all concerned. (In fusion, this is not a limitation, because part of the excess profits of the gainers are transferred to the losers.)

One of the results of our antitrust laws is that collusion is confined to very simple agreements. More elaborate conspiracies require written memoranda and a method of settling grievances, and these are too easily detected. Collusion is, therefore, usually kept on a rather informal basis.

6. Aggression

Sometimes a firm engages in aggressive activity, especially price-cutting, to eliminate competition. It sets a price at which its competitor will lose money, hoping to drive him from the market. Usually this price is unprofitable to the aggressor as well, and the outcome of such a contest depends mainly upon the financial resources of the two companies, not on their true operating efficiency. Such aggression is, therefore, seldom in the public interest. It is generally held illegal under federal antitrust laws and the laws of most states. Many states have laws against selling "below cost," which are aimed at such behavior, although they often miss their target.

These six cases do not exhaust the possibilities. In practice, much effort is devoted to long-distance psychoanalysis of competitors, in an effort to predict their behavior. Nevertheless, extreme competition is so clearly unprofitable for everyone that stable price behavior usually develops. This is usually collusive or quasi-collusive in nature.

QUESTIONS AND STUDY SUGGESTIONS

1. What basic relationships between prices and profits are embodied in Table 40–1? Assuming that firm B holds to a price of $1, explain why firm A's profits will for a time increase as it cuts its price below $1 but will then begin to diminish at prices below 80 cents.

2. Explain the "minimax" strategy and the assumptions upon which it is based. Is this a "conservative" strategy?

3. Explain why oligopolists might be able to realize larger profits through "fusion" than they can by "collusion."

Reading 41

The Economics of the Electrical Machinery Industry

Jules Backman, Research Professor of Economics, New York University

In this reading Jules Backman offers an interesting case study of the electrical machinery industry. We find that the heavy electrical apparatus industry is an oligopoly with large portions of total output concentrated in the hands of a few large firms. Barriers to entry are high because of economies of large-scale production and ample opportunity for product differentiation. Competition other than in price is, however, vigorous, and technological progress has been substantial. Prices in this oligopolistic setting are, of course, administered prices. We view the heavy electrical apparatus industry at two different times in its history: (1) during that period when firms tried to compete on the basis of price and product differentiation and found that the results were "white sales" and near chaos and (2) during a time when the firms secretly colluded to establish prices, rig bids, and divide the market. By implication this selection leaves the reader with a troublesome question: Is price competition possible in this particular kind of market environment? Stated differently: Is private enterprise in this form, unaccompanied by public regulation or private collusion, capable of achieving an allocation of resources which is reasonably efficient from society's point of view?

From Jules Backman, **The Economics of the Electrical Machinery Industry,** New York University Press, New York, 1962, pp. 1–6, 61–65, 84–86, 90, 115–118, 127–138, abridged. Reprinted by permission.

The electric machinery industry is a complex of many related industries. According to the U.S. Bureau of the Census, the industry "includes establishments engaged in manufacturing machinery, apparatus, and supplies for the generation, storage, transmission, transformation, and utilization of electrical energy." Generators, transformers, switchgear, distribution line equipment, and related products are required for the production of electricity. The products using electricity include household appliances, elevators and escalators, factory machinery, light bulbs, radios, and television receivers. In recent years, there has been considerable activity in harnessing nuclear energy and in developing various types of electronic equipment.

The electrical machinery industry is a composite of at least four major product groups. Each of these differs significantly from the other in its economic characteristics. The major product groups are: (1) heavy electrical generating and distribution apparatus used in the production of electric energy; (2) general electrical industrial equipment, such as motors, control apparatus, electrical construction materials, etc., the primary market for which is industry in general; (3) domestic appliances primarily for consumer use: e.g., refrigerators, washing machines, radio and television receivers, heaters; and (4) military electronic and related equipment for aeronautics, astronautics, data-processing, and communications.

This is a multifaceted industry, one which manufactures a host of products used in every phase of our national economy. The degree of specialization of companies varies widely. At one extreme, there are the General Electric Company and the Westinghouse Electric Corporation, the two largest companies in the industry. They participate in many phases of the industry. At the other extreme, companies specialize in the manufacture of one or two products.

HEAVY ELECTRICAL APPARATUS

The major economic characteristics of apparatus sold primarily to the electric utility industry include the following:

1. Electrical apparatus is a durable capital good. The main purchasers are private and public producers of electricity. They are primarily interested in the performance of the equipment because they must provide continuous service. Although the demand for electrical apparatus is subject to cyclical fluctuations, the timing is affected by the purchasing habits of the electric utility companies. Thus, for example, private electric utility construction expenditures rose in 1949 and in 1958, despite the recession in the national economy. On the other hand, declines in such expenditures were recorded in 1950 and in 1955, although the national economy was in a period of recovery. Similarly, additions to installed generating capacity rose in 1949, 1954, and 1958, which were years of recession; such additions were smaller in 1950, 1956, and 1959, which were years of recovery.

2. Sales of electricity generally increase year after year. However, new installations of capacity must be available before such increases take place. Unlike the demand for most products, the demand for electricity must be met instantaneously; utility companies cannot build up surplus supplies of power in periods of low use to meet the demands in periods of high demand. Because of the technology of the industry, capacity must be increased in sizeable steps. Requirements for new capacity must be planned ahead. However, it is not economically feasible to build small plant additions to take care of the immediate prospective increase in demand. Increases in capacity must be substantial if the company is to take advantage of the latest technological developments and install the most economic generating equipment. The result is that capacity is expanded in an irregular step-like pattern by each electric utility. However, there is no way to assure that different customers will so time their orders that the pattern of total demand received by the industry or any company assumes some regularity from year to year.

3. Heavy electrical apparatus usually is produced on order after extended individual negotiations. Under such conditions, considerable time is often required to estimate bids, to agree upon contracts for production, and for installation. Moreover, this tailor-made characteristic of the product also means that output cannot be evened out significantly by a company by producing for inventory.

4. Continuing service after sale and installation is an important characteristic of these products, which often require special engineer-

ing and design. Assurance of good service becomes more important than price in many instances.

5. Competition in the electrical machinery industry emphasizes product changes and differences to a larger extent than in many other industries. Under these conditions, price assumes less importance than nonprice factors such as quality, service, and advances in technology.

6. Large companies are required to produce the major generating installations. The complex nature of many of these products, the continuing service and engineering services required, and the working capital required to finance production which takes a considerable period of time make it impossible for a small company to produce the entire line of apparatus. However, smaller companies may specialize in making some of the components required.

STRUCTURE OF THE INDUSTRY

The structure of the electrical machinery industry is similar to that found in many other mass-production industries: several large companies and a number of smaller ones. In industries which have Big Twos, Big Threes, or Big Fours, it is characteristic of the largest companies to account for a significant proportion of the total volume.

The development of big companies often reflects the technology of an industry. When capital requirements are large and significant benefits can be obtained from mass production, the big company becomes the most efficient instrumentality. In the electrical machinery field, this is the situation prevailing for *heavy apparatus* and *major appliances*.

The largest firm in the industry is General Electric, which had sales of $4,197.5 million in 1960; Westinghouse was in second place with sales of $1,955.7 million. A large number of other companies are far behind Westinghouse in size; none have sales of as much as $1 billion. However, in particular segments of the industry, these other companies may be powerful competitive factors despite the smaller total volume of sales. Thus, Carrier Corporation had sales of $256.8 million in the fiscal year ending October 31, 1960, but these sales were largely concentrated in air conditioning, and, as a result, Carrier was the largest company in that industry.

Some indication of the relative position of each of the four leading companies is found in six of the indictments for antitrust violations handed down by the grand juries in Philadelphia in 1960. The data are summarized in Table 41–1. If the ratios shown bore some approximate relationship to each company's share of total volume, the following pattern is revealed:

General Electric and Westinghouse produced each of the six products. They were first and second largest producers respectively for three products and had equal volume for a fourth product.

I-T-E Circuit Breaker had the largest share for two products; it tied for second once and was the third largest for one product.

Table 41–1.   ALLEGED PERCENT SHARE OF MARKETS IN 1960 GRAND JURY INDICTMENTS

	General Electric	Westing-house	I-T-E Circuit Breaker	Allis-Chalmers	Federal Pacific	Moloney Electric	HK Porter
Power switchgear assemblies	39	35	11	8			
Outdoor oil and air circuit breakers above 1,500 volts	40.3	35		8.8	15.6		10
Isolated phase bus	34	14	42				10
Navy switchgear	20	30	50				
Marine switchgear	40	30	30				
Power transformers	30	30		15		10	

SOURCE: Grand Jury Indictment, Philadelphia, 1960.

General Electric had second place for one product and third place for another.

Allis-Chalmers was in third place for one product and fourth place for two.

For four of the six products, General Electric, Westinghouse, and I-T-E Circuit Breaker were the three largest producers. However, the relative shares of each varied significantly. I-T-E had as much as 50 percent for one product (navy switchgear) and as little as 11 percent for another (power switchgear assemblies). The Westinghouse shares ranged from 14 to 35 percent and General Electric from 20 to 40.3 percent.

These data also indicate that different combinations of large companies are found for important product classes. Thus, although GE and Westinghouse are the two largest firms in the industry, they find themselves faced by a variety of competitors who specialize in particular lines as well as by intensive competition from each other.

Although mergers were of primary importance in the early days of the industry, they have been of minor significance for General Electric and Westinghouse in the past half century. However, mergers have played a significant role in the post-World War II growth of some of the former small companies in the industry.

This industry holds a high proportion of all American patents. However, they have not been used on an exclusive basis for most products. Licenses have been made readily available to all comers, usually on a royalty basis. Patents have played a more important role in connection with lamps than for any other product. In the infancy of the industry, patents were a much more significant force than they have been in later years. To a large extent, the early mergers were influenced by the desire to obtain patents and to avoid lawsuits. In this sense, patents have had a long-run influence on the structure of the industry because they influenced the creation of two dominant concerns.

A review of the data showing concentration by plants and by companies underlines the importance of technological factors in the existing degree of concentration. Technology is reflected in the amount of capital required, the economies of mass production, the importance of continuing large-scale research and development, and the advantages inherent in having one company produce all of the components of an electrical system. These conditions are conducive to higher concentration ratios where the most efficient unit of production is a large-sized plant.

NONPRICE COMPETITION

The electrical machinery industry has been characterized by vigorous nonprice competition from its beginning. Considerable emphasis has been given to product improvement and quality. This has been true for all products, ranging from household appliances to heavy equipment. The electric light bulb, for example, has been steadily improved in quality, performance, and size. The modern refrigerator and transformer are a far cry from their counterparts of a decade ago. New controls have increased the efficiency of the washing machine and have made possible a more scientific use of detergents and water, thus holding down the cost of operation.

Technological improvements have made possible a more effective transmission system which covers a wider area. One result has been to make possible a more efficient use of generating equipment when different parts of an electric utility system reach their peak load at different times of the day or the year. Witness, too, the improvement in the operation of television receivers in the sixteen years after World War II and the accompanying reduction in the number of service calls. To accomplish these results and many others, the electrical machinery industry has been a leader in research and development for many years.

Style changes occur very frequently. The evolution of selected appliances, which are subject to annual model changes, illustrates this point in, for example, the development of the "thin" air conditioning unit, a far cry from its bulky predecessor. Similarly, the ability to install larger units in the home without the need to install heavier electric lines acted to lower the cost of obtaining an operating unit. These developments undoubtedly reduced the opposition to the installation of air conditioning in many households.

Great strides also have been made in improving the quality of various electrical products. In 1940, a TNEC [Temporary National Economic Committee] report emphasized that refrigerators had improved sealed units, perfected cabinets, better insulation, and vast internal changes. In more recent years, many new features have been developed including "frost-free" refrigerators. In the early 1930s, up to 90 percent of the refrigerators were of the four to five cubic feet variety. By the mid-1950s, these small units had virtually disappeared, and close to one half of the models were more than ten cubic feet in size. As a result of the continued improvements in technology, the refrigerator of today has made its counterpart of not-too-many years ago completely obsolete. General Electric has pointed out that "the high degree of technology and volume achieved in the mass production of refrigerators has enabled a reduction in the price of General Electric refrigerators from about $46 per cubic foot in 1948 (when a basic innovation in refrigerator design was introduced) to about $35 in 1960, along with constantly better quality, style and features." This comment is applicable to the experience of other companies as well. It is equally applicable to such items as television sets, radios, washing machines, dryers, and dishwashers. The development of FM radio has given the listener greater fidelity of sound and more enjoyment.

The companies compete in providing various types of services for electrical apparatus. These range from assistance in planning the most efficient units to meet the needs of an electric utility system to prompt repair service in the event of breakdowns. Westinghouse Electric Corporation, for example, developed its Powercasting program to aid potential customers plan their future growth.

Considerable effort and expense have been devoted to building up brand names for consumer products. By creating a public image of reliability, the various companies have sought to pre-empt sections of each appliance market. This area of competition is reflected in the slogans or mottos of the two leading companies, "You Can Be *Sure* If It's Westinghouse" and the General Electric statement that "Progress Is Our Most Important Product." It is also reflected in guarantees of performance which are made for most products.

The intense competition in these nonprice areas has developed because market pressures make it essential to meet the prices of competitors with identical or closely substitutable prod-

ucts. The pattern of nonprice competition in the electrical equipment industry has necessarily been one consequence. In this respect the industry has not been unique. With allowance for special differences of products, it is the same pattern which has developed in most American industries.

PRICES AND PRICE LEADERSHIP

Prices in the electrical machinery industry are administered. Because of the nature of markets and business organization, the administered price is the only feasible one. This is particularly true in an industry in which technological requirements make large aggregations of capital necessary and limit the number of companies or plants which can produce the product.

There are many factors which a price official must consider and evaluate when he administers prices: economic characteristics of product, competition, demand, costs, legal factors, political factors, and public relations. The importance of the combinations of these factors utilized varies for different products produced by a company and for the same product over a period of time. There is no way in which these factors can be fed into a computer to determine the "right" price. It is the informed judgment of the price maker which fuses these several factors into a final decision concerning price. Pricing is an art, not a science.

Price leadership is found in many segments of American industry. It is particularly important for products which are standardized or are considered to be completely substitutable for each other. Under these conditions, each firm recognizes the probability that price cuts will be met by rivals and is concerned over the possibility that rivals will *not* match increases. A company generally will be reluctant to raise or lower prices in the absence of a major change in the economic conditions affecting that product. This change may be a significant rise in labor costs, changes in raw material costs, large increases or decreases in demand, or other developments which have an impact on the industry. Whatever the reason, it is the judgment of the price leader which generally determines the timing and magnitude of the price change.

In the electrical equipment industry, price leadership is characteristic for many products, including steam turbine-generators, power transformers, circuit breakers, switchgear, appliances, and other products. While General Electric often is the price leader, there are exceptions. For example, on January 23, 1961 Allis-Chalmers reduced the prices on feeder voltage regulators by 15 percent; a week later General Electric made a similar reduction. Some companies may not follow the leader at all times. Thus, in the spring of 1961 General Electric raised the price of bus and switch insulators by 3 percent. *Electrical World* reported:

Lapp Insulator Co. said last week that it would stay with its present prices. Earlier, I-T-E Circuit Breaker Co. had said it wouldn't go along with the GE move because it felt the increase would be discriminatory against small power switching equipment manufacturers who have to buy insulators from other companies.

Many examples are also found in the consumer goods segment of the electrical equipment industry. For example, late in May 1957 General Electric increased prices of its 1958 line of home laundry equipment because of product improvements and higher costs. A few weeks later Westinghouse also increased its prices of washers and dryers, citing increased cost as the reason. Early in July, Frigidaire raised its home laundry equipment prices. Kelvinator followed suit later in July.

Early in July 1960, General Electric lowered the prices for four models of refrigerators. A few weeks later Frigidaire cut its prices, and soon thereafter other manufacturers reduced their prices.

Sometimes a company may be the price leader for some products but not for others. The Kaplan study reported that "General Electric does not regard itself as a price leader for all the products it makes. . . . The company thinks of itself particularly as a price follower in the small appliance field."

Consistent matching of the prices of one firm by other sellers may and usually does develop without any agreement and without coercion by one firm over others; by itself it is not prima-facie evidence of conspiratorial price-fixing. Each firm acting independently in its own interest may follow the leadership of another firm.

PRICING ELECTRICAL APPARATUS

Pricing policy usually is related to, and significantly influenced by, the economic characteristics of a product. Many types of electrical apparatus are custom-built. Power transformers, generators, switchgear, and power circuit breakers, for example, often require thousands of hours of design and production time, most of them requiring high skills. Although the components of many types of apparatus may be mass-produced, the final product must be custom-tailored to the needs of the electric utility which is placing the order. In connection with the sale of such apparatus, electrical machinery companies often must engage in considerable negotiations concerning requirements and intended application of product, as well as price, before a transaction is consummated.

Most electrical apparatus is destined for electric utilities which are publicly regulated. Their purchasing is carefully scrutinized by public utility commissions because the capital equipment they buy becomes part of the rate base and hence influences the level of electric rates. Moreover, the utilities are staffed with competent engineers who become fully aware of the alternative types of equipment available and the relative performance of each.

A. D. H. Kaplan and his associates described General Electric pricing in this area as follows: "If the problem is the installation of a turbine-generator or a battery of turbine-generators for a large utility operation, the price develops out of months of consultation with the customer, the primary consideration being the latter's requirements on fuel costs and operational efficiencies. Specifications may be developed in terms of a combination of generators that will make it possible to provide the power at a final cost not in excess of a given figure adopted as a target for efficient operation."

In bidding for large projects, the usual practice of electrical machinery companies is to determine an aggregate cost by adding together the "book prices" of components and then to apply a general discount or multiplier against the resulting total. When the pressure for business grows, the discounts are increased, and vice versa. Published price sheets indicate the changes in "book prices."

Pricing also is influenced by the irregularity

of orders placed by the electric utility companies. The nature of this equipment is such that electric utilities increase their capacity periodically rather than continuously. There may be long periods when the level of new orders is relatively low. During such lulls—and particularly when the backlog of orders is shrinking—electrical machinery companies may cut prices sharply in order to maintain production. One manifestation is the development of "white sales" which may result in a backlog of unprofitable business. In 1955, Gwilym A. Price, then president of Westinghouse, was reported to have stated, "In heavy equipment, for instance, the fight for business became so intense last January that prices were slashed as much as 50 percent. We cut along with the rest in order to protect our position in the industry. As a result some of the business we took then won't show any profit." Under these conditions, the irregularity of demand plays a bigger role than costs.

Both domestic and foreign competition are important in pricing heavy electrical equipment. It was reported that General Electric reduced the price for hydrogenerators by 10 percent "in recognition of competitive conditions in the market place." This apparently referred to both foreign and domestic competition. When Allis-Chalmers lowered the prices of steam turbine-generators in October 1959 a company spokesman said the action was taken "to keep our prices in line with the lower prices announced this week by other manufacturers." In establishing these prices, it appears that competitive factors also play a bigger role than costs.

Nonprice factors often are of greater importance to the customer than price. Design, efficiency, and service (including repairs and supplying required components) are particularly important.

These products have been characterized by tremendous technological change. As the needs of the dynamic electric utility industry have expanded, electrical equipment companies have designed larger and more efficient types of apparatus and have developed more efficient manufacturing techniques. In the process, significant cost savings have been effected and passed on to the customers. That the impact of technological change has been a powerful force in the pricing of apparatus is indicated by the decline in costs per unit during a period of price inflation.

The custom-made nature of electrical apparatus results in unique problems in pricing as compared with the products of most other industries and with other electrical machinery products.

"White Sale" Price-cutting

On several occasions the market for heavy electrical equipment has been affected by severe price-cutting. When such price-cutting gets out of hand, it is described as a white sale. One such period developed early in 1955. To understand these developments it is important to keep in mind the economic characteristics of heavy equipment, particularly the tendency of buyers to bunch orders.

The nature of electric utility production facilities is such that increases in capacity must take place in sizable steps and must be planned several years in advance. Accordingly, orders for heavy electrical equipment are placed at irregular intervals by the individual electric utility companies. After the orders are placed, it may take two or three years before delivery is made. Periods of low orders, therefore, do not coincide with periods of low production. When orders on the books are so rapidly filled that order backlogs shrink, there is considerable pressure to obtain new orders to assure production in the future.

It is against this background that the 1955 experience must be considered. In the last half of 1953 and in 1954, there was a relatively low level of orders placed because of the business recession. *Electrical World* reported that 1954 was a buyer's market for the first time in years. It estimated in December of that year that utility purchases of generating equipment were expected to decline in 1955. The result was intensive pressure to induce new orders. According to *Electrical World*, January 1955 witnessed "one of the biggest breaks of the equipment market in decades." *The Wall Street Journal* referred to "the wave of heavy price cutting by manufacturers of turbines, transformers and other heavy electrical equipment which reportedly reached 'price war' proportions in January this year." The price-cutting reportedly began in capacitors and transformers and then spread to other types of equipment. It was reported that many prices were cut up to 50 percent.

Various reasons were advanced for the white sales, including the following:

1. Utility buyers were reported to believe the sales were started as an incentive to get future orders on the books.

2. Foreign manufacturers alleged the white sales were an attempt to drive them from the market.

3. Some observers blamed foreign competition, which could bid lower prices due to favorable labor costs.

Leading companies disclaimed responsibility for initiating the white sales. Westinghouse stated, "We didn't start it. . . . We've been holding our heads wondering how it all happened so fast." General Electric stated that "the GE company discovered that its competitors were without exception offering drastically reduced prices. . . . What the company has been attempting to do is to meet the competition as we have found it." *Iron Age* reported: "Even to the industry it's not clear why prices were cut."

During the white sale, a large volume of orders was booked. Westinghouse was reported as stating that during January and February the company booked "more orders for heavy power equipment than in all of last year, but at lower prices." In its 1955 annual report, the company reported that "new orders for heavy power apparatus increased substantially over 1954."

Effects of Price-cutting

Cut-throat competition among heavy electrical equipment manufacturers would in the long run lead to a number of unfavorable developments, according to an analysis in *Electrical World*. These include

1. Elimination of "extra" services provided utilities (engineering assistance, system studies, technical information).

2. Charges for extra services.

3. Reduction or elimination of research and development expenditures by manufacturers.

4. Reduction in the quality of equipment to minimum specifications.

5. Elimination of any plans for the expansion of productive facilities.

6. Elimination of unprofitable product lines.

7. A reduction in the number of suppliers.

These would indeed be serious consequences to an industry such as electric utilities which faces a period of major expansion and requires new technological break-throughs in order to meet anticipated demands. Potential white sales affect the pricing of heavy apparatus and provide a constant threat to price stability.

Obviously, the solution for this problem cannot take the form of illegal price-fixing and market-sharing agreements which the heads of the leading electrical companies properly have publicly deplored and condemned. Rather, each company must evolve pricing policies designed to yield prices which are fair to seller and buyer alike. As part of this program, a company's officials should understand the conditions under which they may reduce a price (usually to meet a competitor's price or to obtain a particularly valuable piece of business) and the maximum concession that can be negotiated rather than forego an order. They should be prohibited by company policy from bidding below that minimum level. I-T-E Circuit Breaker Co. appears to have adopted a policy along these lines in March 1961. If each leading company develops such a policy, stability could return to these markets because the smaller concerns have neither the capacity nor the financial resources to supply all demand at the lower prices.

THE PHILADELPHIA ANTITRUST CASES, 1960

In 1960, twenty-nine electrical machinery companies and forty-six company officials were indicted by grand juries for fixing prices and rigging bids on various types of heavy electrical apparatus between 1956 and 1959. A total of twenty indictments were handed down.

Different combinations of companies produce these products. Usually four or more companies, covering substantially the entire industry, and some individuals were indicted for their actions in connection with a specific product. The products fell into two categories: (1) those for which prices were fixed, and (2) those which were subject to various forms of allocation of market, noncompetitive bidding, and price-fixing.

The manner in which prices were fixed, bids controlled, and markets allocated may be illustrated by *power switchgear assemblies*. According to the indictment, five companies and twelve individuals were involved. It was charged that at least twenty-five meetings were held between the middle of November 1958 and October 1959 in various parts of the country. The manner in which the market allegedly was allocated was described as follows:

At these periodic meetings, a scheme or formula for quoting nearly identical prices to electric utility companies, private industrial corporations and contractors was used by defendant corporations, designated by their representatives as a "phase of the moon" or "light of the moon" formula. Through cyclic rotating positioning inherent in the formula one defendant corporation would quote the low price, others would quote intermediate prices and another would quote the high price; these positions would be periodically rotated among the defendant corporations. This formula was so calculated that in submitting prices to these customers, the price spread between defendant corporations' quotations would be sufficiently narrow so as to eliminate actual price competition among them, but sufficiently wide so as to give an appearance of competition. This formula was designed to permit each defendant corporation to know the exact price it and every other defendant corporation would quote on each prospective sale.

At these periodic meetings, a cumulative list of sealed bid business secured by all of the defendant corporations was also circulated and the representatives present would compare the relative standing of each corporation according to its agreed upon percentage of the total sales pursuant to sealed bids. The representatives present would then discuss particular future bid invitations and designate which defendant corporation should submit the lowest bid therefor, the amount of such bid, and the amount of the bid to be submitted by others.

In connection with the meetings and understandings described above, precautionary measures were adopted by representatives of defendant corporations to avoid detection, such as minimizing telephone calls, avoiding leaving notepapers in hotel rooms where meetings were held and avoiding social contacts among such representatives in the hotels where meetings were being held. In addition, code numbers identifying defendant corporations were used in documents effectuating the "phase of the moon" formula referred to above.

There were variations from the above outlined procedure for other products but the effects were allegedly the same; a rotation of low bids, allocation of available volume, and fixing of prices.

Soon after the indictments were handed down, several defendants pleaded guilty, while others attempted to plead *nolo contendere*. Attorney General William P. Rogers opposed the *nolo* plea on the ground that "these indictments charge as serious instances of bid-rigging and price-fixing as have been charged in the more than half-century life of the Sherman Act." However, in December 1960, in connection with the criminal actions, the government and the companies involved agreed to pleas of *nolo contendere* to thirteen indictments and guilty to seven others.

The court found that "this is a shocking indictment of a vast section of our economy. . . ." In addition to heavy fines ($1,924,500) levied on the companies involved, seven jail sentences were imposed upon high-level executives of three companies. Soon after the pleas had been made, the companies involved were subject to a series of damage suits by the federal government, municipal governments, and electric utility companies.

The government brought civil actions as well as criminal actions against the electrical machinery companies. Consent decrees, under which a company promises to eliminate prohibited activities, often are adopted to settle civil actions. Several companies signed such a consent decree for power switchgear assemblies. In addition to the abandonment of prohibited practices, the decree provided that the signatory companies are bound to refrain from "selling at unreasonably low prices with the purpose or intent, or where the effect is, or where there is a reasonable probability that the effect will be, substantially to injure, suppress or stifle competition or tend to create a monopoly."

This is a paradoxical situation. After terminating a conspiracy which allegedly was intended to hold up prices and bringing damage suits on that theory, the government insisted upon the inclusion in the consent decree of a restriction against "unreasonably low prices."

QUESTIONS AND STUDY SUGGESTIONS

1. What are the peculiar characteristics of the demand for heavy electrical apparatus?

2. Describe the characteristics of the heavy electrical apparatus industry using the following criteria: (*a*) the number of sellers and their concentration; (*b*) the barriers to entry confronting new firms; (*c*) the extent of product differentiation; (*d*) the economies that arise from large-scale production; and (*e*) the kinds and amount of nonprice competition.

3. "Prices in the electrical machinery industry are administered. Because of the nature of markets and business organization, the administered price is the only feasible one." What is an administered price, and why is it the only feasible price? What factors must a price administrator consider when he sets price? To what extent is he subject to *mutual interdependence* and *uncertainty* in the heavy apparatus industry?

4. What is a "white sale"? Why do they appear periodically in the heavy electrical apparatus field, and what are their effects on firms in the industry? Why isn't price leadership or some other form of *tacit* collusion a suitable means of preventing white sales?

5. Why did members of the heavy electrical apparatus industry conspire to fix prices, enter noncompetitive bids, and divide the market by colluding? What methods did they employ to achieve these ends?

6. "The number of firms is too small to allow the market to determine prices. Cut-throat competition is not acceptable to producers. Price leadership and other forms of open collusion are not possible, given the nonstandardized nature of the product. Cartels, price fixing, etc. are illegal." What are the policies the government might adopt in dealing with the heavy apparatus industry to achieve prices near the competitive level and conformity with the antitrust laws without the ever-present threat of ruinous price warfare?

Reading 42

The Pricing of Social Goods

Stephen Enke, Professor of Economics, Duke University

Price-output decisions encounter new complexities when one moves from such private goods and services as launderettes, hosiery, and electrical equipment to social goods such as transportation and communication facilities, dams, irrigation projects, and so forth. In this reading Stephen Enke discusses the characteristics of social goods and analyzes the mechanics and consequences of three alternative pricing policies: (1) pricing to maximize profits, (2) pricing to cover total costs, and (3) marginal-cost pricing. We find that there may be economic justification for charging a price which does not cover total costs of production. This leads to a final and even more perplexing issue: What criterion should one adopt in deciding whether to construct social goods in the first place?

Governments and other public authorities invest as well as private entrepreneurs. And every decade sees them owning and operating more and more enterprises. A crucial question is, in providing these useful goods and services, should they make investment calculations that are fundamentally different from those of profit-seeking capitalists?

SOCIAL OVERHEAD CAPITAL

Governments of underdeveloped countries invest quite substantially in what is termed "social overhead" capital. Transportation and communication are among the most important forms of this. Specific projects may be marine docks, railroad lines and rolling stock, or an extended telephone and telegraph system. But multipurpose river dams and irrigation canals are also high on the list. Not to be overlooked are more traditional objects of investment such as local public utilities—water, sewage, and electricity—and schools and hospitals.

A government, when investing in social overhead capital (SOC), is not limited to maximizing profits in the sense that it seeks receipts having a greater present value than that of the disbursements it must make. If government is to economize in its use of the nation's resources, and this is especially important in poor countries, it must do this and more. In fact, government must make investment calculations more complex than those of a private capitalist.

DISTINCTION BETWEEN REAL AND MONEY COSTS AND BENEFITS

But what exactly should a government try to maximize when it is investing the economy's resources on behalf of the nation? In some sense it should consider "real" costs rather than money disbursements and "real" benefits rather than money receipts. In any country there are numerous reasons why money costs and receipts—both in the aggregate and at the margin—may not be commensurate with real costs and benefits, respectively.

Welfare economics provides numerous and

From Stephen Enke, **Economics for Development,** © 1963, pp. 283–289. Reprinted by permission of Prentice-Hall, Inc., Englewood Cliffs, N.J.

familiar examples of disparities that exist between the benefits and injuries that an entrepreneur can occasion for society and the revenues and expenses that fall upon him as a consequence of these same acts. For instance, a factory may pollute the surrounding air, so that a great deal of money and resources must be spent in the local community for extra washing and cleaning. But this might be of little concern to a private owner of such a factory unless he has to pay extra wages to induce workers to live in such a locality. A government factory, it is to be hoped, would invest resources to reduce air pollution if this cost less than the extra expense the public would otherwise have to bear for additional washing and cleaning. It may very well be more economical to prevent the dirt from entering the atmosphere than to remove it from people and clothing later. If so, and the pollution is abated, more of the real costs of the enterprise are included in the money cost curves of the public project. Alternatively, if it is not more economical to prevent air pollution in this case, the public enterprise must *imagine* that the indirect costs of washing and cleaning are included in its cost curves.

Conversely, there are numerous instances of free enterprises that incidentally provide some useful goods and services free, so that their receipts curves understate the total benefits they supply the public. Suppose a private company which booms logs for towage by sea to a sawmill constructs a breakwater so that its log booms can be assembled in protected water. Such a breakwater will also benefit fishing boats and small coasting vessels. But the private lumber company, in constructing the breakwater, does not consider these incidental benefits unless it has authority to levy anchoring charges. A government sawmill would presumably *estimate* the fees that might be levied, and include them in a hypothetical receipts curve, even though never actually assessed.

In underdeveloped countries it is often maintained that almost any new enterprise is likely to provide all sorts of free advantages over and above the services that are sold. A private utility company may dam a river in order to produce and sell electric power, but there may be no ready means of collecting compensation from the people who live downstream and are no longer subject to flood damage. A government highway may be worth far more than the extra fuel tax it collects as a consequence. In both cases, a socially worthwhile product may not be undertaken because it does not seem to "pay" financially. This is because the full value of the services has not been transmuted into money receipts. Some of the most important examples, either from an unwillingness or an inability to collect for all services rendered, are provided by investments in social overhead capital.

PRICING POLICIES FOR GOVERNMENT ENTERPRISES

The receipts of a government project, the buyers' surplus that it occasions, and the value of the benefits it provides without charge, all depend on the price policies it adopts. The apparent "worth" of this or that project is determined by the price it charges. Hence a major problem when considering government projects that provide goods and services that can be sold is: What pricing policy should be followed? For instance, even if government can estimate real receipts and expense curves, should it attempt to maximize a sort of social profit by equating marginal real costs and marginal real receipts? Is the only proper difference between a private and public concern that the former considers only explicit money costs and receipts whereas the latter should make decisions on the basis of all real costs and receipts—including those that do not accrue to the concern itself?

There is certainly very little agreement regarding the answer to this question. There are people within the underdeveloped countries who demand that government projects be operated so as to maximize profits for reinvestment in the public sector, and this seems to be the pricing policy of government steel mills in India. Others propose that government enterprises charge the lowest prices that will meet all variable and fixed cost; this is the policy adopted by many public power authorities, including those that operate the Kariba Dam in Rhodesia. Finally, but only among economists, there is a demand for "marginal cost pricing"—that is, output should be such that marginal costs equal the demand price.

These three contrasting policies can best be understood in terms of an example and a diagram. Suppose government is contemplating the construction of a harbor, with wharves and cranes for handling cargo, and has decided to make some uniform charge for every ton of cargo loaded or unloaded at the main wharf by crane. Light coastal cargoes are not charged if handled by ships' crews and without assistance from the port authority. Two interacting questions are (1) what charges to make per ton of liable cargo, and (2) whether the project should be approved at all.

In Fig. 42–1, the horizontal axis represents tons of cargo loaded or unloaded, and the vertical axis represents dollars. There is a uniform marginal cost (MC) of $1 per ton of cargo handled by crane. Curve D is the estimated commercial demand; at lower prices it is assumed that more cargo will pass through this port than through either of the two other harbors on the coast. From Curve D a marginal revenue curve (MR) can be derived. In this particular case the MC curve is also the average variable cost (AVC) curve. Fixed costs are $750,000 a year. The vertical distance between Curve AVC and the average total cost (ATC) curve is the average fixed cost, including annual debt service.

Maximizing Profits

The first policy of maximizing profits would entail a charge of $3 per ton, as it is estimated that 500,000 tons a year would then be han-

dled by the port authority, and marginal receipts would equal the marginal cost of $1 a ton. There are profits of $250,000 a year. The project pays, is financially sound, and is in all respects a banker's delight.

Price Equals Average Costs

However there will be a demand—especially from importers and exporters—that the port authority set the lowest charges that will still cover all costs. After all, why should government extort the greatest possible profit from its own people, so long as it can meet all operating expenses and cover its fixed costs on schedule? In other words, assuming it estimates the same demand schedule, the commercial community may agitate for a $2 charge. If 750,000 tons a year materialized, the total revenue would cover all operating costs and the balance would exactly meet fixed costs of $750,000 a year. A few analysts might even note that although the government would no longer have a profit of $250,000, users would have extra free services worth from $500,000 to $750,000 —at no cost to them.

Price Equals Marginal Cost

Sophisticated economists, to the horror of the financially conservative, might suggest a third

Figure 42–1.   Alternative pricing policies for public sector projects.

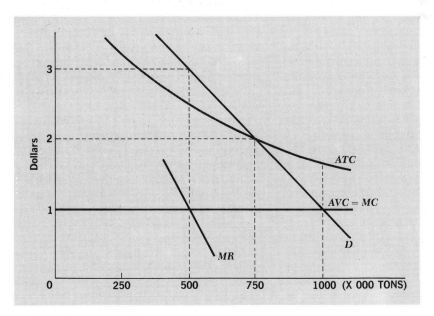

policy of setting a price that will result in an output equating marginal cost to marginal use value. Given current income distribution, the marginal use value is indicated by Curve D. Specifically, they would propose a charge of $1 a ton, as the resultant volume of freight (1,000,000 tons presumably) will produce a marginal use value equal to the marginal cost of $1. The extra freight handled at the lower price, which is 250,000 tons additional, has a use value of from $2 to $1 a ton. The value of the extra use of the port facilities by paying customers is hence about $375,000 and the value of the extra resources used is $250,000, so that the economy has gained $125,000 net. Aggregate fixed costs are unaffected. Of course there may be an annual loss, and in this case it is $750,000 a year. But economists may blandly propose that this be met in the case of a public project from the treasury's general revenue fund. It would be folly, in their view, to make the project self-financing, as this would require a charge of $2 a ton. And at such a "high" price, many persons would not use the port facilities, although the use value to them would be greater than extra resource costs.

The rationale of marginal cost pricing is most evident in short-run cases where the main investment has already occurred. If the wharves have been constructed, and the cranes installed, and so forth, the resources used are lost forever. They are a sunk cost. The problem now is to use these existing facilities as economically as possible. And this means lowering the charge and increasing use until the last ton handled adds use value equal to added resource expense. Public projects should have pricing policies different from those of private concerns—assuming that they can and do distinguish between marginal revenue and demand price—for the government is presumably trying to maximize not private, but social profit.

The important economic consideration is that any enterprise, whether publicly or privately operated, finance itself in a way that makes the most economical use of its facilities. This means that it need not always cover all its fixed and variable costs from charges that vary proportionately with the extent it is used. A price sufficient to meet all costs may limit use to a volume at which the marginal use value exceeds marginal costs. The facility will then be underutilized. The balance of costs must be met from another source—in most in-

stances the government. Taxpayers will meet those costs of a public concern that users do not. Private concerns can be bullied or persuaded into adopting marginal costs pricing by price ceilings or subsidies.

CRITERIA FOR INVESTMENT

What should be the long-run criterion for determining whether or not to invest in a project that has not yet been constructed? Various formulae are possible depending upon the assumed prevalence of monopoly and competition in the domestic economy. The most conservative test, and especially appropriate in competitive economies where highly differentiated products comprise only a small fraction of national income, is that the project could be rendered self-financing. Is there some price, however socially undesirable, that would result in enough volume so that total receipts covered total variable and fixed costs? If so, the project is economical *a priori*, even though this particular price is never charged and marginal cost pricing is adopted instead.

However, in interpreting this long-run criterion, public authorities must realize that total receipts obtained at each possible price may be less than the project's use value. Many people who benefit may escape paying, either because they use the good or service illegally, or because the process of collecting from them may be more expensive than it is worth. In the port facilities example, for instance, it was assumed that vessel owners did not pay for loading or unloading cargo alongside if they did not use the cranes. The harbor and dock were a free service for them under this circumstance. But this use value should be included as part of the project's worth even if this service is enjoyed *gratis* and so never collected.

Inclusion of this real but nonmonetized use value may make all the difference in deciding whether or not to go ahead with a project under consideration. Suppose, reverting to the last example, fixed costs had been not $750,000 but $1,250,000 a year. There would then be no price and quantity combination, given the commercial demand curve, that would yield enough revenue to cover all costs. Diagrammatically, this new average total cost curve (ATC') would lie entirely above the demand curve, and the project would never be undertaken by a private concern. However, the full use value is given not by the usual demand schedule but by a demand curve (D') that includes the use value enjoyed by those who do not use the cranes and so do not pay. Curve D' may lie above ATC' at some combination of quantity and price. The long-run decision for a public concern should be to go ahead and construct the facility. And this is so even though everyone knows that after completion the uniform charge will be one dollar, vessels not using the cranes will not pay, and there will be an annual loss of over a million dollars.

QUESTIONS AND STUDY SUGGESTIONS

1. What bearing do discrepancies between (a) real and money costs and (b) real and money benefits have upon the price policies of private and public enterprises? Upon resource allocation for the entire economy?
2. Discuss the alternative pricing policies which government might apply to social overhead capital, indicating in each instance possible advantages and disadvantages.
3. If a policy of marginal-cost pricing is adopted, total receipts will typically not cover the total cost of the social overhead capital. How, then, does government decide whether investment in specific projects is economically justifiable?

Reading 43

Monopoly and the Process of Creative Destruction

Joseph A. Schumpeter, late Professor of Economics, Harvard University

One of the main arguments in the defense of market structures comprised of large monopolistic firms is that such industries are more conducive to technological progress than are smaller firms in more highly competitive industries. This reading is the classic statement of this view. If we want better (less costly) production methods, new products, and improvements in existing products, we allegedly need large firms to undertake the prerequisite research and development activities. Furthermore, technological progress constitutes a most fundamental competitive force in the capitalistic system. Technological progress is a "perennial gale of creative destruction" which "strikes not at the margins of the profits and the outputs of the existing firms but at their foundations and their very lives."

From **Capitalism, Socialism, and Democracy**, 3rd edition, by Joseph A. Schumpeter, pp. 81–86. Copyright, 1950 by Harper & Brothers. Reprinted by permission of Harper & Row, Publishers.

The theories of monopolistic and oligopolistic competition and their popular variants may in two ways be made to serve the view that capitalist reality is unfavorable to maximum performance in production. One may hold that it always has been so and that all along output has been expanding in spite of the secular sabotage perpetrated by the managing bourgeoisie. Advocates of this proposition would have to produce evidence to the effect that the observed rate of increase can be accounted for by a sequence of favorable circumstances unconnected with the mechanism of private enterprise and strong enough to overcome the latter's resistance. However, those who espouse this variant at least avoid the trouble about historical fact that the advocates of the alternative proposition have to face. This avers that capitalist reality once tended to favor maximum productive performance, or at all events productive performance so considerable as to constitute a major element in any serious appraisal of the system; but that the later spread of monopolist structures, killing competition, has by now reversed that tendency.

CAPITALIST REALITY

First, this involves the creation of an entirely imaginary golden age of perfect competition that at some time somehow metamorphosed itself into the monopolistic age, whereas it is quite clear that perfect competition has at no time been more of a reality than it is at present. Secondly, it is necessary to point out that the rate of increase in output did not decrease from the nineties from which, I suppose, the prevalence of the largest-size concerns, at least in manufacturing industry, would have to be dated; that there is nothing in the behavior of the time series of total output to suggest a "break in trend"; and, most important of all, that the modern standard of life of the masses evolved during the period of relatively unfettered "big business." If we list the items that enter the modern workman's budget and from 1899 on observe the course of their prices not in terms of money but in terms of the hours of labor that will buy them—i.e., each year's money prices divided by each year's hourly wage rates—we cannot fail to be struck by the rate of the advance which, considering the spectacular improvement in qualities, seems to

have been greater and not smaller than it ever was before. If we economists were given less to wishful thinking and more to the observation of facts, doubts would immediately arise as to the realistic virtues of a theory that would have led us to expect a very different result. Nor is this all. As soon as we go into details and inquire into the individual items in which progress was most conspicuous, the trail leads not to the doors of those firms that work under conditions of comparatively free competition but precisely to the doors of the large concerns —which, as in the case of agricultural machinery, also account for much of the progress in the competitive sector—and a shocking suspicion dawns upon us that big business may have had more to do with creating that standard of life than with keeping it down.

PROCESS OF CREATIVE DESTRUCTION

The essential point to grasp is that in dealing with capitalism we are dealing with an evolutionary process. It may seem strange that anyone can fail to see so obvious a fact which moreover was long ago emphasized by Karl Marx. Yet that fragmentary analysis which yields the bulk of our propositions about the functioning of modern capitalism persistently neglects it. Let us restate the point and see how it bears upon our problem.

Capitalism, then, is by nature a form or method of economic change and not only never is but never can be stationary. And this evolutionary character of the capitalist process is not merely due to the fact that economic life goes on in a social and natural environment which changes and by its change alters the data of economic action; this fact is important and these changes (wars, revolutions and so on) often condition industrial change, but they are not its prime movers. Nor is this evolutionary character due to a quasi-automatic increase in population and capital or to the vagaries of monetary systems of which exactly the same thing holds true. The fundamental impulse that sets and keeps the capitalist engine in motion comes from the new consumers' goods, the new methods of production or transportation, the new markets, the new forms of industrial organization that capitalist enterprise creates.

The contents of the laborer's budget, say from 1760 to 1940, did not simply grow on unchanging lines but they underwent a process of qualitative change. Similarly, the history of the productive apparatus of a typical farm, from the beginnings of the rationalization of crop rotation, plowing and fattening to the mechanized thing of today—linking up with elevators and railroads—is a history of revolutions. So is the history of the productive apparatus of the iron and steel industry from the charcoal furnace to our own type of furnace, or the history of the apparatus of power production from the overshot water wheel to the modern power plant, or the history of transportation from the mailcoach to the airplane. The opening up of new markets, foreign or domestic, and the organizational development from the craft shop and factory to such concerns as U.S. Steel illustrate the same process of industrial mutation—if I may use that biological term—that incessantly revolutionizes the economic structure *from within,* incessantly destroying the old one, incessantly creating a new one. This process of Creative Destruction is the essential fact about capitalism. It is what capitalism consists in and what every capitalist concern has got to live in. This fact bears upon our problem in two ways.

STATICS VERSUS DYNAMICS

First, since we are dealing with a process whose every element takes considerable time in revealing its true features and ultimate effects, there is no point in appraising the performance of that process *ex visu* of a given point of time; we must judge its performance over time, as it unfolds through decades or centuries. A system—any system, economic or other—that at *every* given point of time fully utilizes its possibilities to the best advantage may yet in the long run be inferior to a system that does so at *no* given point of time, because the latter's failure to do so may be a condition for the level or speed of long-run performance.

Second, since we are dealing with an organic process, analysis of what happens in any particular part of it—say, in an individual concern or industry—may indeed clarify details of mechanism but is inconclusive beyond that. Every piece of business strategy acquires its true significance only against the background of that process and within the situation created by it. It must be seen in its role in the perennial gale of creative destruction; it cannot be understood irrespective of it or, in fact, on the hypothesis that there is a perennial lull.

But economists who, *ex visu* of a point of time, look for example at the behavior of an oligopolist industry—an industry which consists of a few big firms—and observe the well-known moves and countermoves within it that seem to aim at nothing but high prices and restrictions of output are making precisely that hypothesis. They accept the data of the momentary situation as if there were no past or future to it and think that they have understood what there is to understand if they interpret the behavior of those firms by means of the principle of maximizing profits with reference to those data. The usual theorist's paper and the usual government commission's report practically never try to see that behavior, on the one hand, as a result of a piece of past history and, on the other hand, as an attempt to deal with a situation that is sure to change presently—as an attempt by those firms to keep on their feet, on ground that is slipping away from under them. In other words, the problem that is usually being visualized is how capitalism administers existing structures, whereas the relevant problem is how it creates and destroys them. As long as this is not recognized, the investigator does a meaningless job. As soon as it is recognized, his outlook on capitalist practice and its social results changes considerably.

PROGRESS AND COMPETITION

The first thing to go is the traditional conception of the *modus operandi* of competition. Economists are at long last emerging from the stage in which price competition was all they saw. As soon as quality competition and sales effort are admitted into the sacred precincts of theory, the price variable is ousted from its dominant position. However, it is still competition within a rigid pattern of invariant conditions, methods of production and forms of industrial organization in particular, that practically monopolizes attention. But in capitalist reality as distinguished from its textbook picture, it is not that kind of competition which counts but the competition from the new commodity, the new technology, the new source of supply, the new type of organization (the largest-scale unit of control for instance)—competition which commands a decisive cost or quality advantage and which strikes not at the margins of the profits and the outputs of the existing firms but at their foundations and their very lives. This kind of competition is as much more effective than the other as a bombardment is in comparison with forcing a door, and so much more important that it becomes a matter of comparative indifference whether competition in the ordinary sense functions more or less promptly; the powerful lever that in the long run expands output and brings down prices is in any case made of other stuff.

It is hardly necessary to point out that competition of the kind we now have in mind acts not only when in being but also when it is merely an ever-present threat. It disciplines before it attacks. The businessman feels himself to be in a competitive situation even if he is alone in his field or if, though not alone, he holds a position such that investigating government experts fail to see any effective competition between him and any other firms in the same or a neighboring field and in consequence conclude that his talk, under examination, about his competitive sorrows is all make-believe. In many cases, though not in all, this will in the long run enforce behavior very similar to the perfectly competitive pattern.

FAULTY ILLUSTRATIONS

Many theorists take the opposite view which is best conveyed by an example. Let us assume that there is a certain number of retailers in a neighborhood who try to improve their relative position by service and "atmosphere" but avoid price competition and stick as to methods to the local tradition—a picture of stagnating routine. As others drift into the trade that quasi-equilibrium is indeed upset, but in a manner that does not benefit their customers. The economic space around each of the shops having been narrowed, their owners will no longer be able to make a living and they will try to mend the case by raising prices in tacit agreement. This will further reduce their sales and so, by successive pyramiding, a situation will evolve in which increasing potential supply will be attended by increasing instead of decreasing prices and by decreasing instead of increasing sales.

Such cases do occur, and it is right and proper to work them out. But as the practical instances usually given show, they are fringe-end cases to be found mainly in the sectors furthest removed from all that is most characteristic of capitalist activity. Moreover, they are transient by nature. In the case of retail trade the competition that matters arises not from additional shops of the same type, but from the department store, the chain store, the mail-order house and the supermarket which are bound to destroy those pyramids sooner or later. Now a theoretical construction which neglects this essential element of the case neglects all that is most typically capitalist about it; even if correct in logic as well as in fact, it is like *Hamlet* without the Danish prince.

QUESTIONS AND STUDY SUGGESTIONS

1. Why does Schumpeter reject the traditional (static) conceptions of competition and monopoly?
2. Summarize Schumpeter's view of capitalistic progress and the role played by oligopolistic and monopolistic firms in achieving this progress.
3. What is the "perennial gale of creative destruction"? What is its significance?

Size of Firm, Monopoly, and Technological Progress

Daniel Hamberg, Professor of Economics, University of Buffalo

Joseph A. Schumpeter's view (Reading 43) that monopolistic markets are characterized by technological progress is by no means universally accepted. Daniel Hamberg critically appraises this position in Reading 44, making several basic arguments. (1) An examination of sixty-one important inventions since 1900 reveals that the majority of them were the work of individual inventors and relatively small firms. (2) Much of the research funds of large firms is ultimately provided by the Federal government in connection with national defense. (3) While large firms in some industries (chemicals, electrical equipment, and petroleum) have been progressive, large enterprises in other industries (cigarettes, aluminum, and steel) have been decidedly less so. More generally, Hamberg doubts that large size and monopoly power are prerequisites to technological advance. Smaller firms operating under the stimulus of competition may be an even more fertile source of new processes and products.

For a number of years we used to be treated to the defense of giant, plural-unit corporations with monopoly powers, on the grounds that these were needed to achieve the economies of mass production made possible by modern technology. This argument always suffered from a certain lack of conviction, though, if for no other reason than the fact that in numerous cases the giant firms represented amalgamations of other firms that by any measure had been large and efficient corporations unto themselves; witness, for example, the absorption of Carnegie Steel by United States Steel. Empirical support for this argument was also hard to obtain. Other reasons centered on the widespread belief that most of the economies of mass production were to be found in the large-scale plant, as opposed to the large firm. This belief seemed to gain support from the efforts of some of the largest firms to decentralize many of their operations to the point where individual plants or subdivisions were encouraged to compete with one another.

NEW DEFENSES OF BIGNESS

Failing to carry the day on "cost" grounds, the defenders of giant corporations and monopoly power have more recently been treating us to another brand of argument. Starting with the pronouncements of the late Professor Schumpeter in the thirties and forties, we have been told that monopoly, far from being undesirable, is actually advantageous when economic progress is taken into consideration. In general, the case rested on the thesis that substantial monopoly power creates an environment propitious to both capacities and incentives for innovation. We shall examine this argument in the second half of the present paper.

From **Employment, Growth and Price Levels:** Hearings before the Joint Economic Committee, Congress of the United States, 86th Cong., 1st Sess., Washington, 1959, part 7, pp. 2337–2353, abridged. Statistics updated by editor.

First, however, we want to deal with another form of sanction of big business and monopoly power that has captured the popular imagination. This comparatively new apologia may be set forth as follows:

The independent inventor is now passé. In his place have come the giant corporations as the cradles of invention; only these great firms possess the resources to finance the skilled teams of scientists and engineers, working in splendidly equipped laboratories, that are now the providers of new production methods and new products. In short, inventions are believed no longer to originate in cold, barren garrets; instead, they are now the product of institutionalized research carried on by teams of experts working on preassigned projects whose results are preordained.

Not only has the independent inventor been swept aside by the invention of new ways of inventing, the argument continues, but the small- and medium-size firms are also losing out in this process. Those who may be concerned about the monopoly powers of the giant corporations are assured that this is a small price to pay for the contributions to technology, and consequent improvements in our living standards and overall power, that the corporate giants are now making.

The above is an important and influential line of thought, and no doubt many readers will find themselves in agreement with it. Nevertheless, although there is undeniably a basic element of truth in this view, it is easily, and indeed has been, greatly exaggerated. It will be my task in the first half of this paper to try to place some perspective on this issue and to sound some warning notes against too ready acceptance of the argument of the preceding two paragraphs, both on the grounds of what is and what ought to be.

A good way to go about this task is to seek the answer to four related questions:

1. Is it true, really, that technical development is now the exclusive preserve of the teams of scientists and engineers working in the research laboratories of the giant concerns?

2. Do the large corporations in fact finance the bulk of modern research activity?

3. Has large size per se been a guarantee of serious interest in research, so that we have reason to look to an important offset in the form of progress to the monopoly powers of the giant firms?

4. To what extent is large business size a necessary condition of modern research, and under what conditions?

The answers to these questions should not only cast in a true light the respective roles of the giant firms, the small- and medium-size ones, and the independent as sources of invention, but they may also tell us something about the reputed need for large-size firms in the modern realm of inventions.

Sources of Inventions

As we have noted, the belief that large business size and economic progress go together rests considerably on the conviction that invention is now the exclusive domain of the giant corporation. How accurate is this view? A recent study of 61 important inventions made since 1900 discloses that more than half were the product of independent inventors, working alone, unaffiliated with any industrial research laboratories. Among these were such diverse inventions as air conditioning, automatic transmissions, bakelite—the first commercial plastic—power steering, catalytic cracking of petroleum, the cottonpicker, cellophane, the gyrocompass, the helicopter, the jet engine, quick freezing, streptomycin, insulin, and the continuous casting of steel. Stainless steels were discovered almost simultaneously by an independent inventor and a member of a research laboratory.

In addition, several important inventions have been the product of research conducted in the laboratories of small- to medium-size firms. These include terylene—one of the great synthetic fibers—the crease-resisting process for fabrics, DDT, the continuous metal-casting process, as well as the continuous hot-strip rolling of steel sheets and shell molding.

In short, a total of 40 inventions out of the group of 61 selected as a sample of important inventive activity since 1900 have been the product of research carried on by the independent inventor or in the research laboratories of relatively small firms. Assuming the sample of 61 inventions is reasonably representative of major inventive activity in the current century, these figures certainly cast serious doubt on the thesis that technological progress is now the bailiwick of the large numbers of research workers employed in the great laboratories of the big firms.

All this is not meant to denigrate the contributions of the industrial laboratories of the large firms; the latter have been responsible for some very important inventions. Nylon, of course, was the product of the immense research facilities of the Du Pont laboratories, and if these did not discover cellophane—an individual did that—they were responsible for the development of its present moisture-proof qualities. The General Motors laboratories discovered Freon refrigerants and tetraethyl lead and were responsible for the final developments of the diesel-electric locomotive that made it commercially feasible—although the work had already been done by two small firms that were absorbed by General Motors, along with some of the most experienced workers in the field. The fabulous transistor was the product of the Bell Telephone laboratories, and so on. Altogether, about 11 of the 61 important inventions mentioned earlier may be traced to the work of teams working in the industrial laboratories of large firms.

Yet even in many of these cases, like television, silicones—materials whose characteristics remain unchanged through wide variations in temperatures—and plexiglass, much of the basic research had already been performed by individual inventors working alone or in laboratories of small firms or specialized research laboratories. All this evidence combined seems to tell us that those who believe that the great industrial research laboratories of the giant firms are now the primary leaders along the path of technical advance in our brave new world have a seriously distorted view of things. There is little doubt that the laboratories are much more important in this century than they were in the last one, but apparently they are a far cry from having become the chief source of (qualitatively important) inventions.

Statistics on Research Expenditures

It might be well to look at some of the data on expenditures for research to place the role of large business-financed research in better perspective. First let us note that in the United States in 1968, about $25 billion were spent on research and development. Of the $25 billion figure, at least a half and possibly as much as two-thirds was spent by the Federal government, mostly for defense purposes. Over half of Federal spending was used to finance research and development carried on in the private sector of the economy. This information explains why more than half of private research is found in the aircraft, electronic and electric equipment, atomic energy, and guided missile industries.

What inferences can we draw from these data? For one thing it seems clear that the prodigious increase in corporate research and development spending since 1940, about which so much has been heard, has been largely the result of government financing for defense reasons. Further, most of this spurt in research activity has been concentrated in relatively few industries, largely those with defense connections. That is to say, most manufacturing industries and firms have not shared in this spectacular growth in spending on research and development. In fact, other data show most manufacturing firms, large and small, carry on very little of this activity; they concentrate on manufacturing.

Even in the relatively few industries where corporate research is carried on in a big way, in view of the stimulus that they have received from Federal financing, what can we expect from them in the future? Some may assert that war preparations are here to stay, so that we can look forward to a continued strong interest in research from these groups, and the large firms, with their wonderfully equipped laboratories and skilled research personnel, will lead the way into the technological future. In part, the element of truth in this assertion depends on the length of time cold—and hot—wars will indeed remain with us, and this is a political question beyond our purview. It also remains to be seen to what extent defense-connected industries hold the torchlight to future technical developments.

Others will insist that even if the Federal government steps out of the financing picture, the firms who are now spending on research in a big way will get in the habit of doing so, and will continue to do it in the future. Again, this may or may not be true. Certainly, there is room for some skepticism. Inviting caution on this point are the number of instances of firms that were quite aggressive in their research interest and spending at one time and lapsed into a state of semisomnolence at another. Once the government stops footing the bill, there is always the possibility that the comptrollers and accountants, with their everlasting myopic attitudes toward research, will find continued large-scale spending in this direction wasteful and expendable. This, too, has happened before, and it can happen again.

Large Size and Interest in Research

Among those who believe that large size and technical progress have become as one, there seems to be the implicit notion that all or most giant firms have become sponsors of industrial research. Our previous discussion of the comparatively small proportion of important inventions since 1900 emanating from the giant corporations should be enough to cause strong skepticism on this score. Beyond that, we need only to note a number of important industries dominated by very large firms where interest in research has traditionally been at a minimum. The steel industry is a notable case in point. Since the turn of the century, this industry—particularly the largest firms—has not been noted for its progressiveness. Virtually all the important recent advances in the methods of producing primary steel have come either from outside the industry or from small firms within the industry. Continuous hot strip rolling and the oxygen converter were developed by small firms; continuous casting and planetary mills were created by independent inventors. The same was largely true of the evolution of processes for using taconite ores—low-grade ores constituting an almost unlimited supply of iron. And as noted above, in some of these cases the large firms have strongly resisted the adoption of these new techniques.

But there is no need to dwell on the steel industry. It has been said of the cigarette industry, than which it is difficult to find larger size and more concentrated production, that its firms are almost totally innocent of any serious interest in research. In the equally if not more concentrated auto industry, it is fair to say that most of the recent engineering improvements have come from without the large firms of this industry. Many, like the new suspension systems, were pioneered by small European concerns, and others, like the automatic transmissions and power steering, were largely the results of the work of independent inventors. Again, during the years when the aluminum industry was a virtual monopoly of Alcoa, two of the three most important advances in production methods originated outside the industry. In the basic metal industries generally, where firms tend to be quite big, relatively little is spent on research. The same is true of the food products and agricultural machinery industries, both dominated by large firms. And so on through such similar industries as linoleum, plumbing equipment, meat products, distilled liquors, and so forth.

Certainly there are industries where the typical firm is large and interest and spending on research intense, such as the aircraft, heavy electrical equipment, chemicals and petroleum. But again, note that the first two of these have been the recipient of heavy government financing. More important, however, the large number of cases that can be cited where large firms have by no means been in the vanguard of developing technology is proof enough that large size per se is no guarantee of large-scale spending on research and development and exceptional progressiveness. The fact that manufacturing industries where very large firms predominate have displayed no greater increases in output per man than other manufacturing industries is additional testimony to this fact. So is the tendency of large companies to get into new fields by absorbing smaller ones who have already made substantial progress and possess the men with know-how. General Electric got into the electric range and electric clock fields in this way, as did General Foods in moving into the fozen food market, and General Motors in becoming the chief producer of diesel-electric locomotives, to name but a few examples.

Large Size: A Necessary Condition for Research?

The discussion in the last section indicates that large size is clearly not a sufficient condition for interest and spending on research in the modern world. On the other hand, can it be said that large size is still a necessary condition? Would breaking up the large corporations, for example, be tantamount to depriving us of the major source of research into new techniques and products that will pave the way for future economic progress? In a sense, our earlier examination of the sources of inventions implies a negative answer to this question. But the persistence of unsubsidized research in certain industries, like the chemical and petroleum refining industries, both characterized by very large firms, suggests that in some cases there may indeed be some connection between expenditures on research and size of firm.

This connection seems to lie in fields of research or invention where the path to success is not a systematic one, but rather rests on a protracted and expensive series of experiments and tests. The element of chance assumes a large role as the researchers play a hunch that on the basis of known properties of certain elements or compounds—or soil and bacteria cultures—other compounds or molds—as in the cases of the antibiotics—with desirable properties can be found. Or often, a long series of tests may be performed in the mere hope of discovering unknown properties of certain compounds that will yield useful applications. A knowledge of science may be helpful in narrowing the range of experiments that must be performed in these cases, but perhaps only from 100,000 to 10,000 experiments.

This information may come as a surprise to many who believe that modern science and technology has lost its, supposedly, "hit or miss" qualities of the past, and is now on such a systematic basis that its results are foreordained. Yet a number of important discoveries have been made in recent decades that have been matters of chance observation arising in the course of a search among many possibilities. These discoveries include such products as tetraethyl lead, Freon refrigerants, Duco lacquers, polyethylene, penicillin, streptomycin, and numerous others.

The significance of research of this type for the problems at hand is not hard to discern. When inventions or discoveries involve innumerable observations from a long series of experiments, teams of research workers, with ample and sometimes elaborate research facilities at their disposal, may provide the fastest and most efficient way of achieving results. For the ground to be covered can sometimes be methodically divided between different workers, and teamwork may be of greater value since the accumulation of negative results is one method of finally identifying the correct line of attack. Here, then, the financial resources of the big firms may be required to provide both the facilities and the teams of workers. Moreover, where the element of chance is great, the large firm is in a better financial position to absorb the costs of the many failures involved before success is achieved.

However, we must not exaggerate the potential of the large firm in this respect. For one thing, the kind of expensive experimentation just described appears to apply mainly to chemical and related inventions. For another, this type of research is not new, and has been successfully conducted in the past by individuals or small teams of workers utilizing a bare minimum of equipment. This was true in connection with the discovery of the first aniline dye and the vulcanization of rubber in the previous century, for example, and of Freon refrigerants, tetraethyl lead, and nylon in the 20th century. In fact, some of the very large firms operate a number of small laboratories rather than one large one.

The foregoing discussion should be sufficient to raise serious doubts that the great industrial laboratories are now the repositories of research and invention in the Western World that they have been made out to be and to caution against the glib tendency to identify large firms with serious research interests. This discussion should also prompt us to guard against glib assumptions that large teams of organized scientists and technicians working under close administration guidance, with their tasks and goals carefully preestablished, are indeed the best approach to invention. It certainly remains to be demonstrated that there is a definite correlation between size of research organization and quality as well as quantity of inventive achievement. On the contrary, it is disquieting to hear of the number of research administrators who remark on the amount of piddling that goes on in the great laboratories and the heavy spending on marginal improvements designed to maintain patent controls. And students of invention have often commented on the number of truly important inventions that have been the work of individuals unassociated with an industry and thereby able to approach its problems with a completely fresh and detached outlook.

MONOPOLY AND ECONOMIC PROGRESS

As remarked at the beginning of this paper, there are many who claim not only that the giant firm is needed to undertake research in the modern era, but that the substantial degree of monopoly power that large size usually confers is equally vital to economic progress. Far from being exorcised by the existence of significant monopoly power, these people see in it a definite advantage aiding our quest for technical progress and higher living standards. This advantage is felt to outweigh by a considerable margin the losses from oft-admitted monopolistic powers. So, without further ado, let us see of what fabric this argument is made.

Is Progress Engendered by Monopoly?

The arguments favoring monopoly power as a source of progress fall into two categories. One is that the capacities of the enterprises with significant monopoly power are more likely to lead in the direction of progress than those enmeshed in the environs of pure competition. The other argument views a strong element of monopoly power as an absolute stimulus to progress.

1. *Capacities for innovation.* Dynamic and imaginative entrepreneurs are not likely to be found in pure competition, for the very nature of this market structure tends to be too inhibitive, limiting as it does the activities of the firm to pure production decisions. There is no room for aggressive price and sales policies, no leeway for "creative" product variation, and no outlet for original and striking advertising campaigns. These are indeed cold and uninviting surroundings for the energetic and fertile businessman, galvanized for action and impatient to try out new ideas.

Moreover, because the monopolistic firm is apt to be large in size, it will be in a good position to afford to employ executives with the traits just described, men with the capacities to originate and develop new ideas and ways of doing things. In addition, monopolistic power is frequently the result of superior entrepreneurial ability, ability that can be counted upon to continue to drive for new methods and new products in an effort to enhance monopoly power, perhaps, but still redounding to the benefit of society.

Furthermore, and probably more important, monopoly profits are a principal source of funds to finance research and to finance new equipment implementing discoveries. Expenditures for research are also a very risky type of investment, and the protection that monopoly power affords acts as an inducement to spend on research, because the firm feels a measure of security from the knowledge that it will likely be the sole possessor of the new inventions it produces. Ample proof of this is found in the demonstrably heavy concern with research in concentrated industries and, within these, in the largest and more monopolistic concerns. This last is a highly questionable statement, as previously indicated.

2. *Incentives to innovate.* Probably the most important aspect of the monopoly *cum* progress argument is associated with the matter of incentives. Monopoly power is said to be an indispensable adjunct to the willingness of the firm to invest in the production and sale of new and untried products and techniques of production. Investment of this type, i.e., innovational investment, is often very risky and expensive. It runs the risk of buyer resistance, of long and expensive sales campaigns to overcome this resistance, and possibly of ultimate failure. Expensive investments in new plant and equipment may be required, often preceded by equally expensive periods of experimentation and development. As a result, the excess profits associated with substantial monopoly power are a necessary inducement to innovation. Without the protective shield of such monopoly power, or contrariwise, with the prospect of easy and quick imitation and vigorous competition, the incentive to undertake these expensive risky innovations would evaporate. Vigorous competition in the innovative process would cause this process to wither on the vine. Monopoly power in this connection is the very life-giving air on which economic progress thrives.

Monopoly as a Restraint on Economic Progress

As usual, there are at least two sides to every question, and this is no less true on the issue of the role of monopoly power in the innovation process. For one thing, it would be an egregious mistake to identify the growth of monopolistic power with superior entrepreneurial ability. In some cases, such as the Ford Motor Co., there doubtless has been a large element of this superiority behind the accrual of such power to giant firms. But looking back over the past, particularly to the great merger movements in the period around 1900 and in the 1920s, we find that the greatest source of impetus to these movements originated in the desire to curb competition and from the great profits for the promoters of these mergers. Today, such things as tax considerations, desires to assure sources of supply or market outlets, or product diversification seem to be fostering mergers, rather than any unusual entrepreneurial talents—at least of the type that necessarily bodes well for technical progress.

Moreover, quite the opposite from being a convenient vehicle for the exercise of the talents of the dynamic and imaginative entrepreneur, the large corporation can lead, and has led, to developments not conducive to the risk taking that is associated with innovation. Chief among these is the emergence of bureaucratic organizations of officials to carry out the multiple, complex functions inherent in modern large-scale enterprise. The bureaucrats of the large corporations, usually cloaked with substantial monopoly power, develop a strong sense of security about their jobs, a career attitude toward managerial positions, that make it imperative to be a good organization or team man, to follow the accepted rules of action and behavior. These are not the qualities of the prospective innovator. Risky ventures are avoided that might destabilize existing market situations and threaten the position of the entrenched managerial bureaucracies, which operate better in a stable, rather than a changing, environment. These bureaucracies tend to become instruments of resistance to, not promoters of, change.

Moreover, it must be remembered that innovations that are substitutes for existing products and processes involve losses from the scrapping of existing plant and equipment. Firms protected by monopoly power may be expected to try to avoid such losses by postponing innovation until the existing capital goods have considerably depreciated. Why render obsolete with a new innovation what may have been painfully built up in the past? And this is no less true of firms that spend large sums on research than of those who do not. In fact, for the former, much of their research may be aimed at the protection of existing monopolistic strength, as well as the avoidance of capital loss through obsolescence—by obtaining patents ahead of others threatening the firm's entrenched position. Scrutiny of the innovational behavior of the electric lamp, radio and television, railway locomotive, and telephone industries, among others, discloses that innovations of competitive products have occurred only after long periods of market exploitation

of old products. The investigations of a number of writers have brought them to the conclusion that new firms are very often needed if radically new innovations are to take place; this has even been true in industries where the established firms have had reputations for progressiveness, such as the electric lamp and telephone industries.

This information should not be unexpected. Innovation is certainly expensive and risky. The intelligent entrepreneur is all too aware of this, particularly if he has recently experienced the trials and tribulations of innovation and market consolidation. Following this experience, a period of quiescence is apt to be the most attractive situation. With good profits, monopoly powers that may insulate well against potential competition, executives are more prone to refrain from innovation, to be content with protecting the fruits of past efforts. They are hardly likely to want to render obsolete soon afterward with a new innovation what may have been painfully built up in the past.

COMPETITION AND INNOVATIONAL INCENTIVES

These problems do not arise when there is active and intense competition, although not necessarily pure competition. The adoption of new techniques or products by some firms under competitive conditions literally forces the rest to follow suite, to abandon its existing equipment and write off the losses, or else run the risk of being undersold or losing customers to the new products being introduced by the competitors. In addition, a firm without significant monopoly power, whose share of the market is small, will find the adoption of the latest techniques and products especially attractive as a means of underselling competitive firms and invading their markets. For the losses from scrapping existing equipment will seem rather minor compared to the profits to be garnered from the enlargement of its markets. It is the monopolistic firm, with a sizable portion of the market, that finds losses on sunk capital large compared with prospective profits from further broadening of its market share.

Likewise, competition, in contrast with strong monopoly situations, is ordinarily associated with freedom of entry, with the full freedom of new firms to enter an industry with new and cheaper techniques or new, substitute products. The new firm, too, is likely to be a more aggressive innovator. By definition, it has no vested interest in maintaining the capital values of existing plant and equipment, no vested interest in maintaining existing markets. It will want to take advantage of the latest techniques and equipment, and in doing so will force the existing firms to fall in line or be outsold.

Monopoly, on the other hand, obstructs the entry of new firms. Sometimes it does this by deliberate action, as by threatening destructive price competition, patent shelving, and expensive and drawn-out patent litigation, controls over supplies of important materials, etc. At other times, the mere strength of the monopolistic firm's hold on the market may act as a strong deterrent to the entry of new firms.

Perhaps the outstanding feature of active, intense competition in connection with the innovating process is the persistent pressure it exerts to search for and adopt innovations that would otherwise be delayed if introduced at all. It is sometimes said that strong monopoly power is not necessarily inconsistent with innovation. Despite what was said above, there are large firms that can and do have vigorous managements vitally interested in research and development, of sanguine outlook and adventurous spirits, and constantly willing to exploit new ideas in the market place. This is true; there are indeed firms with such managements. But we have also seen that there are many firms, with much more monopolistic power, whose managements have not been of this ilk.

The advantage of active, intense competition lies in the fact that it does not leave innovative ability and behavior to pure chance. The persistent pressures from competition provide a compelling force to innovate or fall behind and perhaps eventually disappear altogether. Competition is also the proper stimulant to prevent firms from seeking "the quiet life," from being content to reap the fruits of past efforts and rest on their laurels. If it is true that modern managements of large corporations are not profit-mad, grasping ogres, anxious to maximize earnings, it follows that the drive for profits is no longer the reliable spur to innovations it was once thought to be. Competition again, however, does not rely on the chance existence of a strong drive for profits. It provides an inspiration to innovate all its own.

In reply, it is often argued that even firms with apparently substantial degrees of monopoly power are not immune to strong competitive pressures. There have been dramatic struggles even in monopolistic, or oligopolistic, markets; new firms have overcome obstacles in the past and encroached seriously upon monopolistic markets; interindustry competition among otherwise monopolistic firms producing substitute goods has often waxed hot, and so on. In brief, competition is an ubiquitous and pervasive force from which no firm can ever completely cut itself off and enjoy peace and tranquility.

There may be a strong element of truth in this view, although there certainly have been protracted periods during which many large firms have been able to enjoy peace and quiet. Irrespective of the truth of these remarks, however, they can hardly be regarded as a defense of monopoly power. They merely show that despite its existence elements of competition may make their presence felt. This sounds like a very good case for enlarging the area in which competition is allowed to operate, that is, for weakening the forces of monopoly.

QUESTIONS AND STUDY SUGGESTIONS

1. Explain the "cradle of invention" argument for big business. Does available empirical evidence substantiate this position?
2. What do statistics on research spending reveal about the financial sources of technological progress?
3. Is large size a sufficient condition for modern research? A necessary condition? Explain.
4. For what reasons might one argue that a monopolistic firm has a greater capacity and incentive for technological advance than does a purely competitive firm? What counterarguments can be made?
5. Comment: "The advantage of active, intense competition lies in the fact that it does not leave innovative ability and behavior to pure chance."

Reading 45

The Harvest Labor Market

Lloyd H. Fisher, late Professor of Political Science, University of California

Reading 45 is an intriguing case study of the "structureless" harvest labor market in California as it existed shortly after World War II. The simple tools of supply and demand serve as penetrating analytical devices which reveal the workings of this market. Harvest labor, because of the piece-rate method of payment, is in effect homogeneous. There are no unions, no personal ties between employer and employees. No significant skills are required, and capital equipment is not extensively used. The demand for harvest labor is highly seasonal and concentrated within a relatively short period of the year. The quantity of harvest labor supplied is not believed to be very sensitive to small changes in the wage rate. Indeed, beyond some level, higher wage rates may cause less labor to be supplied. These supply and demand conditions have actually resulted in wage rates for harvest laborers which are substantially below those of industrial workers. Prejudice, obstacles posed by labor unions in industry, and the easy entry of migrant workers into the agricultural labor market are all important reasons why the price system has not functioned so as to reduce or eliminate these wage rate differentials. We encounter in this selection an excellent illustration of how the market forces of demand and supply determine a particular wage rate and how economic and noneconomic obstacles to labor mobility sustain substantial wage differentials.

California has a slightly shady reputation among students of agriculture. The well-cherished notion of the husbandman tending his soil, of intimacy between man and the productive urge of nature, although less and less easy to document in any major farming area, is most difficult to discover in California.

Measured by value of product, there are proportionately more large farms in California than in other states, and a far larger proportion of its farms are operated by hired managers; but it is neither size nor absentee ownership which gives to California agriculture its particular character. If that which is most distinctive about California agriculture were to be compressed into a single sentence, it could best be done by simply reversing a familiar phrase: Farming in California is a business and not a way of life.

Most of the agricultural commodities produced anywhere in the United States are to be found in California; but there are particular specialties of the state, and of these California produces most of the nation's supply, e.g., grapes, raisins, lemons, oranges, olives, figs, lettuce, cotton, and so forth.

These are crops which cannot be handled by family labor, either with or without a hired man. Even on the smallest farms the labor requirements of the harvest far exceed the family

From Lloyd H. Fisher, "The Harvest Labor Market," **Quarterly Journal of Economics**, November, 1951, pp. 463–491, abridged. Reprinted by permission.

supply available. Ten acres of peaches, tomatoes, or apricots cannot be harvested without a force of seasonal farm laborers. The characteristics of the agricultural labor market in California are created only in part by the prevalence of large-scale farming enterprises or by the corporate structure of some farm businesses. Small farms are as dependent as large farms upon seasonal hired labor, resident owners as dependent as absentee corporate owners. The harvest labor market is primarily a function of specialization in labor-intensive crops, and the intense seasonal demand for labor which results.

The major labor-consuming operation on the farm is the harvest, and no other aspect of agricultural production approaches it in the quantity of labor which it employs. The effect of specialization on the individual farm is, therefore, an intense demand for labor during a limited period of time. Add the similar specializations of a large number of farms in the same area, and the number of harvest workers required multiplies many times, while the time period during which they are required grows no greater. Add to this the perishability of most of the major California crops—peaches, pears, grapes, tomatoes—and the time period during which workers are demanded becomes very short and the tolerance narrow. On one day the apricots are too green to be picked; with a turn in the weather the crop must be harvested in a week or ten days or the remaining apricots will have spoiled. The pattern of over-all demand for agricultural labor that emerges is characterized by extreme seasonal fluctuation.

The great bulk of the casual work force in agriculture is Mexican and native white. In certain crops, notably asparagus and lettuce, the Filipino is prominent. Since the war Negroes, originally attracted by the shipyards and aircraft factories as much as by cotton, have become increasingly important in the seasonal agricultural labor force.

THE STRUCTURELESS MARKET

Agriculture in California is peculiarly well suited to accommodate and usefully employ labor of almost any description. The market is without any structure of job rights or preferences. Not only are unions virtually nonexistent but there is literally no relationship between employer and employee upon which any

claims to recurrent employment might be built. To the employer the harvest hand is anonymous; he has not even a social security number for identification. To be sure, the farmer has preferences, but these are racial preferences. The Filipino is preferred because Filipinos are presumed to be skilled agricultural workers. The Mexican is preferred to the white because of a presumption that he is less "independent." The Negro is least favorably regarded.

The anonymity of the harvest workers is expressed in the racist folklore of California growers. Rationalizations of an earlier day have become the firm convictions of the present. As California farmers pressed their claims for Japanese immigration, Mexican immigration, and Filipino immigration, the argument was that American workers would not accept field work; what was required was "stoop labor" or "squat labor." What was actually being sought was cheap labor, but the euphemism has come to be transmuted into a firm belief in racial aptitudes. The distinctions recognized among agricultural workers are largely confined to age, sex, race or nationality, and place of origin.

There is, then, no structure provided by skills. The tasks of the harvest hand in a literal sense require little learning and little judgment. There is, to be sure, an element of judgment in knowing which bolls of cotton are fully developed or which fruit is ready for picking, but this is quickly learned. There is an element of skill in the harvesting of asparagus or of lettuce, but this comes to be the specialized task of those possessing the skill, and the market does acquire structure for these few crops; but the great majority of harvest jobs require no such skill.

There are important advantages to a structureless market. It can employ virtually any type of labor and is therefore able to accommodate itself to a wide variety of situations. Paradoxically, the market for harvest labor is organized to maintain the advantages of disorganization. One of the central mechanisms of such a market is the use of piece rates as a method of payment. If time rates were employed, it would be essential to distinguish among individuals as to their competence. The difference between an efficient and inefficient worker would bear importantly on cost and a means of distinguishing among workers would have to be found. But the piece rate is the most common form of compensation in the

California harvest. Consequently, labor costs are equalized as between efficient and inefficient workers. Differences in skill, age, and sex become matters of relative indifference, provided only that the elementary distinction between a ripe grape or a ripe peach and a green one can be communicated. Thus California agriculture is able to provide productive employment for men, women, and children, for the experienced and inexperienced, for alcoholic derelicts from the "slave" markets, and for the skilled Filipino, at a labor cost per unit of output which does not vary widely.

The absence of mechanization is a final necessary condition of a structureless market. In those harvest enterprises such as potatoes, sugar beets, and grain, which depend upon machine methods, the necessary relationship between the character of the machine and the laborers associated with it impose a structure of numbers and of skills upon the working force. In the nonmechanized harvests, within very broad limits, it is a matter of relative indifference how many workers are hired. The advantage tends to be with the greatest numbers, for the more quickly accomplished is the harvest the more nearly minimized is the risk of inclement weather. The presence of capital equipment, particularly in the form of harvest machinery, imposes limits on the number of workers and involves requirements of skill which are not present in the hand harvest.

The general conditions of an unstructured market, then, are fivefold: (1) there must be no unions with their usual accompaniment of seniority, preference of employment, and other limitations upon access to the labor market; (2) there must be an impersonal relationship between employer and employee, lest informal obligations and various types of moral tenure develop; (3) the productive employment must be largely unskilled so that it becomes accessible to a large and unspecialized labor force; (4) the method of compensation must be by unit of product rather than by unit of time; (5) the operation must employ little or no capital or machinery.

Until very recently the market for seasonal labor in California met these requirements closely. But mechanization is on the increase. The potato harvest is largely mechanized. Machinery has been widely introduced into the sugar harvest. The cotton picker is increasingly employed in the cotton fields of the San Joa-quin Valley. The bulk of harvest operations remains nonmechanized. The cotton, grape, and tomato harvest and the harvest of tree fruits account for the vast majority of casual seasonal employment. With the rapid increase in the use of the cotton picker and the development of mechanical aids to fruit picking, the amount of capital employed is undergoing a significant change.

DEMAND FOR HARVEST LABOR

With the exception of the 1930s, California farmers have had an apparently insatiable demand for harvest labor. A common charge against California farmers—and labor contractors as well—is the charge that they have used labor wastefully; that owing in large part to their incontinent demands, the agricultural labor market has been chronically flooded with surplus workers. Sometimes the charge has been made that the policy was a deliberate one, designed to depress agricultural wages, with a large part of the economic costs and all the social costs of the policy borne by relief agencies and the casual workers themselves. That an oversupply of labor has a depressing effect on wage rates is undoubtedly true, but to consider this the chief motivation in the farmers' demand for labor is so oversimplified as to be fundamentally erroneous. The lowering of wage rates where it occurs is as much an effect as it is an objective of oversupply. The true incentives for "flooding" the labor market lie elsewhere. The demand of farmers for more labor than an objective observer would agree they require is a rational response to the peculiar circumstances of the harvest, and is largely independent of the effect that the supply of labor may have upon its price.

THREE ASSUMPTIONS

To place the essential elements of the farmer's employment decisions in proper focus, a few simplifying assumptions will be made. The first assumption is that the harvest operation is a separate economic enterprise, and that decisions made relative to it are independent of earlier decisions as to what and how much would be planted, the amount of fertilizer employed, the degree of cultivation, and so on. To be sure, these decisions have been guided by expectations of yield, price, and labor costs.

These decisions once made, however, the harvest decisions become almost totally independent of them. The farmer confronts a situation in which the fixed costs of his operation are irrelevant, and past variable costs are likewise irrelevant. His concern now is with the cost of harvesting (and perhaps marketing) on the one hand, and the price he will receive, on the other.

The second assumption is that the total harvest cost is labor cost. This is in close accord with the facts in nonmechanized operations. There are minor harvest costs incurred in addition to labor costs in most crops: tomatoes require lugs; peas, hampers; tree fruits, ladders and containers; and cotton, burlap sacks; but these items of capital are inexpensive, and variations in the number of such items employed would have an insignificant effect upon the shape of the average cost curve of harvesting.

The third assumption is that the labor employed is compensated at piece rates. Again this is in substantial accord with the facts. Where farmers employ supervisory help paid at hourly or monthly rates, the number of such foremen is a negligible part of the total labor force. Furthermore, where labor contractors are employed, the supervision of field labor is an almost invariable service rendered by the contractor to the grower.

If the harvest is a separate, or at least a separable, economic enterprise, we must then inquire into the special influences bearing upon the harvest enterprise which motivate or affect the employment decisions.

Although the seasonal character of demand for agricultural labor is inherent in the structure of the agricultural economy itself, in the series of crops which have proved profitable, and in the growing seasons which are characteristic of them, the problem is seriously aggravated by the fact that the farmer's incentives are entirely in the direction of more intense demand than crop and climate require. Here is the explanation for the persistent reports of labor shortage while no crops spoiled, for the chronic "flooding" of agricultural labor markets in California, for the universal experience of all who have dealt with the mercurial problem of estimating the farmer's demand for labor. The farmer's demand is more or less as he states it. He can, by and large, provide some employment for most of the workers he calls for. He could also harvest his crop with many

less. So long as the cost of recruiting additional labor remains negligible and the cost of unemployment is borne by the community, and so long as the piece-rate system prevails, the farmer will continue to demand a larger number of workers for a shorter period of time in preference to a smaller number of workers for a longer period of time.

WAGES OF HARVEST LABOR

Meaningful comparisons between the wages of harvest labor in California and wages in non-agricultural occupations are exceedingly difficult to make. Notwithstanding these difficulties, the comparison has been made. The Department of Agriculture publishes figures on a daily wage of agricultural workers, and the Bureau of Labor Statistics published figures on common labor rates in industry which were discontinued in 1940. The most recent date, therefore, for which the comparison is available is July, 1940. On that date the daily wage of the farm laborer in California was reported to be $2.85, and the daily wage of the common laborer in California industry was $4.72. The divergence between the wage rate of the two groups is doubtless greater than is shown, since the conventional working day in agriculture is nine hours and in industry only eight.

Even though this statistical evidence is not impressive, the differential between agricultural wages and the wages of unskilled industrial workers is in fact substantial. Undoubtedly this differential is much greater in periods of unemployment than in periods of full employment. The evidence is quite clear that the wages of agricultural labor in California rose much more rapidly during the war than did those of industrial workers; but at no point in recent history has the wage disparity been eliminated.

It is a commonplace of economic theory that if laborers were free to move from the lower paying jobs in agriculture to the common labor jobs of industry, such differentials in wages and earnings could not persist. The differences in wages as between manufacturing employment and agriculture would be eliminated as workers moved out of the harvests and into manufacturing enterprises and wages tended toward the same level in both markets. But labor markets seldom, if ever, exhibit these characteristics of the market of economic theory, and not merely because union organization has intervened. The relatively high degree of union organization in nonagricultural enterprises in California is but one among other and more important influences which have kept agricultural wages in California substantially below the lowest wages offered in manufacturing industries within close geographic proximity.

The explanation is to be found in three sets of causes, each operating to depress the wage rate of agricultural workers. The first of these is the relative immobility of agricultural workers as between agriculture and industry, and the second is the accessibility of the agricultural labor market to all groups of workers because of its unorganized character. The third is the high development of organization among agricultural employers. The first and second will be discussed here because of their obvious bearing on the supply of harvest labor. The third will not be treated here.

Segregation and Immobility

Agricultural workers, although highly mobile within agriculture, are relatively immobile as between agriculture and nonagricultural employment. There is perhaps no better instance than the California harvest of a field of employment in which workers are free to move from job to job and from area to area within a single market, without significant impediment from market institutions. In the earlier discussion of the characteristics of a structureless market, it was emphasized that neither union organization nor the informal preferences which grow out of regularized employment relations constitute any bar to movement. There is neither a structure of skills nor the regulating effects of a time-rate system of payment to place limits upon the movement of workers from farm to farm, or upon the substitutability of one worker for another. Community attachment, seniority, pensions, opportunity for advancement, and all the other elements in the attachment of a worker to a job are totally absent. Furthermore, the very character of the productive process ordains that jobs shall be of very limited duration. Surely the conditions making for fluidity and mobility of labor could not readily be duplicated in any other set of economic enterprises. This is, as far as mobility is concerned, as close to the "ideal type" of the perfect labor market as one is likely to encoun-

ter, and consistent with the "ideal types," wage rates are generally uniform, or nearly so, for comparable tasks within the seasonal agricultural labor market. But the freedom to move from farm to farm is a characteristic of agricultural employment only. There is no similar freedom to move from farm to factory.

There are two major obstacles to the movement of labor between agriculture and industry. The first of these is prejudice. However mixed the motives of California employers, agricultural employment has been open to the Oriental, the Mexican, Filipino, and Negro, whereas much of industry has been closed to them. The result has been a form of segregation in which agricultural employers have clearly benefited from a labor force which has been relatively immobile, with the single exception of the war years when the demand for planes and ships was so great that industrial employment was open to all comers. The consequence of this immobilization has been to relieve agricultural employers of the necessity of competing with industry for their labor supply.

To the influences tending to segregate and immobilize agricultural labor, and therefore to depress its wages below industrial wages, must be added labor organization in the industrial labor market. Labor unions are approximately as serious a barrier to the movement of agricultural labor into industrial occupations as are employers. Not only does race prejudice enter importantly in the determination of who shall be eligible for employment in those jobs which unions control, but the natural restrictionist policies which trade unions adopt undoubtedly keep the labor supply relatively more scarce in industrial occupations than in agricultural employment. One major element, then, in the maintenance of large wage differences between agricultural and industrial employment is the set of obstacles to movement from agriculture to industry imposed by race prejudice on the one hand and union restrictions on the other.

Accessibility of the Market

With industrial labor enjoying the relatively protected market which unions provide, agricultural employment is open to almost any who would try it. Not only is its large colored and Mexican labor force handicapped in its access to industrial employment, but it is subject to substantial expansions of supply from at least four sources.

In any period of depression and substantial unemployment in the cities, industrial labor seeks and finds employment in the harvest, reducing the volume of employment available to the permanent agricultural labor force and exerting a depressing effect upon wages.

The constant stream of migrants to the Pacific Coast contributes an annual increment of considerable size to the agricultural labor force. The unprotected character of the harvest labor market, together with its tendency to prefer larger numbers of workers for shorter periods of time, make of agricultural employment a way station for many migrants to California who may have no intention of remaining agricultural workers. A substantial proportion of each year's migration contributes labor to the harvests for a season or two while it seeks a higher level of economic opportunity.

A third source of labor, used ordinarily only in periods of serious shortage of labor, is the rural town in a farming area. A number of factors combined to give the farmer a privileged position in the community and a special claim upon the townspeople of his area. In large part the economic activities of the town are built upon the farming areas. A serious crop loss would have grave consequence for the enterprises of the town. For all these reasons, rural towns will frequently mobilize to meet a shortage of harvest labor. The community, under the leadership of the local banker or the Chamber of Commerce, will declare a three-day holiday, and with a good deal of ceremony symbolizing the unity between farm and town, the employed workers in the town will turn to in the fields and speed the harvest. Local boards of education are usually cooperative, also adjusting the opening and closing of school years, and in some cases the schedule of daily classes, to the needs of the harvest. To the extent that a shortage of labor might otherwise bring forth a high wage, the cooperation of the rural communities and schools makes the higher wage less necessary.

The fourth major source of labor to supplement the normal supply is labor imported by the Federal government in response to representations of need by California farmers. The chief source of this supply is Mexico, with fewer numbers, ordinarily not destined for California, coming from the West Indies.

SUPPLY CURVE OF HARVEST LABOR

It is a widespread belief among growers in California that increases in wages are a highly inefficient means of increasing the supply of agricultural labor. Although wage increases are not uncommon during years in which the labor supply is short enough to threaten some crop spoilage, farmers are more likely to turn to various programs of labor importation than to increases in the wage rate as a means of increasing the supply of labor. The relative advantages of a program of importation, so long as transportation costs are borne by either the government or the worker, are clear enough. But apart from the inherent desirability of securing labor for less, there is some substance in the growers' argument that an increase in wages will not of itself produce an increase in the supply of labor within the harvest season.

For an increase in wages to be effective in augmenting the supply of labor, one of two conditions is necessary. There must either be an available supply of labor in other occupations which can be attracted into agricultural employment as a result of the increase in wages, or the existing agricultural labor force must offer more labor from those already employed or those unemployed in response to the incentive of higher wages.

The first condition is theoretically present but practically absent. The difference between agricultural wage levels and those prevailing in nonagricultural occupations is probably so large that the wage increase necessary to make agricultural employment an attractive alternative would be psychologically, if not economically, out of the question. Furthermore, the new relationship between agricultural and nonagricultural wages would need to stand decidedly in favor of agriculture in order to compensate for the disagreeable character of the work, its low social status, and its extremely seasonal nature.

On the second point the evidence is by no means decisive, but what there is again tends to support the growers' position that an increase in wage rates will not bring forth a larger, and may result in a smaller offering of labor by the agricultural work force. This is to suggest that the labor supply curve may develop a negative inclination somewhere within the relevant range of wage rates. If very substantial increases in agricultural wage rates would attract few if any recruits to the labor force from other occupations, in any single season, then the shape of the labor supply curve will be determined by the response of the existing agricultural labor force and the voluntarily unemployed to a variation in the wage. The voluntarily unemployed may be ignored, since it is extremely unlikely that there is available to the harvests any significant number of persons who are unemployed because their evaluation of leisure is too great to seek employment in agriculture at prevailing wage rates, but not so great that an imaginable increase in the rate would not bring them forth. The response of the agricultural labor force to an increase in wages then becomes the decisive element in the shape of the labor supply curve. Such evidence as there is suggests that an increase in wages probably does diminish the total labor offered.

There are at least two characteristics of the agricultural labor force that would support the view that the curve of labor supply may become negative in slope [backward bending]. The first of these is the fact that a substantial proportion of the labor force is family labor— wives and children who supplement the earnings of the chief wage earner by working with him in the fields. The second is the supposition, which is probably correct, that many agricultural laborers have psychologically adjusted to a low level of living and have developed relatively fixed income objectives.

For that portion of the labor force which is composed of women with domestic obligations (wives and mothers) and children of school age, membership in the labor force is largely involuntary, made necessary by the low level of family earnings when only the husband is employed. As wages and income rise, there is reason to believe that family labor is withdrawn from the market. If wages rise sufficiently, family labor will be withdrawn com-

pletely, thus diminishing the total amount of labor offered in response to a higher wage.

The supposition of fixed income objectives upon the achievement of which leisure becomes highly valued and labor is withheld is essentially without verification. It is a widely observed fact in the San Joaquin Valley that whole communities of agricultural laborers have grown up in areas where income expectations are low, and that the level of living and presumably the standard of living of the agricultural workers who reside there have adjusted to the low income. During the war ample employment opportunities yielding much larger incomes were readily available, but much of the agricultural labor force remained in the "shacktowns" which they had built, and more or less voluntarily forewent opportunities for wartime earnings. It obviously does not follow that a higher wage offered within the areas of the "shacktowns" would cause a decline in the labor offered by adult males. It would not, however, increase the supply, and such change as might result would be more likely to be negative than positive.

Counterbalancing these tendencies somewhat is the debilitating effect of poverty upon the labor force itself. Malnutrition, high incidence of disease, greater mortality, and premature aging all tend to diminish the available labor. To the extent that higher wages would moderate these tendencies, a healthier and therefore a larger working force would result.

The sum of all these tendencies suggests at the very least that higher wages would result in no increase in the supply of labor and quite conceivably could diminish it somewhat. So, at any rate, the farmers believe, and the conviction is widespread that a rise in wages is no remedy for a general shortage of labor, although it may serve to divert labor from one farmer's harvest to that of another.

QUESTIONS AND STUDY SUGGESTIONS

1. Discuss the major supply and demand characteristics of the California harvest labor market.
2. What is meant by a "structureless" labor market? What specific conditions does such a market presume?
3. Describe in detail the demand for harvest labor. Why is it that California farmers seem to demand much more labor than is apparently required to accomplish the harvest? Explain: "The lowering of wage

rates where it occurs is as much an effect as it is an objective of over-supply."

4. What factors account for the substantial wage differentials between the farm laborer and the common industrial laborer in California?

5. Why is it believed that higher wages might not increase, and might even decrease, the quantity of harvest labor supplied?

Reading 46

Of Profit and Loss

John Davenport

Profits, both positive and negative, play a key role in a capitalistic econ-omy: they govern the allocation of scarce resources among competing uses. Reading 46 is a succinct summary of the character of profits and the relationship of profits to uncertainty. The author cautions against "current fallacies" surrounding such concepts as "excessive" and "rea-sonable" profits and the ill-advised economic policies which these notions imply.

"The business of America is business," re-marked Calvin Coolidge, and ever since so-phisticates have been ridiculing the Sage of Northampton, Mass., for his cheap and materi-alistic view of his country. They are, in their way, right. For the business of the United States, from its founding through the first half of the twentieth century, has obviously been more than commercial profit and loss. The "national purpose," however defined—and it is a term that needs careful definition—cannot be confined within the narrow limits of the count-ing house or the factory. Yet in justification to Coolidge it may also be said that without busi-ness and the businessman there never would have been the America which we know today,

and the implementation of the national pur-pose would remain academic small talk. As John Chamberlain has shown in *The Enter-prising Americans*, a history of American en-terprise from colonial times forward, it is the businessman and the risk-taker who in large measure built up this country's agriculture, developed its early manufacturing facilities, laid down the rails between two oceans, ush-ered in the age of mass production, developed the wonders of electricity and communication, and now stand behind its defenses and probe into outer space. Without its Pepperrells, Cabots, Whitneys, Fords, Rockefellers, Trippes, and Sarnoffs, the American continent might have lain potentially rich yet fallow. These and

From John Davenport, **The U.S. Economy**, Henry Regnery Company, Chicago, 1964, pp. 48–55. Reprinted by permission.

many other men were the economic decision-makers. To borrow a phrase from Edison, they "pushed the system."

BUSINESSMEN AND WORKMEN

So pervasive, indeed, has been and is the influence of business enterprise that it is and has always been difficult to define its outer limits. "We are literally all workers," remarked Amos Lawrence expansively in the 1850s, "and the attempt to get up a workingman's party is a libel upon the whole population." Just so, it might be said that everybody who takes part in the creative process of production is a businessman; and attempts to define business as the province of corporate tycoons is an affront to common sense and common observation. It is the essence of the market economy to bind together and to coordinate all types of human effort; and if one observes any particular job in progress—say, the tearing down of an old, and the erection of a new, building—it is difficult to say where the creative function of the workman, the foreman, the manager, and the entrepreneur or businessman begins and leaves off. They are all for the moment engaged on a particular bit of "business" which will, it is to be hoped, eventually serve the community, and the transaction of this business, at the time at least, seems one and indivisible.

Nevertheless, for purposes of analysis it is possible to draw a dividing line which separates out the economic role of the workman and the paid supervisor from that of the businessman or entrepreneur proper. It is found if one asks the simple question: who will suffer the *loss* if the contracting firm in question fails to finish the job on time or in some other way botches the job, and who, alternatively, will make the *profit* if all goes according to schedule and plan? Not the workman, for he will be paid his wages as long as the job continues. Not the salaried supervisor, for he likewise will get his reward. The answer, of course, is that it is the owners of the contracting firm who will reap the rewards or suffer the disappointments of success or failure. It is they who have laid out the money to bring the mason, the carpenter, and the electrician to the spot; it is they who have contracted for a steady flow of materials—concrete, steel, lumber, brick; and, it is they, more importantly, who rent or buy the tools necessary for the undertaking—the pneu-

matic drills, the bulldozers, the soaring, swaying cranes. All these things represent costs—some variable, some fixed—which, it is hoped, will total something less than the final price for erecting the building. If this hope or gamble proves correct, there will be a residual profit. If it proves incorrect there will be loss, and the firm, if it can withstand the strain, will have to turn to another contract to make good the deficiency.

SOURCES OF PROFIT

While this no doubt is an oversimplification of how the construction industry operates, it nevertheless allows us to define the nature of business enterprise with a fair amount of precision. While business in broadest definition is the creative process of making things, business in narrower definition is the act of *organizing* the means of production in a way that will ultimately satisfy buyers or consumers. The reward for undertaking the risks of such organization is profit, defined as the evanescent and residual margin of return between cost and selling price. The word "evanescent" is used advisedly, for in a purely static economy profits as defined above would not long exist. If consumer tastes remained constant, on the one hand, and if no technological developments or inventions occurred, on the other, then there would soon be no room for profits (though there would always be need to pay for supervisory skills). But in the real world such static conditions are never long present. The buying tastes of the public do change from moment to moment and from year to year. New inventions come forward which obsolete old ways of doing things. It is the business of business and the businessman to cope with these changing conditions, and to put them to use in the expectation of profit return.

Put in another way, profit or loss is the result of *uncertainty* about the future which changing tastes and new technologies inevitably create. If everybody were sure today about what would happen tomorrow, there would be no special place for the entrepreneur, and nothing left over for the profit residual. If, to take an extreme example, one were sure this year that there would be demand next year for exactly 100,000 Buick cars priced at $3,400, and if no changes occurred in the costs of making cars, then all risks of manufacturing Buicks would disappear, and costs, including payments for wages, management, and capital, would equal selling price. But such certainty is never present, either on the selling side or the manufacturing side, and the producer in fact always takes a chance which, if correct, is duly rewarded. As the economist Ludwig von Mises has put it: "What makes profit emerge is the fact that the entrepreneur who judges the future prices of the products more correctly than other people do buys some or all of the factors of production at prices which, even from the point of view of the future state of the market, are too low. Thus the total costs of production —including interest on the capital invested—lag behind the prices which the entrepreneur receives for the product. This difference is entrepreneurial profit."

PROFITS AS A RESIDUAL SHARE

Profits are thus something quite different from other shares of the national income and, on analysis, are not really a share at all, and certainly not a fixed share. They are rather something left over after all other factors have been accounted for. The biggest share of national income logically goes for wages and salaries, which are straight payments for work done or contracted for. Another share of the national income goes for interest, which is the reward, not for risk-taking, but for the willingness of some people to wait and to forego consumption today for a larger reward tomorrow. These lend out their money at short term or at long term, as the case may be, to entrepreneurs who will put it to work. Interest is thus wholly vital to capital formation, but it is a payment that, short of default by the borrower, does not vary from the 4 percent or 6 percent promised on the bond. Even dividends, in so far as they represent a normal return on capital tied up in a business, are regarded by economists as something different from "pure" profits, which are, to repeat, something left over after all capital, as well as wage and managerial costs, are paid.

Profits in economic theory are thus something smaller and less calculable than what is shown under this head in the familiar national income statistics, but these latter are nevertheless revealing. For they indicate, as one would expect, that profitability is subject to enormous fluctuations up and down. In 1963, for instance, corporate profits in the U.S. after taxes were reported at $24.6 billion. But in 1932, at the pit of the great depression, profits were actually negative to the tune of $3.4 billion. Some businesses, of course, continued to make money. But in the system as a whole, losses far outran profit. As long as there is any production at all, some wages and salaries will be paid. Profits, however, enjoy no such immunity, and the reward of risk-taking may turn into loss when the market fails to fulfill the expectations of the risk-takers. Fundamentally, the U.S. is not a profit economy. It is a *profit-and-loss* economy, and those who do not emphasize this fact have grossly misrepresented the nature of the so-called "capitalist" system.

MARX ON PROFITS

Such misunderstanding has been widespread, and attack on profits has come from many quarters. The boldest attack was launched by Karl Marx, who argued that profits were a so-called "surplus value," extorted from the hide of the workingman by greedy capitalists for no useful service performed. But this overlooks the fact that the worker cannot create any "surplus value" over what he receives. The value of his work is his wage, which is fixed by the supply and demand for his services. In many cases, this wage would be nonexistent or far lower than it is today were it not that the proper materials and tools have been brought together through which his work can be performed. It is in risking his money for the assembly of these tools, which by definition are scarce, that the entrepreneur performs his most important function from the point of view of the worker and from the point of view of society itself. For the tools have to be made and paid for before wages, or in any case high wages, will be forthcoming. In an advanced economy, production is always "roundabout," involving a large number of steps, such as the erection of a plant or factory, before final goods can come off the line. The more roundabout the process of production becomes, the more need there is for someone to bear the risks of organizing it. The alternative to a profit-and-loss economy is not, as Marx supposed, a worker's paradise. The alternative is either the attempt by government to organize production through total centrist planning or, in the telling phrase of economist Frank Knight, just plain "chaos."

PROFIT FALLACIES

More current fallacies about profits, and so about business enterprise, are the notions that profits can, on the one hand, be "excessive" and, on the other, that they can be fixed at some "reasonable" level. The first idea runs like a red thread through many political investigations, but has little to commend it. If a business has, for instance, brought forward a new invention which greatly reduces costs, it will for the time being earn profits far in "excess" of its competitors, but such excess is simply a signal that still more capital is needed in this line of production. Under conditions of competition within the industry, or, indeed, of inter-industry competition, this new capital will tend to be forthcoming, and the "excessive" profits of the firm originating the invention will under competitive conditions soon be whittled down. The collateral notion, sometimes put forward by businessmen themselves, that while profits should not be excessive, still they should be "reasonable" is equally specious, and can perhaps be even more harmful. For if businesses are to be guaranteed a "reasonable" profit, it will surely not be long before the state or the trade unions assume the task of trying to figure out what this reasonable reward should be. This is an open invitation to reduce all business to the status of the public utilities, with commissions set up to regulate them. The fact is that no business has a "right" to any given level of profits, any more than it has the "right" to any given level of prices. It should charge "what the market will bear," confident that, if it has correctly judged the market and its own costs, some profit may be forthcoming to itself while others may no doubt be taking losses.

QUESTIONS AND STUDY SUGGESTIONS

1. How are profits distinguishable from the returns to other resources?
2. Explain specifically how profits are related to uncertainty. Why does the author contend that the United States is a *profit-and-loss* economy?
3. On what grounds does the author argue that notions of "excessive" or "reasonable" profits are fallacious?

Reading 47

Education: Private and Social Benefits

Burton A. Weisbrod, Professor of Economics, University of Wisconsin

One of the inherent shortcomings of the market system is its failure to take into account fully all of the benefits and costs associated with the production or consumption of a commodity. Reading 47 emphasizes the

Reprinted with permission of the copyright owners, the Regents of the University of Wisconsin, from Burton A. Weisbrod, "Investing in Human Capital," **The Journal of Human Resources**, Volume I, Number 1, 1966, the University of Wisconsin Press.

substantial social benefits associated with education. In addition to such private benefits as the higher incomes and lower unemployment rates which accrue to the immediate consumers of education, education provides the business community with a more productive labor force and yields savings to taxpayers in the areas of crime prevention, law enforcement, and welfare programs. Furthermore, education is essential to the maintenance of competition, to the shaping of socially desirable attitudes and behavior, and to the efficient functioning of political democracy. Professor Weisbrod recommends that government take action to see that the public is well informed about the long-run benefits of investment in human capital; to supplement the private capital market in making loans and grants to students; and to alter tax policy so as to encourage greater expenditures on education.

Properly conceived, education produces a labor force that is more skilled, more adaptable to the needs of a changing economy, and more likely to develop the imaginative ideas, techniques, and products which are critical to the processes of economic expansion and social adaptation to change. By doing so—by contributing to worker productivity—the education process qualifies handsomely as a process of investment in human capital.

ECONOMIC VALUE OF EDUCATION

In analyzing the economic value of education, it is useful to view education as an industry—a user of resources and a producer of outputs. An economy has limited resources and cannot produce all the goods and services we would like to have. Therefore, efforts should be expanded to identify and to measure the values of the education industry's outputs, as well as the costs of all the resources it uses. It is not enough to exhort the virtues of education. While some urge that education merits added support, others press for more resources for health, while still others are urging the expansion of efforts to improve diets or housing, or construct more parks or wider and safer highways.

Unhappily, we must make choices. If they are made without recognition of the full benefits and costs of alternative uses of resources, we are not likely to choose wisely. Within this context, the following sections are devoted to what is known, and to what is not known, about the forms and magnitude of benefits from educational investments in human resources. Private and public benefits will be examined.

By "benefits" of education I mean any of three types of effects: those that increase production possibilities, such as increased labor skills; those that reduce costs and thereby make resources available for more productive uses, such as the reduced crime and law enforcement needs that education may bring by enhancing earnings; and those that increase welfare possibilities directly, such as development of public-spiritedness or social consciousness.

PRIVATE BENEFITS FROM EDUCATION

Direct economic gains to individuals from education are sizeable. Two measures of these gains are the greater incomes and the smaller unemployment rates which added schooling seems to bring. Data for the United States (Table 47–1) present an impressive picture of the favorable relationships between an individual's educational attainment, his subsequent income, and the prospects for his unemployment.

But let me digress with some words of caution. With reference to the income-education relationship, it is probably not true that the high school dropout in the United States, for example, could increase his annual income from around $4,800 to $5,400 (Table 47–1), if only he would complete high school. We frequently forget the selection process by which some young people complete more schooling than others. In general, those students who do not drop out are more able, more ambitious, more anxious to learn, and come from families with better job "connections"—all of which assist in lifting their incomes. We cannot be sure how much of the additional incomes associated with additional education is attributable to these fac-

Table 47–1.   INCOME AND UNEMPLOYMENT BY YEARS OF SCHOOLING COMPLETED IN THE UNITED STATES

Years of schooling completed	Median income, males, age 25 and over, 1959	Unemployment rate, March 1962 (percent)
Elementary:		
8 years	$3,892	7.2
High School:		
1–3 years	4,846	8.3
4 years	5,441	5.1
College:		
1–3 years	5,978	3.7
4 years	7,388	1.5

SOURCES: *U.S. Census, 1960*; and U.S. Department of Labor.

tors, and how much is attributable to the schooling itself. The monetary returns from investment in education are doubtless noteworthy, but they are probably not as large as the data in Table 47–1 suggest.

Caution is also required in interpreting the dramatic data on unemployment rates in the table. It is not unusual to find young people being advised not to quit school partly on the ground that their chances of being unemployed would be reduced if they remained. This approach is too simple. If, by the wave of a magic wand, the entire U.S. labor force could have been endowed with a college education, would the over-all unemployment rate of 6.0 percent in March 1962 have been reduced to only 1.5 percent (Table 47–1)—the rate for college graduates? I think not.

Education alone does not create jobs. It can, however, help cut unemployment by enhancing the matchability of labor-force skills with employer needs. When the task is attaining and maintaining full employment, education is not an adequate substitute for effective government fiscal and monetary policies and high levels of consumer and business demand. However, it is a valuable complement. Let us not expect too much from education, particularly in the short run. Its economic value lies primarily in its contribution to individuals' productive *potential,* rather than in its contribution to the economy's success in achieving that potential.

Having digressed to point up the dangers of over-stating gross economic benefits from education, let me also note that there are important costs as well as benefits of education to

students and their families. Costs include more than cash payments. They also include the earnings and production *foregone* because potentially productive people are in school (or in the hospital or physician's office in the case of investments in health), instead of on the job. In fact, a recent estimate for the United States indicates that the costs of high school and college education in the form of foregone income exceed by more than 50 percent the costs incurred directly by the schools.

Still, when *all* costs are considered, and when an allowance is made for the non-educational factors affecting schooling, our best available evidence for the United States is that formal education does pay in the direct form of enhanced employment opportunities and, thus, of greater incomes. Education is an investment which produces at least as great a financial return as does investment in corporate enterprise—around 10 percent for college, and even more for high school and elementary school.

But the profitability of education does not rest alone on its productivity-increasing or money-income-increasing benefits. Some of the value of education accrues to the individual in other forms. The fruits of literacy—an output of elementary education—include the value of its non-market use. Thus, to cite an illustration which closely touches many of us, if a man prepares his own income tax return, he performs a service made possible by his literacy. Were this service provided through the market, it would be priced and included in national income. Assuming that 50 million of the 60 million personal income tax returns being filed each year in the United States are prepared by the taxpayer himself, at a value of $5 per return, a rough estimate of the annual market value of the tax return services performed by taxpayers for themselves is $250 million. Obviously, this is only one minor form of return from literacy. But it is in addition to the benefits from elementary education which accrue in money form.

SOCIAL BENEFITS FROM EDUCATION

If students were the only beneficiaries of schooling, the broad public support for education would probably wither. But as valuable as education is privately, it is even more valuable publicly. Its benefits take diverse forms which extend well beyond the individuals who receive it.

For one thing, education has an important intergenerational value. When today's students reach adulthood, their children will gain by virtue of the informal education received at home. Much learning takes place at home, where the child's attitude toward school is also largely shaped. Better educated parents are more likely to raise children who recognize the value of education, in terms of job opportunities, as well as in terms of cultural opportunities.

This means that the social value of educating women is not zero, even if they never enter the labor force to utilize the skills developed in school. It is a mistake to say that education has value to society only when additional earnings and *marketable* production result. If we think of an "investment" as involving future as distinguished from current returns, then education has an investment component in the form of these intergeneration benefits.

Another group of beneficiaries from education is employers, who have a financial interest in the education and training of their employees. An employer's job would be much more difficult and expensive if he had to work with an illiterate and untrained labor force or had to educate and train his own workers.

Education also affects taxpayers in general, who pay—directly or indirectly—for the consequences of the lack of education. For example, insofar as lack of education leads to employment difficulties and crime, the costs of crime prevention, law enforcement, and social unrest—with the related welfare costs—will tend to be high.

These costs, however, may not fall upon taxpayers in the community or area having responsibility for the child's education. The migration of poorly educated people whose behavior patterns and educational attainments differ greatly from those prevailing in the areas they migrate to may necessitate additional effort and expense to permit the migrants to adjust to the new school conditions, if they are children, or to the new social and economic conditions, if they are adults. Thus, *residents of areas of in-migration have a stake in the education of children in the areas of out-migration.* People in the U.S. North have a stake in education in the South. In general, people who are or may be in the same fiscal unit with an individual have a financial stake in the investment in his human capital.

The nation as a whole reaps a return from education through the process of economic growth. In an important study of *The Sources of Economic Growth in the United States*, Edward Denison estimated that 21 percent of the growth of real national income per person employed between 1929 and 1957 was attributable to the greater education of the labor force, while another 36 percent was attributable to the "advance of knowledge," much of which is associated with educational advance.

BROAD SOCIAL BENEFITS

We have seen that some of the social benefits from education are enjoyed by individuals and groups that are reasonably identifiable. But some of the benefits are distributed so broadly that the nature of specific beneficiaries is obscure. These general social benefits are not less important by virtue of their pervasiveness.

For example, literacy is of value not only to the individual possessing it and to employers, but to the entire society. Without widespread literacy, the significance of books, newspapers, and similar information media would dwindle; and it seems fair to say that the communication of information is of vital importance to the maintenance of competition and, indeed, to the existence of a market economy, as well as to the maintenance of political democracy.

Education is, after all, much more than a means of raising productivity or otherwise bringing financial returns. It is also a means of inculcating children with standards of socially desirable attitudes and behavior and of introducing children to new opportunities and challenges. In a free society, it helps to develop greater awareness of, and ability to participate effectively in, the democratic process.

No statistics can be marshalled to "prove" that education itself brings about a stronger democracy, but the relationships between people's educational attainments and their participation in activities that help make a democracy strong are striking. For one thing, education appears to develop in people a sense of citizen duty. Measuring attitudes toward the importance of voting on a five-level scale, interviewers from the Survey Research Center of the University of Michigan found that only 25 percent of the grade school graduates were classified in the top level, while 50 percent of the high school graduates and 60 percent of the college graduates achieved it. None of the college graduates was in the bottom level, though 2 percent of the high school graduates and 12 percent of the grade school graduates were. Similarly, favorable effects of education have been found in its relationship with the degree of political participation. Moreover, the percentage of persons who actually do vote increases with educational attainment.

The brevity of this discussion does an injustice to the important and sometimes subtle ways that education strengthens democratic institutions. No attempt has been made here to be thorough in an area where economists probably have little to contribute. Instead, the objective has been simply to recognize the fact that some—and possibly the most important—forms of social benefits from education may defy monetary valuation.

We have found that the social benefits from education take many forms and accrue widely through time and space. Some of the benefits from education—and much of what has been said about education also applies to health and other forms of human investments—are not realized by people in the area which financed the investment. Because the location of gains from some human-resource investments are determined by population movement, the process of migration is a process of spatial shifting of those gains. This produces not only an interstate or interprovincial stake in effective policies of human-resource development, but an international stake as well.

The diversity and complex diffusion of benefits from investments in human capital raise important issues as to how education should be financed and what role government should play generally in the development of human resources.

PUBLIC POLICY

The education system produces many forms of benefits. Some interesting issues arise, once we recognize that there are external benefits from education—benefits to people other than the immediate recipients. For one principle of financing expenditures is that those who benefit from some expenditure should pay for it. Even a partial use of this taxation principle would call for attempts to identify various groups of direct and indirect beneficiaries from investments in human capital and to assess charges in recognition of the distribution of benefits. I do not mean to suggest that the benefit principle should necessarily prevail in financing investments in human capital. However, since many benefits from education are very broadly dispersed, the application of this principle would, in fact, require broad financial support for education and other such investments.

This paper has underscored the need for social recognition of the process of human-resource investment. The previous pages have developed the views that education and health are not merely consumer-type expenditures, but are investments in human-resource productivity; and that benefits from these investments do not merely accrue just to the persons in whom they are made, but extend to other persons as well. Now it is appropriate to focus attention on the responsibility of government in this area.

To begin with, there would be a significant role for government in the human resource field, even if there were no external benefits—even if all benefits accrued to the individual. One reason is that, with particular respect to education, important decisions are made by young people, who may be poor judges of their long-term interests. Dropping out of high school may seem wise to a youth impatient to increase his earnings, but the wisdom of the decision becomes less obvious with the passage of time.

Of course, additional schooling is of value only to those who have the requisite ability and attitude toward learning. There may be little that society can do about a student's ability, but it may be able to shape his attitude toward schooling. This is the goal of many contemporary programs to prevent high school dropouts, in which well-trained guidance counselors can play an especially vital role. And *government has a responsibility to see that, through counselors and otherwise, people are fully informed about the long-run benefits from education, health, and other forms of investments in people.*

A second reason for public concern about the adequacy of private investment in human resources involves the ability of individuals to finance these investments. In education, a proper student attitude and the necessary intellectual ability are not sufficient; financial ability is also required. The costs of obtaining adequate education rations its use among low-income families. With respect to schooling, this would be true even if education, from elementary school through university, were "free." As noted above, much of the real cost of schooling is not the out-of-pocket expense, but the income lost by the student. In a poor family, the immediate pressure upon the youngster to augment family income—foregoing investments in his own human capital, if need be—may be enormous.

To some extent, the financial hurdles to private investments in human capital by low-income persons can be overcome by borrowing. But one should not forget the real obstacles to obtaining a loan for educational purposes through the private market. The capital market conventionally provides loans for the purchases of tangible assets which, if necessary, can be taken over by the lender. Loans for education and for other forms of investment in human capital have a special characteristic. The fruits they produce are intangible—they are embodied in people. Therefore, the asset cannot be attached by an unsatisfied lender. This fact limits the availability of private loans for financing education or other human capital investments. *Government can help to overcome limitations in the private capital market through programs of direct aid, loans, and guarantees of private loans to facilitate investment in people.*

But government responsibility surpasses the need to improve capital markets and provide counseling. It must help the nation to recognize that the benefits to *society as a whole* which result from investment in human resources exceed the direct benefits to the *individual* in whom the investment is made. It must help the nation to recognize that a society bent on economic growth—on raising living standards and erasing poverty—is a society committed to change; and change requires a creative, adaptable, and efficient labor force capable of creating innovations and adjusting to new, often unforeseen, skill requirements. A rigid labor supply is a formidable obstacle to change.

Education can contribute mightily to economic growth by meeting the needs for flexibility and adaptability. But this implies a greater emphasis on the teaching of *basic* techniques and concepts and on the postponement of a student's specialization until late in the educational process. It also implies that the distinction between "vocational" and "general" education may in reality be a great deal more fuzzy than conventional usage suggests. In a world of changing technology and skill requirements, the training that appears to be "general" today may be extremely and directly useful in the world of work tomorrow. Similarly, education that appears today to be of direct vocational value may not only be obsolete later, but its narrowness may intensify the difficulties of adjusting to future manpower demands.

In recognition of the broad social and economic interest in investment in human capital, particularly through education and health, *it is appropriate and desirable for government policy to encourage individuals to invest more in themselves than they otherwise would, and perhaps in somewhat different ways.* For example, a teen-ager may prefer not to continue in school, but the rest of society may prefer that he does, since, as we have seen, it will suffer in many ways if his education, training, and health are not satisfactory.

Today, tax laws provide greater incentives for investment in physical assets than for investments in human capital, because the former are more generally depreciable as a business expense than are the latter. *Reconsideration of tax policy so as to redress the imbalance is warranted.* Similarly, the tradition that the cost of a school building or a hospital is a "capital" cost—which can "appropriately" be financed by borrowing—while the cost of salaries for the teachers or medical personnel in that structure is a non-capital expenditure, leads to an unfortunate emphasis on *construction* relative to *instruction* in the school and elaborate equipment relative to additional personnel in hospitals. Education expenditures other than on buildings and equipment also represent investments—less tangible but no less real than the investments in classrooms. *Government should recognize by its words and deeds the breadth* *of the investment concept and should help lower-level governments and private decision-makers to recognize it also.*

QUESTIONS AND STUDY SUGGESTIONS

1. What is the justification for arguing that education is an "investment in human capital"?
2. What are the basic private benefits from education? State and discuss the relationships between (*a*) education and income, and (*b*) education and unemployment.
3. What is the "intergenerational value" of education? How do employers and taxpayers benefit from education?
4. What is the justification for the contention that education should receive "broad financial support"? Discuss the limitations of the private capital market with respect to education. How can these limitations be overcome? How might tax laws be revised in view of the social benefits from education?

Reading 48

Environmental Pollution and Social Costs

Robert U. Ayres and Allen V. Kneese, Resources for the Future

Reading 47 was concerned with the situation wherein a product or service —education, in this case—yields benefits beyond those accruing to immediate consumers. Where social benefits are significant, the market fails to allocate sufficient resources to the production of such goods and services. Reading 48 is a general appraisal of the opposite case of market failure, that is, the situation where the production of consumption of certain goods imposes "externalities" or social costs upon consumers or firms. More specifically, residual wastes pollute the environment and impose costs upon third parties who are external to the market transaction. The basic economic problem involved can be quite succinctly stated. If producers and consumers are not forced to take social costs into account, "not only

From **Federal Programs for the Development of Human Resources:** Papers submitted to the Subcommittee on Economic Progress of the Joint Economic Committee, 90th Cong., 2d Sess., Washington, 1968, pp. 627–635, abridged.

will the environment be called upon to receive an excessive amount of residuals but the demand for natural resources inputs will exceed the optimum."

We find it useful initially to view environmental pollution and its control as a materials balance problem for the entire economy. We start with a highly simplified schematic of how the goods and residuals production process works, as indicated in Figure 48–1.

Final goods in the schematic can be either consumer goods like food and autos, or intermediates in the productive process. The inputs to the system are fuels, foods, and raw materials which are partly converted into final goods and partly become waste residuals. Except for increases in inventory, final goods also ultimately enter the waste stream. For the sake of simplicity and also because it isolates the problems of greatest significance for urban areas, we will ordinarily begin our consideration of the materials flow after the basic fuel, food, and raw materials have been produced by mines, farms, forests, and wildlife areas, but before they enter into processing. It must be noted, however, that this does neglect some significant discharges of wastes into the environment—mine tailings, acid mine drainage, and salt water pumped up with crude oil, for example. However, the streams included are the most relevant ones for urban environments.

In an economy which is closed (no imports or exports) and where there is no net accumu-lation of stocks (plant, equipment, inventories, consumer durables, or residential buildings), the amount of residuals which is inserted into the natural environment must be approximately equal to the weight of basic fuels, food, and raw materials entering the processing and production system, plus oxygen taken from the atmosphere. This result, while obvious upon reflection, leads to the rather surprising and even shocking corollary that residuals disposal —in terms of sheer tonnage—is an even larger operation than basic materials production.

VALUE IN THE MARKET

To deal meaningfully with the policy issues presented by discharge of residuals to the environment, it is important to have a concept of the functioning of the economy. While the American economy is a mixed one with heavy doses of public production and regulation, the best simple model for understanding its basic functioning and for providing a benchmark against which to measure its performance is the "competitive market." This is really an abstract, theoretical model of how choices concerning resources use are made in a decentralized decisionmaking system, where markets are competitive, and the individual decisionmakers

Figure 48–1.   Schematic of the goods-residuals production process.

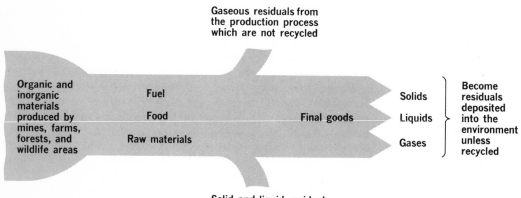

(industries and individuals) act rationally to maximize their private benefit from whatever decisions they take. If we accept two basic assumptions, that is, that the overall distribution of income is justifiable on ethical grounds and that individual preferences should be satisfied to the maximum extent possible given the distribution of income, a normative or "standard-setting" value is attributable to the outcome of the market process. Such a decentralized decisionmaking system will, by definition (subject to the foregoing assumptions), produce maximum welfare: the optimum mix of goods and services which can be procured within the specified income constraints. This process has been analyzed in great detail by economists but Adam Smith, who in the 18th century was perhaps the first to perceive clearly the possibility of an economic system functioning in this way, graphically described the process as the market's "invisible hand." The importance of this perception remains undiminished, even today, for it serves to isolate for us and permit us to understand the basic functioning of a decentralized economy—the organization of production so as to produce what each consumer wants within the limit of his income.

Like all models, the one we have just discussed is an abstraction from reality. But it helps us to identify the ideal functioning of a decentralized system and to isolate and forecast the effects of departures from such an ideal system.

MARKET FAILURES

That things do not actually work out in the way specified by the idealized model will surprise no one who is exposed to the day-by-day operations of the economy. Many reasons for less than perfect operation of the economy are discernible. The particular aspect of "market failure" that concerns us in this paper arises from the fact that what the consumer buys and uses (we carefully avoid saying "consumes"), or what a business firm uses in the way of inputs, is only one aspect of the overall disposition of resources. Large residuals remain at each stage of processing and those that are not recycled become wastes, as do the "final" goods themselves when they become worn, broken, or obsolete. We have already seen that the total weight of these is greater than the weight of fuels and raw materials initially introduced into

the productive process. The environment has a certain limited capability to absorb these wastes without harmful effects, but, once the ambient residuals density rises above a threshold level, they become involuntary and unwanted inputs to other production processes or to final consumers.

At this point the automaticity of the market as an allocator of resources breaks down, in the sense that supply and demand—as expressed through a market mechanism—is not the only vehicle for determining what is received by consumers and what is used as inputs in business firms. There are flows of some goods and services that come to the consumer or business whether he wants them or not and without his paying for them or being able to avoid them by making a payment. The activities of an economic unit thus generate "real"—as contrasted with price or monetary—effects that are external to it. The economist refers to these as external effects or "externalities."

Among the clearest and most important sources of such externalities are the waste residuals resulting from production processes and consumption activities. It is apparent that the downstream water user, be he a recreationist or a manufacturer, can usually not control the quality of water he receives as return flow from upstream users, and the quality of this water is often degraded by residuals discharged into it. The breather of the air is usually not in a position as an individual to have any substantial impact on the quality of the ambient air by exercising his demand in a market. Similarly to the extent that chemical residuals are introduced into the environment after use, affected parties will find them in their food, air, and water, whether they want them or not, and they cannot avoid them by exercising a demand in the market.

The distorting effects of such externalities on resource allocation and use have been analyzed in considerable technical detail by economists. The basic problem which results can be expressed rather simply, however. A society which relies completely on a decentralized decisionmaking system and in which significant externalities (environmental overloadings) occur, as they do in any society which contains significant concentrations of population and industrial activity, will find that certain resources are not used optimally.

The capacity of the natural environment to

assimilate residual waste is extremely valuable. To eliminate completely all residuals—as in a spacecraft—would be an immensely costly process; indeed, as the materials balance view shows, it necessarily implies completely recycling of *all* waste materials, which cannot be seriously contemplated.

But on the other hand, if no price or other use restriction is put upon the assimilative capacity of the environment, it will be used too much—and thereby abused. For example, when the assimilative capacity of a stream is exceeded, significant external costs appear: fish which have value for recreation and commerce will die, industrial plants and municipalities will have to treat their intake water more elaborately, etc. These are real costs which are external to the waste discharger and, since he does not bear them, he does not consider them in his decisionmaking. He will not design his manufacturing processes to take account of them; he will use too much of certain inputs, which have particularly large external costs; he will not recycle except where an internal economic benefit is apparent; he will not control waste in the production process closely enough; he will not treat his effluents, even though doing these things might involve a smaller cost than is subsequently imposed on third parties. Similarly, the consumer will purchase insufficiently durable goods and—like the industrial producer—practice insufficient recycling; for example, he will not purchase returnable or reusable containers to an optimum extent. Under these conditions, not only will the environment be called upon to receive an excessive amount of residuals but the demand for natural resources inputs will exceed the optimum.

CONTROLS AND ENVIRONMENTAL MANAGEMENT

If we wish to realize the very great advantages of decentralized decisionmaking mechanisms—in other words the market—we must find appropriate ways to control these external environmental effects. That means that in some fashion the external costs imposed by residuals discharged to the environment—be they liquids, solids, or gases—must be weighed against, and balanced with, the costs of controlling the amount of these residuals including any external costs which may result from increased levels of residuals in one environmental medium as a result of control exercised in another.

There are two potentially workable ways whereby decisions on how much to produce and how to produce it—and similarly for consumption—can be induced to take better account of all the costs and benefits—private and external or social—flowing from the economic activity in question.

The first is to "internalize" the problem so that a single economic unit will take account of all the costs and benefits associated with the external effects. One way to do this is to enlarge the size of the economic unit. Where external effects are limited in scope, there tends to be some incentive for merger, because—as we implied earlier—overall costs can be reduced, and overall net gains increased, when the external costs are properly taken into account. For example, combining a rolling mill with a blast furnace in an integrated plant facilitates the recycling of "home" scrap and saves on fuel and combustion residuals. But waste products are often so widely propagated in nature and affect so many diverse interests that the merger route is not feasible. Also the decisions of individuals and households bear upon the extent to which external costs occur and these decision units are not subject to merger in the usual business sense.

The second approach is closely related to the first but it involves the formation of a cooperative agency or governmental authority to induce (or require) systematic "internal" consideration of all costs and benefits by changing the framework within which the individual or firm would otherwise be operating. This is sometimes achieved by mutually negotiated restraints, but more frequently by external regulations enforceable at law. For example, certain emission standards may be required for automobile exhausts. There are numerous examples of public agencies placing regulations on economic activities such as production, purchase, and sale of property or goods to limit the external effects involved. Another means which is usually preferred by economists, but little used in practice, is to put an actual price (or tax) on the externality-causing activity. Thus, a tax on sewage effluents which is related to the quality and quantity of the discharge, or a surcharge on the price of fuels with high sulfur content which is meant to take account of the broader costs to society external to the fuel-using enterprise, are examples of this approach. This procedure uses economic incentives to allocate the resource (the waste assimilative capacity of the environment) similar to those generated where market mechanisms can balance costs and returns.

Internalization of external costs by one means or another presents complex problems, but even the best techniques for doing this cannot guarantee that environmental quality will be managed in the most economical way; that is, in such a fashion that the combined cost of controlling or alleviating the ill effects of residuals, plus the external damages imposed by uncontrolled final discharges, is minimized. In Figure 48–2 this optimum level is shown at point X, which is defined mathematically as the point where the slopes (the derivatives) of the cost and benefit functions are equal. But for this to be the true economic optimum, the costs of residual control must be the lowest possible for a given level of control. In this connection, it is important to recognize that in most, if not all, fields of environmental quality management there are potentially effective and efficient measures which cannot be achieved either by setting standards or by imposing taxes upon the activities of individual

decisionmakers that cause externalities (discharge residuals). In other words, there are potentially efficient environmental quality control measures unavailable to the individual firm, or even the individual municipality, not to mention the individual person.

Examples of such measures are reservoir regulation of the low flow of rivers to improve their residuals assimilation capacity, land-use restrictions to achieve a similar objective as regards the atmosphere (or "airshed") over an area, or coordinated solid waste disposal for a megalopolitan region as a whole. Economic efficiency requires that such measures be executed on a geographic scale which would normally encompass a number of political subdivisions, and our society is institutionally ill-equipped to accomplish this. Moreover, existing institutions for environmental management have no machinery or authority to allocate the external cost associated with residuals (or other external effects) to the originating activities, or—indeed—even to identify them unambiguously. This is true even when air, water, and solid wastes control are each considered in isolated categories and very much more so when the integral interdependencies between them are recognized.

Figure 48–2.   The optimum level of residual reduction.

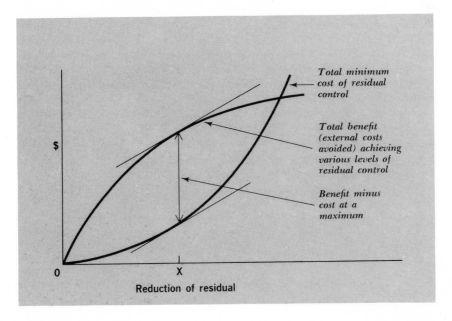

Total minimum cost of residual control

Total benefit (external costs avoided) achieving various levels of residual control

Benefit minus cost at a maximum

$

0   X

Reduction of residual

QUESTIONS AND STUDY SUGGESTIONS

1. Discuss social costs as an external effect. What is the nature of the allocative problem to which social costs give rise?

2. What are the two basic means of correcting resource allocation for social costs?

3. Discuss the problem of environmental control in terms of Figure 48–2. Why is it not desirable to reduce waste residuals to zero?

Reading 49

The Economic Organization of a Prisoner of War Camp

R. A. Radford

The basic institutional feature of capitalism—its reliance upon a system of markets and prices—is frequently taken for granted as it unobtrusively allocates resources, determines incomes, and distributes goods and services. Indeed, it is difficult to achieve the historical perspective requisite for a full appreciation of the important economic functions performed by the price system. In this reading R. A. Radford, an observant inmate of a German prisoner-of-war camp during World War II, provides us with invaluable insights about the evolution and operation of a market system. Here we observe in miniature a price system having the same general characteristics, encountering the same problems and disturbances, and performing essentially the same functions as the infinitely more complex price system of modern capitalistic societies.

After allowance has been made for abnormal circumstances, the social institutions, ideas and habits of groups in the outside world are to be found reflected in a Prisoner of War Camp. It is an unusual but a vital society. Camp organisation and politics are matters of real concern to the inmates, as affecting their present and perhaps their future existences.

One aspect of social organisation is to be found in economic activity, and this, along with other manifestations of a group existence, is to be found in any P.O.W. camp. True, a prisoner is not dependent on his exertions for the provision of the necessaries, or even the luxuries of life, but through his economic activity, the exchange of goods and services, his standard of

From R. A. Radford, "The Economic Organization of a P.O.W. Camp," **Economica**, November, 1945, pp. 189–201, abridged. Reprinted by permission.

material comfort is considerably enhanced. And this is a serious matter to the prisoner: he is not "playing at shops" even though the small scale of the transactions and the simple expression of comfort and wants in terms of cigarettes and jam, razor blades and writing paper, make the urgency of those needs difficult to appreciate, even by an ex-prisoner of some three months' standing.

Nevertheless, it cannot be too strongly emphasised that economic activities do not bulk so large in prison society as they do in the larger world. There can be little production; as has been said the prisoner is independent of his exertions for the provision of the necessities and luxuries of life; the emphasis lies in exchange and the media of exchange.

Everyone receives a roughly equal share of essentials; it is by trade that individual preferences are given expression and comfort increased. All at some time, and most people regularly, make exchanges of one sort or another.

Although a P.O.W. camp provides a living example of a simple economy which might be used as an alternative to the Robinson Crusoe economy beloved by the textbooks, and its simplicity renders the demonstration of certain economic hypotheses both amusing and instructive, it is suggested that the principal significance is sociological. True, there is interest in observing the growth of economic institutions and customs in a brand new society, small and simple enough to prevent detail from obscuring the basic pattern and disequilibrium from obscuring the working of the system. But the essential interest lies in the universality and the spontaneity of this economic life; it came into existence not by conscious imitation but as a response to the immediate needs and circumstances. Any similarity between prison organisation and outside organisation arises from similar stimuli evoking similar responses.

The following is as brief an account of the essential data as may render the narrative intelligible. The camps of which the writer had experience were Oflags and consequently the economy was not complicated by payments for work by the detaining power. They consisted normally of between 1,200 and 2,500 people, housed in a number of separate but intercommunicating bungalows, one company of 200 or so to a building. Each company formed a group within the main organisation and inside the company the room and the messing syndicate, a voluntary and spontaneous group who fed together, formed the constituent units.

Between individuals there was active trading in all consumer goods and in some services. Most trading was for food against cigarettes or other foodstuffs, but cigarettes rose from the status of a normal commodity to that of currency. RMk.s existed but had no circulation save for gambling debts, as few articles could be purchased with them from the canteen.

Our supplies consisted of rations provided by the detaining power and (principally) the contents of Red Cross food parcels—tinned milk, jam, butter, biscuits, bully, chocolate, sugar, etc., and cigarettes. So far the supplies to each person were equal and regular. Private parcels of clothing, toilet requisites and cigarettes were also received, and here equality ceased owing to the different numbers despatched and the vagaries of the post. All these articles were the subject of trade and exchange.

THE DEVELOPMENT AND ORGANISATION OF THE MARKET

Very soon after capture people realised that it was both undesirable and unnecessary, in view of the limited size and the equality of supplies, to give away or to accept gifts of cigarettes or food. "Goodwill" developed into trading as a more equitable means of maximising individual satisfaction.

We reached a transit camp in Italy about a fortnight after capture and received ¼ of a Red Cross food parcel each a week later. At once exchanges, already established, multiplied in volume. Starting with simple direct barter, such as a non-smoker giving a smoker friend his cigarette issue in exchange for a chocolate ration, more complex exchanges soon became an accepted custom. Stories circulated of a padre who started off round the camp with a tin of cheese and five cigarettes and returned to his bed with a complete parcel in addition to his original cheese and cigarettes; the market was not yet perfect. Within a week or two, as the volume of trade grew, rough scales of exchange values came into existence. Sikhs, who had at first exchanged tinned beef for practically any other foodstuff, began to insist on jam and margarine. It was realised that a tin of jam was worth ½ lb. of margarine plus something else; that a cigarette issue was worth several chocolate issues, and a tin of diced carrots was worth practically nothing.

In this camp we did not visit other bungalows very much and prices varied from place to place; hence the germ of truth in the story of the itinerant priest. By the end of a month, when we reached our permanent camp, there was a lively trade in all commodities and their relative values were well known, and expressed not in terms of one another—one didn't quote bully in terms of sugar—but in terms of cigarettes. The cigarette became the standard of value. In the permanent camp people started by wandering through the bungalows calling their offers—"cheese for seven" (cigarettes)— and the hours after parcel issue were Bedlam. The inconveniences of this system soon led to its replacement by an Exchange and Mart notice board in every bungalow, where under the headings "name," "room number," "wanted" and "offered" sales and wants were advertised. When a deal went through, it was crossed off the board. The public and semipermanent records of transactions led to cigarette prices being well known and thus tending to equality throughout the camp, although there were always opportunities for an astute trader to make a profit from arbitrage. With this development everyone, including nonsmokers, was willing to sell for cigarettes, using them to buy at another time and place. Cigarettes became the normal currency, though, of course, barter was never extinguished.

The unity of the market and the prevalence of a single price varied directly with the general level of organisation and comfort in the camp. A transit camp was always chaotic and uncomfortable: people were overcrowded, no one knew where anyone else was living, and few took the trouble to find out. Organisation was too slender to include an Exchange and Mart board, and private advertisements were the most that appeared. Consequently a transit camp was not one market but many. The price of a tin of salmon is known to have varied by two cigarettes in 20 between one end of a hut and the other. Despite a high level of organisation in Italy, the market was morcellated in this manner at the first transit camp we reached after our removal to Germany in the autumn of 1943. In this camp—Stalag VIIA at Moos-

burg in Bavaria—there were up to 50,000 prisoners of all nationalities. French, Russians, Italians and Jugo-Slavs were free to move about within the camp: British and Americans were confined to their compounds, though a few cigarettes given to a sentry would always procure permission for one or two men to visit other compounds. The people who first visited the highly organised French trading centre, with its stalls and known prices, found coffee extract—relatively cheap among the tea-drinking English—commanding a fancy price in biscuits or cigarettes, and some enterprising people made small fortunes that way. (Incidentally we found out later that much of the coffee went "over the wire" and sold for phenomenal prices at black market cafés in Munich: some of the French prisoners were said to have made substantial sums in RMk.s. This was one of the few occasions on which our normally closed economy came into contact with other economic worlds.)

The permanent camps in Germany saw the highest level of commercial organisation. In addition to the Exchange and Mart notice boards, a shop was organised as a public utility, controlled by representatives of the Senior British Officer, on a no profit basis. People left their surplus clothing, toilet requisites and food there until they were sold at a fixed price in cigarettes. Only sales in cigarettes were accepted—there was no barter—and there was no higgling. For food at least there were standard prices: clothing is less homogeneous and the price was decided around a norm by the seller and the shop manager in agreement; shirts would average say 80, ranging from 60 to 120 according to quality and age. Of food, the shop carried small stocks for convenience; the capital was provided by a loan from the bulk store of Red Cross cigarettes and repaid by a small commission taken on the first transactions. Thus the cigarette attained its fullest currency status, and the market was almost completely unified.

It is thus to be seen that a market came into existence without labour of production. The B.R.C.S. may be considered as "Nature" of the textbook, and the articles of trade—food, clothing and cigarettes—as free gifts—land or manna. Despite this, and despite a roughly equal distribution of resources, a market came into spontaneous operation, and prices were fixed by the operation of supply and demand. It is difficult to reconcile this fact with the labour theory of value.

Actually there was an embryo labour market. Even when cigarettes were not scarce, there was usually some unlucky person willing to perform services for them. Laundrymen advertised at two cigarettes a garment. Battle-dress was scrubbed and pressed and a pair of trousers lent for the interim period for twelve. A good pastel portrait cost thirty or a tin of "Kam." Odd tailoring and other jobs similarly had their prices.

There were also entrepreneurial services. There was a coffee stall owner who sold tea, coffee or cocoa at two cigarettes a cup, buying his raw materials at market prices and hiring labour to gather fuel and to stoke; he actually enjoyed the services of a chartered accountant at one stage. After a period of great prosperity he overreached himself and failed disastrously for several hundred cigarettes. Such large-scale private enterprise was rare but several middlemen or professional traders existed. The padre in Italy, or the men at Moosburg who opened trading relations with the French, are examples: the more subdivided the market, the less perfect the advertisement of prices, and the less stable the prices, the greater was the scope for these operators. One man capitalised his knowledge of Urdu by buying meat from the Sikhs and selling butter and jam in return: as his operations became better known more and more people entered this trade, prices in the Indian Wing approximated more nearly to those elsewhere, though to the end a "contact" among the Indians was valuable, as linguistic difficulties prevented the trade from being quite free. Some were specialists in the Indian trade, the food, clothing, or even the watch trade. Middlemen traded on their own account or on commission. Price rings and agreements were suspected and the traders certainly co-operated. Nor did they welcome newcomers. Unfortunately the writer knows little of the workings of these people: public opinion was hostile and the professionals were usually of a retiring disposition.

One trader in food and cigarettes, operating in a period of dearth, enjoyed a high reputation. His capital, carefully saved, was originally about 50 cigarettes, with which he bought rations on issue days and held them until the price rose just before the next issue. He also picked up a little by arbitrage; several times a day he visited every Exchange or Mart notice board and took advantage of every discrepancy between prices of goods offered and wanted. His knowledge of prices, markets and names of those who had received cigarette parcels was phenomenal. By these means he kept himself smoking steadily—his profits—while his capital remained intact.

Sugar was issued on Saturday. About Tuesday two of us used to visit Sam and make a deal; as old customers he would advance as much of the price as he could spare then, and entered the transaction in a book. On Saturday morning he left cocoa tins on our beds for the ration, and picked them up on Saturday afternoon. We were hoping for a calendar at Christmas, but Sam failed too. He was left holding a big black treacle issue when the price fell, and in this weakened state was unable to withstand an unexpected arrival of parcels and the consequent price fluctuations. He paid in full, but from his capital. The next Tuesday, when I paid my usual visit he was out of business.

Credit entered into many, perhaps into most, transactions, in one form or another. Sam paid in advance as a rule for his purchases of future deliveries of sugar, but many buyers asked for credit, whether the commodity was sold spot or future. Naturally prices varied according to the terms of sale. A treacle ration might be advertised for four cigarettes now or five next week. And in the future market "bread now" was a vastly different thing from "bread Thursday." Bread was issued on Thursday and Monday, four and three days' rations respectively, and by Wednesday and Sunday night it had risen at least one cigarette per ration, from seven to eight, by supper time. One man always saved a ration to sell then at the peak price: his offer of "bread now" stood out on the board among a number of "bread Monday's" fetching one or two less, or not selling at all—and he always smoked on Sunday night.

THE CIGARETTE CURRENCY

Although cigarettes as currency exhibited certain peculiarities, they performed all the functions of a metallic currency as a unit of account, as a measure of value and as a store of value, and shared most of its characteristics.

They were homogeneous, reasonably durable, and of convenient size for the smallest or, in packets, for the largest transactions. Incidentally, they could be clipped or sweated by rolling them between the fingers so that tobacco fell out.

Cigarettes were also subject to the working of Gresham's Law. Certain brands were more popular than others as smokes, but for currency purposes a cigarette was a cigarette. Consequently buyers used the poorer qualities and the Shop rarely saw the more popular brands: cigarettes such as Churchman's No. 1 were rarely used for trading. At one time cigarettes hand-rolled from pipe tobacco began to circulate. Pipe tobacco was issued in lieu of cigarettes by the Red Cross at a rate of 25 cigarettes to the ounce and this rate was standard in exchanges, but an ounce would produce 30 home-made cigarettes. Naturally, people with machine-made cigarettes broke them down and re-rolled the tobacco, and the real cigarette virtually disappeared from the market. Hand-rolled cigarettes were not homogeneous and price could no longer be quoted in them with safety: each cigarette was examined before it was accepted and thin ones were rejected, or extra demanded as a makeweight. For a time we suffered all the inconveniences of a debased currency.

Machine-made cigarettes were always universally acceptable, both for what they would buy and for themselves. It was this intrinsic value which gave rise to their principal disadvantage as currency, a disadvantage which exists, but to a far smaller extent, in the case of metallic currency;—that is, a strong demand for non-monetary purposes. Consequently our economy was repeatedly subject to deflation and to periods of monetary stringency. While the Red Cross issue of 50 or 25 cigarettes per man per week came in regularly, and while there were fair stocks held, the cigarette currency suited its purpose admirably. But when the issue was interrupted, stocks soon ran out, prices fell, trading declined in volume and became increasingly a matter of barter. This deflationary tendency was periodically offset by the sudden injection of new currency. Private cigarette parcels arrived in a trickle throughout the year, but the big numbers came in quarterly when the Red Cross received its allocation of transport. Several hundred thousand cigarettes might arrive in the space of a fortnight.

Prices soared, and then began to fall, slowly at first but with increasing rapidity as stocks ran out, until the next big delivery. Most of our economic troubles could be attributed to this fundamental instability.

PRICE MOVEMENTS

The general price level was affected by other factors. An influx of new prisoners, proverbially hungry, raised it. Heavy air raids in the vicinity of the camp probably increased the non-monetary demand for cigarettes and accentuated deflation. Good and bad war news certainly had its effect, and the general waves of optimism and pessimism which swept the camp were reflected in prices. Before breakfast one morning in March of this year, a rumour of the arrival of parcels and cigarettes was circulated. Within ten minutes I sold a treacle ration, for four cigarettes (hitherto offered in vain for three), and many similar deals went through. By 10 o'clock the rumour was denied, and treacle that day found no more buyers even at two cigarettes.

More interesting than changes in the general price level were changes in the price structure. Changes in the supply of a commodity, in the German ration scale or in the make-up of Red Cross parcels, would raise the price of one commodity relative to others. Tins of oatmeal, once a rare and much sought after luxury in the parcels, became a commonplace in 1943, and the price fell. In hot weather the demand for cocoa fell, and that for soap rose. A new recipe would be reflected in the price level: the discovery that raisins and sugar could be turned into an alcoholic liquor of remarkable potency reacted permanently on the dried fruit market. The invention of electric immersion heaters run off the power points made tea, a drug on the market in Italy, a certain seller in Germany.

In August, 1944, the supplies of parcels and cigarettes were both halved. Since both sides of the equation were changed in the same degree, changes in prices were not anticipated. But this was not the case: the non-monetary demand for cigarettes was less elastic than the demand for food, and food prices fell a little. More important however were the changes in the price structure. German margarine and jam, hitherto valueless owing to adequate supplies of Canadian butter and marmalade, acquired a new value. Chocolate, popular and a certain seller, and sugar, fell. Bread rose: several standing contracts of bread for cigarettes were broken, especially when the bread ration was reduced a few weeks later.

In February, 1945, the German soldier who drove the ration wagon was found to be willing to exchange loaves of bread at the rate of one loaf for a bar of chocolate. Those in the know began selling bread and buying chocolate, by then almost unsaleable in a period of serious deflation. Bread, at about 40, fell slightly; chocolate rose from 15; the supply of bread was not enough for the two commodities to reach parity, but the tendency was unmistakable.

The substitution of German margarine for Canadian butter when parcels were halved naturally affected their relative values, margarine appreciating at the expense of butter. Similarly, two brands of dried milk, hitherto differing in quality and therefore in price by five cigarettes a tin, came together in price as the wider substitution of the cheaper raised its relative value.

Enough has been cited to show that any change in conditions affected both the general price level and the price structure. It was this latter phenomenon which wrecked our planned economy.

PAPER CURRENCY—BULLY MARKS

Around D-Day, food and cigarettes were plentiful, business was brisk and the camp in an optimistic mood. Consequently the Entertainments Committee felt the moment opportune to launch a restaurant, where food and hot drinks were sold while a band and variety turns performed. Earlier experiments, both public and private, had pointed the way, and the scheme was a great success. Food was bought at market prices to provide the meals and the small profits were devoted to a reserve fund and used to bribe Germans to provide grease-paints and other necessities for the camp theatre. Originally meals were sold for cigarettes but this meant that the whole scheme was vulnerable to the periodic deflationary waves, and furthermore heavy smokers were unlikely to attend much. The whole success of the scheme developed on an adequate amount of food being offered for sale in the normal manner.

To increase and facilitate trade, and to stimulate supplies and customers therefore, and secondarily to avoid the worst effects of deflation when it should come, a paper currency was organised by the Restaurant and the Shop. The Shop bought food on behalf of the Restaurant with paper notes and the paper was accepted equally with the cigarettes in the Restaurant or Shop, and passed back to the Shop to purchase more food. The Shop acted as a bank of issue. The paper money was backed 100 percent by food; hence its name, the Bully Mark. The BMk. was backed 100 percent by food: there could be no overissues, as is permissible with a normal bank of issue, since the eventual dispersal of the camp and consequent redemption of all BMk.s was anticipated in the near future.

Originally one BMk. was worth one cigarette and for a short time both circulated freely inside and outside the Restaurant. Prices were quoted in BMk.s and cigarettes with equal freedom—and for a short time the BMk. showed signs of replacing the cigarette as currency. The BMk. was tied to food, but not to cigarettes: as it was issued against food, say 45 for a tin of milk and so on, any reduction in the BMk. prices of food would have meant that there were unbacked BMk.s in circulation. But the price of both food and BMk.s could and did fluctuate with the supply of cigarettes.

While the Restaurant flourished, the scheme was a success: the Restaurant bought heavily, all foods were saleable and prices were stable.

In August parcels and cigarettes were halved and the Camp was bombed. The Restaurant closed for a short while and sales of food became difficult. Even when the Restaurant reopened, the food and cigarette shortage became increasingly acute and people were unwilling to convert such valuable goods into paper and to hold them for luxuries like snacks and tea. Less of the right kinds of food for the Restaurant were sold, and the Shop became glutted with dried fruit, chocolate, sugar, etc., which the Restaurant could not buy. The price level and the price structure changed. The BMk. fell to four-fifths of a cigarette and eventually farther still, and it became unacceptable save in the Restaurant. There was a flight from the BMk., no longer convertible into cigarettes or popular foods. The cigarette re-established itself.

But the BMk. was sound! The Restaurant

closed in the New Year with a progressive food shortage and the long evenings without lights due to intensified Allied air raids, and BMk.s could only be spent in the Coffee Bar—relict of the Restaurant—or on the few unpopular foods in the Shop, the owners of which were prepared to accept them. In the end all holders of BMk.s were paid in full, in cups of coffee or in prunes. People who had bought BMk.s for cigarettes or valuable jam or biscuits in their heyday were aggrieved that they should have stood the loss involved by their restricted choice, but they suffered no actual loss of market value.

PUBLIC OPINION

Public opinion on the subject of trading was vocal if confused and changeable, and generalisations as to its direction are difficult and dangerous. A tiny minority held that all trading was undesirable as it engendered an unsavoury atmosphere; occasional frauds and sharp practices were cited as proof. Certain forms of trading were more generally condemned; trade with the Germans was criticised by many. Red Cross toilet articles, which were in short supply and only issued in cases of actual need, were excluded from trade by law and opinion working in unshakable harmony. At one time, when there had been several cases of malnutrition reported among the more devoted smokers, no trade in German rations was permitted, as the victims became an additional burden on the depleted food reserves of the Hospital. But while certain activities were condemned as antisocial, trade itself was practised, and its utility appreciated, by almost everyone in the camp.

More interesting was opinion on middlemen and prices. Taken as a whole, opinion was hostile to the middleman. His function, and his hard work in bringing buyer and seller together, were ignored; profits were not regarded as a reward for labour, but as the result of sharp practices. Despite the fact that his very existence was proof to the contrary, the middleman was held to be redundant in view of the existence of an official Shop and the Exchange and Mart. Appreciation only came his way when he was willing to advance the price of a sugar ration, or to buy goods spot and carry them against a future sale. In these cases the element of risk was obvious to all, and the con-venience of the service was felt to merit some reward. Particularly unpopular was the middleman with an element of monopoly, the man who contacted the ration wagon driver, or the man who utilised his knowledge of Urdu. And middlemen as a group were blamed for reducing prices. Opinion notwithstanding, most people dealt with a middleman, whether consciously or unconsciously, at some time or another.

There was a strong feeling that everything had its "just price" in cigarettes. While the assessment of the just price, which incidentally varied between camps, was impossible of explanation, this price was nevertheless pretty closely known. It can best be defined as the price usually fetched by an article in good times when cigarettes were plentiful. The "just price" changed slowly; it was unaffected by short-term variations in supply, and while opinion might be resigned to departures from the "just price," a strong feeling of resentment persisted. A more satisfactory definition of the "just price" is impossible. Everyone knew what it was, though no one could explain why it should be so.

As soon as prices began to fall with a cigarette shortage, a clamour arose, particularly against those who held reserves and who bought at reduced prices. Sellers at cut prices were criticised and their activities referred to as the black market. In every period of dearth the explosive question of "should non-smokers receive a cigarette ration?" was discussed to profitless length. Unfortunately, it was the non-smoker, or the light smoker with his reserves, along with the hated middleman, who weathered the storm most easily.

CONCLUSION

The economic organisation described was both elaborate and smooth-working in the summer of 1944. Then came the August cuts and deflation. Prices fell, rallied with deliveries of cigarette parcels in September and December, and fell again. In January, 1945, supplies of Red Cross cigarettes ran out: and prices slumped still further; in February the supplies of food parcels were exhausted and the depression became a blizzard. Food, itself scarce, was almost given away in order to meet the non-monetary demand for cigarettes. Laundries ceased to operate, or worked for £s or

RMk.s: food and cigarettes sold for fancy prices in £s, hitherto unheard of. The Restaurant was a memory and the BMk. a joke. The Shop was empty and the Exchange and Mart notices were full of unaccepted offers for cigarettes. Barter increased in volume, becoming a larger proportion of a smaller volume of trade. This, the first serious and prolonged food shortage in the writer's experience, caused the price structure to change again, partly because German rations were not easily divisible. A margarine ration gradually sank in value until it exchanged directly for a treacle ration. Sugar slumped sadly. Only bread retained its value. Several thousand cigarettes, the capital of the Shop, were distributed without any noticeable effect. A few fractional parcel and cigarette issues, such as one-sixth of a parcel and twelve cigarettes each, led to momentary price recoveries and feverish trade, especially when they coincided with good news from the Western Front, but the general position remained unaltered.

By April, 1945, chaos had replaced order in the economic sphere: sales were difficult, prices lacked stability. Economics has been defined as the science of distributing limited means among unlimited and competing ends. On 12th April, with the arrival of elements of the 30th U.S. Infantry Division, the ushering in of an age of plenty demonstrated the hypothesis that with infinite means economic organisation and activity would be redundant, as every want could be satisfied without effort.

QUESTIONS AND STUDY SUGGESTIONS

1. What forces seemed to have had the greatest bearing upon the complexity and sophistication of the economic organization of the POW camp?
2. Explain the evolution and tribulations of the cigarette currency and the use of Bully Marks. What factors were responsible for changes in prices?
3. What was the role of entrepreneurial services in the POW camp? What was the impact of "technological progress" upon prices?

Reading 50

Resource Allocation and the Principle of Equal Advantage

Kenneth E. Boulding, Professor of Economics, University of Colorado

Reading 50 by Kenneth E. Boulding deals with essentially the same subject matter—the price system—as does Reading 49. But now our discussion takes the form, not of a case study, but rather an abstract, generalized treatment couched in terms of the more sophisticated jargon and analytical tools of the economist. Boulding explains how the competitive price system tends to negotiate reallocations of resources which are appropriate to changes in consumer tastes (or changes in technology or resource supplies). Here we envision resource suppliers, motivated by the principle of equal advantage, rendering decisions which, through the functioning of the price system, bring about socially desirable changes in the size of affected industries and in the allocation of the means of production.

In any advanced economic system there exists a high degree of *specialization* of resources. That is to say, our resources—labor, land, equipment—are divided among a large number of different industries. Each industry puts out a product or a group of related products which it exchanges for the product of other industries. It is no exaggeration to say that the principal problem of economic life is to determine *how big* each of these industries, these specialized employments of resources, shall be. How much of each commodity should be produced? How many men should be employed in each occupation? How much land should be devoted to corn? to cabbages? to skyscrapers? These are the fundamental questions of economic life, and all economic systems are attempts to answer them.

In the completely "planned" economy—the extreme case of which would be a slave society governed by a small class of rulers—these questions are decided by the will of the ruler. The dictator of a totalitarian communist state decrees that a steel factory shall be built, and it is built, no matter what the feelings and desires of those who build it or of those who will use its products. The general of an army disposes of the resources at his disposal without inquiring whether Private A likes cooking or Private B likes killing.

In a "free" economy this is not so. A free economy is an economic system in which any individual is allowed to put the resources which he owns to any use he thinks fit, provided he does not thereby violate the property rights of others. In such an economy there is no "economic dictator" who decrees that so many men shall become barbers and so many lawyers, or that so many acres of land shall be used for corn and so many for houses. Nevertheless, the interacting wills of all the individuals in such a society succeed in effecting an apportionment of resources among the various employments.

PRINCIPLE OF EQUAL ADVANTAGE

This apportionment is governed by a principle which we may call the *principle of equal advantage*. It may be stated thus: If the owners of any resources think that they can be put to better advantage in some other use than the one in which they are employed, these resources will be transferred from the less advantageous to the more advantageous use. The process of transfer will generally have the effect of making the occupation *into* which resources have been transferred *less* advantageous than before; it will make the occupation *out of* which resources have been transferred *more* advantageous than before. As long, therefore, as there are people who believe that the resources they own, whether these be their own bodies or some other object, will yield them a greater advantage in an occupation different from that in which they are at present employed, then resources will be transferred from one occupation to another. In this statement, it should be noticed, we use the word "advantage" deliberately, for it includes both monetary and nonmonetary advantages. We do not assume that people are moved only by differences in monetary reward. Indeed, as we shall see, permanent differences in monetary rewards between different occupations may be explained by assuming that people are in fact moved by nonmonetary considerations.

EQUILIBRIUM: ADVANTAGES EQUAL IN ALL EMPLOYMENTS

A position of "equilibrium" in the distribution of economic resources means a situation in which there is no tendency for resources to move from one occupation to another, on balance. In equilibrium, that is to say, the proportion of resources devoted to the various industries does not change. A state of perfect competition is assumed. This means, among other things, that there are no restrictions on the migration of resources from one occupation to another. Under these circumstances the economic system will be in equilibrium only when the advantage derived from the employment of resources in all occupations is the same. For if this were not so, resources would move from the occupations of low advantage to those of high advantage. This movement would raise the advantage in the former occupations and lower the advantage in the latter, until all occupations offered equal advantages. At this point there would be no incentive to a further transfer of resources, and the system would be in equilibrium.

Example: The Distribution of Doctors

We may illustrate this principle first by a simple example. How does it come about that the number of doctors in any one town is roughly proportionate to its size and wealth? How does it happen that a village of 2,000 people may have only four doctors and a town of 20,000 people may have forty? There is no authority of government which sets out to achieve this desirable result; there is no official who says to the medical students, as they come fresh from the schools, "Lo, you must go to Oskaloosa and you to Kankakee." It is the operation of the great and universal principle of equal advantage which brings this about. It is evident that as a general rule the more doctors there are in any one town, the less advantageous will be the lot of each. If there are four doctors practicing in a village, the incursion of a fifth will unquestionably bring down the average remuneration of doctors in that village, unless the newcomer strikes a wholly new demand for his services. The incursion of a sixth will bring that remuneration down still further; a seventh might bring all the doctors to scraping, and an eighth to penury. On the other hand, if one doctor leaves a community, the remuneration of the others is likely to increase. There may be exceptions to this rule, but we shall not consider them now, for in the mass they will clearly be unimportant.

Consider, then, the situation of a young doctor just starting out in practice. Where is he most likely to go? To a place which is already overstaffed with doctors? Surely not. He will seek a place where doctors are relatively few, and where therefore their remuneration may be expected to be relatively high. Similarly, if a doctor residing in a place where there is a surplus of doctors hears of an opportunity in a place which has too few, he will be likely to take the opportunity, because thereby he may hope to better himself. Even in so altruistic a profession as that of medicine, therefore, it is the "advantage motive" which by its slow but persistent pressure constantly pushes doctors out of places where there are too *many* to make what they consider an average living, into places where they are so *few* that they make what is considered a better than average living. This force does not act rapidly. Indeed, for long periods we may find places which have too many doctors and places which have too few. But like the pressure of water on the rocks in a stream, even though it does not always cause change immediately, it infallibly determines the direction of change when it comes. Just as we never find streams washing stones uphill, so we never find the force of advantage pushing people from occupations which they think are better into those which they think are worse.

ALLOCATION OF RESOURCES IN GENERAL

The same principle applies, in a rather more complex manner, to the distribution of resources in general. Is an industry unprosperous? That is a sign that it is "too big" relative to what it ought to be. Is an industry abnormally prosperous? That is a sign that it is "too small" relative to what it ought to be. What will happen? Resources will leave the unprosperous industry. Firms in that industry will close down, workers will be thrown out of employment or forced to accept low wages; profits and wages will be low and unemployment may be high. Consequently, the industry will decline. Those workers who can get out will do so. The workers who die off will not be replaced, for the new, young workers will not be attracted into the declining industry. Capitalists who can get their capital out of the industry will do so, and new capital will not flow in. Consequently, the output of the industry will be smaller. If the underlying conditions of demand and supply do not change, the price of the product of the industry will rise. If, then, the industry decreases in size sufficiently, its prosperity will rise until it is "normal" once more. Then the decline will cease. The industry will be in equilibrium.

Now imagine an industry which is unusually prosperous. Profits are high, wages are high, it is easy to get employment. What will be the result? Workers will be attracted into it, and new firms will enter it. Its output will increase, and therefore the price of that output will fall. The industry will become rather less prosperous. It will continue to expand until it becomes just "normally" prosperous, when it will cease to attract resources into it and will stop growing. It will then be in equilibrium.

ADJUSTMENTS OF THE WHOLE SYSTEM

We must therefore picture the industries of our economic system: some declining under the shadow of adversity, some expanding under the sun of prosperity, some perhaps remaining stationary. But the expanding ones will not expand forever, for the very prosperity which induced their expansion will decline as the industry grows. Likewise those which contract will not contract forever, for by their very contraction they tend to rectify the situation which made them unprosperous.

RESULTS OF A CHANGE IN TASTES

We can illustrate this process best, perhaps, by considering the effects of a change in the things which ultimately determine how resources are divided. Consider a system which is in equilibrium—that is to say, all industries are just normally prosperous, no industry is more prosperous than another, and therefore there is no tendency for resources to move from one industry to another. Now suppose that there is a change in the tastes of consumers— for instance, that a change in fashion causes a marked shift in consumers' demands from silk goods to cotton goods. The results of this shift will depend on the period of time taken into account. We may consider three broad stages. First, there is the immediate, or *"impact" effect*. Second, there are the changes which will take place during the period of adjustment, or the *adjustment effects*. Third, there is the effect on the final position of equilibrium; this is the *final effect*.

In considering these effects we shall assume that the other factors affecting economic life remain unchanged. In fact this will never be the case. Nevertheless, this assumption is necessary in order to separate the effects of the particular change in tastes which we are considering from the effects of all other independent changes.

The Impact Effect

In considering the impact effect we shall assume that over a very short period of time the supply of both cotton and silk is perfectly inelastic [that is, the amount supplied is completely unresponsive to a price change]. Let us also assume that there is no holding of supplies for future sale, so that all that is produced in a given "week" must be sold in that week. These assumptions are rather unrealistic, but they can be relaxed at a later stage. We are considering the effects of a known shift in demand from silk to cotton, which takes place in a certain "week," and which persists thereafter indefinitely. This situation is represented in Figure 50–1.

In Figure 50–1a, dd' is the demand curve for cotton in the week before the change. That is, it shows the quantity of cotton which will be bought in that week at each hypothetical price. The total quantity of cotton coming on the market to be sold in that week is represented by os. It will have to be sold at a price sp. The perfectly inelastic supply curve for that week is ss'. Now suppose that in the next week the demand for cotton has risen to ee'. The quantity coming into the market is assumed to be unchanged. The price at which that quantity can be sold, however, has now risen to sq.

Similarly, in Figure 50–1b the original demand for silk is DD', the weekly quantity of silk coming into the market is OS, the inelastic supply curve for silk is SS', and the new, decreased demand for silk is EE'. The result of the fall in demand is a fall in the price from SP to SQ.

The impact effect of a shift in demand from silk to cotton is therefore a fall in the price of silk and a rise in the price of cotton. These new prices will persist as long as the demands remain at their new levels, and as long as the quantities coming onto the market in each week do not change.

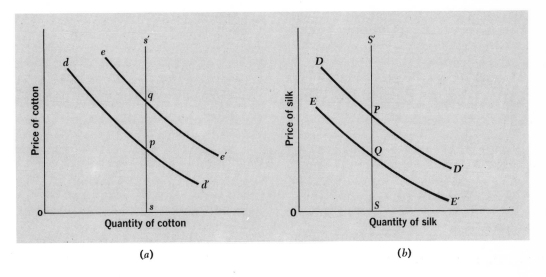

Figure 50–1.   Impact effect of a shift in demand.

Intermediate Effects

However, the quantities coming onto the market *will* change. Under the stimulus of a high price of cotton new producers will enter the cotton industry, new workers will find employment in producing cotton, new land will be put down to cotton, and new cotton factories will be built. The output of cotton will increase. In each "week" after the initial change in demand an increase may be expected in the quantity of cotton placed on the market. This increase may be very slow at first, for it takes time before the effect of a higher price will show itself. Producers cannot enter an industry in the twinkling of an eye; plans have to be made, new fields must be plowed, new men must be trained, new warehouses and factories must be built, new machines must be constructed. All this takes time. Nevertheless, there will be a persistent tendency for the quantity of cotton placed on the market in each week to increase. But this increase will not go on forever, because if the demand remains unchanged at ee', the price in successive weeks must fall. This is illustrated in Figure 50–2a. Again, dd' is the old demand for cotton, and ee' is the new, increased demand. The quantity placed on the market in the week of the change is os_0. The price at which this quantity sells, after the rise in demand, is s_0q_0. Under the stimulus of this high price, however, in the next week a slightly larger quantity, os_1, will

be placed on the market. This will sell at a rather lower price, s_1q_1. In the second week a still larger quantity will be placed on the market, os_2. This will fetch a still lower price, s_2q_2. So, as the weeks go by, the quantity placed on the market will increase under the stimulus of the high price, but the very increase in the quantity supplied will bring about a steady decline in the price.

Final Effects

This movement, however, will not go on forever. As the price falls, the force which makes for an increase in the weekly quantity supplied will also decline. Eventually there will come a week, f weeks from the initial change, when the force of expansion has worked itself out completely. The cotton industry will then be just normally profitable again, and the weekly quantity supplied, os_f, will show no tendency to increase in successive weeks thereafter. The price will be s_fq_f. This is the normal price under the new conditions. It is the price at which, when all necessary adjustments have been made, the industry will neither expand nor contract. The point q_f therefore, must lie on the "normal" supply curve for cotton, ll', for any point on the normal supply curve shows what rate of production will be permanently maintained, without tendency to rise or fall, at the price which it indicates. Similarly, as the point h_0 represents the point of long-run equi-

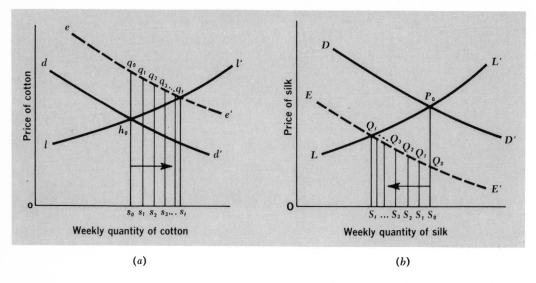

Figure 50–2.   Intermediate and final effects of shifts in demand.

librium before the change in demand, this point also must lie on the normal supply curve. The output os_f and the price $s_f q_f$ represent, therefore, the final effects of the original change in demand, the point q_f being the point of intersection of the new demand curve with the normal supply curve ll'.

In an exactly similar manner we can analyze the effects of the change in demand on the silk industry in Figure 50–2b. In the week of the change there is a quantity OS_0 placed on the market and selling at a low price, $S_0 Q_0$. This low price will cause a decline in the industry. The output of successive weeks will fall from OS_0 to OS_1, OS_2, etc. This decline, however, will not go on forever, for as the output declines the price will rise from $S_0 Q_0$ to $S_1 Q_1$,

$S_2 Q_2$, etc. As the price rises the industry will become relatively less unprosperous, and the force making for its decline will weaken. Finally, the output reaches OS_f, sold at a price $S_f Q_f$, at which the industry is once more normally profitable, and the decline will cease. The normal supply curve, LL' as before, must pass through points P_0 and Q_f.

The final results of a shift in demand from silk to cotton, then, are (1) a rise in the price of cotton; (2) a fall in the price of silk; (3) a rise in the output of the cotton industry, due to an increase in the quantity of resources devoted to cotton production; (4) a decline in the output of the silk industry, due to a decrease in the quantity of resources devoted to silk production.

QUESTIONS AND STUDY SUGGESTIONS

1. Define: (a) the principle of equal advantage and (b) equilibrium. Explain how the principle of equal advantage functions as a mechanism for achieving equilibrium in the allocation of resources.
2. Explain why the adjustments which occur in prosperous and unprosperous industries are self-limiting.
3. Suppose that a technological breakthrough in the manufacturing of cotton goods lowers the costs and therefore substantially increases the supply of cotton goods. Explain the resulting adjustments in terms of the "impact," "intermediate," and "final" effects. What effects might this breakthrough have upon the silk industry? Explain.

PART FOUR

DOMESTIC ECONOMIC PROBLEMS

Reading 51

The New Competition

Fortune Magazine

The editors of *Fortune* contend in this reading that, despite evidence of industrial concentration, there is adequate competition among business firms today. This competition, however, is not synonymous with the pure competition envisioned by economics textbooks. It is argued by *Fortune* that there exists a "new competition," in the development of new products and productive techniques, in quality and service, and through advertising. Furthermore, the self-restraint which businessmen practice in price setting and profit seeking, coupled with "the brooding omnipresence" of the antitrust laws, suggests that monopoly power, where it exists, will not likely be exerted. While not "pure," the new competition is held to be "workable," as is evidenced in the rising productivity and high standard of living in the United States.

Here is a nation that is the home and sanctuary of free competitive enterprise, distinguished from all other nations for such determined adherence to the principles of competition that it has written them into the law of the land with a constitutional force. Virtually every American businessman, manager or owner, big or small, producer or distributor, uses the word "competition" habitually and usually sincerely in describing American capitalism. So do his employees, and so do editors, journalists, and even labor leaders.

But here also is a nation about whose competitiveness many "objective" and professional observers are very dubious. Certainly the country's economists, the men whose job it is to describe, analyze, and interpret the economy, do not talk of competition as businessmen do. Many seem to deny that the word competition has much relevance in the twentieth-century U.S.A.

In his *American Capitalism*, Harvard's J. K. Galbraith makes what is perhaps the most

sweeping statement so far. He says in effect that there is no competition in the classic sense, and hasn't been for years. Real competition has all but disappeared and oligopoly, or a few big sellers—the "Big Three," "Big Four," and so forth—dominate American markets. The economy is workable because big concentrations of industrial power almost automatically beget "countervailing power"—other concentrations of power organized against one another—which tends to prevent abuse. But the time has come, says Dr. Galbraith, to call an economic fact an economic fact, and to cast out "this preoccupation with competition."

The paradoxes of modern American capitalism are not lost on "realistic" Europeans. Probably few things amuse the sophisticated French businessmen and the cynical German industrialist more than the "romantic" American attempts to demonopolize the Continent. The British, too, are amused. On December 15, [1951] the London *Economist* chaffed the "evangelical" American businessmen for

Reprinted from the June, 1952, issue of **Fortune Magazine**, by special permission; © **Time, Inc.**

preaching competition and practicing something else. The Kremlin, of course, harps endlessly on its old well-worn theme that *all* American business is monopolistic.

If the concept of competition has no relevance today, why does the American businessman stubbornly insist that competition is the heart of the enterprise system? Is he hypocritical or merely naive? Is it possible, on the other hand, that he is right? For the good of the national psyche, for the honor of the national reputation—and last but not least for intelligent administration of the antitrust law—it is time to try to resolve this great paradox of the new American capitalism.

THE NEW CAPITALISM

The paradox arises in the fact that American capitalism in the past fifty or sixty years has experienced a profound transformation. It *is* a new capitalism, and the period of change coincides with the rise of the big modern corporation with large aggregations of capital and nationwide markets. This corporation changed the pattern of the critical producing areas of the economy from one of many sellers to one of few sellers and more recently to few buyers. The corporation, moreover, is usually run by paid managers who, in the long-term interest of their company, are forced to be responsible not only to stockholders but also to employees and to consumers.

One result of this change is that the word competition no longer means what it once did. American business today, and particularly Big Business, is practicing a new kind of competition. This competition is not *Fortune's* invention. It has been developing for more than fifty years, and although it is belittled by many economists, a growing number of respected ones have espoused it. And most businessmen have a very good idea indeed of what it is.

They know for one thing that the "new competition" has been a stunning success, especially when measured in terms of delivering a standard of living to the consumer. Could "classic" competition have done any better? As businessmen see it, that's a fair question, the only question. They ask to be judged by results, not by theory. If they tend to grow apoplectic when they are discussed in learned papers as "monopolists" or "oligopolists," it is because they *know* the U.S. is competitive.

As buyers and sellers, businessmen recognize this new competition in terms of such things as prices that respond to market pressures, products that are constantly being improved, and choice for the buyers. They apply such standards pragmatically, not only because they are unfamiliar with formal economic thought but because they know all too well how markets change with industries, products, companies, regions, and from year to year or even month to month. This approach is more or less what the new competition amounts to. It is also more or less what modern economists think of when they talk about "workable" competition. M. A. Adelman of M.I.T., for instance, suggests that workable competition exists when non-collusive rivalry occurs with a sufficient number of alternates open to both buyer and seller.

What causes the great paradox is that most of the economists and experts who have until recently shaped the accepted notions of competition do not describe it that way. Competition to them is a way of life that can be defined fairly rigidly. They conceive of competition in terms of the grand old original or classic model of Adam Smith and his followers.

THE GRAND OLD MODEL

Now this model is based on a great and wise principle, verified by the experience of man through the ages and back into the abyss of time—the principle that the people of the earth, if they know what's good for them, should never trust their welfare to the discretion of a powerful few. Thus competition is a free society's main safeguard against economic injustice. It drives people to produce more rather than less because it enables them to make more money by producing more to sell for less. It tends to make the best use of resources. It is both a regulator and a spur, and its ultimate benefactors are people as consumers.

On these general truths the early British economists reared an ideal superstructure. Its chief characteristic was a market with many sellers turning out practically the same product, and with no seller large enough to have any power to control prices. Competition was assumed to occur by price alone; supply and demand, the impersonal forces of the market, "the hidden hand," automatically regulated the price of everything, including the price of labor. Everybody got no more or less than he deserved, and resources were used with maximum efficiency.

The model was natural and just. It was infinitely superior to socialism in that it recognized the validity of individual incentive. Because it was comprehensive and fundamental, it became the academic model. When pedagogues expounded capitalism to their pupils, they expounded it in terms of the classic model.

But like many great concepts it was a model of perfection rather than of reality, even in its time. It was set up when no one wielded great economic power. Although the concept of the market and the law of supply and demand retained their validity, the notion that competition was effective only when many sellers competed by price alone gradually lost relevance.

Even in the U.S., the only nation that continued to take the model seriously in the twentieth century, the ideal of many sellers went by the board. Large companies grew up swiftly, both by internal growth and by acquisition and merger. The U.S. antitrust laws, of course, were inspired by and partly based on the classic model. But they at first punished only clear conspiracies and accomplished monopolies. And although the Clayton and its subsidiary acts were passed to *prevent* monopoly by catching it in its "incipiency," confusion and irresolution prevented the new law from being effective until the middle 1930s, and even then it did not reform the economy in its image. It could do nothing about the prorationing of the state commissions, which in effect decides the level of the world's oil prices. It could do relatively little about the price "leadership" of big companies—the judgment of the leader, who posts prices in response to his "feeling" about the market, replaces the impersonal forces of the classic market.

The law, finally, could do nothing about the rise of Big Little Business, Big Agriculture, and Big Labor, which proceeded to use political means to gain what Big Business had gained by political and economic means. They not only emulated but outdid Big Business. All three carried their war to the citadel itself, amending the antitrust laws to exempt themselves from many if not most of the effects of price competition.

The classic economists realized that their model was not working well; the last of the great classicists, Alfred Marshall, made due allowances for the fact that competition in practice was bound to be imperfect. The classicists nevertheless went on preaching and teaching orthodox theory because they believed and still believe it provides them with valid principles for measuring a free, competitive society. Let the U.S. strive for perfect competition, they say in effect, and it will be likely to remain tolerably competitive.

THE PRAGMATIC STANDARD

The new competition is an approach, not a model: it cannot be, or certainly hasn't been, rigidly defined. It does not cast aside the classic model. It simply retains the basic principles and discards as much of the model as is necessary to make it consistent with reality. It has no use for collusion, monopoly, or deliberate restraints of trade. But it puts the consumer's interest ahead of theory, and shuns perfect competition for the sake of perfect competition. It makes allowance for the fact that the American economy has delivered to people the benefits that perfect competition was calculated to give.

Therefore, it does not hold that business, to bring maximum benefit to consumers, must necessarily consist of many small sellers competing by price alone. It does not hold that the rivalry of a few large sellers necessarily means economic injustice. And it does not necessarily think of competition as the impersonal, pervasive force of the classic model, but grants it can be, in the words of Michigan's Clare Griffin, "conscious and personal." It corresponds roughly to the businessman's pragmatic description of competition. And in terms of such a concept, the businessman who talks sincerely of our competitive way of life is right. Just look at our economy today.

To begin with, that economy is too complex to encompass with a few generalizations. It is a matter of considerable doubt, for example, whether a relatively few large companies—"the oligopolists"—do "rule" the nation's prices and markets. Professor George Stigler, author of "The Case Against Big Business" in last month's *Fortune,* is an outstanding classicist, and certainly cannot be accused of partiality to Big Business. But even he estimates that only 20 percent of the industries he was able to classify with inadequate data were, in 1939, represented by what he defines as unregulated monopoly or oligopoly. It is his thesis that competition, even judged by the classic model, has been increasing, not decreasing, over the years.

Professor Clair Wilcox of Swarthmore also challenges easy assumptions about oligopoly, but from the standpoint that most figures on concentration are irrelevant. "Meaningful conclusions as to the structure of markets," he insists with considerable plausibility, "are not to be obtained until someone devises a product classification that groups goods according to the readiness with which one can be substituted for another."

Therefore he denounces the habit of judging the whole economy in terms of manufacturing, which after all accounts for less than two-fifths of unregulated, nonbanking private enterprise. Breaking down the consumer's expenditures, by categories, he finds strong evidence that "oligopoly" does not dominate the market.

Clair Wilcox's emphasis on the consumer is much to the point. The consumer has an immense choice of goods and prices; even in the wilderness he has the mail-order catalogue. American retailing is often highly competitive by almost any standard, sometimes almost by that of the classic model.

Not only do retailers compete briskly, they force manufacturers that supply them to price their products competitively. This is an example of what Dr. Galbraith terms "countervailing power"—the idea that big sellers cannot control markets if buyers are strong enough, nor buyers if sellers are strong enough. Sears, Roebuck and the A & P can buy almost anything at the lowest market prices because they buy so much—just as the motor industry is able to buy steel at a competitive price because it is a big buyer, and labor unions can sell their members' services at good prices because they are so well organized.

Countervailing power, however, is plainly not a substitute for competition, as Dr. Galbraith seems to imply it is. Without a concept of competition translated into public policy, this power can be a monopolistic force—as it is in Europe, and indeed as it is for the American labor unions that wield power *as* power because they are exempt from antitrust. But countervailing power, plus the competitive principle, does result in delivering to the consumer the benefits that classic competition was presumed to bring.

NOT CLASSIC BUT EFFECTIVE

Many manufacturers, of course, need no direct pressure to be competitive. Certainly most makers of new consumer products don't. The frozen-orange-juice industry is compelled by circumstances beyond its control to be so competitive it hurts badly. And, of course, garment manufacturers must compete incessantly or go out of business. They do not gang up to fix production or prices. None dominates the market. Their marginal costs often equal—and sometimes exceed—their prices. What keeps them from being an example of classic competition is David Dubinsky and his I.L.G.W.U., which has insulated garmentworkers from the wage market.

And the consumer today certainly enjoys a wonderfully competitive market in appliances, radios, and television sets. Most are made by a fair number of manufacturers, none of whom can control the market, at least not for very long. These durables are today easy to get into (and to fail in, too). Prices are flexible at the retail level, which is where price counts. And they are flexible at the retail level because manufacturers allow for price competition when they set the markup.

Only two years ago, remember, manufacturers were assuring people that they would never again be able to buy a first-line, eight-foot refrigerator for less than $250 or a sixteen-inch television set for less than $350. Today they are both selling at about $150. It is certainly hard to describe as monopolistic and therefore antisocial an economy whose refrigerator industry has sold the astonishing number of 48 million units since 1940; whose radio industry has sold the even more astonishing number of 188 million units since 1922; whose television industry has sold some 18 million units in five years. The competition that made this possible may not have been classically perfect, but who will deny that it has been effective?

This kind of competition, moreover, does not seem destined to wither away but to increase as the nation's productivity increases and the nation's selling apparatus is pressed to get rid of the goods. Buying or countervailing power will surely come into greater play. Retailers will press manufacturers for better buys; manufacturers will press suppliers for cheaper raw materials and components.

Thus the chances are good, unless retailers gang up and legislate sweeping fair-trade laws, that the consumer will continue to buy most of his soft and durable goods, accounting for perhaps 25 percent of his expenditures, as cheaply as he could were they made and sold under the classic model. (At least no one can demonstrate otherwise.) And although many farm prices are exempt from market forces, the competition of the food chains will doubtless continue to give the consumer a good break on the 30 percent or so of his income that he spends on food.

THE "OLIGOPOLISTS"

Now what about Big Business itself—the "oligopolistic" unregulated industries like autos, steel, chemicals, cigarettes, rubber, oil, tin cans, and so forth—wherein a few big sellers are said to rule the markets? To begin with, none is describable as a true monopoly. Their prices usually respond to the market; prices may be "sticky" at times but they do move. These industries offer a choice to the buyer (and seller), and they are constantly improving the quality of their products. Many are subject to countervailing power. And all are subject to the pressure of public opinion.

By classic theory, of course, they are presumed to get a higher price for goods than "perfect" competitors. Prices no longer "rule" them; they "rule" prices. But thanks to the American preoccupation with competition, this phenomenon is often inconsequential even when it is true.

Price leadership occasionally takes the form of "dominant firm" leadership—i.e., one or two firms hold the price umbrella steady, regardless of market conditions. Such instances can be—and are—dealt with by antitrust law. But price leadership often is evidence of competition of the new kind. It can be observed as the "barometric" leadership practiced in the oil and rayon industries. "The leader bears the onus of formally recognizing market conditions," as an oil-industry spokesman describes it. Eugene Holman, president of the Jersey Co., explains it further: "You paste your price on a wall, but you can't be sure it'll stick." Sometimes the leader's prices don't stick. In 1947, after President Truman's plea to keep prices steady, Esso Standard tried to hold the line as smart public relations. But it could not hold the line, at least for very long.

RULE OR RUIN

Another demonstration of big business' ability to "rule" prices was offered by the motor and steel industries, which after the war held prices considerably below the point where market forces alone would have carried them. The classic argument is that prices should be left to find their own level, not only to encourage more production, but to ration what is available "by the purse." But letting prices find their own level, with the restrictions then prevailing, probably would not have resulted in an appreciably greater production. And rationing by the purse, which is theoretically the best way to ration anything, would have created a storm of angry protests from consumers (as the auto dealers' practice of rationing by the purse in fact did).

The motor industry, indeed, could argue without double talk that genuine *competitive* considerations dictated that prices be held. The fundamental purpose of competition after all is not to throw the economy into a tailspin, but to make it function naturally, to dispense economic justice to the consumer. Classic price competition in motorcars after the war might have meant a precipitous rise followed by an equally precipitous drop, and then perhaps by serious economic disruptions and certainly by economic injustice. The restraint of the motor industry thus seems justified from the short-term view of a competitor seeking public approval and the long-term view of an industry cast in a workably competitive mold.

Whether big business is bigger than it needs to be for efficiency and technical progress is a proposition that can be argued endlessly, but there is little doubt that without modern "oligopoly" much of our immense technical progress would not have occurred. Modern research and development not only demand a lot of money which big companies have; the prospect of making unusually good or "monopoly" profits from research and development before competitors get in the field is what drives big companies to do the research and development.

Thus it can be argued that this incentive, which results from product or "quality" competition, brings society more benefits than classic price competition would have. If the chemical industry, for example, had cut prices to the bone as soon as costs declined, it today might be charging more for its products than it is.

Certainly "quality" and service competition indulged in by big companies cannot be summarily dismissed, as it is in strict classic theory, as a wasteful if cheap substitute for price competition. The plain fact, verified by anyone who compares consumer goods of thirty years ago with those of today, is that quality competition has given him more for his money.

THE UTILITY OF LUXURY

And the plain fact, verified every day by anyone who travels anywhere, eats or drinks in any save the meanest places, or buys anything at retail, is that much service competition is not wasteful unless anything remotely "luxurious" is defined as wasteful. Free delivery and other amenities may add nothing to the national stock of goods. But in a nation whose rising standard of living is measured in terms of rising services, they are an important part of life.

Even in capital-goods industries, anything but an example of classic competition, much real competition is evident as service competition. A small specialty steel company, for example, may quote the same prices as the big companies. But it goes to considerable trouble and expense in tailoring shapes and preparing metal content to the special needs of its customers.

And what about big-business advertising and selling? Many economists say they are economically wasteful methods of bolstering monopoly position and thus excluding potential competitors by differentiating between goods that in fact have little difference. "We may assume," writes Arthur Burns in his *Decline of Competition,* "that sales pressure by one or more firms in an industry has no effect on total demand—it merely shifts demand from one seller to another. . . ."

This might be true in a threadbare society hardly managing to keep body and soul together. It might also be true in a model society inhabited by clairvoyant manufacturers who always make the right things and by consumers who promptly buy up everything as soon as it is produced. But in this realm of comparative plenty, most people have more money than they need for subsistence, and are "optional" and therefore arbitrary and erratic spenders. Advertising and selling provide the

only means of persuading them. And advertising and selling may provide an important means of keeping over-all consumption up to production, thus helping to prevent oversaving and the consequent deflation.

POWER AND SELF-RESTRAINT

Modern American capitalism, finally, exhibits a kind of long-term drive to behave as if it were competitive even when it is not driven by countervailing power or the impersonal forces of classic competition. It is a fact that businesses often tend to go on expanding sales whether profits are immediately maximized or not. As M. Adelman says of the A & P, it tries not for the largest possible profit over a planned period but for the best possible position at the end of it. "They recognize," says economist J. M. Clark, "that it is bad business to sacrifice future growth to an exorbitant rate of present profit, even if the curves on paper would permit it."

One reason it does so is that it understands the advantages of adjusting itself to public opinion and the moral climate of the times. Big business is more and more run by professional men whose primary aim is to keep their companies strong, and who therefore cannot exploit the rest of the country. As *Fortune* has put it, the American manager "is part of a group that enjoys power only so long as it does not abuse it—in other words, precisely so long as it does not exercise power the way men and groups of men used to [exercise it]."

"CREATIVE DESTRUCTION"

Another reason companies take the long view is that they sense or understand that in the U.S. economy no one's place is secure. Research and a free-money market have seen to that. Well-heeled companies, no longer beholden to Wall Street, plow back their earnings and constantly look for new things to get into. No company is safe in a field that is too green, uncrowded, or technically backward. General Motors is not only the largest auto maker; it is the largest refrigerator maker; and because the locomotive industry fell behind the times, G.M.'s Electro-Motive Division is now the largest locomotive maker. Crosley is not only a large refrigerator maker but a large television maker. "Anybody today can make anything," one manufacturer puts it, and it's not much of an exaggeration.

Industrial research, furthermore, is providing hundreds of new products that can substitute for older ones—nylon for silk, aluminum for steel and copper, plastics for leather, wood, metals, etc. The laboratory, today, is the great creator of competition.

No one's place is secure, finally, because the consumer has a great many choices and enough money to indulge the luxury of making them. Thus autos compete with fur coats, television sets with furniture, food with gasoline, and so on all down the line. Any manufacturer who wants to achieve volume must sell at a price that overcomes the competitive pressure of the other dissimilar goods.

On such facts the late Joseph Schumpeter based his notion of the "creative destruction" of capitalism. He argued that actual competition is perhaps less important than the threatened competition of the new technology, the new market, the new product. In the long run, he said, this threat "may enforce behavior very similar to the competitive pattern. It disciplines before it attacks. The businessman feels himself to be in a competitive situation even if he is alone in the field." In the short run Schumpeter noted what we already have digressed upon: precisely because corporations can look forward to good profits for a while, they risk big money for research and technological progress.

Such analysis has been attacked as a plea for letting well enough alone and giving up the fight for a competitive economy—and it is probably true that the country will not stay competitive by itself. But this argument would be valid only if the antitrust laws were not very effective.

"THE BROODING OMNIPRESENCE"

Taking everything together, one of the most important reasons why the U.S. economy is competitive is the "contradictory," "impotent," and yet on the whole profoundly effective body of antitrust laws. They were inspired by and based on the classic model, and their contradictions and failures are those of the model itself. They have won comparatively few victories, and some of these, like the basing-point, Alcoa,

and Morton Salt decisions, raise as many difficult questions as they answer.

But the law's greatest achievement is not what it has done, but what its "brooding omnipresence" has induced business to do voluntarily. As the saying goes, it has made the ghost of Senator Sherman an ex officio member of every board of directors in the land. No businessman of consequence makes price, employment, advertising, acquisition, or expansion policies without considering whether or not they will violate the law. "I can't even write to a friend in a competing company," laments one company economist, "and ask him any information pertaining to the business, even if it has appeared in print."

THE ECONOMIC APPROACH

A good case can be made for tightening up some parts of antitrust law and enforcing it more vigorously. But an even better case can be made for the proposition that the law applies the classic model too literally. In general, it lacks an economic approach to what are essentially economic problems. In its preoccupation with "maintaining" competition, as ordained in the various amendments to the Clayton Act, it has tended to produce an opposite result, i.e., to protect competitors from the effects of competition. The recent Alcoa decision has laid it down in effect that business can violate the law merely by growing up to bigness and achieving the *power* to violate the law. And the Federal Trade Commission's stand that identical pricing and "conscious parallelism" are the same as collusion if their consequence is substantially to lessen competition has set a legal basis for prosecuting bona fide competitors.

The concept of the New Competition— "workable" competition—provides not a hard-and-fast definition but an approach to the problem of keeping competition effective. The job of formulating new policies is not easy. But it is not impossible.

Dr. Galbraith, for example, suggests a plausible rule of thumb: let the government encourage countervailing power when that power opposes existing market power, let it even create countervailing power where it is needed; and let it attack market power that is opposed by no countervailing power. As Michael Hoffman of the New York *Times* remarks, that is pretty much what antitrust does now. But Dr. Galbraith's suggestion has merit, and might well be studied by lawyers, prosecutors, judges, and analysts of antitrust policy.

Another and more carefully worked out guide is offered by Clare Griffin in his *An Economic Approach to Antitrust Problems*, recently published by the American Enterprise Association. He details five economic performance tests that he thinks should be used in deciding when to prosecute, how to determine penalties, what to legislate, and how to judge. The tests: (1) Is the company or industry efficient? (2) Is it progressive? (3) Does it show a reasonable and socially useful profit pattern—i.e., are its profits the reward of efficiency and progress rather than the result of artificial advantages? (4) Does it allow as much freedom of entry as is consistent with the business? (5) Is it well suited for defense?

Such tests place a heavy responsibility on the discretionary powers of the authorities, and may assume more intelligence and all-around judgment than the authorities possess. But the tests are apt and carefully thought out, and should not be overlooked. They or similar economic tests will have to be applied if antitrust law is to shape competition to benefit the people whom the creators of the classic model themselves intended it to benefit: the consumers.

QUESTIONS AND STUDY SUGGESTIONS

1. Describe the "grand old model" of capitalism. Contrast this model with the "new competition." What specific defenses are made of the present structure of American industry?

2. In what specific senses are the "oligopolists" said to be competitive? Explain: "Price leadership often is evidence of competition of the new kind."

3. Carefully evaluate in terms of Reading 51: "There can be little doubt that without modern 'oligopoly' much of our immense technological progress would not have occurred."

4. Why do American firms "take the long view"? Of what significance is this? Why are the antitrust laws deemed "effective" in view of the fact that the government has won relatively few legal victories under antitrust?

Reading 52

Rationalizing the "Inevitable": The Case against Business Monopoly

Walter Adams, Professor of Economics, Michigan State University
Horace M. Gray, Professor of Economics, University of Illinois

The validity of *Fortune*'s position (Reading 51) is challenged by Walter Adams and Horace M. Gray who, in Reading 52, contend that the new competition is an "elaborate rationalization of monopoly." Starting from the position that American industry is not now sufficiently competitive, Adams and Gray make four major arguments. (1) The movement toward a more competitive economy does not require a permanently increased role for government in the economy. (2) The existence of business monopolies cannot be justified on technological grounds; many existing firms could be made much smaller without sacrifice of productive efficiency. (3) Existing market forces and countervailing power do not effectively hold business monopoly in check. (4) The "soulful corporation" is more mythical than real; a firm having monopoly power "must either act like a monopolist or cease to be one." In short, the arguments in defense of monopoly, such as those comprising the new competition, are held to be a rationalization of business monopoly which is both "specious and unsound."

Until recently in our history it was generally agreed that government had a positive duty to maintain competition, and that intervention to achieve this end was eminently desirable and socially beneficent. This was a cardinal tenet of the liberal faith and the antitrust statutes were regarded as a basic feature of our constitutional system, commanding in the economic sphere almost the same veneration as the Bill of Rights in the area of civil liberties. This tradition, however, has been seriously eroded by the combined impact of two forces: (1) the widespread fear of totalitarianism generated by the rise of communism, fascism, and various forms of socialism; (2) the sustained propaganda of Big Business designed to capitalize on this fear. The latter seeks, first, to clothe Big Business with all the virtues ordinarily attributed to competitive business and, second, to identify all direct governmental intervention, however

beneficial or limited in scope, as a prelude to totalitarianism.

FEAR OF BIG GOVERNMENT

Thus, the public is led to believe that a positive program for the promotion of competition is not necessary and, still worse, is potentially dangerous. Big Business, according to its self-serving propaganda, is doing everything that competition could do—in fact, much more; if government, pursuing the will-o'-the-wisp of free competition, should break up existing concentration, the efficiency and productivity of the economy will be adversely affected. Furthermore—and this is the clinching argument—the implementation of such a program would necessitate a great, sprawling, corrupt, inefficient, irresponsible, and tyrannical bureaucracy. This Big Government would interfere with business continuously and across the board, stultifying individual initiative and creating such a state of chaos and stagnation that to avoid collapse it would eventually be forced to take over all private business. This last step would usher in the Slave State—some form of socialism in which all human freedom would be extinguished. Confronted with the prospect of this Orwellian horror, those who cherish freedom should resist to the utmost such fatuous interference with private business. Far better it is to bear the minor ills we have than court disaster by attempting to cure them.

This misstatement of the problem tends to induce confusion, an attitude of fear and resignation, and a paralysis of social action. One of the most basic values of free competition is that it *minimizes* governmental intervention. The simplest, most limited, most unobtrusive form of intervention is that required to establish free competition: once established it can be maintained with a minimum of subsequent control. Given such minimal support, competition is a viable, self-perpetuating system within which men can conduct their economic activities free from dictation by government. It is an institutional arrangement consistent with limited government, not Big Government. Those who would stand this proposition on its head and make it appear that the maintenance of competition requires Big Government and eventually leads to totalitarianism misread the lessons of history. Actually, it is excessive concentration and the resulting aggressions of private monopoly that necessitate Big Government to alleviate the tensions, insecurities, and social conflicts inherent in such a system. Unless government is powerful enough to do this, the society is threatened with collapse from internal stresses. The most expeditious means to avert the necessity for Big Government, then, is to maintain effective competition and maximum individual freedom.

It must be recognized that in an economy which has reached an advanced stage of concentration, the restoration of competition, in its initial stages, will require some pretty drastic reversals of public policy and some vigorous action by government. It would be naïve and self-deceptive to believe otherwise. But this initial necessity does not call for big, all-pervasive, potentially dangerous government as a permanent institution. The process of transformation can and should be gradual; the means

highly selective and specific to the circumstances.

TECHNOLOGICAL IMPERATIVES

Fear of Big Government, in this context, is merely one facet of the modern rationalization of monopoly, which conceals a secret admiration for power and a decline of faith in competition. Were faith not wanting we would quickly discover political means to restore competition without risking the dangers of oppressive government. Many factors have contributed to the erosion of public faith in competition, but of all these the most persistent and deadly is the belief that modern technology requires a high degree of economic concentration for its effective utilization. This is the modern American version of economic determinism. Technology, by this reckoning, is a dynamic, material force which operates by natural laws of its own being and exercises imperatives consistent with its organic requirements. It is external to man and beyond human control; its imperatives are exacting, inexorable, and deterministic. In a society that depends on production by the employment of advanced techniques, technology becomes the principal dynamic factor and the principal determinant of institutional organization. All institutions— economic, political, social, and cultural—must conform to the imperatives of technology. There is no escape from this necessity short of complete renunciation and a return to a pre-technological mode of production, which is, by the same reasoning, impossible because man's value system is also determined by this same technology. Man thus becomes a prisoner of the machine and of the values dictated by the machine.

Because modern technology requires for its successful operation large aggregates of capital, integration of related functions, centralized planning and direction, an abundant supply of raw materials, extensive markets, and continuous research, it follows that large-scale organizations are necessary. In short, technology being what it is, economic power must be concentrated if maximum efficiency and productivity are to be attained. And the latter must be attained for, in this scheme of values, they are the ultimate objectives of the system. By this reasoning, competition, with its small-scale, decentralized, uncoordinated production, is technologically obsolete. It violates every imperative of advanced technology; moreover, it is motivated by individual self-interest and directed toward the goal of individual freedom, both of which are incompatible with the values of technology. By this logic, it is inevitable, then, that competition must decline and be supplanted by large-scale organizations in all sectors of the economy where modern technology is applicable. This is a natural, organic evolution predetermined by technological imperatives and, hence, inevitable. Laws that interfere with this evolution, in a vain attempt to preserve competition, are—according to the determinists—foolish and futile; they can at best only retard the process, not stop it; to the extent they succeed in retarding the movement they are per se obnoxious because they deny society the benefits that otherwise would accrue from improvements in efficiency and productivity.

This technological determinism is today the principal obstacle to any rational program for the restoration of competition. It has seriously undermined, if not destroyed beyond hope of rehabilitation, public faith in the efficacy and viability of competition; it has created in the public mind a mood of resignation to the inevitability of monopoly; it has even aroused the timorous hope that this predestined unfolding of historic process may after all be good, progressive, and dynamic, that it may prove compatible with human freedom, that the productive power thereby unleashed may redound to the benefit of all mankind, and that the possessors of this great power may in some mysterious way attain grace and develop a sense of social responsibility. In short, the doctrine of technological determinism has corroded the traditional faith in competition and fortified the pretensions of the monopolist that, on this account, he represents the wave of the future.

TECHNOLOGICAL DETERMINISM REFUTED

Surprisingly enough, however, this doctrine is no more than an unproved assertion. Its advocates have never successfully sustained the burden of proof. They have not demonstrated that technology is a necessary and sufficient explanation of economic concentration. They have not adduced evidence which is both scientific and convincing. On the contrary, a critical examination of the data reveals that technology

has not in fact been a deterministic force and that numerous factors have contributed to the concentration of economic power. Technology, it seems, is but one of many interrelated forces, which, operating in conjunction and unidirectionally, have made economic concentration *possible,* not *necessary* or *inevitable.* Moreover, it is the *control* of technology and of technological development, not the technological process itself, which exercises deterministic effects on the structure of the economy. Failure to make this distinction between monopoly control of technology and the inherent nature of the technological process is a source of much confusion and frequently leads to the erroneous conclusion that technology causes, requires, or necessitates monopoly for its effective utilization.

Given modern technology, the crucial question is not "do firms have to be big?" but rather "*how* big must a firm be to operate efficiently?" In the iron and steel industry, for example, few would deny that a firm must be big both horizontally (i.e., in any one branch of the industry) as well as vertically (i.e., in successive stages of operation). Nevertheless, it is doubtful whether the combination of spatially and functionally separate plant units yields any significant economies. To be sure, efficiency might require integrated operations at Gary *or* Pittsburgh *or* Birmingham; but is there any technological justification for combining these functionally independent plant complexes under the administration of a single firm?

Consider for a moment that U.S. Steel's Gary plant alone is bigger than all the plants of Jones & Laughlin (the nation's fourth largest steel producer) combined. This inevitably raises the question whether Jones & Laughlin, and such other substantial enterprises as National Steel, Youngstown Sheet & Tube, Armco, and Inland Steel, are big enough to be efficient. If they are, then certainly U.S. Steel's Gary plant—standing on its own feet and divorced from the industrial family of U.S. Steel—should also be capable of efficient operation. The same applies to U.S. Steel's integrated units at Pittsburgh and Birmingham. Severing these plants from the head office in New York City should hardly result in a loss of efficiency.

It may not be unreasonable to suggest, as *Fortune* did, that there are areas in American industry where an unmerging process among the giants can contribute both to increased efficiency and more vigorous competition. Put differently—in the parlance of the cautious and conservative scholar—it is clear that modern technology requires big plants and big firms; but there is no scientific evidence that it justifies the Brobdingnagian size of many of our big business enterprises. There is no proof yet made available by the technological determinists that industrial giantism (as distinct from mere bigness) is the *sine qua non* of technical efficiency and the optimum utilization of the industrial arts.

Moreover, it is misleading to argue that a high degree of industrial concentration is the price of technological progress. It is not enough to point to the highly concentrated petroleum industry and say that it is progressive while condemning the intensely competitive bituminous coal industry as technologically backward. Such comparisons do not provide a sound basis for judgment. Other comparisons are more relevant. Thus it is noteworthy that, in highly concentrated industries like steel and meat packing, the increase in output per man-hour has been somewhat less than spectacular.

If modern technology is indeed an imperative, if it inevitably makes for giant size, does it justify conglomerate as well as horizontal and vertical integration, and if so, how much? Is it technological determinism which explains the expansion of General Motors into the locomotive and electric appliance field? Is it technological exigency which compels control of Western Electric by A. T. & T.? Is it technological exigency which compels control of specialization and militates in favor of continuous and apparently unlimited diversification? If technology is an imperative force which inevitably leads to industrial giantism, why do so many dominant firms resort to tying contracts, exclusive dealing, price discrimination, and similar practices to maintain their market position? Why, for example, must American and Continental Can be allowed to tie the sale of their cans to the leasing of closing machinery? Why must the United Shoe Machinery Corporation be allowed to engage in full-line forcing and the knowing and willful infringement of competitors' patents? Why must the major oil companies be allowed to tie up retail gasoline dealers through requirement contracts? Why must General Electric be allowed to fix the retail price at which its patent licensee may sell

his product? Why must du Pont be allowed to retain its hegemony in chemicals, tires, and automobiles if it does not "exercise" the control it has and if the parts of its empire are operated as independent units? If technology automatically forecloses small and medium-sized business from certain industries, why is there such great fear of compulsory patent licensing? Would it not be safe for industrial giants to offer patent licenses to any and all comers upon payment of reasonable royalties (which permit the inventor to recoup his investment plus a reward for risk) if the smaller rivals were incapable of taking advantage of the new technology?

In the absence of convincing evidence on these scores, one is entitled to suspect that technological necessity is merely a convenient and persuasive rationalization for monopoly aspirations. Perhaps the onrush of modern technology makes giantism inevitable; but before we believe this the determinists must make their case. No longer do we accept the notion that poverty is the will of God, that human misery is inevitable, that a better life must await the hereafter. Is there any more reason to embrace the unproved assertion of technological determinism which would condemn us to the despair and tyranny of a monopoly world?

NATURAL CHECKS AND BALANCES

Those who accept monopoly as the predestined fate of industrial society ordinarily feel constrained to allay the public fear of concentrated economic power by demonstrating that, after all, it is not as dangerous as commonly supposed. The fear of monopoly, it is held, exists only in the mind's eye, being an irrational cultural residue from an earlier period. An objective examination of modern business performance in areas of high concentration, we are told, reveals powerful limiting factors which effectively prevent monopolistic abuses and protect the public interest. Many such forces are operative but in general they fall into two broad classes—natural market forces and social pressures that condition the attitudes and behavior of corporate management. The effectiveness of the former will be examined briefly in this section.

In the market, monopoly power confronts a formidable array of limitations, such as: interindustry competition, oligopolistic rivalry, potential substitutes, technological innovations, consumer attitudes and preferences, countervailing power groups, and the ever present threat of antitrust prosecution. The impact of these external forces, combined with the internal pressure of overhead costs, precludes the unlimited exercise of monopoly power and compels the monopolist, notwithstanding his strategic market position and his motivation, to behave in a manner generally consistent with the public welfare. If, oblivious of these limitations or in defiance of them, he attempts to exploit fully his market advantage, he courts disaster, for his conduct will stimulate those hostile forces that have it within their power to effect his undoing. In like manner, if he fails to serve the public interest in respect to attractiveness of products, comparability of prices, and quality of service, his market position and the economic power associated with it will be undermined by more aggressive and less monopolistically disposed producers. Thus, in the long run, monopoly power, according to this view, is an illusion—a frail, limited, transient phenomenon, existing precariously in a hostile market environment, the dynamic character of which effectively restrains its theoretically dangerous potentialities and compels it, contrary to its inherent inclination, to serve the public welfare.

COUNTERVAILING POWER:
A BALANCING FORCE?

The currently popular theory of countervailing power, developed by John Kenneth Galbraith in his brilliant *American Capitalism*, is based upon a special, and somewhat narrower, adaptation of this generalized market approach. Instead of relying on the combined effect of all forces that might conceivably restrain the exercise of monopoly power, Galbraith would depend on those which operate on one side of the market—i.e., the defensive or countervailing pressures exerted by suppliers, distributors, labor, and farmers. His own admittedly too dogmatic statement of the proposition is that: "Private economic power is held in check by the countervailing power of those who are subject to it. The first begets the second." Monopoly at one point in the market, it is assumed, will stimulate other business interests, not consumers generally, to organize countervailing

power by means of which to checkmate and neutralize the first monopoly. This struggle for power and survival among producer groups results in a sort of balance-of-power equilibrium throughout the economy and to a large extent nullifies the exercise of monopoly power by any particular interest. If by any chance this equilibrium is disturbed, and adversely affected groups are unable by their own efforts to organize countervailing power, government should intervene on behalf of the weaker interest to restore the balance. Such intervention, Galbraith affirms, is no different in principle from steps to strengthen competition; it renders the economy more capable of autonomous self-regulation and lessens the need for over-all government control.

There is no disposition here to deny that monopoly power is somewhat restrained by interindustry competition, oligopolistic rivalry, technological innovations, and countervailing market forces. Monopoly is never omnipotent and rarely is it as bad in practice as economic theory might have us suppose. Being subject to some checks and balances, it occasionally yields satisfactory results in terms of economic performance. Nevertheless, as Professor Lewis has pointed out, "results alone throw no light on the really significant question: have these results been *compelled* by the system . . . or do they represent simply the dispensations of managements which, with a wide latitude of policy choices at their disposal, happened for the moment to be benevolent or 'smart'?" Clearly, the mere absence of identifiable extortion or restriction is no proof that monopoly is under effective control. If we are to consider the discipline of the market place "effective or workable, or even acceptable, in any significant, lasting sense, it must not only permit, *it must compel the results we want by the necessary and continuing operation of its processes*. . . . Satisfactory results which happen but which, equally, might not have happened are not good evidence of the successful working of an economic system. . . . The *process* by which results are achieved and assured is the very essence of an economic system." And one mark of a desirable economic system is its ability *systematically* and *predictably* to compel economic decisions and economic results which are in the public interest.

It is not enough, therefore, to say that monopoly is subject to limiting market forces.

Such forces are, to some extent, ubiquitous. They exist in a socialist state where the steel monopoly is a check on the aluminum monopoly, and where the trades union congress offsets the power of the central industry planning board. They are present, in some degree, in a fascist corporate state as well as in a sovietized society. However, the mere presence of these forces, and their operation in a general way, do not transmute monopoly into an instrument for the public good. They do not prevent the emergence of economic power concentrates, nor do they assure their neutralization and eventual destruction. The persistence of these power groups is at least presumptive evidence that general market forces are either nonexistent or too weak to be decisive.

Countervailing power is, at best, a supplement to—rather than a substitute for—competition. It cannot long survive in the absence of competition, nor does its operation afford any clear and administratively feasible guidelines for public policy. Moreover, countervailing power is frequently subverted by vertical integration, collusion, and top-level financial control. The suggestion that these inherent defects can be remedied by governmental intervention on behalf of the weaker party, as per Galbraith's theory, is quite unrealistic. It rests on the untenable assumption that government is an autonomous, monolithic, self-contained organism—that political power always checkmates economic power by intervening on the side of the underdog. Unfortunately this is no more than a fond hope. Experience indicates that economic interest groups are today largely politicized units, making their claims upon and through the institutions of government. Experience demonstrates that all too often economic power attracts, even demands, the support of political power and that constant vigilance is needed to prevent a combination of the two.

DOCTRINE OF THE CORPORATE SOUL

These natural market restraints and countervailing power, it is held, are supplemented by powerful social pressures which condition the behavior of corporate management. Under these pressures corporate executives have acquired "a new sense of social responsibility"—in brief, "a corporate soul," to use Mr. Berle's delightful fiction. Gone are the robber barons with their "public-be-damned" attitude and

their ruthless, irresponsible exploitation of monopoly power. By contrast, modern corporate management is aware of the social responsibilities of power, sensitive to public opinion, and solicitous of meriting public approbation. It is restrained by deference to prevailing social ethics and by its own professional code.

This is the ultimate rationalization of monopoly—the prelude to final legitimization, which is the goal of all aspirants for monopoly power. It is admittedly a difficult concept because, transcending the objective phenomena of the market place, it involves subjective valuations of human nature and certain metaphysical assumptions concerning the perfectability of man. If, either through social experience or salvation by grace, man can sublimate his baser impulses and so perfect his nature as to attain some higher level of altruism and social responsibility, then why cannot the managers of Big Business exercise their great economic power for the common good? Why cannot they, in fact, become their brother's keeper? This is a challenging and appealing thought, particularly in a society traditionally committed to the idea of human perfectibility and social progress. Because it appears to be consistent both with our assumptions about human nature and our aspirations for social betterment, it has great value as a propaganda device to reconcile concentration of economic power and social welfare. In the long run, it is the ultimate justification, for unless those who possess great economic power can convince the public that their intent is beneficent and their behavior socially responsible, their position is untenable.

ARE MONOPOLIES "SOULFUL"?

But how valid is the conclusion derived from these premises? Can it be safely assumed that those who possess great economic power will, from some newly acquired sense of social responsibility, exercise that power in a manner consistent with the public interest? Without in any way abating their faith in the general perfectibility of man, and conceding some improvement in corporate behavior, the authors must answer "no." The issue is not the nature of man and his potentialities for improvement viewed in the abstract and without regard to the social environment. Rather, it is a question of the institutional organization of society and of human response under given institutional conditions. One set of institutions will tend to sublimate man's baser impulses and to stimulate those creative faculties that make both for self-improvement and greater service to society. Another set of institutions will tend to have the opposite effect, accentuating the worst features of human nature and stifling the best. Monopoly is such an institution. The first law of concentrated economic power is to survive—to maintain itself; the first responsibility of those charged with the management of such power is to preserve it, social ethics to the contrary notwithstanding. This means that any given concentration of power, to survive, must be greater than the market forces arrayed against it, and that its imperatives for survival must take precedence over other values.

Monopoly arises in the first instance from the unrestrained pursuit of private advantage, or from the corruption of government, or from the two in conjunction. Men driven by such compelling forces, habituated to the ruthless quest for power and contemptuous of democratic government, are not likely, on attaining their goal, to experience a miraculous conversion and become paragons of civic virtue. Furthermore, a society too weak or too indifferent to prevent such manifestations of antisocial behavior in the original instance is not likely, after power is once concentrated, to restrain the subsequent exercise of it. Even if a monopolist were personally disposed to moderate his behavior and assume the role of a benevolent steward he could not, for he must exercise his economic power continuously and effectively lest it slip from his grasp. The imperative of survival is so compelling that one who wields monopoly power has no personal choice in the matter; he must either act like a monopolist

or cease to be one. Thus the nature of the institution itself precludes the possibility that "a new sense of social responsibility" among corporate executives will suffice to reconcile excessive concentration of economic power with the public interest. To accept and legitimatize monopoly on the basis of such wishful thinking would, in the opinion of the authors, constitute an egregious folly, the ultimate consequences of which would involve a substantial surrender of economic freedom.

CONCLUSION

We come, then, to the final conclusion that the elaborate rationalizations of monopoly encountered in the recent literature are specious and unsound. They represent labored efforts to escape from a dilemma created by false assumptions. If free competition be abandoned as obsolete, unworkable, and undesirable; if socialism be rejected out of hand on both economic and ideological grounds; and if "free private enterprise"—never clearly defined but by implication something akin to the status quo —be regarded as a binding commitment, then there is no alternative other than to accept the existing economic organization with all its imperfections. This is what the apologists for monopoly do, but all too frequently they fail to state their premises explicitly. It is the view here that the premises underlying this whole fabric of rationalization of monopoly are fallacious. Competition is neither technically obsolete nor economically unworkable. It can be made to function with reasonable effectiveness over most of the economy if appropriate public policies are followed.

QUESTIONS AND STUDY SUGGESTIONS

1. Carefully explain (a) the fear of Big Government, (b) technological determinism, (c) market checks and balances, and (d) the corporate soul as arguments in the defense of business monopoly.
2. What specific criticisms do the authors employ in attacking each of these defenses? Evaluate these criticisms.
3. Which defenses of business monopoly do you consider to be most valid? Least valid? Justify your answers.
4. Explain and evaluate: "The first law of concentrated economic power is to survive—to maintain itself. . . ."

Reading 53

The Social Responsibilities of the Businessman: Two Views

The "soulful corporation" controversy, touched upon in Readings 51 and 52, is examined in a broader philosophical context in Reading 53. Here we encounter two sharply contrasting views. Richard Eells argues that the modern corporation has responsibilities to society which neither the law nor self-interest require it to meet. Corporations have responsibilities not only to stockholders but also to employees, suppliers, customers, and society as a whole. It is these diverse responsibilities which underlie the emerging business philosophy of the United States. Theodore Levitt offers a diametrically opposed view of corporate responsibilities. He insists that corporations should concentrate more on profit making and less upon their alleged social responsibilities. "Welfare and society are not the corporation's business. Its business is making money, not sweet music." The pursuit of profits will simultaneously lead to better business performance and to the maintenance of a pluralistic society.

First View: The Nature of Corporate Responsibility

Richard Eells, Adjunct Professor, School of Business, Columbia University

The proposition that the modern corporation is amoral, without any ethical rights or duties, must be rejected at the outset. Few indeed would attempt to defend such a position. As a matter of fact, practically every business leader today hastens to affirm the contrary. At the least there are basic legal rights and privileges that all prudent corporate executives recognize in their capacity as fiduciaries of the property they administer. The institution they preside over is itself a thing of value to be preserved and protected as surely as the physical properties of the corporation. In the older phraseology, it was a "body corporate and politic," indicating that in some way the peculiar integration of human resources authorized by the corporate charter bore a close and intimate relation to society as a political entity. The act of incorporating was and is, in legal theory at least, a public act, and an incorporated body clearly has certain obligations toward the incorporating authority: the State.

But this leaves us far from an answer to the broader issue of social responsibilities. If the corporation is responsible to society, there must exist some claim, or series of claims, on society's part which requires the corporation to perform and deliver. A responsibility entails obligation, and the existence of an obligation is likely to raise issues concerning enforceability upon the obligator. Is the modern corporation obligated to society to do or not to do certain things?

From Richard Eells, **The Meaning of Modern Business,** Columbia University Press, New York, 1960, pp. 70–75, abridged. Reprinted by permission.

And if so, what remedies lie at hand, or ought to be prescribed, to permit society to get specific performance from the modern corporation?

LEGAL AND ECONOMIC RESPONSIBILITIES

It is not specifically legalistic concepts that most people have in mind when they talk broadly of the public responsibilities of the corporation. They are thinking, rather, of the ethical principles that ought to govern the relationships between the corporation and society, the economic problems that arise when corporate enterprise dominates the business scene, and the political issues that have to be faced when public policy must deal with "corporate power." They are concerned about the impact of the corporation upon the individual and the possibilities of reconciling Big Business, Big Labor, and Big Government with the integrity of the human personality and other values so deeply rooted in our culture.

The legal responsibilities or duties of a company are enforceable in courts and administrative agencies. Economic responsibilities, on the other hand, are often thought of as automatically enforceable through the market system. Some would limit the company's social responsibilities to areas of expedient action alone. The legal counselor may occasionally sense incipient restrictive law in prevailing public opinions and attitudes. He may even advise that legally nonenforceable obligations be assumed on a voluntary basis to forestall public legislative action. The public relations counselor may sense the need for certain actions on the part of a company—or forbearance in contemplated action—to garner valuable good will. Social responsibilities of this order are simply a case of enlightened self-interest.

SOCIAL RESPONSIBILITY

But there are other kinds of public and social responsibility. The conviction that this is so appears within the corporation itself. Many business leaders are motivated by the desire to undertake corporate burdens of a truly altruistic character. It can be argued that decisions of this nature, made by corporate officers, actually divert the corporate usufruct to purposes which favor the "public" at the expense of specific contributor-claimant groups whose interests may have priority. Who is to say, for example, whether a corporate contribution to a college is an altruistic or an expedient act—and if the latter, in whose interest? Is it in the interest of the corporation in the long run, or in the interest of the security holder who hopes to send his children to college next year on earnings from dividends? In the opinion of many, both the share owner and the corporation as an entity have social responsibilities that demand from wealth accumulators such as the business corporation, contributions both of knowledge and money to society generally. Not a few business leaders themselves share this opinion.

Climate Nurturing Social Responsibility

One reason for this is that the corporation has become an institution with pervasive influence on its members. As Frank Tannenbaum has so persuasively argued, "institutions tend to stake out a unique role for themselves. They each tend to make an imperative and undeniable claim upon the social body. They each take captive a given section of the population, and set their stamp upon it, and hold onto it. . . . Institutions quite unconsciously create orders of men." Undoubtedly, every institution tends to mold the ideas, shape the characters, and determine the status of its members. The modern corporation is no exception to these general observations. It is this institutional tendency that has launched the Organization Man literature and created the current notion that to identify with a big economic organization is ultimately to lose identity altogether.

But what has been forgotten in the heat of the discussion is that the man makes an impact on the organization, else the social responsibility question might never have been raised at all. A corporation has no human values, save those which are vested in the men who administer it. And it might well be argued that it is as a result of the professionalization of management that the corporation is asked to render to society in value terms something of what society has contributed in the way of human energy and human know-how.

Many today see in the corporation a nucleus of "power" and demand that it use that power "justly." The corporation has, in this sense, a social responsibility to conform to the dominant ethical code, even though to do so may be expensive. Many declare that there are corporate obligations that have nothing to do with the expediencies of good will or the profit position of a company. Managers often share this belief. Businessmen thus internalize society's dominant values as premises for policy decisions which cannot correctly be called ego-oriented in any narrow entrepreneurial sense.

Thus, there would seem to exist a category of social responsibilities which is clearly distinguishable from the ordinary legal and economic obligations of the firm. That there is a widely felt sense of these broader responsibilities of the corporation is undeniable. The causes of this feeling are not easy to determine. Perhaps it is because the social leadership of business has been challenged in so many parts of the Western world, and businessmen sense an increased urge for public approval. Managers of large corporations, it is often alleged, are anxious to prove to the public that their enterprises are socially useful, above and beyond an exclusive profit-making function.

There is said to be a widespread managerial fear of hostility toward big business, especially among some intellectual leaders. The managerial class, it is pointed out, has become defensive in the face of gradual encroachments upon its role as the responsible director of enterprise. Labor unions have moved in from one side, and government from the other. Not least, the examples of totalitarianism abroad challenge businessmen to assume leadership in fields which might otherwise be taken over by public government.

Emerging Business Philosophy

Whatever the complex of forces and causes, we have a milieu that favors socially responsible business institutions. This climate of social responsibility is sensed by corporate management. It is real and pervasive, and it is central to the emergent philosophy of business in this country.

Yet when one comes to the practical problem of describing these responsibilities in day-to-day operational terms that managers can grasp, difficulties arise. This is because current statements of social responsibilities consistently lack substance. In its relations with customers, including dealers and distributors, the corporation is bound by specific legal obligations;

beyond these it is assumed that certain undefined principles of fair dealing apply even though they are not enforceable by any court. In its relations with plant communities, there is no legal standard by which one may judge the decisions of management to reduce its payrolls or to leave the community; yet the failure to take into account the economic health of the community as a whole in such decisions is often regarded as a failure to meet unspecified community responsibilities. One could go on through the list of those groups with which a corporation maintains working relations and point to a great variety of things that a company perhaps ought to do, or ought not do. Agreement on specifics, however, is painfully difficult.

To assess properly the nature of such responsibilities as these is obviously one of the functions of management. It is a difficult assignment, and one which requires imaginative thought and perceptive awareness of the future. Two things we can be reasonably sure of: this is not a static age, and the modern corporation is not a static institution. Nor are the responsibilities of the corporation unalterable. They are in constant change. The obligations of the large managerial enterprise already have altered so much that they bear little resemblance to those of the individual entrepreneur of the earlier free enterprise economy. Gradually they have taken on characteristics of the responsibilities of all comprehensive institutions. Yet the large industrial corporation is still a *private institution* and not at this point in time a microcosm of the Great Society. It is a pooling medium of a mixed economy but certainly not the agency of a collectivistic national regime. It represents, however, a great diversity of interests in the community, and the scope of these interests seems to be expanding.

The trend of change is in the direction of acquiring more and more responsibility toward larger and more diverse sectors of the community. The corporation, as an institution, develops an intricate maze of interrelationships with other institutions. As this change occurs, there is a strong tendency to move away from older concepts of the business firm, with primary responsibility to its owners, and toward the concept of a multifunctional institution with diffused responsibilities.

Second View: The Dangers of Social Responsibility

Theodore Levitt, Lecturer, Graduate School of Business Administration, Harvard University

Concern with management's social responsibility has become more than a Philistinic form of self-flattery practiced at an occasional community chest banquet or at a news conference celebrating a "selfless example of corporate giving" to some undeserving little college in Podunk. It has become a deadly serious occupation—the self-conscious, soul-searching preoccupation with the social responsibilities of business, with business statesmanship, employee welfare, public trust, and with all the other lofty causes that get such prominent play in the public press.

THE NONPROFIT MOTIVE

Contrary to what some uncharitable critics may say, this preoccupation is not an attitudinizing pose. Self-conscious dedication to social responsibility may have started as a purely defensive maneuver against strident attacks on big corporations and on the moral efficacy of the profit system. But defense alone no longer explains the motive.

Before long something new was added to the ideological stockpile of capitalism. "Social responsibility" was what business needed, its own leaders announced. It needed to take society more seriously. It needed to participate in community affairs—and not just to take from the community but to give to it. Gradually business became more concerned about the needs of its employees, about schools, hospitals, welfare agencies, and even aesthetics. Moreover, it became increasingly clear that if business and the local governments failed to provide some of the routine social-economic amenities which people seemed clearly intent on getting, then that Brobdingnagian freewheeling monster in far-off Washington would.

So what started out as the sincere personal viewpoints of a few selfless businessmen became the prevailing vogue for them all. Today pronouncements about social responsibility issue forth so abundantly from the corporations that it is hard for one to get a decent play in the press. Everybody is in on the act, and nearly all of them actually mean what they say! Dedication reverberates throughout the upper reaches of corporate officialdom.

The talk about social responsibility is already more than talk. It is leading into the believing stage; it has become a design for change. I hope to show why this change is likely to be for the worse, and why no man or institution can escape its debilitating consequences.

Dangerous Power

At the rate we are going there is more than a contingent probability that, with all its resounding good intentions, business statesmanship may create the corporate equivalent of the unitary state. Its proliferating employee welfare programs, its serpentine involvement in community, government, charitable, and educational affairs, its prodigious currying of political and public favor through hundreds of peripheral preoccupations, all these well-intended but insidious contrivances are greasing the rails for our collective descent into a social order that would be as repugnant to the corporations themselves as to their critics. The danger is that all these things will turn the corporation into a twentieth-century equivalent of the medieval Church. The corporation would eventually invest itself with all-embracing duties, obligations, and finally powers—ministering to the whole man and molding him and society in the image of the corporation's narrow ambitions and its essentially unsocial needs.

Now there is nothing wrong as such with the corporation's narrow ambitions or needs. Indeed, if there is anything wrong today, it is that the corporation conceives its ambitions and needs much too broadly. The trouble is not that it is too narrowly profit-oriented, but that it is not narrowly profit-oriented *enough*. In its guilt-driven urge to transcend the narrow limits of derived standards, the modern

From Theodore Levitt, "The Dangers of Social Responsibility," **Harvard Business Review**, September–October, 1958, pp. 41–50, abridged. Reprinted by permission.

corporation is reshaping not simply the economic but also the institutional, social, cultural, and political topography of society.

And there's the rub. For while the corporation also transforms itself in the process, at bottom its outlook will always remain narrowly materialistic. What we have, then, is the frightening spectacle of a powerful economic functional group whose future and perception are shaped in a tight materialistic context of money and things but which imposes its narrow ideas about a broad spectrum of unrelated noneconomic subjects on the mass of man and society.

Separate Functions

Business wants to survive. It wants security from attack and restriction; it wants to minimize what it believes is its greatest potential enemy—the state. So it takes the steam out of the state's lumbering engines by employing numerous schemes to win its employees and the general public to its side. It is felt that these are the best possible investments it can make for its own survival. And that is precisely where the reasoning has gone wrong. These investments are only superficially *easy* solutions, not the best.

Welfare and society are not the corporation's business. Its business is making money, not sweet music. The same goes for unions. Their business is "bread and butter" and job rights. In a free enterprise system, welfare is supposed to be automatic; and where it is not, it becomes government's job. This is the concept of pluralism. Government's job is not business, and business's job is not government. And unless these functions are resolutely separated in all respects, they are eventually combined in every respect. In the end the danger is not that government will run business, or that business will run government, but rather that the two of them will coalesce, as we saw, into a single power, unopposed and unopposable.

The only political function of business, labor, and agriculture is to fight each other so that none becomes or remains dominant for long. When one does reach overwhelming power and control, at the very best the state will eventually take over on the pretense of protecting everybody else. At that point the big business executives, claiming possession of the tools of large-scale management, will come in, as they do in war, to become the bureaucrats who run the state.

The final victor then is neither government, as the representative of the people, nor the people, as represented by government. The new leviathan will be the professional corporate bureaucrat operating at a more engrossing and exalted level than the architects of capitalism ever dreamed possible.

The functions of the four main groups in our economy—government, business, labor, agriculture—must be kept separate and separable. As soon as they become amalgamated and indistinguishable, they likewise become monstrous and restrictive.

TENDING TO BUSINESS

If businessmen do not preach and practice social responsibilty, welfare, and self-restraint, how can management effectively deal with its critics, the political attacks, the confining legislation—that is, the things which have induced it to create its own private welfare state? The answer is fairly simple: to perform its main task so well that critics cannot make their charges stick, and then to assert forthrightly its function and accomplishments with the same aroused spirit that made nineteenth-century capitalism as great as it was extreme.

If the public wants protection against the uneven consequences of all-out capitalism, let it run to its unions and to government. If business wants protection against unions and government, let it fight for its cause on the open battlefield of manful contention—on the front of economic and political pressures. We are not back in the age of the robber barons, with its uneven matching of economic and political functional groups. Business, government, and unions are now each big and powerful enough to take care of themselves. As Mao Tsetung once prescribed for China, "Let all flowers bloom together; let rival schools of thought contend."

The Pursuit of Profits

Business will have a much better chance of surviving if there is no nonsense about its goals —that is, if long-run profit maximization is the one dominant objective in practice as well as in theory. Business should recognize what government's functions are and let it go at that, stopping only to fight government where government directly intrudes itself into business. It should let government take care of the general welfare so that business can take care of the more material aspects of welfare.

The results of any such single-minded devotion to profit should be invigorating. With none of the corrosive distractions and costly bureaucracies that now serve the pious cause of welfare, politics, society, and putting up a pleasant front, with none of these draining its vitality, management can shoot for the economic moon. It will be able to thrust ahead in whatever way seems consistent with its money-making goals. If laws and threats stand in its way, it should test and fight them, relenting only if the courts have ruled against it, and then probing again to test the limits of the rules. And when business fights, it should fight with uncompromising relish and self-assertiveness, instead of using all the rhetorical dodges and pious embellishments that are now so often its stock in trade.

Practicing self-restraint behind the cloak of the insipid dictum that "an ounce of prevention is worth a pound of cure" has only limited justification. Certainly it often pays not to squeeze the last dollar out of a market— especially when good will is a factor in the long-term outlook. But too often self-restraint masquerades for capitulation. Businessmen complain about legislative and other attacks on aggressive profit seeking but then lamely go forth to slay the dragon with speeches that simply concede business's function to be service. The critic quickly pounces on this admission with unconcealed relish—"Then why *don't* you serve?" But the fact is, no matter how much business "serves," it will never be enough for its critics.

The Strenuous Life

If the all-out competitive prescription sounds austere or harsh, that is only because we persist in judging things in term of utopian standards. Altruism, self-denial, charity, and similar values are vital in certain walks of our life— areas which, because of that fact, are more important to the long-run future than business. But for the most part those virtues are alien to competitive economics.

If it sounds callous to hold such a view, and suicidal to publicize it, that is only because business has done nothing to prepare the community to agree with it. There is only one way to do that: to perform at top ability and to speak vigorously *for* (not in defense of) what business does.

In the end business has only two responsibilities—to obey the elementary canons of everyday face-to-face civility (honesty, good faith, and so on) and to seek material gain. The fact that it is the butt of demagogical critics is no reason for management to lose its nerve—to buckle under to reformers—lest more severe restrictions emerge to throttle business completely. Few people will man the barricades against capitalism if it is a good provider, minds its own business, and supports government in the things which are properly government's. Even today, most American critics want only to curb capitalism, not to destroy it. And curbing efforts will not destroy it if there is free and open discussion about its singular function.

To the extent that there is conflict, can it not be a good thing? Every book, every piece of history, even every religion testifies to the fact that conflict is and always has been the subject, origin, and life blood of society. Struggle helps to keep us alive, to give élan to life. We should try to make the most of it, not avoid it.

Lord Acton has said of the past that people sacrificed freedom by grasping at impossible justice. The contemporary school of business morality seems intent on adding its own caveat to that unhappy consequence. The gospel of tranquility is a soporific. Instead of fighting for its survival by means of a series of strategic retreats masquerading as industrial statesmanship, business must fight as if it were at war. And, like a good war, it should be fought gallantly, daringly, and, above all, *not* morally.

QUESTIONS AND STUDY SUGGESTIONS

1. Carefully contrast the two views on the social responsibilities of businessmen, specifying the rationale underlying each. To which view do you subscribe? Why?

2. Do the two authors differ more on the goals of "the good society" or on the means of achieving these goals? Explain.

3. According to the first view, what factors have nurtured the social responsibility of business corporations? According to the second view, by what means should nonprofit objectives be achieved?
4. Evaluate and explain: "It is simply not possible for a corporation, faced with severe competition for markets and circumscribed by primary obligations to its stockholders, to assume broad social responsibilities."

Reading 54

Toward a Realistic Farm Program
Committee for Economic Development

Probably no domestic economic problem has caused so much controversy, elicited so many suggested solutions, and resulted in so many policy failures as has the farm problem. Readings 54 and 55 present two vastly different approaches to the problems faced by American agriculture. In Reading 54 the Committee for Economic Development (CED) presumes at the outset that our current policy of supporting farm incomes through price supports has been unsuccessful—farm prices and incomes continue to lag, surpluses of agriculture commodities continue to accumulate, and the entire farm program has become increasingly expensive. The CED therefore proposes to return to free, market-determined farm prices through the gradual elimination of price supports. If accompanied by a substantial reallocation of human and land resources from agriculture, this restoration of free markets will result in lower average farm prices but higher average farm incomes. In the process, the overallocation of resources to agriculture, which in reality is the core of the farm problem, will be alleviated or corrected. Other facets of the CED's program include (1) special assistance programs for the very low-income farmer, (2) the use of price supports to iron out short-run fluctuations in agricultural prices, and (3) the establishment of an Agricultural Board to advise the Secretary of Agriculture and help insulate farm policy from undue political pressures.

From Committee for Economic Development, **Toward a Realistic Farm Program,** New York, December, 1957, pp. 24–43, abridged. Reprinted by permission. Statistics updated by editor.

The objective of a realistic agricultural program, that is, a program that tends in fact to assist the farmer to gain a better livelihood, give public outlays a definite, practical goal, and to serve the national objectives of economic growth, high employment, economic use of resources and over-all Free World strength, must be to create conditions in which the commercial farmer can live with free markets without undue risk.

The approach to this objective lies in three simultaneous lines of attack: one directed at reducing presently existing surplus stocks of farm products; one at bringing resources devoted to agriculture into balance with demand, at prices that yield reasonable returns; and the third at bringing farm prices to the levels at which output can be sold without government support. No one of these lines of action is independent of the others if we are to solve the farm problem without imposing unfair hardships on farmers.

REDUCING SURPLUSES

The task of moving surplus stocks out of government storage into consumption, both at home and abroad, is not an easy one for it must be done so that interferences with normal market outlets are held to a minimum.

Donations of farm surpluses to meet unfilled needs at home or abroad, where purchasing power is lacking, are laudably motivated. However, these disposal efforts—especially the barter program—can infringe upon commercial markets. Such transactions are of no net help so far as our surpluses are concerned because they merely take the place of what would otherwise be commercial sales of our crop product. Moreover, unless very carefully carried out, they may be self-defeating, because where such disposal efforts cut across agricultural trade lines they provoke retaliatory, restrictive measures by other countries that produce the same commodities for export. Thus, our efforts to dispose of our surpluses through donations abroad can limit our commercial markets and sow ill will among our friends and allies.

The recent emphasis given to surplus disposal by export has stimulated interest in various two-price systems. These schemes seek to maintain a higher price domestically than in the world market, or otherwise to shield our unrealistic agricultural prices from competitive world prices. Thus, they allow farmers to keep on producing at high rates at government-supported prices while excesses over consumption at the support price are disposed of under special arrangements at lower prices.

It does not seem to be generally understood that any sale abroad at lower prices than those maintained at home constitutes dumping. We have laws designed to prevent such dumping in our country. Most other nations also have means of counteracting such operations whenever they want to. Added difficulties arise from the fact that other exporting nations have surpluses of some of the same products and naturally become concerned lest our export programs infringe on what they regard as their right to share in foreign markets.

Further, bargain sales abroad generate new restrictions on imports of the products involved and of finished goods made from the products. Price cutting consequently hampers our efforts to expand world trade and to free it from hobbling controls.

It is a very basic objection to the two-price system that it discriminates against the American consumer, who is asked to pay high prices for products we sell cheaply abroad, while we continue to ask the American consumer to pay, in taxes, to support prices that discriminate against him.

For these and other reasons, two-price arrangements will not solve our surplus dilemma. They are simply another form of seeking to postpone the inevitable reduction of output, and return to market prices.

Restrictions on imports are suggested by some as a means of relieving the pressure of surpluses. But the U.S., as the leading nation of the Free World, has international obligations it cannot afford, and in its own best interest, to shirk. Among these is development of expanded international trade on a multilateral basis, carried on primarily by private rather than government enterprise. The temptation to resort to added import restrictions because of temporary situations, must be resisted, and every means used to expand legitimate and desirable trade by reducing tariffs and other trade barriers the world over.

Expansion of domestic consumption through the school lunch program and donations to improve the diets of low-income families have support as another means of lessening surpluses. Better nutrition and health are important public concerns. But, as we have already stated, they are objectives best approached via a vigorous and expanding economy, not by way of surplus disposal. Therefore, such programs have limited usefulness in the task of adjusting agricultural productive capacity to demand.

It is evident that the difficulties of moving our surplus stocks into consumption, at home and abroad, are so great—while production continues to increase—as to make the effort at best illusory, and in many cases harmful.

We shall only be able to free ourselves of this burden without harmful effects if we make room for disposal of our surpluses by cutting production under demand while surpluses exist.

PRICE SUPPORTS

It would be difficult to imagine more convincing evidence than we have already offered that the present system of trying to help farmers through price and income supports is futile, in fact harmful to the farmer, since his income position—in a prosperous, growing economy—has been worsening steadily.

It is plain that further use of price and income supports as they are now used can only encourage further production of surpluses; increasing, and increasingly pointless, tax outlays; a growing misallocation of needed resources of people and materials, and ever stronger pressures for disposal of surpluses in ways that conflict with other national objectives and policies.

Any program, therefore, sincerely intended to assist the farmer must include provisions for getting away from the price-income support system.

The farmer's permanent well-being, and that of the public and of the nation, can only be served by a farm program that allows the farmer to share in national prosperity and growth, and to retain freedom to make his own economic decisions, under the influence of the forces of supply and demand. The farmer must be able to live, prosperously, with market prices, otherwise his position in the economy is insecure.

Price supports, and allied measures seeking to help the farmer by supporting his income, should be *gradually* withdrawn. A five-year withdrawal period seems reasonable, but having a definite schedule and time goal is more important than the number of years allotted to the task.

During this transition, or withdrawal period, we should empty our government warehouses of their surplus holdings. Whether the government should hold any stocks of farm goods at all depends on considerations of national security not related to our farm programs.

LOWER PRICES, HIGHER INCOMES

Gradual withdrawal of price supports, while essential, cannot be the whole of a farm program. All of the people now in commercial agriculture, using all of the land, machinery and other resources they are now using, could not earn reasonable incomes at free market prices for their products. That is why the program must include effective steps to reduce the number of people and the amount of other resources engaged in agriculture. With less resources devoted to agriculture, and smaller production, prices will not have to fall so far to reach unsupported levels. And with fewer people in farming, per capita farm income will be higher.

Lower average prices can be made consistent with higher average income.

The key, of course, is to get farm production, and the number of farm producers, balanced with demand for farm output. This means vigorous, adequate transitional measures to reduce the resources applied to agriculture, to the point where the people and land remaining in farming earn competitive returns.

This is no different from conditions in any other industry, where total output must be in line with demand, and the number of producers cannot be so large that the income from their total product is insufficient, shared among them, for a satisfactory return.

So long as the resources of land and people we devote to agriculture is realistic in terms of demand, farm products must take on values consistent with the values of other products, and the income from farm production will therefore give producers a livelihood comparable to earnings in other industries.

That is, when farm output is not excessive, or spread over an excessive number of producers, the farmer's income position will be secure, for his product is necessary to life.

Our recommendation is for *withdrawal*—except in special, temporary circumstances we discuss later—of price-income supports. Flexible price supports are not a substitute for this withdrawal. Flexible supports, certainly, are preferable to high, rigid supports. But, unless by flexibility we mean a definite move to free market prices away from artificial prices that encourage excessive use of resources in agriculture, flexibility cannot solve the basic problem, which is overproduction of farm goods.

REDUCING OUTPUT

Where curtailment of production is necessary —and this is the case in most instances of crops now supported—how is production to be reduced, keeping in mind the objective of freedom of choice of production by farmers?

The answer, as we have already indicated, is, we believe, to pay farmers to reduce voluntarily the amount of resources now devoted to surplus production. These resources are chiefly land and people.

The use of public funds for this purpose is justified by the fact that a considerable share of agricultural maladjustments is an outgrowth of the magnificent success of farmers in meeting World War II needs, and the subsequent failure of public policies to help the farmer cut back output. It must be kept in mind that the difficulties of adjustment of over-all production by individual action in agriculture, typified by small production units, are immense. Public expenditures for resource shrinkage are also justified by the interest taxpayers have in reducing the drain on the budget of current price support and disposal activity. However, the public is entirely within its rights in demanding solid accomplishments in return for its investment.

The reduction of resources, and hence of output, has a double goal:

Over the long run, enough resources must be taken out of production to keep output in balance with long-term market demand. This can be done by encouraging the shift of some land now producing products in surplus to less intensive uses. An example is the shift in the southwest from wheat to grazing. Other land should be taken out of farm production entirely; some of it could well be used for timber production.

Over the short run, enough additional resources should be taken out of production so output will fall below normal market demand, thus giving us an opportunity to draw down on existing surpluses. For this temporary purpose, some of the best land should also be retired, as the goal is a quick and substantial reduction of current output. Once stocks are down to manageable proportions, the good land can be restored to production.

STABILIZING INCOME

We have mentioned instability of income, springing from such causes as unexpectedly favorable growing conditions or general economic reversals making for sudden wide swings in farm product supply or demand as one of the major problems of commercial farmers.

Public policy should be able to mitigate the effects upon farmers of this type of instability, arising from causes over which they can exert no control. *This is the proper area for use of price and income support authority,* and the government should have standby power to use such assistance, under proper conditions and limits.

It should be clearly recognized that improper use of price and income supports can only lead us back into the impasse of today, in which public policy defeats itself, creating insecurity rather than security for the farmer, burdening the taxpayer uselessly and distorting the use of the nation's human and material resources.

Consequently, price and income supports must be used only temporarily, and in ways that avoid re-accumulation of burdensome stocks of agricultural goods. Further, they should not attempt to replace the market in the making of agricultural prices.

These support actions should take the form of loans based on expected normal prices, so that when the temporary dislocation is past the loans can be liquidated by sale of the crops given as security, thus avoiding new, permanent accumulations of surpluses in the hands of the government.

Such assistance should serve as a guard rail, not as an income or price crutch.

LOW-INCOME FARMERS

It is useless to try and solve the problems of the low-income farm group by means of price supports. The group does not produce enough to be assisted much by price rises, no matter how extreme.

These are farm families who generally have too little land and too few other productive resources to earn more than a subsistence level of living, if that, solely out of farming. Outside the relatively modest Rural Development Program sponsored by the Department of Agriculture, this problem is not being attacked. It really should not be viewed, primarily, as a farm problem. It is a social problem calling for entirely different approaches than the income problem of commercial farmers.

We may have underestimated the ability and willingness of low-income farmers to respond to better opportunities elsewhere. A report by the Census Bureau estimates a drop of 1,816,-000 in the farm population from April, 1956 to April, 1957. This means that about one out of 11 farm dwellers moved to an urban area during the period—one of the greatest such changes in Census Bureau history. In addition to plentiful job opportunities, the new social security retirement program for farmers undoubtedly played a role in the 1956–57 shift by speeding the retirement of farmers reaching 65. The farm population fell by almost 600,000 between 1966 and 1967.

While much has been accomplished through such forces to lessen the number of low-income farmers, much remains to be done. We must recognize that this group includes some who are physically or otherwise incapacitated from earning the means of a decent standard of living in farming or elsewhere. This group will require continuing assistance.

Solutions depend on a determination of how many in this group, with proper training and adequate resources of land and equipment, could achieve a satisfactory income. We do not have this basic information.

An analysis of those now in the low-income agricultural group who are better fitted to attain a satisfactory standard of living in some other vocation is also needed. After determining those who might shift from agriculture, means must be found for bringing their attention to the job opportunities available through Federal and state employment services. In many cases, these will be outside the individual's state of residence. In some cases, financial assistance may be advisable to cover transportation and immediate cash requirements for those having job opportunities available at a distance from their own locality.

THE AGRICULTURAL BOARD

The farm problem, like other economic problems touching the public interest, is a legitimate subject for economically informed political debate and difference. It is neither wise nor practical to suggest that it should be "taken out of politics." However, it is practical to suggest that farm policy, when it has been established, should be protected against depredations in the form of pressures for exceptions or privileges not consistent with over-all goals.

To this end, we have suggested an advisory Agricultural Board, responsible to Congress, to work with the Secretary of Agriculture in implementing the general policy and particular programs agreed upon.

The Board should be composed of outstanding citizens to be appointed, by the President, for staggered, long terms, in the way the Board of Governors of the Federal Reserve System is made up.

It would be the job of this Board to preserve the integrity of agricultural policy adopted by the Congress, to preserve the good relation of that policy with the general workings of the economy, and to move particular programs as rapidly as possible toward their goals. The Board should report regularly to the Congress.

It is essential that the Board, although advisory, should be effective. Its advice should not be fumbled into procedural limbo, or ignored. To this end, we recommend that the Board be authorized to give formal standing to its recommendations, when it deems this desirable, and that the Secretary of Agriculture be required to report, within reasonable time, to the Congress what action he has taken with respect to formal recommendations of the Board, and, if he has not conformed to the Board's formal recommendations, be required to explain his stand, or call for new legislation if he desires to conform but cannot for reasons of existing law.

An effective farm program must be flexibly and selectively administered. A Board such as we are recommending will inspire confidence in the fairness and meaningfulness of a program that must be so administered.

We suggest that, among other things, the Agricultural Board should concern itself with policy as to:

What crops during the transitional period of approach to free market prices should receive price support, for how long, at what levels and in what manner?

What crops, also during the transitional period, should continue to be offered under the two-price system, and when and how use of the double-price standard can be abated?

The types of land to be retired from agricultural production, in what regions, at what prices, under what system of bidding and acceptance, and what other use may be made of the land.

Continuation of acreage allotments, and the manner and pace of discontinuation.

What research is most consistent with the economic position of agriculture?

CONCLUSION

We have outlined in this statement a program, or collection of interlocking programs, that we believe will be of real benefit to the farmer, to the public at large, and to the nation as a whole.

Our program means getting resources—people and land—out of agriculture and freeing farm prices. The higher average farm incomes resulting from dividing farm income among fewer operators will make many farm towns more prosperous. But the flow of people out of agriculture will decrease the trade of other rural towns. This is part of the relocation necessary to a solution of our agricultural problems. It cannot be avoided, but it can be mitigated by the same means—information and training—we have suggested for assisting low-income farmers into better livelihoods. We think public agricultural policy should include this type of assistance.

For the producers of farm equipment and supplies, such as fertilizers, a successful farm program will mean bigger markets, because a successful program means more farms in the prosperous category, and more farms of larger average size.

Prosperous, larger farms will be efficiently operated farms, making optimum use of fertilizers and of productive equipment. The farms that will be taken permanently out of production are not the farms using significant amounts of either. Except in the short run, our program requires more emphasis upon the redirection of *people* from agriculture to better opportunities elsewhere than it does upon retirement of land.

The specific benefits we look for are:

Genuine and lasting improvement in the economic position of farmers, by bringing demand and production into balance at market prices profitable to the farmer, with supplemental programs to assist farmers who cannot make a good living on the farm into industries where they can broaden their economic horizon.

Public release from the expense of farm income and price support policies that have demonstrably failed, and in fact worsen the very problems they are intended to solve, with the substitution of outlays that, in our opinion, will solve the farmer's basic difficulties and will thus have a foreseeable end.

A needed re-allocation of the nation's human and material resources, so that we can make quicker progress in our efforts to raise our standard of living, while providing for our national security.

QUESTIONS AND STUDY SUGGESTIONS

1. Why might it be difficult both domestically and internationally to give away existing agricultural surpluses? What objections might be raised to the "two-price system"?

2. Why does the CED reject price supports and advocate the return to free markets? How are free-market prices to be determined at levels which will provide higher average incomes to farmers? Explain in particular how lower farm prices and higher farm incomes might be consistent objectives.

3. Why does the CED regard (*a*) the instability of farm incomes and (*b*) the very low-income farmer as special and quite distinct aspects of the long-run farm problem? What special policies does the CED suggest in each case?

4. What are the purposes and functions of the proposed Agricultural Board?

Reading 55

Bargaining Power for Farmers?

Daniel I. Padberg, Professor of Agricultural Economics, Cornell University

As the political power of farmers has diminished in recent years, farmers and farm organizations have become increasingly interested in improving their economic status through "collective action" or "direct bargaining power." The National Farm Organization (NFO), which was organized in 1955, has been an aggressive exponent of collective bargaining for farmers. Various NFO "holding actions" for livestock and milk have focused a great deal of attention upon the idea of farmers bargaining collectively with food processors. The holding actions have also made clear some of the difficulties involved in achieving effective market power for farmers. In Reading 55 Professor Padberg takes a broad look at the bargaining power concept as it might be applied to agriculture. He concludes that the functioning of bargaining in agriculture might be substantially different than is the case in the labor market.

To advocate a system of farmer bargaining is to advocate replacing the market price system. Market price has been the basis of farmer incentives and coordination as well as the basis of income distribution in agriculture. Since replacing the market price system is a very basic and fundamental change, careful consideration should be given to alternative methods of coordinating economic activity and regulating income distribution.

VEHICLES FOR ECONOMIC COORDINATION

There are three basic ways to coordinate economic activity. One important way is through the exchange method. In this approach to coordination, members of the economic community essentially are thinking positively. They say to each other, "you do something nice for me and in turn I'll do something nice for you." This type of system works best where it is clear to all parties that each benefits from the exchange. Prices are generated from these exchanges which are used as a system of signals that coordinate the economic activities of production, distribution and consumption.

Another way of coordinating economic activity may be called the integrative method. In this system, a firm or organization is created which takes responsibility for performing several economic functions. Within this integrated organization, the coordination of product flows from one function to another is effected by administrative decision. The main reason for the increasing importance of the integrative method of coordination comes from its greater efficiency. Often costs can be reduced by combining several functions in an administratively coordinated organization rather than through several separate organizations which buy and sell from each other.

A fruit or vegetable canning or freezing operation may illustrate the point. Within such an operation, several separate functions are performed in an assembly line type of setting. Product is received and inspected, washed,

From **Farm Program and Farm Bargaining:** Hearings before the Committee on Agriculture and Forestry, 90th Cong., 2d Sess., Washington, 1968, pp. 486–494, abridged.

peeled or prepared, packed, and cooked or frozen. Product moves through this line rapidly and systematically. Instead of all of these functions being performed by one organization, each function could be performed by a separate firm. This would require, however, a buying and selling operation between each stage or function. Cost would be higher in the unintegrated system for two reasons: product could not be handled as rapidly or systematically and buying and selling required special skills and additional time and effort. While this is an extreme example, the same general principles are causing increased integration between agricultural production and marketing. Integrative coordination is clearly increasing and largely for efficiency reasons.

A third method of coordinating economic activity may be referred to as the "threat system." The "threat system" is somewhat analogous to the exchange system, but it involves negative thinking. In this method of coordination one party says to another, "If you don't do something nice for me, I'll do something nasty to you." Threat is a bad word. Nobody likes to be threatened. Further, the threat has no meaning unless the threatener has power to fulfill the threat. The American tradition is a tradition of freedom. For that reason, we do not like threats or power. Both tend to erode freedom.

Although the threat method of coordination is not a comfortable part of our political and economic ideology, changes in the Twentieth Century American economy made it essential. As many economic functions which had earlier been performed in households were integrated into factories, individuals became workers rather than small businessmen. Their economic returns were not determined in an open exchange situation, it was arbitrarily determined by the factory or millowner. The factory increased the productivity of the worker, but denied him an open market for his services. The almost immediate result was severe abuses. These abuses were not corrected until the threat was developed and made effective by labor unions.

Coordination in Agriculture

Integration of many types is increasing in agriculture. Backward integration by retailers is increasing significantly in several areas. Many products including livestock and fruits and vegetable are moving directly from producer to retailer—bypassing the conventional open market system. Feed companies are very big in the poultry industry. Meat companies are doing more feeding in both the poultry and livestock industries. Why is this happening, and what does it mean?

These developments represent a significant movement away from the exchange method of coordinating economic activity. They're occurring for efficiency reasons. There is certainly nothing wrong with efficiency. In fact, it's as much a cornerstone of the American economic ideology as any concept. While we may all agree that the integrative system is an efficient way to coordinate agricultural production and marketing activity, does it establish a fair value for the farmers' services and the productivity of resources owned by farmers?

While these tendencies toward integration may increase deficiency and reduce costs, therefore benefiting society, benefits to farmers are usually minimal. Efficiency has increased vastly in broiler production probably as a direct effect of integration. As a result, our consumers eat much more poultry meat at much lower prices. Feed companies have sold a lot of feed with minimum selling cost and effort. But the economic returns to the land, labor, and equipment which farmers contributed to this enterprise show little improvement. Farmers' economic returns more nearly resemble the farmers' alternatives in less organized industries than the productivity of the industry to which he contributes. So the productivity benefits which from integration are typically retained by the integrator or passed on to society.

Competitive Pressures in the Food Industry

Farmers often find themselves negotiating price directly with packers or other integrators. This negotiated price is very different from a market price. A market price is determined by the impersonal forces of supply and demand. Negotiated prices arise in a person to person confrontation and therefore reflect relative strengths of negotiators. For this reason, the element of threat is always present in price negotiations. In order to understand the formation of negotiated prices, we must take into consideration the competitive pressures generated throughout the whole system.

It has often been observed that the traditional seat of power in the food distribution system was the processor. He bought unstandardized products from unorganized farmers. He created standardized, branded and differentiated products. Then he sold them to consumers through unorganized retailers. He was the only organized part of the system. The coordinating functions he performed were so essential to marketing that he was in a position to reap most of the benefits—he was uncontested.

It has been frequently pointed out that more recent changes have moved the seat of power to the food retailer. The retailer has become consolidated and organized. He occupies a strategic position—near the consumer. The most significant capability resulting from the power of large retailers has been their ability to integrate and organize the supply operations serving stores. Lower costs thus achieved have been translated into lower prices generally and particularly on "retailer branded" items. In this way large retailers have gained consumer acceptance and have grown rapidly.

The primary impact of retailer power is focused on the supply industries. These organizations force price down—not up. The large chains are not superior merchandisers and they have no significant barriers against competition from smaller retailers. Their power and acceptance rests on undercutting prices of retail competitors. This force partially explains why food prices and farm prices have advanced less rapidly than other prices during the post-war years. This competitive power balance retarded the passing on of cost increases to consumers. This pressure of increasing costs at retail and at the processor level presses very hard on farm price.

The impersonal operation of open markets have traditionally protected farmers from the market power balance of the distribution system. As we see integrative devices eliminating markets, farmers are negotiating directly and personally with buyers. In this situation the force and power generated in other parts of the distribution system has direct bearing. Farmers have no protection from it. Farmers do not have a choice between market prices or the "threat system." Integration denies the market price alternative. Negotiated prices are threat prices.

THE LABOR-MODEL ALTERNATIVE

As basic changes in the agricultural marketing complex gradually unravel the exchange system through which market price coordinated the activity of farmers and established their income, we must look for new methods of coordination and income distribution. Probably the most common method for replacing market price is by substituting collective bargaining concerning price and non-price terms of trade. The advantage of collective action has been to increase bargaining power of economic units which were small by virtue of the nature of the functions they perform (labor). By increasing the power of workers relative to units which were large, by virtue of the functions they perform (manufacturing, etc.), income has been redistributed in the favor of the workers.

The labor model has been attractive because most people think that bargaining strength should be more equal than the size of economic unit—which largely relates to the function performed. The large size of a manufacturing plant does not make its management better people or the management function more essential than the laborer and the function he performs. Technology is what makes the plant large. This is a part of the heritage of all of us. It should not be used by some to exploit others. Collective action on the part of workers leads to greater equality of opportunity among our people than the uninhibited combination of technology and economic incentives.

Collective representation of workers' interest has been a more attractive solution to the problems created by the industrial revolution than direct government control of prices, wages and benefits. Most people consider collective bargaining by labor to be closer to a competitive system than to a socialistic system. In this regard it has been a compromise. It has mitigated the abuses caused by concentrations of economic power resulting from technology and industrialization leaving more competitive flexibility than probably any other system for protecting labor.

Collective Bargaining in Labor

Against this background of national experience many people are asking the question, "Can bargaining in agriculture do what bargaining in labor has done?" In order to approach an answer to this question, we must first carefully identify how bargaining has worked for labor. The first and foremost result of bargaining in labor has been to increase wages, improve benefits and modify working conditions. Collective action has superceded the market price mechanism. There is no question in my mind that the results which flow from collective bargaining have been a significant advantage to the laborer.

Collective bargaining by labor has stimulated automation and reduced employment in affected industries. By defining labor as scarce and expensive, employers have been motivated to use less of it and to find ways, where possible, to substitute machines for men. An important point to note here is that when labor increases its price—or wage rates—it is the employer who prohibits the flow of competing labor into this field. The employer simply does not hire the additional workers who are inclined to respond to the higher wage rates. In fact, the typical employer reaction is to find ways to use less labor rather than more as wages increase.

Labor bargaining has stimulated investment and economic growth. As firms invest in new equipment and new methods to mitigate higher wages, jobs are created to provide the new and better equipment. The new and better equipment increases productivity. Higher productivity, accompanied by higher wages, in turn stimulates demand. In this regard labor does not necessarily get a smaller slice of the same employment pie when it increases its wages. In fact, to the extent that investment results from higher wage contracts, the whole employment pie may be larger. In an economy dominated by technical development and the continuing availability of new processes and methods and equipment, labor bargaining may stimulate rapid adoption and therefore the economy's standard of living.

Bargaining in labor has also affected the efficiency of operations in the short run. While there may be some instances where negotiated settlements concerning working conditions have increased operating efficiency within firms and industries, the more common occurrence is that efficiency has been reduced. Featherbedding and clinging to obsolete commission rates, no longer appropriate in relation to current pro-ductivity rates, are examples where collective bargaining has made the economic system less flexible and denied progress and efficiency which was possible.

In summarizing these points, it is fair to point out the laborer's motivation and interest has been clearly in higher wages, more benefits and more convenient and comfortable conditions. They take little interest in efficiency, largely because efficiency has no direct payoff for them. The payoff for laborers is limited to wages, benefits and conditions. On the other hand, increased efficiency is the major motivation of the employer. His costs bear a direct relationship to his income. Actions taken by the employer to invest in new methods and reduce labor and other costs has, in the long run, reduced or mitigated the effects of higher wages and less efficient work rules and in the end stimulated economic growth and development. In this situation, the labor union is dependent upon the employer for two things: 1) the establishment of entry barriers to protect the supercompetitive wage rates and 2) investment in equipment and new methods which bring the productivity of union members up to the new higher wage rate.

Application to Agricultural Marketing

Can we expect similar developments to result from agricultural bargaining? Can we "tear a page from the labor book" and apply it directly to agriculture? If we look at the bargaining environment in agriculture, several contrasts to the labor situation are apparent. The first contrast is essentially one of bargaining mechanics. Any effort to bargain for higher farm prices must be accompanied by some effective barrier to entry of competing and undercutting supplies—whether these supplies come from within the bargaining region, from other producing regions, or other producing nations. While excesses in the supply of labor are excluded by employers and cared for by the government, excesses in supply of farm products place a powerful downward pressure on farm prices. Full supply contracts provide some opportunity to plan for a disciplined supply within the bargaining region. But it must be accompanied by protection from supplies from other regions and nations.

Another contrast results from the meaning of

substitution among factors of production and the meaning of substitution of final products. You can make an automobile with less labor and more equipment. The addition of more and better equipment makes the labor more productive and therefore more valuable. Creating the extra equipment also creates more jobs for labor. While food products can be substituted in and out of the market, the effects are very different. If you make a chicken pie with less chicken, the addition of potatoes and carrots does not compensate for the reduction in chicken. No consequence of this substitution expands the market for chicken; rather it can only reduce it. Making chicken scarce and expensive does not stimulate the growth of the economy. It merely means that we are going to be eating less chicken.

Another important contrast between the bargaining situation in agriculture and labor is the position of "efficiency and cost savings" as a negotiating motive and incentive. While labor finds its payoff in wages, benefits, and working conditions only, farmers—who have production costs—increase their income as they are able to negotiate procedures or methods which reduce these costs. For this reason, methods and procedures which increase the efficiency of the entire system may be important among the bargainable issues in agriculture where labor bargaining has not included this dimension to any significant degree.

Market Price Has Two Functions

As we look over just these three contrasts between the agricultural situation and the labor situation it becomes rather clear to me that farmer bargaining may go—in fact *must* go—quite a different direction than has evolved in labor bargaining. This is not really surprising. Market price has two major functions. One is the coordination of economic activity and the other is income distribution. It is quite natural to observe that when labor bargaining supercedes the price mechanism, its emphasis is primarily on income distribution. This is true for two reasons. First, the supply of labor is coordinated more by religious, sociological, cultural and family attitudes and traditions than economic stimuli and second, as we have seen earlier, there exists an effective supply control mechanism outside the bargaining unit which

results from the actions of the employer. These two factors leave labor quite free from the normal role of price in coordinating economic activity (free from the "supply response" problem) and allow them to move directly into securing and increasing benefits.

In the case of agriculture, we do not find such a one-sided coin. If we are to replace the market mechanism with a system of negotiated prices, we cannot move directly for increased benefits and disregard the coordinating role which price has performed. The price system has served to guide production and consumption although it may not be the best coordinator. In fact there are many demonstrations that it does a poor job in its role as a coordinator. When we take a continuously abundant supply of feed grains and convert it into too few hogs one year and too many hogs the next, we are doing a very inadequate job of coordinating this sector of the economy. Farmers can't meet the increasing costs of labor, land and equipment from the erratic returns which result from this lack of coordination, and consumers complain bitterly as well.

Bargaining as an Instrument of Coordination

These thoughts and observations lead me to the following hypothesis: Farmer bargaining may yield its greatest benefits by improving the coordinating functions of price while labor bargaining has emphasized primarily the income distribution aspects of price. If this hypothesis proves true, and I expect it will, we may need a massive job of redefining some terms. Bargaining has come to mean—in almost everyone's mind—negotiations for income shares. If farmers work together under new permissive legislation to improve coordination in the production and distribution of food products and stabilize and increase the economic returns to farming, this will be a process very different from anything we have seen in labor bargaining. Perhaps we should call it "collective action" rather than "bargaining." I would define collective action as a system of negotiations which replaces both the coordinative functions and the income distribution functions of the price system.

Let's lay some of the major characteristics and problems in agricultural marketing up against this hypothesis to see how they all fit in. A list of these characteristics and problems probably should include at least the following:

A. *Factors affecting income distribution:*

1. While most of the small farmers earn lower rates of return on their land, labor and capital than firms in other parts of the economy, most of the larger farms which produce two-thirds of our agricultural output earn rates of return as high or higher than typical of other parts of the economy.

2. Farmers need *stability* of income to meet the interest and payments on the rapidly increasing debt burden which is associated with the modern capital-intensive agriculture.

3. Agricultural labor wage rates are increasing rapidly and are destined to continue significant increases in the future. Farmers need a way to systematically pass on these and other cost increases to the consumer.

B. *Factors affecting coordination:*

1. Better coordination of food production, processing and distribution can significantly reduce costs and significantly increase the usefulness of food products to final consumers.

2. Consumers buy products on the basis of convenience, status color, taste, texture and many other nonprice factors. Price is less effective, therefore, in stimulating consumers to use up excessive surpluses or in rationing consumers in cases of scarcity.

3. Violent price fluctuations, as seen in pork products over the past few years, undermine consumer confidence in the food industries. The inability of farmers to control their industry appears to the consumer to be a case of price fixing and market manipulation.

4. Central public wholesale markets for farm products are rapidly disappearing from the scene. It is more efficient to move products from the large commercial producer to the processing plant or retailer. The function these markets performed in openly setting prices is largely lost and must be replaced with something.

5. Functions wholesale markets perform in sorting out product specifications among buyers have largely been transferred back to the farm. In many cases farmers now produce to specifications for their individual buyers. Low quality products which cannot be kept off the market often undermine prices received by farmers who make every effort to meet the needs and demands of their buyers.

6. The chaotic and undisciplined nature of many markets for farm products generates a sense of discouragement and futility in many of the most alert, sensitive and capable farm producers. Industries from which they purchase inputs have power, discipline and good performance as do the industries to which they sell. Farmers see the power and organization of these outside influences encroaching upon their traditional prerogatives and making them captives. Farmers need a system of coordination through which they can participate in the shaping of their own destiny.

Income Distribution Considerations

The situation regarding distribution of income indicates that the case for *substantial* price increases is virtually groundless. While there are many disadvantaged small farmers, two-thirds (68.3%) of farm output in 1966 came from farms with $20,000 gross income or greater. These larger farms earn higher rates of return on their resources invested than is typical for the economy generally. The small farmers with only a trickle of output would not materially benefit from higher prices. This is particularly true for the smaller two-thirds of all farmers who produce only 14.6 percent of all output. Prices high enough to help these small farmers would be excessive for the larger commercial farming operations which produce the bulk of our food supply.

The case for more stable farm prices is impelling. This is particularly true for the large, capital-intensive farming operation which is our primary provider. As farm labor is paid higher wages which stimulate the use of more large and expensive equipment, the debt burden of commercial agriculture will increase. While commercial farmers do not deserve substantial price increases, they do deserve *dependable* prices on which to plan investments in more efficient and productive operations.

Farmers also deserve a price system which *they* can adjust to accommodate changes in their costs. Our national policies of cheap farm labor—which included slavery, open immigration and braceros—have been terminated. Society is demanding better conditions and better wages for farm workers. If farm labor is a necessary part of our economy, people providing it should not be second class citizens compared to people providing other necessary functions. In responding to this demand, farmers incur increases in their costs. Farmers must be allowed to pass these (and other) costs on to society in the form of higher prices.

In the past farmers who depended on the market price system could increase their prices only to the extent that some of their numbers quit or were forced out. That transition may not be too difficult for the subsistence farmer who has little debt. Since the bulk of today's food comes from the large, commercial, debt-burdened operation, price adjustment by economic suicide is generally unsatisfactory. Commercial agriculture deserves dependable prices and the opportunity to adjust them to accommodate cost increases.

Coordination Considerations

Consideration of coordinating the agricultural economy leads to some fundamental observations. The concept of "supply and demand" as the primary explainer of economic activity is probably becoming less relevant as our economy becomes technically complex and as consumers become affluent. Production requires planning which goes beyond the guidance given by price—the price which identifies the product usefulness to consumers. A great deal of planning and investment must be done before there is a product or a price. Among the items which must be planned is how to offer the product to an affluent consumer.

Nor is the consumer guided by price alone. In time past, the housewife gladly shifted from scarce and dear commodities to abundant and cheaper food in order to provide necessities to her family. Now, her family has long since passed the threshold of necessities and one of her concerns is to complete shopping quickly so it won't interfere with the leisure activities which are an important part of her life. Convenience features alone may be more important than price in affecting her purchases. Variations in taste, texture, flavor and color must now be produced in the plant rather than the kitchen. This never ending variety of products, which adds up to several thousands of items in the typical supermarket, is a partner to affluence.

Price is not the dominant influence guiding consumption. Purchases based on living patterns, convenience, variety or other non-price factors continue when farmers underproduce

and are very hard to stimulate when farmers overproduce. Since price was not much of a factor in their original purchase decision, consumer behavior does not change much when price changes. We cannot expect affluent consumers to diligently correct all of the farmers' mistakes by constantly changing their consumption habits. Probably the most prized dimension of affluence is being extricated from the discipline of responding to price.

As the production process grows more complex and consumers become more affluent, the need for planning and coordinating devices which go beyond price is increased. As this need increases, instability and uncertainty of production and prices will represent an increasing loss to society. Better coordination—pertaining to quantity, time and quality discipline—through production, assembly, processing, storage, distribution and merchandising can better serve the consumer, the food marketing industry and the farmer.

Farmer Bargaining Objectives

Realistic bargaining objectives of farmers would include massive programs to improve supply discipline and modest price increases. This combination of activities would substantially improve farm income by increasing prices and reducing costs. While this balance of emphasis between the coordination and income distribution functions matches the needs and problems of agriculture very well, it is not the emphasis most often considered. Farmers most often see bargaining only as a way to bypass the "market" and substantially raise prices. In the first place, this won't work because of the "supply response" problem and in the second place it isn't warranted in view of the nature of returns to commercial farms. It is only by putting the first emphasis on supply discipline that modest price increases can be attained. From society's point of view, a disciplined supply will be worth more than an uncontrollable one.

PUBLIC POLICY TOWARD FARMER BARGAINING

It seems clear that the future of agriculture will be characterized by increasingly effective supply discipline. The remaining question is what body will be given such authority. My choice is an elected group of farmers with legal powers to discipline the actions of their industry. This would require comprehensive permissive legislation guaranteeing fairness in election of representatives and regularizing procedures for financing and settling disputes.

My reasons for favoring farmers being disciplined by farmers are few and uncomplicated.

1. It will be more flexible and competitive than a government oriented system.

2. It gives farmers some control over their destiny.

3. While a government oriented system may be necessary, that extreme degree of regulation should be sought *only* after actual experience shows the more flexible system inadequate.

My analysis of the problems of agriculture and the possibilities of farmer bargaining leads to the desirability for a heavy emphasis on co-ordination. It is now necessary to consider what type of policy could encourage bargaining emphasis in that direction.

Probably the most important prerequisite for coordination is information. Information concerning quantities to be marketed, location and delivery time is often inadequate. Improvements usually require better cooperation of *farmers*. Efforts to improve information by government, industry and other groups have often been rendered ineffective by farmer indifference.

Allowing farmers to conduct price bargaining without basic market information would be chaos. Obtaining and maintaining current market information should be made a necessary condition for bargaining of any kind.

Diversion programs, such as often used with market orders, should be available to bargaining groups. These programs allow the seller to discriminate between markets of different characteristics. The most important result is that quantities and timing of deliveries can be adjusted to the needs of the most important market with other markets or non-use taking up the slack.

Another possibility which should receive careful consideration is granting the elected representatives enough authority to conduct compulsory bargaining in non-price terms of trade only. Any bargaining concerning price would have to be voluntary in nature. The power of the government would enforce all negotiated settlements concerning diversion decisions and non-price terms, but no coercion would be possible concerning price. This alternative would emphasize coordination and supply discipline and thereby enable voluntary price bargaining to be more effective than ever before. On the other hand it would make clear to all farm industries that farmer bargaining is very different from labor bargaining.

QUESTIONS AND STUDY SUGGESTIONS

1. Compare the exchange method, the integrative method, and the "threat system" as means of coordinating economic activity. Which is most relevant to American agriculture?

2. Can we expect bargaining or "collective action" to yield results in agriculture comparable to those which collective bargaining has brought about in labor markets?

3. Distinguish between the income distribution and the coordination aspects of negotiated prices. Why does Professor Padberg believe that bargaining by farmers will "yield its greatest benefits by improving the coordination functions of price"?

4. What are the problems involved in implementing a program of bargaining for farmers?

Reading 56

The Social Utility of Collective Bargaining

John T. Dunlop, Professor of Economics, Harvard University

Both the desirability and viability of collective bargaining as an institution
have been widely questioned in recent years. In Reading 56 John T.
Dunlop reviews some of the major allegations against collective bargaining
—it is a source of community strife and conflict; a distorter of wages,
prices, and the allocation of resources; a source of inflation; a means of
stifling managerial efficiency; and a kind of industrial dictatorship over
members—and raises relevant counterarguments. The author's overall
position is that collective bargaining is "one of our more successful distinctive American institutions." Yet important challenges to collective
bargaining lie ahead, because society has imposed new obligations and
new standards of performance upon it. Professor Dunlop is fearful that
these new obligations and standards may weaken collective bargaining in
fulfilling its traditional functions of determining wage rates, establishing
industrial work rules, and providing means for the settlement of labor-
management disputes.

The American public does not well understand the role of collective bargaining. It is dangerous for a society to distort and misconceive so widely the purposes, operations and limitations of so basic an institution. It is no less inimical to the future of organized labor and management. John Mitchell, the great leader of the miners at the turn of the century, wrote: "In the long run, the success or failure of trade unions will depend upon the intelligent judgment of the American people." Alfred Marshall concluded his analysis of trade unions in the early 1890s: "Public opinion, based on sound economic and just morality, will, it may be hoped, become ever more and more the arbiter of the conditions of industry." These judgments are no less relevant today in shaping the future of collective bargaining and highlighting the decisive role of public opinion.

The social utility of collective bargaining, or any institution for that matter, is to be appraised fundamentally by reference to alternative ways of performing the same functions in the society. What are the central purposes of collective bargaining? What are the major alternatives in our industrial society for achieving these purposes? How is collective bargaining to be judged in comparison to other institutions which involve conflicting interest of individuals and groups, such as local governments, the press, medical care, universities, and Congress?

PURPOSES AND ALTERNATIVES

In our industrial relations system, collective bargaining purports to accomplish three major functions: (*a*) it is a system to establish, revise and administer many of the rules of the work

A. H. Raskin & John T. Dunlop, "Two Views of Collective Bargaining" from Lloyd Ulman, editor, **Challenges to Collective Bargaining** by The American Assembly, © 1967, Columbia University, New York, New York. Reprinted by permission of Prentice-Hall, Inc., Englewood Cliffs, New Jersey.

place; (*b*) it is a procedure to determine the compensation of employees and to influence the distribution of the economic pie; (*c*) it is a method for dispute settlement during the life of agreements and on their expiration or reopening, before or after, resort to the strike or lockout. These are basic purposes which every industrial society and economy must somehow perform.

The major competitors to collective bargaining are three: these decisions may be made unilaterally and posted by management subject to competitive and political limitations; they may be imposed by a labor organization which specifies the conditions on which it will furnish or maintain labor services; they may be decided in one form or another by governmental fiat. Even when decisions are made unilaterally, they are influenced by a variety of constraints: managements must accommodate within limits to the labor market, and government decrees must meet the tests of acceptability and the market within limits in order to survive. There are various combinations or compromises among these three broad alternatives, and our present system of collective bargaining is one.

There is no doubt a role today as always for the prophet wailing against the evils of the system and the reformer who reminds us how far our institutions fall short of perfection. Every conspicuous strike brings forth a rash of editorials and articles. Wrote A. H. Raskin in 1959:

> The steel companies and the United Steelworkers of America have become standard-bearers in what amounts to an outbreak of class warfare—low-voltage, non-violent, but none the less destructive in its implications for industrial democracy and an economy calculated to serve the consuming public, as well as its dominant power blocs . . . And these potential explosions are merely the most dramatic in a series of equally dismaying indications that something is seriously awry in the system of collective bargaining that is our main reliance in keeping labor disputes from wrecking our free economy.

There is much in contemporary collective bargaining, as in other aspects of American life, which generates frustration, alarm and disenchantment. But we would do well to concentrate upon the hard questions of the alternatives, the realistic choices, for major changes or for continuing tinkering with our system of industrial relations.

THE DEBATE: PRO'S AND CON'S

The popular debate about collective bargaining has been conducted with reference to five main issues, or five groups of charges and defenses:

1. Strife vs. Peace—The charge is made that collective bargaining exhausts the parties and the community in strife and conflict. Unions are depicted as the most powerful organizations in the community in that they, and they alone, can deprive the community of essential goods and services.

The defense is made that the extent of strife in collective bargaining is declining, and there is even talk of the withering away of the strike. The average level of strike activity in the six years 1960–65, as a percentage of working time, was one-half the level of the preceding decade. The extent of violence in labor disputes has been very materially reduced over the past generation. The occasional withdrawal of services or a lockout is said to be inherent in the free market, a refusal to buy or sell. In fact, the community has never been seriously hurt by a work stoppage. The alternatives to collective bargaining are likely to prove of greater mischief to the community.

2. Economic Distortion vs. Standardized Competition—The detractors of collective bargaining contend that it leads to labor and management combining against the public interest. Producers combine to push up wages and prices against the interests of the consumer. Moreover, the allocation of resources in the economy is distorted so that there are too few workers at too high wages in organized sectors and too many workers at too low wages in sectors without collective bargaining. The national product for everyone is lower as a result.

The defenders argue that collective bargaining "takes wages out of competition" and compels employers to compete among each other on the basis of managerial efficiency rather than on their capacity to depress wage rates. It places competing employers on an equal basis and assures that competitors are confronted with the same price for labor services.

3. Disruptive Inflation vs. Plea of Not Guilty
—Charles E. Lindblom wrote that "Unionism is not disruptive simply because it causes inflation and unemployment, for these are problems in a non-union economy as well. Rather it is disruptive because it will cause an amount of lasting unemployment or a degree of continuing inflation which will become so serious that the competitive price system will be abandoned in the search for remedies." The experience with incomes policies in Western countries suggests that free collective bargaining, full employment and a reasonable degree of price stability are incompatible.

The proponents of collective bargaining plead not guilty to the charge of constituting a significant independent influence creating inflation. The finger should be pointed rather to monetary or fiscal policy of governments or to high profits which may appropriately stimulate larger wage demands. The relative stability of labor costs in manufacturing over the past five or six years is cited to support this defense.

4. Stifle vs. Stimulate Management—The indictment is made that collective bargaining constricts management with a variety of artificial rules leading to excessive manning, inefficient operations and loss of prerogatives essential for an enterprise to grow and adapt in a dynamic economy. In the absence of collective bargaining management would be more efficient and productivity would grow faster. On the other hand, according to the late Sumner Slichter,

Unions have greatly improved the management of American enterprises by accelerating the shift from personal management to management based upon policies and rules, and they have given the workers in industries the equivalent of civil rights. The strong upward pressure of unions on wages has been an important influence stimulating technological change and raising real wages—though other influences have been even more important.

Collective bargaining procedures facilitate orderly introduction of change.

5. Union Dictatorship vs. Industrial Democracy—The advent of the union at the work place is seen by its critics as installing an arbitrary union boss over the members to replace the management boss over the employees. The union officer is depicted as having vast powers over the member in disposing of grievances

and setting wages and other conditions of work.

Collective bargaining is described, in contrast, as the introduction of industrial democracy at the work place. Through elected representatives, the individual worker participates in the determination of wages and working conditions. Our labor organizations are among the most democratic of institutions in the society; indeed, they may be much too responsive to the immediate wishes of the rank and file on wage and technological displacement issues. The Landrum-Griffin law has accentuated these problems by making union officers even less willing to take unpopular positions with the rank and file.

These conflicting views on collective bargaining are not readily reconciled. There are no doubt individual collective bargaining relationships which can be found to fit each of the above conflicting categories. In a large country with more than 150,000 agreements diversity should not be surprising. Some of these pro's and con's arise from inherent conflicting tendencies within collective bargaining. Some tension and inner conflict is normal to institutions as well as to personalities. Some of these opposing appraisals involve appeals to contending social and economic values—price stability, economic growth, full employment, industrial peace, union democracy, distributional equity and freedom from government regulation. These goals are scarcely entirely compatible, and a degree of one can be achieved only at the price of giving up a degree of another. Finally, some of the popular views sketched in opposition are simply in error or are gross oversimplifications.

It is perhaps foolhardy for anyone to state an over-all appraisal in capsule form. Professor Slichter once put it this way:

Our system . . . gives the American worker better protection of his day-to-day interests than is received by workers anywhere else; it puts American employers under greater pressure than the employers of any other country to raise productivity; and, though it gives unions a wonderful opportunity to whipsaw employers, it gives employers a freedom to bargain which they like and for which they seem willing to pay a big price. Hence, we seem justified in being grateful that we have been favored by fortune and perhaps also in taking modest pride that we have pursued opportunist policies with considerable flexibility and good sense.

My own summary appraisal would state that our collective bargaining system must be classified as one of the more successful distinctive American institutions along with the family farm, our higher educational system and constitutional government of checks and balances. The industrial working class has been assimilated into the mainstream of the community, and has altered to a degree the values and direction of the community, without disruptive conflict or alienation and with a stimulus to economic efficiency. This is no mean achievement in an industrial society.

THE FUTURE OF COLLECTIVE BARGAINING

In recent years the community has placed new obligations on collective bargaining, and recent public criticism of collective bargaining basically involves the issue whether still additional constraints and obligations are to be imposed upon this institution. Beyond the central purposes of collective bargaining noted at the outset of this paper—rule making at the work place, compensation setting, and disputes settlement—an expectation is being developed for imposing four new qualities of performance and new purposes on collective bargaining: (a) Collective bargaining is now to be conducted by labor organizations which are expected to adhere to new standards of democratic procedures to insure more immediate response of officers to the rank-and-file. (b) The results of collective bargaining are expected to meet new standards of efficient performance. The test of long-term market survival is not enough; regardless of the preference or power of workers and their unions, excessive manning and inefficiencies are to be rooted out. As Professor Taylor has commented: "Featherbedding, which once upon a time had such happy connotations, has been remade into a general call to arms not simply against preferred treatment but for denial to labor of some kinds of leisure and job security which is treasured by so many of us in managements and the professions." (c) The results of collective bargaining are to conform further to stabilization guideposts promulgated by government without consultation and without labor and management assent. (d) Not only should the public health and safety be protected in industrial conflict, but

the public convenience should not be disrupted. The reaction to recent airline and newspaper stoppages is illustrative.

A central question is whether these new expectations can reasonably be achieved by collective bargaining or whether such new social purposes can be attained only through other institutions. Can collective bargaining stand the additional stresses and strains? What changes would be required in collective bargaining? If these new standards prove to be incompatible with collective bargaining as it has been operative, how much of each shall we give up? It is important to be clear that such questions are concerned with the long-run adaptability of collective bargaining, with institutional changes in managements and employer associations, in labor organizations, in the mechanisms of bargaining as well as in public policy.

While the history of collective bargaining impresses one with its viability and adaptability, public regulation of collective bargaining agreements which sets aside terms and conditions mutually agreeable to the parties has not been very successful even in the face of strong regulatory measures. A number of provisions of the Taft-Hartley Act concerning payments for services not performed, hot cargo clauses and union security are illustrative. The new expectations for collective bargaining, particularly those relating to stabilization, efficiency and public convenience may be largely unattainable if the community pursues policies of full employment so vital to the disadvantaged, foreign aid, military operations and maintains the price of gold. This is not to say that collective bargaining results in gross inefficiency, rampant inflation or widespread serious inconvenience. In my view this is not so. But the new expectations may be so high as to be unattainable except under stringent government regulation which is itself also unacceptable except in all-out war. Drastic changes imposed on collective bargaining to meet these new standards may well make the institution impotent to perform those functions it now does so well.

The community needs to be clearer about the limitations of collective bargaining; one may admire or condemn an institution without regarding it as a cure-all. It is not primarily an institution to cure the poverty problem; it may make a small contribution but it also can make the problem worse. It is not primarily effective to treat the issues of civil rights, although it may also make a contribution. It is not primarily an instrument to treat the problems of unemployment, although there are some interrelations. H. A. Turner and H. Zoeteweij have said: "The public interest in over-all economic stability is not a consideration that can be expected to play an important role in the work of wage negotiators, especially where the bargaining unit is small . . . or even in industry-wide bargaining. . . ." The public debate on collective bargaining would benefit from recognizing what the institution does well and what is beyond its range.

TOUGH CHOICE

In the inter-relations between collective bargaining and the community, not all of the adjustments are on the side of collective bargaining. The community has some tough choices to make. The community must learn that it cannot expect all good things; it must learn to give up desired, but second ranked, objectives. Free collective bargaining, democratic unions, industrial peace, full employment, improvement in the position of the disadvantaged, price stability, balance in the international accounts, the present price of gold, freedom from governmental controls etc. are simply not fully compatible. The relative priorities and preferences the community assigns to these objectives will be crucial for the future of collective bargaining. For example, the British government had to choose in 1966 between a degree of devaluation and a measure of stern controls over collective bargaining. There are a growing number of economists in this country who would advocate a floating dollar in international money markets. The abandonment of our present international money policy would provide collective bargaining with more elbow room.

No doubt there are many different scales of preferences. It is my estimate, however, that the dominant view of the American community, as expressed in the political process, is that a degree of freedom in collective bargaining and in the setting of both wages and prices at the margin is more expendable than a closer approach to full employment, more jobs and higher incomes for Negroes, a degree of price stability, the Vietnam expenditures and the price of gold.

My own preferences would be to give up first some of the exaggerated views of union democracy expressed in the spirit of the Landrum-Griffin statute. Among other steps, international union officers should be expressly authorized, with the approval of the international union executive board, to sign collective bargaining agreements without ratification of the employees directly affected. This practice is now used in some unions, but the expression of public approval of a greater degree of international union control would help to have some constraining influence. Changes in the structure of bargaining in many industries would also help. My preferences would then be to give up some of our present commitment to exchange dollars and gold at a fixed price. Even should limited steps be taken in these two directions, my view is that our economy operating at a level of activity yielding 3 percent unemployment or so is likely to require appreciable changes in the institutions which make wage and price decisions, including collective bargaining, in order to keep price increases within limits deemed to be tolerable by the political processes of the community.

In making such choices it is imperative the community understand and appreciate much better both the functions and limitations of collective bargaining.

QUESTIONS AND STUDY SUGGESTIONS

1. What are the "central purposes" of collective bargaining? What are the major alternative means of achieving these purposes?
2. What are the five areas of debate with respect to the functioning of collective bargaining? Has collective bargaining performed effectively in these areas?
3. Discuss the new goals and new "qualities of performance" which society has imposed upon collective bargaining. Explain: "Drastic changes imposed upon collective bargaining to meet these new standards may well make the institution impotent to perform those functions it now does so well."

Reading 57

The Right-to-Work: Pro and Con
Bruce S. Warshal

The "right-to-work" controversy has been perhaps the most persistent bone of contention between labor and management in the entire post–World War II period. Section 14(b) of the Taft-Hartley Act of 1947 permits the individual states to pass legislation prohibiting the union shop, under which all workers in a plant or firm are required to be union members. A number of states—particularly in the South and Mid-plains—have passed such laws. Management contends that these laws protect workers from being coerced into union membership. Unions hold that the so-called right-to-work laws deprive unions of the status and security which are essential to constructive labor-management relationships. Reading 57 provides us with a succinct discussion of the entire range of arguments for and against the right-to-work laws which have evolved under Section 14(b) of Taft-Hartley.

The Taft-Hartley law in 1947 outlawed the closed shop which required that an employer hire only workers who had obtained union membership. Through control of its membership, the closed shop, in essence, allowed the union to be its hiring agent.

Under the Taft-Hartley law Congress did allow the union shop employer to hire non-union labor, but after a specified period (usually 30 days) the employee must join the union or lose his job. As part of a compromise, Congress included Section 14(b) which allowed states to outlaw the union shop. Nineteen states have implemented this option and, under the catch-phrase "right-to-work," have decided that the only legal shop arrangement is the open shop, where a nonunion worker can work side by side with a union member.

Not all arguments pro and con are accepted by every protagonist; but a review of some of the major and more plausible points will at least enable us to withstand the propaganda onslaught.

"MORAL" ARGUMENTS

There are many variants among the moral arguments, but they all rest on moral indignation or the superior moral position of free choice over compulsion.

Management claims that it is immoral to force a worker to join a union against his will. It violates his free choice. The unions counter that right-to-work laws are immoral (and, of course, undemocratic) for they do not allow the majority of the working force to establish legitimate work rules. Both sides flavor the moral arguments by lining up their clerical authorities. Management has presented some prominent Jesuit educators while the unions countered with six Ohio bishops. Ministers and rabbis abound on both sides.

From Bruce S. Warshal, " 'Right-to-Work,' Pro and Con," **Labor Law Journal**, March, 1966, pp. 131–137, abridged. Reprinted by permission.

Actually, the whole moral argument boils down to the problem of coercion. No one can deny that the union shop coerces a worker to join the union, but the unions maintain that coercion is the fundamental basis of organized society. Man is civilized when he learns to coerce his fellow-man intelligently. Every time we stop for a red light we are coerced. Coercion is evil only when it goes beyond reasonable limits. Management maintains that the union shop coerces unduly, while the unions maintain that it creates reasonable and necessary work rules in an industrial society where the majority of the workers have voted to join the union.

LEGAL ARGUMENTS

The earliest legal argument in the field against a union shop is freedom of contract. It is heard today in a more sophisticated presentation: the Norris-LaGuardia Act of 1932 outlawed the "yellow-dog" contract under which the worker had to sign an agreement not to join a union in order to obtain employment. Now it is only proper in balancing bargaining power that compulsory union membership should not be a condition of employment. The unions answer that this neglects the most important factor concerning freedom of contract—that is, the equality of the contracting parties. There was not a true bargain made under a "yellow-dog" contract since the employee was abruptly told what to sign. The unions argue that since there is equality of bargaining strength between labor and management, a true bargain is struck when a union security agreement is written.

The freedom of contract argument is one of those elusive things that can be used by both sides. It can be said that every employer should have the freedom of contract to sign a union shop clause, and the right-to-work laws deprive him of that right.

A legal argument of more substance was put forth by the Nebraska Supreme Court in declaring that the union shop violates the First Amendment because it deprives the employees of their freedom of association. In reviewing the case, Justice Douglas wrote for the Supreme Court that "on the record there is no more infringement or impairment of First Amendment rights than there would be in the case of a lawyer who by state law is required to be a member of an integrated bar." Even

though the Supreme Court ruled for the unions, one can still find this argument being bandied about.

POLITICAL ARGUMENT

Although it is clear that the union shop per se does not violate one's constitutional rights, the problem becomes more difficult when compulsory union dues are used to support political candidates to whom the dues-payer may object. In other words, management would claim that it is illegal to force a worker to contribute his dues money to support political ideas that are inimical to him. The unions counter that once the dues money is collected, they have every right to spend it for protection of the organization, thereby protecting the union's collective bargaining strength. Few would deny that political activity is basic defense to a union; but management does present a serious constitutional issue. One should not lightly dismiss forced contributions to political campaigns.

The Supreme Court did pass on this issue under the Railway Labor Act, which regulates labor relations in place of Taft-Hartley in its specialized area. The Court did not outlaw the union shop where dues money was used for political activity; rather, it ordered the lower court to devise a remedy that would reduce dues payments by the objecting members in the same proportion as the political expenditures of the union. Thus the protection of the union shop is afforded the union while the members' constitutional rights are protected. There is no guarantee that this solution will be applied to unions under the Taft-Hartley Act, but the possibility is present.

A common pro right-to-work argument is that there is now a concentration of union power that is dangerous to the stability of the nation, and this power is consolidated by the union's control over all employees under a collective bargaining contract. As the argument runs, it is not anti-union. It merely claims that the unions have too much power and right-to-work laws hold this power potential in check without destroying the collective bargaining functions of the unions.

This is an argument that can easily be exaggerated or can deteriorate into crass anti-unionism. During the debates on the Landrum-Griffin Act one Senator declared that Jimmy Hoffa had more power "than any other man in the United States, except perhaps the President of the United States." David Dubinsky, Walter Reuther, and other prominent labor leaders are the subjects of extensive pamphleteering on union power. Management claims that the unions have outspent them 5 to 1 on the right-to-work issue alone, and that this, in itself, is an indication of union power.

The unions, in retort, claim that they are far from having the power that management attributes to them. Financially, the assets of all the national unions combined do not equal that of one giant corporation, such as Prudential Life Insurance or A.T.&T. Even in liquid assets, any one union, even the most powerful, could not compare with giant management.

The unions further argue that three-fourths of the work force is still unorganized and 40 percent of labor's strength is in only 11 states. With the increase of the working force and the relative numerical stability of the union movement, the proportion of the unionized work force is actually decreasing. Any way you look at it, the unions claim, they do not have overwhelming economic power.

DISCRIMINATION

Union discrimination is a fact that few can deny. Proponents of right-to-work laws claim that opening up many jobs without the need of union membership would benefit Negro and other minority workers who could not obtain union membership.

The unions argue that a union can be nothing better than its membership. There is no magic in a collective organization that transforms prejudiced people into civil rights advocates. This is not a problem inherent in the labor movement, but rather in society. To assume that where discrimination exists in union membership, that without this membership requirement the Negro would gain employment, neglects the factors in the community and the workshop that would still be present to exclude Negro workers. A manager of a plant in an area where prejudice runs high would exclude the minority worker to maintain "plant morale." This has to do with individual relationships—not with the union.

But this union retort does not satisfy the conscience of the pro-union liberal. Some union leaders freely admit that unions do have a positive responsibility to rid themselves of any vestiges of discrimination. They point to the fact that union discrimination is not prevalent and is confined to a relatively few unions, primarily in the building trades. These same union leaders fully support legislation, some already enacted, to meet the discrimination issue head-on. Title VII of the Civil Rights Act of 1964, which was supported by labor, outlaws discrimination in unions. Labor leaders claim that right-to-work laws cannot eliminate hard-core discrimination, and, of course, have the defect of being anti-union.

CORRUPTION

We have all read of union corruption. Before the passage of the Landrum-Griffin Act, the investigation by the McClellan committee uncovered theft, embezzlement, sweetheart contracts, and other forms of corruption on a grand scale. Proponents of right-to-work laws claim that they afford at least a partial remedy since they allow the workers to resign from the union in protest, and that this pressure on the union leader will keep him honest. It is not an anti-union argument because management maintains that right-to-work laws can undermine and destroy trade unionism only insofar as the union leadership has lost the confidence of its membership.

The unions retort that corruption in the labor movement has been overdramatized. Scores of business executives are arrested annually without any of the fanfare accompanying the accusation against any single labor leader.

Without becoming embroiled in the arguments over the extent of corruption, the issue has been met directly by the Landrum-Griffin Act, which provides extensive financial regulation over unions. The most that the proponents of right-to-work laws can now claim is that where Landrum-Griffin fails, right-to-work laws afford the worker the chance to escape from corrupt union control.

DEMOCRACY

The union movement as a whole cannot boast a long history of democratic procedures. Removal charges against workers are often appealable to an executive council comprised of the very same officers who originated the charges. One brazen example of lack of democracy was a

national union which held its seventh convention in 1911 and its eighth convention thirty
years later, in 1941.

Proponents of right-to-work use the same
argument here as they did for corruption—the
worker should be given a chance to register his
protest and get out of the union.

The unions answer that it is true that there
have been undemocratic procedures within the
labor movement, but one must remember that
mass unionization began with the Wagner Act
of 1935, and the movement has had a short
time to grow up. Remember that as late as
1876 (the Hayes-Tilden election) a Presidential election in the United States was conducted
under legally doubtful conditions. Also, since
the Landrum-Griffin Act, union democracy has
been strictly regulated. Where the act does not
apply, courts have been vigorous in implementing union democracy. Some unions, such as the
United Auto Workers, have created an outside
review board as the ultimate appeals body for
all internal disciplinary measures.

In 1966 fraud in union elections was uncovered in the International Union of Electrical
Workers, where it was found that James B.
Carey, incumbent president, was elected with
the help of stuffed ballot boxes. When Carey
was apprised of what his supporters had done,
he resigned his position. Charges of fraud were
hurled by both sides during the recent United
Steelworkers election which unseated incumbent president David McDonald. But, the
unions would maintain, in both these instances
democracy prevailed. This is a sign of the times
in union democracy.

COMMUNISM

Communism in the labor movement is a charge
heard less often these days than ten or fifteen
years ago, when the AFL-CIO was actively
fighting a group of unions it had expelled because of Communist infiltration. But the more
right wing supporters of right-to-work still use
this charge, and it is not uncommon to see
Reuther or other prominent union leaders
branded Communist by the extreme right.

Assuming that Communist elements exist in
the United States labor movement, the next
question is whether right-to-work laws are the
best means by which to counteract these elements. Again, right-to-work proponents claim
that the worker should be able to register his

protest by being able to withdraw from the
union. It is now time to review this argument
in connection, not only with Communism, but
with corruption and undemocratic practices as
well. Do workers actually use their right to
withdraw as a check on the excesses of union
leadership? If they do not, right-to-work laws
have little effect on these three problems.

Empirically, workers have not withdrawn
from notoriously corrupt, undemocratic, and
Communist unions when they have had a
chance. Although under constant fire for its left
wing politics, Harry Bridges' International
Longshoremen's and Warehousemen's Union
(ILWU) is stronger than ever. On the East
coast the International Longshoremen's Association (ILA) came under serious charges of corruption. The AFL-CIO established a rival
"clean" union and the National Labor Relations
Board conducted a certification election. The
workers chose to stay with the ILA, and the
rival union was dissolved.

The Teamsters Union, under heavy attack in
recent years, has not only not diminished in
size in right-to-work states but has increased,
as in non right-to-work states. A worker does
join and remain in allegedly corrupt, undemocratic, or Communist unions when he should
be registering his protest against unsavory
union leadership, according to right-to-work
backers.

Why does the worker remain in a tainted
union? Why don't right-to-work laws succeed
in this field? The probable answer is that the
worker is unsophisticated. He isn't interested
in the larger problems of union reform. He is
only interested in whether the union is to his
advantage. If the union produces for him, he
doesn't care if the officers "take a little for
themselves." If the union does not produce, its
officers can be uncorruptible, democratic, and
100 percent anti-Communist, and yet it will not
command the worker's loyalty.

MUTUAL CONFIDENCE

Anti right-to-work forces claim that these laws
sap any mutual confidence that may have existed between management and labor, since the
unions believe that right-to-work is a union
busting device. The mobility of the American
work force is high, and some union locals report complete membership turnover within a
few years. Under these conditions, the unions

maintain, right-to-work laws are aimed at too vital a part of trade unionism. Without security provisions many unions must expend the major part of their time re-recruiting members. The unions buttress this argument by showing that the major advocates of right-to-work have been organizations that in the past have not exactly looked with favor upon union growth.

The supporters of right-to-work counter that the facts show that these laws do not break unions, and that aggressive unions prosper in right-to-work states as well as in states without these laws. The labor relations student would comment that the major issue is not what actually has happened, but what the labor leader thinks will happen. If the labor leader is convinced, contrary to empirical evidence, that right-to-work laws break unions, then there is an undermining of mutual confidence.

FREE RIDER

The unions claim that the worker who refuses to join the union is a free rider, since the union is obliged by law to bargain for the entire work force. The nonmember gets all the benefits of union representation without paying dues. Management retorts that the nonunion member under a right-to-work law is not a free rider, but a forced rider, since the union demands that it bargain for the entire work force. The union, in turn, maintains that the law must provide, as it does, for the union to represent all workers, union and nonunion, for if each worker were able to bargain individually, the employer could discriminate against the union by maintaining two wage scales—one for the union and a higher one for nonunion workers. Under this arrangement it would not be long before the union would be mustered out of the plant.

Once again, the important consideration is not whether the nonunion worker is a free rider or a forced rider, but what the workers believe the case to be. When nonunion employees work side by side with union employees there is bound to be friction if the union workers believe the nonunion workers are free riders. This friction runs counter to the aim of our national labor policy, which places industrial stability as its prime objective.

SECURITY

Probably the most important argument against right-to-work is that it undermines the union leader's sense of security, forcing him to become overly aggressive in his contacts with management. This is distinct from the problem of mutual confidence, for the labor leader may have complete confidence in management, but still he must constantly prove the value of the union to a membership which can withdraw at any time, under a right-to-work law. Thus, issues which would never have been raised in a union shop are pressed all the way through the grievance procedure. The union leader becomes most responsive to the vocal and often irresponsible minority, which can withdraw its union membership at will.

The same effect is discernible over the bargaining table. The union is obliged to ask for more and press for more in order to please the vocal minority. It is such pressure on a labor leader that leads to otherwise avoidable strikes. Neither union nor management gain in this situation.

CONCLUSION

To conclude, right-to-work laws have not had the effects that are feared by labor leaders. On the whole, the power position of neither side has changed to an appreciable extent. The major disadvantage of these laws is that they force the union leader to be overly aggressive, thus disturbing tranquil labor relations. It may be fair to say that the proponents of right-to-work would not spend the time and money that they do merely to support freedom of contract. They must believe that right-to-work laws will alter the power structure in union-management relations. Someone should enlighten them.

QUESTIONS AND STUDY SUGGESTIONS

1. Precisely what are "right-to-work" laws? Do you feel they are properly named?
2. Briefly summarize the arguments for and against right-to-work laws.

What single union argument and what single management argument do you feel is most valid in this controversy? Why?

3. Do you feel that a high degree of union security, for example, a union shop, is an important prerequisite to constructive labor-management relations?

Reading 58

Migrant Farm Labor: A Case Study of Poverty

Truman Moore

Though there may be legitimate disagreement about the extent of poverty in America, there is a consensus that the social, cultural, moral, and physical impact upon those afflicted with poverty can be devastating. This reading is a vivid case study of poverty among migrant farm workers. Their's is a world of tar-paper shanties, the exploitation of both adult and child labor, and a self-perpetuating cycle of disease, squalor, ignorance, and despair. Here is a grim and depressing portrayal of people who are "always goin' someplace, but . . . never get noplace."

Across America there are tens of thousands of migrant camps. They are in the valleys and in the fields, on the edges of cities and towns. Some are half deserted. Some are behind barbed wire and even patrolled by armed guards. Migrant camps are within commuting distance of Times Square, under the vapor trails of Cape Kennedy, and surrounded by missile sites in the Southwest. They have names like Tin Top, Tin Town, Black Cat Row, Cardboard City, Mexico City, The Bottoms, Osceola (for whites), Okeechobee (for blacks), and Griffings Path.

THE TAR-PAPER CURTAIN

Negroes from the Black Belt are dismayed by camps they find up North. Okies and Arkies who migrate today find camps much like those the Joads found in *The Grapes of Wrath*. You can drive from New York to California and never see a migrant camp. You have to know where to look. To borrow a popular analogy, a tar-paper curtain separates the migrants from the rest of America.

Let us look at a typical migrant camp which we will call Shacktown. Shacktown is owned

From Truman Moore, "Slaves For Rent: The Shame of American Farming," **The Atlantic Monthly**, May, 1965, pp. 109–122, abridged. © 1965 The Atlantic Monthly Company, as taken from **The Slaves We Rent**, published by Random House.

by a corporate farm, one of whose foremen is in charge of the camp. "But mostly," he says, "we just turn it over to the people to run for themselves." In other words, no one collects garbage or maintains the camp in any way. The camp is built on the grower's sprawling farm. It cannot be reached without trespassing, and several signs along the road remind the visitor of this fact. Even finding it is difficult. Local residents are suspicious of outsiders who are interested in migrant camps. Requests for directions are met with icy stares.

Shacktown was built about fifteen years ago. No repairs to speak of have been made since then. Most of the screen doors are gone. The floors sag. The roofs leak. The Johnsons, a Shacktown family, have a six-month-old baby and five older children. "When it rains," says Mr. Johnson, "it leaks on our bed and all over the room. At night when it rains, we have to stand up with the baby so he don't get wet and catch pneumonia."

All the rooms in Shacktown are the same size, eight feet by sixteen. When the Johnsons moved in, they found they needed much more space. They sawed through the wall, a single thickness of one by six inch pine, and made a door to the next cabin, which was not occupied. The exterior walls are unpainted and uninsulated. They keep out neither wind nor rain, sight nor sound. Cracks between the boards are big enough to put your hand through. There is no privacy, and the Johnsons, like most Shacktown families, have learned to live without it. The windows are simple cutouts with a hatch propped open from the bottom. Some have a piece of clothlike screening tacked on.

The only touch of the twentieth century in the Johnsons' cabin is a drop cord that hangs down from the ceiling. It burns a single light bulb, plays a small worn radio, and when it works, an ancient television set that Mr. Johnson bought for ten dollars, through which they get their only glimpse of urban, affluent America.

Although there are trees nearby, the camp is built on a barren red-clay hill, baked by a blazing summer sun. There are four barrack-type frame buildings, divided into single rooms. Behind the barracks are two privies, both four-seaters. The door to the women's privy is missing, but the rank growth of weeds serves as a screen. There are no lights, and no one uses the toilets after dark. The Johnsons use a slop jar at night. It is kept in the kitchen and used for garbage, too.

There is virtually no hope of keeping out the flies that swarm around the privies. But one county health inspector found an unusual way of getting the growers interested in the problem. The inspector would drop by the grower's house just before lunch and ask to see the migrant camp. When they came to the privy, the inspector would throw a handful of flour over the seats, which invariably swarmed with flies. On the way back to the house, the inspector would manage to get invited to stay for lunch. At the table he would remark, "Well I'm sure glad you asked us all to lunch." And there crawling around on the fried chicken would be a floured, white-backed privy fly.

During most of the season in Shacktown there will be several full- or part-time whores. The going price is $3.00. Prostitution thrives behind open doors. Venereal diseases are sometimes epidemic. In a crew near Morehead City, North Carolina, one woman infected ten men in the course of three days. Six out of eight crews working in the area had at least one syphilitic.

There are two hasps on the Johnson's door in Shacktown. One is for the family to use. The other is for the grower. If the rent is not paid, the family will find when they return from the field that they have been locked out. Some growers provide cabins free. Some charge according to the number of able-bodied workers. Rents run from as low as $10 a month to as high as $50.

The Johnsons, like most Shacktown families, do their own cooking. But grocery shopping is not easy. There is a small cracker-barrel store near the camp, run by the grower, but the prices are a third higher than in town. "We got a ten-cent raise," says Mr. Johnson, "and everything in the store went up a quarter. He wants us to buy from him or move out. It don't seem right."

Cooking is done on a small, open-flame, unvented kerosene stove which serves as a heater in the cold weather. Fires and explosions are not uncommon. The cabins are not wired for electric heaters; natural gas is not available. Bottled gas requires a deposit and an installation fee. Asked if the tenants didn't suffer from the cold nights, the camp manager replied,

"Oh, heat's no problem. You'd be surprised how hot it gets in one of them little cabins with so many people."

For most of the year the cabins are miserably hot. Refrigeration is nonexistent, and perishable foods seldom find their way to the migrant's table. The baby's milk sours quickly, and he is given warm Coke. Good water is always scarce in Shacktown. Between the long buildings there is a single cold-water tap. The faucet leaks, and there is no drainage. A small pond has developed, and the faucet is reached by a footbridge made of boards propped on rocks. This is the only water in camp.

Just keeping clean is a struggle. Water must be carried in from the spigot, heated over the kerosene stove, and poured into the washtub. In the evening, the oldest children are sent out with buckets to stand in line for water. Sometimes when the line is too long, the Johnsons buy their water from a water dealer, who sells it by the bucket. "We get some of our water down the road about five miles," says Mrs. Johnson. "Sometimes I get so tired I'd just like to go in and die. We have to boil the water and then take it to the tub to wash the clothes. We have to boil water for washing dishes. The last camp we was in had a shower, but you had to stand in line for it half a day, especially in the summer."

CHILDREN OF THE HARVEST

Inspectors from the Department of Labor find children working illegally on 60 percent of the farms they inspect. And no one knows how many hide in the woods when it "looks like rain." No one really knows how many migrant children there are. Estimates run from 100,000 to 600,000. The most frequently used figure is 150,000. One survey in the olive groves of California showed that nearly three-fourths of the workers were children. An Oregon survey showed the importance of the child's labor to the family. There the average migrant worker earned $32 a week during the weeks he worked. But his wife and children together earned $48. In some crops women and children do more than half the harvest work.

The birth of the migrant child will most likely be in a migrant shack or, at best, in the emergency room of a county hospital. His nursery is the field and his toys the things that grow there. A few camps have day-care cen-

ters. There are twenty-four such registered centers in the United States, with a total capacity of less than a thousand children.

The migrant child may never develop any idea of home. His family is never in any place long enough, and home to him is wherever he happens to be. He seldom sees a doctor. It is almost certain that he will have pinworms and diarrhea. Other common ailments untreated are contagious skin infections, acute febrile tonsillitis, asthma, iron deficiency anemia, and disabling physical handicaps. A poor diet condemns the child from the start. A report on a camp in Mathis, Texas, showed that 96 percent of the childen had not drunk milk in six months. Their diet consisted mainly of cornmeal and rice. A doctor commenting on the report said there was evidence of ordinary starvation. The migrant child is prone to scurvy, rickets, and kwashiorkor—a severe protein deficiency. Some reports have put the incidence of dental abnormalities at 95 percent, and others said that bad teeth were universal.

Epidemics, like the one in the San Joaquin Valley a few years ago, take a heavy toll. Shigellosis, a form of dysentery, had been rampant in the valley for years. The infant mortality rate was extremely high. Within a short time, twenty-eight babies died of dehydration and malnutrition. The migrant child is also prey to a host of diseases now rare in the nonmigrant world: smallpox, diphtheria, and whooping cough. A medical survey in California showed that two-thirds of the children under three years of age were never immunized against diphtheria, whooping cough, lockjaw, or smallpox. Two-thirds of the children under eighteen had not received polio shots.

Children have worked on farms since the first farmer had a son, and it has always been considered part of the rural way of life. But there is a difference between the farmer's boy doing his chores and the migrant child topping onions and digging potatoes. The two are blurred together in the minds of people outside agriculture. The blurring gets help from such spokesmen as North Carolina's Congressman Cooley, who enunciated the Blue Sky Doctrine: "There are no sweat shops on the farms of America," he said. "On the farms of our nation, children labor with their parents out under the blue skies."

Under the blue skies of Idaho, a twelve-year-old girl got her ponytail caught in a potato-digging machine. It ripped off her scalp, ears, eyelids, and cheeks. She died shortly afterward in a hospital. On a farm in California, a ten-year-old girl came back from the fields exhausted from a day's work. She fell asleep on a pile of burlap bags as she waited for her parents. As other workers returned from the fields, they tossed the empty bags on the stack, and the little girl was soon covered up. A two-ton truck' backed across the pile and drove off. They did not find her body until the next day.

If children were mangled in steel mills, there would be a storm of public protest. But death and injury on the mechanized farms seem to pass unnoticed. Under the blue sky of the farm factory is no place for little children. Agriculture is one of the three most hazardous industries. In California alone, more than five hundred agricultural 'workers under the age of eighteen are seriously injured every year.

The migrants who follow the harvest are the only people in America who are desperate enough for this work to take it. Their children will be another generation of wanderers, lost to themselves and to the nation.

NOTHING BUT DESPAIR

The Brent family is typical of many thousands of migrant families. They were forced off their land in Georgia. They blundered into the migrant stream when the owner combined it with five other "mule and nigger" farms. One afternoon a placard appeared in the window of the filling station–grocery store near their home. It offered "employment opportunities" in the harvest in Homestead, Florida. The family was desperate for work. They loaded their household goods into their 1940 Dodge and started for Homestead.

After a long, hot, and dusty trip, they stopped in Belle Glade, north of Homestead, where the harvest was under way. Once there, they found plenty of work, and the whole family went to the fields. In a month it was all over. They never got to Homestead. Work was finished there, too. They realized, too late, that they would have to go where the crops were. They sold their car and joined a crew headed for Pennsylvania. They had become migrants.

Crew leaders and roving bus drivers make recruiting drives into the South, and many workers enter the migrant stream this way. The promise of "a hundred dollars a week and live in a ho-tel" sounds good. A favorite target of the recruiters is the debt-ridden tenant family. Cash earnings and a place to live are heady inducements.

Some families enter the stream to search for a better place to live. One member will go on the season to look around up north or out west. Still, many of them wind up in the rural slums that lie at the fringes of the suburbs across the land. There are, for example, many Negroes from North Carolina living in Riverhead, Long Island. They came with migrant crews first and later brought their families.

Settling is a slow and difficult process. A Long Island woman explained it this way: "A man comes along with a crew and picks a place to settle down. Next season, he may come back with another of the men in the family. If they decide it's OK, he'll come next year with his wife. At the end of the season, they stay in Riverhead. No one wants to hire a migrant because they're supposed to be wild and unstable; no one will rent him a house for fear he'll tear it up. So the first place the family lives is a real chicken house. If he finds a job, he can move his family out of the exmigrant slum into a regular slum. After that, he's got it made. A lot of them don't, and they get stranded. Sometimes the husband has to leave so the wife can get welfare."

The valleys of California and Arizona and the suburbs of the Middle West are filled with the cabin slums of Mexican-Americans, Negroes, and poor whites trying to settle down. After a few years a migrant who cannot escape the stream is broken by it. The poverty, anxiety, homelessness, and isolation wear away his spirit. It is this apathy that is often called acceptance and makes people say, "They like things that way."

"We're always goin' someplace," said a sandy-haired Oklahoma migrant, "but we never get noplace." In a tired, flat voice, an old woman in a Michigan field put it only a little differently: "I been ever' place, and I got no place."

A migrant minister in a Belle Glade camp asked a woman in his camp church if she was going on the season again. "I don't know. Ever' year I go up broke, and I come back broke. I don't know why I go even."

A migrant in Arkansas sat on the steps of his one-room cabin. For an hour he had talked about where he had been, and the things he had done to keep his family alive. Suddenly it seemed as if the memory of the years crushed him. "I get sick of the world sometimes and ever'body in it. I don't know what's goin' to happen. Used to make a livin' pickin' cotton. Then they started bringin' in them Mexicans by the truckload. Now they're gettin' them machines every day."

Few urban Americans have any awareness of this vast impoverished army that tramps through their country to bring the crops in from the fields. It cannot be seen except as a broken-down car or bus here, a truck there, a ragged crew working somewhere off in a field.

But the harvest cycle yields its own fruits: ignorance, poverty, death, and despair. Until we see the connection between migrancy—the corpses piled up on the roadway, the children left to the darkness of ignorance and illiteracy, the despairing, destitute families groping for a way to live—and the bountiful supply of fruits and vegetables on every corner fruit stand or in every supermarket, no changes will come. Without this understanding, no war on poverty can hope to win more than a few skirmishes.

QUESTIONS AND STUDY SUGGESTIONS

1. Briefly describe the plight of the migrant farm worker and his family. Why don't migrant workers seek alternative, and more remunerative, employment opportunities?
2. What specific policies or programs would you recommend to improve the economic status of the migrant farm worker?

Reading 59

The Social Policy of an Opulent Society

Harry G. Johnson, Professor of Economics, University of Chicago

The whole philosophy of social policy in the United States is the subject of criticism in this reading. Harry G. Johnson charges that our ideas with respect to social policy have not been adjusted to the fact that our society has evolved from an economy of scarcity to one of relative abundance. The emergence of a highly interdependent, affluent society has been the result of dynamic change, characterized by fluctuations in income and employment. Our philosophy of social policy, however, suffers from an

From Harry G. Johnson, **Money, Trade and Economic Growth**, George Allen & Unwin, Ltd., London, 1962, pp. 180–183, 186–187, 189–195, abridged. Reprinted by permission.

obsolete and naïve view of the relationship between the individual and society; in short, our social policy is unrealistically based upon an "individualistic conception" of society. The author, therefore, sets forth several principles upon which an improved social policy might be constructed.

In the past ten years or so our ideas about the nature of the society in which we live have been changing rapidly. We have become aware that we are an opulent society, by any comparative or historical standard, and that we are becoming progressively more opulent as time goes on, as a more or less automatic consequence of the way our economic institutions function. At the same time, we have become aware that the ultimate sources of our large and growing wealth are very different from what the conventional wisdom of our times would have us believe; that they are to be found not in the individual parsimony and hard labour of our public imagery but in the accumulation of capital and application of technical progress by corporate enterprises and the acquisition of increasing skill and knowledge by individuals—the accumulation of human capital.

Our ideas about social policy have not been adapted to the facts of life in the opulent society. Our approach to social policy is still dominated by an individualistic conception of our society that might have been appropriate, or at least the best that could be managed, in the early stages of development of modern industrial society, but is certainly not appropriate now. This individualistic conception of society is most in evidence in the opposition of various sections of public opinion, notably business groups, to the spending of public money for almost any social purpose—what one might call the rugged individualism of the directors' dining room, the prestige advertisement, and the expense-account business convention. But it also permeates the social security and welfare services that have been built up in spite of the rugged individualists.

REALITIES OF OPULENCE

Now, I want to make it perfectly clear at the outset that I am not urging in any sense against the liberal democratic ideal of individual self-development in a free society. On the contrary, my arguments will rest on that idea. What I am arguing against is the naïve and unrealistic view of the relation of the individual to society on which we attempt to base the expression of that ideal in our social policy. We assume, in effect, that ours is a simple, stable, and relatively unchanging society, in which the normal individual arrives at maturity equipped with the capacity and knowledge to make the most of himself. We do assist him to take a place in society by providing a free education up to the secondary level and forcing him to accept it up to a certain age; we have been forced grudgingly to recognize contingencies—unemployment, old age, large family size and most recently hospital expenses—for which the individual may be unable or unwilling to provide; and we recognize that some individuals may be incompetent or unlucky enough to need help. But we assume that, by and large, the individual can and should be expected to cope with the society in which he lives; and that the society will operate efficiently if he is left, and preferably forced, to do so.

The realities of life in the opulent society are, I suggest, far different from the simple model on which our social philosophy is based. Far from being simple and easily comprehensible to the average person, our society is one of tremendously complex interdependence between people each of whom is specialized on a small part of the process of production, distribution and exchange. It is this specialization that provides our high standard of living. Far from being stable and relatively unchanging, our society is characterized by irregular, unpredictable growth and change; indeed, its basic dynamic principle is growth through change, change introduced by any person or firm that sees a profit in it. It is this freedom to introduce change that keeps our standard of living rising.

FAMILY DECISIONS

Complexity and dynamic change are the characteristics of the opulent society and the source of its opulence. But it takes only a little thought to realize how seriously these characteristics undermine the assumption of individual responsibility and capacity to cope with society. At this point I should stop talking about the individual, who is a nineteenth-century political fiction elaborated when only *men* counted for anything in society, and start talking about the family, which is really our basic social unit. In our individualistic system the family is entrusted with economic responsibilities that are of crucial importance to the welfare and progress of the opulent society. It is the basic spending unit, whose decisions determine whether increasing opulence will raise the quality of life or debase it; the income it has to spend is obtained by selling the services of its members and their property, so that its decisions in this regard determine both its income and the efficiency with which its human and non-human capital is used; and it determines the amount and type of education acquired by its children, so that collectively it determines the size and quality of the stock of human capital bequeathed to the next generation.

In a complex, rich, growing and changing society these are all difficult decisions requiring a high degree of knowledge, intelligence and foresight, and also the ability to command capital. The capacity of the family to undertake these responsibilities effectively is limited to start with by its small size as an economic unit and by its mode of formation. Its capacity is further limited by the fact that our free society prohibits it from dealing in what is usually its most important asset, human capital, with the same freedom as it can deal in nonhuman capital: you cannot sell your daughter into slavery to keep the family from starving, and you cannot sell your son to someone who will invest in his education. The small economic size of the family also makes its welfare dependent to an important extent on the physical and social environment in which it lives, and over which it has little control. Finally, the narrow economic base of the family, its dependence for income on the sale of the services of its head or heads, renders its income and welfare extremely vulnerable to the human risks of illness, accident, and death, and the economic risks resulting from either the freedom for change that the opulent society allows, or the inability or incompetence of the government to stabilize the economic system.

TWO RISKS: CHANGE AND FLUCTUATIONS

There are in fact two sorts of economic risk to family income inherent in the structure of the opulent society. The first is due to the fact that the opulent society is built on the principle of freedom to introduce change if it seems profitable to do so, regardless of the effect on the value of other people's sources of income. The second arises from the fact that such a system is subject to fluctuations in aggregate income, prices, and employment that are difficult for the government to manage, and that may be aggravated by incompetence or wrongheadedness on the part of the managers. It seems to be asking a great deal too much to expect the family to bear the consequences of these kinds of risks, and to assume that it is capable of guessing when it selects occupations for its children what the probability is that twenty or thirty years later automation will be invented, the Japanese will learn to use modern technology, or the governor of the central bank will decide that it is more important to stop inflation than to maintain an adequate level of employment. Nor is unemployment insurance by itself an adequate form of protection of family income against these risks, since it amounts to little more than forcing the worker to save a part of his income to fall back on when he becomes unemployed.

PRINCIPLES OF SOCIAL POLICY

The argument I have been presenting seems to me to lead to some general principles of social policy. Let me state these principles, and elaborate a little on what concrete measures they might lead to.

1. The first principle is that the complexity and changefulness of the opulent society are such that the individual citizen may need, and ought to be provided with, assistance of a variety of kinds if he is to make the most of the opportunities it provides him. The first need is for as good an elementary and secondary education as the individual can absorb. The free provision of such education is our accepted way both of equipping the child to take a place in our complex economic system and of compensating, in part or least, for the inequalities of family circumstance into which children are born. But it needs to be recog-

nized that in the opulent society an increasing part of the real cost of education is the earnings foregone by going to school instead of to work, a cost which may put severe pressure on poor children to drop out of school even though the advantages to themselves and society of further education are great; accordingly society should be ready to assume the financial burden of maintaining school children, as well as of paying the cost of teaching them. The second need is for social provision of a wide variety of expert informational, welfare, and counselling services to help the individual and family to manage their affairs as intelligently and successfully as possible; in this connection it needs to be recognized that a rising standard of living entails increasing use of consumer durables, and demands increasingly the ability to understand and manage credit. A third need is for appreciation of the severity of the demands that life in the opulent society makes on those who participate in it, and recognition that those who for one reason or another are unable to meet these demands ought not to be treated simply as contemptible failures, but should instead be treated as casualties of the struggle for progress.

2. The second principle is that in an urbanized industrial society an important part of the process of raising the standard of living consists in the progressive improvement of the standards of services and amenities provided collectively, and of the quality of the environment. A community in which the schools look like factories used to look and the factories like schools ought to look, in which the decay and squalour of city centres forces people to risk their lives and blood pressures commuting miles from and to cosy homes in cheerlessly regimented suburbs, and in which the pollution of local beaches forces them to drive hundreds of miles in search of water fit for people and fish to swim in, can hardly be said to be employing its opulence wisely. Nor can anyone seriously believe that urban and rural slums are an appropriate training ground for responsible citizens of the opulent society. The opulent economy concentrates people in metropolitan agglomerations and gives them increasing leisure for enjoyment. The welfare of the opulent society requires the social provision of the collective requirements of decent living, restraint on the private propensity to poison one's neighbour's pleasure, and progressive improvement of the social environment of private living through town planning, slum clearance, and imaginative public works.

3. The third principle is that since the society is founded on the belief that individual freedom to introduce change serves the social good, the society and not the individual member should assume the costs that this freedom may impose on other members when these costs become unreasonably high. Beyond a certain point, the society collectively should bear the economic risks imposed on the family by dependence on the sale of its services, because society itself creates those risks. The same principle should extend to the personal risks, though there the reason is that these risks are the only major remaining risks to family welfare in a properly functioning opulent society. What I am arguing for here is the reversal of the social insurance principle. In the opulent society, the average family should be able to bear the costs of short-term unemployment or minor illness and accident, by drawing on family savings or borrowing against future earning power. It is the prolonged loss of earnings from technological or structural unemployment or unemployment due to depressed business conditions, and the combined high expense and loss of earnings from severe illness or accident, that is disastrous to family finance. And these are precisely the contingencies that cannot be covered by insurance, whether private or social. Instead of providing unemployment benefits for a limited period after the individual has become unemployed, and eventually casting him off to depend on his own resources and public assistance, social policy should provide benefits beginning after the individual has been unemployed for some time, and increasing in amount towards the level of his normal income in employment as he remains unemployed. At some stage it should be recognized that the unemployed individual is a victim of anti-inflationary policy or of economic change; in the former case he should be supported until the government is prepared to restore full employment, in the latter he should be compensated by being retrained or provided with an adequate pension on which to retire. Instead of leaving the individual to bear the risks of unlimited medical expenses, social policy should hold him responsible for a first slice of the costs propor-

tioned to his ability to pay, and bear the remaining costs of providing the medical care he needs up to a socially-determined standard. In addition, social provision should extend to replacing the income lost by prolonged illness or incapacitation, on the same plan as I have suggested for loss of income by unemployment.

4. The fourth principle is that the opulent society ought to apply to its social policy the same principles of rational calculation, innovation and exploitation of technical progress as it applies in its productive system. Let me illustrate what I mean by three examples. First, take education: this is by far our most important capital-goods-producing industry, yet it is very doubtful that it is carried on with anything like the efficiency of a commercial enterprise. Its selection of material for processing is strongly influenced by the irrelevant consideration of family capacity to pay, though it should be possible to design some form of enforceable long-term education loan to support poor but promising students, or at least to take some notice of the fact that an educated man generally will produce substantially more future tax revenue for the state than an uneducated man. Its standards of pay are set by political decision, its methods of teaching by academic tradition, and the proportion of the student's year devoted to it is an inheritance from our agricultural past; very little attention is paid to the fact that an opulent society progressively raises the value of labour—including students' time—and cheapens the cost of capital equipment. And it is very doubtful indeed that it allocates its output among products on the basis of sufficiently detailed and long-range forecasts of demand for them, or builds enough flexibility into its products to make them as adaptable to an uncertain future as they should be.

Second, take medical care. The rising cost of medical care has created the chief threat to family security in the opulent society, and constitutes one of the main obstacles to generous social provision of medical care. One cause of the high cost of medical care is the high cost of doctors' services. This in turn is the consequence of allowing the medical profession to govern the standards and duration of medical training. The progressive raising of standards has had the effect of greatly increasing the investment of money and foregone earnings required by a medical education, an investment the returns on which must be recouped from the fees the doctor charges his patients; further, the great cost of the investment and the uncertainty of the returns has restricted the supply of doctors, so that the average rate of return on a medical education is appreciably higher than that on almost any other comparable educational investment. A rational approach to investment in medical training would aim at reducing the cost of the investment by specializing doctors at an earlier stage and fixing the standard of basic training at what society could afford to pay for, and by carrying investment in medical educations to the point at which the rate of return was brought down to the average for the economy. It would also remove the conflict between the doctor's professional responsibility and his private interest inherent in the fee system, by putting doctors on salary or fixing standard prices for standard treatments.

Third, take the problem of relief of depressed areas. Sentiment strongly favours methods that leave the people in the area, and that aim at creating employment opportunities that otherwise would not exist there, to avoid the social and human problems of moving the people elsewhere and to reconcile aid with the ethic of self-respecting independence. The trouble with this type of policy is that it generally results in creating self-perpetuating pockets of low-quality living that continue to require public support. It would frequently be much cheaper over the long run to invest very large sums in moving people out of such areas and establishing them in more prosperous areas where they, or at least their children, could become full participants in the opulent society.

ANTICIPATED OBJECTIONS

Those are the principles that I believe should govern social policy in the opulent society. Before concluding, I should comment briefly on two objections that will doubtless be raised to any and all applications of them.

Taxes

The first objection is that such a policy costs money, and taxes are too high already. High taxes are often blamed on social security and welfare expenditure, though in fact the present level of taxes is accounted for to a great extent by defense expenditure and by our habit of financing wars by borrowing rather than taxation—two activities that probably contribute more to the security of the upper classes than they cost them in taxes. But more expenditure on social policy would undoubtedly require more tax revenue.

The main economic objection to high taxes is the incentive they give to tax avoidance. This problem and the revenue problem could to a significant extent be solved simultaneously by tightening up on business expense allowances and treating capital gains as income subject to tax; and additional taxes, including a tax on advertising and heavier taxes on gifts and inheritances between generations, could be easily justified. But the dilemma that more extensive social measures require more taxation is fundamentally a consequence of our antiquated way of financing governmental activity. Though government plays an important role in creating and maintaining the conditions under which wealth is created and income is earned, we allow the wealth and income to accrue as private property, and finance the government by taxing back the money after it has passed into private hands. I suggest that a more sensible way of conducting public finance in an opulent society would be to give the government a direct participation in the income of the economy, rather than a tax claim on it. One way of moving in this direction would be to accumulate the proceeds of inheritance taxes in the form of a government portfolio of ordinary shares and industrial bonds, instead of spending them as current income.

Initiative

The second objection is the allegation that any extension of social security will sap the initiative and enterprise on which the competitive system depends. To that there are two answers. One is that an opulent society can afford to tolerate some inefficiency and waste in its social policy just as it does in its household consumption. The other is that there are good reasons for thinking that increased social security will increase and not reduce the initiative and enterprise of the individual in our society. One such reason is the characteristic ethos of the opulent society itself—an ethos of professional expertise and responsibility, of pride in applying intelligence and ingenuity to the solution of problems, of doing one's job well, of looking for opportunities to assume more responsibility. Educated people are not driven by the fear of failure but by the challenge of accomplishment and they work best when they have the security to concentrate on the job they are qualified to do. Another, and to me more cogent, reason is that if social policy does not provide people with the security they want they will not simply do without it. They will try to provide it by whatever means they can, and usually the means they choose reduce the efficiency, flexibility, and progressiveness of the economy. Trade unions enforce restrictive practices; companies form price agreements; workers and executives alike demand that their company provide health and pension plans, thus tying themselves to that company; industries unable to meet foreign competition demand tariff protection; depressed areas demand discriminatory treatment. The result is an inefficient social security system and an inefficient economy. And whatever one thinks of an inefficient social security system, an inefficient economy is undesirable. In the first place, we face a challenge to our high standard of living from the spread of industrialization and modern technology around the world. In the second place, we have an obligation to share the fruits and techniques of our opulence with the underdeveloped nations. And finally, we are nowhere near the point of satiation with the good things that enrich and civilize life.

QUESTIONS AND STUDY SUGGESTIONS

1. Why should the social policy of a wealthy society differ from that of a relatively poor society?

2. What difficulties and risks must families face in their decision making?

3. What principles of social policy does the author suggest? How are these principles justified and defended?

Social Security Re-examined

Paul L. Poirot, Managing Editor, *The Freeman*

The merits and demerits of our social security system have been debated since its inception in the 1930s. Readings 59 and 60 are a part of this debate. Both articles are critical of the system—but with a difference. The overall theme of Reading 59 is that an individualistic conception of security based upon self-reliance is obsolete. But in the present reading, Paul L. Poirot takes the position that each extension of the social security system entails a departure from the basic principles upon which personal security is based. He argues that, unlike private saving or a private insurance program, the social security system is based upon a redistribution of income from the productive to the unproductive members of society through compulsory taxes. These taxes, he contends, are ultimately paid in their entirety by employees and will involve smaller payouts to the current labor force than would the same amount expended upon private insurance. More important, the social security program, as a major aspect of the welfare state, tends to undermine the institutions of private property and voluntary exchange. The author advocates a return of the responsibility for old age security to the private sector.

In a sense, it might be said that the Social Security program of the United States is the best in the world. At least, it would be difficult to name another country in which so high a proportion of persons over 65 years of age can retire in such comparative luxury at taxpayers' expense. Many older persons are simply amazed at how well they can manage on their Social Security payments, while the more skeptical of those now approaching or already beyond retirement age continue from long habit to make other provisions—to save on their own—for those lean years in later life.

The tenacious American tradition of private saving and investment in productive property largely explains why a system of socialized security might appear to function more effectively in the United States than in most other countries. Economically advanced and comparatively prosperous industrialized societies can bear a great deal of socialistic intervention that would be unthinkable in undeveloped countries. The question is: "How much intervention can be borne in the United States?"

ILLUSIONS TO BE EXPOSED

In examining that question, let us first clear away any possible illusions concerning the Social Security program. It should be obvious to all by now that Social Security is in no sense of the word a savings program whereby a portion of a person's property is set aside to be returned to him for use at some later date. Nor is Social Security at all like an insurance program with several persons pooling their savings

From Paul L. Poirot, "Social Security Re-examined," **The Freeman**, November, 1965, pp. 53–59, abridged. Reprinted by permission.

in some cumulative fashion to cover contingencies and catastrophes that might befall certain members at indefinite future dates.

In other words, Social Security involves no fund or stockpile of goods and services from which portions may be drawn. It is purely and simply a compulsory income tax; property is taken from nearly all productively employed persons and redistributed—sometimes to those same persons, but primarily to others—according to a formula based on present and past earnings of the recipients. Social Security is nothing but the compulsory redistribution of property on a day-to-day basis.

WHO PAYS?

A second possible illusion has to do with the incidence of the tax. Who is really paying it? This seems reasonably clear in the case of "self-employed" persons; but otherwise, there is the widespread misconception that the employer pays half of it. The harsh economic fact, of course, is that the Social Security tax is, to the employer, just another part of the cost of hiring labor. If he didn't hire the man, he wouldn't have to pay the tax. But if he could hire without paying the Social Security tax, one of three things must happen: (1) he could hire more help for the same total wage cost; (2) he would be obliged by competition among employers to pay higher wage rates to get the help he needs; or (3) he would be obliged, again by competition, to sell his products at lower prices in order to clear the market. In any event, with rare and strictly temporary exceptions, the saving to any employer—if he were relieved of Social Security tax liability—would be passed along to employees either in the form of increased wages or in the form of reduced prices for goods and services in the market place. In effect, then, the employee does pay all of the Social Security tax levied on his account, including the half he might have thought his employer was contributing.

The foregoing also should help to clear up the illusion that Social Security offers something-for-nothing to everyone. It is true, in strictly materialistic accounting terms, that some of the early beneficiaries under the program were eligible for heavy windfalls at ratios of 20:1 or higher. But it is also true that scarcely any person now under 50 years of age stands a chance of getting back with interest his "investment" in Social Security. Some will have to pay for the multi-billion-dollar windfall accruing to those early beneficiaries. The youngsters are the ones now scheduled for generous portions of nothing-for-something—at an annual cost of $746 a year on any job paying $6,600 or better, when the "health and welfare" tax presumably "levels off" at 11.3 percent. Though precise calculations are impossible for any program that is subject to the whims of politics, it appears now that a young man just entering the labor force could, for the same amount, buy from private life insurance companies two or three times as much old-age security as his Social Security taxes are scheduled to yield.

In the face of these stark realities, how can such a program retain its popularity among Americans? The answer apparently may be attributed to another illusion about the nature of things in general and economics in particular.

"ECONOMICS" OF REDISTRIBUTION

The material abundance flowing from the competitive market economy following the industrial revolution has led some so-called economists to the erroneous conclusion that the problem of production has been solved. The "new economics" is primarily concerned with the redistribution of wealth so that society may be able to consume all that it is capable of producing. They see that the wants of individuals are unending, but seem to overlook the continuing scarcity of means to satisfy such wants. Market prices, to them, are but barriers to the deserving poor; and they reject the first rule of the market: that a buyer must first have something to offer in exchange. But to take the property of those who have earned it by efficiently serving others, for redistribution to those who offer nothing in exchange, can only be accomplished by compulsory methods.

COERCION AND THE "NEW ECONOMICS"

Thus, the "new economics" calls for government action to break down the institutions of private property and voluntary exchange. Goods and services are to be allocated, not by competitive market pricing, but by the coercive measures of the "welfare state." The false premise is that producers will keep on "coming to market" with useful goods and services, despite the certainty of being confronted there by armed bands demanding something for nothing.

This is the illusion of the "new economics," perfectly exemplified by the Social Security program. There is no denying the desirability of security for older persons; almost everyone would like that. But one of the quirks of human nature is that a great many individuals will not voluntarily forego current spending and consumption in order to save or put aside enough of their own property to yield a decent living after they have retired from the labor force. So, if all people are to be guaranteed an income in old age, it will be necessary to force people to pay for this.

Dr. J. K. Galbraith, among others, has observed this tendency of persons to use their property primarily for the things they want most; and he refers to the result as the "affluent private sector" of the economy. On the other hand, noting that a great many persons neglect spending for the things he believes they ought to want—such things as providing for income during old age—he finds this "public sector" relatively starved.

As the financial statements of a great number of life insurance companies will attest, there are persons perfectly willing to save for their old age; and it is a profitable business to serve those willing customers. Many other types of business also efficiently and profitably cater to the wants of those who desire to save and invest in productive private enterprise as a source of future income. But there is no profit to be had in supplying a commodity or service to persons who are unwilling to pay for the item. Businessmen won't and can't voluntarily continue such an operation. So, if old-age security is to be guaranteed to those who do not choose to pay for it, the losing operation will have to be conducted in "the public sector," taking property from those who have earned it, for redistribution to others—by force.

SUBSIDIZED POVERTY

Now, we are gaining considerable experience under the "public sector" in the United States, with government at all levels currently spending for us some two-fifths of our total earnings.

Much of this "public sector" spending, of course, goes for our education—some $40 billion a year of tax monies. And there are those who contend that education specifically, and the advance in knowledge generally, together account for nearly half of the growth of "real national income." If that were true, it would represent a sizable dividend from the "public sector." However, there is one small problem in that the better educated we become, the less we seem to be able to care for ourselves in our old age and other times of adversity. The "public sector" spending for social welfare payments of all kinds has now climbed to $47 billion a year. Some $17 billion of that goes for payments under the Old Age, Survivors, and Disability Insurance (OASDI) feature of the Social Security program. But, unfortunately, the need for other types of social welfare seems to increase even faster than the need for Social Security. The conclusion would seem to be that the starvation of the "public sector" is of a type that is aggravated by feeding it; the subsidizing of poverty increases it.

To question the propriety of various government spending programs is not to deny the usefulness of education and the advancement of knowledge nor to malign the charitable instincts of those who wish to devote their own resources to the assistance of others. But a reasonably educated person cannot escape the fact that the wherewithal of capital formation and the means for charitable undertakings both stem from the same source; namely, the savings of productive individuals. The accumulation of a surplus of personal property beyond one's immediate needs is the foundation of capitalism and the only true foundation upon which principles and practice of charity can stand.

This is the reason why true charity cannot flow from the compulsory processes of government. To promote the welfare of one person at the expense of another is no contribution to the general welfare. The framers of the Constitution of the United States sought to guarantee the rights of individuals to own property. They understood that whatever government can do to secure those individual rights to property is a contribution to the general welfare—and that no government can promote the general welfare in any other manner.

When government resorts to the tactics of a Robin Hood, it has ceased to be a protector of property or a guarantor of security. Instead, it becomes the instrument of plunder by which one citizen or special interest group may loot the earnings and savings of others. Government cannot create security in this fashion, by taking one man's earned security and giving it to others in accordance with politically determined need; it only destroys security.

What starts out as a popular pastime of soaking the rich turns into a program of taxing everyone who works for a living. And as socialism advances, the weak and dependent find themselves competing with the youthful and strong who also have been driven by hunger to the public trough. Such competition in sheer desperation is far more ruthless than that which is sometimes frowned upon in the open market. When people lose respect for the lives and property of one another, then the weak and dependent may expect to be early victims of murder and theft.

SELF-RELIANCE IS BEST

If the less productive members of a society truly seek security, let them rally to the defense of the freedom of choice and freedom of action of those who work for a living and who are personally productive. Let them voluntarily deal with one another in a market place kept free of compulsion. Such voluntary trading directs the instruments of production and· the means of economic security into the hands of those most capable of serving all mankind. It stimulates every individual to develop his own talents to their maximum productivity. It encourages saving instead of squandering. The free market, and not its displacement by governmental controls, is the only route to the kind of personal security which makes for harmonious social relationships.

A feeling of personal security depends upon something more than the legal guarantee of a handout in time of need. Security is an attitude not necessarily satisfied by an "equal share" or even by an abundance of material goods and services. To be truly secure is to be without cause for anxiety, and that kind of security stems from the mind of an individual who knows that he has done his very best with what was properly his own. Such security is fed by one's respect for the rights of others to life and property, a respect upon which is based one's own claim to those rights.

The same time-weathered code of ethics which advocates honoring one's father and mother recommends respect for the life and livelihood—the private property—of others. To violate any part of that code destroys the meaning of the rest of it. Society cannot enforce a law which guarantees security to the aged by denying the producer the right to the product of his own efforts. The best that society can do is to give the individual a chance to honor and respect his elders. This means allowing the individual his choice concerning the use to be made of his own life and his own productive efforts. It is possible for an individual to honor and respect others who are tolerant of his freedom to choose. But rare indeed is the individual who can extract love and honor from others by compulsory means!

Such things as love, respect, honor, and justice in the relationships between persons are measurable and meaningful only to the extent that individuals voluntarily reject an opportunity to dislike, disrespect, dishonor, or deal unjustly with others. And old-age security also falls into that category. Since a weak person cannot force a strong person to help him, it would seem wise to put the appeal on some basis other than coercion. This means retrieving the responsibility for old-age security from the hands of government.

QUESTIONS AND STUDY SUGGESTIONS

1. What basic differences does the author envision between private and social insurance? Why does he hold that private insurance is a "better buy" than public insurance for those now in the labor force?
2. According to the author, why is the social security program a threat to the institution of private property?
3. Which of the two contrasting views of the social security system presented in Readings 59 and 60 conforms more closely with your personal views? Why?

Reading 61

Proposed: A Guaranteed Annual Income

Robert Theobald

The guaranteed annual income (GAI) has been one of the most contro-versial proposals of the decade. Robert Theobald was one of the earliest proponents of the GAI. The essence of his position is that rapid techno-logical progress, as reflected in automation or cybernation, will result in a sharp curtailment of jobs. But automation will also give rise to economic abundance. These two facts make it essential that society create some means of providing income unrelated to work; that is, the "job-income link" must be broken. Theobald proposes the GAI as an "absolute con-stitutional right" and suggests that it be implemented through the existing personal income tax. He contends that the GAI is a desirable substitute for the "mosaic of measures" which now constitute our welfare system.

The evidence is overwhelming. The United States and the other rich countries will shortly have the technological capability to install a productive system based primarily on *machine* power and *machine* skills within the next two decades; market forces will compel both gov-ernment and business to use cybernated equip-ment. Since the beginning of the industrial revolution we have witnessed a growing re-placement of manpower by machine power, but man's skills were still essential to the utilization of machine power. The coming replacement of man's skills by the machine's skills will destroy many jobs and render useless the work experi-ence of vast numbers now employed. The pos-sibility of obtaining employment in one of the restricted number of new fields will depend to a very large extent on the level of skill and education of the job applicant. It follows that the decline in job opportunities will be most severe for those who perform repetitive tasks and whose work can most easily be done by machines. This conclusion implies the *com-plete* breakdown of our present socioeconomic system, which depends on the ability to pro-vide jobs for all who require them. The resul-ting situation is paradoxical. We are going to be able to produce more goods than ever be-fore and we therefore have the ability to pro-vide a standard of living compatible with the maintenance of human dignity for everybody. However, because we still believe that the in-come levels of the vast majority of the popula-tion should depend on their ability to continue working, over 20 percent of the American population is exiled from the abundant econ-omy and this percentage will grow, rather than decline, in coming years.

The meaning of the evidence is clear: our existing socioeconomic system is outmoded by abundance. A collective judgment must now be made on the issue of whether or not we are willing simply to await a disastrous demonstra-tion of the correctness of the evidence.

BREAKING THE JOB-INCOME LINK

What practical steps need to be taken in order to reap the benefits of the scientific and tech-nological revolution rather than its destructive growths? It is the attempt to keep the economy growing fast enough to provide jobs for all that harnesses man to the juggernaut of scientific and technological change and that keeps us living within "a whirling-dervish economy dependent on compulsive consumption." *This book proposes the establishment of new principles specifically designed to break the link between jobs and income. Implementation of these principles must necessarily be carried out by the government as the sole body concerned with every member of society and with the adequate functioning of the total socioeconomic system.* W. H. Ferry has enlarged on the necessity for "due-income" principles:

Abundance may compel social justice as conscience never has. The liberated margin [those unable to find work] will have to get "what is its due." This means developing a basis of distribution of income which is not tied to work as a measure. For decisions about "dueness" will have to be made without economic criteria; at least without the criterion of what members of the liberated margin are worth in the employment market, for there is no such market for them.

In order to ensure that government concern with the total socioeconomic system would not outweigh its responsibility to every member of society, a due-income from government should be given as an *absolute constitutional right,* for unless this is guaranteed the government would have the possibility of developing the most extreme form of tyranny imaginable. During the process of implementation of the due-income principles, the number of people obtaining the totality of their living expenses from the government would increase rapidly; if the right to these incomes could be withdrawn under *any* circumstances, government would have the power to deprive the individual not only of the pursuit of happiness but also of liberty and even, in effect, of life itself. This *absolute* right to a due-income would be essentially a new principle in jurisprudence. Most present constitutional rights can be curtailed when the over-all good of society is held to require this; however, the right of an individual to a due-income could not, in itself, endanger the state.

It is clear that any attempt to break the stranglehold of the job-income link will have to be made with the interests of both the individual and society kept firmly in mind. There is now a growing awareness that in recent years the interest of the individual has been subordinated to the drives of the economy, and that this subordination is withdrawing the values of freedom and human dignity from the lives of a significant proportion of the American population.

BASIC ECONOMIC SECURITY

The need is clear: the principle of an *economic floor* under each individual must be established. This principle would apply equally to every member of society and carry with it no connotation of personal inadequacy or implication that an undeserved income was being received from an overgenerous government. On the contrary, the implication would clearly be one of responsibility by the total society for ensuring that no member of the society lived in a manner incompatible with the standards acceptable to his fellow men merely because he lacked purchasing power. In this respect his position as a member of society would be secure; such a principle should therefore be called *Basic Economic Security* (BES).

Basic Economic Security can be best regarded as an extension of the present Social Security system to a world in which conventional job availability will steadily decline.

We will need to adopt the concept of an absolute constitutional right to an income. This would guarantee to every citizen of the United States, and to every person who has resided within the United States for a period of five consecutive years, the right to an income from the federal government sufficient to enable him to live with dignity. No government agency, judicial body, or other organization whatsoever should have the power to suspend or limit any payments assured by these guarantees.

BES IN OPERATION

We can first examine how entitlements to BES might be established. One of the fundamental principles of the present United States tax system is the "exemption" of part of an individual's income from taxation. At its inception, this exemption ensured that taxes would not be paid on that portion of income required to provide a reasonable standard of living. However, the government lost sight of this original aim when increasing the tax load to pay for World War II, and the value of the exemption has been *further* reduced since the end of World

War II by the effects of inflation. The original aim of the federal tax exemption should be restored and exemptions should be raised immediately to a level which would guarantee an untaxed income adequate for minimum subsistence. Those whose incomes from earnings or from capital did not reach this level would then be entitled to receive federal government payments sufficient to raise their incomes to this level and ensure their Basic Economic Security.

At what levels should these BES entitlements be set initially? Two factors must be taken into account in making this decision: first, the necessity of providing an income adequate for minimum subsistence for everybody; and second, the necessity to prevent the overburdening of the administrative operation at the beginning of the scheme. The full economic implications of any particular level of BES entitlements would probably have to be worked through on computers, but it might be expected that a level of $1,000 a year for every adult and $600 for every child would in fact be feasible levels to use as a starting point for calculations.

So long as entitlements are only adequate to allow minimum subsistence, it seems appropriate that the exemption pattern should be *very* simple and probably this split between adults and children would be sufficient. When incomes were raised to a level adequate to allow human dignity, the question of introducing a declining level of exemptions for families with more than two or three children would have to be seriously considered. Indeed, there would have to be detailed examination, at this time, of the degree of complexity that would be desirable in the pattern of exemptions; for the monetary cost of supporting a six-year-old child is very different from that of a fourteen-year-old, while the cost of living varies widely from place to place. On the other hand, the amount of government verification necessary would increase if the pattern of exemptions were made more complex.

REPLACING SOCIAL SECURITY

BES would be very simple to operate compared to the present mosaic of measures—Social Security, unemployment compensation, welfare, "stamp plans," subsidies to housing—which have been introduced at various times in the past to meet the same goal. Payments under BES would progressively take the place of these schemes. Recalculations of BES entitlement, based on the individual's total income record of the year, would be made annually; the entitlement payments would be made weekly. Although this simplicity of operation is attractice, it nevertheless appears necessary to add one complication, which is probably required both to secure equity in the early stages of the scheme and also to encourage acceptance. Although soon after the introduction of the plan, many recipients of BES would come to depend on BES payments for their total income, others would continue to receive private income from their market-supported work or would have some interest payments on their savings. (We will use "private income" to cover both income received from a conventional market-supported job and income received from interest on savings throughout this discussion.) In calculating BES payments, the amount of this private income should not simply be deducted from the BES entitlement so that those with private income and those without receive the same total income. Instead, those with private income should be entitled to additional payments in the form of a premium, thus raising the level of their total entitlement. The size of the premium could only be determined after extensive study—a figure of 10 percent is here adopted for purpose of discussion. Thus any family (or individual) with some private income of their own would not only receive payments to make up the difference between their private income and their regular entitlement under BES, but also a premium of 10 percent of the value of their private income.

To take an example, let us examine the case of a man with a wife and two children. The family's exemptions of $1,000 for each adult and $600 for each child add up to a BES entitlement of $3,200. If the family received no private income of their own, their total income would simply be the $3,200 from BES. However, if they received private income amounting to $2,000 during the year they would have a total income of $3,400—$2,000 of private income, $1,200 of makeup payments to reach the BES entitlement of $3,200, *plus* $200 accruing to them as a 10 percent premium on their private income of $2,000.

QUESTIONS AND STUDY SUGGESTIONS

1. Discuss and explain: "Abundance may compel social justice as conscience never has."
2. Why does the author advocate the guaranteed annual income *as an absolute constitutional right?*
3. Explain how the GAI might be administered through the Federal personal income tax. Do you favor the GAI as a substitute for our existing social welfare programs?

Reading 62

Income Without Work

Henry Hazlitt

Reading 62 is a critique of the guaranteed annual income proposal. Henry Hazlitt questions the basic assumption that technological progress will give rise simultaneously to growing unemployment and economic abundance. The author argues that an income guarantee would seriously undermine incentives to work and thereby threaten the growth of total output. Furthermore, we should expect the actual cost of the GAI to be substantially greater than that predicted by its proponents. This is so for two reasons. On the one hand, many low-income workers may be induced by the GAI to quit work, and the cost to society will be a gross national product which is less than it would be otherwise. On the other hand, Hazlitt feels it is highly unlikely that existing welfare programs will actually be dismantled if an income guarantee is adopted; there will be no cost saving as a result of "phasing out" our existing social security programs.

The fears of permanent unemployment as a result of technological progress are as old as the Industrial Revolution in the late eighteenth and early nineteenth century. They have been constantly reiterated in the last thirty-five years and as often completely refuted. It is sufficient to point out here that not only has the average unemployment of slightly less than 5 percent in the last twenty years not been growing, and that two-thirds of the jobless have usually remained so for periods of not more than ten weeks, but that the total volume of *employment* in the United States has reached a new high record in nearly every one of these years.

From Henry Hazlitt, "Income without Work," **The Freeman,** July, 1986, pp. 20–36. Reprinted by permission.

Even if it were true, as the authors of the guaranteed income proposal contend, that the American free enterprise system will soon become so productive that more than anybody really wants can be produced in half the time as now, why would that mean the disappearance of jobs? And how could that justify half the population's, say, being forced to work forty hours a week to support the other half in complete idleness? Why couldn't everybody work only in the mornings? Or half in the mornings and the other half in the afternoons at the same machines? Or why could not some people come in on Mondays, others on Tuesdays, and so on? It is difficult to understand the logic or the sense of fairness of those who contend that as soon as there is less to be done some people must be supported in idleness by all the rest.

"AN ABSOLUTE RIGHT"

But that is precisely the contention of the advocates of the guaranteed annual income. These handout incomes are to be given as "an absolute constitutional right," and not to be withheld "under *any* circumstances." This means that the recipients are to continue to get this income not only if they absolutely refuse to seek or take a job, but if they throw the handout money away at the races, or spend it on prostitutes, on whiskey, cigarettes, marijuana, heroin, or what not.

UNREALISTIC COST ESTIMATES

How much would a guaranteed-income program cost the taxpayers? This would depend, of course, on how big an income was being guaranteed.

The following estimates of the cost to the taxpayers of different guarantees have been made:

For a "minimum maintenance" level of $3,000 a year: total cost, $11 billion a year.

For an "economy" level of $4,000: $23 billion a year.

For a "modest-but-adequate" level of $5,000: $38 billion a year.

These figures are huge, yet they are clearly an underestimate. For the calculations take it for granted that those who could get government checks of $3,000 to $5,000 a year, as an absolute guarantee, without conditions, would continue to go on earning just as much as before.

Who is, in fact, going to take the smelly jobs, or any low-paid job, once the guaranteed income program is in effect? Suppose, as a married man with two children, your present income from some nasty and irregular work is $2,500 a year. Comes the income guarantee, and you get a check in the mail from the government for $630. This is accompanied by a letter telling you that you are entitled as a matter of unconditional right to the poverty-line income of $3,130, and this $630 is for the difference between that and your earned income of $2,500. You are happy—for just a day. Then it occurs to you that you are a fool to go on working at your nasty job or series of odd jobs for $2,500 when you can stop work entirely and get the full $3,130 from the government.

So the government would, in fact, have to pay out a tremendous sum. In addition, it would create idleness on a huge scale. To predict this result is not to take a cynical view, but merely to recognize realities. The beneficiaries of the guaranteed income would merely be acting sensibly from their own point of view. But the result would be that the fifth of the population now judged to be below the poverty line would stop producing even most of the necessary goods and services it is producing now. The unpleasant jobs would not get done. There would be less total production, or total real income, to be shared by everybody.

SOMEONE MUST PAY

If "*everybody* should receive a guaranteed income as a matter of right," who is to pay him that income? On this point the advocates of the guaranteed income are either beautifully vague or completely silent. The money, they tell us, will be paid by the "government" or by the "State." "The State would acknowledge the duty to maintain the individual."

The state is a shadowy entity that apparently gets its money out of some fourth dimension. The truth is, of course, that the government has nothing to give to anybody that it doesn't first take from someone else. The whole guaranteed-income proposal is a perfect modern example of the shrewd observation of the French economist, Bastiat, more than a century ago: "The State is the great fiction by which everybody tries to live at the expense of everybody else."

None of the guaranteed-income advocates explicitly recognizes that real "income" is not paper money that can be printed at will but goods and services, and that somebody has to produce these goods and services by hard work. The proposition of the guaranteed-income advocates, in plain words, is that the people who work must be taxed to support not only the people who can't work but the people who won't work. The workers are to be forced to give up part of the goods and services they have created and turn them over to the people who haven't created them or flatly refuse to create them.

We cannot break the link between jobs and income. True income is not money, but the goods and services that a money will buy. These goods and services have to be produced. They can only be produced by work, by jobs. We may, of course, break the link between the job and the income *of a particular person,* say Paul, by giving him an income whether he consents to take a job or not. But we can do this only by seizing part of the income of some other person, say Peter, from *his* job. To believe we can break the link between jobs and income is to believe we can break the link between production and consumption. Goods have to be produced by somebody before they can be consumed by anybody.

OLD SUBSIDIES NEVER DIE

One of the main selling arguments of the guaranteed-income advocates is that its net cost to the taxpayers would not be as great as might appear at first sight because it would be a *substitute* for the present "mosaic" or "rag bag" of measures designed to meet the same goal—social security, unemployment compensation, medicare, direct relief, free school lunches, stamp plans, farm subsidies, housing subsidies, rent subsidies, and all the rest.

Neither the record of the past nor a knowledge of political realities supports such an expectation. One of the main selling arguments in the middle 1930s, first for unemployment insurance and later for social security, was that these programs would take the place and eliminate the need for the various relief programs and payments then in existence. But in the last thirty years these programs have continued to grow year by year with only minor interruptions.

So not only may we expect that the guaranteed income would be thrown on top of all existing welfare payments (we can expect a tremendous outcry against discontinuing any of them), but that demands would arise for constant enlargement of the guaranteed amount.

INCENTIVES UNDERMINED

We have seen how the guaranteed-income plan, if adopted in the form that its advocates propose, would lead to wholesale idleness and pauperization among nearly all those earning less than the minimum guarantee, and among many earning just a little more. But it would also undermine the incentives of those much further up in the income scale. For they would not only be deprived of the benefits that they saw millions of others getting. It is *they* who would be expected to *pay* these benefits, through the imposition upon them of far more burdensome income taxes than they were already paying. If these taxes were steeply progressive in proportion to income, as is probable, they would discourage long hours and unusual effort.

We know that higher income-tax rates, contrary to popular belief, just don't raise revenue. In the current 1966 fiscal year, individual income taxes are estimated to be raising $51.4 billion (out of total revenues of $128 billion). Yet the tax rates in excess of 50 percent have been bringing in only about $250 million a year—less than 1 percent of total income-tax revenues and not enough to run even the present government for a full day. (In other words, if all the personal income-tax rates above 50 percent were reduced to that level, the loss in revenue would be only about $250 million.) If these rates above 50 percent were raised further, it is more probable that they would raise less revenue than more. Therefore, it is the income-tax rates on the lower and middle incomes that would have to be raised most, for the simple reason that 75 percent of the personal income of the country is earned by people with less than $15,000 gross incomes.

POVERTY FOR ALL

It is certain that high income-tax rates discourage and reduce the earning of income, and therefore the total production of wealth, to some extent. Suppose, for illustration, we begin with the extreme proposal that we equalize everybody's income by taxing away all income in excess of the average in order to pay it over to those with incomes below the average. (The guaranteed-income proposal isn't too far away from that!)

Let us say that the present per capita average yearly income is about $2,800. Then everybody who was getting less than that (and would get just that whether he worked or not) would, of course, as with the guaranteed-income proposal, not need to work productively at all. And no one who was earning more than $2,800 would find it worth while to continue to earn the excess, because it would be seized from him in any case. More, it would soon occur to him that it wasn't worth while earning even the $2,800, for it would be given to him in any case; and his income would be that whether he worked or not. So if everybody acted under an income equalization program merely in the way that seemed most rational in his own isolated interest, none of us would work and all of us would starve. We might each get $2,800 cash (if someone could be found to continue to run the printing machines just for the fun of it), but there would be nothing to buy with it.

THE CURE IS PRODUCTION

One of the worst features of all the plans for sharing the wealth and equalizing or guaran-

teeing incomes is that they lose sight of the conditions and institutions that are necessary to create wealth and income in the first place. They take for granted the existing size of the economic pie; and in their impatient effort to see that it is sliced more equally they overlook the forces that have not only created the pie in the first place but have been baking a larger one year by year. Economic progress and justice do not consist in beautifully equalized destitution, but in the constant creation of more and more goods and services, of more and more wealth and income to be shared.

The only real cure for poverty is production.

The way to maximize production is to maximize the incentives to production. And the way to do that, as the modern world has discovered, is through the system known as capitalism—the system of private property, free markets, and free enterprise. This system maximizes production because it allows a man freedom in the choice of his occupation, freedom in his choice of those for whom he works or who work for him, freedom in the choice of those with whom he associates and cooperates, and, above all, freedom to earn and to keep the fruits of his labor. In the capitalist system each of us, with whatever exceptions, tends in the long run to get what he creates or helps to create. When each of us recognizes that his reward depends on his own efforts and output, and tends to be proportionate to his output, then each has the maximum incentive to maximize his effort and output.

QUESTIONS AND STUDY SUGGESTIONS

1. Why does the author contend that the costs of a guaranteed annual income will be substantially in excess of out-of-pocket costs?

2. In Reading 61 Robert Theobald contends that the link between jobs and income must be broken. On what grounds does Henry Hazlitt argue that the job-income link cannot be broken? Who is right?

3. Analyze: "The only real cure for poverty is production."

Reading 63

The Theory of Social Balance

John Kenneth Galbraith, Professor of Economics, Harvard University

One of the most fundamental and far-reaching domestic issues now debated by economists is that of social balance, the question of whether the economy's scarce resources are properly allocated among private and social goods. In this reading John Kenneth Galbraith contends that our society is plagued by a social imbalance problem. Specifically, Americans spend too large a part of the total income on private goods and an insufficient amount on public goods. The causes of this misallocation of resources are manifold: (1) the demand for private goods is stimulated by advertising and emulation—the demand for public goods is not; (2) the "truce on equality," that is, the unwillingness of proponents of both greater and lesser income inequality to reopen their conflict by levying new taxes for the financing of additional public goods; and (3) inflation, which has the effect of reallocating labor resources from the public to the private sector of the economy. All these causal factors are buttressed by the widely held notion that government spending in and of itself is bad. The total result, Galbraith concludes, is a basic misallocation of resources which results in relative affluence in the private sector and relative poverty in the public sector of the economy.

The final problem of the productive society is what it produces. This manifests itself in an implacable tendency to provide an opulent supply of some things and a niggardly yield of others. This disparity carries to the point where it is a cause of social discomfort and social unhealth. The line which divides our area of wealth from our area of poverty is roughly that which divides privately produced and marketed goods and services from publicly rendered services. Our wealth in the first is not only in startling contrast with the meagerness of the latter, but our wealth in privately produced goods is, to a marked degree, the cause of crisis in the supply of public services. For we have failed to see the importance, indeed the urgent need, of maintaining a balance between the two.

PRIVATE ABUNDANCE, PUBLIC POVERTY

This disparity between our flow of private and public goods and services is no matter of subjective judgment. On the contrary, it is the source of the most extensive comment which only stops short of the direct contrast being made here. In the years following World War II, the papers of any major city—those of New York were an excellent example—told daily of the shortages and shortcomings in the elementary municipal and metropolitan services. The schools were old and overcrowded. The police force was under strength and underpaid. The parks and playgrounds were insufficient. Streets and empty lots were filthy, and the sanitation staff was underequipped and in need of men. Access to the city by those who work there

From John K. Galbraith, **The Affluent Society**, Houghton Mifflin Company, Boston, 1958, pp. 251–256, 258–262, 264–269. Reprinted by permission.

was uncertain and painful and becoming more so. Internal transportation was overcrowded, unhealthful, and dirty. So was the air. Parking on the streets had to be prohibited, and there was no space elsewhere. These deficiencies were not in new and novel services but in old and established ones. Cities have long swept their streets, helped their people move around, educated them, kept order, and provided horse rails for vehicles which sought to pause. That their residents should have a nontoxic supply of air suggests no revolutionary dalliance with socialism.

The discussion of this public poverty competed, on the whole successfully, with the stories of ever-increasing opulence in privately produced goods. The Gross National Product was rising. So were retail sales. So was personal income. Labor productivity had also advanced. The automobiles that would not be parked were being produced at an expanded rate. The children, though without schools, subject in the playgrounds to the affectionate interest of adults with odd tastes, and disposed to increasingly imaginative forms of delinquency, were admirably equipped with television sets. We had difficulty finding storage space for the great surpluses of food despite a national disposition to obesity. Food was grown and packaged under private auspices. The care and refreshment of the mind, in contrast with the stomach, was principally in the public domain. Our colleges and universities were severely overcrowded and underprovided, and the same was true of the mental hospitals.

The contrast was and remains evident not alone to those who read. The family which takes its mauve and cerise, air-conditioned, power-steered, and power-braked automobile out for a tour passes through cities that are badly paved, made hideous by litter, blighted buildings, billboards, and posts for wires that should long since have been put underground. They pass on into a countryside that has been rendered largely invisible by commercial art. (The goods which the latter advertise have an absolute priority in our value system. Such aesthetic considerations as a view of the countryside accordingly come second. On such matters we are consistent.) They picnic on exquisitely packaged food from a portable icebox by a polluted stream and go on to spend the night at a park which is a menace to public health and morals. Just before dozing off on an air

mattress, beneath a nylon tent, amid the stench of decaying refuse, they may reflect vaguely on the curious unevenness of their blessings. Is this, indeed, the American genius?

NATURE OF SOCIAL IMBALANCE

In the production of goods within the private economy it has long been recognized that a tolerably close relationship must be maintained between the production of various kinds of products. The output of steel and oil and machine tools is related to the production of automobiles. Investment in transportation must keep abreast of the output of goods to be transported. The supply of power must be abreast of the growth of industries requiring it. The existence of these relationships—coefficients to the economist—has made possible the construction of the input-output table which shows how changes in the production in one industry will increase or diminish the demands on other industries. To this table, and more especially to its ingenious author, Professor Wassily Leontief, the world is indebted for one of its most important of modern insights into economic relationships. If expansion in one part of the economy were not matched by the requisite expansion in other parts—were the need for balance not respected—then bottlenecks and shortages, speculative hoarding of scarce supplies, and sharply increasing costs would ensue. Fortunately in peacetime the market system operates easily and effectively to maintain this balance, and this together with the existence of stocks and some flexibility in the coefficients as a result of substitution, insures that no serious difficulties will arise. We are reminded of the existence of the problem only by noticing how serious it is for those countries—Poland or, in a somewhat different form, India—which seek to solve the problem by planned measures and with a much smaller supply of resources.

Just as there must be balance in what a community produces, so there must also be balance in what the community consumes. An increase in the use of one product creates, ineluctably, a requirement for others. If we are to consume more automobiles, we must have more gasoline. There must be more insurance as well as more space on which to operate them. Beyond a certain point more and better food appears to mean increased need for medical services. This is the certain result of the increased consumption of tobacco and alcohol. More vacations require more hotels and more fishing rods. And so forth. With rare exceptions—shortages of doctors are an exception which suggests the rule—this balance is also maintained quite effortlessly so far as goods for private sale and consumption are concerned. The price system plus a rounded condition of opulence is again the agency.

NEED FOR PRIVATE-PUBLIC BALANCE

However, the relationships we are here discussing are not confined to the private economy. They operate comprehensively over the whole span of private and public services. As surely as an increase in the output of autmobiles puts new demands on the steel industry so, also, it places new demands on public services. Similarly, every increase in the consumption of private goods will normally mean some facilitating or protective step by the state. In all cases if these services are not forthcoming, the consequences will be in some degree ill. It will be convenient to have a term which suggests a satisfactory relationship between the supply of privately produced goods and services and those of the state, and we may call it social balance.

The problem of social balance is ubiquitous, and frequently it is obtrusive. As noted, an increase in the consumption of automobiles requires a facilitating supply of streets, highways, traffic control, and parking space. The protective services of the police and the highway patrols must also be available, as must those of the hospitals. Although the need for balance here is extraordinarily clear, our use of privately produced vehicles has, on occasion, got far out of line with the supply of the related public services. The result has been hideous road congestion, an annual massacre of impressive proportions, and chronic colitis in the cities. As on the ground, so also in the air. Planes collide with disquieting consequences for those within when the public provision for air traffic control fails to keep pace with private use of the airways.

But the auto and the airplane, versus the space to use them, are merely an exceptionally visible example of a requirement that is pervasive. The more goods people procure, the more packages they discard and the more trash that must be carried away. If the appropriate sanitation services are not provided, the counterpart of increasing opulence will be deepening filth. The greater the wealth the thicker will be the dirt. This indubitably describes a tendency of our time. As more goods are produced and owned, the greater are the opportunities for fraud and the more property that must be protected. If the provision of public law enforcement services do not keep pace, the counterpart of increased well-being will, we may be certain, be increased crime.

The city of Los Angeles, in modern times, is a near-classic study in the problem of social balance. Magnificently efficient factories and oil refineries, a lavish supply of automobiles, a vast consumption of handsomely packaged products, coupled with the absence of a municipal trash collection service which forced the use of home incinerators, made the air nearly unbreathable for an appreciable part of each year. Air pollution could be controlled only by a complex and highly developed set of public services—by better knowledge stemming from more research, better policing, a municipal trash collection service, and possibly the assertion of the priority of clean air over the production of goods. These were long in coming. The agony of a city without usable air was the result.

POSITIVE CASE FOR SOCIAL BALANCE

The case for social balance has, so far, been put negatively. Failure to keep public services in minimal relation to private production and use of goods is a cause of social disorder or impairs economic performance. The matter may now be put affirmatively. By failing to exploit the opportunity to expand public production we are missing opportunities for enjoyment which otherwise we might have had. Presumably a community can be as well rewarded by buying better schools or better parks as by buying bigger automobiles. By concentrating on the latter rather than the former it is failing to maximize its satisfactions. As with schools in the community, so with public services over the country at large. It is scarcely sensible that we should satisfy our wants in private goods with reckless abundance, while in the case of public goods, on the evidence of the eye, we practice extreme self-denial. So, far from systematically exploiting the opportunities to derive use and pleasure from these services, we do not supply what would keep us out of trouble.

The conventional wisdom holds that the community, large or small, makes a decision as to how much it will devote to its public services. This decision is arrived at by democratic process. Subject to the imperfections and uncertainties of democracy, people decide how much of their private income and goods they will surrender in order to have public services of which they are in greater need. Thus there is a balance, however rough, in the enjoyments to be had from private goods and services and those rendered by public authority.

THE DEPENDENCE EFFECT

It will be obvious, however, that this view depends on the notion of independently determined consumer wants. In such a world one could with some reason defend the doctrine that the consumer, as a voter, makes an independent choice between public and private goods. But given the dependence effect—given that consumer wants are created by the process by which they are satisfied—the consumer makes no such choice. He is subject to the forces of advertising and emulation by which production creates its own demand. Advertising operates exclusively, and emulation mainly, on behalf of privately produced goods and services. Since management and emulative effects operate on behalf of private production, public services will have an inherent tendency to lag behind. Automobile demand which is expensively synthesized will inevitably have a much larger claim on income than parks or public health or even roads where no such influence operates. The engines of mass communication, in their highest state of development, assail the eyes and ears of the community on behalf of more beer but not of more schools. Even in the conventional wisdom it will scarcely be contended that this leads to an equal choice between the two.

So much for the influences which operate on the decision between public and private production. The calm decision between public and private consumption pictured by the conventional wisdom is, in fact, a remarkable example of the error which arises from viewing social behavior out of context. The inherent tendency will always be for public services to fall behind private production. We have here the first of the causes of social imbalance.

SOCIAL IMBALANCE AND TRUCE ON INEQUALITY

Social balance is also the victim of two further features of our society—the truce on inequality and the tendency to inflation. Since these are now part of our context, their effect comes quickly into view.

With rare exceptions such as the post office, public services do not carry a price ticket to be paid for by the individual user. By their nature they must, ordinarily, be available to all. As a result, when they are improved or new services are initiated, there is the ancient and troublesome question of who is to pay. This, in turn, provokes to life the collateral but irrelevant debate over inequality. As with the use of taxation as an instrument of fiscal policy, the truce on inequality is broken. Liberals are obliged to argue that the services be paid for by progressive taxation which will reduce inequality. Committed as they are to the urgency of goods they must oppose sales and excise taxes. Conservatives rally to the defense of inequality—although without ever quite committing themselves in such uncouth terms—and oppose the use of income taxes. They, in effect, oppose the expenditure not on the merits of the service but on the demerits of the tax system. Since the debate over inequality cannot be resolved, the money is frequently not appropriated and the service not performed. It is a casualty of the economic goals of both liberals and conservatives for both of whom the questions of social balance are subordinate to those of production and, when it is evoked, of inequality.

SOCIAL IMBALANCE AND INFLATION

Finally, social imbalance is the natural offspring of persistent inflation. Inflation by its nature strikes different individuals and groups with highly discriminatory effect. The most nearly unrelieved victims, apart from those living on pensions or other fixed provision for personal security, are those who work for the state. In the private economy the firm which sells goods has, in general, an immediate accommodation to the inflationary movement. Its price increases are the inflation. The incomes of its owners and proprietors are automatically accommodated to the upward movement. To the extent that wage increases are part of the inflationary process, this is also true of organized industrial workers. Even unorganized white collar workers are in a milieu where prices and incomes are moving up. The adaptation of their incomes, if less rapid than that of the industrial workers, is still reasonably prompt.

The position of the public employee is at the other extreme. His pay scales are highly formalized, and traditionally they have been subject to revision only at lengthy intervals. In states and localities inflation does not automatically bring added revenues to pay higher salaries and incomes. Pay revision for all public workers is subject to the temptation to wait and see if the inflation isn't coming to an end. There will be some fear—this seems to have been more of a factor in England than in the United States—that advances in public wages will set a bad example for private employers and unions.

Inflation means that employment is pressing on the labor supply and that private wage and salary incomes are rising. Thus the opportunities for moving from public to private employment are especially favorable. Public employment, moreover, once had as a principal attraction a high measure of social security. Industrial workers were subject to the formidable threat of unemployment during depression. Public employees were comparatively secure, and this security was worth an adverse salary differential. But with improving economic security in general this advantage has diminished. Private employment thus has come to provide better protection against inflation and little worse protection against other hazards. Though the dedicated may stay in public posts, the alert go.

The deterioration of the public services in the years of inflation has not gone unremarked. However, there has been a strong tendency to regard it as an adventitious misfortune—something which, like a nasty shower at a picnic, happened to blight a generally good time. Salaries were allowed to lag, which was a pity. This is a very inadequate view. Discrimination against the public services is an organic feature of inflation. Nothing so weakens government as persistent inflation. The public administration of France for many years, of Italy until recent times, and of other European and numerous South American countries have been deeply sapped and eroded by the effects of long-continued inflation. Social imbalance reflects itself in inability to enforce laws, including significantly those which protect and advance basic social justice, and in failure to maintain and improve essential services. One outgrowth of the resulting imbalance has been frustration and pervasive discontent. Over much of the world there is a rough and not entirely accidental correlation between the strength of indigenous communist parties or the frequency of revolutions and the persistence of inflation.

POSTWAR ATTACK ON PUBLIC SERVICES

A feature of the years immediately following World War II was a remarkable attack on the notion of expanding and improving public services. During the depression years such services had been elaborated and improved partly in order to fill some small part of the vacuum left by the shrinkage of private production. During the war years the role of government was vastly expanded. After that came the reaction. Much of it, unquestionably, was motivated by a desire to rehabilitate the prestige of private production and therewith of producers. No doubt some who joined the attack hoped, at least tacitly, that it might be possible to sidestep the truce on taxation vis-á-vis equality by having less taxation of all kinds. For a time the notion that our public services had somehow become inflated and excessive was all but axiomatic. Even liberal politicians did not seriously protest. They found it necessary to aver that they were in favor of public economy too.

In this discussion a certain mystique was attributed to the satisfaction of privately supplied wants. A community decision to have a new school means that the individual surrenders the necessary amount, willy-nilly, in his taxes. But if he is left with that income, he is a free man. He can decide between a better car or a television set. This was advanced with some solemnity as an argument for the TV set. The difficulty is that this argument leaves the community with no way of preferring the school. All private wants, where the individual can choose, are inherently superior to all public desires which must be paid for by taxation and with an inevitable component of compulsion.

The cost of public services was also held to be a desolating burden on private production, although this was at a time when the private production was burgeoning. Urgent warnings were issued of the unfavorable effects of taxation on investment—"I don't know of a surer way of killing off the incentive to invest than by imposing taxes which are regarded by people as punitive." This was at a time when the inflationary effect of a very high level of investment was causing concern. The same individuals who were warning about the inimical effects of taxes were strongly advocating a monetary policy designed to reduce investment. However, an understanding of our economic discourse requires an appreciation of one of its basic rules: men of high position are allowed, by a special act of grace, to accommodate their reasoning to the answer they need. Logic is only required in those of lesser rank.

Finally it was argued, with no little vigor, that expanding government posed a grave threat to individual liberties. "Where distinction and rank is achieved almost exclusively by becoming a civil servant of the state . . . it is too much to expect that many will long prefer freedom to security."

With time this attack on public services has somewhat subsided. The disorder associated with social imbalance has become visible even if the need for balance between private and public services is still imperfectly appreciated.

Freedom also seemed to be surviving. Per-haps it was realized that all organized activity requires concessions by the individual to the group. This is true of the policeman who joins the police force, the teacher who gets a job at the high school, and the executive who makes his way up the hierarchy of Du Pont. If there are differences between public and private organization, they are of kind rather than of degree. As this is written the pendulum has in fact swung back. Our liberties are now menaced by the conformity exacted by the large corporation and its impulse to create, for its own purposes, the organization man. This danger we may also survive.

Nonetheless, the postwar onslaught on the public services left a lasting imprint. To suggest that we canvass our public wants to see where happiness can be improved by more and better services has a sharply radical tone. Even public services to avoid disorder must be defended. By contrast the man who devises a nostrum for a nonexistent need and then successfully promotes both remains one of nature's noblemen.

QUESTIONS AND STUDY SUGGESTIONS

1. What is social imbalance? Why is it an economic problem? Discuss the various causes of social imbalance.
2. Why is it argued that the process of political voting fails to achieve even a rough balance between private- and social-goods production?
3. Why is the "debate over inequality" an obstacle to social balance?
4. Explain: "Discrimination against the public services is an organic feature of inflation."

Social Imbalance: A False Issue?

Henry C. Wallich, Professor of Economics, Yale University

Henry C. Wallich takes issue with Galbraith's social imbalance view in this reading. Wallich's basic contention is that, even though one may be irritated with the gadgetry and trivia of private consumption, it does not follow that more public spending is the only or best alternative. "Better private spending is just as much a possibility." According to Wallich, "to talk in terms of 'public vs. private' is to confuse the issue." Indeed, many of our newer wants—provisions for old age, higher education, and medical care—lie in the twilight zone between the public and private sectors and are not exclusively social goods. Furthermore, the rate of increase in spending for many of society's "new needs," for example, research and social security, has increased dramatically in recent years. And, finally, there exists a "balance-of-forces" effect in the public sector which makes it easier to negotiate across-the-board increases in public spending than to realize selective increases. The net result is that the expansion of "low priority" public programs must be accepted to achieve the desired expansion in "high priority" public programs; in short, the public dollar is subject to a substantial "discount."

Public needs are underfinanced while private tastes are overindulged—that is the proposition.

The two parts of the proposition seem neatly to complement each other—too much of one, therefore too little of the other. In fact they don't. It is one thing to be irritated by certain manifestations of our contemporary civilization —the gadgets, the chrome, the tailfins, and the activities that go with them. It is quite another —and something of a *non sequitur*—to conclude from this that the only alternative to foolish private spending is public spending. Better private spending is just as much a possibility. My contention here will be that to talk in terms of "public vs. private" is to confuse the issue. More than that, it is to confuse means and ends. The choice between public and private money is primarily a choice of means. The sensible approach for those who are dissatisfied with some of the ends to which private money is being spent, is to specify first what other ends are important and why. Having determined the ends, the next step is to look to the means. That is the order in which I propose to proceed here.

WHAT IS WRONG WITH PRIVATE SPENDING?

One may share the irritation of the new social critics as they look upon some of the fluff and the floss on our standard of living. My personal feelings can be characterized by noting that I have a 1951 car and no TV. The critics may want to bear in mind, however, that not all the money in this country is spent by people for

From Henry C. Wallich, " 'Private vs. Public': Could Kenneth Galbraith Be Wrong?" **Harper's Magazine,** October, 1961, pp. 12, 14, 16, 22, 25. Reprinted by permission.

whom life begins at $25,000. The median family income is $5600. Would these critics of the affluent society want to try living on much less than that? When Galbraith inveighs eloquently against switchblades, narcotics, and other phases of juvenile delinquency, he deserves the support of all right-thinking representatives of what he calls the "conventional wisdom." But are the sources of these aberrations more intimately tied to affluence or to poverty? The exponents of the new social criticism may also want to remember the outcome of that "noble experiment," Prohibition. It should have taught us that it is futile to become our brother's dietitian. I hope that it has also imbued us with wholesome doubt about the moral right of some members of the community to regulate the lives of the rest.

Irritation with the poor judgment of other people who fail to appreciate one's own more advanced tastes is not new. It was a familiar situation during the 1920s. The critics then quoted T. S. Eliot's *The Waste Land*, and some went off to Paris in search of greener cultural pastures. The feeling behind the new social criticism is not dissimilar. Hence one might suppose that the reaction would likewise turn in a cultural direction. One might expect the critics of contemporary materialism to plead for more intensive preoccupation with things of the mind. Some fits and starts in that direction there have been, to be sure. But they have not been in the main stream of the movement. The principal alternative to private materialism that has been offered to us has been public materialism.

SIGNS OF QUALITY

Obviously, the quality of our culture could be greatly improved by public expenditures for education and support of the arts. The sales of good paperbacks and LPs are encouraging signs. But if contemporary materialism is to be leavened by such pursuits, it will be principally because large numbers of individuals make private decisions to that end. Social criticism is constructive if it helps precipitate these decisions. It obstructs a desirable evolution if it suggests that public creature comforts are the only alternative to private.

But while emphasis on nonmaterial ends seems sadly lacking in the new social criticism, the critics are right in pointing out that new material needs also have been carried to the fore by social and economic evolution—even though they mislabel them as public needs. In the good old days, when this was still a nation of farmers, most people had no serious retirement worries, there was no industrial unemployment problem, good jobs could be had without a college degree, most diseases were still incurable—in short, social security, education, and health care found primitive and natural solutions within the family and among the resources of the neighborhood. Today, these solutions are neither adequate nor usually even possible.

Meanwhile mounting wealth and advancing technology have brought within reach the means of meeting these needs. We can afford to live better in every way—more creature comforts, more leisure, more attention to matters of the mind and the spirit. At the same time we can take better care of retirement, of unemployment, of illness, of education, of the possibilities opened by research, than ever before.

There are indeed new needs. The citizen-taxpayer has his choice of meeting them, as well as all his other goods or services he wants privately, for cash or credit. Or he can buy them from the government, for taxes.

The nation as a whole pays taxes to buy public services as it pays grocery bills to buy groceries. The tax burden may be heavier for some individuals than for others. But the nation as a whole has no more reason to complain about the "burden" of taxes than about the "burden" of grocery bills—and no more reason to hope for relief.

Of the two stores, the private store today still is much the bigger. The public store is smaller, but it is growing faster.

Each store has some exclusive items. The private store sells most of the necessities and all of the luxuries of life, and in most of these has no competition from the government side. The public store has some specialities of its own: defense, public order and justice, and numerous local services that the private organization has not found profitable. But there is a wide range of items featured by both stores: provision for old age, health services, education, housing, development of natural resources.

THE NEW NEEDS

The bulk of the new needs are in this competitive area. The fashionable notion is to claim them all for the public store and to label them public needs. The statistics say otherwise. They say in fact two things. First, the supply of this group of goods and services has expanded very rapidly in recent years; and second, they are being offered, in varying degrees, both by the private and the public suppliers. Let us run down the list.

Provision for old age is predominantly private. The average American family, realizing that while old age may be a burden, it is the only known way to achieve a long life, takes care of the matter in three ways: (1) by private individual savings—home ownership, savings deposits, securities; (2) by private collective savings—life insurance, corporate pension funds; and (3) by public collective savings through social security. Statisticians report that the two collective forms are advancing faster than the individual. The increases far exceed the rise in the Gross National Product of almost 80 percent (in current prices) over the past ten years; they do not indicate either that these needs are neglected or that they are necessarily public in character.

Education: the bulk of it is public; but a good part, particularly of higher education, is private. Total expenditures for all education have advanced in the last ten years from $9.3 billion to $24.6 billion ($19.3 billion of it public). Education's share in the national income has advanced from 3.8 percent to 5.8 percent. The silly story that we spend more on advertising than on education is a canard, though with its gross of over $10 billion, advertising does take a lot of money.

Health expenditures are still mainly private. At considerable expense, it is now possible to live longer and be sick less frequently or at least less dangerously. In the past, most people paid their own doctors' bills, although health care for the indigent has always been provided by public action or private philanthropy. Since the war, the proliferation of health insurance has given some form of collective but private insurance to three-quarters of our 182 million people. This has greatly reduced pressure for a national health service along British lines. For the aging, whose health-care needs stand in inverse proportion to their capacity to pay or insure, public insurance has finally been initiated and needs to be expanded. The total

annual expenditure on health is estimated at over $25 billion, a little more than on education. Of this, about $6 billion is public.

So much for the allegation that the "new needs" are all public needs. Now for some further statistics on the public store, which is said to have been neglected. Some of them could make an investor in private growth stocks envious. Research expenditures (mainly for defense and atomic energy) have gone from about $1 billion to over $8 billion in the last ten years. Federal grants to the states have advanced from $2.2 billion to $7 billion during the same period. Social-security benefits rose from $1 billion to over $10 billion. All in all, public cash outlays (federal and state) advanced from $61 billion to $134 billion over ten years, 57 percent faster than the GNP.

For those who feel about public spending the way Mark Twain felt about whiskey, these figures may still look slim. (Mark Twain thought that while too much of anything was bad, too much whiskey was barely enough.) To others, the data may suggest that the advocates of more public spending have already had their way. Could their present discontent be the result of not keeping their statistics up-to-date? In one of his recent pamphlets, Arthur M. Schlesinger, Jr. claims that the sum of the many neglects he observes (including defense) could be mended by raising public expenditures by $10 billion to $12 billion. That is well below the increase in public cash outlays that actually did take place in one single fiscal year, from $118.2 billion in 1958 to $132.7 billion in 1959. In the three fiscal years 1957–59, these outlays went up more than $31 billion, though the advance slowed down in 1960. More facts and less indignation might help to attain better perspective.

Some parts of federal, state, and local budgets have expanded less rapidly than those cited—in many cases fortunately. The massive build-up in defense expenditures from the late 'forties to the 'fifties has squeezed other programs. Unfortunately, on the other hand, some programs that both political parties have favored—including aid to education, to depressed areas, for urban renewal—have been delayed unduly by the vicissitudes of politics. But the figures as a whole lend little support to the thesis that politicians don't spend enough, and that the government store is not expanding fast enough.

THE CITIZEN IN THE STORES

The two stores—private and public—work very hard these days to capture the business of the citizen-taxpayer. Here is what he hears as he walks into the private store:

"The principal advantage of this store," the private businessman says, "is that you can shop around and buy exactly what you want. If I don't have it, I'll order it. You, the consumer, are the boss here. To be sure, I'm not in business for charity but for profit. But my profit comes from giving you what you want. And with competition as fierce as it is, you can be sure the profit won't be excessive."

If the proprietor has been to Harvard Business School, he will perhaps remember to add something about the invisible hand which in a free economy causes the self-seeking of competitors to work for the common good. He will also, even without benefit of business school, remember to drop a word about the danger of letting the public store across the street get too big. It might endanger freedom.

As the citizen turns this sales talk over in his mind, several points occur to him. Without denying the broad validity of the argument, he will note that quite often he has been induced to buy things he did not really need, and possibly to neglect other, more serious needs. Snob appeal and built-in obsolescence promoted by expensive advertising don't seem to him to fit in with the notion that the consumer is king. Looking at the brand names and patents and trademarks, he wonders whether most products are produced and priced competitively instead of under monopoly conditions. The invisible hand at times seems to be invisible mainly because it is so deep in his pocket.

Bothered by these doubts, the citizen walks across the street and enters the public store.

"Let me explain to you," says the politician who runs it—with the aid of a horde of hardworking bureaucrats doing the chores. "The principles on which this store is run are known as the political process, and if you happen to be familiar with private merchandising they may seem unusual, but I assure you they work. First of all, almost everything in this store is free. We simply assess our customers a lump sum in the form of taxes. These, however, are based largely on each customer's ability to pay, rather than on what he gets from the store. We have a show of hands from the customers once a year, and the majority decides what merchandise the store is to have in stock. The majority, incidentally, also decides how much everybody, including particularly the minority, is to be assessed for taxes.

"You will observe," the politician continues, "that this store is not run for profit. It is like a co-operative, run for the welfare of the members. I myself, to be sure, am not in politics for charity, but for re-election. But that means that I must be interested in your needs, or you would not vote for me. Moreover, there are some useful things that only I can do, with the help of the political process, and in which you and every citizen have an interest. For instance, everybody ought to go to school. I can make them go. Everybody ought to have old-age insurance. I can make that compulsory too. And because I don't charge the full cost of the service, I can help even up a little the inequalities of life.

"By the way," the politician concludes, "if there is any special little thing you want, I may be able to get it for you, and of course it won't cost you a nickel."

The citizen has some fault to find with the political process too. He notes that there is not even a theoretical claim to the benefits of an invisible hand. Majority rule may produce benefits for the majority, but how about the other 49 percent? Nor is there the discipline of competition, or the need for profits, to test economy of operation. There is no way, in the public store, of adjusting individual costs and benefits. And the promise to get him some small favor, while tempting, worries him, because he wonders what the politician may have promised to others. The political process, he is led to suspect, may be a little haphazard.

He asks himself how political decisions get to be made. Sometimes, obviously, it is not the majority that really makes a decision, but a small pressure group that is getting away with something. He will remember that—after payments for major national security and public debt interest—the largest single expenditure in the federal budget is for agriculture, and the next for veterans.

THE EXPANDING BELT

Next, the citizen might consider the paralyzing "balance-of-forces" effect that often blocks a desirable reshuffling of expenditures. The allocation of public funds reflects the bargaining power of their sponsors, inside or outside of the government. A classical example was the division of funds that prevailed in the Defense Department during the late 'forties. Army, Navy, and Air Force were to share in total resources in a way that would maximize military potential. By some strange coincidence, maximum potential was always achieved by giving each service the same amount of money. It took the Korean War to break this stalemate.

What is the consequence of the balance-of-forces effect? If the proponents of one kind of expenditure want to get more money for their projects, they must concede an increase also to the advocates of others. More education means more highways, instead of less; more air power means more ground forces. To increase a budget in one direction only is as difficult as letting out one's belt only on one side. The expansion tends to go all around. What this comes down to is that politicians are not very good at setting priorities. Increases in good expenditures are burdened with a political surcharge of less good ones.

The last-ditch survival power of federal programs is a specially illuminating instance of the balance of forces. If a monument were built in Washington in memory of each major federal program that has been discontinued, the appearance of the city would not be greatly altered. In contrast, when the Edsel doesn't sell well, production stops. But the government is still reclaiming land to raise more farm surpluses and training fishermen to enter an occupation that needs subsidies to keep alive. Old federal programs never die, they don't even fade away—they just go on.

The citizen will remember also the ancient and honorable practice of logrolling. The unhappy fate of the Area Development bill illustrates this admirably. As originally proposed, the bill sought to aid a limited number of industrial areas where new jobs were badly needed. It got nowhere in the Congress. Only when it was extended to a large number of areas with less urgent or quite different problems, were enough legislators brought aboard to pass it. Because of the heavy political surcharge with which it had become loaded, the President vetoed the bill. A bill was finally enacted early this year, long after aid should have been brought to the areas that needed it.

Finally, the citizen might discover in some dark corner of his mind a nagging thought:

Any particular government program may be a blessing, but could their cumulative effect be a threat to freedom? He has heard businessmen say this so often that he has almost ceased to pay attention to it. He rather resents businessmen acting the dog in the manger, trying to stop useful things from being done unless they can do them. He is irritated when he hears a man talk about freedom who obviously is thinking about profit. And yet—is there any conclusive rebuttal?

THE CITIZEN'S FAILURES

The citizen would be quite wrong, however, if he blamed the politician for the defects of the political process. The fault lies with the process, or better with the way in which the process, the politician, and the citizen interact. The citizen therefore would do well to examine some of his own reactions and attitudes.

First, when he thinks about taxes, he tends to think of them as a burden instead of as a price he pays for a service. As a body, the nation's taxpayers are like a group of neighbors who decide to establish a fire department. Because none is quite sure how much good it will do him, and because each hopes to benefit from the contribution of the rest, all are prudent in their contributions. In the end they are likely to wind up with a bucket brigade.

But when it comes to accepting benefits, the citizen-taxpayers act like a group of men who sit down at a restaurant table knowing that they will split the check evenly. In this situation everybody orders generously; it adds little to one's own share of the bill, and for the extravagance of his friends he will have to pay anyhow. What happens at the restaurant table explains—though it does not excuse—what happens at the public trough.

Finally, in his reaction to public or free services, the citizen takes a great deal for granted, and seldom thinks of the cost. Public beaches mistreated, unmetered parking space permanently occupied, veterans' adjustment benefits continued without need—as well as abuses of unemployment compensation and public assistance—are some examples. This applies also, of course, to privately offered benefits, under health insurance, for instance. The kindly nurse in the hospital—"Why don't you stay another day, dearie, it won't cost you anything, it's all paid for by Blue Cross"—makes the point.

By removing the link between costs and

benefits, the political process also reduces the citizen's interest in earning money. The citizen works to live. If some of his living comes to him without working, he would be less than rational if he did not respond with a demand for shorter hours. If these public benefits increase his tax burden so that his over-all standard of living remains unchanged, the higher taxes will reduce his work incentive. Why work hard, if much of it is for the government?

THE POLITICAL DOLLAR AT A DISCOUNT

These various defects of the political process add up to an obvious conclusion: the dollar spent by even the most honest and scrupulous of politicians is not always a full-bodied dollar. It often is subject to a discount. It buys less than it should because of the attrition it suffers as it goes through the process, and so may be worth only 90 cents or 80 cents and sometimes perhaps less. The private dollar, in too many cases, may also be worth less than 100 percent. But here each man can form his own judg-

ment, can pick and choose or refuse altogether. In the political process, all he can do is say Yes or No once a year in November.

The discount on the public dollar may be compensated by the other advantages of the government—its ability to compel, to subsidize, to do things on a big scale and at a low interest cost. Whether that is the case needs to be studied in each instance. Where these advantages do not apply, the private market will give better service than the political process. For many services, there is at least some leeway for choice between the private and public store—health and retirement, housing, research, higher education, natural-resource development. Defense, on the other hand, as well as public administration, public works of all kinds, and the great bulk of education—while perhaps made rather expensive by the political process —leave no realistic alternative to public action.

The argument I have offered is no plea to spend more or less on any particular function. It is a plea for doing whatever we do in the most effective way.

QUESTIONS AND STUDY SUGGESTIONS

1. Contrast in detail Professor Wallich's view of the social imbalance problem with that provided by Professor Galbraith in the previous article. Carefully note major points of disagreement. Do these two authors differ more as to ends or means? Explain.

2. What evidence is provided to support the contention that "the new needs" of society are not inherently in the public sphere and that they have not been generally neglected?

3. Compare the characteristics of the "private store" and the "public store," designating the advantages and shortcomings of each to the consumer.

4. What is the "balance-of-forces" effect? What is its relevance to any discussion of the general question of the economic role of government and the more specific problem of achieving social balance? Do you believe the public dollar is spent at a "discount"? Why might private dollars also be spent at a "discount"?

5. In what specific ways does Professor Wallich suggest that the citizen might examine his attitudes toward paying taxes and receiving public services?

6. Do you adhere to Professor Galbraith's view or to Professor Wallich's view of the social imbalance issue? Justify your position.

Reading 65

Recommendations for Improving the Socioeconomic Status of Negroes

National Advisory Commission on Civil Disorders

The Report of the National Advisory Commission on Civil Disorders, chaired by Governor Otto Kerner of Illinois, is a penetrating and detailed analysis of the character, causes, and implications of the race riots of the summer of 1967. Reading 65 consists of excerpts from the summary of the Report which bear most directly upon the economic status of Negroes. The Commission makes a number of pointed and far-reaching recommendations to improve the Negro's position with respect to employment, education, and housing. Our existing welfare system, which the Commission argues is "designed to save money instead of people," is also the target of extensive recommendations for reform.

Although there have been gains in Negro income nationally, and a decline in the number of Negroes below the "poverty level," the condition of Negroes in the central city remains in a state of crisis. Between 2 and 2.5 million Negroes—16 to 20 percent of the total Negro population of all central cities—live in squalor and deprivation in ghetto neighborhoods.

THE CULTURE OF POVERTY

Employment is a key problem. It not only controls the present for the Negro American but, in a most profound way, it is creating the future as well. Yet, despite continuing economic growth and declining national unemployment rates, the unemployment rate for Negroes in 1967 was more than double that for whites.

Equally important is the undesirable nature of many jobs open to Negroes and other minorities. Negro men are more than three times as likely as white men to be in low-paying, unskilled or service jobs. This concentration of male Negro employment at the lowest end of the occupational scale is the single most important cause of poverty among Negroes.

In one study of low-income neighborhoods, the "subemployment rate," including both unemployment and underemployment, was about 33 percent, or 8.8 times greater than the overall unemployment rate for all United States workers.

Employment problems, aggravated by the constant arrival of new unemployed migrants, many of them from depressed rural areas, create persistent poverty in the ghetto. In 1966, about 11.9 percent of the nation's whites and 40.6 percent of its nonwhites were below the "poverty level" defined by the Social Security Administration (currently $3,335 per year for an urban family of four). Over 40 percent of the nonwhites below the poverty level live in the central cities.

Employment problems have drastic social impact in the ghetto. Men who are chronically unemployed or employed in the lowest status jobs are often unable or unwilling to remain with their families. The handicap imposed on children growing up without fathers in an at-

From **Report of the National Advisory Commission on Civil Disorders**, Washington, 1968, pp. 6–7, 10–13, abridged.

mosphere of poverty and deprivation is increased as mothers are forced to work to provide support.

The culture of poverty that results from unemployment and family breakup generates a system of ruthless, exploitative relationships within the ghetto. Prostitution, dope addiction, and crime create an environmental "jungle" characterized by personal insecurity and tension. Children growing up under such conditions are likely participants in civil disorder.

By 1985, the Negro population in central cities is expected to increase by 72 percent to approximately 20.8 million. Coupled with the continued exodus of white families to the suburbs, this growth will produce majority Negro populations in many of the nation's largest cities.

The future of these cities, and of their burgeoning Negro populations, is grim. Most new employment opportunities are being created in suburbs and outlying areas. This trend will continue unless important changes in public policy are made.

In prospect, therefore, is further deterioration of already inadequate municipal tax bases in the face of increasing demands for public services, and continuing unemployment and poverty among the urban Negro population.

THREE CHOICES

Three choices are open to the nation:

We can maintain present policies, continuing both the proportion of the nation's resources now allocated to programs for the unemployed and the disadvantaged, and the inadequate and failing effort to achieve an integrated society.

We can adopt a policy of "enrichment" aimed at improving dramatically the quality of ghetto life while abandoning integration as a goal.

We can pursue integration by combining ghetto "enrichment" with policies which will encourage Negro movement out of central city areas.

The first choice, continuance of present policies, has ominous consequences for our society. The share of the nation's resources now allocated to programs for the disadvantaged is insufficient to arrest the deterioration of life in central city ghettos. Under such conditions, a rising proportion of Negroes may come to see

in the deprivation and segregation they experience, a justification for violent protest, or for extending support to now isolated extremists who advocate civil disruption. Large-scale and continuing violence could result, followed by white retaliation, and, ultimately, the separation of the two communities in a garrison state.

Even if violence does not occur, the consequences are unacceptable. Development of a racially integrated society, extraordinarily difficult today, will be virtually impossible when the present black ghetto population of 12.5 million has grown to almost 21 million.

To continue present policies is to make permanent the division of our country into two societies; one, largely Negro and poor, located in the central cities; the other, predominantly white and affluent, located in the suburbs and in outlying areas.

The second choice, ghetto enrichment coupled with abandonment of integration, is also unacceptable. It is another way of choosing a permanently divided country. Moreover, equality cannot be achieved under conditions of nearly complete separation. In a country where the economy, and particularly the resources of employment, are predominantly white, a policy of separation can only relegate Negroes to a permanently inferior economic status.

We believe that the only possible choice for America is the third—a policy which combines ghetto enrichment with programs designed to encourage integration of substantial numbers of Negroes into the society outside the ghetto.

Enrichment must be an important adjunct to integration, for no matter how ambitious or energetic the program, few Negroes now living in central cities can be quickly integrated. In the meantime, large-scale improvement in the quality of ghetto life is essential.

But this can be no more than an interim strategy. Programs must be developed which will permit substantial Negro movement out of the ghettos. The primary goal must be a single society, in which every citizen will be free to live and work according to his capabilities and desires, not his color.

GENERAL RECOMMENDATIONS

No American—white or black—can escape the consequences of the continuing social and economic decay of our major cities.

Only a commitment to national action on an

unprecedented scale can shape a future compatible with the historic ideals of American society.

The great productivity of our economy, and a federal revenue system which is highly responsive to economic growth, can provide the resources.

The major need is to generate new will—the will to tax ourselves to the extent necessary to meet the vital needs of the nation.

We have set forth goals and proposed strategies to reach those goals. We discuss and recommend programs not to commit each of us to specific parts of such programs but to illustrate the type and dimension of action needed.

The major goal is the creation of a true union—a single society and a single American identity. Toward that goal, we propose the following objectives for national action:

Opening up opportunities to those who are restricted by racial segregation and discrimination, and eliminating all barriers to their choice of jobs, education and housing.

Removing the frustration of powerlessness among the disadvantaged by providing the means for them to deal with the problems that affect their own lives and by increasing the capacity of our public and private institutions to respond to these problems.

Increasing communication across racial lines to destroy stereotypes, to halt polarization, end distrust and hostility, and create common ground for efforts toward public order and social justice.

We propose these aims to fulfill our pledge of equality and to meet the fundamental needs of a democratic and civilized society—domestic peace and social justice.

RECOMMENDATIONS: EMPLOYMENT

Pervasive unemployment and underemployment are the most persistent and serious grievances in minority areas. They are inextricably linked to the problem of civil disorder.

Despite growing federal expenditures for manpower development and training programs, and sustained general economic prosperity and increasing demands for skilled workers, about two million—white and nonwhite—are permanently unemployed. About ten million are underemployed, of whom 6.5 million work full time for wages below the poverty line.

The 500,000 "hard-core" unemployed in the central cities who lack a basic education and are unable to hold a steady job are made up in large part of Negro males between the ages of 18 and 25. In the riot cities which we surveyed, Negroes were three times as likely as whites to hold unskilled jobs, which are often part time, seasonal, low-paying and "dead end."

Negro males between the ages of 15 and 25 predominated among the rioters. More than 20 percent of the rioters were unemployed, and many who were employed held intermittent, low status, unskilled jobs which they regarded as below their education and ability.

The Commission recommends that the federal government:

Undertake joint efforts with cities and states to consolidate existing manpower programs to avoid fragmentation and duplication.

Take immediate action to create 2,000,000 new jobs over the next three years—one million in the public sector and one million in the private sector—to absorb the hard-core unemployed and materially reduce the level of underemployment for all workers, black and white. We propose 250,000 public sector and 300,000 private sector jobs in the first year.

Provide on-the-job training by both public and private employers with reimbursement to private employers for the extra costs of training the hard-core unemployed, by contract or by tax credits.

Provide tax and other incentives to investment in rural as well as urban poverty areas in order to offer to the rural poor an alternative to migration to urban centers.

Take new and vigorous action to remove artificial barriers to employment and promotion, including not only racial discrimination but, in certain cases, arrest records or lack of a high school diploma. Strengthen those agencies such as the Equal Employment Opportunity Commission, charged with eliminating discriminatory practices, and provide full support for Title VI of the 1964 Civil Rights Act allowing federal grant-in-aid funds to be withheld from activities which discriminate on grounds of color or race.

The Commission commends the recent public commitment of the National Council of the Building and Construction Trades Unions, AFL-CIO, to encourage and recruit Negro membership in apprenticeship programs. This commitment should be intensified and implemented.

RECOMMENDATIONS: EDUCATION

Education in a democratic society must equip children to develop their potential and to participate fully in American life. For the community at large, the schools have discharged this responsibility well. But for many minorities, and particularly for the children of the ghetto, the schools have failed to provide the educational experience which could overcome the effects of discrimination and deprivation.

This failure is one of the persistent sources of grievance and resentment within the Negro community. The hostility of Negro parents and students toward the school system is generating increasing conflict and causing disruption within many city school districts. But the most dramatic evidence of the relationship between educational practices and civil disorders lies in the high incidence of riot participation by ghetto youth who have not completed high school.

The bleak record of public education for ghetto children is growing worse. In the critical skills—verbal and reading ability—Negro students are falling farther behind whites with each year of school completed. The high unemployment and underemployment rate for Negro youth is evidence, in part, of the growing educational crisis.

We support integration as the priority education strategy; it is essential to the future of American society. In this last summer's disorders we have seen the consequences of racial isolation at all levels, and of attitudes toward race, on both sides, produced by three centuries of myth, ignorance and bias. It is indispensable that opportunities for interaction between the races be expanded.

We recognize that the growing dominance of pupils from disadvantaged minorities in city school populations will not soon be reversed. No matter how great the effort toward desegregation, many children of the ghetto will not, within their school careers, attend integrated schools.

If existing disadvantages are not to be perpetuated, we must drastically improve the quality of ghetto education. Equality of results with all-white schools must be the goal.

To implement these strategies, the Commission recommends:

Sharply increased efforts to eliminate de facto segregation in our schools through substantial federal aid to school systems seeking to desegregate either within the system or in cooperation with neighboring school systems.

Elimination of racial discrimination in Northern as well as Southern schools by vigorous application of Title VI of the Civil Rights Act of 1964.

Extension of quality early childhood education to every disadvantaged child in the country.

Efforts to improve dramatically schools serving disadvantaged children through substantial federal funding of year-round compensatory education programs, improved teaching, and expanded experimentation and research.

Elimination of illiteracy through greater federal support for adult basic education.

Enlarged opportunities for parent and community participation in the public schools.

Reoriented vocational education emphasizing work-experience training and the involvement of business and industry.

Expanded opportunities for higher education through increased federal assistance to disadvantaged students.

Revision of state aid formulas to assure more per student aid to districts having a high proportion of disadvantaged school-age children.

RECOMMENDATIONS: THE WELFARE SYSTEM

Our present system of public welfare is designed to save money instead of people, and tragically ends up doing neither. This system has two critical deficiencies:

First, it excludes large numbers of persons who are in great need, and who, if provided a decent level of support, might be able to. become more productive and self-sufficient. No federal funds are available for millions of men and women who are needy but neither aged, handicapped nor the parents of minor children.

Second, for those included, the system provides assistance well below the minimum necessary for a decent level of existence, and imposes restrictions that encourage continued dependency on welfare and undermine self-respect.

A welter of statutory requirements and administrative practices and regulations operate to remind recipients that they are considered untrustworthy, promiscuous and lazy. Residence requirements prevent assistance to people in need who are newly arrived in the state.

Regular searches of recipients' homes violate privacy. Inadequate social services compound the problems.

The Commission recommends that the federal government, acting with state and local governments where necessary, reform the existing welfare system to:

Establish uniform national standards of assistance at least as high as the annual "poverty level" of income, now set by the Social Security Administration at $3,335 per year for an urban family of four.

Require that all states receiving federal welfare contributions participate in the Aid to Families with Dependent Children—Unemployed Parents program (AFDC-UP) that permits assistance to families with both father and mother in the home, thus aiding the family while it is still intact.

Bear a substantially greater portion of all welfare costs—at least 90 percent of total payments.

Increase incentives for seeking employment and job training, but remove restrictions recently enacted by the Congress that would compel mothers of young children to work.

Provide more adequate social services through neighborhood centers and family-planning programs.

Remove the freeze placed by the 1967 welfare amendments on the percentage of children in a state that can be covered by federal assistance.

Eliminate residence requirements.

As a long-range goal, the Commission recommends that the federal government seek to develop a national system of income supplementation based strictly on need with two broad and basic purposes:

To provide, for those who can work or who do work, any necessary supplements in such a way as to develop incentives for fuller employment;

To provide, for those who cannot work and for mothers who decide to remain with their children, a minimum standard of decent living, and to aid in the saving of children from the prison of poverty that has held their parents.

A broad system of supplementation would involve substantially greater federal expenditures than anything now contemplated. The cost will range widely depending on the standard of need accepted as the "basic allowance"

to individuals and families, and on the rate at which additional income above this level is taxed. Yet if the deepening cycle of poverty and dependence on welfare can be broken, if the children of the poor can be given the opportunity to scale the wall that now separates them from the rest of society, the return on this investment will be great indeed.

RECOMMENDATIONS: HOUSING

After more than three decades of fragmented and grossly underfunded federal housing programs, nearly six million substandard housing units remain occupied in the United States.

The housing problem is particularly acute in the minority ghettos. Nearly two-thirds of all non-white families living in the central cities today live in neighborhoods marked with substandard housing and general urban blight. Two major factors are responsible.

First: Many ghetto residents simply cannot pay the rent necessary to support decent housing. In Detroit, for example, over 40 percent of the non-white occupied units in 1960 required rent of over 35 percent of the tenants' income.

Second: Discrimination prevents access to many non-slum areas, particularly the suburbs, where good housing exists. In addition, by creating a "back pressure" in the racial ghettos, it makes it possible for landlords to break up apartments for denser occupancy, and keeps prices and rents of deteriorated ghetto housing higher than they would be in a truly free market.

To date, federal programs have been able to do comparatively little to provide housing for the disadvantaged. In the 31-year history of subsidized federal housing, only about 800,-000 units have been constructed, with recent production averaging about 50,000 units a year. By comparison, over a period only three years longer, FHA insurance guarantees have made possible the construction of over ten million middle and upper-income units.

Two points are fundamental to the Commission's recommendations:

First: Federal housing programs must be given a new thrust aimed at overcoming the prevailing patterns of racial segregation. If this is not done, those programs will continue to concentrate the most impoverished and dependent segments of the population into the central-city ghettos where there is already a critical gap between the needs of the population and the public resources to deal with them.

Second: The private sector must be brought into the production and financing of low and moderate rental housing to supply the capabilities and capital necessary to meet the housing needs of the nation.

The Commission recommends that the federal government:

Enact a comprehensive and enforceable federal open housing law to cover the sale or rental of all housing, including single family homes.

Reorient federal housing programs to place more low and moderate income housing outside of ghetto areas.

Bring within the reach of low and moderate income families within the next five years six million new and existing units of decent housing, beginning with 600,000 units in the next year.

To reach this goal we recommend:

Expansion and modification of the rent supplement program to permit use of supplements for existing housing, thus greatly increasing the reach of the program.

Expansion and modification of the below-market interest rate program to enlarge the interest subsidy to all sponsors and provide interest-free loans to nonprofit sponsors to cover pre-construction costs, and permit sale of projects to nonprofit corporations, cooperatives, or condominiums.

Creation of an ownership supplement program similar to present rent supplements, to make home ownership possible for low-income families.

Federal writedown of interest rates on loans to private builders constructing moderate-rent housing.

Expansion of the public housing program, with emphasis on small units on scattered sites, and leasing and "turnkey" programs.

Expansion of the Model Cities program.

Expansion and reorientation of the urban renewal program to give priority to projects directly assisting low-income households to obtain adequate housing.

CONCLUSION

One of the first witnesses to be invited to appear before this Commission was Dr. Kenneth B. Clark, a distinguished and perceptive scholar. Referring to the reports of earlier riot commissions, he said:

I read that report . . . of the 1919 riot in Chicago, and it is as if I were reading the report of the investigating committee on the Harlem riot of '35, the report of the investigating committee on the Harlem riot of '43, the report of the McCone Commission on the Watts riot.

I must again in candor say to you members of this Commission—it is a kind of Alice in Wonderland—with the same moving picture re-shown over and over again, the same analysis, the same recommendations, and the same inaction.

These words come to our minds as we conclude this report.

We have provided an honest beginning. We have learned much. But we have uncovered no startling truths, no unique insights, no simple solutions. The destruction and the bitterness of racial disorder, the harsh polemics of black revolt and white repression have been seen and heard before in this country.

It is time now to end the destruction and the violence, not only in the streets of the ghetto but in the lives of people.

QUESTIONS AND STUDY SUGGESTIONS

1. Compare unemployment rates and income levels for whites and Negroes. Explain the Commission's contention that employment is the key to both the Negro's present and his future.

2. What are the Commission's basic criticisms of our present welfare system? What factors are primarily responsible for the substandard housing of many nonwhites?

3. Briefly summarize the Commission's recommendations in the areas of (a) employment, (b) education, and (c) housing.

The Problems of Urbanization

Council of Economic Advisers

The United States is now primarily an urban nation, and further population shifts from rural areas to cities are anticipated. Furthermore, we find in this reading that the structure of large cities has also been changing: both people and businesses are moving from the "central cities" to outlying suburban areas. These changes have given rise to serious problems of economic, social, and political adjustment. Unskilled and relatively uneducated migrants from rural areas find they have meager job opportunities in urban areas; a cumulative process of urban blight has deteriorated many central city areas; there is a growing need to revitalize and develop efficient mass-transit systems; problems of air and water pollution have grown increasingly acute; recreational facilities have diminished quantitatively and deteriorated qualitatively, and so forth. Because these problems transcend the individual political units which comprise metropolitan areas, the CEA recommends "area-wide metropolitan planning" in coping with the social costs and complexities of urbanization.

Today, America is an urban nation. In 1960, 125 million people, 70 percent of our population, lived in urban places—places with a population of 2,500 or more. Half a century earlier, less than half of our people resided in urban areas. And the forces promoting urbanization are not likely to abate. By the year 2000 over 250 million people, 4 out of 5 of the population, are likely to be urban.

Moreover, the urban population is increasingly concentrated in metropolitan areas—clusters of cities and suburbs and their nearby hinterlands. New York, the largest, had 10.7 million people in 1960. Altogether, one-third of the U.S. population lived in 24 metropolitan areas containing a million or more people. Another 30 percent lived in the remaining 188 metropolitan areas. But 10 million of the urban population still live in the smaller towns that are not part of metropolitan areas.

CHANGING STRUCTURE OF URBAN AREAS

The rapid growth of population in our metropolitan areas has been accompanied by major changes in the locational patterns of life and work. The growth of cities has long taken place primarily by outward movement at the fringes. During the postwar period this process has been characterized by its speed and its tendency to take place beyond the boundaries of central cities. Between 1940 and 1960, the share of the metropolitan population living in central cities fell from 63 percent to 51 percent; the population of central cities rose by only 12 million, while the metropolitan population outside central cities rose by 28 million. Between 1950 and 1960, the central cities of 14 of our 15 largest metropolitan areas lost population.

The flight to the suburbs has been motivated by a desire for more space, fresh air, and pri-

From **Economic Report of the President, 1965,** Washington, January, 1965, pp. 146–155.

vacy, and by a desire to escape from the social disorganization of the city. It has been facilitated by high postwar incomes, by the ready availability of federally guaranteed mortgage credit, and by the automobile.

Many businesses also have been moving from central cities. Retail businesses and, to a lesser extent, wholesale businesses have followed the population to the suburbs. Manufacturing industries have been growing much faster in the suburbs. By 1960, half of the jobs in manufacturing in metropolitan areas were outside the central cities.

A major reason for the migration of manufacturing industries is their desire for space. Expansion is difficult and costly in the central city locations, and modern technology places a premium on continuous one-floor operation. The rise of trucking, and, in many instances, the decreasing dependence on bulky raw materials, have tended to free manufacturing industries from the need to locate near railroads, rivers, and harbors. More widespread ownership of cars by workers has also increased the flexibility of plant location.

There has been continued concentration in central cities of financial, legal, and specialized business and consumer services. Cultural and educational facilities, central office administration, and governments have also shown preference for expansion in central city locations.

By and large, the transformation from rural to urban and from urban to metropolitan areas has been consistent with the search for greater economic opportunity and higher economic rewards. Urban areas offer far more opportunities for high-paying jobs and urban people enjoy higher incomes. With some exceptions, our largest metropolitan areas rank near the top in this respect. But in the wake of this transformation have come serious problems of adjustment: for the rural areas, adjustment to decline; for the central cities, adjustment to change in population structure and economic base; and for the suburbs, adjustment to rapid growth.

Existing institutions have responded only partially to the rapid growth and changing economic structure of our large cities. Many public and private efforts are already devoted to our urban problems, but the time is ripe for a more comprehensive response. Our concern is both with the disadvantaged in the city and with the quality of the physical environment.

HUMAN PROBLEMS OF THE CITIES

Rural-urban migration has created problems of adjustment for the migrants and for the areas receiving them. Existing urban educational systems, social groupings, and economic structures have been unable to absorb smoothly the rapid influx of the poor, uneducated, and unskilled among the rural migrants.

Many have found it difficult to adjust to the new economic and social environment. Because they lack skills, they are handicapped in an industrial society which is increasingly replacing unskilled labor with skilled labor and machines. They become victims of impersonal business fluctuations which affect most heavily the younger, the less skilled, and the nonwhite workers. And if unemployed, they cannot fall back for food and shelter on the extended family system of a traditional rural society.

As middle and upper income groups have fled to the suburbs, central cities have been left with a disproportionately large share of the poor. This situation has been aggravated by racial discrimination which often restricts nonwhites to the older neighborhoods of central cities.

Poverty, lack of education and skills, and irregular employment stifle incentives for self-improvement and lead to social disorganization. Family breakup, alcoholism, drug addiction, rising crime rates, and illegitimacy have become major problems in our cities. Children in such environments, left to their own resources at an early age, quickly assume the ways of the preceding generation, perpetuating the process of poverty. Society must pay the costs through waste of human resources, increased public welfare expenditures, and decay of our social fabric.

The human problems are aggravated by the inadequacies of the physical environment. The accommodation of a large population at very high densities in cities which were shaped in an earlier technological era produces living conditions with little privacy or amenity.

URBAN DECAY

The blight and decay that afflict large parts of central cities are clear and visible. Part of what we see is another reflection of poverty: poor people cannot afford adequate, attractive housing. Another part results from the decreased dependence of industry and trade on central city locations.

But blight in cities tends to be cumulative. The older structures concentrated near the city center lose their economic usefulness as the functions of the downtown areas change. Extensive conversion, rehabilitation, and reconstruction are needed. If a few buildings need to be replaced or renovated in an otherwise prosperous area, the market provides private developers and builders with sufficient incentives to undertake the work. However, when a pattern of decay permeates a large area, the dilapidation of neighboring buildings reduces the profitability of improving a particular property. A large area must then be improved as a single unit, and the cost and difficulties of acquiring and redeveloping a large tract of central city land are likely to deter private investors from the undertaking. In such cases, there is need for public policies to assist the private market in developing property for new and improved uses.

Although inadequate housing is by no means the only aspect of urban blight, it is the most important. Ten percent of all urban households —about 3.8 million families—live in housing that is dilapidated or lacking such amenities as plumbing facilities, piped hot water, and kitchen or cooking equipment. Inadequate housing is particularly acute for nonwhites: only 7 percent of urban white families live in inadequate housing, compared with 32 percent of urban nonwhites.

In many U.S. cities, the process of urban blight is worsened by discrimination against nonwhites. Discrimination in housing markets provides a captive market for dilapidated slum dwellings. Large profits can be made by under-maintenance, since Negroes are virtually deprived of access to adequate housing. The situation is sometimes aggravated by inadequate enforcement of building codes and public health statutes. The success of any effort to upgrade urban housing standards will depend on the elimination of racial barriers.

Commercial and industrial structures also become obsolete. The failure to maintain these facilities reflects in part the greater attraction of suburban locations. Here, too, it is sometimes difficult for normal market processes to avoid cumulative deterioration, and achieve conversion to new uses.

AREA-WIDE PROBLEMS

The large metropolitan area typically consists of a central city and several smaller suburban communities. In dealing with many of the public services of the metropolitan area, it is desirable to take a broad view encompassing the needs and preferences of all the constituent communities. This is true in some instances because there are important economies that can be achieved by acting in concert; in others, because decisions taken in isolation by a particular community may have undesirable side effects on its neighbors. Thus, as metropolitan areas grow in size and diversity there is greater need for some area-wide coordination and planning.

Land Use

Efficient use and aesthetic development of the limited land resources are major problems facing almost all urban communities. Private uses compete with each other and with public facilities for space. Individual land use decisions affect the value of neighboring properties and the general environment. These effects can be given adequate weight only if a broader social view is taken, through appropriate taxation, zoning, and other regulations.

In metropolitan areas, zoning and other land use restrictions need to take into account the needs of the area as a whole, together with the special problems of the individual communities. Each community in isolation will zone its land use to suit itself, frequently banishing the less desirable uses to outskirts remote from its center and residential areas, but possibly near the living areas of neighboring communities. If the area is to have an efficient transportation system and if enough land is to be set aside for recreational purposes in convenient locations, a metropolitan perspective must be added to local land use decision.

Transportation

The movement of people and businesses to the suburbs has greatly increased the burdens on our urban transportation systems. Part of this increase has been due to commercial traffic— the result of expanded economic activity. The greatest part, however, has been due to the growth of commuting between places of residence and employment. People are commuting longer distances, and more are crossing city boundaries. During the 1960 Census week, nearly one-fourth of the 39 million workers employed in our metropolitan areas commuted across the limits of the central city.

By no means all urban traffic moves into the city in the morning and out in the evening. As much as 29 percent of commuting across central city limits takes place in the opposite direction. The decentralization of retailing, manufacturing, recreation, and other activities has meant that travel patterns have increased in variety and complexity.

Commuters in most areas travel to and from work by automobile. This has led to massive investment in streets and highways and in parking facilities. As roads have been extended and improved, more individuals have been encouraged to commute by automobile, and congestion has continued. This has stimulated a revival of interest in mass transportation.

An effective transportation system involves a combination of individual and mass transit. The advantage of the automobile is its flexibility and convenience in terms of time and place of travel, number of people, and cargo. The advantage of public transit lies in its lower cost, more economical use of space, and broader availability to persons unable to rely on automobiles. But no one system can do the job alone.

In many areas, patronage of public transportation has declined drastically; between 1952 and 1962, revenue passengers carried by buses and streetcars in the United States dropped by 41 percent; and 194 transit companies were abandoned between 1954 and the end of 1963. The loss of patronage raises unit costs, requiring higher fares to break even, and leading to further shrinkage of patronage. Railroads subject to the same process have abandoned many commuter routes. With the advent of the automobile, some decline in patronage of public transportation was inevitable. Yet it might not have been as great under a program of more balanced public development of individual and mass transportation. While billions of public funds have been spent on roads and streets, the mass transit systems have not been able to attract private capital, nor have the central cities been able to invest sufficiently to keep them from deteriorating.

Clearly, the transportation problems of a metropolitan area transcend individual communities, whether they be the central city or the suburbs. An effective transportation system for the metropolis should permit people to move easily both between and within the suburbs and central city. Individual communities working in isolation to solve their local traffic problems are more likely to provide a patchwork than a logical system of connecting routes. Thus, area-wide planning is required if an effective transportation system is to be devised and coordinated.

Waste Disposal and Water Pollution

The growth of urban population, commerce, and industry has led to a rapid rise in the use of water. Little water is actually consumed in most uses for which it is withdrawn. Most of it is returned to some natural body of water, usually with some waste or other deterioration in quality. If the quality has not deteriorated too much, the water is available for reuse. Water in major rivers is reused several times before it reaches the sea.

Since most of the costs of pollution are borne by downstream users rather than by those who generate the wastes, municipalities and industry have little incentive to treat waste adequately before discharge. The result is that the collection and treatment of waste lag behind water use. In 1962, about 20 million more people were served by municipal water supply than by waste treatment systems. Much industrial waste is discharged without treatment, and between 1950 and 1960 the discharge of industrial organic waste to streams increased by 30 percent.

The discharge of pollutants is concentrated in urban areas and is increasing as time passes. More effective regulations and enforcement will be necessary to achieve cleaner streams and lakes. Another policy instrument that may be of value is a system of fees for the discharge of effluent. Such fees, if feasible, would confront polluters with the social costs of their actions and would encourage them to reduce pollution.

Air Pollution

Air pollution, like water pollution, results from excessive discharge of wastes, often the result of incomplete combustion. Pollutants are discharged into the air by industries, households, and municipalities. The automobile is probably the largest single source of air pollution; California has adopted a law prohibiting the sale of cars without pollution control devices, and other states are considering similar action.

Discharge of pollutants has increased rapidly with the growth of population and industry. More than half of all U.S. urban communities are affected by air pollution. One-quarter of the population live in communities in which air pollution is a major problem.

Air pollution is at best a public nuisance, at worst a source of serious damage to health and property. Although more research is needed, relatively inexpensive methods are already available for the control of most pollutants. As with water pollution, economic incentives are lacking. The cost of air pollution is borne mainly by the community at large rather than by those responsible for the pollution. It can be reduced by more effective regulation or, for major polluters, by discharge fees.

Open Spaces and Outdoor Recreation

Although people value open spaces in urban areas, there is no market on which they can register these preferences. It would not be feasible to create such a market because of the difficulty of imputing or confining benefits from urban open spaces to particular individuals. There is a strong temptation for hard pressed local governments to maintain their tax base by abandoning open spaces to developers, by routing new roads through parks rather than through developed areas, and by making inadequate additions to the available open space as the population expands.

The amount of open space per person is small and probably declining in the larger metropolitan areas. In addition, the provision of State and country parks within driving distance of metropolitan areas is lagging behind the growth of these areas, and most of our Federal recreational facilities are remote from the major population centers.

But with incomes rising and leisure time increasing, the demand for outdoor recreation is growing rapidly. Many city parks are now used nearly to capacity, and visits to State parks have increased by 123 percent in the last decade. The Outdoor Recreation Resources Review Commission projects a tripling of over-all demand for outdoor recreation facilities by the year 2000.

FEDERAL PROGRAMS FOR URBAN AREAS

During the past thirty years, the Federal Government has been developing programs of assistance—to individuals, to business, and to State and local governments—that contribute to the improvement of the urban environment and to the alleviation of the social, developmental, and financial problems of urban areas. Among the most important of the existing programs to improve the physical environment are aids to public housing, urban renewal, highways, mass transit, waste treatment, airports, and hospitals. The human problems of the city are approached through national programs for education, health, welfare, and social insurance, and to combat poverty.

These measures have made great contributions to the development of urban life. But the rapid growth of metropolitan areas has compounded or changed the nature of many of these problems and created new ones. New knowledge—partly gained from the mistakes of the past—can be brought to bear. It is now evident that new directions in Federal policy are needed in these efforts.

Most important is Federal encouragement of area-wide metropolitan planning, to assure the development of integrated systems of land use, of transportation, water supply, sanitation, and pollution control. Some Federal programs now require local coordination in the provision of physical facilities. But even if some area-wide coordination is achieved in individual functions such as transportation or sanitation, an effectively integrated pattern of development cannot emerge unless the several functions are brought into a common focus. This can only be achieved if there is some method of taking an area-wide, comprehensive point of view, which brings together all levels of government and pertinent private organizations to evolve a metropolitan area plan.

Metropolitan area planning is no panacea. Each community has its own preferences and problems, and its local government is best able to discern them. Nor does metropolitan planning directly augment the resources available to meet the rapidly increasing needs. It is clear, however, that fragmentation of legal jurisdictions has proceeded too far in many of our metropolitan areas. The Federal Government has a responsibility to promote planning to assure that public needs are met efficiently and that the federally aided local public programs will, indeed, produce a more livable and efficient urban environment.

Because the allocation of land to various purposes is so fundamental to the future pattern of a metropolitan area, the Federal Government should continue to give some help to promote better land use planning. While decisions about land use will remain mainly a local matter, research and the spreading of information to improve zoning techniques are desirable.

As the metropolis grows in area and density, it is particularly difficult to preserve open spaces for recreational and aesthetic purposes. The Federal Government already aids localities to acquire open lands, and this program is a logical part of a greater emphasis on metropolitan planning.

One way of avoiding congestion in the metropolitan area is to bring homes, community services, and jobs closer together in smaller and more self-contained communities. Federal aids to urban areas need to be adapted to this promising new approach.

The Federal Government has a responsibility to reexamine and improve its existing programs. Urban renewal is rapidly transforming many of the blighted downtown areas of our cities to new and more productive uses, thereby helping to reverse the downward spiral of malfunction and decay. However, despite an increase in the efforts to find adequate housing for the persons displaced by the tearing down of slums, it is evident that these efforts are still not wholly successful. Experience has shown that much of the land made available through urban renewal in downtown areas is drawn into commercial and high rent residential uses. The Government therefore must take further steps to augment the supply of low and medium rent housing in the city. The recent emphasis in urban renewal on rehabilitation of existing residential units should make a contribution to this need; and the Federal sharing of costs of code enforcement begun last year should help to stem the decline of gray areas.

The FHA and VA mortgage guarantee programs have greatly increased the supply of middle-income houses and are among the main forces behind the growth of suburbs. The public housing program has sought to provide low-income housing, and in recent years housing assistance for middle-income families has been a major program innovation. But we need to test out more flexible methods of providing housing assistance for families of different incomes, under which families are not forced to move out of their homes when their incomes rise above a specified level.

The impact of governments on the private decisions which mainly determine the development of metropolitan areas is large. The value of land in alternative uses depends on government decisions on zoning and transportation. The commuter's decision to use a particular transportation system depends on the cost he must pay. The extent of air and water pollution depends on the willingness of governments to impose regulations. Federal, State, and local methods of taxation help to determine the profitability of slums and of their rehabilitation.

As public policy seeks to improve the livability of metropolitan areas, it must be keenly aware of its effects on private incentives and behavior. The development of our metropolitan areas will always be primarily determined by private actions. Wise government policies will promote private efforts that improve the quality of urban life and will provide incentives which channel private decisions toward an efficient use of resources.

QUESTIONS AND STUDY SUGGESTIONS

1. What are the social costs of urbanization? Explain why the presence of these costs might make it difficult for private developers to counter urban decay.

2. Why does the CEA put great stress upon area-wide planning and "a metropolitan perspective" in meeting urban problems?

3. Discuss the relative advantages and disadvantages of automobile and public transportation in urban areas.

Reading 67

The Economic Consequences of Disarmament

Surendra J. Patel, Economic Commission for Europe, United Nations

What might be the economic impact of disarmament? Could the economically advanced nations readily reallocate the 10 percent or so of their resources now devoted to arms production to useful alternative employments? Or is unemployment and stagnation to be the consequence of disarmament? This reading presents a basically optimistic view of the economic implications of disarming. Disarmament is certain to pose significant problems of economic adjustment. But appropriate application of stabilization and reallocation policies by the advanced nations could result in the economic wherewithal to raise the level of private consumption and the output of social goods domestically and expand the production of capital facilities domestically and in the underdeveloped nations of the world. In short, disarmament is a potential economic boon to mankind which can be realized through international cooperation and farsighted planning.

Throughout the history of humanity, chiefs, kings, emperors, and nation states have all relied on warfare to protect and, if possible, to expand their domination. Major advances in techniques have often found their first application in means of conquest—no less true today than at the height of the power of ancient Egypt, Sumer, China, India, and Peru. The continuing reliance on weapons of warfare has now as never before reached the point of logical absurdity. Armaments in the arsenals of the major powers are capable of annihilating most of mankind. Realization that war between them could no longer serve as an instrument of national policy is spreading. And yet, arms are being piled up. Like the miserly person hiding under the floor the savings he would neither use nor bequeath, nations are adding to an ever-expanding stockpile of weapons even a small part of which is adequate to destroy all, including themselves.

There is now an accumulation of technical knowledge which in an outburst of half an hour of insanity could devastate almost all animate objects, the product of patient evolution over the ages. But if wisely utilized, it also has the potential to overcome in half a century the age-old afflictions of mankind—squalor, poverty, want, and disease. Humanity is thus being steadily pressed to choose between half an hour of insanity or half a century of farsighted international cooperation.

A disarmed world would presuppose political accommodations among nations. Continued heavy military expenditures have become almost an economic habit, acting like a tranquilizer for national nervousness born of insecurity. To re-deploy the resources now devoted to armaments would create important problems of adjustments for individuals, countries, and the entire world economy.

In pursuance of the General Assembly resolution 1516 (XV), a group of experts was appointed by the United Nations to study the problems of transition to a disarmed world. In its report, *The Economic and Social Consequences of Disarmament,* the group was "unanimously of the opinion that all the problems and difficulties of transition connected with disarmament could be met by appropriate national and international measures."

This article draws heavily upon the findings of the consultative group. Their unanimity of views was underlined by Acting Secretary-General U Thant, in his preface to the report. He stated: "It is a source of profound gratification to me, as I am sure it will be to all governments, that, on a subject that has until recently been so beset by ideological differences it has now proved possible for a group of experts drawn from countries with different economic systems and at different stages of economic development to reach unanimous agreement."

MAIN FEATURES OF MILITARY EXPENDITURES

The Burden of Armaments

A study of the economics of disarmament requires an assessment of the resources which are at present devoted to military expenditures. On the basis of the available data, the U.N. consultative group suggested that the world appears to be spending roughly $120 billion annually on military expenditure. This is equal to about 8 to 9 percent of the world's annual output, or to at least two-thirds of the entire national income of the underdeveloped countries. It is close to the value of the world exports of all commodities, and slightly lower than the total resources that are devoted to net capital formation in the whole world. Nearly 20 million men now serve in the world's armed forces. When other persons occupied directly or indirectly in servicing the needs of these armies are added to them, the total may well run over 50 million.

The volume of resources devoted to military expenditure during the last decade of relative peace is indeed impressive. The world has spent more on the instruments of international intimidation in this short period than on education since the beginning of the age of enlightenment three centuries ago. Total military expenditures in the last ten years amounted to nearly $1,200 billion. This sum is about seven times the annual income and seventy times the annual net investment of the underdeveloped countries. As a rough and ready estimate, it may be suggested that if it were devoted to the economic development of these countries, it could have raised the volume of their reproducible assets in industries and in the modernized sectors twelvefold, and their total capital assets nearly threefold. Their annual per capita income could have been raised three times. Poverty could thus have become a pastime for the historians, and later for the archeologists.

Concentration of Defense Outlays

The heavy military burden is not spread evenly all over the world. It is concentrated in only a handful of countries, and within each of them in a limited number of sectors of employment and geographical locations.

The United Nations group of experts estimated that only seven countries—Canada, Western Germany, France, China, USSR, UK, and the United States—account for nearly 85 percent of them. At the other end of the spectrum, the underdeveloped countries are responsible for nearly five percent of the world total. All of them together spend for this purpose nearly as much as the United Kingdom alone. Military expenditures are, in fact, much more heavily concentrated in a few countries than world income or investments.

Among the major military powers, production as well as employment depending on military ends is also highly concentrated in a few industrial sectors—for example, munitions, electrical machinery, instruments and related products, and transport equipment (including airplanes and missiles). More often than not such dependence is centered in a particular locality or region within a given country.

Most of the underdeveloped countries devote less than four percent of their resources to military expenditures. A large part of these consists of payment of salaries and provision of food and clothing for the armies. The resources that these countries devote to military hardware are relatively small and a significant portion of it is often financed from abroad. Disarmament would therefore have a relatively limited direct impact on the flow of physical output in these countries. (The influence of world disarmament on their exports is, however, a very important consideration, which is discussed later.) Insofar as some countries have to spend their own precious foreign exchange resources to import military equipment, disarmament would enable them to transfer these to imports of much needed capital equipment.

THE EXPERIENCE OF POSTWAR DISARMAMENT

The elimination of armaments from national arsenals would obviously depend on political understanding among the major powers. But the man in the street is often concerned about whether countries can really afford to disarm. This genuine concern symbolizes the individual fear of losing a job without finding another. It focuses attention at a national level on the apprehensions about maintaining full employment in countries which may have become used to armaments as an economic drug. There is also uncertainty about whether the economic and political leadership which so readily allocates resources for military purposes would be equally willing, ready, and prompt to divert them toward much more beneficial social and other ends.

An advance analysis of the problems involved in the process of transition to disarmed economies is therefore of considerable importance. Drawing on the experience of such a transition at the end of the second world war can set the stage for the discussion of the problems which countries with different economic systems and at different stages of economic growth would now face in the event of disarmament.

During the closing years of the last war, many countries devoted nearly half their resources to mutual destruction. The number of men in uniform and the real volume of military expenditure were four times as high as today. The destructive preoccupations of these years left in their trail the terrible signs of sick humanity—millions dead and mutilated; homes, hospitals, and factories destroyed; productive assets paralyzed; communications dislocated; the network of trade disrupted; currencies without confidence; and people in despair. And yet, huge armies were quickly demobilized with almost no rise in the level of unemployment. Plants producing armaments were rapidly turned to the output of articles of everyday use. The visible scars of war were soon healed.

The experience of conversion may be illustrated by some examples. In 1946 the military expenditure in the United States was reduced to just about one-fifth of the level of only one year before. Between August 1945 and June 1946, over nine million men gave up the army uniform for civilian clothes. In the United Kingdom, seven million persons engaged either in the army or in servicing it were released in a matter of sixteen months. But in both the countries a very rapid expansion of output for civilian purposes opened up sufficient employment opportunities so that unemployment, contrary to the predictions of many economists, increased but little. In continental western Europe, war destruction and dislocation was much greater. Most commodities were in short supply. Inflationary pressures were severe. Confidence in currencies was shaken. But in eighteen months after the end of the hostilities, industrial output rose to the prewar level nearly everywhere, except in western Germany and Italy.

The Soviet Union and the eastern European countries had suffered most severe human and material losses. Vast numbers of peoples were moved far away from their normal place of residence. Despite these incredible handicaps the prewar level of industrial output was reached or surpassed by 1948.

The destruction, devastation, and dislocation caused by the war were very severe. The total resources devoted to the war were far greater than at present. But the destructiveness of the war was more than matched by the resilience of the economies. This process of very rapid conversion has provided the countries with a valuable experience. Referring to the measures adopted during the process of conversion, the United States government stated that "Tried measures such as these would be under active consideration again in the event of the acceptance of a disarmament program."

The ease as well as the rapid pace of the conversion at the end of the war was no doubt due to special circumstances. A decade and a half of the great depression and the war had created a vast backlog of demand for both consumption and investment. Liquid savings in the hands of the population and enterprises were devoted to buying things as soon as they became available. The major concern of economic policy was to curb, rather than to maintain—let alone to stimulate—effective demand.

This particular difference between the early postwar and the present setting was sharply underlined by the recession which was associated with the reduction of about $10 billion in military spending in the United States between 1953 and 1954. Governments are now aware that the special factors of postwar conversion are no longer present. The government of the United States, for instance, stated:

Despite the mildness of the 1954 recession it now is clear that fiscal and monetary policies might have been applied with more vigor. The reason they were not is that the decline in defense spending following the Korean war was not treated by the policymakers as a major demobilization requiring strong compensatory action. For this reason the 1953–54 period does not provide a significant guide to the behavior of the American economy in a disarmament program during the 1960s.

It may be expected therefore that this awareness would prove conducive toward adopting effective measures during future disarmament.

TURNING SWORDS INTO PLOWSHARES

Mankind's first step towards a disarmed world would not be like sailing in already charted waters. They would encounter a number of new problems while turning the swords into plowshares. Attention may be drawn to three of them which merit advance study: the maintenance of the overall level of economic activity or, in more familiar words, avoiding a recession or a depression which would increase unemployment; minimizing and counteracting the adverse economic effects in particular industries, localities, or regions caused by the elimination of certain activities serving military uses; and overcoming the disturbance that a decline in the military demand for certain imported materials may cause to the economies which depend on them for their foreign exchange earnings.

Avoiding a Recession

How would the reduction in military expenditure be carried out? The answer to this question would, to a large extent, determine whether it would lead to a recession or give additional stimulus to economic growth. If reduction in military expenditures leads to a fall in overall purchasing power, there is little doubt that it will reduce the level of economic activity and increase unemployment. But it

would hardly be a tribute to the calibre of economic management if falling demand were to culminate in a recession. On the other hand, if a reduction in military expenditure were balanced by an equivalent expansion of other forms of demand, there need be no short fall in overall demand. The offsetting expansion could take the form of increases in personal consumption, private investment, and public expenditure for domestic ends, as well as for foreign aid to the developing countries. The task of economic policy would be to ensure an expansion in other sectors which would offset the decline in military expenditures.

Since the great depression, considerable advances have been made in solving the problem of maintaining effective demand in the private enterprise economies.

The various instruments of policy that could be used to sustain the level of economic activity include the reduction of income taxes, indirect taxes on mass consumption goods, measures to stimulate investment, reduction of public debt, and expansion of government expenditure. Following an analysis of the relative merits of these, the experts concluded that "disarmament need not therefore increase the difficulty of economic stabilization in the industrialized private enterprise economies."

In the centrally planned economies, the major economic decisions concerning consumption, investment, and public expenditures are coordinated through a central plan. The maintenance of the level of economic activity during the processes of conversion in these countries would therefore "be simply a matter of economic efficiency of planning techniques," according to the report. For one form of expenditure, such as military outlays, could be substituted other forms, such as investment, consumption, and foreign assistance. The precise manner of allocating resources among these forms would be determined by "the physical adaptation of plants producing armaments to the production of goods for civilian use," suggests the report.

Structural Problems of Conversion

Even when the countries succeed in maintaining the overall level of economic activity during the conversion, they would be faced with important problems of adjustments in specific industrial sectors and geographical areas. In some cases, the adaptation might be relatively easy: for instance, a shift from the production of tanks to tractors, of military to civilian aircraft, of naval vessels to merchant ships. The changes in the plant and equipment, and in the number and in the skills of the employees would be small in these cases. On the other hand, there would be instances where disarmament would necessitate major adjustments in the pattern of output and employment in specific economic fields or regions. Many sectors of employment, for instance the ordnance factories or the armed forces, might be eliminated completely. The people employed in these would have to seek work in other sectors, often located at different centers. It would thus involve the movement of people to different locations.

Hypothetical estimates about the changes in employment called forth by complete disarmament, under various assumptions concerning reallocation of resources, have been prepared for two countries—the United States and the United Kingdom. These calculations suggest that if the processes of disarmament were spread over a number of years "the change per annum would be only a fraction of the total." In countries with labor shortages, disarmament would release manpower for accelerating economic growth.

The group of experts also analyzed a number of special problems arising from the concentration of military effort in certain sectors and areas. These related to adaptation of skills to peacetime requirements: problems of assistance to particular enterprises, industries, and localities heavily oriented to military use; and reorientation of research and technological development. In general they were of the opinion that the resources released by disarmament would be so large that, given advanced planning and vigorous policy, it should be possible to overcome these dislocations.

Influence on Foreign Trade

Disarmament would reflect a lessening of international tensions, a rebuilding of confidence between the private enterprise economies and the centrally planned economies, and would improve the economic relations between them. This would contribute to the expansion of trade between them, and higher economic activity in the wake of disarmament would also help expand international trade in general.

An acceleration of economic growth would also stimulate the demand for primary products. But in some countries the fall in military demand for particular commodities might cause difficulties. Military expenditures account for a significant part of demand for many primary products, such as copper, tin, nickel, lead, zinc, and petroleum, and their prices are very sensitive to changes in demand. The combined unfavorable influences of a decline in the volume of demand as well as in prices could affect adversely those countries whose exports consist largely of these items.

Since the fall in military demand would be offset by a rise in civilian and other forms of public demand, the experts felt that disarmament would have only a small effect on the overall demand for these commodities. Should particular difficulties be faced by some countries, however, they emphasized the need for special aid to them:

For many of the countries mainly dependent on the export of primary commodities, a percentage decline in their export earnings which might appear small arithmetically could cause grave damage. For example, a six percent drop in their average export prices, were it to take place, would imply for the underdeveloped countries a decline in foreign exchange earnings equivalent to something like one-half of all official economic grants and loans currently received from abroad in a year. Recessions in activity in the industrial countries have caused declines of this order of magnitude in the recent past. Concerted international action would therefore be required to prevent any such decline in their prices and incomes of the primary producing countries as a result of disarmament.

A DISARMED WORLD

What would be the economic image of a disarmed world? Its shape would largely depend on the alternative uses toward which the resources released from armaments were directed. Many of the most urgent needs of mankind have so far remained unsatisfied because precious resources were turned to destructive purposes.

Alternative Uses for Resources Devoted to Armaments

The resources released from armaments can be used for many purposes, such as raising levels of personal consumption, expanding productive capacity, social investment, and aid to under-developed countries. These claims are not only interlinked—in the sense that an increase in one depends upon an increase in another—but they are also competing. While disarming, it would therefore be necessary for each country to establish a scale of priorities based on its needs and consistent with the possibilities of satisfying them.

Since social investments have often given way to the claims of military expenditures, it is of some relevance to give an idea of the wide scope that exists in this field. After thousands of years of cold and dreary winter, the arrival of springtime of mankind—a century of the machine age—has so far mainly helped raise levels of living only in the industrial countries. Most of mankind is still ill-fed, ill-clad, ill-housed, and illiterate. But even in the richest countries of the world, there are widespread deficiencies in capital for such social investment.

The National Planning Association estimated that to carry out the existing public programs of development and improvement in the United States, the present public expenditure of about $30 billion per year would have to be more than doubled—a vast sum indeed. Urban centers are expanding rapidly. In the Soviet Union, the housing problem remains acute. "The growth of the urban population in the Soviet Union during the past few years is considerably in excess of the estimates," said Premier Khrushchev in his report to the twenty-second congress of the Communist party. The conditions of urban living, as reflected in the existence of slums, bad housing, poor community services, delinquency, paralysis of city traffic, and inadequate sanitation, are deteriorating.

The world's needs for development and conservation of natural resources are immense. It has been estimated for the United States that water resource development alone would require federal expenditures amounting to nearly $55 billion up to 1980; nonfederal programs would need as much as $173 billion. Huge nature-transforming projects in various parts of the world are awaiting execution. In the underdeveloped countries many important multipurpose schemes could be carried out if adequate resources were available.

Even in the richest countries, there is room for improvement of the medical and health services. In the rest of the world, they are simply inadequate. Mortality rates of infants and of pregnant mothers are high. Millions of people still suffer from diseases that would be easy to cure or prevent if adequate resources were available. The age of enlightenment has so far seen its full fruition only in the industrially advanced countries, and even there scope for expansion of higher educational facilities is wide indeed. More than half the population in the rest of the world is still illiterate, unable to decipher the magic of the written word.

There are many other ventures that can be carried out adequately only through the international cooperation of many countries. Audacious undertakings remain today merely paper plans because of lack of mutual confidence among nations and availability of resources. A few of them may be cited: a worldwide network of meteorological stations, telecommunications, air transport; utilization of atomic energy for peaceful purposes; space research to widen the horizons of the universe within man's reach; exploration of the Arctic and Antarctic; control of desert locusts, which continue to devastate crops in Africa and western Asia, through the establishment of highly mobile international brigades; research into the earth's interior; and, above all, joint programs to put an end as rapidly as possible to hunger and poverty in the industrially less developed countries.

Drawing pointed attention to the vast magnitude of the major needs of mankind that have so far remained unsatisfied, the United Nations experts concluded that "the resources freed by disarmament would not be large enough for the many claims upon them. . . . It seems abundantly clear that no country need fear a lack of useful employment opportunities for the resources that would become available to it through disarmament."

International Aid to Developing Countries

Perhaps the most important advantage of disarmament would accrue to the developing countries. So far they have benefited only marginally from the vast advances in modern science and technology. Two-thirds of the world population in these countries produce only about one-fifth of the world output. Per capita income for this overwhelming majority of mankind is only one-tenth of that in the industrial countries. International attention and growing concern for their poverty has so far done little to narrow the economic distance that separates the rich and poor countries. The rate of growth of per capita output in the poor countries over the last twenty years has remained lower than in the rich ones.

To narrow this vast and growing gap, the growth rate of the poor economies has to be raised significantly above that of the rich ones. The United Nations experts emphasized that "the responsibility for initiation and intensification of development efforts will continue to lie entirely with the governments and peoples" of the underdeveloped countries. But many of these countries would be faced with grave shortages of foreign exchange if they were to embark on ambitious plans for raising the volume and the rate of capital formation in their economies.

The flow of foreign assistance to these countries can be increased manifold once the industrial countries have eliminated armament expenditure. The United Nations experts, however, warned that "because the competing claims in developed countries are also urgent, there is a serious possibility that the financial resources released by disarmament might be rapidly absorbed by purely national aims. It is therefore desirable that an appropriate proportion of these resources should be allocated to international aid in its various forms simultaneously with their use for domestic purposes."

The impact of a large increase in international aid (as a result of disarmament) to the developing countries may be illustrated by a hypothetical example. If the total capital flow from the industrial countries, both in the east and the west, were to rise to $15 billion a year, this would amount to a little more than one percent of their combined gross national product. It would be a small share of what they spend at present upon armaments. But this sum is nearly twice as high as the total volume of machinery and equipment that is being imported every year by all the underdeveloped countries. Even if half of this sum were to be spent exclusively on expanding the imports of machinery and equipment in these countries, it would form a basis for doubling the present level of investment.

The influence of such a rise in investment on the growth rate of the economy would perhaps be more than proportionate, since proper management of investment plans often yields a relatively higher growth rate per each additional unit of investment. But even doubling the growth rate would mean a rise from the present rate of about three percent to six or seven percent. With population increasing at about two percent per year, the per capita rate of growth would rise from just about one percent to as high as four to five percent. At this rate, per capita output in these countries could rise sevenfold to tenfold in fifty years— or nearly equal to the present level in the industrial countries.

The diversion of even a small proportion of the resources devoted to war to assist the developing countries would provide the basis for a final solution of mankind's age-old affliction of squalor, poverty, want, and disease. The choice facing mankind is between half an hour of insanity and half a century of wise international cooperation.

QUESTIONS AND STUDY SUGGESTIONS

1. What is the volume and distribution of world armament expenditure?
2. What are the major economic problems posed by disarmament? What lessons can be derived from reconversion experience following World War II?
3. Analyze the potential economic advantages of world disarmament.

PART FIVE

THE INTERNATIONAL ECONOMY AND COMPARATIVE ECONOMIC SYSTEMS

Reading 68

Toward Freer Trade: The Kennedy Round

Council of Economic Advisers

The economic advantages of human and geographic specialization are well known (Reading 3). Yet for a variety of reasons, substantial tariff barriers have persisted among nations, to the end that free trade and therefore the opportunity to specialize are impeded. Since the passage of the Reciprocal Trade Agreements Act of 1934, the United States has played a major role in the reduction of international trade barriers. Reading 68 describes the background, accomplishments, and shortcomings of the Kennedy Round of tariff reductions, which was completed in the summer of 1967. Aside from the specific reductions achieved, the Kennedy Round is highly important in that it sustains the trend toward freer trade which began in the mid-1930s. In looking to the future, the CEA holds that "a liberal commercial policy is the only rational policy for the United States" and urges Congress to resist protectionist pressures.

World trade has grown spectacularly in recent years. Between 1953 and 1966 it expanded by almost two and a half times, while world output of primary and manufactured products doubled. The growth of trade relative to output has been an important factor in making this period the most prosperous one in recorded history. It was fostered by the progressive liberalization of the commercial policies of the major trading nations. The United States can take pride in its leading role in this liberalization.

The Kennedy Round was the sixth venture at multilateral trade negotiations undertaken by the GATT [General Agreement on Tariffs and Trade] since its creation in 1947. The growth of regional trading blocs in Europe and elsewhere introduced a special urgency and significance to the latest negotiations. The major nations of Europe had divided themselves into two trading groups, the EEC [European Economic Community] and the EFTA [European Free Trade Association]. Each group provided for eventual free trade among its members, accompanied by a continuation of tariffs and other restrictions against nonmembers. While these organizations have many desirable features, they can pose a threat to the development of more liberal trading relations among nations that belong to different groups and between group members and nonmembers like the United States.

The United States' response to this challenge was the passage of the Trade Expansion Act of 1962 which became the stimulus for the Kennedy Round. This act permitted the President greater flexibility in bargaining for lower tariffs and provided for adjustment assistance to American workers and business firms that might be injured as a result of tariff concessions. The negotiations were formally begun in May 1964 and were concluded after many difficulties on June 30, 1967. Although some problems could not be adequately overcome within the Kennedy Round, a remarkable degree of tariff reduction was achieved. The results have been widely and accurately acclaimed as a major accomplishment.

From **Economic Report of the President, 1968,** Washington, February, 1968, pp. 187–191.

FEATURES OF THE AGREEMENT: INDUSTRY

The agreement includes tariff concessions covering about $40 billion of world trade; the United States gave concessions on about $8.5 billion of its imports while concessions by others cover the same amount of U.S. exports. Tariff reductions of 50 percent were applied to numerous manufactured products and significant but smaller reductions were applied to many others. For the four largest participants —the United States, the EEC, the United Kingdom, and Japan—the weighted average reduction of tariffs on manufactured products was about 35 percent. The U.S. tariff reductions will generally take effect in five equal annual installments, the first of which became effective on January 1, 1968. Some of our trading partners took a similar step at the same time, but others will wait until midyear and then make 40 percent of their reductions.

Certain manufactured products required special negotiations; these included chemicals, cotton textiles, and iron and steel. Chemical products posed a particularly difficult problem, which was resolved by making two separate agreements. The first is incorporated in the multilateral tariff-reducing agreement providing for a stipulated unconditional reduction of chemical tariffs by the United States and other countries.

The second is conditional upon legislative action by the United States to remove the special valuation method now applied by U.S. tariff regulations on benzenoid chemicals. Under legislation adopted in 1922, when the American chemical industry was still in an "infant" stage, the U.S. tariff rate for competitive benzenoid chemicals is applied to the price of similar products made by domestic producers rather than to the actual price of imports. If the United States adopts the normal valuation practice on these items, certain of its major trading partners will further reduce chemical tariffs and will also lower some nontariff barriers.

FEATURES OF THE AGREEMENT: AGRICULTURE

Agricultural products were also considered in the Kennedy Round and proved to be especially troublesome. However, significant tariff concessions were finally agreed upon. Those by other nations cover about $870 million of U.S. exports. Our concessions covered about the same amount of U.S. imports. The other major accomplishment in agriculture was the negotiation of a grains agreement. It provides for a higher minimum price for wheat than existed under the old International Wheat Agreement, and involves an increase of about 15 percent in U.S. export prices. It also provides for a multilateral food aid program equivalent to 4.5 million tons of cereals a year, of which the United States would contribute 42 percent.

While these steps are encouraging, the degree of restriction remaining on international trade in agricultural products—particularly through nontariff barriers—still greatly exceeds that on manufactured goods. Nevertheless, the Kennedy Round went further than previous negotiations in the agricultural area. Furthermore, the principle embodied in the food aid agreement may have great significance over the long run, because it recognizes that responsibility in the international war on hunger extends to all countries, not just to the United States and the other major food exporting nations. If the world's need for food should outrun supplies in the year ahead, this agreement could become the pattern for an international corrective program.

The United States made particular efforts to reduce tariffs on products of special interest to less-developed countries. It granted concessions on more than $900 million of such products without attempting to obtain full reciprocity.

Another element in the Kennedy Round package was the successful negotiation of an international antidumping code. This accord is consistent with existing American laws which safeguard our industry, and it commits our trading partners to insure fair procedures to American exporters. Also a part of the negotiation, a three-year extension of the long-term cotton textile arrangement was concluded.

CONSEQUENCES OF THE TARIFF REDUCTIONS

The amount of existing trade covered by tariff cuts in the Kennedy Round does not reflect the potential expansion of trade which is one of the key benefits of the tariff reductions. New U.S. export opportunities will be created. Moreover, American producers will experience lower costs as a result of reduced tariffs on many inputs. The welfare of American consumers will be enhanced by lower prices of goods of both domestic and foreign origin.

Exports

American exports will be stimulated from two sources. First, as tariffs abroad are reduced, our exporters will have an opportunity to compete on a more equal footing in the domestic markets of foreign producers. Second, the tariff advantage in favor of member nations over nonmembers within the EEC and EFTA will be reduced, thereby enabling American exporters to compete more effectively in these large markets. For example, because the EEC tariff on pumps and compressors will be reduced from 12 to 6 percent when the Kennedy Round reductions are completed, German pumps will have only a 6 percent preferential edge over American pumps in the Dutch market as compared to the 12 percent they now enjoy.

Inputs

A second major gain from the Kennedy Round will come from the reduction of American tariffs on materials and components used by American manufacturers. Both the imported items and the competing domestic materials will be cheaper, and production costs will thereby be reduced. As a consequence, the competitive position of American manufacturers using these inputs will be improved in both export and domestic markets.

To cite only one example, tariffs on a wide range of steel alloying materials will be progressively reduced. This should reduce the costs of producing alloy steels, and of machine tools, machinery and equipment manufactured from such steels, thus strengthening the competitive position of our machinery industries in export markets.

Consumer Goods

The Kennedy Round also provides benefit to American consumers from U.S. tariff reductions. Consumers will enjoy reduced prices on imported goods and also on American products that compete with imports. If the full reduction is passed on, for instance, the 50 percent

drop in tariffs on wooden furniture is the equivalent of price reductions of 5 to 10 percent. Further, in the climate of more liberal trade, foreign producers will be encouraged to market new products to American consumers.

Adjustment Strains

A full evaluation of the impact of the Kennedy Round must recognize that there may be some adverse effects as well. The increases in imports resulting from reduced U.S. tariffs can cause discomfort for certain American industries. Imports, however, still amount to only 3 percent of our GNP, and can hardly pose insuperable adjustment problems, even in the short run. The overwhelming majority of American industries that face brisk competition from imports can adjust in stride. American business knows how to respond to shifting domestic and international competitive pressure, and its responses are generally beneficial to the entire economy. But a few American industries may need help to meet the competitive challenge; and that aid should be given through temporary Government support to improve efficiency. Adjustment assistance is essential to meet the limited costs the Kennedy Round may impose in a few areas while maintaining its large benefits for the entire Nation.

LEGISLATIVE TASKS

The 1962 Trade Expansion Act provided for adjustment assistance in cases of injury arising from tariff reductions, but the legislated criteria for eligibility have proven to be excessively restrictive. These criteria can and should be liberalized without opening the door to possible abuse, and the President is asking for the necessary congressional action to this effect.

Assistance for workers includes the payment of readjustment allowances directly to those who are obliged to seek alternative employment as a result of tariff reductions. The allowances can also be paid while workers are taking part in on-the-job training. The Government can also provide for testing, counseling, training, and placement services to promote a swift and smooth transfer. Adjustment assistance can be provided to injured firms to permit them to adapt their product lines or lower their costs in order to meet new competitive conditions. Such a solution within the affected firms is particularly desirable because it avoids dislocation in the employment of workers and in the use of capital. The offices of the Department of Commerce can make technical assistance available. Financial aid can be provided through loans or loan guarantees. Tax relief is offered through extension of the provisions of the Internal Revenue Code for the carryback and carry-forward of business losses.

A second urgent legislative requirement is the elimination of the American selling price system. This action is needed to assure the full benefit of lower chemical tariffs abroad and to win important concessions on certain foreign nontariff barriers, as well as to provide the United States with a uniformly rational valuation system.

It is essential that Congress *not* enact legislation that would reverse or jeopardize our long-term efforts and policies to promote liberal trade. Bills were introduced into the Congress in 1967 to impose new legislated quotas on textiles, apparel, steel, meat and meat products, mink furs, lead and zinc, groundfish fillets, baseball gloves and mitts, consumer electronic products, scissors and shears, hardwood plywood, ferro-alloys, potash, flat glass, ball and roller bearings, and stainless steel flatware. Other bills sought to tighten restrictions on petroleum and petroleum products and dairy products. The value of the imports covered by specific bills amounts to over $6 billion. If general quota provisions were adopted along lines proposed in some bills, $12 billion or more of imports would be affected.

If enacted, quota bills could severely harm our economy in several ways. Quotas would deprive American producers and consumers of flexible import supplies that help to moderate shortages. Quotas also would exert upward pressures on prices at a time when price stability is a critical national objective. Furthermore, protected American industries would be insulated from competitive forces abroad. Many of these industries need the invigorating influence of foreign competition, and should not be permitted to relax behind high protective barriers.

Finally, and perhaps most seriously, our exports would certainly suffer from quota restrictions on imports. Some exports would be lost simply because importing countries would have less foreign exchange. But more importantly, foreign governments would surely take advantage of their rights under the GATT to retaliate against whichever American products they may choose. In the end, we would have sacrificed the interests of more efficient industries and businesses for the sake of protecting less competitive elements in the economy; we would have jeopardized the creation of higher paying jobs in order to preserve low-wage jobs; and we would have traded international cooperation for international economic warfare. A move toward protectionism would also hurt our balance of payments. The rising trade surplus counted upon to help achieve payments equilibrium would be impossible in a world of widespread trade restrictions. For all of these reasons a liberal commercial policy is the only rational policy for the United States.

QUESTIONS AND STUDY SUGGESTIONS

1. What is the relationship of the Trade Expansion Act of 1962 to the Kennedy Round of tariff negotiations?
2. Summarize the basic accomplishments of the Kennedy Round. Explain the contention that, as a result of tariff reductions realized in the Kennedy Round, "American exports will be stimulated from two sources."
3. What is the relationship between the Kennedy Round and our balance of payments deficit?

Reading 69

Import Quotas for Petroleum: Two Views

As indicated in Reading 68, the tariff reductions realized in the Kennedy Round stimulated considerable pressure upon Congress to impose new import quotas upon steel, textiles, meat, dairy products, petroleum, and a wide variety of other products. Import quotas can have an even more restrictive effect upon trade than tariffs, in that quotas put an outright limit upon the quantity of a product which can be imported while tariffs do not. Specifically, quotas usually limit imports of a commodity to some fixed percentage of recent domestic production. The two views which comprise Reading 69 debate the merits of a bill (S. 2332) introduced shortly after the conclusion of the Kennedy Round. The proposed legislation is designed to limit petroleum imports to 12.2 percent of domestic production.

Petroleum Import Quotas: First View

Joe McGuire, President, Independent Oil Producers & Land Owners Association, Tri-State, Inc.

Mr. Chairman, the Independent Oil Producers & Land Owners Association, Tri-State, Inc., is an association whose membership consists of producers, landowners, and other independent businessmen directly serving the oil industry in the States of Illinois, Indiana, and Kentucky. This area is also referred to as the Tri-State Basin, and is one of the oldest oil producing areas in the United States. The objective and purpose of IOPLOA is to provide a collective voice for the independent oilman, who continues to contribute substantially to the industry in our area.

Our association wishes to go on record as wholeheartedly supporting S. 2332 and we hereby commend Senator Russell B. Long and the cosponsors of this bill for assuming the responsibility and leadership to provide legislation so vital to the security of our Nation and so necessary to the health of the domestic oil industry.

OIL AND NATIONAL SECURITY

It is the unanimous position of our association that the recent Mideast crisis has clearly dem-

onstrated the danger to our national security of overreliance upon foreign sources for crude oil. The fact that such a situation did occur twice within an 11-year period is unimpeachable evidence of the necessity to maintain a safe margin of domestic reserves. The oil import program, as implemented by the Trade Expansion Act of 1962, has failed to accomplish its stated purpose. During the past 10 years, the period estimated to exhaust our proven domestic reserves has declined from 13.5 years to 11.5 years. We are now consuming approximately the same amount of oil annually as is discovered. With domestic consumption rising and domestic exploration declining, this reserve figure can only decline further unless and until adequate programs are adopted which will provide the essential stimulus and incentive to induce the domestic oilman to renew his search for oil. We believe that the imposition, through legislation, of a 12.2 percent quota as a ceiling on foreign imports is one such program.

It is recognized that the interest and security of the Nation as a whole is the overriding reason to stabilize oil imports. There are other

From **Import Quota Legislation:** Hearings before the Committee on Finance, 90th Cong., 1st Sess., Washington, 1967, part 1, pp. 296–299, abridged.

factors which affect the overall problem to which this hearing is addressed and it is to these that we confine our remarks.

DECLINE OF DOMESTIC INDUSTRY: CAUSES

The oil industry in the Tri-State is composed primarily of numerous small independent operators. It has, until recent times, been a healthy and vibrant industry and has made a significant contribution to the overall economy of our three member States. For the past 10 years, however, we have witnessed a steady decline, as demonstrated by the fact that where there were employed over 50,000 persons in the Tri-State in the production of oil and gas there are now less than 13,500 so employed, based upon 1966 figures. Production has declined steadily from over 360,000 barrels of oil per day to approximately 250,000 barrels of oil per day. The number of active rotary drilling rigs operating in this area was 200 and has declined to the present time to less than 40, and wildcat drilling for oil is down 80 percent, all of the foregoing declines being over the past 10 years.

One of the more serious problems of the oil industry in our area is the loss of technical personnel to other industries. This is caused by the decline in exploration activity and our inability to meet average wage scales due to the economic conditions imposed by excessive imports. This type of personnel, so necessary to our industry in the search for reserves, requires years of education and experience to be effective. The time element necessary for the education and training of these technicians would not be available to our industry in the event of a national emergency.

The foregoing represents in capsule form the present state of the oil industry in the Tri-State area.

It is a matter of public knowledge that demand for crude oil, as well as consumption of crude oil products, has risen in the past 10 years. On the other hand, while the price index of almost every commodity and service used by the oil producer has risen, the price of crude oil has declined slightly.

Thus, faced with constantly rising costs of every commodity necessary to explore for and produce his sole product, and an eroding price for his sole product, the independent oil man has been caught in a rising cost spiral which is forcing many to leave the industry.

Contributing significantly to this situation is the importation of foreign crude oil which has saturated the rising demand for crude oil products, and has helped to deteriorate the price paid for domestic crude in an otherwise rising economy. That foreign crude oil is cheaper, in the total analysis, may be argued. That foreign crude oil will always be available is problematical. That foreign crude oil has created a problem involving our national security is fully recognized. That foreign crude oil is undermining a previously healthy and necessary domestic industry is undeniable.

Another important factor contributing to the present plight of the domestic oil industry is the lack of capital available to the domestic oil producer. The basic reason for this withdrawal of investment capital is the lack of incentive, or, to put it another way, the lack of profit potential. If he is unable to attract such investment he will be forced to curtail, if not eliminate, further exploration, and must then confine his activity to the production and liquidation of those reserves he may have already found.

QUOTAS AS A REMEDY

To restore the domestic oil industry to a healthy status will require a return to the marketplace where supply and demand will govern the pricing of both crude oil and crude oil products. Sufficient incentives will have to be provided to the domestic oil man to induce him to return to the high-risk activity of searching for oil. Additionally, investment capital will have to be attracted, and to do so in our free enterprise system will require, at the very least, a reasonable chance for a reasonable profit. We think that S. 2332, imposing a 12.2-percent quota limitation on foreign imports and phasing out all exceptions heretofore created, is a giant step in the right direction. Without such protection, we firmly believe the domestic industry will witness an even more dramatic rate of decline in the immediate future than has been the case in the recent past.

We heartily commend the sponsors of this legislation, urge its passage, and pledge our support and assistance wherever possible.

Petroleum Import Quotas: Second View

Franklin M. Fisher, Professor of Economics, Massachusetts Institute of Technology

The argument that quotas on petroleum imports enhance the security of the United States is a false one. To ensure the preservation of domestic oil supplies in the event of a petroleum crisis, the United States should import freely and reduce consumption of domestically produced oil. While it is true that this would sharply curtail petroleum exploration, it is not true that petroleum *discoveries* would be so greatly affected as to make domestic reserves decrease substantially if at all. Further, it is clear that the United States is in no danger of running out of oil. If it is desirable for strategic purposes to ensure that some oil reserves are kept in a readily producible state, this should be done by stockpiling reserves in the ground analogous to the treatment of other strategic materials. It should not be done by keeping gasoline and other oil prices high at the expense of American consumers.

In fact, the main effect of oil import quotas is the maintenance of high prices and the subsidization of various relatively inefficient domestic producers at the expense of the American motorist. Quotas should be discontinued, not written into law.

QUOTAS AND NATIONAL SECURITY

The basic argument put forward in favor of oil import quotas is one of national security. It is argued that free imports of oil make us reliant on foreign sources which may be (and have been) cut off or diminished in the event of an emergency. By limiting imports, we free ourselves from international political blackmail (principally by the Arabs). I believe this argument to be false. The imposition of oil import quotas does not advance the security of the United States and it unduly penalizes American motorists.

It is obvious that for the national security argument for oil import quotas to be right, it must be so for somewhat subtle reasons. If free imports lead to heavy use of imported oil and a cutback in domestic production displaced by

imports, the natural conclusion is that domestic oil will not be used up so fast and there will be more of it around in the event of an emergency than would be the case if imports were limited and domestic production expanded. If one wants to have a strategic material on hand for crises, a reasonable way to behave is to stockpile it and use foreign sources in non-crisis situations, not to use up domestic supplies faster. This is United States government policy with respect to most other strategic materials.

This argument is realized by quota proponents. They claim that the true situation is as follows:

A. Domestic supplies of crude oil in the ground change when oil is produced (a subtraction) and when new oil is discovered (an addition).

B. Free imports will reduce domestic production and thus indeed reduce the rate at which we subtract from known oil reserves.

C. However, free oil imports will also reduce the price of crude oil. This will reduce the incentive to exploration for and discovery of oil. Exploration is very sensitive to such incentives and will fall off drastically.

D. This will greatly reduce additions to oil reserves through new discoveries and

E. The net result of the two effects will be a reduction in oil reserves.

This fairly complicated argument is not ridiculous, but it is almost certainly completely false. A good deal of recent quantitative research (mine and others) has shown that while oil exploration is indeed rather sensitive to price, the *discovery* of new crude oil supplies is not so sensitive as exploration. The principal reason for this is that higher prices lead prospectors to drill many fields that would be too small to be worth drilling at lower prices.

Indeed diminishing returns to oil exploration induced by higher prices tend to set in rather quickly. The best estimate of the effects of a price increase seems to be that a ten percent price increase (other things equal) leads to

From **Import Quota Legislation:** Hearings before the Committee on Finance, 90th Cong., 1st Sess., Washington, 1967, part 1, pp. 372–374.

about a sixteen percent increase in the number of wildcat wells but only about a nine percent increase in discoveries. Whether this means that discoveries are sufficiently sensitive to prices to make the pro-quota argument true is not clear. What is clear is that such sensitivity is not so obviously high as to make that argument highly persuasive. (In this connection, it is worth noting that the supposed high sensitivity of oil discovery to economic incentives is used to buttress any special treatment for crude oil producers, principally the percentage depletion provisions of the tax laws. It is not a strong buttress.)

Moreover, whatever the effects of free imports on oil discoveries, and even if new oil discoveries were to cease altogether on the abandonment of quotas, the United States is in no danger whatever of running out of oil. This is so for three reasons:

A. Proved reserves of crude oil are sufficient for about 10–12 years production at current rates. (This figure has been roughly constant for a long time.)

B. Proved reserves are a deliberately conservative estimate of the amount of oil in known oil fields and pools. They measure oil in place in such fields close to existing wells and available pretty much without further exploration. The total amount of recoverable oil in already discovered deposits is at least 1.3 times proved reserves (thirteen years supply, and I am being conservative here).

C. Production of crude oil from oil shale is technologically feasible. There is at least forty years supply of such oil in known deposits (but it would be somewhat more expensive to produce than domestic crude out of the ground).

D. And, of course, in the event of a prolonged oil crisis, exploration would rise sharply.

A good argument as to national security is that whatever the long-run supplies of oil, an emergency requires that oil be readily available (although the nature of crises since World War II may suggest that the ability to produce more oil *in a great hurry* is not of primary importance). This makes points B–D irrelevant in the short run. Further, the possible need to keep oil supplies readily available may require that the industry not shut in known fields, but keep them in a state ready to produce as well as keeping in being the capacity to produce already known proved reserves in a hurry. To the extent that such very short-run considera-

tions are indeed important, however, it is obviously efficient and appropriate for the government to stockpile producible oil in known fields by buying up fields or developing fields on federal lands (these are quite substantial) or to directly subsidize such stockpiling. (One way to do this is by paying producers in fields closed down as a result of import competition to maintain those fields and their equipment in a state of readiness.) It is both inefficient and inequitable to subsidize the entire domestic industry by keeping gasoline prices high. For no other strategic material do we engage in such inefficient action in place of direct stockpiling. The question should be consciously studied (or existing studies used) and direct action taken to stockpile readily producible oil in the ground if this turns out to be necessary. There is no reason to do this at the expense of every motorist by limiting imports of efficiently produced cheap petroleum (largely produced by American firms, by the way).

REAL EFFECTS OF QUOTAS

The national security argument for quotas is thus respectable and bogus. The real effects of quotas are the maintenance of high domestic prices and the protection of relatively inefficient domestic oil producers. The system works as follows.

For reasons of conservation, crude oil production is exempted from the effects of the anti-trust laws and interstate shipment of crude oil produced outside of state conservation limitations is prohibited. In practice, when the market for petroleum weakens, state conservation authorities (principally the Texas Railroad Commission) limit production far below the levels which would be dictated by conservation considerations. However such limitations are rationalized, their effect is the adjustment of production to demand and the maintenance of relatively high prices for crude petroleum and petroleum products. In particular, state production restrictions limit production from efficient, low-cost high-production wells very severely. This keeps prices artificially high and inefficient, high-cost producers in business. In recent years, there has been an abundance of domestic oil and production has been kept far below capacity.

Obviously, this system could not work if low-cost foreign oil were freely imported. It is thus greatly in the interest of the domestic oil producers to limit such imports. It is not in the interest of the United States as a whole, nor is it in the interest of most of its citizens.

CONCLUSIONS

A. Import quotas on petroleum should be abandoned, not written into law. They do not advance the security of the United States and they penalize the American motorist for the benefit of domestic oil producers.

B. A study of the advisability of stockpiling readily producible oil in the ground should be undertaken and such stockpiling done by direct action in the cheapest possible manner.

C. The present practice of maintaining oil prices at an artificially high level under the guise of conservation should be abandoned. Although free imports should go a long way toward accomplishing this, Congress should consider whether direct legislation toward this end would be appropriate.

QUESTIONS AND STUDY SUGGESTIONS

1. "Import restrictions upon petroleum are vital to the national security of the United States." Do you agree? Defend your position.
2. Evaluate the two views with respect to the impact of the proposed import quotas upon the rate of discovery of new crude oil supplies in the United States. Which view do you feel is more accurate?
3. In your opinion is S.2332 an economically desirable piece of legislation? Justify your answer.

Reading 70

Resolving the Payments Deficit: The Government's Program

Lyndon B. Johnson, President of the United States

This reading and the following three are all related. All deal with the United States's balance of payments problems and the means by which it can be resolved. Reading 70 summarizes the solution to our payments deficits as viewed from the White House. On January 1, 1968, following the British devaluation of the pound and a worsening of the United States's payments position, President Johnson outlined a program designed to resolve our payments deficit. Specific aspects of the program include mandatory restrictions on direct investment abroad by American firms; restraints upon

From President Lyndon B. Johnson, **Statement by the President on the Balance of Payments,** Washington, January 1, 1968.

foreign lending by American banks; discouragement of nonessential travel abroad by Americans; and minimization of the foreign exchange costs of maintaining American troops in Europe. It is hoped that our trade surplus can be widened by measures which reduce nontariff barriers to American exports and promote foreign travel in the United States. Reading 71 is a critique of the President's proposals.

I want to discuss with the American people a subject of vital concern to the economic health and well-being of this Nation and the free world.

It is our international balance of payments position.

The strength of our dollar depends on the strength of that position.

The soundness of the free world monetary system, which rests largely on the dollar, also depends on the strength of that position.

To the average citizen, the balance of payments, and the strength of the dollar and of the international monetary system, are meaningless phrases. They seem to have little relevance to our daily lives. Yet their consequences touch us all—consumer and captain of industry, worker, farmer, and financier.

More than ever before, the economy of each Nation is today deeply intertwined with that of every other. A vast network of world trade and financial transactions ties us all together. The prosperity of every economy rests on that of every other.

More than ever before, this is one world—in economic affairs as in every other way.

Your job, the prosperity of your farm or business, depends directly or indirectly on what happens in Europe, Asia, Latin America, or Africa.

WHERE WE STAND TODAY

The health of the international economic system rests on a sound international money in the same way as the health of our domestic money. Today, our domestic money—the U.S. dollar—is also the money most used in international transactions. That money can be sound at home—as it surely is—yet can be in trouble abroad—as it now threatens to become.

In the final analysis its strength abroad depends on our earning abroad about as many dollars as we send abroad.

U.S. dollars flow from these shores for many reasons—to pay for imports and travel, to

finance loans and investments and to maintain our lines of defense around the world.

When that outflow is greater than our earnings and credits from foreign nations, a deficit results in our international accounts.

For 17 of the last 18 years we have had such deficits. For a time those deficits were needed to help the world recover from the ravages of World War II. They could be tolerated by the United States and welcomed by the rest of the world. They distributed more equitably the world's monetary gold reserves and supplemented them with dollars.

Once recovery was assured, however, large deficits were no longer needed and indeed began to threaten the strength of the dollar. Since 1961, your government has worked to reduce that deficit.

By the middle of the decade, we could see signs of success. Our annual deficit had been reduced two-thirds—from $3.9 billion in 1960 to $1.3 billion in 1965.

In 1966, because of our increased responsibility to arm and supply our men in Southeast Asia, progress was interrupted, with the deficit remaining at the same level as 1965—about $1.3 billion.

In 1967, progress was reversed for a number of reasons:

Our costs for Vietnam increased further.

Private loans and investments abroad increased.

Our trade surplus, although larger than 1966, did not rise as much as we had expected.

Americans spent more on travel abroad.

Added to these factors was the uncertainty and unrest surrounding the devaluation of the British pound. This event strained the international monetary system. It sharply increased our balance of payments deficit and our gold sales in the last quarter of 1967.

THE PROBLEM

Preliminary reports indicated that these conditions may result in a 1967 balance of payments deficit in the area of $3.5 to $4 billion—the highest since 1960. Although some factors affecting our deficit will be more favorable in 1968, my advisors and I are convinced that we must act to bring about a decisive improvement.

We cannot tolerate a deficit that could threaten the stability of the international monetary system—of which the U.S. dollar is the bulwark.

We cannot tolerate a deficit that could endanger the strength of the entire free world economy, and thereby threaten our unprecedented prosperity at home.

A TIME FOR ACTION

The time has now come for decisive action designed to bring our balance of payments to—or close to—equilibrium in the year ahead.

The need for action is a national and international responsibility of the highest priority.

I am proposing a program which will meet this critical need, and at the same time satisfy four essential conditions:

Sustain the growth, strength and prosperity of our own economy.

Allow us to continue to meet our international responsibilities in defense of freedom, in promoting world trade, and in encouraging economic growth in the developing countries.

Engage the cooperation of other free nations, whose stake in a sound international monetary system is no less compelling than our own.

Recognize the special obligation of those nations with balance of payments surpluses, to bring their payments into equilibrium.

THE FIRST ORDER OF BUSINESS

The first line of defense of the dollar is the strength of the American economy.

No business before the returning Congress will be more urgent than this: to enact the Anti-Inflation Tax which I have sought for almost a year. Coupled with our expenditure controls and appropriate monetary policy, this will help to stem the inflationary pressures which now threaten our economic prosperity and our trade surplus.

No challenge before business and labor is more urgent than this: to exercise the utmost

responsibility in their wage-price decisions, which affect so directly our competitive position at home and in world markets.

I have directed the Secretaries of Commerce and Labor, and the Chairman of the Council of Economic Advisers to work with leaders of business and labor to make more effective our voluntary program of wage-price restraint.

I have also instructed the Secretaries of Commerce and Labor to work with unions and companies to prevent our exports from being reduced or our imports increased by crippling work stoppages in the year ahead.

A sure way to instill confidence in our dollar—both here and abroad—is through these actions.

THE NEW PROGRAM

But we must go beyond this, and take additional action to deal with the balance of payments deficit.

Some of the elements in the program I propose will have a temporary but immediate effect. Others will be of longer range.

All are necessary to assure confidence in the American dollar.

TEMPORARY MEASURES

Direct Investment

Over the past three years, American business has cooperated with the government in a voluntary program to moderate the flow of U.S. dollars into foreign investments. Business leaders who have participated so wholeheartedly deserve the appreciation of their country.

But the savings now required in foreign investment outlays are clearly beyond the reach of any voluntary program. This is the unanimous view of all my economic and financial advisers and the Chairman of the Federal Reserve Board.

To reduce our balance of payments deficit by at least $1 billion in 1968 from the estimated 1967 level, I am invoking my authority under the banking laws to establish a mandatory program that will restrain direct investment abroad.

This program will be effective immediately. It will insure success and guarantee fairness among American business firms with overseas investments.

The program will be administered by the

Department of Commerce, and will operate as follows:

As in the voluntary program, over-all and individual company targets will be set. Authorizations to exceed these targets will be issued only in exceptional circumstances.

New direct investment outflows to countries in continental Western Europe and other developed nations not heavily dependent on our capital will be stopped in 1968. Problems arising from work already in process or commitments under binding contracts will receive special consideration.

New net investments in other developed countries will be limited to 65 percent of the 1965–66 average.

New net investments in the developing countries will be limited to 110 percent of the 1965–66 average.

This program also requires businesses to continue to bring back foreign earnings to the United States in line with their own 1964–66 practices.

In addition, I have directed the Secretary of the Treasury to explore with the Chairmen of the House Ways and Means Committee and Senate Finance Committee legislative proposals to induce or encourage the repatriation of accumulated earnings by U.S.-owned foreign businesses.

Lending by Financial Institutions

To reduce the balance of payments deficit by at least another $500 million, I have requested and authorized the Federal Reserve Board to tighten its program restraining foreign lending by banks and other financial institutions.

Chairman Martin has assured me that this reduction can be achieved:

Without harming the financing of our exports;

Primarily out of credits to developed countries without jeopardizing the availability of funds to the rest of the world.

Chairman Martin believes that this objective can be met through continued cooperation by the financial community. At the request of the Chairman, however, I have given the Federal Reserve Board standby authority to invoke mandatory controls, should such controls become desirable or necessary.

Travel Abroad

Our travel deficit this year will exceed $2 billion. To reduce this deficit by $500 million:

I am asking the American people to defer for the next two years all nonessential travel outside the Western Hemisphere.

I am asking the Secretary of the Treasury to explore with the appropriate Congressional committees legislation to help achieve this objective.

Government Expenditures Overseas

We cannot forego our essential commitments abroad, on which America's security and survival depend.

Nevertheless, we must take every step to reduce their impact on our balance of payments without endangering our security.

Recently, we have reached important agreements with some of our NATO partners to lessen the balance of payments cost of deploying American forces on the continent—troops necessarily stationed there for the common defense of all.

Over the past three years, a stringent program has saved billions of dollars in foreign exchange.

I am convinced that much more can be done. *I believe we should set as our target avoiding a drain of another $500 million on our balance of payments.*

To this end, I am taking three steps.

First, I have directed the Secretary of State to initiate prompt negotiations with our NATO allies to minimize the foreign exchange costs of keeping our troops in Europe. Our allies can help in a number of ways, including:

The purchase in the U.S. of more of their defense needs.

Investments in long-term United States Securities.

I have also directed the Secretaries of State, Treasury and Defense to find similar ways of dealing with this problem in other parts of the world.

Second, I have instructed the Director of the Budget to find ways of reducing the numbers of American civilians working overseas.

Third, I have instructed the Secretary of Defense to find ways to reduce further the foreign exchange impact of personal spending by U.S. Forces and their dependents in Europe.

LONG-TERM MEASURES

Export Increases

American exports provide an important source of earnings for our businessmen and jobs for our workers.

They are the cornerstone of our balance of payments position.

Last year we sold abroad $30 billion worth of American goods.

What we now need is a long-range systematic program to stimulate the flow of the products of our factories and farms into overseas markets.

We must begin now.

Some of the steps require legislation.

I shall ask the Congress to support an intensified five year, $200 million Commerce Department program to promote the sale of American goods overseas.

I shall also ask the Congress to earmark $500 million of the Export-Import Bank Authorization to:

Provide better export insurance.

Expand guarantees for export financing.

Broaden the scope of government financing of our exports.

Other measures require no legislation.

I have today directed the Secretary of Commerce to begin a Joint Export Association Program. Through these Associations, we will provide direct financial support to American Corporations joining together to sell abroad.

And finally, the Export-Import Bank—through a more liberal rediscount system—will encourage banks across the nation to help firms increase their exports.

Nontariff Barriers

In the Kennedy Round, we climaxed three decades of intensive effort to achieve the greatest reduction in tariff barriers in all the history of trade negotiations. Trade liberalization remains the basic policy of the United States.

We must now look beyond the great success of the Kennedy Round to the problems of nontariff barriers that pose a continued threat to the growth of world trade and to our competitive position.

American commerce is at a disadvantage because of the tax systems of some of our trading partners. Some nations give across-the-board tax rebates on exports which leave their ports and impose special border tax charges on our goods entering their country.

International rules govern these special taxes under the General Agreement on Tariffs and Trade. These rules must be adjusted to expand international trade further.

In keeping with the principles of cooperation and consultation on common problems, I have initiated discussions at a high level with our friends abroad on these critical matters—particularly those nations with balance of payments surpluses.

These discussions will examine proposals for prompt cooperative action among all parties to minimize the disadvantages to our trade which arise from differences among national tax systems.

We are also preparing legislative measures in this area whose scope and nature will depend upon the outcome of these consultations.

Through these means we are determined to achieve a substantial improvement in our trade surplus over the coming years. In the year immediately ahead, we expect to realize an improvement of $500 million.

Foreign Investment and Travel in U.S.

We can encourage the flow of foreign funds to our shores in two other ways:

First, by an intensified program to attract greater foreign investment in U.S. Corporate Securities, carrying out the principles of the Foreign Investors Tax Act of 1966.

Second, by a program to attract more visitors to this land. A special task force, headed by Robert McKinney of Santa Fe, New Mexico, is already at work on measures to accomplish this. I have directed the task force to report within 45 days on the immediate measures that can be taken, and to make its long-term recommendations within 90 days.

MEETING THE WORLD'S RESERVE NEEDS

Our movement toward balance will curb the flow of dollars into international reserves. It will therefore be vital to speed up plans for the creation of new reserves—the special drawing rights—in the International Monetary Fund. These new reserves will be a welcome companion to gold and dollars, and will strengthen the gold exchange standard. The dollar will remain convertible into gold at $35 an ounce, and our full gold stock will back that commitment.

A TIME FOR RESPONSIBILITY

The program I have outlined is a program of action.

It is a program which will preserve confidence in the dollar, both at home and abroad.

The U.S. dollar has wrought the greatest economic miracles of modern times.

It stimulated the resurgence of a war-ruined Europe.

It has helped to bring new strength and life to the developing world.

It has underwritten unprecedented prosperity for the American people, who are now in the 83rd month of sustained economic growth.

A strong dollar protects and preserves the prosperity of businessman and banker, worker and farmer—here and overseas.

The action program I have outlined in this message will keep the dollar strong. It will fulfill our responsibilities to the American people and to the free world.

I appeal to all of our citizens to join me in this very necessary and laudable effort to preserve our country's financial strength.

QUESTIONS AND STUDY SUGGESTIONS

1. Briefly summarize the President's program for correcting our payments deficit. What is the importance of the distinction between "temporary" measures and "long-term" measures?

2. What effects will the program's restrictions on overseas investment and lending have upon the international allocation of resources? Upon the United States's future capacity to export? Explain.

3. Critics of the government's program (Reading 71) hold that it restricts freedom and fails to get at the causes of our payments deficit. Do you agree?

A Critique of the Government's Balance-of-Payments Program

Fritz Machlup, Professor of Economics, Princeton University

In Reading 71 Fritz Machlup, an authority on international economics and finance, raises basic questions as to the efficacy of the government's program to deal with our payments problem (Reading 70). His major criticism is that the program does not embody "real adjustments" in our payments position, but rather offers stopgap measures of a restrictive character. Professor Machlup argues that these measures fail to get at the underlying causes of our payments deficit and that when they are removed, the deficit will reappear. Even in the short run the government's program will be less effective than anticipated. This is so for two reasons. First, other forms of foreign investment abroad can be substituted for the kinds of foreign investment prohibited by the government's program. Second, the restrictions on American investment and travel abroad and the reductions in our overseas military outlays will have indirect and adverse repercussions on the overall payments position of the United States. Professor Machlup recommends a fundamental adjustment of exchange rates. Readings 73 and 74 deal with the advisability of flexible exchange rates as a means of achieving equilibrium in a nation's international balance of payments.

For some 250 years economists studying international finance have known the process of economic adjustment that would remove imbalance and restore balance. This adjustment involves changes in relative prices and incomes in the countries concerned, resulting in changes in the allocation of productive resources and in the international flow of goods and services. The process had originally been conceived as an automatic one, but it can be fully automatic only under monetary institutions that no longer exist. Hence, deliberate adjustment policies are now required to produce the effects which the conceivably automatic mechanism would have produced. These policies do not, however, include every type of measure, including direct controls, that may be instituted for the purpose of removing a payments deficit.

In medicine, no one would doubt for a moment that there is a difference between a surgical operation or some other painful treatment and a disappearance or removal of the need for it. There may be some alternative therapeutic techniques that could remove the need for the painful one; or perhaps the affliction may disappear all by itself. The same possibilities exist for balance-of-payments troubles: with luck, the troubles may go away or some other therapy may make it unnecessary to go through the operations which economists have called the adjustment process. I use the term "compensatory corrections" or "correctives" to indicate those things that are considered as alternatives to the adjustment process.

From **1968 Economic Report of the President,** Hearings before the Joint Economic Committee, 90th Cong., 2d Sess., Washington, part 2, pp. 400–407, abridged.

REDUCING THE PAYMENTS DEFICIT: ALTERNATIVE METHODS

We need even more distinctions. There are measures that do not remove deficits but facilitate financing them. For example, if an increase in interest rates attracts short-term capital from abroad, one may not want to regard this as a credit item in the balance of payments that removes a deficit, but may prefer to regard as a temporary stopgap, a way of financing an existing deficit for a while. (As soon as the attractive interest differential is terminated, the inflow of short-term capital will stop and what has been received will flow back.) In addition, we should separate measures that work on the flow of goods and services from those that work on the flow of capital funds. The adjectives "real" and "financial" can be used for this purpose.

We thus distinguish real adjustment, real correctives, financial correctives, corrective management of government transactions, and external financing.

To *finance* a deficit is to pay for it by reducing the net monetary reserves or by increasing liquid liabilities to foreigners incurred just for this purpose. (If an increase in foreign liabilities arises from an increased foreign demand for dollar balances and other dollar assets, it should be treated as an autonomous capital inflow, as a debt incurred in order to finance a deficit. Unfortunately, we usually lack the information required for this distinction.)

To reduce or remove a deficit by *real adjustment* is to induce such changes in relative prices and incomes as will alter the allocation of real resources and cause such changes in the international flows of goods and services as will improve the current account to match the balance on capital account and unilateral payments. We distinguish aggregate-demand adjustment, cost-and-price adjustment, and exchange-rate adjustment.

Real correctives influence the international flow of goods and services through selective impacts on particular goods, industries, or sectors. *Financial correctives* influence the international flows of private capital funds. *Corrective management of government transactions* may affect government expenditures, loans, and grants to other countries.

REAL ADJUSTMENTS

Economists trained in the classical or neoclassical tradition—the present writer included—have a deep-seated prejudice in favor of real adjustment: (1) It relies largely on market forces rather than selective "interventions" by the state; (2) it is more likely to operate without discrimination, avoiding differential treatment of particular industries or firms; and (3) the chance of its working, of achieving its objectives, is greater.

On the other hand, practical-political considerations militate against real adjustment: (*a*) Policies to check the expansion of aggregate demand are apt to reduce business activity and employment; (*b*) policies to check increases in wage rates and prices are resented by some of the strongest groups in society; and (*c*) policies to adjust foreign-exchange rates are opposed by leaders in business and finance, here and abroad, for reasons good and bad; most understandable is the opposition abroad to a successful adjustment in the flow of goods and services, since it would hurt the business of some of the industries abroad.

Aggregate-demand adjustment is not without advocates among practical men: some highly respected bankers here and abroad advise the United States to "put its house in order" and "halt inflation"; and they intimate that this can be done by means of higher interest rates, higher taxes, and economies in government programs.

Their practical advice is unexceptionable if it refers merely to avoiding inflation of incomes and prices. As a matter of fact, high interest rates, higher taxes, and budget cuts are badly needed to prevent a further deterioration of the imbalance of payments. But it would be far too optimistic to expect that containment of further expansion would restore external balance, especially since the major industrial nations of Europe are likewise pursuing anti-inflationary policies, some even more successful than the United States.

If the conservative advice goes beyond mere avoidance of inflation and suggests in effect that aggregate demand in this country be *reduced* to such a level that our imports fall and exports rise sufficiently for the export surplus to match all other outflows of dollars—

then the advice is not acceptable. A deflation of such force could have well-nigh catastrophic consequences for domestic employment and world trade.

Real adjustment by means of demand deflation in the United States is out of the question; adjustment by means of demand inflation abroad is not likely to be accepted, nor would it be advisable. Now, if the adjustment of levels and structures of costs and prices cannot be expected to occur either through reductions in the United States or through increases abroad, the only remaining possibility of real adjustment lies in alignments of foreign-exchange rates. Yet, the resistance to any moves in this direction seems too strong to allow it to be contemplated. I shall, however, not be inhibited and will return to this only chance for a workable adjustment.

PARTIAL DEVALUATIONS

Among real correctives the policies most appealing to advocates of selective measures are what I have for years called "disguised partial devaluations of the dollar." Open and uniform devaluation being ruled out, measures are recommended to reduce the value of the dollar for particular purposes or in chosen sectors of the economy.

The United States has resorted to such makeshifts several times. For example, it devalued, not formally but in effect, the dollar used for foreign military expenditures. This was done by trying to save foreign exchange whenever the cost of buying at home was at first not more than 25 percent, later 50 percent, above the cost in foreign currencies calculated at the official exchange rate. In other words, in decisions whether to buy abroad or at home, foreign currencies were to be given a higher value than would correspond to the official parity.

Through tying foreign aid to purchases of our products, the United States reduced the value of its foreign-aid dollar. Countries receiving aid had to buy in this country even if they could have bought at lower prices elsewhere. It cost some of them about 30 percent more, which corresponds to a devaluation of the aid-dollar by about 23 percent.

In July 1963, the United States began taxing purchases of foreign long-term securities at a rate of 15 percent. This is the equivalent of devaluing the dollar used for buying foreign securities. This partial devaluation, designed to reduce capital outflows, is a financial, not a real, corrective.

Last month, in January 1967, the administration proposed a tax on foreign travel and tourism, which would be the equivalent of devaluing the tourist's dollar. In addition, there are nonofficial proposals for taxes or tariff-surcharges on imports—the equivalent of devaluing the dollar for imports—and for subsidies or tax-refunds on exports—the equivalent of lowering the price of the dollar to foreign buyers of our exports.

If these disguised devaluations of the dollar were uniform, affecting proportionally all imports, all exports, and all other international transactions, they might work indiscriminately and perhaps efficiently. As it is, however, they are selective, disproportionate, and inefficient. They discriminate against some sectors and in favor of others, distort the structure of prices and the allocation of productive resources, and are usually incapable of effecting their purpose.

Partial devaluations can improve particular items in the balance of payments, but may worsen others in the process, partly because of the substitution of purchases for which the dollar is not "devalued," partly because of foreign and domestic repercussions to the reduction of purchases for which the value of the dollar is reduced.

DIRECT CONTROLS

Partial devaluations have at least one advantage: they work through price incentives and disincentives, and leave the markets essentially free. The bureaucratic mind, however, prefers a more direct approach, a more direct attack on the "item" that has been found irritating or insalubrious: it prefers direct controls, which give to some governmental authority the power to prohibit, to restrict, to license, or to permit, according to its unfailing judgment of what is or is not warranted in the national interest.

Direct controls can be employed as real correctives or as financial correctives of the payments deficit. As real correctives they may involve discretionary subsidies to exporters, quotas and other nontariff restrictions on imports, licensing of foreign travel or fixing the amounts that travelers may spend abroad. As financial correctives they may restrict bank credits to foreigners, direct foreign investment, portfolio investment and foreign loans of various types.

The effectiveness of controls that are not comprehensive, not all-inclusive (as general foreign-exchange controls, comprising all foreign transactions, would be) is limited by the possibilities of avoiding, evading, and circumventing the restrictions. The elasticity of substitution among different forms of capital outflow, for example, is not sufficiently appreciated; there are also those offsetting changes in other items that are classed as repercussions, though in some instances substitutions and repercussions shade into one another.

It should be easy to understand that portfolio investment, bank loans, trade credit, and direct investment may be substituted for one another. Restrict one and you will see the others expand. Yet, many overlook that there is also substitution between foreign and domestic funds. Restrict the outflow of American capital funds and you will see foreign funds withdrawn from the United States.

This is not retaliation or an unfriendly act, but the operation of normal market forces: if American funds are kept from going abroad, interest rates abroad will rise and, naturally, foreign funds will "go home." Or, if American firms are forbidden to use their own money for direct investment abroad, but are permitted to raise foreign funds in foreign markets, foreigners holding American securities may decide to sell them in New York and buy the more attractive new securities offered by the American subsidiaries abroad. Thus, a legitimate outflow of capital takes the place of a forbidden one. Call it repercussion or call it substitution, it severely limits the effectiveness of the financial correctives.

If financial correctives are effective in reducing the outflow of capital, they may induce offsetting reductions in the trade surplus. These repercussions or feedbacks may be small or large, but will rarely be zero. They can be zero only if the reduction in the flow of capital does not affect the use of funds either in the domestic or in the foreign markets. Assume that an American, A, is prevented from lending his money to a foreigner, F; only if A then decides to sit on his money and not to spend, lend, or invest it at all, and if F manages to disburse abroad exactly the same amount of money that he would have disbursed, thanks to the receipt of A's funds, only then will imports and exports be unaffected by the financial corrective. In all probability, A will use some of his funds at home and F will have less to spend abroad, and the United States will have larger imports and smaller exports as a result.

FOREIGN PROGRAMS OF THE GOVERNMENT

In the search for "guilty items" in the balance of payments, foreign disbursements by the U.S. Government are the most popular targets. According to one's political philosophy, one will argue for cutting military expenditures abroad or for cutting foreign aid. The question whether these funds for fighting wars and fighting poverty abroad are desirable expenditures is often confused with the question whether the reduction of these funds would cure the imbalance of payments.

Both hawks and doves are inclined to exaggerate the effects which a reduction of expenditures for military operations in Viet-Nam would have on the payments deficit. If the war ends and military expenditures in Viet-Nam are reduced, there will probably be an increase in economic aid to Viet-Nam, in an effort to rebuild what has been destroyed and to show the world that our intentions all along had been to help the country maintain its freedom and develop its economy. If, nonetheless, total expenditures abroad are reduced when military operations cease, then the Vietnamese will have less money to purchase goods and to import from abroad. The reduction of their imports may not always directly reduce exports from the United States, but through triangular trade and multilateral repercussion our exports may still be affected.

In addition, there is the probability that defense expenditures in the United States will be replaced by expenditures for other purposes. Programs in our domestic war against poverty have been cut because of the rising cost of the war in the Far East. If, with the end of military operations, we escalate expenditures for domestic programs, imports from abroad are likely to increase above the volume they would have otherwise. Hence, with all these repercussions on the flow of goods and services, one must not count on an improvement of the balance of payments by anything near the full amount by which our military expenditures are reduced.

THE INEXORABLE DEFICIT

I may well be accused of undue pessimism. Is there any historical or theoretical support for my warnings about the ineffectiveness of the various corrective measures adopted or proposed? Is the deficit really impervious to all efforts to deal with it through corrective measures?

Our actual experience can really make us rather fatalistic. Year after year, at least since 1960, we have done all sorts of things to work on the balance of payments; we have picked one item after another for special treatment; yet, we have failed. I have prepared a list of quotations from statements by our Presidents and Secretaries of the Treasury expressing their assurances and confident expectations that balance was just around the corner, that the deficit would disappear within the year, or the next one. Yet, the deficit is still with us and one cannot even say that it is substantially smaller than it used to be.

I am not including this list of assurances in my testimony, because to do so would not be charitable. After all, the President and the Secretary of the Treasury were courageously battling a Hydra: they did not realize that for every head cut off two grew in its place. They did not know that you cannot decapitate a Hydra: you have to dehydrate her if you want to get rid of her.

THE NEW BALANCE-OF-PAYMENTS PROGRAM

After seven years of unsuccessful corrective measures, the Government has now embarked on a new program. It is, again, not a program to promote real adjustment in the economic sense; instead, it relies on selective correctives operating on hand-picked items of the balance of payments. The President, the Secretary of the Treasury, and the Council of Economic Advisers hope that the country will save at least $1 billion by a "mandatory program" to restrain direct investment abroad and to bring home larger parts of foreign earnings from past investments; another $500 million by a "tightened program" to restrain foreign lending by banks and other financial institutions; another $500 million by discouraging "nonessential travel outside the Western Hemisphere"; and again another $500 million by reducing the foreign-exchange cost of keeping troops in Europe.

In summary, $1.5 billion are to be saved by financial restrictions, $500 million by a corrective measure operating on the private demand for foreign travel, and $500 by corrective management of government disbursements abroad. The last of these may turn out to be the only continuing saving, if troops are brought back from Europe or if compensating payments are received from NATO allies. The other $2 billion are nothing but stopgaps.

Even if the three stopgap measures succeeded in improving the balance by the full $2 billion, and even if this improvement eliminated the deficit for the time the restrictions are in force, it would not restore balance; it would only suppress imbalance. As soon as the restrictions are lifted, the deficit will reappear, for there is nothing in the program that has any adjusting, remedial or curative effects. The demand for foreign travel will not be reduced over a long period by restricting for a few years the chance of satisfying it. The flow of capital funds from this country to Europe is determined by relative incomes, prices, profit rates, interest rates, and saving ratios. None of these underlying conditions is altered by the restrictions. The flow is likely to resume, perhaps even to broaden, when the restrictions and prohibitions are taken off.

But that these selective controls are only temporary, and that they have no lasting effects, is not all. An additional question arises concerning the effects that they will have even temporarily. The possibilities of substitution and of repercussions must not be disregarded. Permitted outflows may be substituted for the prohibited ones, and repercussions in the trade balance may offset some of the savings achieved in the selected items. I shall presently provide explanations for these warnings. But I must first deliver myself of an observation on the principle of restrictive measures.

As one who has lived many years in Central Europe under all sorts of prohibitions, restrictions, and controls, I have always admired and loved the supposedly indomitable spirit of freedom in this great country. It is a traumatic experience to see the lighthearted sacrifice of several freedoms with the adoption of the program of payments restrictions. I would never have thought that this wonderful country could sink so low as to impose restrictions on foreign travel.

SOME THEORETICAL EXPLANATIONS

But now I must make good on my promise to present explanations for my skepticism concerning the effectiveness of the corrective measures. The explanations are theoretical, but I hope they will not appear esoteric or specious.

I shall use as illustration the restriction of direct investment, which is intended to save $1 billion a year.

There are two extreme positions concerning the effectiveness of such a corrective measure. At one end is the opinion that a reduction of a financial transfer, say by $1 billion, will leave all other items in the payments balance unchanged and merely reduce the financing item, that is, reduce the loss of gold or the increase in liquid foreign liabilities.

At the opposite end is the opinion that reduction in financial transfers by $1 billion will reduce the export surplus by the same amount and hence will leave the deficit, and the need to finance it, unchanged.

I propose to regard the first theory as naive and the second as oversophisticated; both are wrong. The truth lies in the middle, and whether it comes closer to the naive or to the over-sophisticated theory will depend on circumstances. What kind of circumstances control the outcome can be briefly indicated, still with reference to the same illustration, the reduction in direct investment abroad.

If American firms that have for several years been making direct investments abroad are now barred from doing so unless they can raise new capital in foreign markets, it is possible that the increased demand in the foreign capital markets leads to a backflow of foreign capital from the United States. It may be short-term capital or it may be long-term capital that returns to Europe. To repeat the example used before, American firms issuing new securities in a European market may find foreign buyers who secure the needed funds by selling in the New York stock market some of the American shares they have been holding. The incentive

for such a switch from old to new securities is clear: newly issued securities have to be offered at slightly reduced prices. To the extent that this way of financing is used, the restrictive measure by the United States will be ineffective.

Let us assume that the American firms reduce direct investment in Europe but make, within the limits stipulated by the new mandatory restrictions, some investments in Canada which they might not have made otherwise. The addition to the investible funds available in Canada may make it possible for Canadians to engage in the purchase of European securities. This would again constitute substitution of another form of capital flow from the United States to Europe.

Let us assume next that direct investment abroad is in fact reduced by the full $1 billion and that there is no replacement by any other funds going from the United States to Europe. Investment in Europe in preceding years has unquestionably contributed to effective demand and, directly or indirectly via third countries, to purchases of goods and services from the United States. The amount so used may have been relatively small; if so, the feedback from the reduction in investment, resulting in a reduction of American exports, may be small, too. But it will surely be greater than zero.

The next repercussion to be considered is connected with the use the American firms make of the funds which they, but for the restriction, would have invested in Europe. If they use any of these funds for increased investment in the United States, this will amount to an injection of additional funds into the stream of effective demand. Some fraction of any addition to effective demand is likely to show up as an increased demand for imports. The fraction may be small, but not zero.

To the extent that the domestic market, because of the increase in effective demand, becomes more attractive than foreign markets, American firms will be less eager to seek foreign outlets and will divert some of their production from export to domestic sales. It is unlikely that the amounts involved would be very large, but it is just as unlikely that they would be zero.

Increases in our financial transfers to foreign countries have for many years failed to produce equal increases in our export surplus. The same conditions that can explain the incomplete adjustment of the trade balance to increased financial transfers can explain also why reductions in our financial transfers are unlikely to be matched by equal reductions in our export surplus. On the other hand, just as our increased financial transfers have increased our export surplus significantly, so reductions in financial transfers can be expected to reduce our export surplus.

CONCLUSIONS REGARDING THE PAYMENTS DEFICIT

I shall not be so bold as to present my conclusion in the form of a numerical forecast. It is not possible to predict a result determined by so many unknown variables. At this point we do not even know whether the Congress will pass the proposed surcharge on the income tax. This one factor alone can make a difference of about $1 billion in the payments deficit. That is to say, if we get the surtax, and thereby reduce the spending power of individuals and corporations, imports will be smaller and exports larger than if no tax increase is imposed.

But there are too many other factors in the picture to permit anyone to come up with a reliable forecast. Nobody knows, for example, what will happen concerning movements of foreign capital. This item can change either way and in very substantial amounts.

Nonetheless, I believe that conclusions of a qualitative sort can and should be drawn. The two conclusions on which I feel pretty sure are the negative and regrettable ones concerning the effects of the restrictive program. There will not be an improvement of the payments balance by $2.5 billion, as the Administration seems to hope. And whatever improvement will be achieved by the program, it will be only temporary and will not contribute to the adjustment process, will not bring us closer to a solution of our problems.

The widely believed excuse that our military expenditures abroad, chiefly those connected with the war in Viet-Nam, are too large to permit balance in our payments to be achieved, is not justified. Our total financial transfers, inclusive of military expenditures, have been between 2.3 and 1.5 percent of our GNP. This is a modest drain on our resources. There is no reason why a nation should be unable to accomplish a real transfer of such magnitude.

Adjustment of the balance of goods and services to make the real transfer match a financial transfer of around 2 percent of GNP is not an impossible task, provided the adjustment process is allowed to work. I agree that we must not try to do it by depressing domestic incomes and prices. I am afraid that we must not expect our major trading partners to help us sufficiently by means of inflations of their income and price levels. But I see no reason other than superstition and timidity why we should not try to achieve the required relative reduction of our income and price level through adjustments of foreign-exchange rates. The rate adjustment that would achieve the needed adjustment of the trade balance is quite modest and should be negotiable.

I must safeguard myself against misinterpretation. If I speak of adjustment of exchange rates, this does not mean devaluation of the dollar in terms of gold. I do not believe either the desirability or the inevitability of an increase in the price of gold. So let no one confuse exchange rate and gold price.

QUESTIONS AND STUDY SUGGESTIONS

1. What does the author mean when he argues that recent government programs for dealing with our payments deficit have involved "partial devaluations"?

2. Explain the contention that the government's payments program is comprised of "stopgap measures" which will only repress, not correct, our payments deficit.

3. How does Professor Machlup back up his contention that the $2 billion reduction in foreign investment and lending and in outlays for sustaining American troops abroad will have a quantitative impact upon our payments position substantially less than $2 billion?

Reading 72

The Troubling Shift in the Trade Winds
Lawrence A. Mayer

One of the peculiar characteristics of the United States's chronic balance of payments problem has been that its competitive position in world markets has been strong. That is, the United States has enjoyed a substantial export surplus, and its payments deficit has been the result of net public and private capital outflows in excess of its export surplus. The disquieting theme of Reading 72 is that our competitive position in world markets is changing to the end that our export surplus is declining. If it is "permanent," this development will tend to intensify our payments deficit. The author explores the possible implications of a narrowing export surplus for the historical trend toward free trade and suggests devaluation of the dollar as a remedy for United States trade and payments problems.

Among the shocks, strains, and insults inflicted on the U.S. economy in recent months, perhaps the most ominous of all has been a drastic turn for the worse in foreign trade. Beyond its unpleasant short-run effects, this sudden deterioration in the U.S. foreign-trade position has grave implications for the nation's economic future. For many years now, the U.S. has relied on a hefty surplus in merchandise trade with the outside world. This surplus has served to offset, to the extent of several billion dollars a year, the chronic deficits in various other sectors of the U.S. payments account—capital investment, overseas military costs, foreign aid, tourist traffic, shipping. But during the final quarter of 1967 and the first quarter of this year, the once sturdy U.S. trade surplus crumbled.

DETERIORATING TRADE POSITION

What wrecked it was a remarkable surge in imports. Exports have been rising too, but nowhere near fast enough to maintain their lead over imports. The remaining margin of trade surplus has become so thin and frail that an eleven-day dock strike in New York was enough to put U.S. foreign trade in deficit for the month of March. In one sense, moreover, the U.S. began running a deficit some months prior to the strike. A sizable share of U.S. exports is financed by the U.S. Government under foreign aid or other public programs. (Some of these exports, though, would move out anyway if special government financing were not available.) Such government-financed exports now amount to $3.2 billion a year. In the first quarter, the U.S. trade surplus—total merchandise exports minus total merchandise imports—worked out to less than $1 billion, at an annual rate. So apart from the government-financed slice of exports, U.S. foreign-trade accounts showed a deficit at the rate of more than $2 billion a year.

Even when it still enjoyed a substantial trade surplus, the U.S. ran a deficit in its overall balance of payments, and lost a lot of gold as a result. Now, suddenly, the outlook seems

From Lawrence A. Mayer, "The Troubling Shift in the Trade Winds," **Fortune**, June 1, 1968, pp. 77–79, 140, 142, 144, abridged. Reprinted by permission.

much bleaker. The deterioration in the U.S. trade position greatly increases the difficulty of coping with the balance-of-payments deficit.

Another unpleasant consequence of recent trends in trade has been the strengthening of protectionism in the U.S. As more and more industries feel the cutting edge of foreign competition, the demands for protection grow more insistent. That is understandable, but also regrettable. A retreat into protectionism would go against the long-range U.S. commitment to freer trade among nations. What's more, higher tariffs and stricter quotas would invite retaliation against U.S. exports. Rather than slip back in that direction, the U.S. would do better to undertake a persistent campaign against European and Japanese nontariff trade barriers— quotas, export rebates, subtle subsidies, and other arrangements that hinder imports from the U.S. and favor exports to the U.S. The U.S. would have to reduce its own nontariff barriers, but would still come out ahead.

It would be unrealistic, though, to expect even a strenuous fight against nontariff impediments and discriminations to bring about a quick, decisive improvement in the U.S. trade position. The troubles are too basic for that. The crumbling of the export surplus suggests that we may have reached the end of the cushioned era in which we could count on industrial superiority to counterbalance lower wage costs abroad. It also suggests that the dollar may be overvalued in relation to currencies of other major industrial nations. These are unpleasant thoughts, but they are likely to be recurring inescapably in months to come, for those somber trade statistics appear to be signaling a serious and hard-to-reverse decline in the U.S. competitive position in the world.

THE PROBLEM IN PERSPECTIVE

The sharp deterioration in the U.S. trade balance follows upon a gradual loss of ground that began after 1964. In that year, the U.S. trade surplus reached $7 billion, the highest level since 1947. The reason for that good export performance in 1964 is clear enough: it was an extraordinarily prosperous year in Europe and Japan, and demand for imports from the U.S. rose accordingly. After 1964, however, rates of economic growth abroad generally abated, and so did the increase in U.S. exports; they expanded by a comparatively modest 14 percent from 1964 to 1966. The

U.S. economy, meanwhile, picked up momentum, moving on toward full employment and boom-time utilization of industrial capacity— conditions that typically lift demand for imports. Consequently, U.S. imports rose 37 percent between 1964 and 1966, and the trade surplus fell to $3.8 billion. All the while the amount of government-financed exports rose, so the surplus exclusive of government financing dropped sharply, from $4.2 billion in 1964 to $800 million in 1966.

During the first nine months of last year, with the economy somewhat decelerated, U.S. imports showed only moderate growth. In the third quarter, imports ran at a seasonally adjusted annual rate of $26 billion, and exports at a rate of $31 billion, providing, in round numbers, a comfortable spread of $5 billion. But starting in the final quarter, imports whipped ahead, and the trade surplus went into a dramatic decline. In the first quarter of this year the figures went: exports, $32 billion; imports, $31 billion; surplus, $1 billion.

Part of the extraordinary climb in imports can be charged to special factors. Oil imports increased last fall to make up for some of the lag resulting from the Arab-Israeli war. Copper imports jumped because of the U.S. copper strike, and steel imports because of the threat of a steel strike in 1968. But these special factors accounted for only about $800 million of the $2.3-billion increase in imports (at annual rates) in the fourth quarter of last year. And, huge as they were, the enormous imports of steel early this year came nowhere near accounting for the additional rise of $3 billion in the rate of imports during the first quarter of 1968. The combined increase of more than $5 billion within a span of six months largely resulted from a steep rise in imports of manufactured goods—both consumer goods and capital equipment. In other words, the U.S. appears to have become disturbingly vulnerable to import penetration in the very area of economic life where we thought we had special competitive strength.

The rise of imports would seem less ominous if the U.S. export position had more expansionary zip in it. In the global picture, U.S. exports declined from 18.1 percent of total free-world exports in 1960 to 16.6 percent in 1967. And the short-run outlook seems a bit gray. The current economic pickup in Europe will presumably help U.S. exports, but last fall's devaluation by Britain and fifteen other nations will work the opposite way. An unfavorable omen: new orders for exports of U.S. durable goods have held level since mid-1966.

The disquieting trends in U.S. trade have begun to cast a shadow over the seemingly sunny results of last year's Kennedy Round of multilateral tariff negotiations, which reduced tariffs on industrial goods by an average of 35 percent. U.S. protectionists and their congressional supporters, who had been lying doggo during the Kennedy Round, have come to life. They've changed their long-standing strategy of asking for tariff protection and instead are asking for quotas. Pending in Congress at last count were 717 different bills to impose quotas on imports. The battle is being waged even in state legislatures, where members are feeling pressure to pass bills requiring that only American-made products be used in public construction projects. The change in climate is evident in the turnabout of Pennsylvania's Governor Raymond P. Shafer, who vetoed such a measure last year and is supporting one this year.

THE IMPORT SURGE

Basic to any assessment of the U.S. trade problem is a question about the significance of the recent import surge. Is it a temporary aberration, brought on by transient factors, or does it represent something much more disturbing, a shift in the conditions of international trade? The evidence suggests a mixture of both, with enough of the latter to be distinctly worrisome. The world's leading manufacturing nation is now confronting—and may have to confront from now on—a flood of competitive goods from the factories of other nations. Imports of finished goods were 150 percent higher last year than in 1960, and are increasing a lot this year. In 1960 finished manufactures accounted for 35 percent of the dollar value of all imports; these days they account for 50 percent or more.

It is not really surprising that other industrial nations have succeeded in catching up with the U.S. in technology, know-how, and mass-production efficiencies—or at least narrowing the distance. That was to be expected. And U.S. corporations have for years been contributing to the effectiveness of foreign economies by increasing investment and licensing abroad. The outside world, moreover, has greatly expanded its industrial capacity in recent years. So it is natural for the U.S. to be facing greater competition. What *is* surprising is the extent and force of the competition. The startling rise in imports suggests that the catching up has gone faster and spread further than seemed possible just a short time ago.

Industrialization, moreover, has lately been moving ahead in really low-wage economies such as Taiwan, Hong Kong, and South Korea, and this development has already led to a new wave of competition in light manufactures such as textiles and electronic products. If such new competitors keep extending the range of the goods they make, that could mean a lot more import push into the U.S. What's more, it's far from clear that we have seen the full brunt of import intrusion from Europe and Japan.

In the near future, at least, the ability of U.S. industry to compete in the world under these changing conditions may be seriously impaired by accelerated inflation in the U.S. Unit labor costs in manufacturing rose 5.3 percent last year, and another large rise is already in the making for this year. If U.S. costs and prices rise faster than those of other industrial nations, U.S. exports get less and less attractive abroad, and imports get more and more attractive in the U.S. market.

Of the four grand categories of merchandise trade, the U.S. is a net exporter in two, capital goods and food, and a net importer in the two others, consumer goods and industrial materials. What has been happening in recent years is that U.S. net exports of capital goods and foods taken together have been increasing less rapidly than U.S. net imports of consumer goods and industrial materials.

Only a few years ago the Federal Reserve Board published a chart showing that, based on past experience, the normal range for imports lay between 2.7 and 3 percent of gross national product. That standard has now been outmoded, for total imports are currently equal to 3.8 percent of GNP. At present levels of GNP, the extra eight-tenths of a point is adding about $6.5 billion to the annual import bill —a great deal more than last year's entire balance-of-payments deficit.

THE CASE OF STEEL

While imports have increased in many categories of goods, attention has focused especially on steel, textiles, consumer electronics, and autos. Steel presents a classic case of a major U.S. industry that seems increasingly unable to hold its own in the domestic market, much less compete abroad.

Ten years ago the U.S. was a net exporter of steel—exports exceeded imports by a substantial margin. The import climb began in 1959, when imports more than doubled, from $231 million to $574 million, as a result of that year's 116-day steel strike. Since then the trend has been up. Every year, it seems, more U.S. companies buy foreign steel. Imports reached $1.4 billion in 1967—nearly all from Western Europe and Japan—and are headed for another large gain in 1968. In the meantime, U.S. exports of steel have failed to grow; last year the U.S. was a net importer of steel to the amount of $720 million. In the early 1960s the increase in imports consisted mainly of simple products such as wire rods and nails, but later on imports of more advanced steel-mill products—plates, sheets, strip—also rose in volume. Early this year iron and steel imports amounted to about 12 percent of the total volume of U.S. supplies; for the western states the figure was 22 percent.

A widespread impression lingers that many foreign steelmakers have a technological advantage over U.S. companies because they operate newer plants or use newer processes. While that used to be true, the newness factor is no longer very important; about 60 percent of U.S. output is now produced in oxygen-process or electric furnaces, and almost all of the remaining open-hearth furnaces are oxygen-lanced. What is fundamental in the import flood is the enormous expansion of steel-making capacity abroad. Free-world capacity ouside the U.S. has about doubled in the last ten years. As a result, there's a lot of excess capacity, and this is putting tremendous pressure on foreign mills to export—especially to the U.S., the world's biggest market.

Foreign steel companies have some advantages that U.S. steel companies consider unfair. In France, Britain, Belgium, Luxembourg, and other countries, steel producers receive various kinds of subsidies or special treatment from their governments. In Germany the steel companies have organized into four cartel-like groups. Japanese producers likewise cooperate among themselves.

With all this, the U.S. steel industry feels itself sorely pressed, and is one of the most insistent voices asking Washington for import quotas (Crucible Steel is the lone dissenter). To help forestall quota legislation, the Japanese steel industry is promising to hold future increases in its shipments to the U.S. to 10 percent a year. American companies think that's much too high a figure—steel consumption in the U.S. is growing by only 2 or 3 percent a year.

The U.S. steel industry argues with some justification that there are inequities in the competitive situation. And it must be said for the industry that it has been far more burdened than its foreign competitors with strikes or the threat of strikes, which have turned its customers to imports (as is happening again this year). But nevertheless, for a once majestic industry to ask for quotas seems a monumental confession of failure. The steel industry has been a desultory competitor in the international arena. It has until recently been raising prices and has refused to use pricing as a competitive weapon, while foreign steel companies have been cutting export prices—accepting lower profit margins to get added volume. Now U.S. Steel has broken out of the pattern: almost furtively, the company has cut prices sharply on a variety of products to meet foreign quotations. Much of the industry is distressed about this untraditional behavior, but it may be the best thing that's happened in steel for years.

AUTOMOBILE IMPORTS

Especially hurtful to American industrial pride has been the ever increasing rise in imports of foreign passenger cars. This year America will probably import $1 billion worth of cars—far, far ahead of exports. Last year's import bill came to $877 million, against exports of $294 million. The number of cars imported, 697,000, declined a bit from 1966, but the dip was misleading, a fluke of inventory fluctuations; retail sales of imported passenger cars actually reached a record high of 767,000. Sales of imports were even brisker in the first quarter of this year, up an astonishing 43 percent over a year ago. This rise indicates that sales could go above a million units this year.

Imports are taking something more than 10 percent of the U.S. new-car market (about 20 percent on the Pacific coast). Volkswagen, with nearly 60 percent of the import market, sells twice as many cars in the U.S. as American Motors. To meet the competition, U.S. auto makers are trying to expand sales of their own "captive" makes produced abroad, such as the G.M. Opel and the Ford Cortina, but these now account for only 12 percent of all imports.

Here again the foreign advantage seems to lie in style and pricing, and the threat—if it is a threat—seems to go to that matter of declining U.S. ability or desire to compete. Some increase in the imports of sport, novelty, or special luxury cars could be expected in any boomy consumer economy, but the breathtaking rates of increase have come in the price ranges below anything Detroit can (or wants to) offer—e.g., in the Volkswagen and the Toyota. This toe-to-toe challenge to Detroit signals more dramatically than anything else the shifts in the equations of competition.

Of course, as an international competitor, the U.S. fares much better in trucks, buses, and automotive parts and equipment than in passenger cars. Despite the big deficit in autos, total U.S. trade in automotive products last year was about in balance at $2.7 billion each way. That balance, however, represented a considerable deterioration in the U.S. position over the past several years: in 1960, for example, the U.S. ran a $600-million surplus.

CAPITAL GOODS: SOPHISTICATION AND SCALE

The great strength of the U.S. in foreign trade lies in capital goods—usually with a high technology quotient. Here, exports run way ahead of imports. Last year exports of capital goods reached $10.9 billion, compared to $6 billion in 1960. The exports included $433 million worth of electronic computers and parts, about ten times the 1960 amount. U.S. manufacturers also made large gains in aircraft (exports of $790 million last year, excluding military aircraft), broadcasting and related equipment (exports of $555 million), measuring and control instruments ($519 million), industrial engines ($474 million), office machines ($408 million), machine tools ($405 million), heavy electric equipment ($302 million). In this grouping aircraft, of course, promises the brightest future; foreign sales of the airbus are projected to bring the U.S. balance of trade a net gain of several billion by 1980.

Apart from the sophistication of its capital goods, there are several reasons why the U.S. does so well in this field of international trade. The sheer scale of the American economy creates markets for numerous units of large machines (e.g., mining and construction) that it would be uneconomic to make in other countries. Also the U.S. holds a continuing lead in innovation in capital goods, and there is usually an interval before the latest products get produced abroad, even in U.S.-owned plants.

Still, the sobering fact is that U.S. imports of capital goods have been rising at a faster *percentage* rate than exports—albeit from a very small base so that the export surplus in dollars continues to mount. Imports have quadrupled so far during the Sixties, from $700 million in 1960 to $2.8 billion last year. The imports come mostly from Europe, plus a good many from Canada and Japan. Among the biggest gainers have been electric and electronic equipment (imports of $546 million last year), nonelectric machinery ($420 million), machine tools ($232 million), and business machines ($183 million). Import competition in capital goods may well get tougher. While making capital goods requires sophisticated know-how and technology, it also requires a lot of labor, since most capital goods can't be turned out in mass quantities on assembly lines. Accordingly, high wage rates make the U.S. potentially vulnerable even here.

About 45 percent of all U.S. imports fall into the category of industrial materials, which include raw materials as well as such semifinished goods as steel, yarns, and industrial chemicals. Even though the export surplus in industrial chemicals grew to an impressive $1.9 billion last year, the U.S. is losing ground on industrial materials as a whole. Imports came to $11.8 billion in 1967, about $2 billion more than exports. The U.S. is a net importer of, among many other materials, iron ore, lumber, and petroleum. The deficit in petroleum and its products—$1.5 billion last year—would be much larger were it not for import quotas.

SHIFTS IN COMPETITIVE POWER

By and large, the trade figures seem to be indicating some important shifts in competitive power. Some of the shifts are cyclical, reflecting relative rates of inflation or relative amounts of boominess in the various economies, and these, while serious, can be modified by responsible domestic policies and international coordination. But other shifts seem to reflect basic changes that require some re-examination of long-standing assumptions.

There has long been an assumption, for example, that U.S. capital, technology, and large-scale production could more than offset the disadvantages of higher wages and costs. As noted, this advantage is fading faster than we expected. Take the growth of the European Common Market, long and quite properly an objective of U.S. foreign-economic policy. In its great success, the E.E.C. has provided Europeans with all the opportunities for volume production. The bright prospects have brought heavy investment in plants—some of them U.S. owned—with new technologies. So on the face of it, there has been a shift in competitive power. In addition, the reduction of tariff barriers within common market areas—and this applies to all of the regional groupings, including the European Free Trade Association, the Central American Common Market, and the Latin American Free Trade Area—tends to nourish a kind of regional protectionism at the expense of worldwide trade.

Another kind of tacit assumption underlies the U.S. approach to trade negotiations with other nations. The emphasis has fallen on lowering tariffs, but as they have come down, the relative importance of nontariff barriers, new and old, has gone up. Apart from quotas and arbitrary customs rulings, such barriers range from restrictions on trade in agricultural products, through discriminatory government procurement methods, to anti-dumping legislation, which in reality works to impede foreign exporters.

Especially notable are the barriers that foreign countries such as Britain, Belgium, France, and Germany have erected against imported coal to protect their inefficient mining industries. If all these restrictions were removed, the U.S.—a very efficient producer of coal—might be able to export between $2 billion and $3 billion worth a year. At present U.S. coal exports, mainly to Canada, Italy, and Japan, amount to only $500 million a year. Of course, the U.S. sins in such matters as well, but on balance has cleaner hands than those of other industrial nations. William B. Kelly Jr., a member of the U.S. delegation to the Kennedy Round, makes the point that in general "U.S.

restrictions are specifically stated in legislation and in detailed regulations, and officials are given little discretion in their administration." In other countries legislation and regulations are less specific, but the flexibility of action is great. This makes foreigners' trade restrictions hard to take into account and to pin down.

TROUBLE FROM HARMONY

One particular barrier that is assuming new importance for the U.S. is the effect that national tax systems have on international trade. The Common Market is now moving toward large-scale systems of taxes on value added (T.V.A.). France has had one for some time, Germany has just adopted one in full; the other countries will have theirs by 1970. So far as the Six are concerned, this is a step forward in harmonizing their economies, but the immediate effect on the U.S. and other outsiders is adverse. It happens that the General Agreement on Tariffs and Trade allows countries that use indirect taxes—excises, turnover taxes, or T.V.A.—to hinder imports by a "border tax" to match the indirect taxes on equivalent domestic goods. It is also permissible under GATT rules to help exports by rebating taxes on exported goods. For this reason, Germany rebated and levied border taxes that averaged about 6 percent until this year; when it went on a full T.V.A. system on January 1, the levies and rebates jumped to 10 percent.

In the past, when a border tax has been in effect for some time, its distorting effects have been gradually offset by other sorts of changes, such as in relative exchange rates, in tariffs, or in prices. But such compensations are now harder to achieve when border taxes suddenly leap. German officials have themselves estimated that the new jump in their border-tax adjustments is equivalent to a 2 percent devaluation of the German mark. Therefore the U.S., because of its present trade difficulties, is considering putting in its own border-tax adjustment of 2 percent, a rate estimated to be justified by the general level of indirect taxes here. The trouble is that this might invite other countries like Japan, Britain, Canada, and Australia to join the game, and they might impose even larger border taxes than the U.S.

These tangled tax relationships help focus attention on how far from really free trade the world is and may always be. The fact is that the world is made up of mixed economies and not of perfectly competitive ones, because in every country a certain amount of interference with free competition is deemed economically or socially necessary. These interferences—even including health and safety regulations—also affect international trade and are part of the structure of nontariff barriers. Since such interferences will never be completely eliminated, one helpful thing would be to get them and their effects all out into the open and on the same basis. Robert B. Schwenger, a veteran U.S. trade negotiator, has come to the conclusion that it is hopeless to try to negotiate nontariff barriers away completely in the traditional way. Indeed, he proposes that governments abandon the usual system of adversary bargaining for the reduction of trade intervention. Instead, he suggests that intergovernmental examining bodies be set up. By not being in the position of requiring quid pro quo's, they could try to adjudicate which specific interventions are really defensible and necessary, which policies could be harmonized, and which might be dispensable or do more harm than good.

MORE AND MORE THINKABLE: DEVALUATION

Sensitive to the shifts in competitive power, some economists assert that the dollar is overvalued in relation to other important currencies. Professor Paul Samuelson of M.I.T. says he began to suspect as much in 1959, but all through the years that he was an adviser to President Kennedy the topic was *verboten*. Today he is conducting a modest campaign for devaluation.

In practice, devaluation of the dollar in terms of other currencies would be extremely difficult to bring off, and could easily disrupt the international monetary system. But the concept of devaluation (or selective upward revaluation of other currencies) is attractive because the alternative—deflation—is so downright unattractive. Granted that a certain amount of deflation, or disinflation, is necessary right now to cool off an overheated economy, and granted that it is essential to the trade balance for the U.S. to keep its prices competitive. But the amount of deflation that would be required, per se, to drive down prices and bring a readjustment in trade is unthinkable. No sane trading partner would want to see it, and no U.S. citizen concerned with the urban crisis would want the unemployment it would bring. So the idea of a basic readjustment in currency values becomes more and more thinkable.

Certainly it is increasingly clear that if the U.S. cannot restore its long-standing surplus in foreign trade, it will be driven to reduce the relatively free access other nations have to the U.S. market—the world's largest and most important. This would be particularly serious at a time when the less developed nations are asking other countries to open the door to their products. And it would impair even further the ability of the U.S. to supply capital to the rest of the world, a role that already has been hampered by the present controls on foreign investment. And not the least is the handicap a weak trade surplus imposes on U.S. efforts to improve its entire balance of payments. Obviously, a great deal is riding on the ability of the U.S. to raise its exports quickly and to moderate the growth in its imports.

QUESTIONS AND STUDY SUGGESTIONS

1. What are the basic factors underlying the apparent decline in the competitiveness of American goods in world markets?
2. Compare the changing positions of the American steel and automobile industries in world markets. Why has the position of American capital goods industries been less vulnerable to world competition?
3. Discuss "border taxes" as barriers to trade and indicate their impact upon the United States balance of trade and payments.
4. Why are devaluation of the dollar and domestic deflation regarded as alternative means of correcting the United States's payments deficit? What problems are posed by devaluation?

Reading 73

Perspectives on Foreign Exchange Rates

Federal Reserve Bank of Cleveland

This reading is a straightforward discussion of the meaning, significance, and determination of exchange rates. Trade between nations involves two different currencies. Exchange rates—the price of one currency in terms of another—are essential to comparisons of domestic and foreign prices of goods. The level of the exchange rate between two countries affects both the volume and composition of trade between them. In a free market, equilibrium exchange rates are determined by demand and supply and fluctuate in response to changes in demand and supply. However, under the existing international monetary system, nations belonging to the International Monetary Fund are obligated to maintain stable exchange rates. The advisability of maintaining a system of fixed exchange rates is debated in Readings 74 and 75.

What are exchange rates? Why are they important? How are they determined?

Essentially, an exchange rate is a price paid for a unit of one nation's currency in terms of the currency of another. Thus, for example, the U.S. dollar–pound sterling exchange rate may be expressed as approximately £1 = $2.80; that is, it costs $2.80 to acquire one British pound. Similarly, the dollar–*Deutsche mark* exchange rate may be expressed as DM1 = $0.25; that is, it costs $0.25 to acquire one German *mark*. Turning the explanation around, it follows that the price of a dollar in terms of pounds is just a trifle over seven shillings, and four marks will exchange for one dollar.

EXCHANGE RATES AS "LINKS"

Since exchange rates express the price of one currency unit in terms of others, they provide a direct link between the prices of goods and services in different parts of the world. Consider, for example, a men's clothing chain in the United States choosing between purchasing a line of suits from a domestic manufacturer or a similar line from a manufacturer in England. Assume, further, that the decision rests largely upon price, with delivery periods and quality being essentially the same, and tariffs nonexistent. The U.S. manufacturer obviously states his price in terms of dollars. Suppose the wholesale price of suits is set at $52.00 each. The British manufacturer sets a price for his garments in terms of pounds. Suppose he is willing to sell the suits at £18 each. Where should the U.S. clothing chain make its purchase? First the purchasing agent must determine the dollar equivalent of the price in pounds. At approximately $2.80 per pound, he quickly calculates that the price, in dollars, of the British-made garment is $50.40 (18 × $2.80). With transportation and other charges assumed negligible and with no tariff charges, the agent would probably make his company's purchase from the British manufacturer.

Knowledge of exchange rates thus is essen-

From "Some Perspective on Foreign Exchange Rates," **Economic Review**, Federal Reserve Bank of Cleveland, September, 1965, pp. 24–34, abridged.

tial to international trade by enabling traders to compare, in terms of their own country's currency, the effective prices of foreign goods and services. Because commerce between nations is a substitute for mobility of productive factors (natural, human, and physical resources) across national boundaries, it is essential to overall economic efficiency. And because exchange rates are essential to trade, they therefore play an important part in promoting a dynamic and expanding world economy.

In addition to the broad function of enabling international commerce, exchange rates serve two additional specific functions. First, the value and volume of a nation's imports and exports are related to the exchange rate between its currency and the currencies of other nations. Second, the composition of trade (that is, the makeup of imports and exports) is related to the exchange rate between the home currency and those of other nations.

VOLUME OF TRADE

Consider first the relationship between exchange rates and the value and volume of imports and exports. To make matters simple (though at the cost of introducing an element —hopefully not too large—of unreality), assume that prices of goods manufactured in the U.S. (as expressed in dollars) and goods manufactured in Britain (as expressed in pounds) remain stable despite exchange rate movements. Assume further that initially £1 = $2.80. At this rate of exchange between the dollar and pound, traders in the U.S. will import some dollar amount of goods and services from Britain, say $280 million worth. Also, at this rate traders in the United States will export a certain dollar amount of goods and services to Britain, say $280 million worth.

Suppose now the exchange rate becomes £1 = $5.60. Everything else the same, what could happen to U.S. exports to and imports from Britain? Because the dollar price of American-made goods does not change, and because the pound can now command more dollars ($5.60 as against $2.80), the British would find American-made goods and services more attractive (in terms of price) than previously. For example, an American camera, which formerly sold in Britain at £8 ($22.40), would now sell for £4. Britain can thus acquire the same dollar volume of imports from

the U.S. for one-half of what it formerly cost in terms of pounds. In terms of dollars, this country would receive the same amount as before. Almost certainly, however, the British would seek to acquire more American-made goods than before, since the absolute pound price has declined, and since the price of American goods has fallen relative to the price of alternate goods produced in Britain. Thus, the dollar value of American exports to Britain would almost certainly increase.

What of imports from Britain? The dollar price in the U.S. of such imports will rise in proportion to the increase in the dollar price of the pound. Thus, for example, prior to the change, a purchase of an automobile selling for £985 in England would have cost a U.S. importer (exclusive of transportation and other charges) $2,758 (985 × $2.80). A doubling of the dollar price of the pound now doubles the import price of the automobile to $5,516 (985 × $5.60). Because the dollar price of goods imported from Britain would increase both absolutely and in relation to prices of substitute goods produced at home, Americans would likely purchase fewer British goods. But, though possible and perhaps likely, it does not necessarily follow that the dollar value of American imports would decrease. Prior to the increase in the value of the pound, Americans were spending in total, say, £100 million on British goods. Suppose now they decided to purchase fewer British goods and to spend only £80 million on imports. In terms of dollars, however, the outlay increases to $448 million (80 million × $5.60).

COMPOSITION OF TRADE

The preceding paragraphs have attempted to clarify the role of exchange rates in influencing the value and volume of a nation's total imports from and exports to other nations. The following brief discussion deals with the additional role played by exchange rates in influencing the product composition of a country's exports and imports. Consider, in this connection, the hypothetical data in Table 73–1.

The table provides a sample of commodities produced both in the U.S. and Great Britain. The unit of each commodity is that amount costing $1 to produce in the United States (column 1). Column 2 shows the cost in Britain, in terms of British currency units, to

Table 73–1.   PRICES AND EXCHANGE RATES

Commodity	(1) Cost in U.S. in $	(2) In Shillings and Pence	(3) @ £ 1 = $5	(4) @ £ 1 = $4	(5) @ £ 1 = $2.80
Margarine	$1	4/-	$1.00	$0.80	$0.56
Wool cloth	1	4/3	1.06	0.85	0.60
Cotton cloth	1	4/8	1.16	0.93	0.65
Cigarettes	1	5/-	1.25	1.00	0.70
Linoleum	1	5/6	1.38	1.10	0.77
Paper	1	6/-	1.50	1.20	0.84
Glass bottles	1	7/-	1.75	1.40	0.98
Radio tubes	1	8/-	2.00	1.60	1.12
Pig iron	1	9/-	2.25	1.80	1.26
Tin cans	1	10/-	2.50	2.00	1.40

Columns 3 through 5 header spans: Cost in the United Kingdom in dollars

SOURCE: P. T. Ellsworth, *The International Economy,* revised, The Macmillan Company, New York, 1958, p. 262.

produce the same amount of product. Though all commodities appearing in the table are produced in both countries, it is likely that the real costs of some commodities are relatively less in one country than in the other. And, as explained by the law of comparative advantage, it is these commodities which will generally constitute a nation's exports.

The distribution between what a nation imports and what it exports becomes explicit only when an exchange rate is introduced. From a consideration of columns 1 and 2 above, one could hardly tell what commodities each country would export and import. Columns 3 through 5 translate costs in Britain, expressed in terms of shillings and pence, into their dollar equivalents. It can be observed that, at an exchange rate of £1 = $5.00, the first arbitrary exchange rate level, Britain would not be able to export to the U.S. *any* of the commodities in the table. With the exception of margarine, U.S. buyers would be able to purchase American-made goods at lower prices than those of equivalent British-made goods. (The British may still produce these goods for domestic sale, however, because purchase in the United States would involve additional costs— transportation, tariffs, etc.—which could offset their production cost disadvantage.) As the pound becomes cheaper in terms of the dollar, British goods become more and more competitive with equivalent American-made products. Thus, at £1 = $4.00 the British may start

exporting cotton cloth, wool cloth, and cigarettes. At £1 = $2.80 the list of exported products would extend to linoleum, paper, and glass bottles. Thus, the exchange rate markedly affects the distribution of products traded between nations.

EXCHANGE RATE DETERMINANTS

Having briefly explored the meaning of exchange rates and their importance, consideration may now be turned to how exchange rates are determined. As mentioned earlier, the discussion is limited to exchange rate determination under free market conditions. In such a situation the prevailing exchange rate would reflect basic supply and demand conditions. Consider, by way of illustration, the exchange rate between the U.S. dollar and the British pound. In any period the rate of exchange between the two currencies would reflect the relationship between the supply of dollars made available to Britishers by Americans and the demand for dollars by Britishers. Alternatively, it could be said that the exchange rate between the two currencies would reflect the relationship between the supply of pounds made available by Britishers to Americans and the demand for pounds by Americans.

The matter can, perhaps, be made clearer and more precise with the aid of Figure 73–1. The vertical axis measures the price of the pound in terms of dollars. The horizontal axis

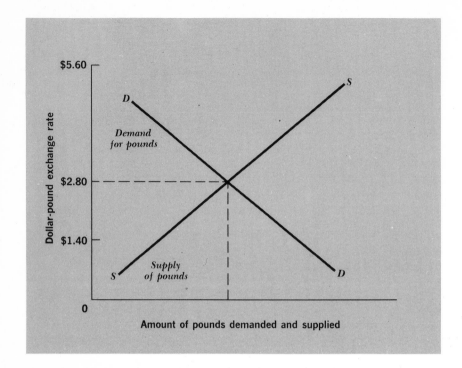

Figure 73–1.   The market for foreign exchange.

measures the amount of pounds supplied and demanded. The *DD* line sloping downward to the right shows a hypothetical relationship between the exchange rate and the demand by Americans for pound sterling. With British prices (fixed in terms of pounds) given, it is reasonable to assume that Americans will want fewer pounds as the price of the pound increases in terms of dollars. The *SS* line sloping upward to the right shows a hypothetical relationship between the exchange rate and the supply of pounds made available by Britishers to Americans. With American prices (set in terms of dollars) given, it is hypothesized that, as the dollar becomes cheaper in terms of pounds (or put otherwise, as the pound becomes dearer in terms of dollars), the volume of pounds made available to Americans, in the course of business dealings, will increase.

Suppose now that the exchange rate were set at £ 1 = $5.60. Could this rate be long maintained, given the hypothesized supply-demand relationships? Probably not, for at this price the supply of pounds would exceed the demand for pounds; not all sellers of sterling will be able to find buyers. The price of the pound would therefore tend to fall. Suppose

the exchange rate were set at £ 1 = $1.40. Could this rate be long maintained in a free market? Probably not, for at this price the demand for pounds, to purchase goods and services or investments in Britain, would exceed the supply of pounds made available. The price of the pound would therefore tend to rise. Only at £ 1 = $2.80 is there an exact coincidence between supply and demand. Thus, £ 1 = $2.80 becomes an "equilibrium" rate of exchange.

This rate of exchange—£ 1 = $2.80—would be an equilibrium rate only so long as changes do not occur in the hypothesized supply and demand relationships. Shifts in these relationships would make the existing equilibrium rate unmaintainable and, hence, necessitate a new equilibrium rate.

Suppose, for some reason, Americans become more willing to spend dollars in Britain, for example, as a result of the recent popularity in this country of a British singing group known as the "Beatles." An increased willingness to acquire pounds would manifest itself in a shift of the demand curve to the right (see Figure 73–2); that is, at each dollar-pound exchange rate, Americans would seek more pounds than

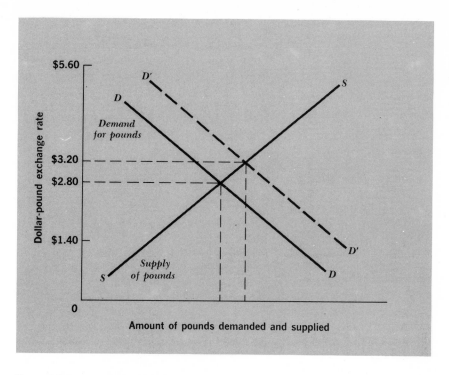

Figure 73–2.   Changes in the demand for pounds.

previously. The existing exchange rate, £ 1 = $2.80, would become unmaintainable; the demand for pounds would exceed the supply of pounds. Unsatisfied demanders of the pound would drive up the pound's price in terms of dollars. Only at some new figure, perhaps at £ 1 ≐ $3.20, would a new equilibrium rate be found.

EXISTING INTERNATIONAL MONETARY SYSTEM

Under present international monetary arrangements, exchange rates are allowed to vary only slightly in response to temporary changes in supply and demand factors; member countries of the International Monetary Fund (IMF) are required to maintain—through buying and selling as needed in the foreign exchange market—stable rates of exchange between their internal currency units and a specified weight of gold. This requirement effectively establishes stable rates of exchange between a member nation's currency and the currency units of other member countries. To illustrate, the U.S. exchanges dollars for gold or gold for dollars for official foreign holders at a price of $35 an

ounce; if Great Britain were to do the same, it would be at a price of £ 12/10s ($35 = one ounce gold = £ 12/10s; and $2.80 = £ 1). Similar relationships can be worked out for all other member countries, although not all countries buy and sell gold in the market.

Though member nations are required to maintain stable rates of exchange between their own currencies and those of other countries, this requirement does not apply in situations where "fundamental disequilibrium" exists. That is, when it becomes evident that the prevailing exchange rate no longer corresponds closely to a market-determined rate reflecting long-term supply and demand forces, the IMF will permit exchange rate adjustments. The IMF, however, has never made explicit, or given substance to, the term "fundamental disequilibrium," though what is *not* meant has been made quite apparent. According to one well-known economist closely associated with the IMF:

No attempt has ever been made—nor perhaps could it be—to define fundamental disequilibrium precisely. But it is clearly intended to exclude merely ephemeral balance of payments disequilibria, due to temporary factors of a seasonal, speculative, or possibly even of a short cyclical type. . . . Moreover . . . it was probably implicit in the articles that exchange rates should be adjusted only at infrequent intervals.

Consider what it means for a nation to guarantee to maintain a fixed rate of exchange between its own currency and a specified amount of gold or, what comes to the same thing, another country's currency, such as the U.S. dollar. The situation facing a hypothetical country like South Morango can be used as an example. Assume that that country has declared that 60.0 units of its currency, the *morang* will exchange for one U.S. dollar, or, put otherwise, that the *morang* is equivalent to 1.667 cents. South Morango has also established fixed rates of exchange between the *morang* and the currency units of all other member countries. To maintain these exchange rates, the monetary authorities in South Morango should stand ready to buy and sell *unlimited* amounts of gold and/or dollars. For example, suppose South Morango was suffering a deficit in its international balance of payments. That is, the demand for foreign currencies to make desired purchases and investments abroad exceeds the supply of such currencies made available as a result of sales (of either goods, services, or long-term debt instruments) by South Morangoans to foreigners. In this type of situation, there would be a *natural tendency*, all things

being equal, for the *morang* to fall in value. To prevent this, and thus maintain the established rate, the authorities must make either gold or dollars available at the official price.

The problem, obviously, is that South Morango can neither print dollars (and for that matter any currency other than the *morang*) nor manufacture gold. Because its reserves of foreign currencies and gold—as those of any nation—are limited, there are constraints as to the magnitude and duration of balance of payments deficits that South Morango could withstand without lowering the value of the *morang* to make purchases in South Morango relatively more attractive. Sufficient monetary reserves (or adequate international liquidity) are essential to any system of fixed exchange rates.

Establishment of the IMF, in 1946, in effect provided additional international liquidity; member countries could now borrow foreign exchange from the Fund to meet temporary deficits. Thus, for example, South Morango would be allowed to borrow up to a specified amount from the IMF to cover a temporary disequilibrium in her payments position. The foregoing points up the fact that international liquidity presently consists not only of gold and foreign exchange, particularly dollars and pounds sterling, but also of borrowing rights on the IMF. Insofar as a system of fixed exchange rates rests upon the existence of adequate international liquidity, the Fund has clearly made such a system more viable than it would otherwise be.

QUESTIONS AND STUDY SUGGESTIONS

1. Why are exchange rates necessary? What causes exchange rates to change in a free market?
2. How would a decrease in the dollar price of pounds affect (*a*) the volume and (*b*) the composition of trade between Great Britain and the United States?
3. Explain the basic characteristics of the present international monetary system, indicating the role of the International Monetary Fund.
4. Explain: "Sufficient monetary reserves . . . are essential to any system of fixed exchange rates."

Reading 74

The Case for Flexible Exchange Rates

Milton Friedman, Professor of Economics, University of Chicago

One feature which makes international trade distinct from domestic trade is that foreign trade requires that one nation's currency be exchanged for that of another. Whether the rate of exchange is market-determined or fixed by some means has important implications for a nation's domestic economy and its balance of payments position. Readings 74 and 75 debate the advisability of abandoning our current system of fixed exchange rates in favor of a system of flexible rates. In Reading 74 Milton Friedman alleges that under the present system of fixed rates our payments deficit can be met only through the loss of monetary reserves or domestic deflation. Deflation is undesirable per se, and the loss of reserves puts severe constraints upon domestic policies. But if exchange rates are made market-determined and therefore freely flexible, these alternatives can be avoided. Gradual market-determined changes in exchange rates, Friedman argues, will automatically resolve balance of payments maladjustments and simultaneously avoid highly adverse effects upon domestic price and employment levels.

Discussions of U.S. policy with respect to international payments tend to be dominated by our immediate balance-of-payments difficulties. I should like today to approach the question from a different, and I hope more constructive, direction. Let us begin by asking ourselves not merely how we can get out of our present difficulties but instead how we can fashion our international payments system so that it will best serve our needs for the long pull; how we can solve not merely *this* balance-of-payments problem but *the* balance-of-payments problem.

A shocking, and indeed, disgraceful feature of the present situation is the extent to which our frantic search for expedients to stave off balance-of-payments pressures has led us, on the one hand, to sacrifice major national objectives; and, on the other, to give enormous power to officials of foreign governments to affect what should be purely domestic matters.

Foreign payments amount to only some 5 percent of our total national income. Yet they have become a major factor in nearly every national policy.

I believe that a system of floating exchange rates would solve the balance-of-payments problem for the United States far more effectively than our present arrangements. Such a system would use the flexibility and efficiency of the free market to harmonize our small foreign trade sector with both the rest of our massive economy and the rest of the world; it would reduce problems of foreign payments to their proper dimensions and remove them as a major consideration in governmental policy about domestic matters and as a major preoccupation in international political negotiations; it would foster our national objectives rather than be an obstacle to their attainment.

To indicate the basis for this conclusion, let

From **The United States Balance of Payments**, Hearings before the Joint Economic Committee, 88th Cong., 1st Sess., Washington, part 3, pp. 451–459, abridged.

us consider the national objective with which our payments system is most directly connected: the promotion of a healthy and balanced growth of world trade, carried on, so far as possible, by private individuals and private enterprises with minimum intervention by governments. This has been a major objective of our whole postwar international economic policy, most recently expressed in the Trade Expansion Act of 1962. Success would knit the free world more closely together, and, by fostering the international division of labor, raise standards of living throughout the world, in- including the United States.

ILLUSTRATION: TARIFF CUTS

Suppose that we succeed in negotiating far-reaching reciprocal reductions in tariffs and other trade barriers with the Common Market and other countries. Such reductions will expand trade in general but clearly will have different effects on different industries. The demand for the products of some will expand, for others contract. This is a phenomenon we are familiar with from our internal development. The capacity of our free enterprise system to adapt quickly and efficiently to such shifts, whether produced by changes in technology or tastes, has been a major source of our economic growth. The only additional element introduced by international trade is the fact that different currencies are involved, and this is where the payment mechanism comes in; its function is to keep this fact from being an additional source of disturbance.

An all-around lowering of tariffs would tend to increase both our expenditures and our receipts in foreign currencies. There is no way of knowing in advance which increase would tend to be the greater and hence no way of knowing whether the initial effect would be toward a surplus or deficit in our balance of payments. What is clear is that we cannot hope to succeed in the objective of expanding world trade unless we can readily adjust to either outcome.

METHODS OF ADJUSTMENT

Suppose then that the initial effect is to increase our expenditures on imports more than our receipts from exports. How could we adjust to this outcome?

One method of adjustment is to draw on reserves or borrow from abroad to finance the excess increase in imports. The obvious objection to this method is that it is only a temporary device, and hence can be relied on only when the disturbance is temporary. But that is not the major objection. Even if we had very large reserves or could borrow large amounts from abroad, so that we could continue this expedient for many years, it is a most undesirable one. We can see why if we look at physical rather than financial magnitudes.

The physical counterpart to the financial deficit is a reduction of employment in industries competing with imports that is larger than the concurrent expansion of employment in export industries. So long as the financial deficit continues, the assumed tariff reductions create employment problems. But it is no part of the aim of tariff reductions to create unemployment at home or to promote employment abroad. The aim is a balanced expansion of trade, with exports rising along with imports and thereby providing employment opportunities to offset any reduction in employment resulting from increased imports.

Hence, simply drawing on reserves or borrowing abroad is a most unsatisfactory method of adjustment.

Another method of adjustment is to lower U.S. prices relative to foreign prices, since this would stimulate exports and discourage imports. If foreign countries are accommodating enough to engage in inflation, such a change in relative prices might require merely that the United States keep prices stable or even, that it simply keep them from rising as fast as foreign prices. But there is no necessity for foreign countries to be so accommodating, and we could hardly count on their being so accommodating. The use of this technique therefore involves a willingness to produce a decline in U.S. prices by tight monetary policy or tight fiscal policy or both. Given time, this method of adjustment would work. But in the interim, it would exact a heavy toll. It would be difficult or impossible to force down prices appreciably without producing a recession and considerable unemployment. To eliminate in the long run the unemployment resulting from the tariff changes, we should in the short run be creating cyclical unemployment. The cure might for a time be far worse than the disease.

This second method is therefore also most

unsatisfactory. Yet these two methods—drawing on reserves and forcing down prices—are the only two methods available to us under our present international payment arrangements, which involve fixed exchange rates between the U.S. dollar and other currencies. Little wonder that we have so far made such disappointing progress toward the reduction of trade barriers, that our practice has differed so much from our preaching.

EXCHANGE RATE FLEXIBILITY

There is one other way and only one other way to adjust and that is by allowing (or forcing) the price of the U.S. dollar to fall in terms of other currencies. To a foreigner, U.S. goods can become cheaper in either of two ways—either because their prices in the United States fall in terms of dollars or because the foreigner has to give up fewer units of his own currency to acquire a dollar, which is to say, the price of the dollar falls. For example, suppose a particular U.S. car sells for $2,800 when a dollar costs 7 shillings, tuppence in British money (i.e., roughly £1 = $2.80). The price of the car is then £1,000 in British money. It is all the same to an Englishman—or even a Scotsman—whether the price of the car falls to $2,500 while the price of a dollar remains 7 shillings, tuppence, or, alternatively, the price of the car remains $2,800, while the price of a dollar falls to 6 shillings, 5 pence (i.e., roughly £1 = $3.11). In either case, the car costs the Englishman £900 rather than £1,000, which is what matters to him. Similarly, foreign goods can become more expensive to an American in either of two ways—either because the price in terms of foreign currency rises or because he has to give up more dollars to acquire a given amount of foreign currency.

Changes in exchange rates can therefore alter the relative price of U.S. and foreign goods in precisely the same way as can changes in internal prices in the United States and in foreign countries. And they can do so without requiring anything like the same internal adjustments. If the initial effect of the tariff reductions would be to create a deficit at the former exchange rate (or enlarge an existing deficit or reduce an existing surplus) and thereby increase unemployment, this effect can be entirely avoided by a change in exchange rates which will produce a balanced expansion in imports and exports without interfering with domestic employment, domestic prices, or domestic monetary and fiscal policy. The pig can be roasted without burning down the house.

DEVALUATION VERSUS FLEXIBILITY

Changes in exchange rates can be produced in either of two general ways. One way is by a change in an official exchange rate; an official devaluation or appreciation from one fixed level which the Government is committed to support to another fixed level. This is the method used by Britain in its postwar devaluation and by Germany in 1961 when the mark was appreciated. This is also the main method contemplated by the IMF which permits member nations to change their exchange rates by 10 percent without approval by the Fund and by a larger amount after approval by the Fund. But this method has serious disadvantages. It makes a change in rates a matter of major moment, and hence there is a tendency to postpone any change as long as possible. Difficulties cumulate and a larger change is finally needed than would have been required if it could have been made promptly. By the time the change is made, everyone is aware that a change is pending and is certain about the direction of change. The result is to encourage flight from a currency, if it is going to be devalued, or to a currency, if it is going to be appreciated.

There is in any event little basis for determining precisely what the new rate should be. Speculative movements increase the difficulty of judging what the new rate should be, and introduce a systematic bias, making the change needed appear larger than it actually is. The result, particularly when devaluation occurs, is generally to lead officials to "play safe" by making an even larger change than the large change needed. The country is then left after the devaluation with a maladjustment precisely the opposite of that with which it started, and is thereby encouraged to follow policies it cannot sustain in the long run.

Even if all these difficulties could be avoided, this method of changing from one fixed rate to another has the disadvantage that it is necessarily discontinuous. Even if the new exchange rates are precisely correct when first established, they will not long remain correct.

A second and much better way in which changes in exchange rates can be produced is by permitting exchange rates to float, by allowing them to be determined from day to day in the market. Under this method, exchange rates adjust themselves continuously, and market forces determine the magnitude of each change. There is no need for any official to decide by how much the rate should rise or fall. This is the method of the free market, the method that we adopt unquestioningly in a private enterprise economy for the bulk of goods and services. It is no less available for the price of one money in terms of another.

ALLEGED DISADVANTAGES REFUTED

Despite their advantages, floating exchange rates have a bad press. Why is this so?

One reason is because a consequence of our present system that I have been citing as a serious disadvantage is often regarded as an advantage, namely, the extent to which the small foreign trade sector dominates national policy. Those who regard this as an advantage refer to it as the discipline of the gold standard. I would have much sympathy for this view if we had a real gold standard, so the discipline was imposed by impersonal forces which in turn reflected the realities of resources, tastes, and technology. But in fact we have today only a pseudo gold standard and the so-called discipline is imposed by governmental officials of other countries who are determining their own internal monetary policies and are either being forced to dance to our tune or calling the tune for us, depending primarily on accidental political developments. This is a discipline we can well do without.

A possibly more important reason why floating exchange rates have a bad press, I believe, is a mistaken interpretation of experience with floating rates, arising out of a statistical fallacy that can be seen easily in a standard example. Arizona is clearly the worst place in the United States for a person with tuberculosis to go because the death rate from tuberculosis is higher in Arizona than in any other State. The fallacy in this case is obvious. It is less obvious in connection with exchange rates. Countries that have gotten into severe financial difficulties, for whatever reason, have had ultimately to change their exchange rates or let them change. No amount of exchange control and other restrictions on trade have enabled them to peg an exchange rate that was far out of line with

economic realities. In consequence, floating rates have frequently been associated with financial and economic instability. It is easy to conclude, as many have, that floating exchange rates produce such instability.

Floating exchange rates need not be unstable exchange rates—any more than the prices of automobiles or of Government bonds, of coffee or of meals need gyrate wildly just because they are free to change from day to day. The Canadian exchange rate was free to change during more than a decade, yet it varied within narrow limits. The ultimate objective is a world in which exchange rates, while free to vary, are in fact highly stable because basic economic policies and conditions are stable. Instability of exchange rates is a symptom of instability in the underlying economic structure. Elimination of this symptom by administrative pegging of exchange rates cures none of the underlying difficulties and only makes adjustment to them more painful.

The confusion between stable exchange rates and pegged exchange rates helps to explain the frequent comment that floating exchange rates would introduce an additional element of uncertainty into foreign trade and thereby discourage its expansion. They introduce no additional element of uncertainty. If a floating rate would, for example, decline, then a pegged rate would be subject to pressure that the authorities would have to meet by internal deflation or exchange control in some form. The uncertainty about the rate would simply be replaced by uncertainty about internal prices or about the availability of exchange; and the latter uncertainties, being subject to administrative rather than market control, are likely to be the more erratic and unpredictable. Moreover, the trader can far more readily and cheaply protect himself against the danger of changes in exchange rates, through hedging operations in a forward market, than he can against the danger of changes in internal prices or exchange availability. Floating rates are therefore more favorable to private international trade than pegged rates.

THE PRESENT PAYMENTS PROBLEM

Though I have discussed the problem of international payments in the context of trade liberalization, the discussion is directly applicable to the more general problem of adapting to any forces that make for balance-of-payments difficulties. Consider our present problem, of a deficit in the balance of trade plus long-term capital movements. How can we adjust to it? By one of the three methods outlined: first, drawing on reserves or borrowing; second, keeping U.S. prices from rising as rapidly as foreign prices or forcing them down; third, permitting or forcing exchange rates to alter. And, this time, by one more method: by imposing additional trade barriers or their equivalent, whether in the form of higher tariffs, or smaller import quotas, or extracting from other countries tighter "voluntary" quotas on their exports, or "tieing" foreign aid, or buying higher priced domestic goods or services to meet military needs, or imposing taxes on foreign borrowing, or imposing direct controls on investments by U.S. citizens abroad, or any one of the host of other devices for interfering with the private business of private individuals that have become so familiar to us.

Fortunately or unfortunately, even Congress cannot repeal the laws of arithmetic. Books must balance. We must use one of these four methods. Because we have been unwilling to select the only one that is currently fully consistent with both economic and political needs —namely, floating exchange rates—we have been driven, as if by an invisible hand, to employ all the others, and even then may not escape the need for explicit changes in exchange rates.

It is not the least of the virtues of floating exchange rates that we would again become masters in our own house. We could decide important issues on the proper ground. The military could concentrate on military effectiveness and not on saving foreign exchange; recipients of foreign aid could concentrate on how to get the most out of what we give them and not on how to spend it all in the United States; Congress could decide how much to spend on foreign aid on the basis of what we get for our money and what else we could use it for and not how it will affect the gold stock; the monetary authorities could concentrate on domestic prices and employment, not on how to induce foreigners to hold dollar balances in this country; the Treasury and the tax committees of Congress could devote their attention to the equity of the tax system and its effects on our efficiency, rather than on how to use tax gimmicks to discourage imports, subsidize exports, and discriminate against outflows of capital.

A system of floating exchange rates would render the problem of making outflows equal inflows unto the market where it belongs and not leave it to the clumsy and heavy hand of Government. It would leave Government free to concentrate on its proper function.

QUESTIONS AND STUDY SUGGESTIONS

1. Explain how flexible or "floating" exchange rates would cause the domestic economy to adjust to a trade deficit. Why does the author reject (a) the drawing down of international monetary reserves or borrowing and (b) domestic price level reduction as means of adjusting to a trade deficit?
2. Why does the author prefer free-market changes in the exchange rate to official government changes ("devaluation") of the exchange rate?
3. Explain: "It is not the least of the virtues of floating exchange rates that we would again become masters in our own house."

The Case for Fixed Exchange Rates

Henry C. Wallich, Professor of Economics, Yale University

Henry C. Wallich takes the position in this reading that flexible exchange rates are unworkable in today's world economy because "their successful functioning would require more self-discipline and mutual forbearance than countries today are likely to muster." It is true that a depreciation of the dollar would tend to increase American exports and reduce American imports, thereby tending to correct an American payments deficit. But other nations might not be willing to tolerate the declines in their exports and the rise in their imports which would face them as the value of their currencies appreciates internationally. In short, freely flexible exchange rates might lead to retaliation by other nations in the form of simultaneous depreciation of their currencies or the imposition of tariffs upon American goods. Other undesirable effects of flexible rates include the possibility that worldwide inflation will be accelerated and that the uncertainty and risks which accompany flexible rates may discourage both international trade and investment.

Let me say at the outset that I conceive of my paper as a defense of fixed rates.

ECONOMICS VERSUS POLITICS?

Flexible rates have achieved a high measure of acceptance in academic circles, but very little among public officials. This raises the question whether we have a parallel to the famous case of free trade: almost all economists favor it in principle, but no major country ever has adopted it. Does the logic of economics point equally irrefutably to flexible rates, while the logic of politics points in another direction?

The nature of the case, I believe, is fundamentally different. Most countries do practice free trade within their borders, although they reject it outside. But economists do not propose flexible rates for the States of the Union, among which men, money, and goods can move freely, and which are governed by uniform monetary, fiscal, and other policies. Flexible rates are to apply only to relations among countries that do not permit free factor movements across their borders and that follow, or may follow, substantially different monetary and fiscal policies. It is the imperfections of the world that seem to suggest that flexible rates, which would be harmful if applied to different parts of a single country, would do more good than harm internationally.

It is quite arguable that the Appalachian area would benefit if it could issue a dollar of its own, an Appalachian dollar which in that case would sell, probably, at 60 or 90 cents. Exports from that region would increase, and unemployment would diminish. A great many good things would happen, but we are also aware of what it would do to the economy of the United States—and, therefore, we do not

From **The United States Balance of Payments,** Hearings before the Joint Economic Committee, 88th Cong., 1st Sess., Washington, part 3, pp. 495–499, abridged.

propose that solution. The question is, Do we want to look upon the world as quite different from the United States, as hopelessly divided into self-contained units where cooperation and efforts to coordinate policies are doomed to frustration? In that case, flexible rates may be the best way to avoid a very bad situation. But should we not try to establish within the world something that begins to approximate the conditions that prevail within a country, in the way of coordination of policies, freer flow of capital and of goods and so try to achieve the benefits of one large economic area within the world? That is what we should try for.

Now to resume: The proponents of flexible rates argue, in effect, that flexible rates can help a country get out of almost any of the typical difficulties that economies experience. This is perfectly true. If the United States has a balance-of-payments deficit, a flexible exchange rate allows the dollar to decline until receipts have risen and payments fallen enough to restore balance. If the United States has unemployment, flexible rates can protect it against the balance-of-payments consequences of a policy of expansion. We would then have less unemployment. If the United States has suffered inflation and fears that it will be undersold internationally, flexible rates can remove the danger.

All of these advantages are quite clear.

Other countries have analogous advantages. If Chile experiences a decline in copper prices, flexible rates can ease the inevitable adjustment. If Germany finds that other countries have inflated while German prices have remained more nearly stable, flexible rates could help to avoid importing inflation. If Canada has a large capital inflow, a flexible rate will remove the need for price and income increases that would otherwise be needed to facilitate the transfer of real resources.

There are other adjustments, however, that must be made in all of these cases. If a country allows its exchange rate to go down, some price adjustments still remain to be made. Furthermore, each time a country makes this kind of adjustment, allowing its exchange rate to decline, other countries suffer. If the U.S. dollar depreciates, we undersell the Europeans. It could be argued that if the U.S. price levels go down instead of the exchange rate, we also undersell the Europeans, and if because of a declining price level we have unemployment

we would be buying still less from them. Nevertheless, there is a difference. A price adjustment tends to be slow and is likely to be no greater than it need be and tends to be selective for particular commodities. In contrast, an exchange rate movement is unpredictable. It can be large—we could easily have a drop of 10 or 20 percent in an exchange rate. It comes suddenly. And it compels other countries to be on their guard.

LIMITS OF TOLERANCE

Why, given the attractions of flexible rates, should one advise policymakers to stay away from them? Since the dollar problem is the concrete situation in which flexible rates are being urged today, it is in terms of the dollar that they must be discussed. In broadest terms, the reason why flexible rates are inadvisable is that their successful functioning would require more self-discipline and mutual forbearance than countries today are likely to muster. Exchange rates are two sided—depreciation for the dollar means appreciation for the European currencies. To work successfully, a flexible dollar, for instance, must not depreciate to the point where the Europeans would feel compelled to take counteraction. I believe that the limits of tolerance, before counteraction begins today are narrow and that a flexible dollar would invite retaliation almost immediately.

In the abstract, the European countries perhaps ought to consider that if the United States allows the dollar to go down, it is doing so in the interests of all-round equilibrium. They ought perhaps to consider that with a stable dollar rate the same adjustment might have to take place through a decline in prices here and a rise in prices there. In practice, they are likely to be alive principally to the danger of being undersold by American producers if the dollar goes down, in their own and third markets. The changing competitive pressure would fall unevenly upon particular industries, and those who are hurt would demand protection.

RETALIATION

The most likely counteraction might take one of two forms. The Europeans could impose countervailing duties, such as the United States also has employed at times. They could alternately also depreciate European currencies along with the dollar or, what would amount to almost the same thing, prevent the dollar from depreciating.

A sudden outflow of funds from the United States, for instance (because of the fear of budget deficits or many other things that could happen), would tend to drive the dollar down. As a result, American exporters could undersell producers everywhere else in the world. It seems unlikely that foreign countries would allow a fortuitous short-term capital movement to have such far-reaching consequences. It would not even be economically appropriate to allow a transitory fluctuation in the capital account of the balance of payments to have a major influence on the current account. Such a fluctuation should not alter the pattern of trade, because the situation is likely to be reversed. Other countries therefore would probably take defensive action to make sure that no industry is destroyed and after several years may have to be rebuilt because of the ups and downs of short-term capital movements.

It can be argued that under flexible rates the effects of such a movement would be forestalled by stabilizing speculation on a future recovery of the dollar. This is possible. It is possible also, however, that speculation would seek a quick profit from the initial drop in the dollar, instead of a longer run one from its eventual recovery. Then short-run speculation would drive the dollar down farther at first. In any case there is not enough assurance that speculators will not make mistakes to permit basing the world's monetary system upon the stabilizing effects of speculation.

FLEXIBILITY AND INFLATION

This points up one probable consequence of flexible exchange rates: A worldwide acceleration of inflation. In some countries the indicated ratchet effect of wages will be at work. If exchange rates go down, wages will rise, and exchange rates cannot recover. In the United States the rise in the cost of imports would not be very important. But the removal of balance-of-payments restraints may well lead to policies that could lead to price increases. The American inflation of the 1950s was never defeated until the payments deficit became serious. Elsewhere, the removal of balance-of-payments disciplines might have the same effect. Rapid inflation in turn would probably compel gov-

ernments to intervene drastically in foreign trade and finance.

I am aware that there is a choice to be made here—more employment or more stable prices. If we pursued more sensible policies and exerted a little more self-restraint, this choice would not be upon us. But if we insist on raising costs and raising prices in the presence of unemployment then this unpleasant choice must be made. It is quite clear that the discipline of the balance of payments has made for a more restrictive policy in this country than would have been followed in the absence of this discipline. It is quite conceivable that the absence of balance-of-payments disciplines would have strong inflationary effects in some countries. In that case governments would be compelled immediately to intervene drastically in foreign trade and finance; in other words, flexible exchange rates would contribute to their own extinction or to exchange control.

UNCERTAINTY AND DISINTEGRATION

The prospect that flexible rates would greatly increase uncertainty for foreign traders and investors has been cited many times. It should be noted that this uncertainty extends also to domestic investment decisions that might be affected by changing import competition or changing export prospects. It has been argued that uncertainties about future exchange rates can be removed by hedging in the futures market. This, however, involves a cost even where cover is readily available. The history of futures markets does not suggest that it will be possible to get cover for long-term positions. To hedge domestic investment decisions that might be affected by flexible rates is in the nature of things impracticable.

The picture that emerges of the international economy under flexible rates is one of increasing disintegration. Independent national policies and unpredictable changes in each country's competitive position will compel governments to shield their producers and markets. The argument that such shielding would also automatically be accomplished by movements in the affected country's exchange rate underrates the impact of fluctuations upon particular industries, if not upon the entire economy. That international integration and flexible rates are incompatible seems to be the view also of the European Common Market countries, who have left no doubt that they want stable rates within the EEC. The same applies if we visualize the "Kennedy round" under the Trade Expansion Act. I think if we told the Europeans that, after lowering our tariffs, we were going to cast the dollar loose and let it fluctuate, we would get very little tariff reduction. They would want to keep up their guard.

If the disintegrating effects of flexible rates are to be overcome, a great deal of policy coordination, combined with self-discipline and mutual forbearance, would be required. The desired independence of national economic policy would in fact have to be foregone—interest rates, budgets, wage and prices policies would have to be harmonized. If the world were ready for such cooperation, it would be capable also of making a fixed exchange rate system work. In that case, flexible rates would accomplish nothing that could not more cheaply and simply be done with fixed rates. It seems to follow that flexible rates have no unique capacity for good, whereas they possess great capacity to do damage.

It remains only to point out that, even in the absence of a high degree of international cooperativeness, a system of fixed exchange rates can be made to work. It can be made to work mainly because it imposes a discipline upon all participants, and because within this discipline there is nevertheless some room for adjustment. The principle sources of flexibility are productivity gains and the degree to which they are absorbed by wage increases. Wages cannot be expected to decline. But their rise can be slowed in relation to the rate of productivity growth, in which case prices would become more competitive relative to other countries. With annual productivity gains of 2 to 3 percent in the United States and more abroad, it would not take many years to remove a temporary imbalance.

QUESTIONS AND STUDY SUGGESTIONS

1. Are flexible exchange rates economically workable but politically unfeasible?

2. Why, according to the author, might flexible exchange rates contribute to inflation in the world economy? To uncertainty and an ultimate disintegration of world trade?

3. Explain: "Flexible rates have no unique capacity for good, whereas they possess great capacity to do damage."

Reading 76

Honduras: Dilemma of Development

William S. Stokes, Professor of Comparative Political Institutions, Claremont Men's College

This reading is an interesting case study in economic underdevelopment. Honduras presents a frustrating picture. Although faced with many problems common to underdeveloped nations—for example, widespread illiteracy, primitive housing, and the lack of basic social capital—Honduras does have the natural resource potential for considerable growth. The country's success in achieving economic progress, however, has been quite unimpressive. In the author's judgment an exaggerated reliance upon public spending as the primary means of expanding production, coupled with overly ambitious social legislation and value patterns inappropriate to rapid growth, has been the cause of Honduras' disappointing performance. Liberal land reform legislation may be the only bright spot on an otherwise dismal development horizon.

When the distinguished leaders of the New Frontier accelerate the expenditure of the $20 billion promised for Latin American development under the *Alianza para Progreso* [Alliance for Progress] program, it is almost certain that Honduras will not be overlooked. This beautiful heart-land republic of Central America provides abundant evidence of economic backwardness.

ECONOMIC BACKWARDNESS

Probably about 50 percent of the homes in the country are floorless mud and wattle huts. Although approximately 83 percent of the people are farmers of one kind or another, only four percent of the total land area is cultivated. Except for the advanced methods of the fruit companies, and a few other farmers, agricultural practices can only be described as primitive. There is only one plow for every 4.3 farms or one for every 14.4 farmers. Most farmers live at elevations of 2,000 to 5,000 feet and grow subsistence crops. Their productivity is so low that few people can leave the farm to produce goods and services in the cities. Sanitary conditions are unsatisfactory, and many people, especially babies, die needlessly. The many illegitimate children (*naturales*) weaken such social institutions as the family. Although UNESCO reported in 1961 that a 40 percent increase in enrollment had taken place in elementary education in the past three years, probably 50 percent of the school-age children of the nation are not receiving any education at all. Many of those in school attend for three years at most. Between 60 and 65 percent of those 10 years or older are illiterate. About one-half of the secondary schools are located in the two cities of Tegucigalpa and San Pedro Sula.

Roads are inadequate. There were only 24 miles of paved roads in 1955, and there are fewer than 100 miles of paved roads in the entire country today with not more than 700 miles of all types of highways in use. No main

From William S. Stokes, "Honduras: Dilemma of Development," **Current History**, February, 1962, pp. 83–88. Reprinted by permission.

highway crosses the country from east to west, and only horse or mule trails can be found in the entire eastern half of the country. The Inter-Oceanic Highway crosses the country from north to south, but parts of it are passable only in dry weather. The railroad lines (fewer than 1,000 miles in use) all operate near the port cities of Puerto Cortés, Tela and La Ceiba and are mainly useful to only one industry—bananas. There is no railroad line to Tegucigalpa, the capital.

Although the hydroelectric potential is estimated at 1,040,000 kilowatts, Honduras has less electric power than any country in the Western Hemisphere except Haiti. No power plant exceeds 5,000 kilowatts in total installed capacity and rates are high. (In 1960, the World Bank loaned $8,800,000 and the United States Development Loan Fund $2,800,000 to the *Empresa Nacional de Energía Eléctrica,* a government agency, to help finance the $14,750,000 Canaveral hydroelectric project near the Rio Lindo. The first unit will yield 27,000 kilowatts and the entire project will have 160,000 kilowatts of generating capacity.)

The magnificent hard woods of the rain forest regions and the splendid stands of soft woods, mainly pine, are inadequately exploited. The known deposits of commercially valuable iron ore (about 50,000,000 tons) in the El Níspero region of Santa Bárbara Department are inaccessible due to lack of roads or railroads. Known deposits of zinc, copper and antimony remain undeveloped. Lake Yojoa, one of the most beautiful bodies of water in the world, offers hunting, fishing and exploring, but its tourist potential is untapped. Ocean resources of the north and south coasts are largely untouched.

Only Tegucigalpa exceeds 100,000 in population. Heavy industry is discouraged by the lack of coal and iron ore, and even light industry is not widely developed. As of January, 1951, there were a total of only 3,836 industrial establishments employing 20,379 people with investments totaling 57,344,551 *lempiras* (2 *lempiras*–$1).

Panama disease and government policy have contributed to the decline of banana production by the United States-owned United Fruit and Standard Fruit Companies. In 1960, about 10 million stems were exported (50 percent of the country's total exports), and 1961 production might equal the 1958 level of 13.5 million stems. However, Honduras exported 21 million stems in 1931. A 69-day strike, the worst in Honduras' history, began on May 3, 1954. At the height of the strike, 38,000 workers were out, 35,000 of them banana company employees. There is evidence that Communists from Guatemala prolonged the strike. The Fundamental Charter of Labor Guarantees, the first broad labor law in Honduras, took effect on February 16, 1955 (providing for minimum wages, maximum hours, collective bargaining, social security and other guarantees). Since that time the fruit companies have faced repeated demands for wage increases, resulting in financial losses which may compel them to leave Honduras. This would be a loss to the country, for in addition to providing a large part of the government's revenues, the companies have offered the highest wages, the best conditions of employment, and most elaborate fringe benefits (education, hospital services, recreation) of any large employer in the country. Perhaps of even greater significance the fruit companies have trained thousands of Hondurans to become skilled workers in various fields.

ECONOMIC DEVELOPMENT

This grim portrayal of economic backwardness can be softened by optimistic review of other data. A strong effort was begun in 1950 to reduce illiteracy, and education continues to receive a large percentage of the yearly budget. The School of Agriculture at Zamorano, founded by the United Fruit Company in 1943, offers free courses in scientific husbandry for 160 students. The country's first income tax law was passed in 1949, and on July 1, 1950, the Central Bank of Honduras (with great control over monetary policy) and the National Development Bank were opened. United Nations technicians studied the forests in 1956 to determine the economic feasibility of a pulp and paper plant which might provide newsprint and paper requirements for all of Central America. In 1961, Congress passed a law establishing forest areas to protect wood, soil and water resources. The International Development Association (an affiliate of the World Bank) extended its first loan to Honduras in 1961, a $9 million interest-free credit to assist in highway development and maintenance. The $13.5 million highway project was also assisted by a $2.5 million loan from the Inter-American Development Bank. When completed, Honduras will have a 62-mile extension of the western highway, linking Puerto Cortés on the Caribbean with El Salvador and Guatemala. The total gross product of Honduras rose 34 percent between 1948 and 1957.

The *Banco Centroamericano de Integración Económica* was established on May 30, 1961, to encourage economic development and strengthen and unify the Central American common market. The United States was expected to provide ultimately $10 million of the authorized capitalization of $16 million. Finally, by 1961, the government had drafted a four-year development program ("Forward toward Progress") designed to exploit natural resources, improve communications, and expand farm production, the financing to come from internal and external sources (the *Alianza para Progreso,* for example).

SLOW GROWTH

On balance, one must conclude that although some developmental progress has taken place, there has been too little at too slow a rate to satisfy the aspirations of both leaders and people. Why has this been so?

I have often heard Latin Americans explain the tremendous productivity and great prosperity of the United States in terms of some single factor, such as fabulously rich resources available for the taking. Productivity is a complicated process, even in simple, preindustrial societies. It never depends upon one single factor. Natural resources (land, water, forests, minerals), capital (factory, farm, equipment, materials, money), and labor (entrepreneurial, managerial, skilled, unskilled) must be brought together to produce the goods and services men desire.

It has already been shown that Honduras is endowed with various types of valuable natural resources. Resources which are lacking can be acquired by purchase or barter from other countries. Honduras has capital. Indeed, there is a far greater capital accumulation in the country than has been used in the past or is being used at the present time. I have personally known wealthy Hondurans who preferred to export their capital rather than invest it in productive activity in their country. Additional capital can, of course, be attracted from outside by appropriate governmental policies.

Honduras has labor. If the cultural anthropologists and the theologians are correct, and I think that they are, the people of Honduras have been blessed with as much intelligence, talent and ability as any people to be found anywhere in the world.

WHAT RETARDS PROGRESS?

It is, therefore, difficult to explain the relative lack of economic progress of Honduras in terms of any one of the factors of land, labor and capital. Instead, there is a fourth factor of productivity and hence economic development which must be considered. This is what can be termed the attitude or value pattern of a people. The attitude or value pattern of a people is a product of historical experience and the conditioning impact of the social and economic institutions with which the individual comes into contact during his life. Thus, in order for land, labor and capital to be used intensively and effectively, individuals must believe that work—growing, making, creating, serving—is a value of the highest order, something most devoutly to be sought. Individuals must believe that hard work, sacrifice and saving—the process of capital accumulation—represents not only a theoretical ideal but a practical guide to day-to-day living. Conversely, the value of leisure must be rendered unimportant or, for a country which wants rapid economic development, eliminated almost entirely from the culture. There are other attitudes and values which act as catalysts to bring land, labor and capital together for the purpose of productivity, but enough has been said for the moment to establish the relevancy of such matters to the economic conditions of Honduras.

Hispanic culture has traditionally emphasized the value of ostentatious leisure (travel, patronage of the arts, ceremonialism in personal relations, oratory, conspicuous consumption). If leisure ennobles, work degrades, and there is generalized contempt for the kind of labor described in such terms as "manual, productive labor," "menial labor," "physical labor," "labor with the hands," "mechanical labor," and "vile employment." Thus, the highest status in society is likely to be accorded those who live in ostentation without labor of any kind. Historically, the attitude or value that leisure ennobles, work degrades, finds its origin in the nature of Iberian society and in the fact that in the colonial period the menial work was performed by the lower-class colored peoples—sometimes slaves. In addition, however, many Latin Americans reasoned that technology, the industrial revolution, and modern-day mechanistic society tended to depersonalize and hence to dehumanize the individual.

The *pensadores* (high level novelists, poets, essayists, intellectuals) attacked utilitarianism and materialism as inimical to the traditional values of Hispanic culture. The great literature of Latin America does not argue that mechanization and technology are values which Latins should seek and adopt. The institutions of higher learning reflect the prevailing feeling. Although education is greatly venerated, it is sought more for prestige than for its values in utility and training. The most popular curriculae are those producing lawyers, medical men, writers, poets, politicians and others who demonstrate by their titles ("Dr.," "Ingr.," "Lic.," "Arq.") that they have nothing to do with the inferior, producing classes.

AN EXCRUCIATING DILEMMA

The *pensadores* and the political leaders of the upper-middle classes cannot ignore the problem of economic development, however. The masses of people everywhere in Latin America have become convinced that the word "progress" should have some meaning for them. Their demands for material improvements have compelled political leadership to consider reforms. This has produced an excruciating dilemma.

Capitalism with its principles of private ownership of both producers' and consumers' goods, private initiative and enterprise, the price system or market mechanism, free, fair competition and the profit incentive is without doubt the most productive economic system the world has ever known. Even in recent decades countries such as West Germany and Japan, which have "turned the clock back" to principles of economic liberalism, have achieved far higher rates of economic growth than countries like India or East Germany which have adopted state interventionism, planning, and socialism. However, the values of capitalism have not been self-evident to élite groups in Latin America. Indeed, there is a vast literature which attacks capitalism. The criticism ranges all the way from extreme assertions that capitalism produces exploitation, parasitism, moral perversion and poverty to more commonly-expressed views that it is inefficient and too individualistic to make possible the human solidarity that people in Hispanic culture seek.

The antagonism of Latin American thinkers for capitalism can perhaps be explained in part by the tradition of mercantilism in Hispanic culture. Mercantilism was an economic theory which was designed to enhance the power of the state. Thus, Latin Americans have been accustomed for centuries to the idea that the state should guide and direct various economic activities and promote and protect public and private monopolistic enterprises. Whereas capitalism is unpopular, various theoretical approaches to state interventionism and collectivism have proved attractive to the intellectuals in the modern period.

KEY ROLE OF PUBLIC SECTOR

Lord Keynes' famous treatise, *The General Theory of Employment, Interest and Money,* was published in 1936 and became known and widely quoted in Latin America almost immediately as a source for ideas on how to achieve rapid economic change. What the great majority of Latin Americans found in Keynes was the following: the reason for inadequate production is inadequate consumption. As private enterprise does not supply enough goods and services at low enough prices to raise the material standards of living of the masses rapidly, it becomes the duty of the state to correct this failure. This the state can do easily and quickly by increasing the purchasing power of the people through state spending. The state should spend on public works and also on the creation of new enterprises. When the state spends, employment for a number of people immediately results. The newly-employed workers have purchasing power they did not have before which they spend, and the recipients spend, and these recipients spend, and so on, multiplying the original "good" at stages along the way. If the state does not have the money to spend, it is then the duty of the state to embark on deficit financing. The state should borrow wherever possible, and if this fails, print paper money.

This may be an inaccurate, even distorted, interpretation of what Lord Keynes was trying to say, but many Latin Americans have believed it. Some have, of course, dealt in a more sophisticated way with the "multiplier" (the idea that investment outlay increases spending power beyond the original amount) and the "accelerator" (the contention that a rise in con-

sumption expenditure induces fresh investment) and the relations between the two.
Political leadership in Latin America has often
acted on Keynesian panaceas to cure economic
ills. Borrowing, deficit financing, public spending and inflation are common almost everywhere in Latin America.

The theory of economic development which
is most popular ,in Honduras at the present
time is that high public investment and rapid
economic growth go hand in hand. By emphasizing only one factor in the productive
process—capital investment—political leaders
free themselves from the unpleasant task of
examining their attitude or value pattern to
determine whether it facilitates or hinders the
union of land, labor and capital required to
produce goods and services.

INCREASED CENTRALIZATION

The new Constitution of 1957 provided for
increased governmental centralization, regulation of the economy, and welfare benefits for
the masses. President José Ramón Villeda
Morales and the Liberal party have attempted
to achieve development by government planning, heavy public expenditures, and deficit
financing. These policies have so far produced,
among other things, a flight of local capital,
unemployment, and rising prices. The new
labor code and social security law (effective
after August 31, 1959) provided for increases
in welfare benefits, such as full pay during illness up to eight months, severance pay on
similar terms, ten weeks at full pay for pregnant women workers, employer-supported nur-
series. The government's policy was to raise
the material standards of living of the masses
by increasing their purchasing power and by
providing them with welfare programs.

However, one cannot buy what is not produced nor enjoy welfare which does not exist.
The present policies of the Honduran government discourage foreign and internal investment and result in decreased production. By
producing less, one does not gain more, regardless of minimum wage laws or social security
benefits. Other Latin American countries have
put into effect similar theories of economic
growth. All have had the same consequences,
and some countries, like Argentina and Chile,
have been brought to the edge of financial
ruin. The "Revolución Nacional" of Bolivia

(1952 to present) has nationalized more than
70 percent of the means of production and
increased the amount of .money in circulation
90 times, but the state has not been able to
operate the public enterprises efficiently or
profitably. Inflation has ruined thousands of
people. Individuals with capital have tried to
save it by removing it from the country. The
United States has been asked to provide the
country with food and large quantities of foreign aid.

As Honduras is an agricultural country,
everything possible should be done to increase
productivity in this field. When the farms can
produce sufficient food for the nation, satisfy
export demands, and provide the towns and
cities with men and women to produce other
goods and services, the country will be on the
way to achieving real development.

LIBERAL LAND REFORM

Although it is not widely known, Honduras
has long enjoyed some of the most liberal and
progressive agrarian laws to be found anywhere. The first land law after independence
was promulgated on March 19, 1829. It provided for the sale of former royal lands. Article
2 of this law limited land sales to 20 units per
purchaser. Although on April 26, 1834, each
buyer was permitted 100 units, the principle of
prohibiting land grabs by a few individuals
was maintained. After 1837, individuals could
accept public land in payment for loans to the
government and public officials could take all
or part of their salaries in land. In 1846, the
government offered to trace ownership and
supply titles to people for a very low fee.

In 1835, a land law expressed concern for
the first time for the very poor who might not
be able to acquire land, even at the low prices
the Government asked. This was followed in
1836 with a law making it even easier for
individuals and societies to buy land. If this
proved impossible then the government would
give land free to communities in the form of
ejidos [coöperative farms]. The right of prescription was recognized in 1872. Anyone who
went into unoccupied national territory and
worked farms there for three years became an
owner and was entitled to a legal title from the
treasury department.

The first comprehensive land law of the
modern period was passed in 1888. Rural com-

munities were granted lands if they needed them at a cost only of the sealed paper and the small fee for surveying. State land could be purchased at low cost, and the law provided for a fair, equitable, and inexpensive system of surveying and granting titles. The law of 1888 was restated, modified and improved in 1898. In 1902, further liberal changes were made. The government embarked on a program of surveying lands, so that individuals could know in advance exactly how much they were going to receive.

The 1924 agrarian law was actually made part of the constitution. The law recognized all the earlier methods of acquiring national lands, and in addition it provided for the donation of land in family lots of 50 acres each free of charge and exempt from municipal taxes. In 1928, the 1924 agrarian law was amended so as to exempt from compulsory military service and fiscal taxes all those who were renting, purchasing or in any other way receiving national land. Such individuals were also allowed to import duty-free machines and tools for agriculture and cattle raising, gas and crude oil, dynamite, construction materials, blooded animals, seeds, insecticides, and medicines.

In 1935 President Tiburcio Carías Andino signed an executive decree establishing a rural colonization plan. Immigrants were invited to come to Honduras to make their homes. The government offered 50-acre plots free of charge, and in addition agreed to supply tools, animals, seeds and other equipment to get started without cost to the individual. The 1936 law was mainly a copy of the statute of 1924 with improvements in wording and administration. The sale of national lands was greatly liberalized, however. In addition, the individual could rent national land for from 5 to 20 cents per acre per year. The principle of limitation of size of landholdings remained. Each individual could only rent 250 acres for agriculture and 1,000 acres for cattle raising. Exception was made if the individual or company could prove that he had the capital and know-how to use larger acreage; if so, in theory he might even receive up to 2,500 acres.

AGRICULTURAL CENTRALIZATION?

Under these and other laws practically all Hondurans—no matter how poor—have been able to own land. With some few exceptions, they have not become wealthy, but the system of family farms has surely tended to modify the authoritarian values of Hispanic culture. Equality, tolerance for the rights of others, and most important of all, a feeling of individual dignity and independence are entrenched in Honduras. In 1961, the *Instituto Nacional Agrario* was empowered to centralize agrarian studies and prepare a reform bill. Will the planners build on the liberal land laws of the past and preserve the family farm or will they move more in the direction of the collective or state farm? Relatively simple technological changes could increase agricultural productivity rapidly in Honduras. The widespread introduction of the iron or steel plow, the horse collar, and the four-wheeled cart would result instantly in dramatic increases in the production of food and fiber. Many people probably would like to impose such changes through centralized governmental authority. However, such changes can also be produced by voluntary means. Almost without doubt the most important contribution any government could make to agriculture in Honduras would be to build roads so that farmers can see the value of producing not only for subsistence but for money in markets within reach.

In a broader sense, Honduras must decide whether to build interventionist and collectivistic policies on the vestiges of the mercantilism of the past or remove many governmental restrictions, restraints, and controls and depend on a free economy. Although Honduras must assume responsibility for its decisions, it is inevitable that a vast spending program such as the *Alianza para Progreso* will bring with it a deep and pervading influence from the United States. In an indirect way, therefore, the United States must bear some of the responsibility for what is to happen in Honduras.

QUESTIONS AND STUDY SUGGESTIONS

1. Briefly describe the current state of economic backwardness in Honduras, noting any considerations which bespeak of future development.

Would it be accurate to say that the single major obstacle to Honduras's development is the absence of "the will to develop"? Explain.

2. Describe the policies adopted by the Honduran government in an effort to achieve economic growth. Do these policies accurately reflect "Keynesian thinking"?

3. Explain and evaluate Professor Stokes's contention that Honduras's emphasis upon the notion that "high public investment and rapid economic growth go hand in hand" is an overly narrow conception of the requisites for economic development. Describe Honduras's land laws and policies. Assess their implications for future economic development.

Reading 77

Economic Development through Birth Control

Stephen Enke, Professor of Economics, Duke University

This reading dispassionately examines the population dilemma faced by most of the world's underdeveloped countries. Increases in their national outputs have been largely offset by population growth, with the result that living standards have remained substantially unimproved. The author applies cost-benefit analysis to birth control and concludes that a dollar used to slow population growth can be one hundred times more effective in raising per capita income than a dollar spent to expand the national output. He concludes that an effective program of birth control is an essential supplement to the developmental programs of the poor nations.

Demographers have been warning governments of the population explosion for almost a decade —with little result. Perhaps the coming famine in India may finally persuade the governments of poor countries to adopt vigorous measures— including the payment of bonuses—to induce couples to have fewer children. In that event, a possible million deaths in the 1960s from malnutrition will not have been in vain.

The past decade of planned economic development in Asia, Africa and Latin America has been a disappointing failure. Domestic production has typically increased three to five per cent in real terms while population has increased two to three percent each year. The small one to two percent increase in income per capita that remains is usually industrial output. Agriculture has been neglected in many development plans, with the result that food production in some countries is actually less

From Stephen Enke, "The Economic Case for Birth Control," **Challenge**, May–June, 1967, pp. 30–31, 41–43. Reprinted by permission.

today than it was five years ago. But there are more mouths to feed.

ARITHMETIC OF POPULATION GROWTH

Too many governments have been reducing the death rate through desirable public health measures while ignoring continuing high birth rates. Today, births continue at an annual rate of from four to four and a half percent of population, while death rates are as low as two percent a year. This leaves a natural increase of two to two and a half percent annually. The result is that the population doubles every 30 to 35 years.

The developed nations of North America and Western Europe began their rapid technological advance 150 years ago, when death rates were not much below the natural birth rate. It is the misfortune of the less developed countries of today that control of epidemics and improvements in sanitation have reduced death rates before true economic development has taken hold. For many countries the only remaining hope is that their families will voluntarily use available contraceptive techniques to reduce births by one-third or more within 10 years or less.

Briefly, if governments wish to raise per capita incomes significantly, they must induce birth reductions within a decade comparable to those that occurred in developed nations during a century. Fortunately, techniques such as the intrauterine coil and the contraceptive pill are now available and are far more effective than anything available to our grandparents. Moreover, whereas sales of birth control devices were once almost universally banned, planned parenthood is now subsidized by the governments of India, Pakistan, Korea, Taiwan and Tunis.

The evils of high birth rates in countries that are *already* overpopulated are obvious enough. Countries such as Egypt do not have enough exports to trade for food imports, and they lack the land and water to feed themselves. A doubling of population can only bring catastrophe. But even "empty" countries with expanses of almost unpopulated forest, such as Brazil and Thailand, cannot afford to increase their populations too rapidly.

Every government aspires to a per capita increase in population of at least two and a half percent a year. But if population keeps increasing at this pace every year, this calls for a quadrupling of gross national product in 30 years. From where can this quadrupled output come?

INPUTS AND GNP

A country's output (GNP) comes from inputs of labor, capital (structures and equipment) and land (natural resources, generally). Other things being equal, a doubling of labor, capital and land would only double national output. Unfortunately, these inputs cannot all double simultaneously. Thus natural resources (land) do not increase at all except insofar as investments in exploration and in technological improvements effectively increase them. A doubling of population will admittedly double the labor force, but this is not enough to double output if capital and land do not double also.

The only hope for an increase in output per head is that new investment and improved technology will prove more than enough to overcome diminishing returns to labor inputs.

Economists have calculated that a doubling of the labor force and a quadrupling of national capital stock (which is difficult to attain in underdeveloped countries where private and public savings range between 5 and 10 percent of GNP) will do little more than double aggregate output over a period of 30 years. "Modernization"—that is, technological advances that increase output per unit of labor or capital input—is essential if families are generally to be better off.

These considerations explain why the *rate* of population increase must be slowed. It takes time to accumulate investments from domestic savings. And it takes time to innovate better methods, equipment and technology. Every country can have larger populations with higher individual incomes—eventually. But meanwhile, the *timing* of changes in labor, capital and innovations is everything.

THE DEPENDENCY BURDEN

High birth rates impose an economic burden in still another way. The percentage of children in a country depends upon the birth rate. Thus a nation whose annual number of births equals or exceeds four percent of its population will typically have 40 percent or so of its inhabitants under 15 years of age and, therefore, unproductive. A halving of the birth rate over several decades could reduce this ratio to roughly 20 percent. With half as many children to support, families can save and invest more; increased output of goods and services will result. It is ironic that the poorest countries, which have the highest birth rates, should carry the highest dependency burden.

INVESTING IN BIRTH CONTROL

In 1965 President Johnson asserted before the U.N. General Assembly that "less than $5 invested in birth control is worth $100 invested in economic development." Since then many persons have wondered what calculations lay behind this estimate. The explanation provides a nice exercise in applied economics.

A common objective of planned economic development is to increase the *ratio* of national output to national population. To accomplish this, the government can spend funds and use resources either to accelerate growth in output or to slow growth in population. Which alternative will raise income per head most? Clearly, this will depend upon whether output or population will respond more in percentage terms to expenditures designed to alter them.

Consider an undeveloped country that has a per capita income of $100 a year, a population of 10 million and a GNP of $1 billion.

Suppose its government invests $1 million each year for 10 years in development projects, which increase output 15 percent a year on an average. At the end of 10 years, the increase in output attributable to the total investment of $10 million will be $1.5 million, or an increase in GNP of .15 percent.

Now suppose this $1 million worth of resources is invested each year in a birth-reduction program. The cost per participant each year will be about $1 if the program stressed inexpensive methods such as the coil and the pill. There will then be a million participants during each year. After 10 years there will have been about 1.5 million fewer births than would have otherwise occurred. This is a reduction, relative to population, of 15 percent.

There can be no question which is the more effective use of the $10 million—a 15 percent reduction in births is 100 times greater change than a .15 percent increase in output. The moral is clear: if the objective is higher income per head, money spent to reduce births will be as much as 100 times more effective

than money invested to raise output. Such an enormous ratio of superiority is seldom encountered when comparing economic policies.

The common sense of all these calculations is simple enough. With modern techniques it costs very little to prevent a birth. A coil costs a penny to make and can be inserted for a dollar. Male sterilization may cost $5 to perform as part of an organized program. The rhythm method, although less safe in practice, costs little by way of instruction. (Although very effective, the pill's cost—over $15 a year—makes it relatively expensive and, therefore, less desirable for programs in really poor countries.)

The alternative to preventing a birth is to support the child thus born. Few children under 15 years of age can earn their keep, even in undeveloped countries. In later life, especially if there are already too many people relative to available capital and land, they will not produce enough to prevent their being a net burden on the economy.

NEGATIVE VALUE OF CHILDREN

Economics may sometimes seem an inhuman as well as a dismal science. Nevertheless, from the viewpoint of the national economy at large, additional children do have a plus or minus monetary value. In point of fact, in almost all poor and backward countries their discounted "worth" is today *negative*.

Consider a thousand possible infants (of randomly selected parents) who would be born this year in some undeveloped country were it *not* for birth control. During their lives, these children would subtract goods and services as consumers and add goods and services as producers. Unfortunately, the present discounted value of these subtractions exceeds the value of these additions.

There are three reasons why such infants have a negative discounted value at time of birth. First, many never survive to a productive age, and hence are never anything but subtracting consumers. Second, because of diminishing returns to labor, the output attributable to the labor of this extra population is less per head than the average output of all labor. Third, additions from production are long postponed, whereas subtractions through consumption start almost at birth.

Accordingly, a typical infant tends to have a negative present worth. This negative worth is roughly 2.5 times income per head in an un-developed country. Thus the value of *permanently* preventing a birth in a typical Afro-Asian country is around $250.

The value of *postponing* a birth from one year to the next is roughly one-fourth that of permanently preventing a birth that otherwise would occur this year. This value of postponing is thus approximately $60 a year, or $5 a month, in a really poor country. It would tend to be proportionately greater in a typical Latin American country where income per head tends to average considerably above $100 a year.

The practical value of calculating these "worths" of prevented and postponed births is that they set a limit on what a government can rationally spend to avoid pregnancies. If 60 percent of all pregnancies result in births—the other 40 percent being "wastage" from miscarriages, abortions, etc.—the worth to government of preventing a pregnancy is about 1.5 times the annual per capita income, while the worth of postponing a birth is about .35 times this income per head.

BIRTH CONTROL PROGRAMS

There is no question that these worths are many times greater than the costs of birth control. Consider the three principal ways in which a government can expend funds to reduce births. First, it can subsidize family clinics, operated primarily to promote the health of mothers and desired children, but at which birth control assistance is also available. Mothers who already have several children are usually most interested in obtaining such help. Such clinics serve not only to prevent unwanted births, but also to strengthen those children already born.

Second, a government can use funds and resources to educate couples on ways to prevent unwanted children. Surveys indicate that a majority of rural parents have little idea of any, save the most primitive, methods of avoiding pregnancies. Even if they have heard of the coil or the pill, they usually have no idea where they can be obtained at low cost or *gratis.*

Third, governments can offer rewards to fertile couples for not having children. Thus some Indian states, such as Madras, have given what is, in effect, a quite inadequate bonus to both the fathers who undergo sterilization and to the "finders" who introduce these volunteers to clinics. Various studies have also shown that it would be economical to pay about $10 three times a year to "exposed" mothers who do not become pregnant over a period of years, as revealed by a simple examination every four months.

Rewards programs are particularly economical because they involve transfer payments of money from taxpayers to participants and thus divert a minimum of resources from production. Moreover, the philosophy of rewards is truly libertarian. Parents who voluntarily limit their families are compensated for the psychic enjoyment they may consequently lose. The general community is saved the adverse incidence of a burdensome increment of population.

The most economical methods of birth control are those that are cheap and effective. At present, the intrauterine coil is the best method for those mothers who can retain it, although sterilization of the male is economically almost as efficient. However, many couples prefer that the woman should be the participant rather than the man, and many women prefer the pill to the coil even though it may be less economic in cost-benefit terms. Others prefer, for reasons of conscience, to practice the rhythm method of contraception. Any government that subsidizes family clinics must, for political reasons, ordinarily offer a wide variety of contraceptive methods.

In most undeveloped countries it is possible to mount a five-year birth control program that will cost about $1 a year per participant if about half of them use the coil, about a fifth elect male sterilization and the balance use condoms or spermicides. A million dollars a year will then finance participation by a million adults a year. And over a five-year period, the $5 million thus spent will have prevented over 1.5 million pregnancies—or over a million births.

Thus the cost of avoiding a birth under such a program comes to about $5. This must be compared with the "worth" of preventing or postponing a birth given above. The ratio of advantage to cost is obvious and certainly considerable.

Of course, the magnitude and cost of any particular birth-reduction program will depend on the goals established by government. Through widespread abortion, Japan succeeded in halving its annual birth rate from 34 to 17 per thousand of population during a single decade following World War II. More humane methods are feasible and preferable, however.

A one-third reduction in birth rates might require that half of all fertile couples practice birth control at any one time. This participating half would probably include a disproportionate number of couples over 25 years of age. Attainment of the one-third reduction goal would require majority use of effective birth control methods.

Approximately 10 percent of the population must be participants in any program designed to cut birth rates by one-third. In a typical undeveloped country, about 16 men and 16 women per 100 of population are fecund and exposed. Some of these 16 women will not be pregnable in any month. Others will be seeking pregnancy. If those fertile women who *cannot* conceive or *want* to conceive are excluded, about eight women (or their partners) per 100 of population remain to practice birth control.

COST OF BIRTH CONTROL

It follows arithmetically that if 10 percent of total population joins in the program at a cost of $1 each per year, the total annual cost of a major birth-reduction program would be about 10 cents per head.

Such amounts are insignificant in terms of many nations' expenditures on economic development. Thus India, with a population approaching 500 million, would have to spend $50 million a year. This is a little over one percent of what is annually spent in and for India to increase production! A survey of a dozen other undeveloped countries indicates that an effective birth control program would require direct expenditures slightly under one percent of planned development expenditures.

This one percent cost needs to be set against the estimate that money used to slow population growth is 100 times as effective in raising income per head as money used to expand output. Thus it appears that most undeveloped countries could obtain as much increase in income per head by diverting $1 out of every $100 used for development as they receive from the other $99 altogether. This amazing superiority demands the attention of policy makers.

Any economist-demographer will recognize that such estimates have a considerable margin of error. They depend upon assumptions about fertility by age, costs of methods, acceptable method mixes and many other uncertain variables. Nevertheless, when dealing with superiorities of 100 to 1, it is most improbable that all the errors will so combine to eliminate the enormous apparent benefits of such national birth control programs.

It is not as though these programs would be substitutes for conventional development investments in transport, irrigation, industry, etc. Indeed, it would be impossible to spend on birth-reduction programs all the funds now invested to expand output in most undeveloped countries. It is simply that of these two *supplementary* approaches, a greater increase in output per head will result from resources used to slow population growth rather than to accelerate production.

Historians of this period may well be critical of those who govern our affairs. With notable exceptions, the government leaders of most underdeveloped countries refuse to act on the obvious facts, whether from fear of vociferous and hostile minorities or from knowledge that benefits from birth reductions will not accrue while they are still in office. The advanced nations, afraid of disturbing known sensitivities, have preferred to make grants and loans for almost any other development purpose so long as it will briefly postpone the coming day of reckoning.

QUESTIONS AND STUDY SUGGESTIONS

1. Why doesn't total output increase proportionately with population growth?
2. What is the "dependency burden"? Why is it important for economic development? Why do children in underdeveloped countries have a "negative present value"?
3. Explain the author's basic conclusion that "money used to slow population growth is 100 times as effective in raising income per head as money used to expand output."

Reading 78

How Much Aid for the Have-not Nations?

John A. Pincus, The RAND Corporation

Reading 78 is a realistic appraisal of the immensity of the problem of aiding the less developed countries. The author flatly concludes that "there isn't enough money to fill the economic gap in any reasonable time period. Even to fill it halfway within a generation is impossible in practice." But there are other gaps—social, political, psychological, and cultural—between the have and the have-not nations. Will a narrowing of the economic gap tend to close the noneconomic gaps? Or must the noneconomic gaps be reduced before development can occur? It is contended, however, that the ultimate gap resides in the perceptions of the issues by rich and poor countries: "The rich [are] too stingy and too free with avuncular ideology, the poor [are] reluctant to abandon their own cherished stereotypes for a harsher reality."

How much, indeed? There have been a number of estimates of the savings gap–the difference between investment levels needed to sustain a specified rate of economic growth and the estimated funds available from a combination of domestic saving and probable capital inflows from abroad. There have also been estimates of the trade gap–the difference between estimated import levels required to maintain the specified growth rate and probable foreign exchange revenues available from a combination of exports and capital inflows.

More recent analysis is based on a so-called two gap approach–in which the larger of the two gaps is applied on a country-by-country basis to emerge with a combined world total. Those estimates that are roughly comparable emerge with a total requirement for anywhere from $10 billion to $20 billion annually by 1970 and $16 billion to $34 billion by 1975. The variation is accounted for by differences in target growth rates in the world economy (ranging in the estimates from 4.1 to 5.5 per-

cent per year for less developed countries), in the behavior of exports and imports, and in assumptions about savings propensities in developing countries and about the relation between investment and changes in output.

A good deal of effort and analytical refinement have been injected into the analysis of less developed country (LDC) requirements for foreign capital, and in the process economists have been able to apply an increasingly sophisticated technique to measurement of the gap. I suggest, however, that further refinements of the aggregate gap analysis are virtually valueless as guides to policy, although they may be of considerable professional interest. Nor are the existing estimates, despite the great differences among them in input of effort and intellectual novelty, of much more value than the casual observation by George Woods that underdeveloped countries could today effectively use an additional $3 to $4 billion annually of capital from abroad. This is not to suggest that Mr. Woods' estimate should

Reprinted from the September–October, 1967, issue of the **Columbia Journal of World Business**. Copyright © 1968 by the Trustees of Columbia University.

be taken any more seriously as a guide to the size of the gap than any of the econometric guesses cited above.

GAPSMANSHIP IN PERSPECTIVE

Gap-estimation exercises are essentially a political arithmetic, a technique for quantifying discontent. They put the seal of rationality on donors' charitable inclinations, or on the aspirations of nations that receive aid. A nation with an average annual income of $150 per head has an economic plan aimed at raising real income by say 3 percent per head per year —a goal that, according to the planners, requires $50 million annually in gap-filling aid. Is there anyone so naive as to imagine that the contentment of one's people or the stability of one's government or social system will be assured by the gap-filling aid endowment?

In the brief silence that follows, let me point out the obvious: the pause ensues because the gap we are dealing with is the one that separates the aspirations of governments and people in underdeveloped countries from their present realities. This gap is not only vast, but multidimensional. It cannot be encompassed by any computations of the margin that separates savings from investment targets or exports from import requirements. This is not to say that it lacks any measurable dimensions; as we shall see, there are some. But first, let me enumerate the components, all of them too obviously interrelated.

The aid requirement is usually discussed in terms of an economic gap. The size of this gap can roughly be measured by the difference between average income in developing countries and that in industrial nations. The economic gap also includes an element of domestic income distribution. Oil-rich countries for example have high per-capita incomes, but very unequal distribution, and an aspect of the economic gap thereby remains unfilled.

Another gap is social. The developing countries aspire to build modern urbanized societies, moving, in the well-worn phrase, from status to contract in social relations.

A third gap is political, reflecting a desire for mass participation in a stable political system, either in the form of parliamentary democracy, or of various forms of state socialism.

A fourth gap is psychological, proceeding from a consciousness of living in nations that are not "modern," where people are less able to utilize the mixed blessings of contemporary technology; of belonging to colonial societies with their heritage of inferior status, often with overtones of racial inferiority; of belonging to social groups that maintain, despite themselves, feelings of inferiority born from the awareness of educational and cultural deprivation.

ULTIMATE HIATUS

Each of these four elements combines to create a situation that might be called a gap in the quality of life. In industrial countries, life is usually long and reasonably healthy; people spend from ten to twenty years as students, developing their intellectual and technical skills. The majority of them are relatively insulated from real poverty. Leisure time and the means to enjoy it are normal constituents of life. Most people, whatever their doubts and insecurities, do not feel that other contemporary societies are clearly superior to modern industrial ones. And finally, with obvious serious exceptions, most people feel that they are able, at least in some degree, to determine their material destiny. By and large, only a tiny fraction of people in poor countries can boast these advantages; and that minority serves to make its countrymen more aware of the gap in the quality of their own lives.

The first five gaps are overlapping differences that many people in poor countries are either directly aware of, or in the case of certain social or psychological elements, express through hostility to the policies of rich nations. The sixth gap, if we can call it one, is often not something that people in poor countries seek to close, despite its adverse effects on the quality of life and on economic standards. This is the gap in population rates. Governments of developing countries would generally prefer to bring population growth down to the levels prevailing in industrial countries, but individuals do not necessarily share this opinion. In many countries, family limitation is far from a universal quest and it would require an obsessive attachment to social goals for people to wish to shorten their own life expectancies as a substitute for family planning.

WHERE DO YOU START?

Now that we know that *multiple gaposis* is a condition of the world community, what does it have to do with how much aid developing countries need? The answer is that it depends on what gaps you want to fill. In terms of costs, the cheapest to fill is probably the population gap. It has been estimated that investments in birth control in India are of the order of one hundred times as profitable as investments in production. But this gap may be hardest of all to fill presently, in view of the existence of the first four gaps. The economic gap means that large families offer a form of social security, while the social gap implies differences in value systems and attitudes vast enough to be incompatible with acceptance of family planning. The political gap includes a frequent reluctance by political leaders to offend long-standing traditions affecting procreation. We should remember that birth control was a political tabu in the United States until very recently. Finally, the psychological gap may often carry with it the feeling that rich countries' proposals for population control reflect a lack of confidence in the poor countries' ability to achieve stable and prosperous societies; therefore, to the underdeveloped countries, foreign subsidy of birth-control efforts may simply be the rich countries' way of announcing that the basic problems are insoluble.

How much would it cost to fill the economic gap? It depends on the time horizon. Filling it halfway at once by raising per-capita incomes to say $1,000 a year, the bill would come to about $1.4 thousand billion, a sum roughly equal to the combined annual gross national product of the industrial countries, and more than two hundred times as much as the current aid flow.

If we rule out levels of philanthropy that reduce donors' incomes to zero, we could work out some equal average level of world income at about $630 per capita (1963), if the rich countries initially transferred about $600 billion annually to poor countries. These sums could naturally be reduced if the returns to investment in developing countries surpassed those in industrial countries. Then according to the implicit view expressed here, aid would flow back toward the original donors.

Neither of these alternatives is likely to win unanimous approval as a method of filling the economic gap. If adopted, they would do little to reduce most of the other gaps. For example, once government-to-government aid, somehow magically extracted from a willing public, starts hitting hundreds of billions a year, the

political rewards that accrue to the dispensers of aid in the recipient countries would become substantial and the prospects for perpetual coups d'état would be enhanced. Nor would there be much systematic incentive to reduce other gaps in an atmosphere of megalargesse.

The reason for introducing these fantasies into the discussion is simply to demonstrate that if the goal is approximate equality of income, sights must be set very high indeed. Even if we forego the vision of instant equality, and aim only at equality with today's levels of income in rich countries after a generation, it means that on the average, per-capita income would have to increase at the rate of 11.5 percent annually over a 20-year period, nine times faster than the current rate. Even to reach current per-capita levels of the rich nations within 50 years, by the year 2017, per-capita GNP in the poor countries would have to increase by 4.2 percent annually, three times as fast as it is now on the average.

$550 BILLION PER ANNUM

How much foreign capital would it take to hit the 20-year target? Initially, we are talking about a $70 billion annual increase in LDC income, compared to a current annual increase of perhaps $8 billion in purchasing-power equivalent. For the 50-year target, the annual GNP increase required would initially be of the order of $25 billion. We can compute the subsequent aid requirement on the following assumptions: (1) foreign capital initially finances all of the increase in growth and is replaced progressively by increased domestic savings; (2) the capital inflows allow LDC economies to build a sufficiently flexible structure to avoid growth restriction stemming from foreign exchange shortages; (3) each dollar invested raises the value of total output by $33\frac{1}{3}$ cents in perpetuity, (4) rates of population growth decline by one-fourth during the period.

All of these assumptions are probably invalid to some degree, but we will simply take the implicit fraud for granted. In the first year of a 20-year program, the LDCs would be saving at their current rate of about $24 billion and rich countries would contribute $215 billion in grants. With marginal savings rates of 20 percent, LDCs would save $41 billion in the second year, rich countries would contribute $240 billion and so on. The 20-year program aimed at bringing LDC incomes to 1965 levels in industrial countries would require an additional capital inflow of $11 thousand billion over the period, or an average of $550 billion per year. One dismaying feature of the 20-year program is that under our assumptions, the 11.5 percent per-capita growth rate requires steady increases in foreign aid, although by 1985, domestic savings in LDCs would be more than one-sixth of GNP, and could thereby sustain a 6 percent rate of growth, unsupported by capital inflows.

In the slightly less fantastic 50-year program, foreign capital requirements would total $2.1 thousand billion, starting at the rate of $93 billion in the first year, and declining to zero after 32 years, averaging $65 billion annually over the period, about seven times the current level of capital flows. If we allow population growth rates to decline by 50 percent instead of by one-fourth, then the required capital inflow is a mere $1.7 thousand billion, averaging $64 billion annually over a 27-year period.

In other words, there isn't enough money to fill the economic gap in any reasonable time period. Even to fill it halfway within a generation is impossible in practice.

For those who remain unconvinced, let's take a look at the success stories of economic development. Economic growth in the past 15 years has been most rapid in a number of Communist countries, plus Japan, Germany, Spain, Greece, Israel, Jordan, Iraq, El Salvador, Nicaragua, Trinidad, Jamaica, Venezuela, Mexico, Thailand, South Korea, and Taiwan. The Communist countries did the job by enforcing a tight squeeze on current consumption, and channeling the savings into investments for capital plant and education. Japan and Germany had the basic skills, and the additional advantages of massive postwar aid, with further stimulus in Japan's case from the Korean war and in Germany's from cost advantages stemming from a large initial labor supply and the growth of the European market.

SMALL IS BEST

When we turn to success stories in developing countries, several points are clear. Table 78–1 lists growth rates, population, per-capita aid, and export growth for the fast-growing countries (6 percent or more annual increase in gross domestic product). First, most of the fast-growing countries are small. Ten of the 13 countries have less than 20 million people. Second, most of them have either received massive U.S. aid, four to fifteen times the worldwide average per capita, or else struck it rich through minerals, tourism, or staple exports. Third, they have been much more competitive in world markets than the LDCs as a whole, as measured by comparative export growth rates. The only sizable countries that have grown rapidly over the 15-year period without much aid are Mexico and Thailand. Mexico benefited substantially from the U.S. market for goods and tourism, and from access to international capital markets to help finance industry; Thailand from rice, tin and a fairly steady growth of all domestic economic sectors.

These "success" stories (with all the problems they still face barely hidden behind the facade of aggregate growth rates) account for only about 6 percent of the people who live in developing countries, and have often been associated with massive aid transfers. If the remaining 94 percent were to receive the same amounts per capita, U.S. aid appropriations would have had to reach $130 billion over the past 16 years, about three and one-half times the actual level of aid. Other donors' contributions (currently accounting for two-fifths of the aid flow) would have had to increase by the same proportions.

This gives us some indications of how much aid the developing countries need. More, much more, if they are to bring their income levels even within hailing distance of current northern levels by the end of this century. On the other hand, from the viewpoint of the industrial countries, the present level of aid seems to be about the right price for the diverse collection of diplomatic, military, economic, and philanthropic benefits they receive in exchange for their outlays. Aid outlays, after rising sharply from the early Fifties through the early Sixties, have stabilized over the past four or five years. The inference is that in view of other claims on rich nations' resources, present aid levels reflect *social opportunity costs* as perceived by donors.

Therefore, as might be expected, donors' and recipients' views diverge. Donors apparently are much less concerned in practice than in theory about the possible dangers stemming from a world permanently divided into rich and poor nations. Recipients, on the other

Table 78–1. **GROWTH OF DOMESTIC PRODUCT, UNDERDEVELOPED COUNTRIES, 1950/1952–1962/64**

Country	Percent GDP growth rate, 1950/52—1962/64	Per-capita U.S. aid, 1949–1965 ($)	Population, 1965 (million)	Trade growth, 1950/52 to 1962/64[2] (percent)
Greece	6.4	207	8.5	3.5
Yugoslavia	7.7	106	19.3	N.A.
El Salvador	6.8	24 (cotton, industry, CACM)	2.8	4.2
Jamaica	7.3	11 (bauxite, tourists)	1.7	12.3
Mexico	5.9	12 (tourists, industry)	39.6	3.7
Nicaragua	6.4	52 (cotton, CACM)	1.6	7.2
Trinidad	8.5	44 (oil, tourists)	1.0	9.6
Iraq	9.4	7 (oil)	7.0	11.7
Israel	10.2	430	2.5	17.0
Jordan	8.2	241	1.9	13.1
Taiwan	7.4	212	12.1	8.8
South Korea	6.1	166	27.6	14.6[a]
Thailand	6.3	15 (rice, tin, maize)	29.7	4.9
All LDCs[1]	4.8	27	1,422.1	3.0[b]

[1] The population totals include only countries receiving U.S. aid. If all LDCs were included the population total would be 2.3 billion; and aid over the 16-year period, on the basis of mid-period population, would total $18 per capita.
[2] Corrected for terms of trade changes (1962 = 100). [a] 1955–1964. [b] 1950–1962.

hand, are much less worried in practice than in theory about the possible harmful social and political effects of excessive dependence on aid from imperialist countries. In fact, they are currently bargaining for preferential trade access to the markets of industrial countries, and higher prices for commodities through international agreements. Both of these, if achieved, are virtually guaranteed to cement their economic and political dependence even more closely than aid, despite the apparently automatic and market-determined nature of the transfers.

Nor have the LDCs invariably demonstrated as much zeal in pursuit of domestic reforms as they have toward revisions in rich countries' aid and trade policies. In his recent study of economic policies toward developing countries, Professor Harry Johnson has demonstrated, with balance and clarity, how the present barriers to LDC growth include not only external constraints (tariff structures that discriminate

against LDCs, immigration controls, restrictions on capital movements, high-cost aid tying, etc.), but also domestic ones (excessive protection, overvalued currencies, ideological attachments to government controls that appear excessive in light of limited administrative skills; fondness for investments that are more monumental than productive; a reluctance to accept foreign private investment, domestic price systems that encourage high-cost manufacturing and discourage agricultural development).

There has been a good deal of discussion of the remedies for LDC defections from economic grace. But since no one, despite all too frequent preconceptions to the contrary, knows all the sure formulas for economic development—or at times perhaps, any of them—we don't know whether the remedies are really remedies, necessary for promoting economic development. Overvalued currencies? Look at the ruble—or, some might say, the dollar. Pervasive government controls over the private sector? Japan's development was built on it. Excessive dependence on handouts (in Hans Morgenthau's quaint phrase, "bum and beggar nations")? Taiwan, Israel, Jordan, South Korea, and the other success stories couldn't have gotten anywhere without passing through a "beggar" stage. Doubts about foreign capital? *Mes chers collègues!*

ABSORPTIVE-CAPACITY HUMBUG

This snowballing of alleged prerequisites to development is related to another concept that has contributed to misspecifying the economic gap. The inability of economically backward nations to use massive capital transfers effectively has been defined in the expression "absorptive capacity," and it has been claimed that LDCs are now getting all the aid they can "absorb." This expression involves a good deal of humbug, so let's try to straighten it out. If the purpose is simply to raise living standards, then absorptive capacity is not a significant barrier. The rate at which investment can be increased is likely to be a barrier, but when investment opportunities are limited, aid can switch over to consumption subsidies which have much more elastic limits. Investment in most countries rarely rises at more than 15 percent per year for prolonged periods, but the rich countries have never really brought their resources to bear on the problem of raising LDC living standards. In the few cases cited in our table, where aid was both massive and effectively administered, most people's preconceptions about absorptive capacity for investment had to be jettisoned. And even then, the rich countries did not fully enlist the capacities of their private sectors.

This is a major weakness in the structure of aid to developing countries, because it is clear that if material progress is the aim, the rich countries have no instrument so effective as the modern corporation. Yet ideological hostilities and ignorance on both sides have prevented any significant progress. U.S. annual manufacturing investments in all developing countries combined is less than its annual investment in Canadian manufacturing. Private investors of all OECD countries combined invest directly about $2 billion annually in developing countries, most of it for mineral extraction. Total rich-country private investment in poor countries is somewhat less than the annual domestic private investment of Belgium.

Not only is absorptive capacity reduced by inability to use private industrial initiatives effectively, and by our natural preference to think small when it comes to voting public funds for foreigners, but it is also narrowed by the habit of using the wrong intellectual framework in thinking about the problem. We often hear that aid is used unwisely in underdeveloped countries, so therefore there is something wrong. Of course there is—the countries are underdeveloped. To apply the economic efficiency standards of Western Europe or North America to gauge the investment performance of LDCs is ridiculous. If they could invest capital as effectively, maintain machinery and equipment as well, administer public and private enterprises as smoothly, they would be rich, not poor. Waste and inefficiency should be looked on as normal companions of an accelerated development effort, not to be encouraged or placidly accepted, but as elements that can only be reduced gradually. Once we realize that different standards of performance are necessary for LDCs, then absorptive capacity becomes a flexible concept indeed, even if confined solely to investment and technical assistance.

So far as the economic gap is concerned, then, I have said that there is no practical way to fill it with the amount of aid that the recipients require. From the donors' standpoint there seems to be no strong urge to raise the ante. What does this imply for the question we started out with—how much aid do developing countries need? The answer seems simple. All they can get, except when countries are too underdeveloped to handle large sums in a hurry (many African nations today might serve as cases in point).

AND NOW, THE OTHER LACUNAE

So far, I've talked as if developing countries needed only economic aid to fill in the distance between present reality and some version of that relentless vision of a good society that dogs us all differently. In a way—a backward one—we might say that filling the economic gap takes care of all the others. This is true only in the restricted sense that all the gaps act to some extent as barriers to bridging the others. If one is overcome, there is *prima facie* evidence that the others are relatively small. They interact, and filling any of them has implications for the state of the others.

REACHING THE SOCIAL MATRIX

But can or should rich countries address themselves directly to the social, political, psychological, cultural elements of the gap, rather than indirectly through economic aid? An economist must tread this ground carefully, and I will be brief. A social anthropologist has tried to answer this question, on the basis of the African experience:

There is much to be gained, and many misconceptions can be avoided, if the economic problem of an underdeveloped community is framed, not in terms of the vicious circle of poverty, Malthusian pressure or inadequate capital formation, etc., but in terms of strategic factors of an ultimate character, namely its social and psychological inertia. . . . Economic development of an underdeveloped people by themselves is not compatible with maintenance of their traditional customs and mores . . . What is needed is a revolution in the totality of social, cultural and religious institutions and habits, and thus in their psychological attitudes, their philosophy and way of life. . . .
    If economic progress is deemed desirable and necessary policy is to be formulated to achieve this end, the cart could in a certain sense be put before the horse, in that economic changes can be utilized to generate the social revolution.

The author seems to be saying that economic instruments, if properly used, may catalyze the social changes that lead to a multidimensional development. Yet we often hear that economic instruments cannot work effectively as agents of change, because they would create unacceptable strains in a rather rigid social system. The impediments to economic growth imposed by the caste system in rural India are often cited as a case in point.

Perhaps the basic point is that students of sociology, anthropology and psychology are in a difficult position. They observe rather clearly the limitations of a strictly "economic" approach to aid, without disposing of the instruments to surmount those limitations.

There are, of course, aspects of aid that do go rather directly to some of the issues of social change. To the extent that technical assistance, foreign training, subsidies to education or the Peace Corps introduce new ways of looking at issues, they may serve as catalysts for the social situation. Of course, they may also disclose strains that serve to solidify resistance to social change.

The approach suggested by the above quotation may in the short run be more practical than any attempt to operate directly on social organizations and attitudes in a world where nationalism reigns and zenophobia is the order of the day. In order to catalyze development, economic aid can be used deliberately with the advice of behavioral scientists as a lever to affect the social matrix.

This proposal has two obvious disadvantages. First, it makes heavy demands on the behavioral scientists: are they confident enough of their knowledge to be sure which catalysts will be positive and which negative in terms of any stated set of goals? Second, since the issues overlap, social change and desired political change may not go hand in hand. If social revolutions are held necessary in some instances, are their political consequences likely to be acceptable to aid donors? I venture to guess that our ability to predict this interaction correctly is limited.

These disadvantages are, in my opinion, probably less than those that have already been incurred by insufficient attention to the non-economic elements in development. A more important role for behavioral science in the planning and review of economic aid would probably benefit the long-run interests of donors, and at the very least make clear to recipients some of the implicit inconsistencies between their modernizing objectives and their existing value systems.

BIRTH CONTROL: PRO AND CON

Finally, a word about the population growth gap. It has been argued that rapid population growth is not necessarily a disadvantage for development—one might cite Israel, Mexico and some of the Central American countries as examples. The challenge of incorporating more people productively may stimulate positive responses, and so on. Larger populations may make possible more division of labor, economies of scale and higher real incomes. Optimum population is a vague concept: the conservationist has one idea, the economist, the sociologist, the politician each another, and so on.

It does seem clear, however, that some countries are clearly adding people too fast to please anyone who takes a national viewpoint. India, Pakistan, China, Ceylon are standard examples. If labor productivity is low, then the benefits from birth control may outweigh the cost manyfold. To an economist, therefore, population control efforts seem well worth subsidizing, even to the point of paying bonuses for limiting births in some LDCs. Governments have often adopted the opposite device—payments to families for bearing children—so that the idea of financial incentives for influencing family size is no novelty. In cases where this is not feasible, or the need for family limitation is less urgent, government subsidy of birth-control information and of the devices adopted seems most desirable. In terms of the criterion of aid requirements, population control may often appear the most effective method for reducing the amount and time span of dependence on foreign capital.

We are a long way from felicity in the relations between rich and poor countries. There is a heritage of mistrust, reinforced by the LDCs' knowledge that they are dependent on rich countries for technological progress, for economic and technical assistance and often even for the exemplars of society's cultural standards, both popular and elite. In this hothouse of resentment and dependence, we can expect a luxuriant growth of hostility, rationalized on ideological grounds, and easily utilized as elements of broader international power conflicts.

There is no easy way around these difficulties. No levels of aid that now seem likely can accomplish the reconciliation. For that matter, there is no guarantee that vast increases in aid would reduce the resentments for long.

The obvious answer seems to be found in the political cliché—"if you can't beat them, join them." The rich countries could deliberately adopt policies aimed at fostering the social revolutions that may appear to be necessary conditions of development. As a practical matter, it may be doubted whether such policies would have much content. It is one thing to announce support for revolutionary social and economic change. It is another thing to effect those changes by the machinery of intergovernmental relations. Nor is it likely that the rich capitalist countries would support regimes that insisted on drastic redistributions of wealth; yet the present distribution of property and power in certain Latin American countries is alleged, for example, to be inconsistent with the goal of effective progress in economic development.

BITTER CHOICE

Therefore, in many cases, the choice is between providing aid where the political or social conditions are inopportune and not providing aid at all. Haiti and the Philippines may be cited as examples. In one case, donors have all but suspended aid, as an indication of political mistrust. In the other, aid has been continued because the political consequences of no aid were assumed to be more unfavorable to donors' interests. In neither case is there much hope for rapid development, in the absence of major political and social changes. Yet it is clear that neither the withholding nor granting of aid has been a major element in contributing to those changes. This is not to say that aid can never be an effective political weapon— the recent history of Brazil and Indonesia offers testimony enough. But we may well close by asking whether the changes so induced, favorable as they may be to donors' immediate political interests, really do much to overcome the underlying social and economic weaknesses that made the weapon effective. The endless rotation of fragile regimes seems to be a trademark of many poor countries. As long as they are so easily juggled, it is evident to me that, in those countries at least, the more enduring accomplishments of foreign aid remain largely prospective.

The ultimate gap of course lies in rich and poor countries' perceptions of the issues. Donors hypothesize a relationship among political stability, economic growth catalyzed by aid, and donors' self-interest. In fact, economic growth and political stability are often inconsistent. So the dilemma is genuine, if it is true (as I doubt) that political stability in LDCs is always preferable to political instability. Furthermore, donors try to limit the application of this hypothesis by invoking absorptive capacity and LDC economic derelictions to rationalize inadequate aid levels.

Recipients, on the other hand, have tended

to follow the normal and convenient device of putting the blame on Dad. If only aid were bigger, trade concessions greater, rich countries less neo-colonial, then, brothers, then. . . .

In fact, of course, all parties are to some extent at fault—the rich too stingy and too free with avuncular ideology, the poor reluctant to abandon their own cherished stereotypes for a harsher reality. We need great men on both sides to bridge this ultimate gap of communi-cation—the most delicately fashioned bridge of all, its cables spun from a treasury of goodwill, its roadway built on wisdom in the affairs of men and states, its pillars sculpted from the rock of common material interests. It remains an open question whether any of us will ever attend the ribbon-cutting ceremony for this particular construction. If we do, our careers would be rewarded with an unexampled fe-licity.

QUESTIONS AND STUDY SUGGESTIONS

1. Describe the multidimensional character of the gap between the aspira-tions of the underdeveloped countries and their present status.
2. What are the costs of closing the economic gap? Will the closing of the economic gap be sufficient to close the noneconomic gaps between the developed and underdeveloped countries?
3. What are the general characteristics of those less developed countries which have achieved rapid growth? What are the external and domestic constraints to growth which underdeveloped nations face?
4. Is "absorptive capacity" a constraint on the progress of the less devel-oped nations? Explain.

Reading 79

Economic Planning in France
Bernard D. Nossiter

Most of us are inclined to think of the various economies of the world as being clustered rather closely around the poles of American capitalism and Russian communism. In this reading Bernard D. Nossiter reminds us that there exists an almost unlimited number of ways by which a society might cope with the economizing problem. Indeed, considerable effort has been expended in some countries to combine the better features

From Bernard D. Nossiter, **The Mythmakers**, Houghton Mifflin Company, Boston, 1964, pp. 194–203, abridged. Reprinted by permission.

of the market economy and the centrally planned economy. France has reshaped its economy in terms of "indicative planning." This new planning accepts the existing institutional framework and is designed to be a means by which the economy can actually realize its growth potential through the essentially voluntary cooperation of all major segments of the economy.

One reason for the enthusiasm with which the new planning has been adopted is that it has the obvious virtue of leaving existing institutions largely intact. It seeks to improve their performance rather than uproot the structure. Economists understandably hunger to bring their models to life, to create a world of atomistic, competitive firms and atomistic, non-unionized workers all performing the intricate minuet composed by Adam Smith and his successors. Scholars of other disciplines, statesmen, politicians and plain citizens have a greater (and perhaps more realistic) respect for the tenacity of institutions and a better understanding of the great forces that called them into being. The new style of planning takes the world pretty much as it finds it. It accepts the concentration of markets, dominated by a handful of firms, that characterizes most modern industry. It sees a host of possible advantages, technological and political, that flow from this order. It accepts the existence of unions in the labor market and regards them as potentially fruitful organs of economic production and political expression.

The new philosophy of planning, however, suggests that these great institutions have no divine mandate to order their own affairs, and thus the affairs of society at large, without let or hindrance. Nor does it pretend that, left to themselves, they will behave just like the atomistic enterprises and workers of the classical world. Instead, the new planners say: let us, with a maximum of inducement and a minimum of coercion, through a diet more heavily laced with carrots than with sticks, harness the energies of these great institutions to socially desirable ends. These ends shall be determined by citizens generally, or, more accurately, their representatives.

"INDICATIVE PLANNING"

The most striking characteristic of the new planning is its generally noncoercive nature. It is planning by assent. In contrast with the directed, compulsory planning of the commu-nist world, the French call the new style, "indicative planning."

In skeleton form, indicative planning follows this pattern. A group of government economists tentatively select a plausible rate of growth for their nation's economy. This rate, perhaps 5 percent a year, is based on two central elements: population forecasts of the probable growth in the labor force and the likely pace at which the productivity of these workers will increase at full employment. Then, combining past experience and possible future policies, the technicians draw up a model or projection of the economy's broad outlines four or five years in the future.

This model might spell out the likely shape of spending by households, by government and by industry. In trade-dependent Europe and Japan, it would include forecasts of imports and exports. The model gives a quantitative picture of consumption and investment, private and public. In other words, it is a projection of the broad sectors that make up national income accounts.

This statistical sketch of a possible future is then examined by key representatives of industry, labor, farmers and consumers and by officials from government agencies that make decisions affecting the economy. They accept, reject or modify the growth target; they criticize and adjust the projections for the broad sectors of the account. Once agreement is reached on this outline of the economy, on the great economic aggregates, it is translated into meaningful terms for individual industries and ministries.

In each major industry, leading businessmen, union executives, government officials and public representatives calculate the model's implications for their specific area of interest. This is not altogether remote from practice in the United States where, for example, executives of General Motors calculate the firm's investment, employment and raw materials needs on the basis of their private forecast of the economy's future shape. In Europe, however, industrialists—collaborating with other branches of society—estimate their industry's requirements on the basis of a common forecast.

The projections of the individual industries are then reconciled; bottlenecks are spotted; inconsistencies are, hopefully, eliminated. A new picture or model of the future economy is then drawn up. Government tax, trade, subsidy and other policies needed to achieve the targets are tentatively mapped out. The projection is given final shape by the nation's cabinet and sent to the legislature for debate. Here, a last look is taken at the projections that both predict and help determine the future division of the economic pie.

The legislators need not concern themselves with technical details (Has enough coal been provided for the expected level of steel production? How accurate is the projection for the number of youths entering the labor force?), but with larger issues of social policy. Does the model leave a big enough role for private enterprise? Should the public sector be enlarged? If so, should there be more or less emphasis on schooling, parks, roads?

The model is then adopted and becomes The Plan.

PROJECTIONS AS GUIDES

The plan does not embody orders, mandates or directives to private firms and to unions. Instead, the projection is a guide to their decisions and to those of the government. It is not a collection of piecemeal guides like those that large corporations and government agencies now draw up for themselves in the United States. It is a coherent, integrated projection on which the major groups in society have agreed.

Since it lacks sanctions, does an indicative plan make any difference? Is this merely an empty exercise in forecasting with no consequences? In Western Europe and Japan the answer is clear. There is general agreement that planning exerts an important and beneficial influence over the great decisions made by industry, unions and the government.

FRENCH PLANNING

A look at some specific indicative plans will make clearer why this belief, an odd one by the standards of many American economists, has taken hold. Such an examination will also underscore some of the pitfalls in planning,

demonstrate how far the actual techniques depart from our idealized sketch, and perhaps offer some answers to America's economic and political dilemmas.

The best known version of planning by assent, the form most carefully studied by Britain, is the French. The construction of the fourth plan, for the years 1962 through 1965, shows how the method works.

The heart of the system is the Planning Commission, a small group of government economists, engineers and other technicians. This body was told by the government to draw up sketches of the economy for 1965 that would embrace several objectives. These included: full employment, balance in France's international accounts and a modest start on improving the quality of modern life. More specifically, this last goal meant shifting some resources from private consumer goods to public investment for an attack on noise and polluted air.

THE GROWTH GOAL

Aided by experts from the Ministry of Finance, the Commission outlined in early 1960 some alternative models. These assumed yearly rates of economic growth of 3 percent, 4.5 percent and 6 percent. The 6 percent model was discarded on the grounds that it would dangerously strain France's balance of foreign payments.

The alternative models were then discussed with the Economic and Social Council, a body representing the nation's principal interest groups. The Council urged a high rate of growth and recommended special emphasis on education, research, health and housing.

Armed with these reports, the government picked a 5 percent growth rate for the plan's tentative target. The Commission then drew up a more detailed sketch of the 1965 economy, projecting the probable levels of investment, consumption, imports, exports and other broad categories of the national income. It took one more step. Utilizing the input-output technique the Commission calculated how much each of about twenty principal industries would buy and sell from each other in an economy of the size forecast in the model. These estimates were made for mining, iron and steel, electricity, chemicals and the like.

Here, then, was a reasonably detailed blueprint of the possible shape of the French economy in 1965. Was it practical? Were reasonable estimates made of the required investment, employment and materials, of the likely output in each of the industries?

THE MODERNIZATION COMMISSIONS

These questions were answered by the twenty-five Modernization Commissions. These bodies were dominated by industrial and financial leaders but they also include representatives of unions, farmers and other private groups. In the fourth plan, there was one Modernization Commission for each of twenty industries and five Commissions that cut across industry lines to deal with broad questions like labor skills and financing.

The Modernization Commissions made further refinements in the estimates. From their deliberations, too, came a new, overall growth target. The government was persuaded that 5.5 percent was more desirable than a 5 percent pace to insure full employment. However, the projections for each industry now did not mesh as neatly, one with another, as the more abstract blueprint drawn up earlier by the Planning Commission. So the chairmen of the Modernization Commissions and the planning officials met with each other to iron out the differences.

The Economic and Social Council was then called back into session to approve a final version. At last, the National Assembly—largely a rubber stamp in De Gaulle's Fifth Republic—was handed the plan for debate.

IMPLEMENTATION

French officials like to stress that the Planning Commission and other government organs have no power to compel any firm to abide by the plan. The government can't allocate materials to cooperative companies and deny them to firms that balk. In a formal sense, nobody is bound by the blueprint. But the government is far from powerless in France or anywhere else in the modern world. Indeed, the French government's power to induce cooperation is much greater than the federal government's in the United States.

A significant portion of the French economy is owned and operated by the state. The government runs the gas, electricity, coal, com-

munications and air and rail transportation industries. Important banks and insurance companies are nationalized. Government firms explore, develop and distribute oil; the Renault auto company is state-owned. If these enterprises alone adhere to the plan, they increase the prospect that it will be fulfilled.

In the private sector, the state exercises a powerful influence over investment. The government directly invests public funds in private enterprises; it invests indirectly by controlling the lending policies of the nationalized banks; and before any firm can float a sizeable issue of bonds, it must receive the government's consent. Only firms profitable enough to finance their expansion out of their own earnings can afford to disregard the suggestions and advice of the government.

In addition, the government has a battery of forces in reserve to compel cooperation. Price controls have been largely lifted since 1957, but the power to impose them remains. An industry's leaders could be persuaded to follow the plan through fear that otherwise controls over their products would be reimposed. The government can also dispense subsidies and tax privileges to encourage good behavior. In sum, the Planning Commission itself may not be able to order and direct but the government can exert much more than a hortatory influence over key private decisions.

EFFECTIVENESS

But the question still remains: How effective has the plan been? There is no doubt about the French boom. The decade of the 1950s marked the fastest growth in the French economy in a century, a full 33 percent higher than the pace in the United States. In the past, French manufacturers typically practiced industrial Malthusianism, curbing investment and plant capacity to prop up prices, erecting cartelist and protectionist walls around firms. They have now been transformed into one of the world's most expansive and growth-minded business communities. Nevertheless, one distinguished scholar, Professor Charles Kindleberger of MIT, concludes that planning played little part in this, that "the basic change in the French economy is one of peoples and attitudes."

But what forces created the new men and the new attitudes? Kindleberger himself says: "French planning is in some important respects the opposite of planning. Knowledge of income and industry projections and faith in the inevitability of expansion are communicated to firms at intra- and inter-industry meetings. This is perhaps the most powerful effect and one which has a faint resemblance to a revivalist prayer meeting."

Fundamental Strength

The faintly derisive tone of this estimate obscures one important strength of indicative planning. Collaborative forecasts, reinforced by the government's commitment to full employment and growth, encourage businessmen to believe that there will be an increasing demand for their products. Secure in the knowledge that key firms are acting on more or less the same assumptions of growth, convinced that the projections have a degree of realism and consistency that would not exist if each firm made its own separate projection, French businessmen have become much more willing to invest in expanded capacity and modern equipment. This willingness, supported by the state, tends to be self-justifying. For the very act of increased investment increases incomes and productivity, thereby creating faster growth.

Disadvantages

This is not to say that French indicative planning is flawless. For one thing, the broad-based democratic direction implied in the idealized model has not been realized. The Modernization Commissions, for example, are heavily weighted with business and financial leaders; unions have a very modest share in the discussions. In the third plan, the French government enlisted nearly four management representatives for every labor member.

The businessmen taking part in these discussions would indeed be a transfigured breed if they did not draw up a plan that to some extent protected each participating firm and divided up market shares. Undoubtedly, planning aids the survival of some less efficient firms that would go under in pure competition. But neither in the United States nor anywhere else in the world does pure competition exist. The characteristic live-and-let-live competition of the few in America tends toward the same result as discussion among competitors. At the very least, under indicative planning the public interest conditions some of these private decisions.

Other Advantages

There are some other dividends. The government's day-to-day economic policy making, whether broad-gauged fiscal and money policy or the narrower focus of a nationalized coal industry, is much more likely to be consistent. This is because government officials join with private decision makers, in selecting targets and making forecasts. In the United States, for example, the Federal Reserve System, dominating monetary policy, may be pursuing a deflationary course at the very moment when the Administration is pressing for higher employment and growth. With indicative planning, the French are less likely to run into this kind of paralyzing contradiction.

Finally, the technique offers a good vantage point for taking account of the quality as well as the quantity of economic life. This is reflected in the French decision to make a start, however hesitant, on expenditures for dealing with such industrial side effects as noise and air pollution.

Critics of planning often observe that targets are rarely hit on the nose, that the vagaries of human behavior, changes in technology and changes in prices yield results that the planners don't foresee. This is true but may not be nearly as important as the critics argue. It is probably more important to correctly calculate the direction of change, up or down. On this score, the French have done quite well. For example, the second plan for 1954 through 1957 projected increases of 25 percent for gross domestic output, 30 percent for industrial production and 28 percent for investment. The actual results were increases of 28 percent, 46 percent and 41 percent. In the third plan for 1958 through 1961, these three targets were undershot by a range of 3 percent to little more than 6 percent. Again, however, the direction of the change and its general magnitude were on target.

One point is clear; the peculiar mix of planning and private enterprise, of state stimulus and free decision making represents an abandonment of doctrinaire, either-or approaches in economic policy making. It is the kind of experiment that led the chairman of the steel industry's Modernization Commission to declare: "On n'est plus dans le pays de Descartes; on est plus près du pragmatisme des Anglais."

QUESTIONS AND STUDY SUGGESTIONS

1. What is "indicative planning"? Is such planning compatible with a capitalistic system?
2. Explain the mechanics of economic planning in France, emphasizing the roles of the planning Commission and the Modernization Commissions.
3. Briefly assess the strengths and weaknesses of French economic planning.

Reading 80

An Economic Profile of Communist China
Arthur G. Ashbrook, Jr.

Interest in China derives from the sheer size of its economy and the fact that it represents a case study in economic development through the application of Communist techniques and institutions. This reading is an historical survey of the economic successes and shortcomings of Communist China. The author discusses the restoration of order and rehabilitation of the economy after the Communists came to power in 1949 and the substantial economic growth realized under Soviet-type planning in the mid-1950s. However, the excesses of the Great Leap Forward, the adverse effects of poor harvests, and the Sino-Soviet ideological rift have all contributed to China's current economic difficulties and forced substantial changes in economic policy in the early 1960s. The future course of China's economy under the Proletarian Cultural Revolution remains uncertain.

Since the establishment of Communist control over Mainland China in 1949, Mao Tse-tung and his lieutenants have tried to catapult China into the company of modern industrial nations. The ultimate objective of Mao's economic policy is political and military power. If, as Mao says, all power grows out of the barrel of a gun, there must be an arsenal to furnish the gun. Industrialization for Communist China, therefore, has meant first the building up of basic heavy industry—steel, coal, electric power, and petroleum refining—and then the building up of machinery and armament production. The culmination of this effort to date has been the three nuclear explosions in the Western desert.

From Arthur G. Ashbrook, Jr., "Main Lines of Chinese Communist Economic Policy," in Joint Economic Committee, **An Economic Profile of Mainland China,** Washington, February, 1967, pp. 15–44, abridged.

REHABILITATION, 1949–52

On October 1, 1949, the Chinese Communists under Mao Tse-tung established the People's Republic of China with its capital at Peking. The military and political triumph was complete. The new leadership immediately set about to transform China into a modern industrial nation that would dominate Asia and command the respect of the whole world.

Economic policy was seen, not as an end in itself, but as a means of furthering Chinese Communist military and political power at home and abroad. Economic policy for this period of rehabilitation (1949–52) was therefore part of the general Communist policy of consolidating power at home and laying the groundwork for the thoroughgoing transformation of Chinese society.

The economy inherited by the new regime was a shambles. Since the fall of the Manchu dynasty in 1911, extensive areas of China had been wracked by revolution, war lordism, civil war, foreign invasion, and flood and famine. Industry and commerce had almost come to a standstill in major urban centers. The industrial base in Manchuria had been looted by the U.S.S.R. of more than $2 billion worth of machinery and equipment. Dams, irrigation systems, and canals were in a state of disrepair. Railroad lines had been cut and recut by the contending armies. Inflation had ruined confidence in the money system. And, finally, the population had suffered enormous casualties from both manmade and natural disasters and was disorganized, half starved, and exhausted.

The first general aim of economic policy after the Communist takeover was the establishment of economic law and order. The brutally direct command structure of the Communist regime was especially well suited to carrying out this objective, and in a remarkably short time the new government had suppressed banditry; restored the battered railroad system to operation; repaired and extended the badly neglected system of dikes; replaced the graft-ridden bureaucratic system of local government with apparently incorruptible Communist "cadres"; introduced a stable currency and enforced a nationwide tax system; begun an extensive program of public health and sanitation; and provided a tolerably even distribution of available food and clothing.

Control over the Commanding Heights

The restoration of the workaday activities of peace went hand in hand with the establishment of central economic planning and control in Communist China. Whereas political and military control went down to the smallest village and last urban block, economic control at first was concentrated on the commanding heights of the economy, such as the railroad system, the banking system, and steel and other key industries. However, for the Communist regime this control was merely a prelude to the thoroughgoing transformation of the economy into a command economy patterned after the economy of the U.S.S.R.

An example of how control from the center gradually tightened is to be found in the organization of agriculture. In the early years of the regime perhaps 2 million rural landlords and rich peasants were slaughtered as enemies of the revolution, and the land was divided up among the poorer peasants. However, the peasants were not long left undisturbed. Mutual aid teams were formed under the pressure of the Communist command structure; groups of peasants pooled their labor at various seasons but with no sharing of income or property. Later, lower level cooperatives were set up; land was used jointly but each peasant received income from the land he had contributed. The next stage was the higher level agricultural producer cooperative (APC), similar to the Soviet collective farm, in which land was owned collectively and brought no income to the former owner. In 1958 there was the super-collective or commune.

Appraisal of Performance

Chinese economic policy in the period of Rehabilitation (1949–52) gets full marks for drawing all China together in one national economic unit and laying the groundwork for the transformation of the economy to a Soviet-type command economy. The objectives of this period—the establishment of economic law and order, the seizure of the commanding heights of the economy, and the restoration of existing productive facilities—were all achieved.

A major economic result of the successful rehabilitation was a temporary relaxation of the jaws of the Malthusian trap. Up to the time of the new regime, the familiar checks of war, famine, and disease had kept the population within the bounds of current food production. Now suddenly, the new regime had welded the country into a national unit and had greatly increased the effective capacity and the output of the economy. Production temporarily was in excess of minimum consumption needs. There now existed the possibility for net investment which could build up industry and provide support for agriculture, science, exports, more industry, and so on. There was even the prospect for urbanization, and, ultimately, a fall in the birth rate.

But the regime had to move fast. All the fertile land in China was already in use and was already being worked intensively. Very little additional output would result from applying more labor to the land, once the non-recurring gains of peace had been achieved. Furthermore, the elementary discipline in health and sanitation that the regime quickly imposed on the country led to a sharp drop in the death rate; the Malthusian trap would quickly close again in the absence of rapid and large-scale industrialization. In this matter the Chinese Communists were victims of their own success. Through their public health program and their ability to get food to disaster areas, they kept people alive. Although the leadership was ruthless enough, if it so wanted, to let millions starve in order to import military equipment and industrial facilities essential for the production of modern armaments, there were practical political reasons why Parson Malthus' dismal remedies were not open to them.

THE FIRST FIVE-YEAR PLAN, 1953–57

The first stage (1949–52) had seen the new government consolidate control over the economy, restore the small industrial base, and provide a minimum ration of food and clothing for the population. The second stage, the period of the First Five-Year Plan (1953–57) was the beginning of forced-draft industrialization in the Soviet style. Economic policy was directed to the rapid expansion of capacity and output in basic industrial commodities—steel, coal, electric power, petroleum, cement, and the rest. Concurrently, a beginning was made in the machine building and armaments industry. In transportation, the completion of a

major bridge at Wuhan linked up the rail systems of north and south China: a major program of double tracking existing rail lines was undertaken; and new lines were pushed toward the remote provinces of the west. Agriculture had the threefold task of feeding the rapidly growing population (including the new urban population), supplying large quantities of raw materials to industry, and providing exports to pay for imports of military and capital equipment and industrial raw materials.

Selection of the Soviet Model

It was natural that the Chinese Communist leadership should look to the U.S.S.R., the first Communist state, for its economic strategy. In political ideology and economic objectives, the U.S.S.R. in many respects was the only model for Communist China to follow. An even more compelling reason was that the U.S.S.R. stood ready to support China in its industrialization, and Soviet aid was especially effective because it was to be received in one huge politicoeconomic bundle. As Mao Tse-tung put it in September 1956, "We must be good at studying. We must be good at learning from our forerunner, the Soviet Union. . . ."

The features of Soviet-style industrialization that Communist China adopted were—

The notion of a central economic plan covering a 5-year period and prescribing rates of growth for major industrial and agricultural products as well as rates of growth for all other branches of economic activity.

The principle that investment should have priority once minimum defense and consumption needs had been met; also, a corollary principle that in the event of lags in the plan, additional resources would come out of the hide of the consumer and only *in extremis* out of the military establishment.

The precept that investment in industry should outrank investment in agriculture and that, within industry, investment in heavy industry should be several times as great as investment in light industry.

The policy of running the whole economy at full throttle, that is, of pressing managers and workers to increase physical output to the outermost limits of capacity.

The reliance on a centralized organization of production, under which large ministerial bureaucracies ran each branch of industry (steel, coal, petroleum, etc.) from offices in Moscow or Peking.

Under a series of agreements that began in 1950, the U.S.S.R. agreed to transfer to Communist China in the course of three 5-year plans (1953–67) (1) a package of 300 industrial plants worth a total of about $3 billion, (2) a high proportion of the whole spectrum of Soviet technology, and (3) the administrative know-how necessary for running a modern economy. By the end of 1967, Communist China was to have 300 modern steel mills, electric powerplants, machine-tool plants, aircraft plants, chemical plants, electronics plants, and agricultural machinery plants. All these plants would be dovetailed together as suppliers and customers of one another—for example, the Soviet plans for Chinese industrialization presumably had steel mills "coming in" at the right time to supply newly commissioned machine-tool and agricultural equipment plants.

Chinese Communist economic policy, then, was to rely on Soviet economic assistance for a rapid-fire development of Chinese industry. On what terms was this assistance to be paid for? In return for Soviet machinery and equipment, China exported to the U.S.S.R. specialty foods, textiles, and processed ores, notably tin, antimony and tungsten.

Agriculture as a Holding Operation

The Chinese Communists did not try to begin the large-scale mechanization of agriculture in the First Five-Year Plan period and this was sound economic policy. Industrial effort had to go toward expanding the industrial base. Machines in agriculture would only displace men, not raise output. And there were plenty of men.

Agriculture was to continue to benefit in this period from the restoration of peace and the establishment of a strong central government. Continued improvement in flood control and irrigation systems depended on the organization and discipline of large bodies of men; the new government was well-suited for this kind of task. Of course, it could not prevent dips in production caused by flood and drought but it could reduce losses and take care of the victims.

Another major line of improvement in agriculture was largely beyond the capacity of the economy in this period; namely, the develop-

ment and application of improved techniques of production, especially the increased use of chemical fertilizers and the introduction of superior strains of rice and other crops.

Appraisal of Performance

In this period also, the Chinese Communist leadership should be graded high for its economic policy and its economic achievements at this stage of its development. The proof is in Table 80–1's production figures for basic industrial items, at the beginning and at the end of the plan.

In addition to a several fold increase in the production of major industrial products, the Chinese Communists with Soviet help also—

Modernized and increased the capacity of major branches of industry.

Trained thousands of skilled and semiskilled industrial workers.

Laid the groundwork for a Soviet-type planning and statistical system.

Obtained sufficient growth in agriculture to keep up with the growth of population.

The economic policy of the First Five-Year Period of "learn from the Soviet Union" was an excellent choice, given the Chinese Communist military and political goals and given the practical alternatives. If the Malthusian trap were not to close, industrialization had to be achieved without delay, had to be conducted on a tremendous scale, had to be simple to administer, and had to be achieved at low cost measured in terms of the food and raw materials China would have to export. The Soviet-sponsored industrial program met all these criteria.

By the end of the First Five-Year Plan period Communist China had achieved an enviable momentum in economic development. This momentum was translated into high morale and enthusiasm among a large part of the population.

THE GREAT LEAP FORWARD, 1958–60

The Chinese Communist leadership intended to follow up the successful First Five-Year Plan (1953–57) with a Second Five-Year Plan (1958–62). The new plan was superseded in early 1958, however, by the Great Leap Forward, a complete turnabout in Chinese Com-

Table 80–1.   PRODUCTION OF BASIC INDUSTRIAL GOODS IN MAINLAND CHINA, 1952–57

Item	Unit	Output 1952	Output 1957
Crude steel	Million metric tons	1.35	5.35
Coal	Million metric tons	66.5	130.7
Petroleum	Million metric tons	.44	1.46
Electric power	Billion kilowatt-hours	7.3	19.3
Cement	Million metric tons	2.9	6.9
Sulfuric acid	Thousand metric tons	190	632

munist economic policy. The Great Leap Forward was an ill-conceived scheme to drive the Chinese economy ahead at a much faster pace; output in industry and agriculture was to be doubled and redoubled in a few short years; seemingly regardless of the effect on men, machinery, and quality of output. Instead of the grateful acceptance of the dour Soviet model of economic development, the new era was marked by fanaticism and sloganeering. "Politics must command economics." "Produce more, faster, better, and more economically." "Catch up with Great Britain in the production of steel and other industrial commodities in 15 years" (later the time span was shortened to 10 years).

Two seemingly contrasting explanations of the Great Leap are available. The first holds that the leadership was so encouraged by the results of the First Five-Year Plan that it was inspired to greatly step up the pace of the economy. The second holds that the leadership was so discouraged by the results of the First Five-Year Plan in relation to China's enormous economic problems that it lashed out in a bit of frustration to get immediate solutions to these problems.

Economic Theory behind the Great Leap

The Great Leap concerned much wider issues than economics. Mao and his colleagues have a vision of Chinese society as it should be. The yearnings of the individual Chinese for rest, privacy, and a little more food play no part in this vision. All human and material resources are to be devoted to making China a world power. The Great Leap was to have speeded up this process.

The first major tenet of the economic theory behind the Great Leap was that China's vast population was—contrary to the Malthusian theories of the bourgeois economists—an eco-

nomic asset. As Liu Shao-chi put it, "Man should be viewed as a producer rather than a consumer." The more people, the more hands to build socialism. This point of view could hardly be more in error in a country pushing hard against the limits of its existing agriculture to obtain food. A distinction is necessary between the *huge size* of China's population and the rate of growth which adds *tremendous annual increments* to the population. Both aspects are disadvantageous. The huge size is a disadvantage because of the imbalance created between land and capital on the one hand and population on the other. Once China's land suitable for agriculture is being busily worked, a doubling of the labor force will not double output from the land, because each worker's labor now is being applied in effect to only half as much land.

The rapid growth in population is a related but separate disadvantage. Rapid growth in population means that rapid growth in output of food and clothing is necessary merely to maintain the present low level of living. Increases in production brought about by gradual improvements in agricultural technology and small increases in the amounts of farm machinery and farm structures are offset by the new mouths to feed.

A second element in the economic thinking of China's leaders was that China's population, especially in the countryside, was underemployed a large part of the year. In the rural areas, it was argued there were peak periods of activity during planting and harvesttime but the peasant spent the remainder of the year working far below capacity. Communist organization was the key to the mustering of this unused labor. The off-peak periods could be used for communal labor in constructing dams, repairing dikes, digging irrigation ditches, building roads, and producing industrial or handicraft goods.

The "underemployed" argument was not completely thought out. In the first place, the Chinese peasant family in the framework of the clan village had fashioned over the generations a rhythmic pattern of life, in which many subsidiary activities had been dovetailed in between the peak agricultural periods; the village was largely self-contained and its members carried on such traditional local activities as making clothing, processing food, building housing, gathering fuel, and conducting petty trade; the trade relations with outside markets were small. Given this reality, any attempt by the Communist government to mobilize what appeared to be underemployed people ran the danger of breaking up well-established patterns of economic activity and of losing considerable local economic output. In the second place, the consumption of food over much of China usually provided for bare subsistence, and any attempt to increase the energy output of large numbers of people would cost large additional amounts of food.

In urban areas, the same dubious economic appraisal was made. Housewives, it was argued, could be drawn into industry at practically no cost and the whole of the urban labor force could readily step up the tempo of work. Insufficient attention was paid to the contribution already made by housewives in the form of domestic production and child care.

A third element of the economic theory behind the Great Leap Forward was the emphasis on ideological motivation compared to the "normal" economic elements of material incentives, steady technological advance on the basis of research and testing, and dry accounting and cost control procedures. A fervid faith and vision of the future had brought the Chinese Communists through the rigors of the Long March and to their sweeping triumphs on the Mainland. The dangers of ideological backsliding were always present, and the Soviet-style industrialization was running the danger of glorifying (and paying a premium to) the successful planner, technician, accountant, and engineer—at the expense of the true believer who was exhorted to sacrifice and practice self-denial in the interest of strengthening the state.

Economic Consequences

China had made great strides in industry in the first 8 years under Communist rule but this was not enough. Targets sketched out for a Second Five-Year Plan (1958–62) were swept aside and new Leap Forward targets introduced.

Under standard economic policy, Communist governments call on industry to raise output each year and to bring great new capacity into operation. Output per worker is also supposed to rise at the same time, but often it is only the above-plan expansion of the work force that enables goals to be met. The Leap Forward in China went far beyond this conventional Communist policy toward industry. Industrial output was to be pushed upward in a sort of religious frenzy, almost regardless of the cost in terms of (1) lower quality, (2) exhausted workers, (3) worn-out machinery, and (4) unusable product. Steel produced in thousands of backyard furnaces lay unused or had to be remelted as a charge in other furnaces. Coal dug out of the earth at a furious pace contained large quantities of dirt and rock and could not be used efficiently.

Communist countries have sometimes been able to make spectacular percentage gains in output by concentrating resources and managerial efforts in a narrow sector of industrial output. Agriculture, however, presents a much more difficult problem because normally it is impossible to rapidly increase key resources such as land and water or to rapidly introduce more efficient factory-style methods of production. During the Leap Forward, the Chinese Communist leadership scoffed at these lessons of history and announced that both agriculture and industry would expand at a lightning pace.

The central economic policy for agriculture was the formation of super collectives—or communes—each averaging about 25,000 people. The commune was the multipurpose unit of local administration in rural areas. Not only was it responsible for agricultural production but also for industry (food processing, handicrafts, repair shops, and even little outposts of heavy industry such as the backyard furnaces, trade, water conservation, transport, and the militia). Each commune was supposed to be a large pool of highly motivated workers who could be shifted from one large task to another. The Communist leadership had in mind some crude notion of economies of scale from a unit large enough to tackle, say, major irrigation projects. The commune was the highest form of collectivist agricultural organization yet sponsored by the government. It was to be the vehicle for the transfer of the whole society from socialism to communism, with the resultant abolition of wage differentials.

The Leap Forward in agriculture resulted in the most bizarre statistical event in the whole Chinese Communist administration. Production of grain in the bumper crop year 1958 was announced as 375 million tons, or more than double the 185 million tons of 1957. If this were the case, the population should have had plenty to eat, and indeed some communal messhalls began serving meals on an as-much-as-you-can-eat basis. In August 1959, serious statistical errors by overenthusiastic local officials were admitted and the claim for grain production in 1958 was lowered by one-third, to 250 million tons. This figure was still far too high. To judge from food shortages and other independent evidence, a reasonable estimate for 1958 is about 200 million tons.

The Great Leap Forward penetrated almost every aspect of Chinese Communist life. Technology acquired an ideological dimension. Rank-and-file workers and peasants were urged to create inventions *en masse,* and each local political unit announced that so-and-so many hundreds of inventions had sprung from these untutored sources. Educational standards were sacrificed in two ways. The quality of education was diluted by the introduction of new political indoctrination courses, and the demand for thousands of trained workers to meet skyrocketing plans in industry and agriculture resulted in drastic educational shortcuts.

Withdrawal of the Soviet Technicians

The Soviet leadership was concerned about its political and economic investment in Communist China. The U.S.S.R. was sponsoring a rapid fire but fully realistic industrialization program for China. Thousands of Soviet technicians had gone to China to help; thousands of Chinese technical students had gone to the U.S.S.R. for training. Chinese scientists were even working with Soviet scientists in the nuclear research laboratory at Dubna, near Moscow. Politically, the U.S.S.R. was prepared to use this economic dependence as a lever to gain Chinese adherence to Soviet policies.

In spite of Soviet hints that Chinese continuance of the Leap Forward could jeopardize the Soviet aid program, the Chinese persisted. But as the Leap Forward went on and as general relations between the U.S.S.R. and Communist China deteriorated, the aid program began to suffer. After the purge of Marshal Peng Te-huai in August 1959—ostensibly for criticizing the Leap Forward—Chinese managers and technicians in the new Soviet-aid plants or at the new construction sites began to turn deaf ears toward their Soviet mentors. The Soviet technicians were handed leaflets giving the Chinese side of the Sino-Soviet dispute. Khrushchev moved to exploit Soviet leverage upon the Chinese leadership, and in July 1960 the Soviet technicians were summarily withdrawn from China. They took their blueprints with them. Now it was up to the Chinese, armed with the spirit of self-reliance, to complete the construction projects, to operate already completed plants without Soviet troubleshooters on the production floor, to make their own blueprints, to find their own spare parts, and to balance outputs of all supplier plants against the requirements of user plants.

These things the Chinese could not do, the Leap Forward spirit notwithstanding.

Winter of Discontent, 1960–61

The gap between total production and the subsistence requirements of the people, which had opened after 1949 with the coming of peace, now closed. Two poor harvests in 1959 and 1960 resulted in a dangerous cut in food rations. The winter of 1960–61 marked the lowest point in food rations under the Chinese Communists. It is the only period when visitors to Communist China detected signs of widespread malnutrition. It was a time of greatly weakened resistance to disease, of grave discontent among the population which affected even the army, and probably of numerous outright deaths from starvation. The Great Leap Forward was at an end. A new economic policy was necessary—at once. This new policy is the subject of the next section.

Appraisal of the Great Leap Forward

The Great Leap Forward was a manmade disaster for Communist China. The name of the man was Mao Tse-tung. The formidable economic momentum built up during the first 8 years of the Communist regime was lost. The Leap Forward had no redeeming economic feature:

In agriculture, spurious new methods of cultivation led to unnecessary work for the peasants and lowered the quality of the land; the new communes ruptured proven and efficient production patterns in rural areas and led to poor harvesting and lack of concern for the land.

In science and education, the Leap Forward substituted political rhetoric for laboratory research and careful education; educational standards were diluted and thousands of half-trained people let loose on the economy.

In economic planning and statistics, the new Second Five-Year Plan was superseded by manic Leap Forward planning methods, and statisticians were enjoined to make the figures back up political guidelines; for example, the output of grain in 1958 was reported at nearly double what it really was, and the claim for output of coal covered a great amount of dirt, rocks, and thin air; the fledgling Soviet-style statistical system was swept away, not only because politics command statistics but also because statisticians like other office workers were pressed into service as frontline workers in industry and agriculture.

In economic development—and this was the most unkindest cut of all—the Leap Forward ultimately resulted in the withdrawal of Soviet economic aid; of the 300 modern plants to be built with Soviet help by 1967, about half were in operation when the Soviets pulled out; the Chinese sometimes could not continue operating the completed plants without Soviet troubleshooters and spare parts; much of the capital plant built up over the past 8 years and paid for by down-to-earth sweat and iron rations suddenly became useless.

RECOVERY AND READJUSTMENT, 1961–65

The Leap Forward debacle set the stage for the next period in Chinese Communist economic policy—the period of Recovery and Readjustment, which lasted 5 years—1961–65. The new economic policy was at first one of simple survival but gradually during the period there was recovery in industrial production. The end of the period saw the spectacular success in setting off China's first nuclear devices.

The period of Recovery and Readjustment marked above all a forced retreat from the disastrous economic policies of the Leap Forward period. It marked a change in economic priorities and in the style of economic management. The new economy policy:

Placed first priority on the restoration of food consumption to the subsistence level.

Continued the emphasis on China's development as a nuclear power on the (correct) assumption that available resources were sufficient not only to restore the essential supply of food but also to pay membership dues in the nuclear club.

Simplified economic planning and kept it on a year-to-year basis.

Abandoned the claptrap about the value of China's enormous population and began quiet support for a program to reduce its rate of growth.

Reduced the scope of economic development and indefinitely postponed the day when China would overtake such developed economies as Great Britain, West Germany, and Japan.

Increased Priority for Agriculture

During the period of Recovery and Readjustment, numerous statements appeared in the official press to the effect that economic priorities had been reshuffled and that agriculture and the industries supplying agriculture were now to get top billing. Emphasis was to be placed on insuring the supply of food by concentrating rural labor on the growing of food crops (as opposed to the confusing multiplicity of goals for rural labor under the Leap Forward), by commissioning industry to supply more fertilizer and irrigation pumps to agriculture, and by using scarce foreign exchange to import grain. What had happened was that the Leap Forward had overstretched China's resources and in the process had reduced China's production possibilities at the same time that minimum subsistence requirements were inexorably rising. The Malthusian trap was closing.

A major change in agricultural policy was the almost complete abandonment of the ill-fated communes. Responsibility for production was shifted down to smaller and more manageable units, namely, the production brigade (consisting usually of several villages) or the production team (one village).

In place of the discredited technical campaigns of the Leap Forward for deep plowing and close planting, emphasis now was placed on learning from old farmers. In place of the shortsighted denunciation of private agricultural plots, peasants were permitted to till small pieces of land and keep pigs and fowl; needless to say, this pragmatic concession to individual initiative was of great importance in restoring food production after the bleak winter of 1960–61. In place of the policy restricting petty private trade and handicrafts, more freedom was conceded to market goods locally and to produce farm tools, clothing, and household utensils. These sensible changes in policy, however, merely gave back what the Leap Forward so improvidently had taken away.

Development of Industry on a Narrow Front

In the period of Recovery and Readjustment, the policy for industry was to pick up the pieces, that is, to restore production in those areas of greatest national importance and to restore the quality of output. Instead of a broad program of industrialization, as sponsored by the U.S.S.R. before the withdrawal of Soviet support in mid-1960, the Chinese leadership had to be content with advance on a narrow front.

The new economic policy of this sobering-up period called for industry to support agriculture. Accordingly, the expansion of production and capacity in the chemical fertilizer industry and in certain branches of the agricultural equipment industry had the green light. The production of tractors, combines, and other large farm equipment was not emphasized, and rightly so; fertilizer and pumps for irrigation would increase yields, whereas tractors and combines would only displace men.

A second area of priority for industry in this period was the support of a narrow program of production of modern weapons. The construction and operation of facilities producing nuclear materials, the revival of domestic aircraft production, and the continued production of small arms are cases in point.

In contrast to the situation during the Leap Forward, an appreciable share of Communist China's industrial capacity was left idle during the period of Recovery and Readjustment. This partly was a legacy of the Soviet withdrawal. As industrial production gradually recovered in 1961–65, much of the idle capacity was brought into operation.

Change in Attitude toward Population

The about-face in economic policy in this period included a much clearer appreciation of the danger posed by China's rapidly growing population. Now at last the regime was willing to concede that an attack on the population side of the equation was desirable. However, the regime did not push birth control until near the end of this period. Population in the period rose from an estimated 690 million at the beginning of 1961 to 760 million at the end of 1965, or at an average annual rate of 2 percent.

Appraisal of Results

Economic policy in the period of Recovery and Rehabilitation met the minimum aims of the regime. Communist China drew back from the edges of mass starvation and mass rebellion. Essential food supplies were restored by prompt and continuing imports of grain as well as by concessions to private agriculture that cost the regime nothing economically. Industrial production in many sectors recovered to pre-Leap levels and in some instances—for example, petroleum and chemical fertilizers—showed large increases. Support for China's nuclear program continued, and impressive progress was made, particularly in view of the general political and economic reverses suffered by China. On the negative side, population continued to grow rapidly, and there seemed to be no immediate prospect for obtaining a safe margin of food production.

PROLETARIAN CULTURAL REVOLUTION, 1966–?

The year 1966 opened blandly enough. The economy of Communist China was continuing its steady recovery but with no sign of genuine economic momentum. Industrial production was continuing to increase, but Chinese buyers were continuing to scour the grain markets of the West. There were rumblings in the official press about the resurgence of a capitalistic spirit, especially in agriculture (private plots) and trade (petty merchandising), but the leadership did not seem ready to sacrifice vital food supplies for ideological purity. Economic policy still seemed to reflect the sober and pragmatic spirit of 1961–65.

Launching the Cultural Revolution

But something happened to China on its way to the Third Five-Year Plan—namely, the "Proletarian Cultural Revolution." Erupting in the spring of 1966, this revolution has shaken the political structure of China more violently than the upheavals of 1953 (dismissal of Kao Kang and Jao Shu-shih) and 1959 (the Peng Te-Huai case). The Proletarian Cultural Revolution is a convulsive (and probably final) attempt by the 72-year-old Mao to cast all of Chinese society into a mold of his own pattern which will endure long after his death. Up through September 1966, the Revolution has gone along these lines:

A renewed call to study the "thought of Mao Tse-tung" as the ultimate truth and the ultimate inspiration for solving all problems from selling watermelons to setting off nuclear explosions.

A revived emphasis upon "spiritual" incentives and on the supremacy of political ideology and a corollary denunciation of those who give first place to material incentives and to mere expertness or scientific techniques.

The closing of high schools and universities until their curriculums can be "revolutionized."

An insistence upon a whitewashing of the former Great Leap Forward as an "absolutely correct" course which was the fruit of Mao's thinking.

A revitalized campaign against "bourgeois" and "revisionist" influences, which has been entrusted to teenage activists dubbed "Red Guards."

At the time of writing there are as yet few indications that the Proletarian Cultural Revolution will supersede the Third Five-Year Plan in the way the Great Leap Forward superseded the Second Five-Year Plan in 1958. The aims of the Proletarian Cultural Revolution have been mainly political, and the regime has attempted to insulate the economy from its effects. The Revolution has not taken an even course. It has flared up to claim major victims like Peking's party boss, Peng Chen, and then has quieted down for a time; it has unleashed the youthful Red Guards, who later have been cautioned against overzealousness in punishing enemies of the revolution; it has attacked the spirit of concentration on technical excellence at the expense of personal political involvement and yet has moved to protect leading scientists and managers. On balance, the substitution of ideological cant for logic and reason cannot help but produce economic disruption. The uncertainty is how much.

Outlook for Economic Policy

The food-population problem will continue to be the first item on the agenda in any discussion of Communist China's intermediate-term economic prospects. The agricultural policy inherited from 1961–65 is one of steadily increasing inputs of fertilizer, equipment, and technology and of tolerating small plots, petty trade, and household handicraft production. This policy may be sufficient to feed adequately the growing population, given average weather and continued imports of grain, probably increasing slowly up to say 7 or 8 million tons annually. On the other hand, a new Leap Forward policy that (1) prohibited private agricultural and trading activity on ideological grounds, (2) switched technical leadership back from the old farmers to the ideologues in Peking, and (3) brought the communes back from limbo would lead to a food crisis much more quickly than did the original Leap.

In this connection, one can argue that the present Chinese leadership when things are going well economically adopts political policies that are ruinous economically. Conversely, when things are going badly economically, the leadership takes a pragmatic attitude and temporarily suspends political impediments. This model of the leadership's behavior assumes that its political ideas are sometimes in opposition to China's basic economic well-being—a reasonable assumption. The model leads to middle-of-the-road economic predictions, for if economic affairs are going well, they are pulled back down by political drives, whereas, if economic affairs are going poorly, political impediments are removed and economic activity is pulled up toward the norm.

Another interpretation of the relation between economic and political policies is that the party faithful must periodically be stirred up to move on to the next station on the road to communism or else they settle down at an intermediate point; at the same time, the general population must be goaded into speeding up the work pace and foregoing increases in living standards through appeals to patriotism and national pride.

On the supply side of the food-population balance, then, prospects are for small increases in food production that would more or less match growth in population but with the probability of some rise in imports of grain. These increases would be cut short in the event the leadership went ahead with another Leap Forward or a similarly disruptive ideological convulsion. On the demand side of the food-population balance, population is growing at about 2 to $2\frac{1}{4}$ percent annually. Over the period 1966–70, it is difficult to forecast a population policy that would appreciably lower this rate. After 1970 the population prospects fan out in a wide range of possibilities, mainly because of the dynamic technology of birth control.

Economic policy for 1966–70 almost certainly will include top priority for work on nuclear weapons and their means of delivery. It is noteworthy while the regime has specified that those scientists and technical personnel who have made contributions should be protected from the Revolution, numbers of them must have felt its impact. An attack upon intellectuals as a class—the main target of the Revolution—affects all educated people in China. It is highly probable that the morale and efficiency of hundreds of lesser scientists, managers, economists, and teachers has already suffered. Moreover, the day-to-day business of factories and offices has been disturbed by interminable meetings to indoctrinate people in the new Revolution; so far, the impact has been mainly in urban areas and, by inference, mainly on industry, foreign trade, and science and technology. There are numerous precedents during the previous Leap Forward for great waste of energy in indoctrination and great confusion from disturbing the status of technical specialists.

Again two alternative policies are possible. The more happy policy from industry's point of view would be a continued emphasis on quality and usefulness of output, continued assimilation of the technology of Japan and Western Europe, and continued willingness to be content with political lipservice from the scientists and managers. The less happy alternative would be a shift in the focus of the Proletarian Cultural Revolution to the realm of economic affairs, with intensive indoctrination of scientists and managers and a determined effort to keep out foreign technicians and even foreign machinery. A resumption of large-scale Soviet aid seems a highly unlikely development because the Revolution includes the U.S.S.R. as a key foreign influence to be weeded out.

The industrial outlook for Communist China is less bright if economic policy is viewed as demanding either catching up with the industrial potential of Japan, West Germany, and Great Britain or developing solely from China's own resources. The advances made by China in nuclear technology, petroleum refining, and electronics come at a time when technology throughout the world is advancing geometrically. To be 10 years behind today raises the prospect of being several generations behind in the 21st century. In a relative sense, therefore, China is falling behind in industrial technology. Both the rift with the U.S.S.R. and the periodic rooting out of capitalistic tendencies in the economy assume even greater importance as hindrances to China's industrial progress.

Economic policy in Communist China probably will continue to be subject to wide swings for as long as Mao and other leaders of the "Maoist persuasion" are in control of China. These swings in policy will be greater than the changes in economic activity, because policy is translated into action slowly and imperfectly. For example, there is foot dragging down the chain of command, especially when Peking's policy sacrifices economic well-being for ideological objectives or ignores local interests in favor of national interests. Consequently, there is more continuity and inertia in the conduct of actual economic affairs than a description of highlights in economic policy suggests. China will continue to be a potentially rich but backward and overcrowded nation in which progress will be made only in spotty fashion. Its Communist rulers will continue to face a formidable food-population problem as well as the problem of mastering increasingly complex industrial technology. The leaders seem determined to continue to score successes and to throw away the fruits of success.

QUESTIONS AND STUDY SUGGESTIONS

1. Why did China adopt the Soviet planning model? Explain how Communist China was able to achieve a high rate of economic growth during the First Five-Year Plan (1953–1957).
2. What was the rationale underlying the Great Leap Forward? Why did it fail?
3. What changes occurred in Chinese economic policy following the Great Leap Forward? Briefly discuss the Proletarian Cultural Revolution as it is reflected in economic policy and practices.
4. What is the Malthusian trap? Trace the changes which have occurred in the Chinese government's attitude toward population growth.

Reading 81

Soviet Economic Performance: Past and Future

Joint Economic Committee

This reading evaluates the performance of the Soviet economy under the 1959–1965 seven-year plan and indicates the emerging priorities of the five-year plan for 1966–1970. Soviet economic growth during the 1959–1965 plan fell substantially short of the planned rate; production shortfalls were common to all major sectors of the economy. The performance of the agricultural sector was particularly poor. In general, the Soviet growth rate has been declining since 1958 and is currently on the order of 5 to 5½ percent per year. A growth rate of this general magnitude is projected for the Soviet Union through 1975. The trend in the growth rate of the United States, on the other hand, has been upward, and the projected American growth rate through 1975 is 4 to 4½ percent. Sustained full employment in the United States and the failure of recent Soviet economic reforms (Reading 82) could narrow or eliminate this differential.

The economy of the Soviet Union has been operating within the formal guidelines of a new 5-year plan since the beginning of 1966. However, at the political level, responsibility for the formulation of national policy in the U.S.S.R. has been exercised by a new team of political leaders over a somewhat longer period of time—since October 1964. The latest 5-year plan may, therefore, be legitimately regarded as the economic program of the new leader-

From Joint Economic Committee, **Soviet Economic Performance: 1966–67,** Washington, 1968, pp. 1–5, 8–9, 11–17, abridged.

ship, represented by L. Brezhnev, the General Secretary of the Communist Party, and A. Kosygin, the Chairman of the Council of Ministers of the U.S.S.R. Formal ratification of the current 5-year plan, covering the period 1966–70, was provided by the 23d Congress of the Communist Party of the Soviet Union, at its meeting in Moscow during March–April 1966.

THE BURDEN OF INHERITED PROBLEMS

The economic climate in which the policy objectives and quantitative targets of the new plan were developed was unique in a number of ways. It was a climate heavily influenced by an array of troublesome economic problems left behind by the excessively ambitious 7-year plan, initiated by an overconfident Nikita Khrushchev in 1959 and brought to conclusion, after his removal from power, at the end of 1965. While there were a number of prominent areas of disappointing performance in evidence at the conclusion of the 7-year plan, the failure of the agricultural sector to come up to announced official expectations was most conspicuous. For the new leaders, it must have been a sobering exposure to economic reality to realize that the per capita output of farm products in 1965 remained at the 1958 level, and that, furthermore, in the 3-year period of 1963–65 the U.S.S.R. had to import more than $1½ billion worth of grain from non-Communist countries. The average annual growth rate in agriculture during the 7-year plan period was 1.6 percent, far below the planned yearly rate of 7.0 percent.

Apart from agriculture, there were a number of other economic problems that the new leaders inherited at the time of their accession to power. One especially serious cause for concern, from their vantage point, was the measurable slowdown in the rate of economic growth, a new phenomenon which began to manifest itself in the early years of the present decade. Thus, the gross national product, according to the Western concept, grew during the 7-year plan at an average annual rate of 5.4 percent, as compared with a planned growth rate of 7.4 percent.

Another disturbing development that could not be ignored by the Brezhnev-Kosygin team was the fact that the industries producing consumer goods were not meeting their production targets, while purchasing power in the hands of the population was rising more rapidly than provided for by the planners. This difficulty was reflected in the fact that per capita consumption had fallen short of the target set for it by the 7-year plan, having achieved a rate of growth of 2.7 percent, as against the projected annual increase of 4.9 percent.

The plan for investment, as may be seen in Table 81–1, also fell short of meeting its goal, showing an average yearly margin of growth of 7.5 percent, instead of the anticipated 9.0 percent.

In the field of urban housing, the new leaders also inherited a record of frustrated expectations. New dwelling space built during the 7-year plan came to an average of 80 million square meters yearly, as compared to the 93 million square meters per annum promised by the plan. Moreover, the shortfall of performance, as compared with specific plan targets, was reflected more generally by incontrovertible evidence of a steady decline in the efficiency of the national economy. A variety of calculations made by both Soviet and Western economists clearly indicated that the yield on new capital investment in industry, for example, was considerably lower during the first half of the sixties than in the comparable period of the fifties. During the same period, the productivity of the labor force also showed a weaker growth trend in the economy as a whole as well as in the major sectors of production.

These indicators have been generally interpreted by Soviet economists as reflecting a

Table 81–1.   U.S.S.R.: INDICATORS OF ECONOMIC GROWTH DURING THE 7-YEAR PLAN, 1959–65 (plan versus actual[1]; in percent)

	Average annual rate of growth	
	1959–65	
	Plan	Actual
Producing sectors:		
Gross national product	7.4	5.4
Industry[2]	8.6	7.8
Agriculture	7.0	1.6
Principal claimants:		
Consumption (per capita)	4.9	2.7
Investment (total)	9.0	7.5

[1] 1958 is the base year for the calculations.
[2] The plan indicator is for total industrial output. The indicator for actual growth is for civilian output only.

widespread condition of inertia and indiscipline at the level of the industrial enterprise toward such basic economic criteria as the effectiveness of the production processes in use, technological standard of manufacturing, and quality of the finished product. This condition, in turn, had been traced by the Soviet economic press to the preoccupation of plant managers with the quantitative goals of their production assignments, on which, after all, their reputation and their bonus earnings had come to depend. There was, above all, discouraging evidence of the state of affairs in regards to the efficient operation of heavy industry. The evidence available to the economists showed that the producer goods sector was continuing to devour a growing proportion of its output (over 80 percent) for use in the process of its own expansion, thus releasing an ever smaller share of plant, equipment, and material for consumer goods production. Only 18 percent of the output of the producer goods sector was made available to the consumer goods sector of industry in 1964, as compared with 28 percent in 1950.

For the new leadership, this raised a host of serious problems, pointing to an urgent need to create a better system of incentives for managers and workers alike in order to encourage them to seek more advanced, more sophisticated, and more productive models of equipment for their operations and, ultimately, to show a higher degree of responsibility for the quality and utility of the products manufactured by their enterprise. In light of this need, the Brezhnev-Kosygin political leadership enacted a comprehensive system of economic reform measures in September-October 1965, the main thrust of which was to help improve the system of economic incentives and to make the managers relatively more independent of their superior agencies, more responsible for maintaining a profitable production operation, and better motivated to turn out high quality, salable products.

THE SHAPE OF NEW ECONOMIC POLICIES

Against this background of inherited economic problems the Brezhnev-Kosygin leadership has found it necessary, from the beginning of their tenure of high office, to engage in a far-ranging effort to evolve a new economic policy that would not only regain the economic momentum of the 1950s but would also promise to be more effective in enforcing their own political priorities. However, as soon as they began to cope with the task of formulating a policy reflecting their own preferences, especially in the crucial areas of resource allocation among the recognized major claimants—investment, consumption, and defense—they discovered how intricately these economic decisions were intertwined with the whole fabric of domestic and foreign policy issues. They became aware at once of the hard fact, for example, that a decision on their part to build up the military power of the country at a more rapid tempo would inevitably have a direct negative impact on the consumer, involving not only his current level of economic well-being but also the general long-range outlook for progress toward the improvement of the nation's standard of living. Similarly, it was soon brought home to the Brezhnev-Kosygin regime that by sacrificing present investment in economic growth they could indeed achieve a notable increase in military power in the near term, but not without running the very real risk of having fewer resources at their command to satisfy all claimants, including the military, in the more distant future.

The main economic policy objectives of the new leadership began to reveal their distinctive shape in the provisions of the preliminary draft of the eighth 5-year plan (1966–70), which was discussed and adopted at the 23d Party Congress meeting, in March–April 1966. The new plan, as it finally evolved, was manifestly directed toward the pursuit of the following major goals: (1) obtaining an acceleration in economic growth over the comparatively low rates of increase of annual gains of the early 1960s by increasing productivity in the use of resources; (2) restoring domestic self-sufficiency in regard to the supply of major farm products, especially food grains; and (3) achieving conspicuous gains in the annual supply of goods and services for all principal claimants.

By itself, however, the act of formulating a set of broad economic objectives, through the medium of a new draft plan, did not advance the Soviet regime very far toward meeting the whole range of its rather urgent immediate resource requirements. The evidence is rather clear, for example, that until quite recently the political high command of the country had not made up its collective mind on priorities in the distribution of scarce resources. The vague, oracular language in which allocational policy was discussed throughout 1966 suggested that, if anything, the leadership was anxious to evade certain painful decisions by the simple device of assigning high priorities to several competing goals, including defense, economic growth, and consumption. Thus, for example, Kosygin and other leaders stated on a number of occasions that each of the following constituted "the" most important economic objective: (1) strengthening national defense, (2) raising agricultural production, (3) modernizing industry and raising its efficiency, and (4) improving the lot of the consumer.

In the course of 1967, the continued postponement of action on the adoption of the "final version" of the 1966–70 plan was accompanied by increasing overt signs of controversy, tending to support the presumption that the continued delay in action reflected some serious behind-the-scenes dispute over allocational policies. If, indeed, nearly 2 years were required to hammer out some hard-and-fast decisions about "who gets what," it helps to provide a practical illustration of how difficult it is for a collective political leadership in the Soviet Union to act promptly and effectively in cases involving the resolution of substantive issues.

Events of the more recent past, however, have brought to the foreground a body of evidence to suggest that a consensus of some sort has been reached at the level of the Soviet political high command concerning its shortrun priorities in resource allocation. Although much of the evidence is still sketchy in detail, an examination of the available data at this stage indicates the establishment of the following pattern of resource allocation for 1968, with a probable continuation into 1969–70: (1) a marked increase in outlays for military and space programs; accompanied by a measurable increase in the overall share of GNP allocated to these programs, (2) immediate and large additions to consumer money incomes, (3) a further deceleration in the growth of investment, and (4) a marked cutback in the original plan to allocate large quantities of additional resources to agriculture during 1966–70.

ECONOMIC REFORMS

The current program of administrative reform measures, initiated for gradual adoption by Soviet industry during the autumn of 1965, continues to be implemented by stages, more or less in keeping with the official timetable. This program provides for some decentralization of economic decisionmaking and for a change in the existing pattern of managerial incentives. Under the new dispensation, enterprise managers are allowed somewhat more authority in making decisions of the kind that were formerly made by a higher echelon of officialdom. In addition, they are under instruction to be guided in making these decisions by such criteria as volume of sales, profit, and rate of return on capital. As operational flaws in the reform measures, or obstacles to their implementation, come to the surface, they are often highlighted in the Soviet press with a view to finding solutions and carrying out the needed adjustments.

As expected, there have been occasional reports of opposition to the reform program on the part of elements within the upper strata of the economic bureaucracy (who may be deprived of a share of their power), and even within the structure of the Communist Party. But there is no firm evidence to suggest that a faction within the Politburo may be opposed to the reform. Whether or not support of the reform is universal or wholehearted, however, it appears that the transfer of industrial enterprises to the new system of management will be completed as scheduled by the end of 1968. During 1966, a group of 704 enterprises, accounting for 8 percent of total industrial production, were transferred to the new system. But by the end of the third quarter of 1967, 5,500 enterprises, accounting for a third of industrial production had been transferred; by the end of 1967 nearly 6,000 enterprises were working under the new system.

COMPARATIVE GROWTH RECORD

The general performance of the Soviet economy during the 2 most recent years, in terms of aggregate growth, was consistent with the trend established in the first half of the present decade. Viewed separately, however, the 2 recent years disclose a rather divergent record of performance. For the year 1966, the margin of new growth measured an impressive 7.1 percent. During the following year, according to present provisional calculations, aggregate economic output advanced by an unspectacular 4.3 percent.

As happened so often in the past, the difference in the overall performance of the economy was strongly influenced by the sharp disparity in the contribution made by the agricultural sector. The farm sector enjoyed optimal climatic conditions during the growing season of 1966, as a result of which the year's output of field crops and animal products rose by 10 percent. In the following year, however, weather conditions were far less favorable, thereby inducing a decline in the Nation's farm output by 3 percent. This decline, in turn, had a depressing effect on general economic growth, thus underscoring once more the critical role which agriculture continues to play in the Soviet economy.

If we abstract from the agricultural cycle in order to gain perspective on longer run trends, the results of the last 2 years tend to distribute themselves neatly around a longer run trend for Soviet GNP (Table 81–2). Specifically, by dividing the postwar period into several significant periods, we may observe that the growth of the Soviet economy, which reached a high-water mark during 1955–58, has proceeded by a lower average rate since 1958, appearing to have leveled out at rates between 5 and 5.5 percent.

In regard to its standing in the international growth league moreover, the position of the Soviet Union is no longer one of leadership, as it was in the early and middle 1950s, but it is still relatively strong. While the performance of the United States, for example, has greatly improved since 1961, those of several other major economies, like Germany, Italy, and the United Kingdom, have deteriorated, so that the relative position of the U.S.S.R. has remained unchanged (Table 81–3).

Table 81–2.   U.S.S.R.: ANNUAL AND PERIOD GROWTH RATES OF GNP FOR SELECTED YEARS, 1951–67

Year	Rate	Period[1]	Rate
1958	9.4	1951–55	6.9
1959	4.9	1956–58	7.4
1960	5.2	1959–61	5.8
1961	7.0	1962–67	5.4
1962	4.2		
1963	2.8		
1964	7.9		
1965	6.2		
1966	7.1		
1967	4.3		

[1] Average annual rate.

Table 81–3.   U.S.S.R. AND MARKET ECONOMIES: COMPARATIVE GROWTH RATES OF GROSS NATIONAL PRODUCT FOR SELECTED YEARS, 1956–67 (in percent)

Country	Annual rates						
	1961	1962	1963	1964	1965	1966	1967[1]
U.S.S.R.	7.0	4.2	2.8	7.9	6.2	7.1	4.3
France	4.4	7.1	4.8	6.0	3.5	4.9	3.8
Germany	5.4	4.2	3.4	6.6	4.6	2.6	−1.0
Italy	7.8	6.2	5.5	2.7	3.4	5.8	5.5
United Kingdom	3.5	1.1	4.4	5.6	2.4	1.6	1.5
Japan	15.3	7.8	6.1	15.6	4.0	9.7	12.5
United States	1.9	6.6	4.0	5.3	5.9	5.8	2.6

Country	Period rates (average annual)		
	1956–61	1962–66	1962–67[1]
U.S.S.R.	6.4	5.6	5.4
France	4.9	5.4	4.8
Germany	6.2	4.3	3.2
Italy	6.2	5.1	5.0
United Kingdom	2.9	3.0	3.1
Japan	10.9	8.6	9.5
United States	2.1	5.6	5.1

[1] Preliminary estimates.

FUTURE TREND OF GNP

Currently the dollar value of Soviet GNP is around 48 percent of the U.S. level. The Soviet Union occupies a strong second position among the economies of the world, some 2½ times the size of Germany and Japan, the economies in third and fourth positions (Table 81–4). In per capita terms the Soviet position is relatively lower, with a level some 40 percent that of the United States and about two-thirds of the major economies of Northwestern Europe. Within reasonable margins of error, per capita GNP in the U.S.S.R. is about matched by those of Italy and Japan. This comparison does not apply to any measurement of personal consumption, for the U.S.S.R. would rank lower, given the high proportions of GNP allocated to investment and defense.

As a proportion of the U.S. economy, the greatest gains made by the Soviet economy were accomplished during the fifties. Since 1961 Soviet GNP has reached a proportionate plateau of around 46 to 48 percent. In terms of the absolute margin of the U.S. economy over the Soviet, the minimum difference was reached in 1958. Since then the dollar gap between Soviet and United States GNP has been widening (Table 81–5).

The economic significance of the gap depends on the variable being measured. If GNP is considered as a rough quantification of general economic potential, the comparison in Table 81–5 is appropriate. If the concern is with some concept of consumer welfare, the dollar gap between the two economies would be limited to a comparison of consumption and would show an even wider divergence. If the concern is military potential, the best indicator would be industrial production, in which case the gap would continue to narrow.

The future prospects for the growth of the Soviet economy ultimately depend on the availability of new productive resources and upon the increased efficiency with which they are utilized. Through 1975 it will be assumed that the maximum increase in employment will be set by the projected annual average increase in the number of adults of working age, 1.6–1.7 percent. The rise in capital stock will, as a maximum, be determined by the investment target of 7.9 percent annually of the current 5-year plan. After making provision for a retirement rate of about 2.5 percent per year, a net increase in assets of about 7.5 percent per year is projected.

Projections of labor and capital productivity are based on recent historical analogs. Use of these analogs assumes continuation of the same institutional environments which have prevailed since Stalin's demise. The best productivity performance in the post-Stalinist years occurred in the midfifties, a period of liberalization and correction of the worst Stalinist errors. The least favorable period was during the late Khrushchev years, when the institutional environment became static. If the limits of productivity growth rates are set by the historical experiences of these two eras and the figures be combined with the assumptions of growth in the principal factors of production, employment and capital stock, a GNP growth range of 4.8 to 6 percent per year is obtained. This range should be regarded as a maximum and will likely not be attained if investment continues to fall below plan. A young Soviet mathematical economist using econometric techniques has projected a 5.4 percent growth

Table 81–4.   U.S.S.R. AND SELECTED MARKET ECONOMIES: COMPARATIVE DOLLAR VALUE OF GROSS NATIONAL PRODUCT IN 1966 (market prices; 1966 U.S. dollars)

Country	Ranked by GNP (billions)	Country	Ranked by per capita (dollars)
United States	$743	United States	$3,777
U.S.S.R.	357	Germany	2,382
Germany	142	France	2,217
Japan	134	United Kingdom	2,047
United Kingdom	113	U.S.S.R.	1,532
France	110	Italy	1,408
Italy	73	Japan	1,352

Table 81–5.   U.S.S.R. AND UNITED STATES: COMPARATIVE TRENDS IN DOLLAR VALUES OF GNP IN MARKET PRICES (in 1966 U.S. dollars)

Country	1950	1955	1958	1961	1965	1966	1967[1]
United States	414	508	519	575	711	743	762
U.S.S.R.	132	185	229	272	330	357	372
Difference	282	323	290	303	381	386	390
U.S.S.R. GNP as a percent of U.S.	31.9	36.4	44.1	47.3	46.4	48.0	48.8

[1] Preliminary.

rate for the period, midway within this growth range.

Recent estimates for the United States project the annual rate of growth of GNP through 1975 in a range of 4 to 4.5 percent. The envisaged differential rates of growth between the two economies are thus minor and will likely be narrowed if full employment and technological progress are sustained in the United States and if the over-commitment of resources and institutional stagnation continue to plague the Soviet Union.

QUESTIONS AND STUDY SUGGESTIONS

1. Discuss the performance of the Soviet economy in fulfilling the objectives of the 1959–1965 plan.
2. Discuss the economic priorities which the new leadership of the Soviet Union has established for the 1966–1970 plan.
3. What is the general character of recent Soviet economic reforms?
4. To what extent has the Soviet growth rate slackened in recent years? What factors underlie this decline?

Reading 82

Economic Revolution in the Soviet Union

Marshall I. Goldman, Associate Professor of Economics, Wellesley College

In the late 1950s and the 1960s the Soviet economy encountered a number of interrelated difficulties. In general, as the Soviet economy became more sophisticated and complex, detailed central planning became less workable and less efficient. In particular, the incentive system has caused

From "Economic Revolution in the Soviet Union," **Foreign Affairs,** January, 1967, pp. 319–331, abridged. Excerpted by special permission from **Foreign Affairs,** January, 1967. © Council on Foreign Relations, Inc., New York.

serious distortions in the composition of output and the use of inputs. Furthermore, capital productivity has lagged and Soviet factory managers have been resistant to innovation. Reading 82 is concerned with the character and scope of the economic reforms initiated in the mid-1960s for the purpose of coping with these problems. Whether these reforms will actually increase the efficiency of the Soviet economy depends, first, upon the government's capacity to revise prices so as to reflect with greater accuracy the real value of products and resources and, second, the degree of bureaucratic resistance to the "new look" in Soviet planning.

On the eve of the Fiftieth Anniversary of the Communist Revolution, the Russians embarked on yet another economic revolution. With hardly a word about ideological purity, Premier Alexei Kosygin has announced that by 1968 profits, sales and rate of return on investment will replace fulfillment of quotas as the main standards of success for every Soviet firm. Moreover, Soviet managers will have to pay interest or capital charges for the capital they use. Profits will be divided up in a form of profit-sharing, and some enterprises will even have to pay rent. The economic reforms are matched in their significance, according to one Russian economist, A. Birman, only by the transition to N.E.P. (the New Economic Policy) in 1921 and the launching of the Five Year Plans in 1929–32. Clearly what the Soviets are currently attempting amounts to a repudiation of formerly sacred doctrines.

RECENT ECONOMIC DIFFICULTIES

Why have the Russians picked this juncture to make such basic structural changes? It is not an impetuous action. The call for reform originated with Professor Evsei Liberman in September 1962. This was followed by more than three to four years of active debate and about two years of actual experimentation. During this period the majority of Russian economists came to acknowledge that there was a need for a drastic overhaul. They were obviously shocked when they saw their rate of economic growth fall badly during their Seven Year Plan from 1959 to '65. Most observers came to realize that a long-run upturn in the growth rate would depend on the resolution of some basic underlying problems. What was needed was improvement of day-to-day operating procedures as well as reform of the process by which longer-run changes were made. All of

this would require a more productive use of the country's capital and the stimulation of innovation.

By the early 1960s, the Soviet economy had become a very complicated mechanism and was in serious danger of self-strangulation. The central planners were finding it harder and harder to make efficient decisions without help from factory managers. There were simply too many eventualities for Moscow to be able to plan for them. Yet the central planners continued to insist on detailed control over day-to-day operations. The factory managers were given little authority to deviate from quantitative plans, frequently drawn up a year or more in advance. Moreover, plant managers were often led to produce completely inappropriate items by a misdirected incentive system. The system contained no mechanism for responding to error. Often there was more concern about the bureaucrats than about the factory's customers. It was true that these methods had brought growth in the past, but increasingly output was unrelated to needs.

Growth and change had been obtained in the past largely by pressure and prodding. Because managers and planners were almost always submerged in their daily operating problems and had very short-term goals, the government had to launch campaign after campaign to shake the economy out of its deeply furrowed ruts. This was the only way to move industry to Siberia or force the growth of the chemical industry or the use of natural gas. While such campaigns often accomplished their stated purpose, Soviet observers began to point out that they also involved considerable waste. Invariably all other activities would be halted in order to devote exclusive efforts to the campaign goal. Occasionally a second campaign would then be necessary to right the balance.

The Russians also discovered that their capital productivity had fallen badly. Capital was less productive because of the inefficient operating methods just described. The problem was intensified because capital was treated as a free good. There was no interest or repayment. Consequently, factory managers would try whenever possible to hoard capital, especially raw materials, for their productive needs. In this way they could insulate themselves from the transportation tie-ups and supply bottlenecks that were a hallmark of centralized planning. But in addition to input accumulations, many factories and stores have begun recently to find themselves with stocks of their output which have accumulated unexpectedly because of unsuitability or poor quality.

THE PROBLEM OF INNOVATION

Partially as an effect and partially as a cause of all these factors, little innovation arose from within the factory itself. When the priorities were high enough, as on military and space projects, there could be impressive innovation. But lesser projects produced none of the instant innovation which seemed to characterize Western industry. When innovation came it was often too costly and too late. For instance, Russian officials now admit that during the five years required to work out the production problems of the Ural 4 computer and the Zaporozhets automobile, both had been made obsolete by production advances in the West.

What the Russians needed was some system that would provide them with self-generated flexibility and growth. Only with such a reform could they hope to improve their rate of economic growth, compete more effectively in foreign markets, improve the supply of consumer goods and ameliorate their inventory problem. It would not suffice just to know when to introduce new products; there also had to be some way of knowing when to drop old ones.

For a time many economists thought that the computer would solve all these problems. It was expected that advances in planning and computing technology would eventually make it possible to determine centrally all production, price investment and consumption decisions. The various unknowns would be thrown in and the necessary answers would come parading out in neat formation. Soon, however, even some of the computer specialists came to

realize the impracticality of relying on the computer alone. There were simply too many unknowns for everything to be determined centrally.

ENTER: THE MARKET

Looking around, the Russians saw that in the Western countries, and even in a country like Yugoslavia, the market economy handled day-to-day transactions with a maximum of efficiency and a minimum of regulation. The Russians also saw that the problems of learning and responding were solved when the market economy was combined with something like the American system of competitive enterprise. Whatever shortcomings it may have, business enterprise in the United States responds to "feedback." In such a system, failure to so respond can lead to financial loss for some identifiable group or person. Consequently, managers have a great incentive to respond. The Russians realized that if their problems were to be solved, they would need similar responsive effort and flexibility in their economy.

NATURE OF THE REFORM

What is so radical about the Reform? First of all, the old system of planning and incentives has been scrapped. No longer will factories be assigned quantitative output targets. The first experiments were conducted in May 1964. *Bolshevichka*, a Moscow factory making men's clothes, and *Maiak*, a Gorki manufacturer of women's dresses, became the first enterprises to be evaluated on something other than quantity of production. To stimulate production of items better suited to the customer's needs, the payment of premiums was made dependent on the fulfillment of delivery and profit plans. In January 1965, some heavy-industrial firms in the Ukraine were also permitted to experiment. The scheme grew rapidly and by the end of the year over 400 consumer-goods manufacturers and 3,000 retail stores had been converted to the new system.

In September 1965, Premier Kosygin himself announced that the reorganization would gradually be extended to the whole economy. He ordered the adoption of a slightly revised set of gauges which in addition to profits included rate of return on capital, interest, capital charges and rent. Market research and advertising were also to be more used. To say the least, such economic forms are highly unorthodox by Soviet standards. None the less, as of January 1966, Soviet managers in 43 major factories were to be judged on the fulfillment of sales or profits targets and the rate of return on capital (profits as a percent of capital). These factory managers will have to deduct interest at a rate of .5 to 2 percent on any bank loans they may have. No longer will sums of capital be allocated to them as a gift from the budget for capital already borrowed. These capital charges are to average 6 percent of the enterprise's fixed and working capital. The interest charge and capital charge are to be supplemented by a rent charge, to vary so that firms and mines more favorably located than others will not earn undue profits. All of these charges must be deducted from profits before premiums can be paid or the rate of return calculated. By January 1967, almost one-third of all the country's industrial workers will have been switched to the new incentive system, with the rest of the factories scheduled to be converted by 1968.

Wherever possible, economic standards and charges will be set several years in advance. In this way it is expected that the managers will seek to do their best without fear that their targets will be jacked up the moment they show signs of improved operation. This should free them for more experimentation. Logically they should be more willing to risk the introduction of new processes and products if they know they will not be criticized for making lower profits during periods of innovation and will not have their increased profits taken away from them as soon as they work out the kinks.

Enterprises whose products are already in abundant supply or whose inputs are in short supply will be judged by how well they fulfill their profit plan. It is hoped that this will cause them to produce as efficiently as possible. Firms whose output is in short supply will have to fulfill sales targets. This will insure that such goods will continue to be produced. A sale will not be counted, however, until payment for delivery has been deposited in the bank to the seller's account. Better quality may be stimulated in this way because the buyer will not release his funds until he is satisfied that he has received what he asked for.

In a further effort to increase flexibility, Soviet authorities are introducing new supply procedures. Wherever possible, enterprises are authorized to work out their own purchase and sale agreements without the interference of ministerial authorities. This will ultimately mean the increased use of salesmen, trade fairs, marketing research and advertising. If stocks of merchandise are made readily available in local warehouses, managers should have less reason to hoard supplies in their own private warehouses. Ultimately, it is thought, this could lead to the end of centralized allocations for all but the highest priority goods.

The rate of return is to be used in conjunction with either profits or sales as the second criterion of success. Rate of return is now defined as profit in relation to capital, as Liberman had suggested. Previously when rate of returns (rentabelnost) was discussed, it referred to profit as a percent of cost.

With the new criteria the manager has a strong incentive to cut back on his capital stock. Anything the manager does to reduce the denominator in the profit-to-capital ratio will presumably lead to a more efficient use of capital and a reduction of inventories. But by reducing his capital, the rate of return is further improved because interest and capital deductions will be lower, and therefore profit (the numerator) will be higher. If this curbs the squandering of capital, then capital productivity will be increased and an important goal of the reform will have been achieved.

THREE FUNDS

The net profit that remains after the deduction of interest, capital charge and rent determines not only the rate of return but also the amount that is available for the discretionary use of the factory manager. The manager is entitled to put a specified portion of net profit into three funds—the Incentive Fund, the Cultural and Housing Fund and the Development Fund, all three of them designed to promote the firm's productivity.

Since the size of these funds depends on the enterprise's profitability, they are expected to stimulate the workers' interest in holding down costs more than in the past when extra pay and bonuses ("premiums") depended on the quantities produced. In the new system, fulfillment of targets remains an important factor in calculating the amounts that can be put into the fund, but over-fulfillment is rewarded at a lower rate. This is the reverse of former procedures. According to Liberman, this will stimulate plant directors to seek higher targets in the beginning and not hold back on their efforts.

Managers, engineers and the like will get all their bonuses from the incentive fund, but for the blue-collar workers there will also be some payments from the old wage fund, so that the worker is not penalized if his performance is good but the enterprise fails to be profitable for reasons beyond his control. The size of the bonuses varies from industry to industry and differs according to the situation of the enterprise, but there is a formula that puts a limit on the amount of profits that can be spent this way, in order to be sure that wages do not increase faster than productivity.

The Development Fund is a particularly important one, designed to encourage innovation and investment by the firm itself. The share of profits that can be put into this fund is related to the size of the capital of the enterprise; yearly amortization charges are added to it and also proceeds from the sale of old or surplus capital equipment. Ultimately as much as one-fifth of all the capital investments made in the Soviet Union may come out of the Development Funds of individual enterprises. Liberman sees a connection between this kind of decentralization of investment and the direct incentive payments to workers and managers, because the Development Fund, by increasing the importance of self-financing for each enterprise, gives managers much more control than they had in the past. Moreover, the use of bonuses from the other funds and cultural and housing benefits are also to a considerable extent under their control.

PROBLEMS OF IMPLEMENTATION

No one among Soviet officials pretends that implementation of the Reform will be easy. As Kosygin recently remarked to the Supreme Soviet, there are two immediate problems: poor pricing and bureaucratic resistance. Existing Soviet prices do not adequately reflect the true value of the product. Wholesale prices have not been thoroughly revised since 1955. Supply-and-demand relationships among different commodities have changed markedly

since then. By producing those items which have unduly high prices, factory managers will be able to make unintended profits on an undesired assortment of goods. This could easily provoke the reintroduction of detailed controls.

Kosygin also mentioned that there has been resistance to the Reform by those who fear it will undermine their own positions. "A certain conservatism and lack of initiative," he asserted, "are sometimes displayed in trying to solve a number of matters connected with the operation of the economic reforms." There has been foot-dragging by the ministries of the industries affected. Kosygin declared: "The ministries should not demand an excessive amount of reference notes and information of various kinds from the enterprises." To the extent that ministerial intervention limits a firm's ability to deal through direct contracts, it eliminates the possibility of feedback.

Of course it is not just the bureaucrats who oppose the change. Like their counterparts all over the world, many Soviet managers fear the effects of competition and are reluctant to abandon the relatively tranquil climate of fixed markets and stable production quotas in which they have operated. Finally, like the workers in the movie "The Man in the White Suit," there are many Soviet workers who recognize that increased efficiency will mean layoffs and unemployment.

With such opposition there is a possibility that some or all of the Reform may be suspended. After all, Soviet economic history is filled with the scraps of brilliantly conceived experiments. A real danger exists that the slow pace of the Reform could create such chaos that the entire program might be discredited. Possibly the Reform should have been introduced throughout the economy simultaneously to prevent the distortions that result from piecemeal change. Yet this too could cause trouble.

Some Soviet officials feel that the new interest rate and capital charge will hold back the introduction of new capital. This indicates a misunderstanding of the function of capital charges. A charge for capital should not frustrate investment if the proposed equipment is productive enough to make possible repayment of the capital charge. If it is not productive enough, then the investment should not be made in the first place. It was just because of the absence of such a restraint that capital has been consumed so wastefully in the past. However, just in case the managers do hold back too much on investment, senior officials have the power to exempt new capital from the capital charge until the new equipment is operating at full capacity.

To the surprise of some, the Reform is also creating problems where it was thought none existed. The introduction of economic guides like interest and rent has created a schizophrenic split between Russia's domestic and foreign-trade interests. With their new economic methods, the Russians have begun to reëvaluate their production possibilities. They have discovered that they have not engaged in the most productive kind of foreign trade. Now that they are beginning to recognize the impact of rent and interest, they find that they have seriously underestimated the substantial costs of the capital and land resources involved in expanding the production of their raw materials. As a result they have complained publicly and repeatedly that they have been *subsidizing* their East European allies with such items as oil, iron ore and coal. Naturally this comes as a shock to the East Europeans who have long complained about Soviet *overpricing* of raw materials.

ADMINISTRATIVE EFFICIENCY

Two big questions remain: Will the Reform increase overall administrative efficiency, and will it stimulate the productive innovations so much desired? Undoubtedly there will be improvements on both counts, but will they be enough?

Liberman and the other proponents of the Reform are convinced that decentralization is a necessary step in the right direction. If anything, they feel the Reform will make central planning more effective. They dispute those who worry that the use of direct contracts, wholesalers, market research, advertising and profits will mean the end of central planning or the excessive diversion of natural resources from heavy to light industry. On the contrary, the reformers insist that freeing the planners · from having to deal with so many small details will make it possible for the planning organizations to concentrate their efforts on issues of more importance. No longer will the authorities in Moscow have to worry about such things as whether or not a factory in Novgorod is sending the right size screws to the right factory in Minsk on time. Instead the planners can devote their attention to long-term goals and major investment needs. Where necessary, heavy industry can be protected by use of price adjustments and government subsidies.

By dividing up responsibilities in this way, the planners also hope to make more effective use of computing equipment. Once the central planners are freed to the minutiae of individual plant problems, they should be free to use their computers to project alternative solutions to long-range problems. The reformers also hope that the individual firm will be able to use its own computers to improve its operational efficiency through the use of operations research techniques.

Administrative efficiency, in the final analysis, is dependent on more than the availability of hardware; there must also be well-trained managers. Heretofore the Soviets have used production engineers who have been trained to produce in large quantities and to secure unavailable components. Will it be possible to revise the whole concept of managerial administration so that two generations of quantity-oriented production specialists can be converted into quality-conscious innovators? As the Minister of Education has acknowledged, such a change can hardly take place overnight. In recognition of the urgent need to develop a new breed of manager, open admiration is now expressed for such managerial hatcheries as the Harvard Business School. In fact, a Russian exchange student is now enrolled in Cambridge learning the technique of teaching American business administration.

STIMULATING INNOVATION

Assuming that managerial practices can be improved, will this also stimulate the flow of innovation? Theoretically, the Russian manager should be able to operate as efficiently and be as inventive as his counterpart in the large American corporation. The Reform, with its emphasis on sales, profit and rate of return, is much the same incentive system that is used by such large American corporations as DuPont and General Electric. Similarly, these American corporations permit decentralized investment within certain limits, just as will now be the case in the U.S.S.R. Consequently, like their American counterparts, the new Soviet enterprises should now be able to promote numerous important innovations and move the inventions from their laboratories to the production floor.

Innovation in the United States, however, does not originate solely in the larger corporations. In fact, there are many who argue that much of the American leadership in innovation comes not from the larger corporation, but from the small private enterprise. Despite the growth of large corporate research laboratories, a large proportion of the basic discoveries in the United States continue to come from small firms, which sometimes succeed so well that they turn into large corporations themselves— like Polaroid, Itek or Xerox. It is hard to see how the Russians even with the Reform will be able to avail themselves of this particular kind of innovation.

The phenomenon of the small and creative entrepreneur is possible only where there is private ownership of capital. The man with the idea must be able to solicit financial support for his project from a wide variety of financial sources. It is not enough to have inventors with ideas that are advanced for their day; there must also be a wide variety of financiers around to support them. The more sources of capital there are, the more likely it is that an investor will be found who can appreciate the worth of a particular investment. When the state controls all the society's capital, the sources of capital are sharply reduced. Normally there will be no more than one decision-maker and no court of appeal. If the state's capital controller happens to lack the vision to appreciate a particular invention, no matter how brilliant the discovery may be, it will not move past the idea stage. Innovation also requires a willingness to take a risk and lose. The stewardship of the state's funds, however, generates extreme conservatism, hardly a desirable environment for promoting innovation.

In partial recognition of the handicap associated with state control of capital, the Reform does permit some decentralized investment by the enterprise in the hope that inventors will be able to seek out alternative capital support. Yet even if the single government veto over capital is abolished, there may be a need for something more. To be successful, the Reform must touch off a competitive spark among the country's managers. Whatever its limitations, the phenomenon of competition in the West plays a basic role in stimulating the search for new and better processes and products. While the Soviets are trying to emulate this spirit, it is questionable whether they will be successful in generating it at the enterprise level. There have been some very dynamic nationalized enterprises like Volkswagen. But such firms have made their mark in competitive coexistence with private enterprises. So far it has been very difficult to ignite that inventive spark when all the enterprises in a country are owned by the state.

STATE CAPITALISM?

Radical as the Reform is, it does not herald the advent of capitalism. As the Chinese have been quick to note, however, the use of such tools of the marketplace as profit, interest and rent certainly is not a reaffirmation of Marxism. What is in progress seems to be a determined effort to improve the effectiveness of a form of state capitalism. The dynamic operation of a massive and complex industrial system dictates the use of certain universal techniques. The Russians do not have too much choice; it is like trying to go up the down escalator. As their economy becomes more complicated, it becomes harder and harder to move forward at a rapid rate. Without the Reform, their economy may well be carried backward. With the Reform, they hope it will be able to move forward—at the very least, hold its own.

QUESTIONS AND STUDY SUGGESTIONS

1. Describe in detail recent Soviet economic problems and the reforms to which they have given rise. In particular, what changes in production targets and incentives have been initiated?

2. Why have Soviet planners found it difficult to stimulate innovation at the factory level?

3. What were the consequences of the fact that Soviet planners have treated capital as a "free good"? What incentives do factory managers now have to cut back on the use of real capital?

4. What are the main problems involved in implementing the new economic reforms?